22

Information Systems
A Management Perspective
Second Edition

Steven Alter
University of San Francisco

The Benjamin/Cummings Publishing Company, Inc.
Menlo Park, California ▪ Reading, Massachusetts ▪ New York ▪ Don Mills, Ontario ▪
Wokingham, U.K. ▪ Amsterdam ▪ Madrid ▪ Sydney ▪ Singapore ▪ Tokyo ▪ Seoul ▪
Taipei ▪ Mexico City ▪ San Juan, Puerto Rico

Executive Editor: Michael Payne
Senior Acquisitions Editor: Maureen A. Allaire
Developmental Editor: Rebecca Johnson
Projects Manager: Adam Ray
Art Supervisor: Karl Miyajima
Photo Editor: Kelli D'Angona, Big Picture Research
Manufacturing Supervisor: Janet Weaver
Copyeditor: Robert Fiske, Vocabula Communications
Proofreader: Holly McLean-Aldis
Composition: Bruce Saltzman, Digital Type & Image
Text Designer: Gary Palmatier, Ideas to Images
Cover Designer: Yvo Riezebos

Credits appear following the Longer Cases.

Library of Congress Cataloging-in-Publication Data

```
Alter, Steven.
    Information systems : a management perspective / Steven Alter. --
  2nd ed.
       p. cm.
    Includes index
    ISBN 0-8053-2430-5
    1. Management information systems.  I. Title
  T58.6.A44 1996
  658.4'038'011--dc20                                    95-22579
                                                            CIP
```

1 2 3 4 5 6 7 8 9 10—DOW—99 98 97 96 95

The Benjamin/Cummings Publishing Company, Inc.
2725 Sand Hill Road
Menlo Park, CA 94025

Preface

Searching for a Better Paradigm

The second edition of *Information Systems, A Management Perspective* contains what I think is a new way to synthesize and explain ideas about information systems. This approach grew out of the following challenge:

Assume that I have to give a one hour lecture to a group of business professionals who will later attend an important meeting about a particular information system in their business. Like many business professionals, they understand their business situation and may be familiar with spreadsheets, word processors, or other computer applications but probably have never received training about information systems. My lecture should increase their insight into the particular information system that will be discussed in their meeting. Unfortunately, I face three unreasonable restrictions in preparing my lecture:

- I cannot know what job or business background the business professionals have. They may be system users, programmers, top managers, or anyone else who cares about the system. They may work for a grocery store, an airline, a computer company, or any other organization.

- I cannot know anything about the information system they will be discussing. It may be a telephone voice mail system, a customer billing system, an information system for managers, or any other system.

- I cannot know the agenda of their meeting. They may be reviewing an existing system, evaluating a proposal from a software vendor, or designing a new system.

Is there any way I could accept these unreasonable restrictions and still say something useful?

Accepting this challenge, I cobbled together an initial lecture and gradually improved it by presenting it 22 times at universities and several research institutions. I watched the audience reaction to each presentation, recorded questions and disagreements, and tried to clarify the ideas. When the ideas finally seemed clear enough, I wrote a working paper and asked students to use the approach to analyze an information system in a business. Misunderstandings or omissions in student papers provided feedback that helped clarify the ideas further.

The goal of finding something valuable and general to say about information systems in a single hour-long lecture might sound crazy. However, if I could identify and express the basic ideas, I could then add the real world examples and deeper explanation that would allow this text to achieve its goals: helping students become able to *recognize, describe, analyze,* and *design* information systems from a business professional's viewpoint.

Approach

Integrated throughout the second edition of *Information Systems, A Management Approach* are basic ideas and topics that receive only superficial coverage in most introductory texts. These ideas are expressed in a number of forms:

A revised framework for summarizing an information system

Current business concepts related to total quality management and business process reengineering offer many insights into the relationship between an information system, the work being done, and the results being produced. These ideas were used to update the system framework from the first edition. Aside from information and technology, the new work-centered framework includes the business process being supported, the process participants, the product of the business process, and the internal or external customer.

Use of this revised framework as the basis of a work-centered analysis (WCA) method for business professionals

Introduced in the first few chapters of the book, the WCA method outlines the use of the new framework from five perspectives:

- Architecture (components and how they operate together)
- Performance (how well the system operates)
- Infrastructure (shared resources needed for system operation)
- Context (organizational and technical factors affecting the system)
- Risks (foreseeable things that could go wrong).

Use of the framework from these different perspectives gives students organized, business-oriented guidance for thinking about any information system in an organizational setting.

Emphasis on the basic concepts, such as infrastructure, integration, compatibility, and structure of work

Highlighting basic ideas provides a conceptual core that should be equally applicable ten years from now, when currently dazzling technology may seem as outdated as punched cards seem today. Furthermore, emphasizing these ideas makes the course more approachable and understandable for students because they can relate technology issues to many aspects of their everyday experience.

Frank recognition of successes and disappointments

Like any important part of business, information systems have had their share of successes and disappointments. Numerous examples throughout the text illustrate not only wonderful accomplishments and optimism about future developments but also the human, organizational, and technical problems that are part of any realistic treatment of the field.

Organization of This Book

Each of the parts contains three or four chapters. Although it is preferable to start with the first chapter and at least portions of other chapters in Part I, the book is designed to permit sequencing of the parts in many different orders depending on the instructor's priorities.

Part I: Basic Ideas for Understanding Information Systems

Part I introduces ideas any business professional can use to understand information systems from a business viewpoint. The introduction to Part I presents a framework that can be used to create a system summary to start the analysis of any information system. It defines the term information system and explains the relationship between information technology, information systems, and business processes. Chapter 1 presents seven challenges for business professionals related to different aspects of the framework. Chapter 2 explains the framework in more depth and shows how it can be used to organize a business professional's analysis of an information system. Chapter 3 delves more deeply into business processes, the central element in the framework. Chapter 4 takes a similar look at information and databases. Taken together, these chapters are designed to provide a starting point for analyzing an information system from a business viewpoint. The remainder of the book expands on this introduction.

Part II: Applications and Impacts of Information Systems

Part II discusses the applications and impacts of information systems. Chapter 5 looks at applications and impacts related to communication and decision making, two intertwined elements of every business process. It uses ideas about communication and decision making to explain roles of different types of information systems in both areas. Chapter 6 looks further at roles of information systems in business processes, focusing on ways information systems can be used to improve the efficiency and effectiveness of internal business operations within a firm. Chapter 7 looks at the customer and product and discusses competitive uses of information systems. Chapter 8 looks at participants and covers human and ethical issues related to information systems.

Part III: Understanding the Role of Information Technology

Part III explains aspects of information technology users and managers need to understand to appreciate the relationship between technical advances and the changing nature of business processes. Chapter 9 covers computers and peripherals, with substantial emphasis on underlying ideas rather than merely cataloguing different technologies. Chapter 10 takes a similar approach in explaining software and programming. Chapter 11 looks at networks and telecommunications. Chapter 12 looks at applications usually included under the heading of artificial intelligence along with major limitations of current "intelligent" systems.

Part IV: Building and Managing Information Systems

Part IV closes the book by looking at processes related to building these systems and keeping them operating. Chapter 13 summarizes information system planning, the process by which a firm decides how to allocate its resources among different information system projects, most of which involve operating existing systems rather than building new ones. Since firms build information systems based on these decisions, Chapter 14 explains and compares different types of processes for building and maintaining information systems. Chapter 15 looks at system control and security, the things that must be understood and done to assure that information systems are used effectively, efficiently, and without fraud or crime.

Pedagogical Features

Helping students become more able to recognize, describe, analyze, and design information systems is easier said than done. Even with the recent improvements in texts in this area, many students still find the introductory course boring, overloaded with quickly forgotten technical jargon, and difficult to relate to their personal career goals. Many professors dislike teaching the course for the same reason. This book's pedagogical approach tries to address these problems by focusing on practical ideas any business professional can use for thinking about systems.

This second edition was designed to include features that make it attractive to both students and instructors. It is designed to aid learning by balancing examples, concepts, and details. The effort to articulate the basic ideas more clearly made it possible to reduce the number of chapters from 20 to 15.

An unusual feature of the book is the substantive part introduction preceding each group of three of four chapters. These part introductions identify major themes spanning the chapters that follow. They support continuity across the chapters by highlighting the enduring system-related ideas the book conveys.

All chapters are designed in a consistent format that amplifies the ideas in the text:

Outline and study questions

Each chapter starts with major outline headings plus a set of study questions that also organize the summary at the end of each chapter.

Featured case

Each chapter starts with a featured case that demonstrates the ideas in the chapter and reinforces some of the book's main themes.

System summary diagram

The featured case in every chapter is also summarized using the WCA framework. Repetitive use of this framework shows how the same six elements can be used to think about any information system.

Debate

Following each featured case is a suggested debate designed to encourage active interest and participation by students. Even the technology chapters contain debate topics designed to intrigue students. A similar debate topic follows each of the two application scenarios at the end of the chapters. Since the featured cases and application scenarios are designed to raise a broad range of issues, some instructors may wish to use other debate topics.

Body of the chapter

The body of each chapter aims for a balance between concepts and examples. Concepts are explained in sufficient depth and are supported by real-world examples. Most examples are integrated into the explanations and are not isolated in boxes that disrupt the flow of ideas.

Reality checks

Following major sections in each chapter is a reality check box asking the student to think about how the section's main ideas are related to things encountered in everyday life. The reality checks help counter the common tendency to believe that information systems are technical systems unrelated to the student's life experience. They can also be assigned as homework exercises to support student involvement in the course material.

Art and photographs

The book includes a carefully prepared art and photo program designed to support the ideas being presented. The figures and photos are not just decoration. Each one genuinely reinforces the ideas being explained.

End-of-chapter study aids

The end-of-chapter material starts with a summary keyed to the study questions at the beginning of the chapter. Key terms are introduced in boldface throughout the chapter and are listed following the chapter summary. Review questions encourage the reader to recall some of the important ideas that support the main concepts covered in the chapter. Discussion questions ask the reader to think conceptually about ideas in the chapter.

International vignettes

At the end of each chapter are one or two brief vignettes about information systems built or used outside the United States. Following each vignette are three questions, one encouraging integrative use of the WCA framework to summarize the vignette, one directed at international or intercultural issues, and a third related to the specifics of the particular situation.

Real-world cases

Following the international vignettes are two or three brief real-world cases that discuss interesting situations not mentioned in the body of the text.

Application scenarios

These are descriptions of interesting situations students can analyze using the ideas presented in the chapter. Unlike the featured cases, international vignettes, and real world cases, the application scenarios combine a variety of real world experiences into fictional situations designed to raise important issues, engage the student's interest, and serve as the basis of classroom discussion.

Cumulative case

Each chapter contains a continuation of a cumulative case that runs through the entire book. The case is about an entrepreneurial chain of t-shirt stores that encounters issues discussed in each chapter. The portions of the case included with each chapter are not totally independent but are designed to be independent enough that they can be used even if some of the previous chapters have been skipped.

■ *Transaction processing system and database*

A model transaction processing system supporting the cumulative case is distributed along with the instructor's manual. It is written in Microsoft Access 2.0 and provides opportunities to perform transactions, examine the way a relational DBMS operates, and observe the way transactions affect a database. Some instructors may ask their students to suggest improvements to this model system, and may even ask their students to program those improvements.

■ *Hands-on exercises*

One or more hands-on exercises involving spreadsheets, word processors, and other tools are provided for each chapter.

■ *Longer cases*

A set of six longer cases is provided at the end of the book. These specific cases were chosen because they are interesting and they integrate topics from at least several chapters.

Teaching Supplements

A complete set of teaching supplements is available for instructors who adopt this book. These supplements are designed primarily to enhance the accessibility, versatility, and teachability of the text material.

■ *Instructor's manual*

This supplement was prepared by Professor Linda Behrens of the University of Central Oklahoma. It starts with alternative course syllabi and approaches to teaching with this text. It contains lecture outlines for each chapter, suggestions for teaching each chapter according to the teaching approaches outlined in the introduction, additional study questions, answers to end-of-chapter questions and cases, and transparency masters. These masters are cross-referenced with the lecture notes.

■ *Electronic art masters*

A majority of the book's art has been provided in Adobe Acrobat, along with the Acrobat Reader. Load these electronic masters into your IBM-compatible computer and display them using a screen display device, or print out the image to create conventional transparency masters.

■ *Testbank*

Prepared by Professor William Cummings of Northern Illinois University, the testbank contains 75-100 multiple choice questions per chapter. Each question is labeled as conceptual, definitional, or applied. Each question is also labeled in terms of level of difficulty. The page reference also appears beside each question. An IBM-PC version is also available that gives the instructor the ability to print customized exams.

■ *Videos*

A selection of interesting videos are provided, including the five part series *The Machine that Changed the World*, a compilation of sales demo videos for various products.

▪ Model transaction processing system

This model transaction processing system contains sample transactions, sample standard inquiries, and sample management reports related to the cumulative Custom T-Shirt Case in the text. The system has been created in Microsoft Access.

▪ Internet support

Benjamin/Cummings will provide a variety of supplementary materials via the World Wide Web. Initially, additional real-world cases will be available. Other material that will be available later includes current news, supplementary lecture ideas, and additional cases, exercises, and teaching ideas contributed by users of the book. Instructions for using this Web site will be available from Benjamin/Cummings sales representatives.

Acknowledgments

Many individuals and organizations have contributed to this book, either directly or indirectly. The University of San Francisco supported this book with research assistants, especially Padma Chandrasekaran and Andrea Cunanan. Students in undergraduate, MBA, and executive MBA classes at the University of San Francisco provided an excellent testing ground for both the ideas in this book and the approach for conveying those ideas.

This book benefited greatly from the efforts of many reviewers. Numerous review cycles identified strengths that could be amplified and shortcoming that could be eliminated or minimized. Although it is impossible to respond to every request and answer every criticism (in both books and information systems), and although I am responsible for any confusions or misunderstandings that remain, I did my best to incorporate the many insightful ideas and criticisms provided by the following reviewers:

Linda J. Behrens
University of Central Oklahoma

Harry Benham
Montana State University - Bozeman

Robert Behling
Bryant College

William Cummings
University of Illinois

David Fickbohm
Golden Gate University

Ernest A. Kallman
Bentley College

William Leigh
University of Central Florida

Michael D. Myers
University of Auckland, New Zealand

Leah R. Pietron
University of Nebraska at Omaha

Erik Rolland
University of California

The Benjamin/Cummings Publishing Company, Inc., provided colleagues (and friends) whose professionalism, enthusiasm, and hard work were essential during the lengthy process of writing this book. From the moment he took over this project, Larry Alexander, the senior editor, showed exceptional energy, commitment, and knowledge of both publishing and information systems. Rebecca Johnson, the developmental editor, showed a similar combination of high standards and knowledge. Her analysis of reviews and her detailed comments about chapters were always valuable. Adam Ray, the project manager for production, did exactly what every author hopes a project manager will do. His meticulous organization, knowledge of the subject matter, and mastery of the publishing process made the project flow smoothly. Others who contributed significantly include:

Gary Palmatier, whose attractive book design makes the book easy to use and learn from; Ben Turner Graphics, who translated my sketches into effective artwork; Kelli d'Angona, who found photos that support many important points; Robert Fiske who copy edited the manuscript; Mark Schmidt, Krista Reid-McLaughlin, Karmen Butterer, and Noah Blaustein, who helped coordinate the efforts of the entire team.

Finally, I would like to thank my wife Carol and daughter Emily, who endured yet another lenthy writing process with a totally reasonable number of "never agains." They made me feel guilty, but not too guilty to get the work done. This book is dedicated to Emily because she is wonderful, because I love her, and because it's her turn.

Contents

Chapter 4 Information and Databases   143

Data Modeling 146

Database Management Systems 163

Evaluating Information Used in Business Processes 170

Models as Components of Information Systems 178

Part II: Applications and Impacts of Information Systems   191

Enabling New Forms of Organization, New Ways to Work, and New Ways to Compete 191

II: Understanding the Role of Information Technology   363

Behind the Magic: Basic Ideas Underlying Information Technology   364
Six Basic Functions Performed by Information Technology   364   ■   Representation
of Data and Instructions   364   ■   Translating from Human Intentions to Machine
Instructions   364   ■   Attaining Efficiency and Effectiveness Through Modularity,
Compatibility and Reusability   366   ■   Optimizing Performance Based on Current
Hardware and Software Capabilities   366   ■   Trends and Limitations Related to
"Intelligent" Technology   367

Thinking About Information Technology Performance   367
Difficulty Forseeing the Progress of Technology   370

Chapter 9   Computer Hardware   373

Overview of Computer Systems   376
Basic Model of a Computer System   376   ■   Types of Computers   378   ■
Computer System Architectures   380   ■   The Trend Toward Client-Server
Computing   383

Chapter 7 **Helping Firms Compete through Selling, Pricing, and Product Differentiation**

Part I

Part IV: Planning , Building, and Managing Information Systems   543

Longer Case Studies

About the Author

About the Author of
Information Systems, A Management Approach

Steven Alter is Professor of Information Systems at the University of San Francisco. He holds a B.S. in Mathematics and Ph.D. in Management Science, both from MIT. While on the faculty of the University of Southern California, he revised his Ph.D. thesis and published it as *Decision Support Systems: Current Practice and Continuing Challenges*, one of the first books on this important type of information system. Professor Alter's journal articles have appeared in *Harvard Business Review, Sloan Management Review, MIS Quarterly, Communications of the ACM, TIMS Studies in Management Sciences, Interfaces, Data Processing, Futures,* and *The Futurist.*

Prior to joining the University of San Francisco, he served for eight years as a founding vice president of Consilium, Inc. (CSIM on the NASDAQ stock exchange). His many roles included starting departments for customer service, documentation and training, technical support, and product management. He participated in building and implementing early versions of manufacturing software currently used by major semiconductor manufacturers in the United States, Europe, and Asia. Subsequent product extensions moved these systems into other industries including electronics, pharmaceuticals, specialty chemicals, and aerospace.

Upon returning to academia, Professor Alter decided to work on a problem he observed in industry, the difficulty business people have in articulating what they expect from computerized systems and how these systems can or should change the way work is done. His initial efforts in this area led to the 1992 publication of the first edition of this text. The Preface explains how additional research led to the improvements you will find in this second edition.

When not working, he indulges his love of music by playing cello-piano duets and string quartets. His other hobbies include hiking, skiing, and international travel. Most recently, he celebrated the completion of this manuscript by visiting friends in New Zealand and hiking the Milford Track. He lives in San Francisco with his wife Carol and daughter Emily.

PART I

Basic Ideas for Understanding Information Systems

This text has a very practical purpose: to help you understand information systems from the viewpoint of a **business professional,** a person in a business or government organization who manages other people or performs professional work in fields such as engineering, sales, manufacturing, consulting, and accounting. Understanding information systems from this viewpoint is important to you because personal involvement with information systems is virtually inevitable in today's business world. Many readers will not only use information systems extensively but will also be called on to analyze systems from a business viewpoint, identify their strengths and weaknesses, recommend changes, and participate in their implementation and ongoing improvement.

The four chapters in Part I introduce ideas you or any business professional can use to understand information systems from a business viewpoint. This brief introduction to Chapters 1 through 4 focuses on three major ideas underlying much of what the chapters say:

1. Information systems are systems that use information technology to capture, transmit, store, retrieve, manipulate, or display information used in one or more business processes.

2. Successful information systems help balance six related elements that any business professional can understand from a business viewpoint.

3. Focusing on business processes when thinking about information systems helps business professionals avoid being swept away by technology hype.

This introduction presents these ideas using three diagrams. The first helps define the term *information system.* The second is the work-centered analysis (WCA) framework used throughout the book for understanding systems in business by focusing on the work being done, rather than on the technology. The third shows an information system's location within the WCA framework.

The chapters in Part I explain these ideas in more depth. Chapter 1 uses the WCA framework to organize an overview of seven management challenges this book will help you recognize and respond to during your career. All the book's subsequent chapters contribute to your understanding of one or more of these challenges. Chapter 2 shows how the WCA framework can help organize a business professional's analysis of any business system. Chapter 3 delves more deeply into business processes, the central element in the WCA framework. Chapter 4 takes a similar look at information and databases. Taken together, these chapters are a first step toward being able to analyze an information system from a business professional's viewpoint.

Figure I.1 Information Technology and Information Systems in a Business Context

Information systems are systems that use information technology to capture, transmit, store, retrieve, manipulate, or display information used in one or more business processes. The oval surrounding information systems is light because information systems can sometimes be seen as business processes themselves. Firms consist of interdependent groups of business processes and compete in a business environment.

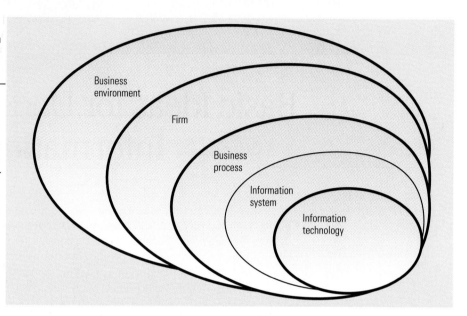

What Is an Information System?

The layers in Figure I.1 illustrate why the term *information system* must be defined along with the terms *information technology* and *business process.* Information systems are systems that use information technology to capture, transmit, store, retrieve, manipulate, or display information used in one or more business processes. Firms consist of groups of business processes and compete in a business environment. More specifically:

- **Information technology** is the hardware and software that make information systems possible. Hardware is the devices and other physical things involved in processing information, such as computers, workstations, physical networks, and data storage and transmission devices. Software is the computer programs that interpret user inputs and tell the hardware what to do. Software includes operating systems, end-user software such as word processors, and application software related to specialized business tasks such as recording credit card transactions or designing automobiles.

- An **information system** is a system that uses information technology to capture, transmit, store, retrieve, manipulate, or display information used in one or more business processes. For example, a department store's bar-code system for collecting data at the point of sale is part of a larger purchasing and distribution system that includes purchasing decisions and physical movement of goods to the stores. Viewed as general-purpose tools, computer programs such as a spreadsheet program or word processing program are not information systems because they do not provide information for specific business processes.

- A **business process** is a related group of steps or activities that use people, information, and other resources to create value for internal or external customers. Business processes consist of steps related in time and place, have a beginning and end, and have inputs and outputs.[1, 2] Examples of business processes in a restaurant include taking orders, cooking food, and preparing a bill. Examples in a factory include manufacturing products, hiring employees, and maintaining equipment. Examples in a doctor's office include making appointments, examining patients, and filling out insurance forms. Each of these business processes consists of a group of related activities that have a beginning and end and have inputs and outputs. Although some business processes such as providing customer service are directed at external customers, many business processes create products or services for internal customers within the organization.

- A **firm** (or government organization) consists of a large number of interdependent business processes that work together to generate products or services in a business environment.

- The **business environment** includes the firm itself and everything else that affects its success, such as competitors, suppliers, customers, regulatory agencies, and demographic, social, and economic conditions.

These terms will be explained in much more depth throughout the book. The key point for now is that information technology has business significance only when it is used as part of an information system that supports at least part of a business process. When people speak about "competing through information technology" what they mean (or what they *should* mean) is "competing through business processes that make especially effective use of information systems that employ information technology."

Framework for Thinking About Any System in Business

A framework is a brief set of ideas for organizing a thought process about a particular type of thing or situation. Any useful framework helps make sense of the world's complexity by identifying topics that should be considered and showing how the topics are related.

Figure I.2 shows a general framework for thinking about business processes and the information systems that support them. We will call this the work-centered analysis (WCA) framework because it is based on the idea that business professionals can and should analyze systems by focusing on the work being done. Work is the application of human and physical resources such as people, equipment, time, effort, and money to generate outputs used by internal or external customers. Work occurs only if product or service outputs are generated for use by internal or external customers.

The WCA framework combines ideas from many sources including total quality management, business process reengineering, and systems theory. It consists of six linked elements:

- The internal or external customers of the business process

- The products (or services) generated by the business process

- The steps in the business process

- The participants in the business process

- The information the business process uses or creates
- The technology the business process uses

Figure I.2 The WCA Framework for Thinking About Any System in Business

The WCA framework consists of six linked elements that can be used for thinking about any information system or other business processes and the information systems that support them.

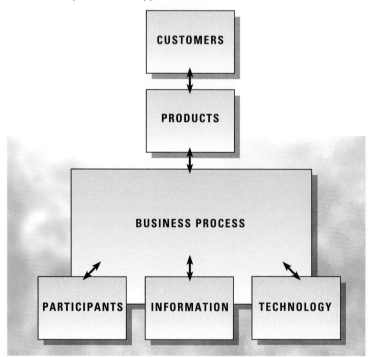

The WCA framework implies that although people sometimes speak of computers as "systems," the system business professionals should focus on is the system performing the work, and this is much broader than just the technology. The WCA framework uses a box to indicate that this system consists of four elements that can be discussed individually: the business process, participants, information, and technology. If processing information plays any role in performing the work, which is almost always the case, part of the system is an information system. Regardless of the role played by its information system components, the system's outputs are the products received and used by its internal or external customers.

All the links in the WCA framework are two-way, implying that the elements should be in balance. For example, the participants should fit the business process, and the product should fit the expectations of the customers. An attempt to automate a collections office demonstrates this need for balance. The long-time manager of collections activities helped system builders design a system that reflected his view of work and eliminated most discretion from the job. A year after the system was in place, turnover had reached almost 100 percent. The new and less educated collectors presented a different set of problems for management and training. Even with the new staff, turnover remained about three times higher than in the rest of the organization.[3]

The two-way links also imply that a change in any area may result in changes in any of the other areas. For example, availability of more powerful technology could affect every other element of the framework. By making more information accessible, the new technology could permit business process changes that in turn affect the skills required of participants and the quality of the product received by the customer.

Except for the arrow connecting customers and products, all the arrows in the diagram are attached to the business process. This implies that the business process is the central focus for a business professional's understanding of a system. If the customer is unhappy with the product, the business process should change. If the participants cannot perform as required, either the business process must change, or they must change through training, motivation, or replacement.

To understand the importance of thinking about "the system" this way, consider an excerpt from a letter written by the admiral who was U.S. Chief of Naval Operations when the U.S.S. Vincennes shot down a civilian Iranian airliner over the Persian Gulf in July 1988 despite using Aegis, the most advanced radar in the world.

> … Contrary to your assertion, Aegis works and it has been so proved. The system, since its introduction, has performed to its full capabilities. More testing has been done on Aegis than on any other system to date. …Other critics, meanwhile, lament that Aegis did not work because it didn't distinguish between the size of an Airbus and the size of an F-14. The fact of the matter is that Aegis is not designed to identify electronically radar contacts by size discrimination.[4]

The admiral viewed "the system" as the Aegis radar and says it performed as designed. But if we think of "the system" as the process of protecting both U.S. military activities and local civilian activities, the system failed, perhaps in part because Aegis could not differentiate between airliners and fighter planes and in part because the user interface was inadequate for the task at hand:

> … The altitude information was not displayed on the main screens, but only on one of various subtables that had to be called up on a smaller screen. There was no indication of rate of change of altitude, not even a choice among ascending, cruising, or descending.[5]

And this interface issue may have been only part of the problem the crew was facing when making a life or death decision for 290 people on the airliner:

> … The crew had been fatigued and stressed by frequent calls to general quarters battle stations. Each time the exhausted crew members went below decks to sleep, another small Iranian patrol boat was spotted carrying potential attackers, and, following combat procedures, again the crew members were called out of their bunks. …Although the radar showed the commercial airliner climbing on a normal flight path, at least one fatigue-stressed CIC [Combat Information Center] operator anxiously and repeatedly told the captain that the "target" was descending.[6]

The decision to fire at a commercial airline resulted from a combination of human, technical, and situational factors. Business professionals thinking about systems need to consider this full range of issues. The WCA framework puts a box around the business process, participants, information, and technology because it views these linked elements as "the system."

Locating the Information System in the Framework

The WCA framework was designed to help business professionals think about any type of business process or system in business, including information systems. When used for thinking about information systems, the framework implies that business professionals should think about the desired business process before they think about the information system supporting that process. Organizations that fail to do this may use information technology to automate a process that is a mess and may end up with nothing more than an automated mess.

But where is the information system in the framework? It may seem surprising that the information system itself is not a separate part of the framework, but this actually makes it easier to think about information systems from a business professional's viewpoint. The framework says the business professional should be thinking about a system that includes a business process, participants, information, and information technology. Within this system, the information system includes the information, the information technology, at least part of the participants' efforts, and at least part of the business process. The information system is therefore the part of the system that happens to use information and information technology. Adopting this viewpoint helps in resisting the tendency to analyze information systems as purely technical systems without regard to why they exist. This tendency is probably one of several key reasons for the ineffectiveness of many information technology applications.

The shaded portions of Figure I.3 separate out the information system in two examples because we still want to know where the information system is in the WCA framework. The first example involves a bank granting student loans and monitoring loan repayments, and the second involves a farm growing crops. Granting and monitoring the loan is mostly processing of information such as identification, qualifications, references, payments, and balance due. Growing crops mostly involves physical action, although it does include some information processing such as recording how much fertilizer is used and monitoring growth during the crop year. The business process for the student loan is information intensive because much of the work involves processing information. The farm uses information, but most of its work in growing the crop is physical work. When a business process is information intensive, most of it is intertwined with an information system.

Note that this discussion has emphasized a business professional's view of the system. In many situations, an information systems (IS) professional would share many of the business professional's concerns but would think about the information system in broader context. For example, an IS professional who builds or maintains the information system for student loans might see the student loan information system as just a part of a larger student-related information system, including applications for admission, payment of fees, and academic records. When working together, business professionals and IS professionals should always recognize that they share some concerns but also have some unique concerns and responsibilities related to their specific roles.

The WCA framework is designed to help business professionals maintain a balanced view emphasizing the issues they truly care about. Attaining this balance is especially important in the light of the hype that accompanies information technology in our society.

Fig. I.3 Identifying an Information System Within a Business Process

The figure uses shading to identify the part of a business process that is actually an information system. The shading shows that the information system is a much larger part of an information intensive business process.

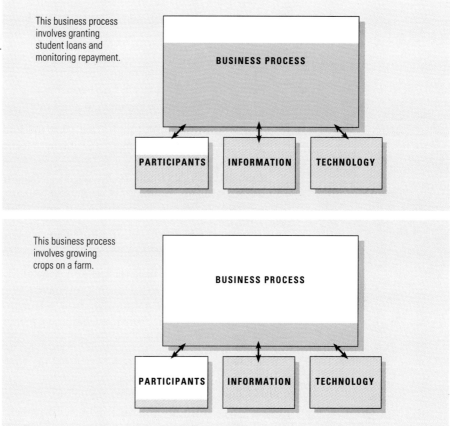

This business process involves granting student loans and monitoring repayment.

This business process involves growing crops on a farm.

Cutting Through Hype and Understanding the Role of Technology

Understanding the true role of technology requires cutting through technology hype. Computer technology has always received more than its share of speculation and hype. In 1952, an early Univac computer used simple statistical methods to "predict" the winner of the presidential election. The next day's newspaper headlines included "Big Electronic Gadget Proves Machines Smarter Than Men."[7] What might have seemed like a giant brain at the time had considerably less computing power than a personal computer you can put in a shopping cart at an office supply store today.

In today's business world, computer mystique has expanded to encompass business and social environments that use computers extensively. Many interesting books, articles, and even advertising supplements to *Business Week* have described the postindustrial society and what businesses must do to succeed in the information age, the age of smart machines, the age of intelligent corporations, the age of total quality, the age of globalization, and the age of continual change and reengineering. Separating hype from reality in these discussions is sometimes difficult, especially since the message is sometimes a loosely disguised infomercial for technology or consulting firms.

Even when no bias is intended, people often exaggerate or misstate the role of technology. "Auto Screws Up" might seem a strange headline for an article about a traffic accident, but here are some examples of what the business press said about computers in 1993 and 1994:

> *Forbes* used "When machines screw up" as the title of an article about a management error, Citicorp's ill-fated decision to sidestep basic loan qualification procedures by using computers to grant mortgages in as little as 15 minutes.[8]

> The *Wall Street Journal* said, "Last year, the budget office said that computer goof-ups were the single biggest problem in its high risk program ..."[9]

> *Business Week* said Deutsche Bundespost Telekom sent a "78 year old pensioner a $10,000 bill for six months of service. Since [her] monthly bill had averaged $35 for the past 18 years, it was clearly a computer error."[10]

> The *San Jose Mercury* said, "Tens of billions in debt owed to the government are uncollectable, experts say, because of slow, inaccurate computers."[11]

> The *New York Times* used "Hopes and Fears of New Computer Organisms" as the title of an article about the first commercial appearance of "intelligent agents," a software technique permitting a user to launch a computerized process that operates through a network to accomplish a preprogrammed task such as making an airplane reservation.[12]

These examples say computers screwed up, goofed up, made errors, were slow and inaccurate, and are becoming organisms. But a careful look at each example would probably show that computers didn't goof up, were neither slow nor inaccurate, and certainly weren't alive. The flaws in business processes were attributed to the computers that probably performed exactly as expected. The real problems were human business decisions related to the design or automation of business processes. Although reporters' misstatements in the face of publication deadlines may not matter very much, they are probably representative of common confusions that make it more difficult to use technology to the fullest.

Another side of the techno-hype problem is the implied or expressed belief that merely having or using the latest information technology makes you smarter. Consider what happened to John Sculley, former CEO of Apple Computer, who wrote in his 1987 biography *Odyssey:* "Technology gives you a good reason not to take anything on faith. Suddenly there is so much information you can almost effortlessly find the facts for your-self. You can explore alternatives. Computing offers you the incentive to become skeptical." But in 1994, Sculley was in court claiming executives at Spectrum Information Technologies had duped him into joining that troubled company. Where was his trusted computer when he was deciding to leave Apple and join Spectrum?[13]

One of this book's goals is to help you see information technology and information systems for what they really are: powerful, valuable tools, but not magic. When applied thoughtfully, these tools can bring important benefits for individuals, organizations, and customers. When misapplied, they can waste tremendous amounts of time, effort, and money.

KEY TERMS

business professional   business process
information technology   firm
information system   business environment

REFERENCES

1. Harrington, H. J. *Business Process Improvement.* New York: McGraw-Hill, 1991.

2. Davenport, Thomas H. *Process Improvement: Reengineering Work through Information Technology.* Boston: Harvard Business School Press, 1993.

3. Zuboff, Shoshanna. "New Worlds of Computer-Mediated Work." *Harvard Business Review*, Sept.–Oct. 1982, pp. 142–152.

4. Trost, C. A. H. "Aegis Has Performed to Its Fullest." *Letter to Editor, New York Times*, Dec. 22, 1988.

5. Neumann, Peter. "Aegis, Vincennes, and the Iranian Airbus." *ACM Sigsoft: Software Engineering Notes*, Vol. 14, No. 5, July 1989, p. 20.

6. Moore-Ede, Martin. *The Twenty-Four-Hour Society: Understanding Human Limits in a World That Never Stops.* Reading, Mass.: Addison-Wesley, 1993, pp. 3–4.

7. Palfreman, Jon, and Doron Swade. *The Dream Machine: Exploring the Computer Age.* London: BBC Books, 1991.

8. "When Machines Screw Up," *Forbes*, June 7, 1993, pp. 110–111.

9. Davis, Bob. "Uncle Sam's Progress: High-Tech Proves to Be High Risk." *Wall Street Journal*, Apr. 12, 1993, p. B3.

10. Levine, Jonathan B. "The Continent's Wake-Up Call." *Business Week*, Dec. 20, 1993, pp. 96–98.

11. Greve, Frank. "Computer Morass Hobbles U.S." *San Jose Mercury*, Mar. 16, 1993, p. A1.

12. Markoff, John. "Hopes and Fears on New Computer Organisms." *New York Times*, Jan. 6, 1994, p. C1.

13. Darlin, Damon. "Absentminded Skeptic." *Forbes*, Mar. 28, 1994, p. 20.

1

System-Related Challenges for Business Professionals

Study Questions

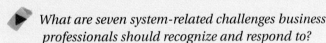

What are seven system-related challenges business professionals should recognize and respond to?

What trends in business processes pose competitive challenges for many firms?

What is total quality management?

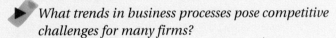

What technological trends have created opportunities for business innovation in the past and promise to do so for the near future?

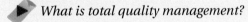

What are some of the special characteristics and enigmas of information?

In what ways do information systems depend on people?

How are infrastructure and context either enablers or obstacles for information systems?

What are the phases of any information system and the alternative system development processes?

Automatic teller machines (ATMs) are common today, but they have been used extensively during only the last 15 years. With current ATMs, depositors can perform common transactions almost any time without going into a bank and waiting for a teller. Externally, an ATM system is a cash dispenser and depository controlled through simple choices the customer keys into a terminal. Behind the terminal, an extensive information system authorizes the transaction, updates customer records, and monitors the ATM itself. Without this type of online system, the business strategy of providing more convenient access to customers and eliminating tellers from simple transactions would have been impossible.

The technology of ATMs grew out of automatic cash machines first developed in Europe and Japan. Chemical Bank installed the first magnetic strip ATM on Long Island, New York, in 1969 and had 39 ATMs in the field by 1975. The initial system was basically a cash machine. It had many problems with fraud because the ATMs were not linked to central computers until 1974 for instant updates of account information.

Citibank studied the pioneering work of other banks and implemented a network of around 500 ATMs in the New York City area in the late 1970s. With its full-service teller machines and special safety enclosures permitting the customer to withdraw money any time of the day or night, the system probably cost at least $250 million. Citibank promoted its ATMs with the slogan "The Citi never sleeps." Thanks to ATMs, Citibank tripled its depositors from 1978 to 1987, increasing its local consumer market share from 4.5 to 13 percent.[1, 2] But other New York banks responded to Citibank by banding together to produce their own network, New York Cash Exchange, or NYCE, which began operations in 1985. Eventually, several national ATM networks permitted people to withdraw money from ATMs in all major cities in the United States and some cities abroad. In 1994, Citibank quietly joined NYCE, whose debit card capabilities enabled customers to transfer money directly from their accounts for purchases at gas stations and supermarkets.[3]

Despite the widespread use of ATMs, ATM fraud has remained a significant problem. PINs (personal identification numbers) provide some security but do not deter pickpockets if the ATM card's owner wrote the PIN on the card. Technically sophisticated thieves have stolen account numbers and PINs by intercepting electronic transmissions between ATMs and central computers. In one unusual case in 1993, a phony ATM machine was placed at a mall near Hartford, Connecticut. It was on wheels, looked temporary, and gave out nothing but apologetic receipts saying that no transactions were possible. But it recorded the customer's ATM card number and PIN number. Using these stolen identifiers, thieves produced counterfeit bank cards and used them to steal at least $50,000.[4] To reduce problems related to PINs, AT&T started testing a voice recognition system for ATMs in mid-1993.[5]

Things sometimes go wrong with ATMs even without fraud because there are many possible points of failure, including the machine itself, the central computer, and the network connecting the ATM to the computer, which could be virtually anywhere. In 1993, customers of 5,000 ATM machines in Texas, Illinois, California, and elsewhere couldn't use them for a week because heavy snows collapsed the roof of the Electronic Data Systems data center in New Jersey.[6] And in 1994, a single incorrect instruction in a computer program caused Chemical Bank's ATM system to subtract each customer withdrawal twice, affecting customers who had withdrawn around $15 million in 150,000 individual withdrawal transactions from Tuesday night through Wednesday afternoon.[7]

DEBATE TOPIC   *Argue the pros and cons and practical implications of the following proposition:*
Businesses and their customers should act as though information systems cannot be trusted.

THIS CASE ABOUT **ATMs** exemplifies many of the issues and concerns stressed throughout this book. ATMs represent a comparatively new technology that has gone from an experiment to an essential business service in fewer than 20 years. Customers take these systems for granted and rely on them. Competitors in consumer banking view them as a competitive necessity. Yet they still fail occasionally despite the great care that banks take in improving these systems and maintaining their reliability.

Figure 1.1 Citibank: Using Automatic Teller Machines

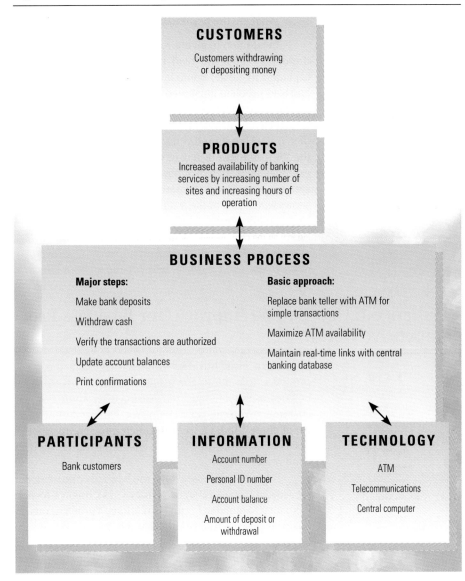

CUSTOMERS

Customers withdrawing or depositing money

PRODUCTS

Increased availability of banking services by increasing number of sites and increasing hours of operation

BUSINESS PROCESS

Major steps:

Make bank deposits

Withdraw cash

Verify the transactions are authorized

Update account balances

Print confirmations

Basic approach:

Replace bank teller with ATM for simple transactions

Maximize ATM availability

Maintain real-time links with central banking database

PARTICIPANTS

Bank customers

INFORMATION

Account number

Personal ID number

Account balance

Amount of deposit or withdrawal

TECHNOLOGY

ATM

Telecommunications

Central computer

This introductory chapter presents an initial summary of key issues raised through-out the book. It does this by identifying and briefly discussing seven management challenges that business professionals face directly or are affected by in their work.

1. How can we improve our business processes in today's competitive world?

2. How can we benefit from technical trends and innovations?

3. How can we achieve maximum benefit from information?

4. How can we extend our human skills and motivate our people?

5. How can we make the most of the surrounding infrastructure and context?

6. How can we recognize and respond to common system-related risks?

7. What are the best business processes for building and maintaining our systems?

In addition to giving you a feeling for the types of issues you will understand more thoroughly after you read this book, this chapter introduces some of the concepts explained in greater depth in every chapter that follows. Doing this helps with a "chicken and egg" problem illustrated by the two-way arrows in the WCA framework presented in the Part I introduction. In combination, those two-way arrows indicate that you can't real-ly understand an information system until you understand something about every aspect of it. But where should you start? This chapter introduces ideas about all six elements of the WCA framework (customers, products, business processes, and so on) plus other essential ideas such as infrastructure, risks, and processes for building and maintaining systems. A small representation of the WCA framework at the beginning of each section shows which part of the framework the section pertains to most directly.

Building on the challenges and examples cited in this chapter, Chapter 2 will show how the WCA framework can be used to organize a business professional's analysis of any specific information system. In terms of an overused analogy, Chapter 1 is a tour of the forest, and Chapter 2 tells you more about how to look at an individual tree.

Challenge 1: How Can We Improve Our Business Processes in Today's Competitive World?

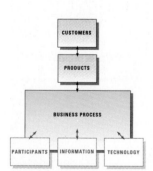

More than ever, business professionals face the challenge of improving business processes to produce the results internal or external customers want. The way many businesses operated just ten years ago, we could easily imagine they were telling their customers "You can get it cheap, you can get it right, or you can get it fast, but you can't get all three." Today's world is much more competitive. Most firms find it increasingly necessary to provide what the customer wants when the customer wants it and at a good price.

Business processes form the basis of competition. A firm's products and services are viewed by customers in terms of cost, quality, responsiveness, reliability, and con-formance to standards and regulations. These characteristics are a direct result of the business process that produces them.

In 1982, this was brought home in an unpleasant way to Xerox, the copier indus-try leader. It discovered that Japanese competitors were selling small copiers in the U.S. market for less than Xerox's manufacturing cost. During the 1980s, Xerox had to change its entire way of doing business to regain its competitive edge.[8] Xerox was not alone. By the early 1990s, major companies such as General Motors, IBM, and Sears were struggling visibly to compete and survive in a rapidly changing business climate. It was not at all obvious that these firms could change their business processes fast enough to continue their decades of success.

To appreciate the theme of improving business processes in a competitive world, we will look at three important trends: global competition, new ways to do business, and total quality management. These trends call for thinking about information systems as an integral part of the way businesses operate, not as an isolated set of technical tools.

Global Competition

Today's business environment is characterized by a trend toward global competition involving competitors anywhere in the world. The geographic proximity of businesses and their customers was more important in the past than it is today. Although proximity still matters to dry cleaners and pizza delivery businesses, direct competitors in many manufacturing, distribution, and service industries may be virtually anywhere in the world (see Figure 1.2).

Global competition even applies at a personal level because information technology makes it possible to bring many types of work to the workers instead of bringing the workers to the work. Wages at the Texas Instruments programming group in Bangalore, India, are low enough that work is done at half of American costs even after the cost of telecommunications. Metropolitan Life's 150 workers in County Cork, Ireland, analyze medical insurance claims forms using knowledge from 18 weeks of training on medicine, the American medical system, and the insurance business. In Jamaica, 3,500 workers connected to the United States by satellite dishes make airline reservations, handle calls to toll-free numbers, and enter data into computer systems.[9] All these jobs involve people who can be considered competitors by Americans capable of doing the same work. Working with programmers on the other side of the globe was once impractical. Today, communication technology has reduced the difficulty of working at a distance.

Figure 1.2 Example of Global Competition

These programmers in India are translating software into Japanese for the American company Digital Equipment Corporation.

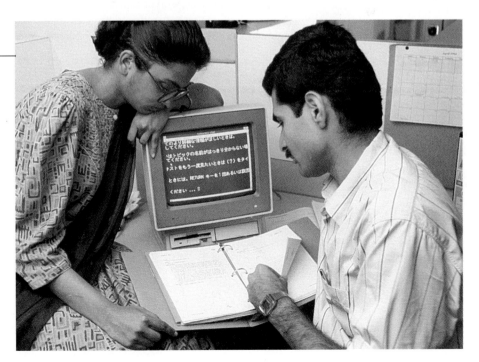

New Ways to Do Business

Many observers of business in the 1980s and 1990s say that the nature of business is changing. New combinations of products and services are appearing; the limitations of geography and time are disappearing; technology is changing rapidly; organizations are becoming flatter and less hierarchical.

New types of products and services

Our contemporary society is often referred to as an **information economy** or age of information or postindustrial society. At the simplest level, this means that more of what people produce is related to information than to physical goods. There is a trend toward increasing the **information content of products,** the degree to which the value of products resides in information rather than in physical objects. As manufacturing becomes more automated, it is increasingly divided between two phases. First is a design phase, which creates a computerized description of the product. Next is a manufacturing phase, which uses the computerized description directly. Since information is easier to change than physical things, manufacturers try to keep the product in the form of information as long as possible into the manufacturing process. As production moves in this direction, more of the value of what is produced is contained in the information needed for production. This trend has swept other areas of manufacturing ranging from automobiles and construction to pharmaceuticals and clothing.

The trend toward feeding product description information into automated factories is gradually changing the logic of both manufacturing and service businesses. When Henry Ford built the first mass-produced automobiles, he told customers they could have any color they wanted as long as it was black. The current trend is toward **mass customization,** the use of mass production techniques to produce customized products or services. It is an attempt to retain the advantages of mass production while providing value related to customization. From the producer's viewpoint, the product or service is mass produced; from the consumer's viewpoint, it is customized. Figure 1.3 shows an example of mass customization. Building these customized bicycles takes 3 hours instead of 90 minutes for a standard bicycle, but profits are much higher than for standard bicycles.[10]

Figure 1.3 A New Way to Build a Bicycle

A subsidiary of Matsushita uses an information system to build customized bicycles in Japan. (a) This photo shows the session in which the customized dimensions of the bicycle are determined. (b) These measurements are entered into a special computer-aided design (CAD) system that creates a diagram that is transmitted directly to the factory.

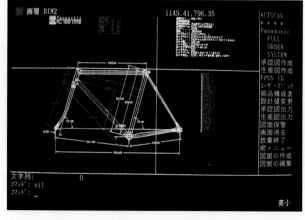

Conquering distance and time

Stanley Davis coined the phrase "any place, any time" to describe the way today's businesses have used information technology and more effective organization to provide what the customer wants, where the customer wants it, and when the customer wants it. Aside from producing what the customer wants, the challenge here is to conquer distance (where the customer wants it) and time (when the customer wants it).

The role of telecommunications in publishing national newspapers such as *USA Today* and the *Wall Street Journal* is an example of how companies have conquered distance. Instead of printing these newspapers in one location and shipping them across the country, publishers use telecommunications to transmit the content and layout of each edition to publishing plants near customers in major metropolitan areas. This is an example of keeping the product in the form of information as long as possible before giving it a physical form.

Businesses have tried to conquer time by slashing both the time to design a product and the time to manufacture it, often by more than 50 percent. This improvement came from reorganizing work flows, removing unnecessary bureaucracy, and using information technology to eliminate redundant work and speed up the necessary work. For example, computer-aided design (CAD) systems can use computerized drawings and parts lists for the previous version of a product as the starting point for designing the next version. Designs may be tested using computerized simulation models to avoid the delay and expense of building physical models or prototypes. On completion, some designs may be transmitted to the factory in a form that can immediately drive numerically controlled machine tools.

Thanks to information systems that track and coordinate sales, inventory, and orders, inventories have been slashed 50 percent or more in both manufacturing and distribution. The enabling technology includes bar coding to identify individual items

Figure 1.4 Automating the Work of Telephone Operators

In telephone systems of the 1930s, switchboard operators at telephone company offices and customer offices plugged in wires to connect telephone calls. Some "experts" thought the number of telephones in society was fundamentally limited by the number of telephone operators who could be hired.

and prevent data errors; data communications to consolidate the information from multiple locations; and rapid computing to convert the raw data into new orders, scheduled receipts, projected shortages, and other information needed to support customer demand with minimal inventory levels. Some economists believe that such tight inventory control even helped flatten the traditional business cycle, which was driven by excessive inventory buildups during periods of high demand followed by nationwide production slowdowns and layoffs when inventories got too high.[11]

Automation of work

Automation is the use of machines to perform tasks that people would otherwise do. Throughout business and society, work is becoming more automated and less labor intensive. This trend has varied effects on people, business, and society (see Figure 1.4).

The science fiction image of automation as something done by a humanlike robot is a far cry from the reality of automation today. Understanding automation requires looking at the particular types of automated tasks. These can be divided into tasks directed at information (such as capturing, transmitting, storing, retrieving, and displaying information) versus tasks directed at physical objects (such as transporting, fabricating, and assembling).

Using computers to automate office work has eliminated many inefficient tasks such as retyping whole pages of a document to insert a few changes. This was accomplished by substituting computerized systems for paper as the primary storage medium and using paper as a display medium. Computerized information systems have automated certain parts of standard business functions such as accounting and purchasing while often creating a more systematic, accurate, and effective way to do things.

Automation in factories has had a dual impact. It has automated the processing of information related to accounting, inventory, quality, manufacturing specifications, and factory communications. In addition, it has automated tasks directed at physical objects. Most of the physical production tasks automated thus far are repetitious, dirty, or dangerous. Examples include welding, spray painting, fabricating metal parts, and assembling circuit boards. Although the trend toward automation is strong in both offices and factories, office automation has progressed faster because office work is so information intensive.

New ways to organize a business

Most large businesses, governments, military forces, and even major religions have traditionally been organized hierarchically. Functions were divided among departments or other groupings based on geography (eastern region versus western region), time (day shift versus night shift), or the type of tasks being performed (manufacturing department versus sales department). Decisions were made at the highest levels and filtered down to the ranks. In this model, much of the interaction and communication occurs in narrow groups within departments.

Forms of organization are changing rapidly because of a combination of successful alternatives and new information technology. Although writers have mentioned new organizational forms for several decades, the competitive need for less hierarchy became apparent with the market success of Japanese companies that were only six layers deep, compared to 12 for some U.S. companies. Flattening the organization became part of a common strategy to avoid delays, respond to customers, bring quality products to the market, and reduce overhead.

Information systems are important tools in the process of organizational downsizing. Readily accessible databases of performance data and other corporate data permit automatic consolidation and summarization of operating results for top managers. Along with competitive pressures and a general movement to give more responsibility to workers, this may cut middle management ranks by 50 percent.

Information systems also change the way people think about the boundaries separating their organization from other organizations. For example, consider the way Milliken, a supplier of fiber products such as towels and rugs, changed the nature of its relationship to some of its retailers. Milliken told the retailers, "If you send us the daily orders for area rugs that you get from the consumer, we will manufacture the rugs and ship them directly to the consumer's home." This gave retailers more incentive to sell Milliken's products because the retailers could reduce their costs by eliminating part of their distribution centers and limiting their inventory to the display items in the showroom.[12]

Total Quality Management

Increasing competition throughout the world has forced most businesses to look at the quality of their products and services. This was especially true in the United States, where many American consumers started to believe (correctly or not) that foreign products had higher quality than corresponding American products.

Although people agree that quality is a crucial competitive issue, quality experts disagree on its definition. Some say that quality is conformance to the engineering specification of what the product or service should be. Viewed this way, quality can be measured as deviations from specifications or as defect rates. Others say that quality is customer satisfaction and that quality can be measured only in terms of the customer's perception. Even with disagreement about the definition of quality, many companies are pursuing total quality management as part of their competitive strategy.

Total quality management (**TQM**) is a business strategy based on three general principles: customer focus, process improvement, and total involvement.[13] The idea of TQM is to identify, analyze, and improve the processes that directly or indirectly create value for the customer. Looking at the three principles more carefully helps us see why few businesses follow TQM wholeheartedly even though the idea of TQM may seem obvious.

Customer focus. Every process in a business has customers, whether **internal customers** (within the firm) or **external customers** (outside the firm). Customer focus means thinking of business processes as ways to satisfy customers by meeting their stated or unstated expectations. Often this is not what happens. Consider what happened when a patient called a medical clinic to schedule minor surgery. The clinic's next available date was about a month away but on a date the patient was unavailable. The patient asked for a date in the following month but was told the clinic didn't schedule that far in advance and to call back next month.[14] This scheduling process may have simplified scheduling tasks inside the clinic, but it certainly didn't satisfy the customer.

Process improvement. Every process can be improved by gathering and using information about how each step is performed and how the steps operate together. The TQM philosophy calls for **continuous improvement** of processes, never being satisfied and always looking for ways to do the work better and produce better outputs. This contradicts the traditional, comfortable idea of being satisfied by meeting performance standards (such as answering 16 phone calls per hour or finding three defective parts per day). Some observers also distinguish between continuous and discontinuous improvement. They view continuous improvement as fine-tuning an existing process, whereas **discontinuous improvement** is totally changing a process. This book contains many examples of both types.

Total involvement. Total quality management requires attention and commitment from everyone in the firm. Making everyone in a firm genuinely responsible for quality requires empowerment of employees. **Empowerment** means giving employees the information, tools, and authority to do their work effectively and to suggest and make changes that improve quality. Truly empowering employees often changes the relationship between employees and their managers. Instead of just following orders, totally involved employees question the way things are done and look for ways to improve how they are done.

TQM principles are easy to state but difficult to instill. Ingrained ideas about the differing roles of management and workers are obstacles to total quality management. Many leading organizations view issues related to these themes as one of their principal challenges. Companies such as General Electric and Xerox have spent years moving toward total quality management.

REALITY CHECK   **The Challenge of Improving Business Processes in a Competitive World**   In this section, we identified global competition, new ways to do business, and total quality management as three aspects of the process improvement challenge to many businesses.

1. Explain why it is or is not likely that you will personally compete for jobs against people who live in other countries.

2. Explain whether any of the new ways of doing business affect you personally as a customer of current businesses.

3. Explain what difference it would make (or has made) if an active TQM program were instituted in an organization you belong to or work for, such as a club, sports team, church, or business.

Challenge 2: How Can We Benefit from Technical Trends and Innovations?

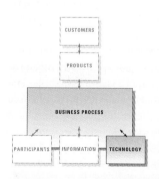

Since the 1960s, key characteristics of computer hardware technologies such as price, reliability, and density have been improving at a rate of 30 to 50 percent per year.[15] Even at a rate of 20 percent, the equivalent of hardware capabilities costing $100 in 1960 would have cost $10.74 in 1970, $1.15 in 1980, and $0.12 in 1990. If automotive technology had improved at that rate since 1960, a new car would cost less than a ticket to a football game, and we could drive across the United States on less than a gallon of gasoline (if gasoline were still used). Most experts believe the current rate of improvement will continue at least through the end of the century.

Technological accomplishments have little meaning for business, however, unless they can be linked to business innovation. The challenge for business professionals is to find ways to improve business processes by using technical innovations. Portable computers, portable telephones, and fax machines are all examples of technologies business professionals have applied successfully in important business innovations in the last decade. Each of these examples demonstrates aspects of trends we will look at next.

Greater Miniaturization, Speed, and Portability

The increasing speed and power of electronic components is the force underlying the immense progress to date in computers and telecommunications. These increases result directly from **miniaturization**, the process of creating smaller electronic components with greater capabilities. Miniaturization of computers started when the solid-state transistor (an on–off device that can represent a 1 or 0) superseded the vacuum tube (an older on–off device). It exploded with the 1959 invention of the **integrated circuit,** a device incorporating multiple transistors on a single silicon chip the size of a fingernail. Integrated circuits were smaller, used less electricity, and were more reliable because they replaced many separate parts that previously had to be wired together (see Figure 1.5).

Figure 1.5 Comparison of a Vacuum Tube and an Integrated Circuit

(a)The first general-purpose computer contained thousands of vacuum tubes, each of which represented a single on–off switch. (b)This Intel Pentium microprocessor contains complex logical circuitry along with the equivalent of 3.2 million transistors.

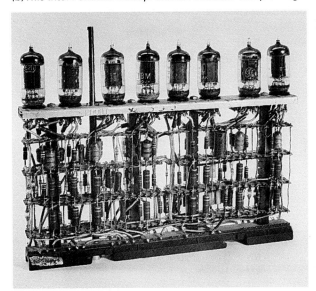

The degree of progress that has occurred through miniaturization of electronic components is difficult to imagine because it defies our normal experience. Normally, back-to-back improvements of 10 percent or 15 percent are viewed as significant achievements. In contrast, Table 1.1 shows that the capacity of computer memory chips has doubled approximately every 18 months for the last 20 years and will probably continue to do so through the year 2000. Four megabit memory chips containing the equivalent of 4 million transistors are commonplace, with 256 megabit chips likely to be available by the year 2000. And this is just one of many aspects of the technical progress that has occurred.

Speed and reliability improvements from miniaturization permitted the development of current computers, VCRs, fax machines, bar code scanners, cellular phones, telephone switches, fiber-optic phone cables, and many other types of information technology. The current rate of progress implies that raw computing power in the year 2000 could be 100 times cheaper than it was in 1990.

The miniaturization of electronic components plus advances in communication technology led to much greater **portability** of computer and communications devices. Devices are portable when their users can carry them around conveniently. Previous generations of computers and telephones were far from portable since early computers required specially air-conditioned rooms, and telephones were anchored in place by wire connections. Just being able to store hundreds of pages of data on a pocket-sized diskette was an important step toward portability, even if the computer remained anchored in place. Today, the equivalent of hundreds of diskettes can be stored on a single CD-ROM.

Although large computers and major telephone installations are still in fixed locations, today's individual users have many choices of portable devices. The first common portable computers were laptops, which business professionals could carry conveniently for use on airplanes and other locations away from the office (see Figure 1.6). Pen computers that look like tablets and have no keyboards are another approach to portability. They permit computer use for certain types of tasks by people who move around continually. Examples include the computers used by parcel delivery drivers for receipt confirmations and those used by field technicians to record residential usage of gas and electricity. Portable telephones demonstrate that telephones no longer must be anchored by wires.

This trend toward portability brings great convenience but also makes it much more difficult to control the flow of information. A single diskette in a person's pocket can contain a company's entire customer list; the hard disk in a laptop computer can store much more information. Risks created by portability are evident from what happened when someone stole a laptop computer from a car parked for five minutes in downtown London in late 1990. The car belonged to a wing commander in Great Britain's Royal Air Force. The laptop contained some of General Schwartzkopf's plans for attacking Iraq. (The commander was court-martialed, demoted, and fined. The computer was returned anonymously a week later.)[18]

Table 1.1 Progress in Memory Chip Capacity Since 1973

For each type of chip up to 1994, the date given is one or two years after its commercial introduction but before its sales peaked and started to decline as the next generation came into use. The date was estimated by combining data on product introductions and product sales patterns.[16, 17] (The term kilobit *refers to approximately 1,000 bits since a kilobit chip actually contains 1,024 on–off units. Similarly, a megabit chip actually contains 1,024 times 1,024 bits.)*

Approximate Date of Widespread Commercial Availability	Type of Chip	Capacity in Number of Bits
1973	1 kilobit	1,024
1976	4 kilobit	4,096
1979	16 kilobit	16,384
1982	64 kilobit	65,536
1985	256 kilobit	262,144
1988	1 megabit	1,048,576
1991	4 megabit	4,194,304
1994	16 megabit	16,777,216
1997	64 megabit	67,108,864
2000	256 megabit	268,435,456

Figure 1.6 Using a Portable Computer to Give Parking Tickets

The portable computer permits the officer to write legible parking tickets and automatically update the city's database of unpaid tickets.

Greater Connectivity and Continuing Convergence of Computing and Communications

Connectivity is the ability to transmit data between devices at different locations. Increasingly, computerized data can be transmitted almost instantaneously nearly anywhere in the world. The scope of connectivity includes interactive communication between people, electronic mail, transmittal of faxes, and transmission of business data between computers. Connectivity is important to businesses because it reduces some of the disadvantages of being separated geographically. It also makes it easier to obtain important business information, much of which comes from outside sources, such as customers and suppliers.

Connectivity means more than just transmitting a signal from one place to another, however. Since many organizations often own hardware and software from a variety of vendors, true connectivity often depends on the ability of these heterogeneous components to work together conveniently and inexpensively, which is often called **interoperability.** Software products that perform the same or complementary functions are often rated in terms of interoperability. For example, the interoperability of two word processing programs is determined by the extent to which a document produced using one word processor looks the same and is handled the same way when it is displayed by another word processor, perhaps on a different type of computer. In this case, interoperability requires compatible internal coding of data, compatible program logic, compatible user interfaces, and compatible communication with storage devices and printers.[19]

The need for connectivity and interoperability has generated customer demand for **open systems,** systems that use clearly described, nonproprietary industry standards available to anyone. Hardware and software buyers insisted on the movement toward open systems, which make it easier to switch hardware or software brands without complete system overhaul. Many hardware and software suppliers have tried to resist because they see open systems as a direct threat to their strategy of providing unique, incompatible capabilities that lock in customers by making brand switching difficult.

Continuing trends toward connectivity and interoperability provide a range of opportunities to compete more effectively. Within the firm, these trends make it easier and cheaper to build information systems and transmit data. Reducing these costs makes it more practical to use information systems to help people work together and to link more effectively with customers.

Greater connectivity supports the continuing **convergence of computing and communications,** whereby communication capabilities became essential to many computer systems, and computing capabilities became essential to communication systems (see Figure 1.8). Consider the way salespeople at many firms use touch-tone telephones to obtain pricing information and enter orders. In these systems, a telephone becomes a data entry terminal for an information system. Similarly, companies deploying computers in branch offices often require communication networks to perform companywide computing tasks such as consolidating results and sharing data. Even within a single building, wireless data transmission between computers can make work more effective (see Figure 1.7). As the overlaps between computing and communications became more apparent, companies combined their previously separate computer and communications staffs to manage this convergence.

Figure 1.7 Example of the Convergence of Computing and Communications

This mechanic is using a portable computer to record information and wireless data transmission to send it to a central database.

Figure 1.8 Convergence of Computing and Communications

The convergence of computing and telecommunications sprang from separate innovations related to telegraphs (1794), telephones (1876), radio broadcasting (1906), television broadcasting (1925), and computers (around 1945). Existing combinations of computers and telecommunications will continue to evolve into new applications in the future.

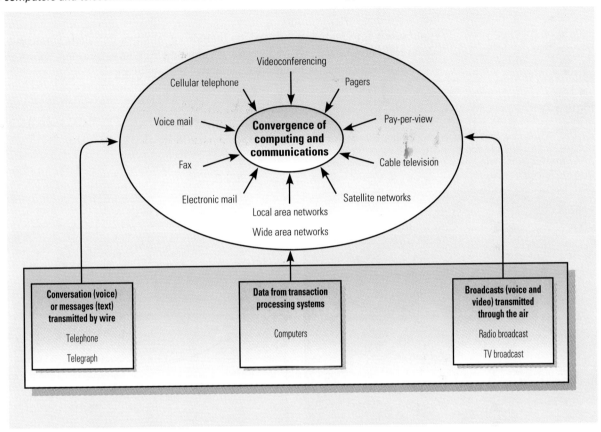

Greater Use of Digitized Information and Multimedia

Information exists in five different forms—formatted data, text, pictures, sounds, and video (sequences of pictures and sound), each of which can be digitized. **Digitization** involves coding the data as an equivalent or approximately equivalent set of numbers. For example, the letters in the word *cab* might be coded 33-31-32 if the coding rule were to add 30 to the position of each letter in the alphabet. Likewise, a picture can be digitized by dividing it into tiny dots on a grid and assigning a number to represent the color and intensity of the dot. Since any type of data can be digitized, any type of data can be stored, manipulated, and transmitted by computerized systems.

The method used to digitize pictures and sounds originally limited the feasibility of processing these types of data on computers. The problem was that digitized pictures and sounds require much more storage and transmission capability than pure text. All the text in this book can be stored on several pocket-sized diskettes, but a single high-resolution photograph could require a similar amount of storage because each square inch of it might be represented by the same quantity of data as an entire chapter of text.

Advances in miniaturization and speed of electronic components made large-scale use of digitized data affordable. These advances started solving the problem by providing processing speeds and storage capacities needed to store, manipulate, and transmit pictures and sounds over telephone lines. This made widespread use of fax machines and videoconferencing economically feasible (see Figure 1.9). These advances also made the extensive use of multimedia feasible. **Multimedia** is the use of multiple types of data within the same application. The first steps toward multimedia involved things such as combining drawing software with word processors. Some current applications for creating presentations include capabilities to handle photographs, sound clips, and video clips. Multimedia is emerging from its infancy and shows great promise for education, entertainment, and business applications.

Figure 1. 9 Applications of Digitized Information

(a) This videoconference relies on technology that digitizes pictures and sounds and transmits the digitized information to remote locations where it is displayed on screens and through loudspeakers.

(b) This computer is being used to produce a multimedia document.

Better Software Techniques and Interfaces with People

The first computerized systems were difficult to develop and use. Today, millions of workers use desktop computers interactively even though they may know little about computer technology. Information is accessible through interactive terminals that can show text and graphics. Interactive techniques for entering and requesting data exist in both business application systems such as inventory and purchasing and end-user tools such as spreadsheets and word processors. Instead of mastering complicated computer languages, users of well-designed systems can often specify new outputs they need by pointing and filling in blanks (see Figure 1.10).

Major advances in the programming languages and techniques for developing programs made these dramatic improvements possible. These advances generally involve permitting programmers (or users) to specify what they want the computer to accomplish rather than every detail of how the computer should store, retrieve, and manipulate the data. The software advances themselves were made possible by the improvements in miniaturization and speed that made computers much more powerful. For example, current spreadsheets contain graphing and analysis features that simply could not operate on early personal computers. Even though we don't know exactly how computers will be used in the future, ongoing advances in both hardware and software make it safe to predict that they will be even easier to use than they are today.

Figure 1.10 Which Interface Is Easier to Use?

Compare the two user interfaces. The one on the left forces the user to remember the files by name, and the names are limited to 8 characters in length. The one on the right permits the user to select the required file, and the filenames are up to 32 characters in length. Which one would you find easier to use?

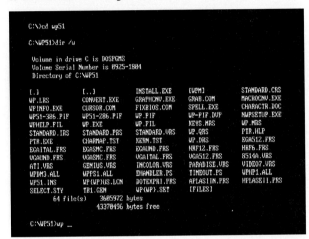
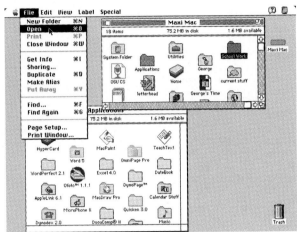

More, but Still Limited, "Intelligence" Built into Devices

For hundreds of years, people have been fascinated by the possibility of building intelligent machines. Despite the enormous progress that has occurred, and despite the hoopla about artificial intelligence, computerized systems are still quite limited. All they can do is follow detailed instructions from people. If a person cannot specify exactly how a task should be done, a computer cannot do it.

The most basic issue is that no one knows how to build genuine understanding and common sense into computerized systems. Even when programmers include every rule, exception, and special case that they and the users can think of, something may still be missing. The system may respond incorrectly or even disastrously when it encounters an unanticipated or poorly understood situation or interaction of factors. When people process information, they usually exercise common sense about what they do and do not understand. When an unanticipated situation arises, they can recognize it as such and respond accordingly. Figure 1.12 represents the difference between human intelligence and what computers can do.

Currently, there is little evidence that programmers will be able to build common sense into computers within the next few decades. Therefore, although computers will be easier to use, any appearance that they are intelligent will probably be superficial. Users will have to be vigilant, remembering that they still own the responsibility for whatever computers produce.

REALITY CHECK **The Challenge of Finding Benefits from Information Technology** In this section, we cited a number of technical trends that enable business innovations.

1. Explain how some of the technical innovations cited have affected you in your everyday life.

2. Identify some of the ways continuation of these trends might affect you in the next five years.

Figure 1.11 Comparing Human Intelligence with What Computers Can Do

Computers are being incorporated into what were previously totally mechanical devices such as coffee makers and automobile brakes. Techniques for interpreting information such as voice and handwriting are being extended. More applications are being developed that handle many types of data. Despite these developments, computerized systems do not yet demonstrate common sense or understanding.

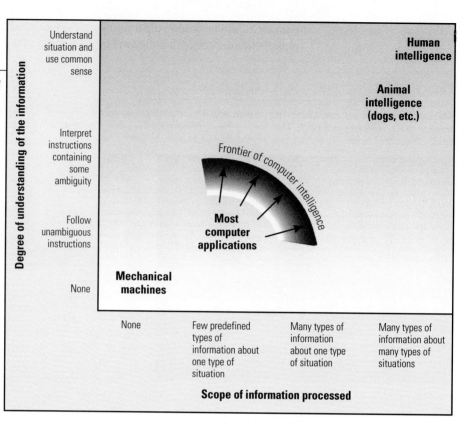

Challenge 3: How Can We Achieve Maximum Benefit from Information?

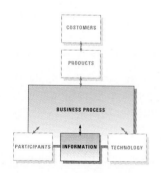

We often take information for granted, but it is an important determinant of how effectively business processes operate. When General Gordon Sullivan, Army Chief of Staff, looked for improvements following the successful military effort in the 1991 Persian Gulf War, he found that 40,000 tractor-trailer-sized containers had arrived in Saudi Arabia with no identifying information. It was necessary to open each container just to find out whether it contained tires, generators, or something else. In addition, there were many over-shipments because supply sergeants traditionally order everything three times in the expectation that two requisitions will go astray in unmarked containers. No more. From now on, containers are bar-coded to list their contents, and sensors signal their location using satellites.[20]

Since business processes depend on information, it is important to recognize some of its special characteristics. We start with the distinction between data, information, and knowledge.

Data, Information, and Knowledge

The distinction between data, information, and knowledge is important for understanding what information systems do and why they are sometimes ineffective. Figure 1.12 shows that data form the basis of information and that knowledge is needed to use information. **Data** are facts, images, or sounds that may or may not be pertinent or useful for a particular task. In our everyday lives, we receive data from newspapers and television, from billboards, and from other people. We are bombarded with so much data every minute that our conscious minds can't possibly pay attention to all of it. **Information** is data whose form and content are appropriate for a particular use. Converting data into information by formatting, filtering, and summarizing is a key role of information systems. People need knowledge to use information effectively. **Knowledge** is a combination of instincts, ideas, rules, and procedures that guide actions and decisions. Helping apply the best available knowledge to decision making is another important role of information systems.

Figure 1.12 Relationship Between Data, Information, and Knowledge

People use knowledge about how to format, filter, and summarize data as part of the process of converting data into information useful in a situation. They interpret that information, make decisions, and take actions. The results of these decisions and actions help in accumulating knowledge for use in later decisions.

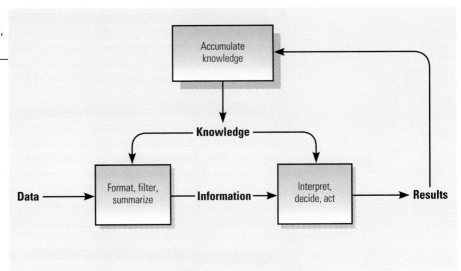

The distinction between data and information is easy to remember. It is cited frequently in explaining why systems that collect vast amounts of data often fail to satisfy managerial information needs. These data constitute information for people performing day-to-day operational tasks such as processing orders but are not useful for managers, who need the data filtered, sorted, and combined in various ways.

There are many methods for converting data into information for decision making. For example, you could select the data pertinent to the situation and remove the irrelevant data. You could combine the data to bring it to a useful level of summarization. You could highlight exceptions that may bias the results or explain more clearly what the data really say. You could display the data in an understandable way. You could develop models that convert data and assumptions into explanations of past results or projections of future results.

In addition to showing the conversion of data into information, Figure 1.12 shows the process of accumulating knowledge and using that knowledge. It says that people act based on their information about the current situation plus their accumulated knowledge about using information for taking action. Actions and their results feed into the process of accumulating more knowledge, which in turn makes people more able both to process data into information and to use that information in the future. For example, this is the process by which medical students become expert doctors. As medical students examine patients, treat them, and observe the results, their medical knowledge deepens.

Special Characteristics of Information

Information has a number of special characteristics related in various ways to the effectiveness of information systems.

Usefulness depends on a combination of information quality, accessibility, and presentation. Usefulness of information starts with quality, expressed in terms such as accuracy, timeliness, and completeness. Even high quality may not ensure usefulness if the information is difficult to access. For example, information on paper in a file cabinet may be useful for looking up individual facts but virtually useless for statistical analysis. And accessibility may not ensure usefulness unless the information can be presented appropriately.

One person's information may be another person's noise. It is not always true that information is power. A splotch on an x-ray might say a lot to a radiologist and nothing to an untrained observer. Likewise, a sharp month-to-month inventory increase might be mysterious to a new analyst but obvious to an expert as a typical pre-Christmas buildup. For information to give you power, you need the knowledge to interpret it and do something with it.

Soft data may be just as important as hard data. Formal information systems provide only part of the information people and organizations need. **Hard data,** clearly defined data generated by formal systems, must often be balanced with **soft data**, intuitive or subjective information obtained by informal means such as talking to people or interpreting rumors or gossip. Hard data is more precise and systematic, whereas soft data is often fuzzy and full of personal viewpoints. If you wanted to find out why your company's productivity varied unexpectedly, you would probably combine analysis of hard data, such as trends in output per labor hour, with use of soft data obtained by talking to different individuals around the company.

Ownership of information may be difficult to maintain. Information is unlike other types of property because it can be duplicated and distributed so easily. John Perry Barlow, lyricist for the Grateful Dead, made this point by describing "the problem of digitized property…If our property can be infinitely reproduced and instantaneously distributed all over the planet without cost, without our knowledge, without its even leaving our possession, how can we protect it?"[21] This issue concerns not only musicians, but also visual artists, authors, computer programmers, and anyone else whose main work product is a form of information.

More information may be better or worse. The combination of computer and communication technology has made much more information available than was ever available before. Even though they lack much specific information that would be important, many business professionals feel overwhelmed with the amount of information they have. This phenomenon is called **information overload.**

Providing the truth on some issues may be a punishable offense. The ancient admonition not to be the messenger of bad news applies to this day. Rubens Ricupero, Brazil's finance minister, seemed to believe this when he made the following off-the-record comment to a television interviewer about economic data: "What is good we take advantage of. What is bad, we hide." Ricupero and the interviewer thought the interview had ended, but the comment was heard around the country because technicians had not terminated the broadcast. Ricupero was forced to resign.[22]

In what is often called the age of information, it might seem ironic that public officials feel obligated to hide or distort information. Consider the way government budgeters commonly project revenues that are too high and expenses that are too low. Developing a government budget is an important process, yet it is often considered impolitic to use realistic estimates. Incentives to hide and distort information certainly exist in many businesses and families as well.

REALITY CHECK **The Challenge of Achieving Maximum Benefit from Information**   In this section, we distinguished between data, information, and knowledge and asserted that information has a number of unique characteristics.

1. Does the distinction between data, information, and knowledge apply to activities or jobs you are familiar with?

2. Which of the unique characteristics of information have affected you, and how have they done so?

Challenge 4: How Can We Extend Our Human Skills and Motivate Our People?

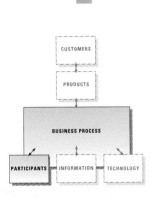

Every aspect of information systems depends on people. People decide what business processes to improve, build appropriate information systems, put them into operation in organizations, and use them. The process of building a system depends on the ability of system builders to collaborate with the users in defining what the system should do. The system's technological adequacy depends on the builders' skills. Successful implementation in the organization depends on whether the users are willing and able to change to the new way of doing things. Whether the system is used to the utmost, used partially, or even misused depends on the users' skills and ambitions.

Conversely, information systems affect business process participants directly and may affect business process customers and stakeholders directly or indirectly. Information systems can make work easier or harder, more interesting or more boring. They can help participants develop new skills or make some of their skills obsolete. They can provide useful information to people or harm people by infringing on their privacy or by providing inaccurate information.

Figure 1.13 Two Views of Participants in Business Processes

When analyzing information systems, one can view participants as a means to an end, or as an end in their own right.

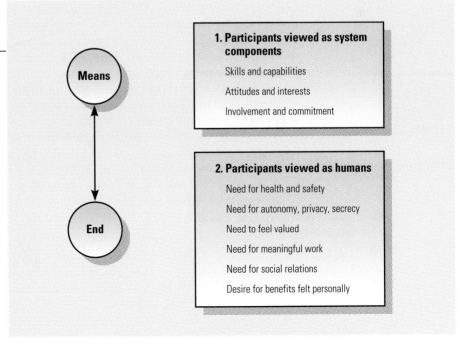

To illustrate both the dependence and the impact of information systems on people, Figure 1.13 views business process participants in two different ways: as a means or as an end. Viewing participants as a means for performing the business processes raises questions such as whether they have the skills and capabilities, attitudes and interests, and involvement and commitment needed to participate effectively. Viewing them as an end raises questions about the effects of business processes on human needs and desires, such as the need for health and safety, autonomy, feeling valued, having meaningful work, and having social relationships.

The tension between viewing participants as a means versus viewing them as an end raises many ethical issues. **Ethical issues** are issues related to whether people are being treated properly whether or not an enforceable law governs the situation. In Chapter 8, we will present an extensive discussion of effects on system participants and of ethical issues in four areas: privacy, accuracy of information, property rights to information, and access to information and information technology. For now, we will look at skills, involvement, and job satisfaction as three aspects of the dilemma of means versus end.

Skills

Skills and training have become a major competitive issue on many levels. As individuals, people compete for jobs based in part on their skills. As businesses, firms compete based on their employee's ability to perform business processes. Even nations compete based on the skills of their people. Many U.S. economists believe that upgrading the skills and literacy of its people is one of the main challenges the United States faces for the future. Maintaining a high standard of living in a world of global competition requires a populace whose skills make them more productive than low-wage workers elsewhere.

Using information systems effectively calls for many types of skills, the first of which is literacy. Many employers have found that productive employees could not adjust to new business processes involving automated equipment because they could not understand the instructions. The same thing happened with some quality initiatives in which companies discovered employees could do everyday work but lacked basic numerical skills needed to analyze quality information. In response, many firms have started basic literacy and math training for valued employees who cannot succeed in today's business processes even if they might have performed well in the business processes of the past.

Information systems can affect skills in many ways. They may increase an employee's skills by supporting ways of doing work that go beyond what was previously possible. For example, people who use computer-aided design (CAD) systems to design buildings or electronic circuits have acquired skills that help them do a higher level of professional work. On the other hand, information systems can bypass or automate previously valuable human skills. This is called **de-skilling.** For example, some argue that automatic pilot systems on airplanes have the effect of de-skilling pilots because pilots have less practice controlling airplanes in the air.

Involvement

Employee involvement is an employee's active participation in performing work and improving business processes. Old-fashioned business processes often treated employees like components of a machine, with the employee following the employer's instructions in return for a wage. This view encouraged employees to be passive, take little initiative, and often view themselves as adversaries of the firm and its management.

In contrast, truly involved employees feel responsibility to improve their work practices with the help of managers and others in the firm. Employee involvement is a key tenet of the TQM movement.

Information systems can directly affect employee involvement. For example, comparative studies of the use of manufacturing data in the 1970s found important differences between Japanese and U.S. factories. U.S. factories tended to aggregate production, scrap, and warranty data into performance measures sent to management for distributing rewards and punishments. Japanese factories tended to maintain detailed data about specific problems encountered by customers. They sent the data to factories to help factory workers identify and solve problems.[23] In U.S. factories, failure to share data meant lost opportunities to use it in a cooperative and motivational way.

In general, information systems can be deployed in ways that increase or decrease employee involvement in their work. Information systems that provide information and tools for employees increase involvement because they reinforce the employee's authority and responsibility for the work. Information systems that provide information to managers or quality inspectors but not their employees can reduce involvement by reinforcing the suspicion that the employee is not really responsible.

Job Satisfaction

Job satisfaction is the degree to which a participant's monetary, professional, and personal needs are met by the job. Information systems can have a positive or negative impact on each facet of job satisfaction mentioned in Figure 1.13. They can make work easier, more interesting, and more enjoyable; can respect people's need for autonomy; can increase skills; can make work more meaningful; and can extend social relations at work. They can also do the opposite in each area.

It may seem surprising to discuss issues about job satisfaction in conjunction with information systems. Yet this area is important because information systems succeed not only on how well they process information, but also on how well they fit into the work environment. However technically brilliant the system may be, it will not succeed if users fight it because it degrades their work life. It is especially important for users and managers to think about these issues because the computer staff may be more concerned about how the technology and the system work in theory rather than its effects on people.

REALITY CHECK   **The Challenge of Extending Human Skills and Motivating People**   In this section, we discussed skills, involvement, and job satisfaction as part of a general discussion of the way systems depend on participants and affect them.

1. Identify any ways computerized systems you are involved in depend on you and other participants.

2. Explain any effects that these systems had on you.

3. Explain why you believe computerized systems will or will not affect you directly in the future.

Challenge 5: How Can We Make the Most of the Surrounding Infrastructure and Context?

Information systems always exist within larger organizational and technical systems that may enable their effective operation or may be obstacles. Infrastructure and context are distinct ways of thinking about the impact of these larger systems.

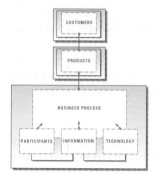

Infrastructure consists of essential resources shared by many otherwise independent applications. A local region's physical infrastructure includes its roads, public transportation, power lines, sewers, and snow removal equipment. Its human and service infrastructure includes police, fire, hospital, and school personnel. A region's physical and human infrastructure can be either an enabler or an obstacle and is therefore a central concern in many business decisions.

Context is the setting within which an information system operates. Its organizational context includes the way the firm is organized; the firm's general approach for sharing information and power; and the firm's policies and procedures related to information, personnel, and business operations. Its technical context is the information technology used by other related information systems in the organization, along with technical standards and policies related to information technology.

Competitive Significance of Infrastructure

Infrastructure affects competition between businesses, geographic regions, and even nations. Inadequate infrastructure prevents business innovation and hurts business efficiency. Consider the way Citibank's Brazilian offices tried to maintain contact with New York in the 1950s and 1960s. Because there were so few international telephone circuits at the time, Citibank staffers would stay on the line and read the newspaper until someone actually needed to speak. Eventually, Citibank Brazil created a job category known as "dialers," whose job was just to dial phones in the hope of establishing a connection.[24] Things have changed vastly in the interim, but the significance of infrastructure as a competitive enabler or obstacle has not changed.

The importance of national information infrastructure is a key motivation for the idea of an "information superhighway" providing most homes and businesses in the United States access to enormous amounts of information. Whether an information superhighway will be built and, if so, whether it will be built and controlled by the government or by private industry remain to be seen.

Information infrastructure raises a broad range of economic, social, and technical issues: Who should pay for infrastructure? Who should have access and at what cost? Which technologies should be used? The economic question often pits telephone companies against cable companies, both of which can provide similar capabilities for major parts of the telecommunications system. The social question is about whether large groups of people will be excluded from using the nation's information infrastructure. The technical question involves issues such as how much data transmission will occur through various wire and wireless technologies.

Importance of Organizational and Technical Context

When analyzing an information system in any business or government organization, comments such as the following are often encountered:

1. The proposed system's technology is much better, but we cannot switch to the proposed system because of the effort required to integrate the new system with our other systems that use the old technology.

2. We are especially enthusiastic about the new electronic mail system because it reinforces our organizational strategy of knocking down barriers between departments.

3. The idea of making manufacturing schedules available to all salespeople through a database sounds great, but it will never fly because our head of manufacturing doesn't want that type of information sharing.

Each of these comments concerns the organizational and technical context a new system must fit into. Even if a system seems to be a wonderful solution to a local problem, the context within which that problem exists may negate the solution. On the other hand, the competitive necessity of increasing speed and flexibility has led to the realization that new information systems and infrastructure are key enablers of the needed changes.

REALITY CHECK **The Challenge of Making the Most of the Surrounding Infrastructure and Context** In this section, we defined infrastructure and context and explained why they can be enablers or obstacles.

1. Identify situations you have encountered in which infrastructure has been an enabler or an obstacle.

2. Identify situations you have encountered in which organizational or technical context has been an enabler or an obstacle.

Challenge 6: How Can We Recognize and Respond to Common System-Related Risks?

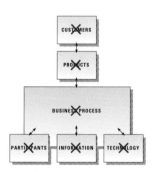

Along with their benefits, automated systems bring risks and vulnerability. Anyone who has called for an airline reservation only to learn that "the computer is down" has felt one aspect of the problem, as has anyone who has typed a document using a word processor but then accidentally erased it without having a backup. The example in Figure 1.14 is just one illustration of the potential size of the errors that can be generated by computerized systems. The overview of risks will be deferred to Chapter 2, in which we will give examples of accidents and malfunctions, computer crime, and project failures as part of our discussion of the WCA method. We will also identify risks related to each of the six elements of the WCA framework. Later, in Chapter 15, we will give more extensive coverage to the topic of identifying and controlling risks.

Figure 1.14 The $68 Billion Tax Bill

To say the least, this woman was surprised when she opened her U.S. income tax bill and saw that she owed $68 billion.

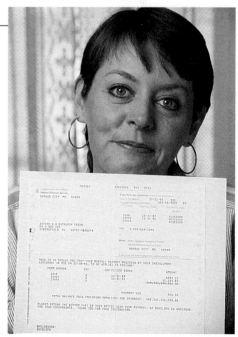

Challenge 7: What Methods Should We Use for Building and Maintaining Systems?

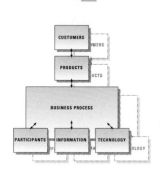

If you think that building systems is basically about programming computers, you might be surprised that programming is less than 20 percent of the effort for most systems. Business professionals need to understand choices in building and managing information systems because they participate directly in these business processes.

We will use two ideas to introduce choices in building and managing information systems. The first is that four project phases apply to any information system: initiation, development, implementation, and operation and maintenance. The second idea is that there are different ways to perform the overall process of acquiring or building an information system. We will look at four approaches, including the traditional system life cycle, prototypes, application packages, and end-user development. We will explain the ideas in more detail in Part IV.

Four Phases of an Information System's Life Cycle

Figure 1.15 shows that any information system, regardless of how it is acquired or built, goes through the phases of initiation, development, implementation, and operation and maintenance.

Figure 1.15 Four Phases of an Information System

The business process of building and managing an information system has four phases. These phases apply to all information systems even though different systems may be acquired using different business processes.

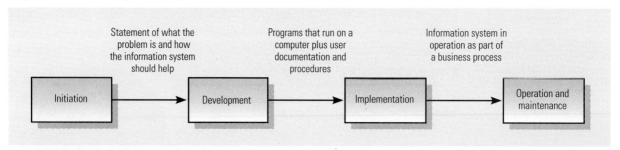

Initiation is the process of defining the need for a system, identifying the people who will use it or be affected by it, and describing in general terms what the system will do to meet the need. In some cases, the initiation phase occurs in response to obvious problems, such as data that cannot be found and used effectively or high error rates in data. In other cases, the initiation phase is part of a planning process in which the organization is searching for ways to improve and innovate, even if current systems pose no overt problems. The conclusion of the initiation phase is a verbal or written agreement about the general function and scope of the desired system, plus a shared understanding that it is technically and organizationally feasible.

Development is the process of transforming general system requirements into hardware and software that accomplish the required functions as well as documentation that explains the system to programmers and users. This phase includes deciding exactly what the system will accomplish and exactly how the computerized and manual parts of the system will operate. If the hardware isn't already in place, development includes purchasing and installing the hardware. Development concludes with thorough testing of the entire system to identify and correct misunderstandings and programming errors. Completion of development does not mean that "the system works." Rather, it means only that the computerized parts of the system operate on a computer. Whether or not the system works will be determined later by how it is used in the organization.

Implementation is the process of making a system operational in the organization. This phase starts from the point when the software runs on the computer and has been tested. Activities in implementation include planning, user training, conversion to the new system, and follow-up to make sure the system is operating effectively. The implementation of a new system may involve a major change in the way organizations or individuals operate. Conversion from the old to the new must be planned and executed carefully to prevent errors or even chaos. For systems that keep track of transactions such as invoices and customer orders, the conversion process requires some users to do double work during a pilot test, operating simultaneously with the old and new systems. Running two systems in parallel helps identify unanticipated problems with the new system that might require system modifications before the system is used fully.

Operation and maintenance is the ongoing use of the system after it has been installed, plus the work done to enhance it and correct bugs. At minimum, the operation of many systems requires that someone be in charge of ensuring the system actually works and provides benefits. Frequently, systems must be changed to address the current business problem rather than one that existed when the system was first built. Eventually, the system may be absorbed into other systems or terminated.

Alternative System Development Processes

Although it would be convenient if there were some "correct," guaranteed method for developing information systems, it is generally agreed that no best method exists. To the contrary, different situations call for different system development processes. Table 1.2 summarizes the approaches.

The **traditional system life cycle** uses a prescribed sequence of steps and deliverables to move reliably from user requirements to a system in operation. These deliverables are related because each subsequent step builds on the conclusions of previous steps. The traditional system life cycle tries to solve a *control* problem by keeping the project on track. This type of process became popular in response to numerous system development efforts that went out of control and either failed to produce a system at all or produced a system that did not solve the users' problem effectively. Accordingly, the traditional system life cycle ensures each step is completed in turn and documented carefully.

A **prototype** information system is a working model of the system built to learn about its true requirements. Firms build prototypes to solve a *knowledge* problem of not knowing exactly what the system should do to solve an important problem. In this situation, the user needs some way to get a feeling for how the system should operate. Accordingly, a prototype is built quickly to help the user understand the problem and determine how a system might help in solving it.

An **application package** consists of commercially available software that addresses a specific type of business process, such as billing customers, accepting customer orders, or keeping track of inventory. Firms acquire application packages to solve a *resource and timing* problem by using a commercially available system that performs most of the functions desired. The in-house information systems staff installs and operates this system instead of programming a system from scratch. Thus, purchasing a system from an outside vendor reduces the development phase to the clarification of objectives, the choice of a system, and the determination of exactly how to use the system. This approach avoids delays in developing systems, limits risks due to business and technical uncertainties, and reduces the resources needed to solve the problem.

End-user development is the development of information systems by end users rather than by information systems professionals. Firms apply end-user development to solve a *responsiveness* problem involving the inability of information systems groups to keep up with individuals' changing information needs. The idea is to allow end users to produce their own applications systems without requiring development by programmers. This is accomplished by giving end users spreadsheets, database packages, report generators, analytical packages, and other tools that can be used by nonprogrammers. End-user development is effective only for systems that are small enough that a systems professional is not needed for system design, programming, testing, and documentation.

Table 1.2 Differences Among Four System Life Cycle Approaches

Life Cycle Approach	Issue Addressed	Summary of Method
Traditional system life cycle	Control	Proceed through a fixed sequence of steps with signoffs after each step and careful documentation.
Prototype	Knowledge	Quickly develop a working model of the system; use the model to gain experience and decide how the final system should operate.
Application package	Resource and timing	Purchase an existing information system from a vendor; customize the system if necessary.
End-user development	Responsiveness	Provide tools and support that make it practical for end users to develop their own systems.

Although there are many technical choices in building and maintaining information systems, users and general managers should have a say in choices about the business process in any particular situation. The four phases and four alternatives just mentioned provide useful background for the chapters that follow because they help you visualize the process of making some of the decisions discussed in these chapters. In the last part of the book, we will explain system building in more depth.

REALITY CHECK   **The Challenge of Finding the Best Processes for Building and Maintaining Systems**   Every information system goes through four phases and can be built and acquired using alternative system life cycles.

1. Use the four phases to describe a project of any type that you have done.

2. Explain why the choice of a system life cycle might or might not matter to the system users.

Chapter Conclusion

SUMMARY

What are seven system-related challenges business professionals should recognize and respond to?

Seven system-related challenges include:

- How can we improve our business processes in today's competitive world?
- How can we benefit from technical trends and innovations?
- How can we achieve maximum benefit from information?
- How can we extend our human skills and motivate our people?
- How can we make the most of the surrounding infrastructure and context?
- How can we recognize and respond to common system-related risks?
- What are the best business processes for building and maintaining our systems?

What trends in business processes pose competitive challenges for many firms?

Global competition, new ways of doing business, and the transition to total quality management all pose competitive challenges. The trend toward global competition means that many long-time advantages related to geographic proximity are no longer as important. This trend has many personal implications since people around the world are now more able to compete for the same work. New ways to do business include new types of products and services, the ability to conquer distance and time when serving customers, and the automation of work. New ways to organize businesses are also becoming a competitive issue as suppliers do more for their customers and boundaries between the supplier and customer change.

What is total quality management?

TQM is a business strategy based on three general principles: customer focus, process improvement, and total involvement. The idea is to identify, analyze, and improve the processes that directly or indirectly create value for the customer. Customer focus means thinking of business processes as ways to satisfy customers by meeting their stated or unstated expectations. Process improvement includes both continuous and discontinuous improvement. Total involvement means that TQM requires attention and commitment from everyone in the firm.

▶ *What major technological trends have created opportunities for business innovation in the past and promise to do so for the near future?*

These trends include:

- Greater miniaturization, speed, and portability
- Greater connectivity and continuing convergence of computing and communications
- Greater use of digitized information and multimedia
- Better software techniques and interfaces with people
- More, but still limited, "intelligence" built into devices

What are some of the special characteristics and enigmas of information?

The usefulness of information depends on a combination of information quality, accessibility, and presentation. What is information to one person may be meaningless to someone else. For some management purposes, soft data such as opinions and gossip may be as important as hard data from formal systems. Compared to physical things, the ownership of information may be difficult to maintain. Obtaining information may be very important in some situations and totally useless in others, such as when people are already overloaded with information. Finally, although people usually say they want correct, complete information, messengers of bad news are often punished.

▶ In what ways do information systems depend on people?

Every aspect of information systems depends on people. People decide what business processes to improve, build appropriate information systems, put them into operation in organizations, and use them. The process of building a system depends on the ability of system builders to collaborate with the users in defining what the system should do. The system's technological adequacy depends on the builders' skills. Successful implementation in the organization depends on whether the users are willing and able to change to the new way of doing things. Whether the system is used to the utmost, used partially, or even misused depends on the users' skills and ambitions. When analyzing an information system, the participants in the system should always be considered in terms of their skills, involvement, and job satisfaction.

▶ How are infrastructure and context either enablers or obstacles for information systems?

Information systems always exist within larger organizational and technical systems that may enable or prevent their effective operation. Infrastructure such as telecommunications and electric power systems enable information systems by providing capabilities these systems need. Conversely, inadequate, excessively expensive, or nonexistent infrastructure can make a potentially valuable information system infeasible. Organizational and technical context can also be an enabler or obstacle by creating conditions making a potentially valuable system easier or more difficult to build and operate effectively.

What are the phases of an information system and the alternative system development processes?

An information system, regardless of how it is acquired, goes through four phases: initiation, development, implementation, and operation and maintenance. These steps occur differently in different system development processes. The traditional system life cycle uses a prescribed sequence of steps and deliverables to move reliably from user requirements to a system in operation. A prototype may be used when it is necessary to build a system to learn more about the true requirements. Firms acquire application packages to solve a resource and timing problem by using a commercially available system that performs most of the functions desired. End-user development is the development of information systems by end users rather than by information systems professionals.

INTERNATIONAL VIGNETTES

Singapore: Building a Trade Network to Promote National Competitiveness

In 1989, Singapore launched TradeNet, the world's most comprehensive trade-related electronic data interchange (EDI) system. TradeNet offers electronic documentation, financing, and logistical support for international trade shipments. Users in the trade sector include government departments such as customs, the port and airport authorities, cargo companies, freight forwarders, shipping and airline companies, banks, and insurance companies.

By 1994, TradeNet served 3,500 companies and handled more than 95 percent of Singapore's export and import trade declarations. The system has saved Singapore's government and businesses an estimated $600 million per year by greatly decreasing the time and effort devoted to trade documentation. Approval for declarations used to be time consuming, involving much paperwork and as long as four days. With TradeNet, a single electronic document can be sent to all relevant government agencies and returned with the necessary approvals within 15 to 30 minutes. This more than halved the time any ship has to remain in port and is believed to be a key to ensuring Singapore remains a port of choice in the Far East.

TradeNet was sponsored by the Singaporean government because it was viewed as important for the nation's competitive advantage as a port of choice in the Far East. Singapore is a small island nation of 2.7 million people located at the tip of the Malay peninsula. It has one major port and one large international airport but no significant natural resources. Although TradeNet is run by a private company, the government played a critical role in its development by marshaling resources, keeping the project on track, and making sure the project redesigned forms and procedures in the trading process instead of just automating the existing process.

> Sources: Konsynski, B. R. "Strategic Control in the Extended Enterprise." *IBM Systems Journal*, Vol. 32, No. 1, 1993, pp. 111–142.
> Mesher, Gene. "Singapore Sings Praises of EDI." *Information Week*, Apr. 11, 1994, p. 70.

- Use the WCA framework to organize your understanding of this vignette and to identify important topics that are not mentioned. (Refer to Figure 1.1 as an example.)

- What issues (if any) make this case interesting from an international or intercultural viewpoint?

- Do you believe any country could build a system like TradeNet and benefit from it?

Italy: Benetton Responds to Local Tastes

One of the world's largest garment companies, Benetton is an Italian firm that operates approximately 5,000 retail stores in more than 75 countries. It works with over 200 suppliers and sells through retail outlets largely owned by outside investors. Benetton's organization and business process emphasize quick response, flexibility, low prices to customers, and excellent service. The range of technologies it uses to accomplish these goals start with proprietary technologies for cutting and dyeing cloth that make it possible to respond quickly to changes in color preferences. Benetton also uses computer networks and computer-aided design systems to plan and coordinate activities among its suppliers and outlets.

Benetton is prohibited by law from requiring point-of-sale terminals in its franchisees' stores, and therefore relies on 73 worldwide agents to gather information from stores. It connects each agent's computer to a central system in Italy to capture demand and order information. To get early demand indications for new products, it uses point-of-sale terminals installed in 20 Benetton-owned outlets in carefully chosen fashion-forward locations in Europe and the United States.

Benetton maintains so much detailed information in its database that it can fine-tune offerings to the demographics and tastes of the customers of each store. Colors, styles, and sizes could be adjusted to the specific characteristics of customers for stores only a few blocks apart.

> Sources: Hammond, Janice H. "Quick Response in Retail/Manufacturing Channels." In Stephen P. Bradley, Jerry A. Hausman, and Richard L. Nolan (eds.), *Globalization, Technology, and Competition*. Boston: Harvard Business School Press, 1993, pp. 185–214.
> Quinn, James Brian. *Intelligent Enterprise: A Knowledge and Service Based Paradigm for Industry*. New York: Free Press, 1992, p. 108.

- Use the WCA framework to organize your understanding of this vignette and to identify important topics that are not mentioned.

- What issues (if any) make this case interesting from an international or intercultural viewpoint?

- Why are information systems important to a firm like Benetton?

REAL-WORLD CASES

Zale Corporation: Making the Most of Damaged Jewelry

Zale Corporation, the world's largest jewelry retailer, has a jewelry processing center in Irving, Texas, that receives around 300,000 pieces of damaged, returned, or repossessed jewelry from its 1,500 stores each year. Previously, Zale melted down these pieces and lost substantial revenue because there was no efficient way to inspect each piece and decide whether it should be repaired. A new computerized system changed that process, and around 58 percent of the jewelry processed using that system could be recycled for sale at discount outlets.

The new system was designed to help gemologists appraise each piece of damaged jewelry and decide what should happen to it. The system identifies each piece of jewelry with a bar code. The gemologist uses digital calipers, a sensitive scale, and personal knowledge to answer a set of structured questions related to the type of jewelry, the type and quality of metal, and the number, type, size, quality, and cut of each stone. If the item originated in Zale's inventory, the descriptive information is filled in automatically from a database, and then changed as appropriate by the gemologist, such as by noting that a stone is missing. For some items, the system provides additional help by retrieving data such as the likely repair cost. The gemologist decides what should be done and sends the item to the appropriate next step.

To help keep the gemologist's hands free, the computer system was originally designed to accept gemologist inputs using a voice recognition system. To "train" the voice recognition system to recognize the highly structured inputs to specific questions, a group of gemologists had given all possible answers to each of the questions. Eventually, the users decided it would be more efficient to enter the data using specially designed keys, and the voice recognition system was bypassed.

Source: Newman, Julie, and Kenneth A. Kozar. "A Multimedia Solution to Productivity Gridlock: A Re-Engineered Jewelry Appraisal System at Zale Corporation." *MIS Quarterly*, Mar. 1994, pp. 21–30.

- Use the WCA framework to organize your understanding of this case and to identify important topics that are not mentioned.
- How did the new system help Zale avoid melting down so much damaged jewelry?

USAA: Providing Excellent Service for Insurance Customers

USAA is a worldwide insurance and financial services company serving primarily present and former military officers and their dependents. One of the largest home and auto insurers, it has 2.6 million members and customers and receives over 300,000 phone calls every day. Its long-term plan in the early 1980s called for modernizing systems and procedures so that information would be stored in computers instead of paper files and so that employees could enter data directly during phone calls without creating millions of worksheets that would have to be routed and filed. From 1984 to 1987, USAA experimented with a prototype system. In July 1987, it selected IBM to install an image system covering over 1,000 terminals. By 1990, all users had access to the image system from their desks, and none of the 25,000 letters received each day were delivered to user areas in paper form. Paper storage could be eliminated only if images of the original documents were legally acceptable. According to the Universal Commercial Code, microfilmed documents were acceptable if the recording was part of normal business, used a permanent medium, and was reproducible in the original size. Since the system was using nonerasable optical disks, it met this requirement.

The system involved much more than just storing a picture of paper documents. Information attached to each electronic document included member number, date received, data filed, line of business, and abstract description. Work flow management software then routed the document to the appropriate USAA organizational unit and to the appropriate work queue within that unit. It also prioritized the documents for distribution to agents. The agents reacted positively to the system because it seemed to assign work fairly and because "you lose that drowning feeling since you do not have that stack of folders staring you in the face."

> Source: Elam, Joyce, and John Sviokla. "The Image Project at USAA." Boston: Harvard Business School, case N9-190-155, 1990.

- Use the WCA framework to organize your understanding of this case and to identify important topics that are not mentioned.

- Why don't all insurance companies use this type of system?

Boeing: Autopilot Malfunctions

A Boeing 747 was flying over Thunder Bay, Canada, when its autopilot system began to malfunction by gradually banking the plane to the right. It was a dark night, and the motion was so gentle that the pilots did not notice the problem until too late. The plane banked 90 degrees, a position in which the wings provided no lift, and it began to dive toward earth. It fell two miles before the pilots could roll the wings and pull out of the dive. A probe by the Federal Aviation Administration found 30 related incidents. After more than a year of intense investigation, engineers could not agree on whether the fault lies in the autopilot system or elsewhere. Boeing said pilots should pay close attention to their job so that they can respond quickly in case the autopilot malfunctions. After all, the autopilot is designed to assist and supplement the pilot's capabilities, not replace them.

> Source: Carley, William M. "Jet Near-Crash Shows 747s May Be at Risk of Autopilot Failure." *Wall Street Journal*, Apr. 26, 1993, p. A1.

- Use the WCA framework to organize your understanding of this case and to identify important topics that are not mentioned.

- Should autopilots be outlawed? Why or why not?

KEY TERMS

information economy	miniaturization	data	context
information content of products	integrated circuit	information	initiation
mass customization	portability	knowledge	development
automation	connectivity	hard data	implementation
total quality management (TQM)	interoperability	soft data	operation and maintenance
internal customers	open systems	information overload	traditional system life cycle
external customers	convergence of computing and	ethical issue	prototype
continuous improvement	communications	de-skilling	application package
discontinuous improvement	digitization	job satisfaction	end-user development
empowerment	multimedia	infrastructure	

REVIEW QUESTIONS

1. How do business processes form the basis of competition?
2. What is meant by an information economy?
3. What are some of the ways businesses have used information technology to conquer distance and time?
4. What do you think are the advantages and disadvantages of automation?
5. What is the difference between continuous and discontinuous improvement?
6. What role do information systems play in organizational downsizing?
7. What is meant by empowerment, and how is it beneficial to businesses?

8. What is connectivity, and how is it beneficial to businesses?

9. How does portability make it difficult to control the flow of information?

pg24 10. What are open systems, and why are some hardware and software suppliers resistant to them?

11. How do continuing trends toward connectivity and interoperability provide opportunities to compete more effectively?

pg28-9 12. What are the distinctions between data, information, and knowledge?

pg30 13. What are the special characteristics of information?

14. In what ways do information systems depend on and affect people?

15. What are some of the ethical issues that should be considered as part of the analysis of an information system?

16. What effects can information systems have on an employee's skills?

17. Why is it important to consider job satisfaction when analyzing information systems?

18. Describe the different methods for developing information systems.

■ DISCUSSION QUESTIONS

1. Explain how the following is pertinent to the topics in this chapter: Louis Gerstner, chairman of IBM and co-author of *Reinventing Education,* says that American education has to change, citing among other facts that U.S. businesses spend $30 billion per year on worker training and lose $25 to $30 billion because of poor literacy among workers. In an annual comparison of 15 selected nations, American 13-year-olds ranked 13th in science and 14th in math, behind South Korea, Taiwan, Hungary, and Slovenia. Yet parents in one Midwestern city were three times more likely to be very satisfied with their child's current level of achievement as were mothers in Asia.[25]

2. It has often been said that the introduction of new technology is never neutral and usually has both positive and negative effects. Think about the seven challenges discussed in this chapter to elaborate on what this statement means.

3. Competition between people, cities, countries, and other groups of people has existed for centuries. Do you believe that computerized information systems are changing the nature of global competition. Why or why not?

4. Quality has been a concern of manufacturers for centuries but has received more emphasis recently. Explain what you think are the main issues related to quality. What do you think determines the success of total quality management?

■ HANDS-ON EXERCISES

1. This exercise reviews basic capabilities of word processors. It assumes a document is provided.

   a. Using the word processor, correct any apparent errors in the document provided.

   b. Make all the following changes without retyping the paragraph: Change the type font and size for about half the paragraph. Underline the first line of the paragraph, italicize the second line, make the third line bold, and make the fourth underlined, italicized, and bold. Save the document under a new name. Quit the word processing program. Check in the directory to make sure the new document was saved. Print the new document, and then delete it.

   c. Open the word processor again, and use the table feature to create a table containing the name, address, and telephone number of five people. Explain how you would do this if the table feature did not exist. Is there any sense in which the table feature of the word processor seems "intelligent?"

2. This exercise asks you to think about how "intelligent" your word processor is. (It uses the same document as the previous exercise.)

a. Start again from the original document provided. Use the word processor's spell checking feature to check the document for errors. Identify any spelling errors the word processor missed, and explain why it missed them.

b. Use the word processor's grammar checker to check the document for errors. Identify any grammar errors it missed, and explain why it missed them.

c. Based on these results, describe how smart the word processor is, and explain any conceivable capabilities that might make it smarter. In particular, ask yourself whether the word processor could understand the document and, if so, how you would know it understood the document.

APPLICATION SCENARIOS

The National Board of Trade

"When they bring computers in here, things will never be the same." Arnold O'Connor had been a successful trader at the National Board of Trade for 20 years. He enjoyed the pressures and excitement of being a trader and had built a prosperous life for himself and his family by owning a seat on the exchange and trading for clients and for his own account. After learning of a proposal to computerize floor trading, he became worried about his future.

The National Board of Trade is one of the largest commodities exchanges in the world and competes with other exchanges on its ability to create the best market for trading. The traditional purpose of these exchanges is buying or selling contracts for future delivery of commodities such as corn or silver at a specific price. Farmers use futures contracts to eliminate the risk that farm prices will drop. Food companies that buy commodities for their manufactured products use futures to eliminate the risk that farm prices will skyrocket. Financial speculators use futures to make money by buying and selling the contracts without ever taking delivery of the goods.

A trade takes place when a buyer's bid price matches a seller's ask price. Trading has traditionally been done using the "open-outcry system," in which traders and brokers work on a large open trading floor called "the pit" and literally yell at each other to convey the latest bid and ask prices. This traditional process has worked for many years, but it takes its toll on the traders, some of whom have had surgery to repair damaged vocal chords. Some traders trade for their own account. Many others perform trades for either financial speculators or businesses wanting to minimize their risk.

The new system will still use open outcry for making trades but will use hand-held terminals to record trades instead of the paper methods of the past. Previously, trades were recorded on small cards collected every half hour and then entered into a computerized accounting system. The handheld terminals will record the trades immediately and transmit them to a central computer by radio waves. The recordkeeping system was motivated partially by the need to handle paperwork more efficiently. The Board's officials didn't like to discuss another reason, complaints that some traders cheated by "front running." On receiving a large buy order, these traders allegedly bought the commodities for their own account at a low price and then sold them to the customer at a higher price.

Recently, the exchanges started analyzing the use of computers to support international trading during the hours when the pits are closed. For these off-hour trades, the open-outcry system can potentially be replaced by several variations of computerized trading. These variations range from totally automatic matching of bid and ask prices to several ways that a person at a terminal could assign bids (offers to buy) to asking prices (offers to sell) and keep the market operating smoothly. Finally, front running will be more difficult with the computerized audit trails that computerized systems can provide. Even so, some skeptics believe that people who want to manipulate prices will figure out ways to do so. The top managers of the

National Board of Trade are convinced that data input using the handheld terminals is the way to go. They frankly aren't so sure that international 24-hour trading will succeed, but they feel they must move in this direction because other exchanges are already doing so. They fear that the National Board of Trade will lose business to other commodity exchanges if it cannot establish itself as a leading-edge user of technology.

O'Connor is concerned that computerization will gradually drive him out of his job. He sees no direct threat from the data collection system but worries that it is just the first step toward ending a very profitable career. He thinks that the overnight trading may show that all the trading can be done through the computer after a few years. He worries about being replaced by a row of people sitting in front of computer terminals in an office in Tokyo and thinks those people may be replaced a few years later by a single big computer somewhere else. Who would have dreamt of this five years ago? O'Connor knows that many other traders share his fears, and none of them knows what to do about it.

1. What are the major business processes in this situation?

2. Consider the seven challenges in the chapter, and explain how each either does or does not apply to this situation.

3. Assume you are the president of the National Board of Trade and that O'Connor has come to your office and expressed his fears. You are not sure about the future of trading either, but you need to respond to him. What would you say?

DEBATE TOPIC   *Use ideas from the chapter to argue the pros and cons and practical implications of the following proposition: O'Connor should not be worried about the new system.*

Metroplex Times-Dispatch: An Electronic Newspaper?

Jenny Birch was tired of hearing her top marketing people say the *Times-Dispatch* was behind the times. During her tenure as publisher, it had become a leader with a respected, well-balanced staff, good advertising revenues, good relations with unions, and efficient production facilities. In fact, the printing plant had just been refurbished two years ago to incorporate the latest printing technology. Data transfer technology was totally up to date, with reporters in the field able to transmit their stories by modem or even by satellite in some instances. The page layout programs the newspaper used were the best in the industry, and the paper's physical appearance was tops.

Yet some of the more aggressive marketing people had started saying that electronic newspapers were right around the corner. "How could they use *electronic* and *newspaper* in the same breath?" she wondered. A newspaper is a physical thing that is easy to distribute, easy to read, and easy to advertise in. Are people going to start carrying computers with them everywhere? Who would want to read a newspaper crunched down onto a tiny computer screen? And who would want to advertise in something like that? Furthermore, hadn't the first attempts to move toward electronic newspapers been miserable failures losing millions of dollars? Despite her doubts, she decided to raise this issue in a brainstorming meeting related to long-range planning.

The head of marketing felt there was no question at all that newspapers would become electronic. The only question in his mind was when that would happen. "But what should we do about that?" Ms. Birch wanted to know. "Should we put out an electronic edition now and bleed for 20 years until newsprint goes out of style? When will enough people have computerized viewing devices so that an electronic newspaper would make sense financially, even assuming we knew how to produce it?" After kicking around various ideas, the group concluded *Metroplex* could not become an electronic newspaper tomorrow because it would lose most of its readership and advertising if it did that. On the other hand, there were things it could do to gain experience with electronic delivery while also making a profit or breaking even.

In addition to publishing the newspaper in its current form, they would take a low-risk step toward electronic distribution by "publishing" an electronic version that would be available over telephone lines. The electronic version would be a supplement, not the main newspaper. It would contain all the articles and advertisements in the existing newspaper but none of its layout. It would be possible to download the entire newspaper or limited parts of it, depending on what the customer wanted. For simplicity, the categories were things like world news, state news, local news, business news, sports, classified ads, and regular ads.

Readers would use the electronic paper in one of several ways. They could simply browse through it. They could also use keywords or categories to pinpoint the specific things they needed. Because the electronic newspaper would not be limited by space and layout constraints, it could contain much more information than the regular newspaper. For example, when a story in the business section mentioned a company, related press releases from that company could be available in their entirety through the electronic newspaper. Furthermore, the electronic newspaper could provide access to every article mentioning that company in the last eight years. Moving in this direction, the newspaper could become more like an information service in addition to being a newspaper. By joining up with other information sources, there is no telling what additional possibilities the newspaper might find.

1. What are the major business processes in this situation, and how would those business processes change if the newspaper were totally electronic?

2. Consider the seven challenges in the chapter, and explain how each either does or does not apply to this situation.

DEBATE TOPIC *Use ideas from the chapter to argue the pros and cons and practical implications of the following proposition: The electronic newspaper doesn't make sense, and Ms. Birch should not pursue it.*

Cumulative Case: Custom T-Shirts, Inc.

It started with a complaint and became a multimillion-dollar company with over 400 outlets and a variety of products and services. Terry Williams and Dale Jones picked up the t-shirts that had been custom printed for the election party and couldn't believe how shoddy they were. "This is the crummiest looking t-shirt I have ever seen. Look at the awkward design and splotchy ink, not to speak of the mismatched colors."

The store manager shrugged. "That is what this product is like. You gave us a design, and we produced it the best we could, and the best any store like this can do. If you wanted a work of art, you should have gone to an art museum."

"Maybe this is the best you can do," Terry thought, "but I'm sure I can do better." And that was the beginning of Custom T-Shirts, Inc. Calling on a background in commercial art and printing, Terry started spending evenings at home experimenting with ways to make customized t-shirts. The breakthrough came at work during a discussion with Pat Olin, who was repairing a laser printer. Terry asked Pat whether there might be some way to use an inexpensive black-and-white laser printer to generate totally controllable patterns that could create vivid color images when heat-pressed onto a t-shirt. Color images from standard black-and-white laser printer seemed impossible at first, but eventually Terry, Dale, and Pat developed a promising four-layer screening technique.

After months of working nights and weekends, they left their jobs to start Custom T-Shirts, Inc. The basic business concept involved the ability to produce a virtually infinite number of different t-shirts using patterns stored on a computer, selected and possibly modified by the customer, printed on demand, and heat-pressed onto the t-shirts. Because the patterns would be stored in the computer rather than on t-shirts in inventory, it would be unnecessary to keep a huge stock of printed t-shirts in expensive rental space. Having the image on the computer meant that the t-shirts could also be customized easily for individuals.

Terry, Dale, and Pat believed they were ahead of the rest of their industry because they saw a new way to use information technology to provide benefits for customers. The idea of genuinely customized t-shirts produced on the spot seemed novel, practical, and expandable into other products such as baseball caps or even uniforms. By using telephones to transfer possible patterns to customers with computers and to get their modifications in return, it might even be unnecessary for some customers to come to the stores. It also might be possible to do large orders at remote sites where the rent would be low. The possibilities seemed huge. Since the four-layer screening technique could probably be patented, they might be able to build a chain of stores using technology others could not copy easily.

The entire business concept depended on technical advances that had occurred in the last decade. Laser printer prices had plummeted. The ability to work with pictures easily on a computer was recent, as was the ability to transmit pictures easily from one location to another. But Terry, Dale, and Pat were also worried about things that might go wrong with computerized systems. They had all used computers, but none of them was close to being an expert. What would happen if the computers essential for their product broke down in the stores?

If they were going to grow to a large chain of stores, part of their challenge would involve staffing and managing the organization. How would they get people to run these stores who would really enjoy doing that work and would find it creative? Should they hire artists as store managers so that customization could be even better? They might be able to charge more for a genuinely custom drawn picture of an individual. Perhaps they should hire store managers who enjoyed working with the public and just occasionally have an artist come to the store for special promotions.

Another aspect of their challenge was to create systems for keeping track of things that happened in the business and making sure people in the stores got adequate feedback about what they had done well and where they could improve. Would they hire an information systems staff to build these systems, or could they buy the systems from vendors? They wondered what were the different ways to build these systems, and what were the risks of each approach.

1. Explain how each of the seven management challenges is or is not pertinent in this situation.

2. Explain how the following ideas from the chapter are or are not reflected in the business they are thinking about: globalization, mass customization, automation, TQM, empowerment, job satisfaction, infrastructure, alternative system development processes.

▪ REFERENCES

1. Diebold, John. *The Innovators*. New York: E.P. Dutton, 1990.

2. Wiseman, Charles. "Attack & Counterattack: The New Game in Information Technology." *Planning Review*, Vol. 16, No. 15, Sept.–Oct. 1988, p. 6.

3. Hansell, Saul. "Citibank Quietly Joins New York Cash Exchange." *New York Times*, June 7, 1994, p. C3.

4. Johnson, Kirk. "One Less Thing to Believe In: High-Tech Fraud at an ATM." *New York Times*, May 13, 1993, p. A1.

5. Ramirez, Anthony. "New Teller Machines That Listen." *New York Times*, Dec. 9, 1992, p. C5.

6. Nash, Kim S. "ATMs Frozen by Blizzard." *Computerworld*, Mar. 22, 1993, p. 6.

7. Hansell, Saul. "Cash Machines Getting Greedy at a Big Bank." *New York Times*, Feb. 18, 1994, p. A1.

8. Kearns, David, and David Nadler. *Prophets in the Dark: How Xerox Reinvented Itself and Beat Back the Japanese*. New York: HarperBusiness, 1992.

9. O'Reilly, Brian. "Your New Global Work Force." *Fortune*, Dec. 14, 1992, pp. 52–66.

10. Moffat, Susan. "Japan's New Personalized Production." *Fortune*, Oct. 22, 1990, pp. 132–135.

11. Gleckman, Howard. "A Tonic for the Business Cycle." *Business Week*, Apr. 4, 1994, pp. 57–58.

12. Blackburn, Joseph D. *Time-Based Competition*. Homewood, Ill.: Business One/Irwin, 1991.

13. Tenner, Arthur R., and Irving J. DeToro, *Total Quality Management: Three Steps to Continuous Improvement*. Reading, Mass.: Addison-Wesley, 1992.

14. Albrecht, Karl. *The Only Thing that Matters: Bringing the Power of the Customer into the Center of Your Business*. New York: HarperBusiness, 1992, p. 29.

15. Benjamin, Robert I., and Jon Blunt. "Critical IT Issues: The Next Ten Years." *Sloan Management Review*, Summer 1992, pp. 7–19.

16. Gelsinger, Patrick, Paolo Gargini, Gerhard Parker, and Albert Yu. "2001: A Microprocessor Odyssey." In Derek Leebaert, *Technology 2001: The Future of Computing and Communications*. Cambridge, Mass.: The MIT Press, 1991, p. 100.

17. Murillo, Luis Eduardo. *The International DRAM Industry from 1970 to 1993*. Ph.D. Thesis, University of California, Berkeley, 1994, p. 539.

18. Reilly, Patrick M. "The Dark Side: Warning: Portable Devices Can Be Hazardous to Your Health." *Wall Street Journal*, Nov. 16, 1992, p. R12.

19. Robertson, Bruce, and Stephen Morse. "Microsoft Word on Four Platforms ... but Not Across Them." *Network Computing*, Aug. 1992, pp. 107–111.

20. Smith, Lee. "New Ideas from the Army." *Fortune*, Sept. 19, 1994, pp. 203–212.

21. Barlow, John Perry. "The Economy of Ideas: A Framework for Rethinking Patents and Copyrights in the Digital Age." *Wired*, Mar. 1994, pp. 85–90+.

22. Brooke, James. "In Brazil, Slip of the Tongue and Campaign Slips." *New York Times*, Sept. 5, 1994, p. A2.

23. Garvin, Donald. "Quality in the Line." *Harvard Business Review*, Sept.–Oct. 1983, pp. 65–75.

24. Wriston, Walter. *The Twilight of Sovereignty: How the Information Revolution Is Transforming Our World*. New York: Charles Scribner's Sons, 1992.

25. Gerstner, Louis V., Jr. "Our Schools Are Failing. Do We Care?" *New York Times*, May 27, 1994, p. A15.

2

Framework and Method for Analyzing Systems in Business Terms

Study Questions

▶ Why is it important to have a framework for analyzing information systems?

▶ In what sense are businesses and business processes systems?

▶ What is the relationship between information systems and business processes?

▶ What six elements can be used for thinking about the role of information systems within business processes?

▶ What are the steps in systems analysis?

▶ How can business professionals use the WCA framework for analyzing information systems?

Wal-Mart is the world's largest and most profitable retailer, with $44 billion in 1992 sales and 380,000 employees. Its growth from a single store in Rogers, Arkansas, to almost 2,000 bright, attractive stores in 43 states is legendary in American business. Sam Walton was central to the legend. He built his empire on a belief in providing value for the customer and empowering employees, who are called associates. The Wal-Mart culture is built on obtaining the most current information about what customers want, getting the best ideas from employees about how to run the stores well, and sharing some of the profits with employees. The way Wal-Mart operates has been a model for General Electric's quest to increase speed and productivity. Jack Welch, CEO of General Electric, said, "Many of our management teams spent time there observing the speed, the bias for action, the utter customer fixation that drives Wal-Mart."[1]

The use of information technology has been an essential part of Wal-Mart's growth. A decade ago, Wal-Mart trailed K-Mart, which could negotiate lower wholesale prices because of its size. Part of Wal-Mart's strategy for catching up was a point-of-sale system, a computerized system that identifies each item sold, finds its price in a computerized database, creates an accurate sales receipt for the customer, and stores this item-by-item sales information for use in analyzing sales and reordering inventory. Aside from handling information efficiently, effective use of this information helps Wal-Mart avoid overstocking by learning what merchandise is selling slowly. Wal-Mart's inventory and distribution system is a world leader. Over one five-year period, Wal-Mart invested more than $600 million in information systems.

Wal-Mart uses telecommunications to link directly from its stores to its central computer system and from that system to its suppliers' computers. This allows automatic reordering and better coordination. Knowing exactly what is selling well and coordinating closely with suppliers permits Wal-Mart to tie up less money in inventory than many of its competitors. At its computerized warehouses, many goods arrive and leave without ever sitting on a shelf. Only 10 percent of the floor space in Wal-Mart stores is used as an inventory area compared to the 25 percent average for the industry.

With better coordination, the suppliers can have more consistent manufacturing runs, lower their costs, and pass some of the savings on to Wal-Mart and eventually the consumer. Some 3,800 vendors now get daily sales data directly from Wal-Mart stores. And 1,500 have the same decision and analysis software that Wal-Mart's own buyers use to check how a product performs in various markets.[2,3]

Aside from computers and telecommunications equipment, the technical basis of the point-of-sale system is the bar-code scanner. Bar-code scanners make it possible to record the sale of each item and make that information available immediately for both reordering and sales analysis. The first use of bar-code scanners occurred in the 1970s. After two decades of experience, accurate inventory tracking using bar-code scanners is a competitive necessity for large grocery stores and retailers.

Consistent with the adoption of any information technology, development and acceptance of bar codes required agreements on standards. The idea of bar-code scanning required that industry develop a universal product code (UPC) system, a standard method for identifying products with numbers and coding those numbers as the type of bar code. The UPC codes that we see routinely today were chosen from a number of alternatives developed by different companies.

As happens with other uses of technology, the use of bar codes has brought a range of problems along with the benefits Wal-Mart and other retailers have realized. The use of bar-code scanners made it unnecessary to stamp the price on every item (except in states that still require this for consumer protection). This reduced costs but also eliminated jobs of some of the clerks who formerly did the stamping. Other problems (not necessarily related to Wal-Mart) were uncovered when a UCLA study of 1,200 purchases at three retail chains in California found mischarges on 5 to 12 percent of the purchases. For example, a researcher was charged a scanner price of $21.99 for a pair of jeans that were marked on sale for $15.44. The ratio of overcharges to undercharges at one chain was as high as 5-to-1. In other words, the majority of the mistakes were overcharges, not undercharges. The Riverside, California, district attorney who prosecuted three retailers for scanner overcharges said, "I don't believe scanners have helped the consumer at all."[4] On the one hand, the productivity of modern retailing depends on bar-code scanners; on the other, the system of updating the prices is imperfect and may even be an opportunity for dishonesty.

Stepping away from the technology and back to Wal-Mart, even its tremendous success has brought some problems. The huge Wal-Mart stores on the outskirts of small towns have overwhelmed many merchants on Main Street. Wal-Mart is so large that it can sell products profitably at prices less than many small-town merchants' cost. Some feel that Wal-Marts have killed the traditional business districts of some small towns. If this is true, consumers in these towns receive the benefits of the best selection and pricing but lose some of the benefits of living in a small town.[5]

DEBATE TOPIC *Argue the pros and cons and practical implications of the following proposition:*
Stores should be required to stamp a bar-coded price on each item or on an attached tag to ensure that customer bills are accurate.

Figure 2.1 Wal-Mart: Making the Most of a Point-of-Sale System

Wal-Mart's point-of-sale system is an essential part of its business strategy of providing a wide range of merchandise at low prices to the consumer.

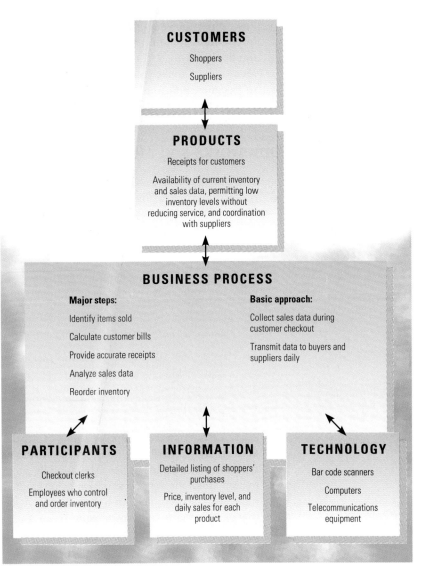

CUSTOMERS

Shoppers

Suppliers

PRODUCTS

Receipts for customers

Availability of current inventory and sales data, permitting low inventory levels without reducing service, and coordination with suppliers

BUSINESS PROCESS

Major steps:

Identify items sold

Calculate customer bills

Provide accurate receipts

Analyze sales data

Reorder inventory

Basic approach:

Collect sales data during customer checkout

Transmit data to buyers and suppliers daily

PARTICIPANTS

Checkout clerks

Employees who control and order inventory

INFORMATION

Detailed listing of shoppers' purchases

Price, inventory level, and daily sales for each product

TECHNOLOGY

Bar code scanners

Computers

Telecommunications equipment

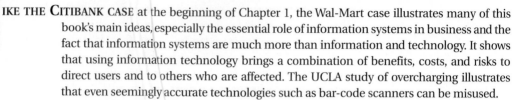

LIKE THE **C**ITIBANK CASE at the beginning of Chapter 1, the Wal-Mart case illustrates many of this book's main ideas, especially the essential role of information systems in business and the fact that information systems are much more than information and technology. It shows that using information technology brings a combination of benefits, costs, and risks to direct users and to others who are affected. The UCLA study of overcharging illustrates that even seemingly accurate technologies such as bar-code scanners can be misused.

Because business professionals need to think about information systems that affect them and their organizations, this book's approach is based on a framework people with virtually any level of technical knowledge can apply. The WCA framework was introduced in the Part I introduction and illustrated in Figure I.2. This chapter describes how to use the framework from five perspectives when studying a specific information system. The first section explains the need for a framework and presents basic business ideas about systems and the value chain. The other sections explain how to use the WCA framework. Like any general method for studying or designing information systems, the ideas presented here and developed throughout the rest of the book are not a cookbook, and you cannot just fill in the blanks. Studying these ideas will not make you an expert in information systems but will improve your ability to recognize information systems, understand their role in businesses, and participate in their development and use.

The Need for Frameworks and Models

This book's goal is to teach you how to analyze information systems from a business professional's viewpoint. It presents many ideas and examples tied together by a framework that helps you create models as part of your systems analysis process. To clarify the basic approach, we will start by defining the terms *framework* and *model*.

A **framework** is a brief set of ideas for organizing a thought process about a particular type of thing or situation. A framework helps people by identifying topics that should be considered and showing how the topics are related. Here are some frameworks you have probably encountered.

- In economics, the concept of supply and demand as an explanation for how markets operate and how people make buying and selling decisions

- In biology, the classification into species, which helps biologists understand relationships between different types of animals

- In sports, the rules that determine how to play the game and what types of actions are permitted

A **model** is a useful representation of a specific situation or thing. Models are useful because they describe or mimic reality without dealing with every detail of it. They typically help people analyze a situation by combining a framework's ideas with information about the specific situation being studied. Figure 2.2 shows examples of how a model can be used. The dummy represents a person in a crash test, permitting testing that would otherwise be impractical or unsafe. Other types of models frequently used in conjunction with automobiles include computerized drawings, wind-tunnel models, and simulators for training drivers. In a less dramatic example in Figure 2.2, managers use the spreadsheet model to decide whether the current plan for next year is adequate. This model supports the decision by providing an organized way to combine past results and assumptions about the future.

Models always stress some features of reality and downplay or ignore others. For example, a scale model of a car could help in seeing what it would look like but might be useless for understanding the effect of the car's shape on its handling during rainstorms. Likewise, the spreadsheet model might emphasize the company president's assumptions about next year's sales but might totally ignore the sales manager's unannounced plan to leave the firm next month.

Figure 2.2 Examples of Models

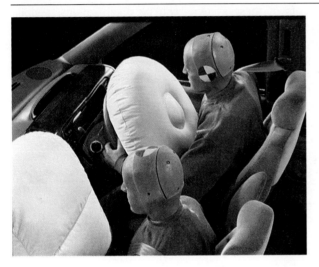

	JAN.	FEB.	MAR.	APR.	TOTAL
SALES	1750	1501	1519	1430	6200
COST OF GOODS SOLD	964	980	932	943	3819
GROSS MARGIN	786	521	587	487	2381
NET EXPENSE	98	93	82	110	383
ADM EXPENSE	77	79	69	88	313
MISC EXPENSE	28	45	31	31	135
TOTAL EXPENSES	203	217	182	229	831
AVERAGE EXPENSE	68	72	61	76	277
NET BEFORE TAXES	583	304	405	258	1550
FEDERAL TAXES	303	158	211	134	806
NET AFTER TAX	280	146	194	124	744

The entire history of science can be viewed as the development and testing of frameworks and models for understanding the world. When people believed that the sun rotated around the earth, they interpreted their observations of the sun, moon, planets, and stars in terms of models based on this framework. Shifting the framework so that the earth rotated around the sun made it easier to understand their observations and led people to examine things they might have never considered otherwise.

Frameworks and models are important in business and society as well as science because they help us make sense of the world's complexity. For example, Figure 2.1 was a simple descriptive model of Wal-Mart's point-of-sale system. It applied the WCA framework to summarize a complex situation involving the work of literally thousands of people. As we will see later in this chapter, that type of summary is only a starting point for analyzing a system.

REALITY CHECK   **Why Are Frameworks Important?** A framework is an explicit set of ideas that helps in thinking about a particular type of situation. Although everyone generalizes from personal experience, the idea of using a framework for thinking about particular types of situations may not be as obvious.

1. Identify some of the frameworks you have studied or used in areas such as government, languages, history, literature, music, sports, or everyday life.

2. Identify situations in which you have disagreed with someone about either the framework that should be used for resolving an issue or the way to use a particular framework.

Viewing Businesses and Business Processes as Systems

The WCA framework starts from basic ideas about systems in general. A business is a system consisting of many subsystems, some of which are information systems.

What Is a System?

A **system** is a set of interacting components that operate together to accomplish a purpose. Systems in our everyday lives range from our bodies' circulatory and digestive systems through our society's transportation and communications systems. In this book, we are concerned with systems that perform work in business and government organizations. The components of these systems can be organizations, people, machines, software, and other systems.

A component of a system that is a system in its own right is called a **subsystem.** Since information systems serve as subsystems of other systems, understanding an information system requires at least some understanding of the larger systems it supports.

A system's **purpose** is the reason for its existence and the reference point for measuring its success. For example, the purpose of the Wal-Mart point-of-sale system is to maintain product availability for customers while keeping inventory costs low. A system's **boundary** defines what is inside the system and what is outside. A system's **environment** is everything pertinent to the system that is outside its boundaries. A system's **inputs** are the physical objects or information that cross the boundary to enter it from its environment. A system's **outputs** are the physical objects and information that go from the system into its environment.

The systems we are concerned with always have subsystems that perform different parts of the work. The division of labor within the system implies that the system must also contain methods for coordinating the separate subsystems. Figure 2.3 shows how information coordinates subsystems in business.

Businesses as Systems Consisting of Business Processes

Figure 2.3 represents a manufacturing firm that differs from Wal-Mart because it both manufactures and sells its products. The figure describes the firm as though it consists of five major subsystems: design, produce, sell, deliver, and service. Each of these subsystems can be divided further into smaller subsystems that are not shown in the figure. Some of those smaller subsystems are information systems that help people perform the work.

The figure shows the suppliers and customers as part of the environment. The inputs into the firm from the environment include parts purchased from suppliers and information such as preferences, orders, and service requests from customers. The outputs to the customers include finished goods and information such as warranties and advice about how to use the product.

The subsystems of the firm in Figure 2.3 are business processes. A **business process** is a related group of steps or activities that use people, information, and other resources to create value for internal or external customers. These steps are related in time and place, have a beginning and end, and have inputs and outputs.[6,7] Figure 2.3 shows that the design process creates the product design for an internal customer, the process of producing the product. In turn, the production process creates finished goods for another internal customer, the delivery process. The delivery process provides finished goods to an external customer.

Figure 2.3 Viewing a Firm as a System

This diagram represents a firm as a system consisting of five subsystems that are business processes: design, produce, sell, deliver, and service.

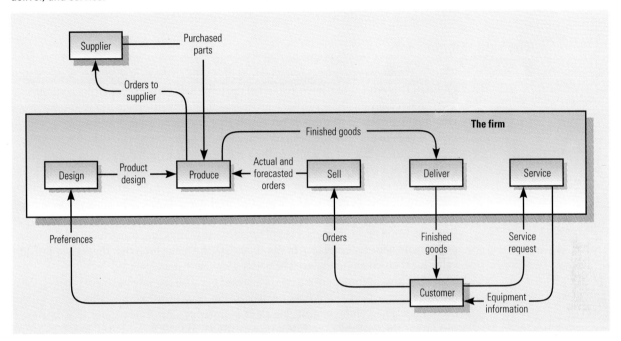

The **scope** of a business process is the specific set of subprocesses and activities it includes. Subprocesses are parts of a process that are processes in their own right because they consist of well-defined steps related in time and place, have a beginning and end, and have inputs and outputs. For example, the process of producing a textbook includes subprocesses such as writing the manuscript, designing the book's layout, producing the artwork, and printing the book. In contrast to the term *subprocess*, we will use the term *activity* to denote more general, often less well-defined things that people do in businesses, such as communicating with others, motivating employees, and analyzing data. In some cases, an important role of information technology is to convert a poorly defined activity into a better defined subprocess that is done in a predictable way and produces consistent outputs. For example, this happens when voice mail is installed to improve message taking.

A process's **value added** is the amount of value it creates for its internal or external customer. For example, the business process "assemble an automobile" starts with the automobile's parts and ends with a completely assembled automobile. From the internal or external customer's viewpoint, the value added is the difference between the value of the components (for the customer) and the value of the assembled automobile.

Scope and value added present a number of immediate design issues for any business process. If its scope is too small, it doesn't add as much value as it might. If its scope is too large, it may be too difficult to understand or manage and may be more effective if separated into smaller processes.

The most obvious question to ask about any business process or step within a business process is whether it adds any value at all. Consider what happened when the employees at a General Electric plant met to identify ways to improve internal processes.

The editor of an award-winning plant newsletter complained that seven approvals were needed before each monthly edition could be released. The plant manager's public response: "This is crazy. I didn't know that was the case. From now on, no more signatures." Producing the newspaper added value for internal customers, but getting signatures added nothing but delay and wasted effort.[8]

The Value Chain

The set of processes a firm uses to create value for its customers is often called its **value chain.**[9] (This is an abbreviated version of the term *value added chain* from economics.) The value chain includes **primary processes** that directly create the value the firm's customer perceives and **support processes** that add value indirectly by making it easier for others to perform the primary processes.

Figure 2.4 identifies some of the processes in a hypothetical restaurant's value chain. These primary processes include purchasing, taking orders, and serving food. Essential support processes not mentioned in Figure 2.4 include cleaning the kitchen, hiring employees, paying taxes, and managing the restaurant. Managing can be viewed as a support process because it is not directly involved with doing the work that provides value for customers. One of the reasons many companies reduced the number of managers per employee in the 1980s was the realization that they could provide value for their customers as well or better with fewer managers.

The idea of the value chain is important because the way business processes are organized in a firm should be related to the way the firm provides value for its customers. The value chain in Figure 2.4 probably does not belong to a fast-food restaurant. In most fast-food restaurants, the customers seat themselves instead of waiting to be seated. In addition, many fast-food restaurants cook the food before receiving the orders and receive payment before serving the food.

Figure 2.4　Primary Processes for a Hypothetical Restaurant

Based on the primary processes shown, this is not the value chain for a fast-food restaurant that cooks food before taking orders.

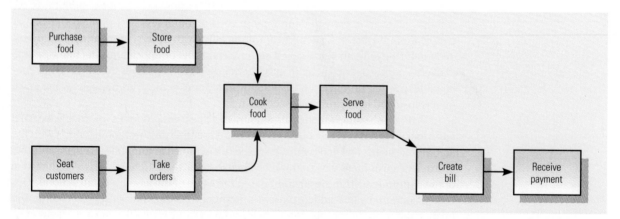

Attaining agreement about a specific way to think about a firm's value chain is an important step in improving business processes. Although a value chain may seem obvious after a good picture of it is produced, the picture is often far from obvious in advance. For example, the value chain in Figure 2.4 leaves out deciding what menu to serve and developing recipes. For some purposes, these might have been the heart of the issue. Deciding what to include and what to exclude requires judgment and careful attention to the purpose of the analysis.

Business Processes and Functional Areas of Business

Large subsystems of a firm related to specific business disciplines, such as production, sales and marketing, and finance, are often called **functional areas of business.** Although businesses were traditionally organized in terms of functional areas, many current business observers agree with the CEO of Allied Signal: "There is a near unanimous opinion forming that in the 1990s we'll be running businesses primarily by customer-oriented processes. We're breaking down the walls that separate finance and manufacturing and engineering and marketing and putting all these functional disciplines into process organizations. We're all looking at how to overhaul those processes."[10] Some AT&T units have started doing annual budgets based not on functions or departments, but on processes such as maintenance of a worldwide network. Its Network Systems Division identified 13 core processes, each of which has an "owner" who focuses on day-to-day operations and a "champion" who makes sure the process remains linked with overall strategies and goals.[11]

Figure 2.5 shows why functional areas are important in many practical situations but are ineffective as a basis for studying information systems. It identifies three types of processes:

- Processes that cross functional areas. Essential processes such as creating a new product, creating a coordinated plan for an entire business, and fulfilling customer orders usually span multiple functional areas. Seeing these processes from the viewpoint of just one functional area is often misleading and contrary to the way today's business leaders want their organizations to operate.

- Processes related to a specific functional area. Other essential processes such as manufacturing products, identifying potential customers, and paying taxes are typically viewed as belonging to a particular functional area. The best way to learn about these processes and the information systems that support them is by learning about the functional area rather than about information systems per se.

- Activities and subprocesses that occur in every functional area. These activities and subprocesses include communicating with other people, analyzing data, planning the work that will be done, and providing feedback to employees. These activities occur very frequently, often use information systems in one way or another, and are not at all unique to a particular functional area.

The existence of these three groups of processes demonstrates that even individuals specializing in one of the functional areas may spend much of their careers involved in business processes that are not unique to that functional area. Furthermore, they may work for firms that deemphasize traditional functional areas by organizing around geographical regions, product groups, or cross-functional business processes, such as fulfilling customer orders.

Since information systems have important effects on all three groups of processes, devoting large sections of chapters to information systems in each of the functional areas would be highly repetitive. Instead, this book focuses on roles of information systems, uses examples in every functional area to explain information system concepts, and provides tables and figures (such as Figure 2.5) to identify common information systems in particular functional areas.

Figure 2.5 Business Processes and Functional Areas of Business

At the top of the figure are business processes that require coordinated effort involving several functional areas. The center shows business processes that typically occur within a particular functional area. The bottom shows business processes and activities that occur in all functional areas.

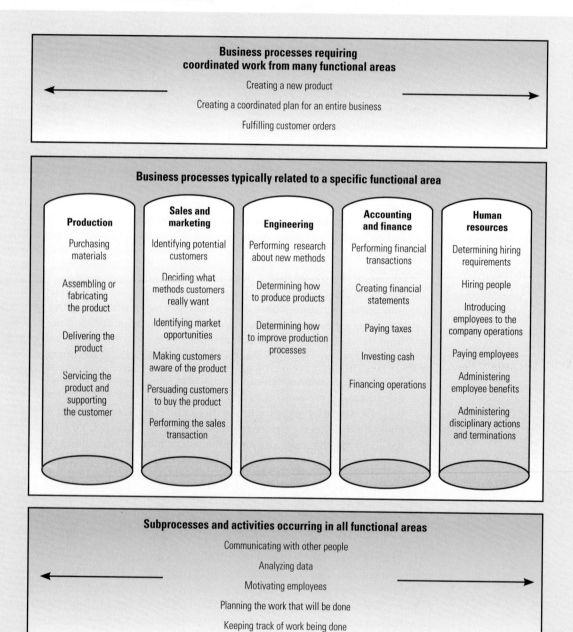

REALITY CHECK   **Describing a Business as a System**   Ideas about systems in general can be used for thinking about how a business operates.

1. Summarize your understanding of the inputs, outputs, and major subsystems of any business you are familiar with.

2. Explain your view of the advantages and disadvantages of dividing any business or government organization into specialized functional areas.

Information Systems and Business Processes

An **information system** is a system that uses information technology to capture, transmit, store, retrieve, manipulate, or display information used in one or more business processes. This definition says that an information system isn't just information technology such as computers or spreadsheets. It isn't just information. It is a system that uses information technology and information. It typically includes people, methods, and procedures for doing things with the information. Understanding an information system requires understanding the way information and information technology are used to accomplish work in a business setting.

Role of Information Systems in Business Processes

Table 2.1 illustrates the difference between information systems and the business processes they support. In each example shown, the information system plays an important role but does not directly affect other significant aspects of the business process.

The vast differences between these representative information systems present a challenge for learning about information systems. Emphasizing differences between systems makes it hard to learn anything other than a bunch of unrelated examples and terminology, whereas emphasizing similarities makes it hard to understand the reality of different types of systems. This is why it is important to use a framework as an organizing approach for thinking about information systems.

Table 2.1 Information Systems as Subsystems of Business Processes

The Information System	The Business Process the Information System Supports	The Aspects of the Business Process not Included in the Information System
Bar-code scanners and computers identify the items sold and calculate the bill	Performing customer checkout	Establishing personal contact with customers, putting the groceries in bags
Airline reservation system keeps track of flights and accepts reservations for customers	Making airline reservations	Deciding where to go and when
Word processing system used for typing and revising chapters	Writing a book	Deciding what to say in the book and how to say it
Interactive system top managers use to monitor their organization's performance	Keeping track of organizational performance	Talking to people to understand their views about what is happening
System that identifies people by scanning and analyzing voice prints	Preventing unauthorized access to restricted areas	Human guards, cameras, and other security measures

Elements of the Framework for Thinking About Information Systems

Figure 2.6 shows the definitions of the terms in the WCA framework introduced in the Part I introduction and used to summarize systems at the beginning of each chapter. The framework will help you understand information systems from a business professional's viewpoint. Both the elements of the framework and the links between them are important. The elements identify the components of the system. The links determine system effectiveness.

Figure 2.6 Definitions of Elements of the WCA Framework

The annotations define each element of the WCA framework. The "system" being analyzed consists of the business process as it is performed by the participants using the information and technology.

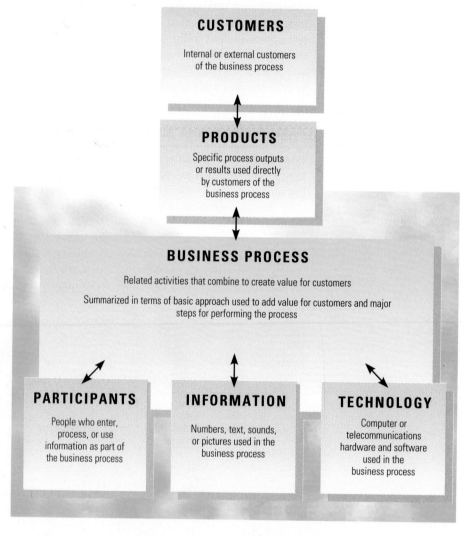

CUSTOMERS

Internal or external customers
of the business process

PRODUCTS

Specific process outputs
or results used directly
by customers of the
business process

BUSINESS PROCESS

Related activities that combine to create value for customers

Summarized in terms of basic approach used to add value for customers and major
steps for performing the process

PARTICIPANTS

People who enter,
process, or use
information as part of
the business process

INFORMATION

Numbers, text, sounds,
or pictures used in the
business process

TECHNOLOGY

Computer or
telecommunications
hardware and software
used in the
business process

All the links in the framework are two-way, implying that all the elements should be in balance. For example, if the process is designed to check and double-check the work of unskilled participants with lackadaisical attitudes, it will probably be seen as an insult by skilled, highly committed individuals. Likewise, if the customers want a product that is cheap and don't care about customization, a process capable of producing a highly customized product may be too expensive. System success relies on participants and managers because they are in the best position to perceive imbalances that reduce system effectiveness and waste time and energy.

In Figure 2.6, the box surrounding business process, participants, information, and technology defines the boundaries of the system that produces the outputs (products) customers receive. Analyzing only things within the boundary would be too introspective, however. The analysis must include the product and customers because the system's purpose is to generate the product for the customer. We will now look at each of the elements in turn.

Customers

The internal and external customers of a business process are the people who use its outputs. **Internal customers** are people within the same firm who work in other business processes that create additional value before the product or service goes to the external customer. **External customers** are people who purchase products or services from the firm, or they may be governmental agencies or other groups that receive information, taxes, or other things from the firm.

External customers are not usually part of the process itself although some business processes have been improved by making customers participants. For example, this is how banks have used ATMs to improve the convenience and efficiency of processes related to depositing and withdrawing money. Similarly, leading distributors such as McKesson and Baxter International have made it easy for their external customers to perform the data input for their internal order entry systems. Benefits from making the customers direct participants in these systems include not only eliminating data entry clerks but also providing customers quicker response about product availability and delivery dates.

Identifying the customer is especially important for internally directed business processes whose benefits are distributed unevenly among several groups of users. Consider what happened with the first version of a major textbook publisher's "sales force automation system." The system permitted salespeople to plan and record their selling activities such as visiting potential adopters at universities and providing sample texts as part of the sales process. Entering the data required a lot of a salesperson's time, but in the system's initial form, most of the benefits went to headquarters, which needed a way to produce better annual revenue projections earlier in the sales-year. Subsequent enhancements were designed to motivate and support the sales force by making them not only data entry participants but also genuine customers of the system.

Having multiple customers with different concerns is a complicating factor in the business process of building many information systems. In one sense, customers of this process are the people who will use the information system. But the information system's staff is also a customer of the process because they will have to maintain and improve the resulting information system over time. Since an information system that might satisfy all the end users' wishes might be a nightmare to maintain, the process of building systems must often reconcile the differing needs of these two sets of customers.

Although everyone recognizes that customers determine business success, people performing internally directed business processes often have difficulty conceding that their internal customers should evaluate their product. For example, information system professionals sometimes believe that their systems are good but that users aren't smart enough to appreciate them. Similarly, managers often believe that they are performing well but that their subordinates aren't listening. Thinking about the customer of management processes may have led firms such as General Electric to institute 360-degree performance reviews in which individuals are reviewed by superiors, peers, and subordinates.[12]

Product

The product is the output of the business process. The product of a business process can consist of tangible things, such as bicycles or canned tuna, or can be services, such as legal advice or housecleaning. The product can emphasize physical things, such as the tuna being purchased or the house being cleaned, or can emphasize information, such as the advice of an attorney.

Both in this book and in everyday business vocabulary, the term *product* is used in two different senses. In the first sense, product refers to "whatever output a business process provides for its customers." This could include any combination of physical things, information, and services. In the second sense, product often denotes things and information provided to the customer as opposed to services performed for the customer.

Customers evaluate products in terms of characteristics such as cost, quality, responsiveness, reliability, and conformance to standards or regulations. Although one or two of these characteristics are often more important than the others in specific situations, separate consideration of each often helps in thinking about ways to improve the product from the customer's viewpoint.

Business process

As defined earlier, a business process is a related group of steps or activities that uses people, information, and other resources to create value for internal or external customers. Business processes consist of steps related in time and place, have a beginning and end, and have inputs and outputs. It is usually helpful to summarize business processes in terms of the basic approach for adding value and the major steps. The basic approach in the Wal-Mart example was to collect data at the time of checkout and to transmit that data to buyers and suppliers daily. The major steps summarize what is being done, such as identifying items sold, reordering inventory, analyzing sales data, and providing accurate receipts.

It is possible to improve a business process by adding, combining, or eliminating steps or by changing the methods used by the steps. For example, Wal-Mart might use different methods for performing one step: recording the information about a sale. Currently, they use bar-code scanners. Previously, they might have written the information on paper or have it printed automatically on a noncomputerized cash register's tape. Changing the method for this one step made it more efficient in addition to making other activities unnecessary, such as gathering and combining the paper records that might have existed.

Participants

Participants are the people who enter, process, or use the information within the system. Unless a system automates a task totally, it must include participants. Participants mentioned in Figure 2.1 include employees who control and order inventory and checkout clerks. A more detailed analysis of the same case would surely reveal others who use information generated by the system, such as store managers and purchasing agents.

The two-way arrow between business process and participants is not an accident. The arrowhead directed toward the participants says that the business process affects the participants. Managing these effects is a crucial issue in developing and implementing information systems. The application of information technology to change business processes may provide personal opportunities and make jobs more interesting and challenging. It may also devalue job skills and make jobs tedious or even obsolete.

The arrowhead pointing toward the process indicates that characteristics of the participants determine what methods are feasible within the business process. Participants with special skills and motivation make it possible to do things that would otherwise be impractical. In contrast, manufacturing firms attempting to move from totally manual to partially automated production methods often discover that many workers lack the literacy needed to read instructions and program the machines. These firms have to provide literacy training to change this characteristic of the workers before they can upgrade to world-class manufacturing processes.

The discussion of customers noted that certain systems such as ATMs are based on a strategy of including customers as participants in the business process. Taking this idea in the opposite direction, there are ways to add value by treating participants as customers of parts of the business process. For example, management information systems were once built assuming managers were their main customers. With the trend toward downsizing and employee empowerment, process participants have become more intensive users of performance data generated by the business process.

Information

The information in an information system can potentially take a variety of forms, including preformatted data items, text, sounds, pictures, and even video. The information in the Wal-Mart case includes the universal product code, price, inventory level, and daily sales for each type of item. The two-way arrow between business process and information indicates that the business process determines information needs, whereas information quality and availability determine what activities and methods are feasible.

Technology

Technology can be defined many different ways. For sociologists, technology includes both tools and methods for using those tools, such as a region's "agricultural technology." For analyzing information systems, it is more useful to separate the tools from the methods. The framework treats business processes as methods and procedures for doing work; it treats technology as tools that either perform work directly or are used to help people perform work. Information technology mentioned in the Wal-Mart case includes bar-code scanners, computers, and telecommunications equipment. The software for the system was not mentioned explicitly although it had to exist for the system to perform the processing described.

A business professional's view of information technology is primarily concerned with whether the technology can support the desired business process and with the long-and short-term costs, risks, and other business implications. A business professional's analysis must include technology but should emphasize technology use in the business process rather than the internal details of technology itself. From this viewpoint, the complexity in information technology is not in technical details but in decisions about exactly how to use it.

REALITY CHECK   **Elements of the Framework**   The WCA framework identifies six elements needed to understand the role of an information system in a business process.

1. Identify these elements in a business process you are familiar with, such as registering for classes, renting a video, or ordering a meal at a restaurant.

2. From a customer's viewpoint, identify the product of the business process, and explain how you would evaluate that product.

Analyzing Information Systems from a Business Professional's Viewpoint

A business professional's view of an information system differs from that of a system builder. A system builder's work is primarily involved with the technical, interpersonal, and managerial tasks required for developing and maintaining information systems. Business professionals often participate in information systems and rely on them heavily but usually consider their own primary roles to be in other areas such as marketing, finance, manufacturing, accounting, or customer service. Their role in building and maintaining information systems is still essential, however. They often participate by analyzing business processes and making recommendations to technical professionals who will design, program, and operate the computerized parts of the system. A business professional's ability to analyze systems will become even more important as system-building tools become more effective for nonprogrammers at the same time that organizations continue to downsize.

General Idea of Systems Analysis

Systems analysis is a very general process of defining a problem, gathering pertinent information, developing alternative solutions, and choosing among those solutions. This general process can be used for a broad range of systems, including information systems, physical systems, and social systems. The details of the process always vary depending on the type of situation being analyzed and the purpose of the analysis. Although different authors express it differently, they are basically prescribing a four-step decision-making process:

1. Define the scope of the system and the purpose of the analysis.

2. Gather information to describe the current situation and identify important issues.

3. Develop alternatives.

4. Select the best alternative.

The version of systems analysis presented here uses these same four steps but fleshes them out with business-specific ideas. It provides guidelines you can follow while analyzing any information system from a business professional's viewpoint. The goal is to understand the situation well enough to articulate how the system operates and how it might be improved. This would help you discuss the system with other business professionals and with systems professionals. Subsequent analysis by systems professionals would often go deeper to understand and organize details needed to develop the system.

Work-Centered Analysis of Systems

The systems analysis method described here can be called the work-centered analysis (WCA) method because it focuses on the work being done rather than on the technology, information, or organization. It applies a single framework from five perspectives necessary for understanding any existing or proposed system in business. As summarized in Table 2.2, the perspectives include architecture, performance, infrastructure, context, and risks.

1. **Architecture** specifies how the current or proposed system operates mechanically by summarizing its components, the way the components are linked, and the way the components operate together. Although the term *architecture* may sound technical, it applies equally to processes, information, technology, and organizations. For example, information architecture is a statement of how information is organized within a system, whereas organizational architecture is a statement of how the people and departments are organized.

2. **Performance** is a business description of how well the system or its components operate. One of the TQM movement's main tenets is that many businesses need better process measurement to guide process improvement. The framework identifies six different elements, each of which can be described and monitored quantitatively or qualitatively as part of the analysis of a system. Because system performance depends on the balance and alignment between system components, improving the performance of just a part of the system may not affect the results if the other parts are left unchanged.

3. **Infrastructure** is the resources the system depends on and shares with other systems. Infrastructure is typically not under control of the systems it serves yet plays an essential role in those systems. For information systems, the technical infrastructure typically includes computer networks, telephone systems, and software for building and operating these systems. The human infrastructure for these systems is the support staff that keeps them operating effectively. Examining infrastructure may reveal untapped opportunities to use available resources, but it may also reveal constraints limiting the changes that can occur.

4. **Context** is the organizational and technical realm within which the current or proposed system operates, including stakeholders, competitive and regulatory issues external to the firm, resources outside the system, and implementation issues related to the organization's policies, practices, and culture. The context may create incentives and even urgency for change but may also create obstacles.

5. **Risks** consist of the foreseeable events whose occurrence could cause system degradation or failure. Since every business situation has some risks, any effort to build or change a system should include identifying foreseeable risks and deciding on either countermeasures or acceptance of the risks.

Systems have external and internal goals related to the perspectives. **External goals** involve generating products whose features (architecture) and performance satisfy the customer. Its **internal goals** include acceptable internal performance, efficient use of infrastructure, operation consistent with context, and acceptable risk.

Table 2.2 Issues Raised by Five Perspectives for Understanding an Existing or Proposed System in Business

Perspective	Key Issues
Architecture	• What are the components of the system that produces the work and uses the work product? • How are the components linked? • How do the components operate together?
Performance	• How well do the components operate individually? • How well does the system operate? (How well is the work performed?) • How well should the system operate?
Infrastructure	• What technical and human infrastructure does the work rely on? • In what ways does infrastructure present opportunities or obstacles?
Context	• What are the effects of the organizational and technical context? • In what ways does the context present opportunities or obstacles?
Risks	• What foreseeable things can prevent the work from happening, make the work inefficient, or cause defects in the work product? • What are the likely responses to these problems?

Figure 2.7 illustrates the steps in the systems analysis process and shows how the framework is used from five perspectives. The steps are as follows:

1. *Determine the scope and purpose of the analysis.* Decide what problem is being solved. The scope of the problem is defined primarily by the scope of the business processes included in the analysis.

2. *Describe the current situation.* Describe the existing system considering five perspectives: how it operates, how well it operates, what infrastructure it relies on, what context it operates in, and what risks affect it. Look at each element of the framework within all five perspectives.

3. *Design potential improvements.* Suggest ways of changing one or more elements to improve the system's performance. Describe potential changes in architecture, and estimate how they will be reflected in the other perspectives, namely, performance, infrastructure, context, and risks. Because the six elements in the framework are linked, architectural changes in any element usually call for corresponding changes elsewhere.

4. *Select among alternatives.* Use the understanding developed through the first three steps to decide what to do. Make the decision considering issues such as tradeoffs, constraints, uncertainties, decision criteria, and feasibility of implementation in the organization.

Several aspects of Figure 2.7 should be noted. First, the figure shows that each step can be performed using the WCA framework. Applying a single framework from many perspectives helps both keep the analysis coherent and avoid excessive attention to tangential issues. Second, the figure shows that the process is iterative, that is, the cycle of steps can be repeated if necessary. This is consistent with the way people typically identify a problem they want to think about and then redefine the problem after gathering information that helps them understand it. Note that the steps in Figure 2.7 are stated as though they apply to a single system. If the situation being analyzed contains several major subsystems, the steps can be used to examine each subsystem separately and then to examine the overall system.

Figure 2.7 Steps in Systems Analysis for Business Professionals

Systems analysis iterates between defining system scope, describing the system, and proposing improvements. The description and improvement stages each use the same five perspectives.

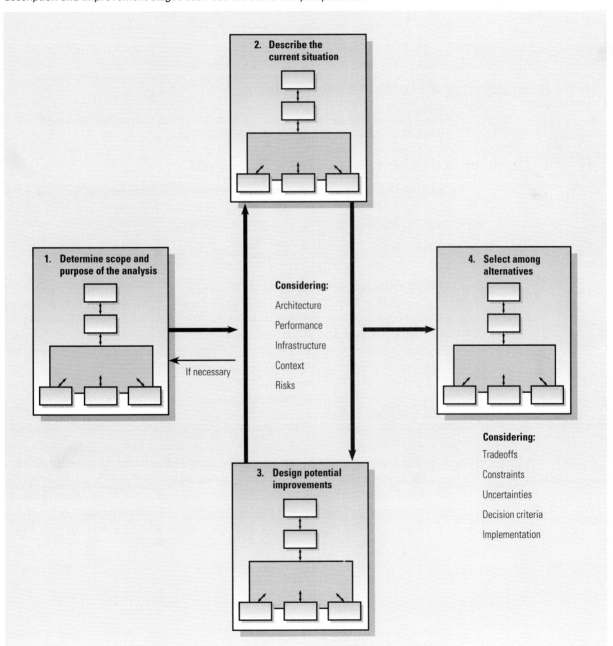

Before we look at the steps in more depth, it is important to think about the purpose of a systems analysis method for business professionals. The purpose of such a method is to provide an organized approach for thinking about systems, not to create a cookbook or straitjacket forcing use of a particular procedure. For example, the fact that five perspectives can be used for describing the current situation, the potential alternatives, and the preferred alternative improvements does not mean that a system write-up must contain numerous repetitions of the framework. The goal here is to provide a way of thinking about systems that can be adapted to any practical situation. Anything unimportant for a particular situation should be deemphasized in that situation.

Steps in Analyzing an Information System

We will now discuss the steps in the WCA method in turn along with figures showing questions and issues that might be raised at each step.

Determining the Scope and Purpose of the Analysis

The first step in any analysis is to identify its scope and purpose. Even though the problem may be redefined later, starting with an initial problem definition helps people organize the analysis, gather information, and engage in dialogue. Figure 2.8 shows how the framework can be used to summarize the scope of the analysis. It identifies major steps in the business process and the general approach that unifies them. It also summarizes the other elements. Figure 2.1 at the beginning of this chapter gave an example of this type of summary.

Any picture of this type is a simplification of reality. It provides only a brief snapshot and leaves out many features that are essential for understanding the situation. On the other hand, it is useful because it identifies six elements you can learn about in just a few minutes when you begin analyzing an information system. As the analysis proceeds, other approaches and ideas can be used to go much deeper.

A starting point for defining the situation being analyzed is to identify the business processes within the scope of the situation. In some cases, this is simple because from a business professional's viewpoint "the system" contains a single business process supported directly by a specific information system. In other cases, a single large information system such as an airline reservation system may support a wide range of business processes, some of which are outside the scope of the analysis. For example, the business professional doing the analysis might view "the system" as the work travel agents do to find the best flights for their customers. In this case, pertinent aspects of the information system include those that help the travel agent specify what the customer wants, identify practical alternatives, or select the best options. Other parts of the information system would be outside the scope of the analysis, such as those that support an airline's overbooking strategies or keep track of requests for special meals.

Describing the Current Situation

Figure 2.7 showed that both the description phase and the improvement phase of the systems analysis process use five perspectives: architecture, performance, infrastructure, context, and risks. We will examine each of these perspectives in turn.

Figure 2.8 Using the Framework to Summarize the Scope of the Analysis

The annotations show some of the topics included when identifying the scope of the analysis. The central issue is what business processes are included.

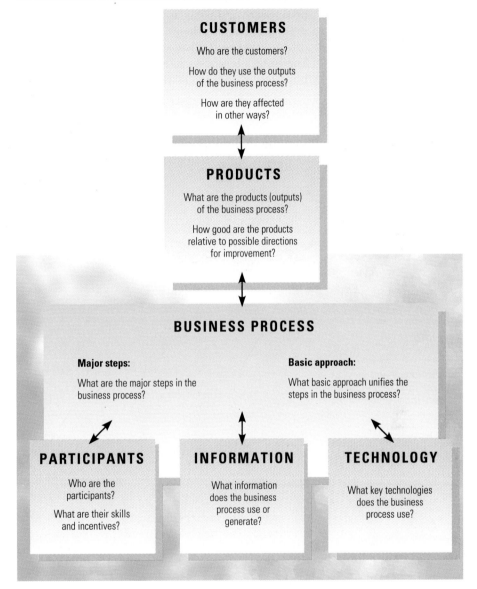

CUSTOMERS

Who are the customers?

How do they use the outputs of the business process?

How are they affected in other ways?

PRODUCTS

What are the products (outputs) of the business process?

How good are the products relative to possible directions for improvement?

BUSINESS PROCESS

Major steps:

What are the major steps in the business process?

Basic approach:

What basic approach unifies the steps in the business process?

PARTICIPANTS

Who are the participants?

What are their skills and incentives?

INFORMATION

What information does the business process use or generate?

TECHNOLOGY

What key technologies does the business process use?

Architecture: System components and how they operate together

Although the term *architecture* often connotes technical topics, we will use this idea in a more general way. From a business professional's viewpoint, architecture is a summary of how a business process operates. It focuses on the components of the business process, how those components are linked, and how they operate together mechanically to produce business process outputs. It is impossible to build an information system without specifying in detail at least the information and technology portions of the architecture.

Figure 2.9 identifies aspects of architecture that business professionals should consider for each of the six elements in the framework. Architecture is not just a technical issue because a knowledgeable user of any system or product needs to know something about its architecture. For example, a driver needs to know what the steering wheel, brake pedal, and lights do and how to use them. In special circumstances, a driver needs to know other things, such as how to use them in a skid or in thick fog. But typical drivers do not need to know exactly how the steering or braking systems work technically. Therefore, a business professional's understanding of architecture might not have to be as deep in some areas as a system builder's understanding.

Figure 2.9 Architecture

Architecture is an overview of the system's components and the way these components are linked to accomplish the system's work.

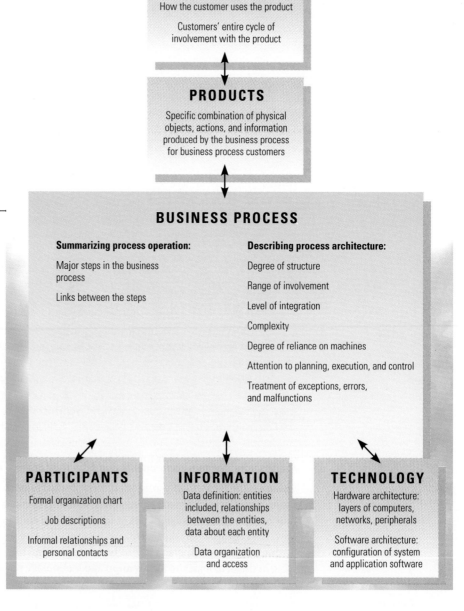

CUSTOMERS

How the customer uses the product

Customers' entire cycle of involvement with the product

PRODUCTS

Specific combination of physical objects, actions, and information produced by the business process for business process customers

BUSINESS PROCESS

Summarizing process operation:

Major steps in the business process

Links between the steps

Describing process architecture:

Degree of structure

Range of involvement

Level of integration

Complexity

Degree of reliance on machines

Attention to planning, execution, and control

Treatment of exceptions, errors, and malfunctions

PARTICIPANTS

Formal organization chart

Job descriptions

Informal relationships and personal contacts

INFORMATION

Data definition: entities included, relationships between the entities, data about each entity

Data organization and access

TECHNOLOGY

Hardware architecture: layers of computers, networks, peripherals

Software architecture: configuration of system and application software

The basic approach for documenting and summarizing architecture is successive decomposition, namely, dividing things in their components and subdividing the components further until the person doing the analysis understands the architecture well enough for his or her purposes. Substantial portions of Chapters 3 and 4 focus on process architecture and information architecture, respectively.

Notice how Figure 2.9 divides architecture for business processes into two separate parts, summarizing process operation and describing process architecture. Summarizing process operation means identifying the major subprocesses and the links between them. This is the beginning of the successive decomposition mentioned previously. Describing process architecture means using conceptual terms such as degree of structure, range of involvement, and integration to think about the nature and characteristics of the process. The goal of the conceptual side is to rise above detailed documentation by asking questions such as whether the process has the right degree of structure, the right range of involvement, and the right integration. We will explain these ideas in Chapter 3.

Performance: How well the system operates

A complete analysis of a system involves more than learning about how it operates mechanically. It also includes qualitative or quantitative measurements evaluating how well the system operates. Figure 2.10 shows how the framework supports this step by identifying characteristics that can be measured and evaluated for each element. For example, quality, accessibility, presentation, and usefulness are key characteristics of information, whereas skills, involvement, commitment, and job satisfaction are important for participants.

The characteristics listed in Figure 2.10 were chosen because they often have direct or indirect impact on business process operation and results. These characteristics should be considered in the analysis because they may lead to ideas for improvement and because natural conflicts between some of them raise important issues. For example, increasing the reliability of a product may not increase the responsiveness perceived by the customer. Increasing product reliability might require a reduction in the business process flexibility. In turn, this might decrease the responsiveness perceived by a customer requesting a minor variation in the product.

Although "more is better" almost always applies for some characteristics such as customer satisfaction and information quality, the right levels of many other characteristics such as capacity, security, and flexibility should be a compromise between problems of excess and problems of deficiency. For example, too much capacity usually means less could have been spent, whereas too little capacity limits process output. Likewise, too much consistency may mean participants cannot use their creativity to respond to changes, whereas too little makes the business process inefficient and the results chaotic. Even in today's breathless business world, shorter cycle times may not always be beneficial. Xerox found that its business process for delivering products was sometimes too fast. Customers cared much less about rapid delivery than about delivery on an agreed on delivery date when they are prepared to receive and install the new equipment.[13]

You might wonder why similar characteristics are assigned to different elements. For example, cost is a characteristic of the product, whereas productivity (which is related to internal costs) is a characteristic of the business process. Similarly, reliability is a characteristic of the product, whereas security is a characteristic of the process. Things are broken out this way because the customer is concerned with the cost of the product (to the customer) but may not care about the productivity of the business process that produced the product. Likewise, the customer is concerned with the reliability of the product but may not feel a direct stake in the security of the business process.

Figure 2.10 Performance

Listed with each element of the framework are performance variables that can be used for measurement and evaluation.

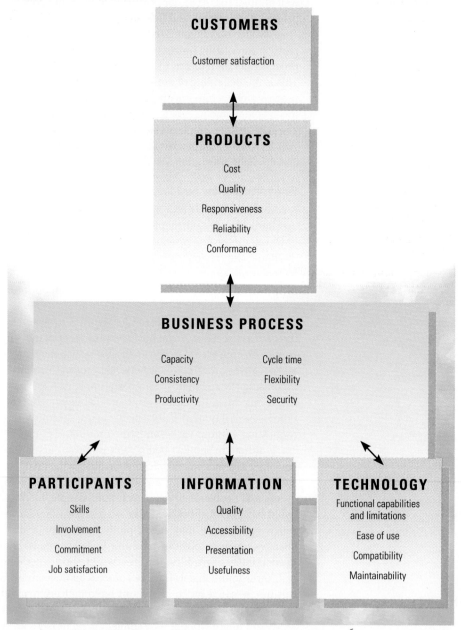

Looking separately at the characteristics of different elements is important because changes or improvements in one area may or may not generate better business process results. For example, enormous amounts of time, money, and effort are wasted improving the quality, accessibility, or presentation of information in ways that have little impact on business process results. Word processors make it possible to edit documents endlessly, often with the net effect of improving their appearance much more than their substance. Spreadsheets on personal computers make it possible to run a model under numerous scenarios without ever thinking about whether those scenarios lead to genuine insight. Management and executive information systems provide enormous amounts of information, much of which may have no impact on decisions.

Finally, notice how each of the characteristics can be described or measured at different levels of clarity. A central tenet of TQM is that measurement is essential for process improvement. Table 2.3 illustrates the nature of such measurements by comparing them with vague descriptions and interpretations for a few characteristics. Notice how the measurements are stated more precisely and quantitatively than the vague descriptions.

Table 2.3 Comparing Vague Descriptions, Measurements, and Interpretations

Characteristic	A Vague Description Related to This Characteristic	A Measurement Related to This Characteristic	An Interpretation Related to This Characteristic
Accuracy of information	The information doesn't seem very accurate.	97.5% of the readings are correct within 5%.	This is (or is not) accurate enough given the way the information will be used.
Skills of participants	The salespeople are very experienced.	Every salesperson has five or more years of experience; 60% have more than ten years.	This system is (or is not) appropriate for such experienced people.
Cycle time of a business process	This business process seems to take a long time.	The three major steps take an average of 1.3 days each, but the waiting time between the steps is around five days.	This is (or is not) better than the average in this industry, but we can (or cannot) improve by eliminating some of the waiting time.
Quality of the business process output	We produce top-quality frozen food, but our customers aren't enthusiastic.	65% of our customers rate it average or good even though our factory defect rate is only .003%.	Our manufacturing process does (or doesn't) seem OK, but we do (or don't) need to improve customer satisfaction.

Infrastructure: Essential resources shared with other systems

Chapter 1 explained that infrastructure consists of essential resources shared by many otherwise independent applications. Figure 2.11 shows some of the infrastructure issues that are often important. As demonstrated by infrastructure failures, such as telephone or electricity outages, and by work stoppages by public employees such as police officers or bus drivers, infrastructure is at least partially beyond the control of people who rely on it.

Just as local regions depend on transportation and communication infrastructure, infrastructure issues are important for information system development and operation. These systems are built using system development tools such as database management systems (DBMSs) and computer-aided software engineering (CASE) systems. Their operation depends on computers and telecommunication networks and on the information system staff. Deficiencies in any element of the hardware, software, or human and service infrastructure can cripple an information system. Conversely, a well-managed infrastructure with sufficient power makes it much easier to maximize business benefits from systems.

Figure 2.11 Infrastructure

Shown with each element of the framework are aspects of human and technical infrastructure that may determine the feasibility of the business process and the usefulness of the product to the customer.

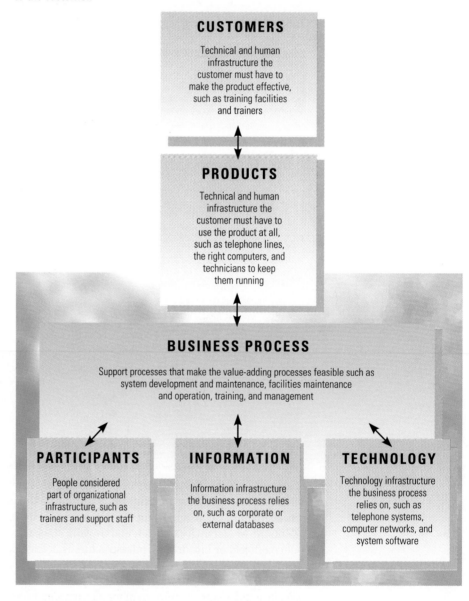

CUSTOMERS

Technical and human infrastructure the customer must have to make the product effective, such as training facilities and trainers

PRODUCTS

Technical and human infrastructure the customer must have to use the product at all, such as telephone lines, the right computers, and technicians to keep them running

BUSINESS PROCESS

Support processes that make the value-adding processes feasible such as system development and maintenance, facilities maintenance and operation, training, and management

PARTICIPANTS

People considered part of organizational infrastructure, such as trainers and support staff

INFORMATION

Information infrastructure the business process relies on, such as corporate or external databases

TECHNOLOGY

Technology infrastructure the business process relies on, such as telephone systems, computer networks, and system software

The human and service side of infrastructure often gets short shrift in discussions of new systems or system enhancements. Business professionals are often surprised at the amount of effort and expense absorbed by the human infrastructure needed to keep information systems operating technically and to train and counsel users. The tendency toward organizational decentralization and outsourcing of many system-related functions makes it even more important to include human infrastructure in the analysis of new systems.

Evaluation of infrastructure is often difficult because the same infrastructure may support some applications excessively and others insufficiently. For example, a telephone network that is fine for voice conversations may be inadequate for video conferencing or data transfer. Likewise, a DBMS that is adequate for small systems developed by end users may be totally inadequate for larger systems with stringent performance requirements.

Critical mass, having enough users to attain the desired benefits, is often a key infrastructure issue since many of the shared benefits are not realized until there are many users. Consider a disagreement about whether the University of San Francisco had an electronic mail system. My research assistant claimed we did, and sent me an electronic mail message to prove the point. I claimed we didn't and pointed to the stack of paper memos cluttering my desk. If electronic mail had been part of our organizational infrastructure, those memos would have arrived via computer. Our electronic mail capability wasn't part of our organizational infrastructure because it wasn't incorporated into our work.

Context: Personal, organizational, and technical environment surrounding the system

Figure 2.12 identifies important aspects of the context surrounding the system, such as external stakeholders, organizational policies and practices, personal incentives, organizational culture, resource availability, business pressures, and laws and regulations. Context, the fourth perspective in the WCA method, is important to consider because the environment surrounding the system may create incentives and even urgency for change but may also create obstacles that make those changes infeasible.

The personal, organizational, and economic parts of the context have direct impact through resource availability. External competitive threats and opportunities increase the attention directed toward systems that address those threats and opportunities. Simultaneously, unavailability or diversion of the human and economic resources needed to build a system or operate it effectively reduces its likelihood of success. Even if the firm has the necessary monetary resources, context factors ranging from historical precedents and budget cycles to internal politics and culture can be stumbling blocks. We will say a bit more about three aspects of the context: incentives, policies and practices, and stakeholders.

Incentives

Personal incentives of system participants are often a key determinant of whether the system will succeed. Regardless of how well designed it appears to be, system participants tend to put little energy into systems that are unrelated to or inconsistent with their personal incentives.

Consider what happened at CompuSys (a disguised name), which manufactures and sells computer systems. During the 1980s, CompuSys had developed a successful system for verifying existing sales orders to be sure they were complete and consistent before shipping the computer to the customer. CompuSys decided to extend that system to generate error-free configurations before even quoting prices to the customer.

An information system was built over several years with the participation of sales reps and eventually produced more accurate configurations than average sales reps could produce. A 1986 survey showed that 75 percent of the reps had tried the information system, but only 25 percent were using it, and that dropped to 10 percent by 1989. An expensive revamping in 1990 resulted in a much more effective user interface, but no change in usage patterns because sales reps had little motivation to use it. They were evaluated and paid based on sales, not on correct configurations. Furthermore, they actually felt disincentives because this information system was not completely linked to a pricing information system and therefore made it more difficult to complete the paperwork for a sale. Building the new information system without considering the participants' incentives wasted a lot of time and money.[14]

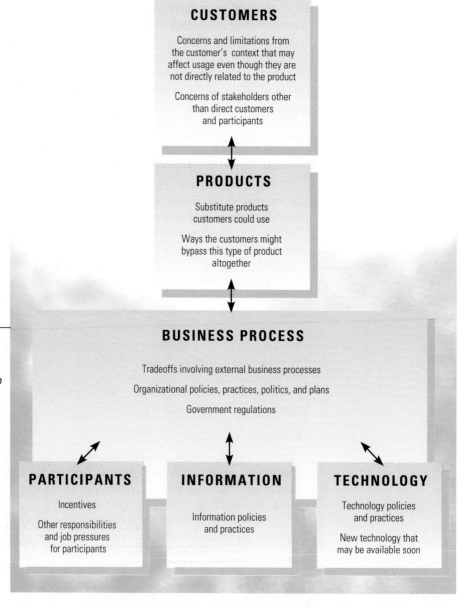

Figure 2.12 Context

Shown with each element of the framework are aspects of the surrounding environment that must be considered, such as stakeholders and practices and policies.

Policies and practices

Every organization has written or unwritten policies and practices that define part of the culture and that govern the way people behave. For example, a new electronic mail system would probably be less effective or would generate unanticipated consequences in a hierarchical firm whose unwritten practices and culture regard communications outside the chain of command as inappropriate. Likewise, a firm's explicit policy about whether electronic mail messages are firm property or confidential might avoid the issues Epson Computer faced when it fired an electronic mail supervisor who had complained that a manager was copying and reading other employees' electronic mail.[15]

Cost-effective information system efforts often require agreed on technical standards and policies. For example, Nynex, parent of New York Telephone and New England Telephone, discovered it could save $25 million per year simply by standardizing to two brands of personal computers instead of 83.[16] Uncoordinated hardware and software purchases and upgrades have wasted huge amounts of time and effort in most large companies and many small ones as well. To avoid this type of situation, even companies with highly decentralized information system activities often maintain central authority over brands and versions of hardware and software that can be purchased and used.

As their staffing thins out, many companies are also searching for appropriate policies and practices related to computing controlled by end users. For example, the pharmaceutical company Syntex found that some essential information systems for monitoring laboratory procedures or communicating critical data to the Food and Drug Administration had been developed by end users and contained no security, backup, or recovery capabilities. A task force including business managers and IS staff members created guidelines for mission-critical information systems. One of the policies said that business managers would be responsible for identifying these systems and making sure they complied with controls and standards.[17]

Stakeholders

Stakeholders other than participants and customers form another important part of the context. **Stakeholders** are people with a personal stake in the system and its outputs even if they are neither its participants nor its customers. Managers playing high-visibility roles as system sponsors or champions are key stakeholders in many strategically important systems because they work for the system's success and ultimately receive some of the credit or blame. Other stakeholders may be affected less directly if a system shifts the balance of power in an organization or works contrary to their personal goals. Information systems that create new communication patterns are likely to have a wide range of stakeholders. For example, new voice mail or electronic mail systems sometimes enhance the visibility and status of individuals with expert knowledge about specific activities and reduce the power of secretaries, middle managers, and others who formerly served as information conduits.

IS staff members are important stakeholders of most information systems since they are responsible for system operation and enhancement. As professionals in the field, they have a deeper understanding than business professionals about what it takes to build and maintain solid information systems. They also have a clearer view of technical relationships between different systems and of policies and practices related to systems. Business professionals shouldn't ignore the technical infrastructure and context issues identified in Figures 2.11 and 2.12, but they should also realize the IS staff is usually much more aware of the technical structure and rationale in both areas.

■ Risks: Foreseeable things that can go wrong

Along with benefits, automated systems also bring vulnerability. Figure 2.13 uses the WCA framework to identify common risks related to each element in the framework. We will look at risks in three areas: accidents and malfunctions, computer crime, and project failures. Chapter 15 will discuss these and related topics along with some of the countermeasures that can reduce IS-related risks.

Figure 2.13 Risks

The annotations within each element of the framework identify risks related to information system problems that occur all too frequently.

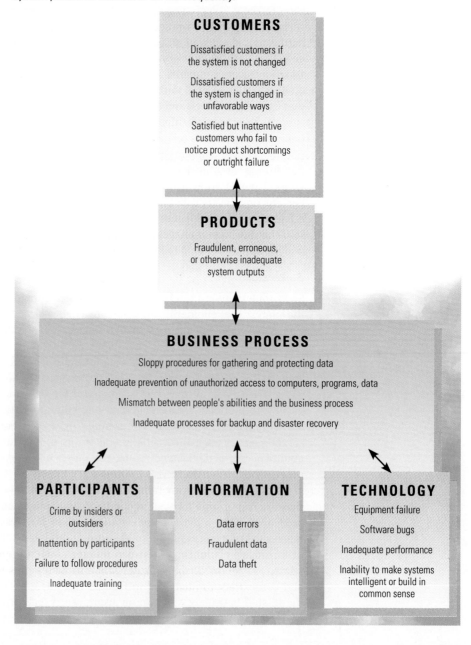

CUSTOMERS

Dissatisfied customers if the system is not changed

Dissatisfied customers if the system is changed in unfavorable ways

Satisfied but inattentive customers who fail to notice product shortcomings or outright failure

PRODUCTS

Fraudulent, erroneous, or otherwise inadequate system outputs

BUSINESS PROCESS

Sloppy procedures for gathering and protecting data

Inadequate prevention of unauthorized access to computers, programs, data

Mismatch between people's abilities and the business process

Inadequate processes for backup and disaster recovery

PARTICIPANTS

Crime by insiders or outsiders

Inattention by participants

Failure to follow procedures

Inadequate training

INFORMATION

Data errors

Fraudulent data

Data theft

TECHNOLOGY

Equipment failure

Software bugs

Inadequate performance

Inability to make systems intelligent or build in common sense

Accidents and malfunctions

Every computerized system has flaws. Some of these involve shortcomings in system design; others are programming errors called bugs. Even a tiny flaw in a carefully tested system can cause catastrophic system failure. Current debugging methods rely on people to identify every condition to test. Since even the best programmers cannot think of everything that could happen, it is impossible to guarantee bug-free systems.

Significant bugs in computerized systems have caused inconvenience and cost money. Some bugs have even been a direct cause of death. An example is a bug in the software that reset an x-ray machine when the operator tried to fix an incorrectly entered setting. Several patients received enormous doses of radiation because of this bug.[18] Although the possibility of bugs must be considered in any project involving software, the danger from software bugs is especially serious in systems controlling processes whose failure could be disastrous. Systems with potential for software disaster include air traffic control, missile defense systems, electrical networks, communication systems, and electronic funds transfer systems.

Although it is important to recognize risks related to bugs, the majority of system failures are caused by human inattention, incorrect data, and failure to follow system procedures. The Chernobyl nuclear accident that contaminated a large area near the city Kiev in the Ukraine illustrates this type of problem. A direct cause of the accident was that the plant operators turned off the nuclear reactor's safety system to test the reactor's response under certain low-power conditions during which reactors of that type tend to be unstable.

Natural disasters such as floods and earthquakes and infrastructure outside the control of business process participants are important sources of accidents and malfunctions. The use of computerized networks has created situations in which even distant infrastructure problems can prevent local business processes operation. For example, the ATM case at the beginning of Chapter 1 mentioned that 5,000 ATMs across the nation shut down for a week because a snowstorm collapsed the roof of an Electronic Data Systems data center in New Jersey.

Computer crime

Damage can also occur when someone uses computers for criminal activity. There are frequent stories in the news about computer hackers, viruses, forgeries, and unauthorized transfers of millions of dollars to overseas bank accounts. A famous computer crime occurred in 1988, when a Cornell graduate student figured out a way to send a computer "worm" across the Internet, a computer network linking many other networks across the world. (Unlike a virus, which attacks and modifies computer programs, this worm made copies of itself and transmitted them through the network.) Although the worm was supposed to spread slowly, it spread rapidly because of a programming mistake and soon infected up to 6,000 computers. Work on these computers slowed to a crawl, and they had to be shut down to remove the worm. One defense-related installation shut down for six days because of concerns it was being attacked by spies. An industry group estimated damages at $96 million in wasted computer time and clean-up effort.[19] The programmer was tried and convicted of a felony.

Annual business losses to computer crime add up to hundreds of millions of dollars. A report by the National Academy of Sciences noted increasing dependence on computers throughout society and cited the future possibility of a systematic attempt to subvert critical computer systems.[20] Clearly, any organization that relies on computerized systems should ensure that they are designed and managed properly.

Project failures

Part of the risk of information systems is that some system development projects never succeed. Some projects end when the original sponsors fail to resolve issues about what problem should really be addressed and how the system should operate. Other projects end when the analysis and programming work fails to produce a set of programs that operate reliably on the computer. Some systems are implemented in organizations only to be rejected by users. Like inadequately serviced automobiles, systems may even fail after going into operation because of insufficient effort to keep them running efficiently and effectively.

A failing project at the insurance company Blue Cross & Blue Shield of Massachusetts unfortunately dragged on for six years, cost $120 million, and almost brought the company to bankruptcy before it was canceled. The system was supposed to provide better service to customers in claims process, billing, and enrollment. The outside contractor that developed the system never received firm priorities on its features. When they finished the claims processing software, managers at Blue Cross added new requests that delayed the project and led to cost overruns. Behind schedule and over budget, the project was scrapped, and the company turned over its computer operation to Electronic Data Systems, another outside contractor.[21]

Designing Potential Improvements

The five perspectives help organize the analysis of an existing system and proposals for improvement. Each of these perspectives can be used for thinking about improvements, but it would be tedious to present five more diagrams roughly equivalent to Figures 2.9 through 2.13. Instead, Figure 2.14 consolidates some of the issues that can be considered when trying to design potential improvements. At the most direct level, Figure 2.14 simply notes that each of the six elements is a potential improvement opportunity. For example, the idea of improving effects on participants or providing better information may lead to a more effective business process and better results. In addition, Figure 2.14 emphasizes the need to go beyond a strictly architectural view of a business situation by looking at the fit between the business process and the participants, information, and technology.

Selecting Among Alternatives

Ideally, selecting among the alternatives should be based on clearly stated decision criteria that help resolve tradeoffs and uncertainties in light of practical constraints and implementation capabilities. The tradeoffs include things such as conflicting needs of different business processes, conflicts between technical purity and business requirements, and choices between performance and price. The uncertainties include uncertainty about the direction of future technology and about what is best for the business. Design decisions are almost never made by formula because so many different considerations don't fit well into understandable formulas.

Realistically, most business professionals cannot answer all questions related to the way work should be done, and they usually need help on questions related to technical issues and constraints. Nonetheless, doing their own analysis using the WCA method clarifies what they would like and leaves them more able to communicate and negotiate effectively both with other business professionals and with the system builders responsible for filling in the technical details and operating the resulting system.

Figure 2.14 Finding Opportunities for Improvement

Listed with each element of the framework are opportunities and issues that should be explored when designing a new or revised system.

CUSTOMERS

What benefits do they receive, and how much do they value what they receive?

Opportunities for additional benefits?

Conflicts between goals and interests of various customers and stakeholders?

Relative priority of various customers and stakeholders?

PRODUCTS

Opportunities to improve the product?

Opportunities to match or exceed customer's expectations?

Opportunities to combine products of different business processes?

BUSINESS PROCESS

Match between the business process and the participants, information, and technology?

Need to reconcile inconsistent goals of different processes?

Opportunities to add, combine, or eliminate steps or business processes?

Opportunities to improve methods used by some steps?

Need to alleviate risks?

PARTICIPANTS

Opportunities to improve effects on participants or extend their skills and interests?

Conflicts between incentives and interests of different participants?

Adequacy of support insfrastructure?

INFORMATION

Opportunities to use or provide better information or knowledge?

Data organization and access meeting all requirements?

TECHNOLOGY

Opportunities to use more efficient technology?

Inconsistencies between different technology requirements?

Adequacy of technical infrastructure?

REALITY CHECK   **Using Systems Analysis in Everyday Life**   The systems analysis process described here is very general. Much of it can be applied in everyday life even though we don't often think of everyday issues in terms of architecture, performance, infrastructure, context, and risks.

1. Identify any nontrivial problem you have had to deal with in your everyday life (not a problem assigned in a course). Describe the way you performed each of the four systems analysis steps in solving this problem.

2. What you really did in your situation may or may not have fallen neatly into these four steps. Explain why it did or did not.

Concluding Comments

You can use the WCA method for analyzing almost any specific business system from a business professional's viewpoint. Although this method has been described as a way of analyzing systems, in this book its ideas also serve as the basis for learning about information systems in general.

The WCA framework and five perspectives emphasize uses of information and information technology within business processes. This reflects the way managers and consultants think about business issues such as total quality management, business process reengineering, and the nature of competition. A key question under all these headings is "what are our business processes and how can we improve them?"

The framework's current form is a compromise between complexity and completeness. The six elements were selected to be as understandable and broadly useful as possible to managers and other business professionals. Other elements that could have received more emphasis include facilities, management, and organization. Facilities, such as computer rooms and wiring closets, were not treated as a separate topic in the framework because issues related to facilities are not typically central to a business professional's understanding of systems. Instead of treating management as a separate highlighted element, the WCA method handles it in two ways, as the planning and control component of a business process or as a separate business process. Likewise, organization is not highlighted in the framework, but it is an important aspect of how the work is organized and of the context surrounding the system.

The WCA method was developed through many iterations. At each point, the ideas and details of the approach were clarified and improved by looking at how employed MBA students used the ideas in analyzing systems in their workplaces. Its current form was designed to help alleviate commonly encountered problems including:

- The difficulty distinguishing between software products and business processes, such as talking about production planning software as though it were the entire production planning process. The business process always includes things other than just the software. This is one of the reasons the framework distinguishes between the business process and the technology.

- The difficulty defining the boundaries of the system, such as difficulty deciding whether the system being studied is the entire sales process or just the part of the sales process that involves determining customer requirements. This is the reason for starting the analysis by using the WCA framework to identify the scope of the system.

- The overemphasis on tiny architectural details, such as explaining a clerical process as a 15-step process instead of a 4-step process, each of whose steps could be subdivided into smaller steps if necessary for the analysis. This is one of the reasons for using the framework in the first place (instead of detailed documentation techniques such as data flow diagrams and flow charts, which we will explain in the next chapter). It is also the reason Figure 2.9 divides the summary of architecture for the business process into two parts, summarizing process operation (by identifying the main subprocesses) and describing process architecture in conceptual terms (such as how structured or integrated the process is).

- The tendency to avoid topics related to system performance, such as saying the information was adequate but not discussing the error rate, or saying a business process was fast but not specifying how long it actually took. This is why Figure 2.10 identifies common performance variables for each of the six elements in the framework.

- The tendency to ignore infrastructure issues, such as talking about implementation without talking about the role of the support staff. This is why Figure 2.11 identifies infrastructure-related topics that are important for many systems.

- The tendency to assume systems will work as planned and frequently to ignore the possibility that things could go wrong within the system or that it could be derailed from outside. This is why Figure 2.12 identifies issues related to personal, organizational, and technical context and Figure 2.13 identifies commonly encountered risks.

Although the WCA method has many uses, it still has limitations. Like any framework or general problem-solving approach, it is not a formula or cookbook. You have to use your own judgment to apply it effectively. It applies most directly when business processes consist of identifiable steps occurring over time and producing a recognizable output. It is not as effective when applied to broad, amorphous activities such as "management" or "communication." For example, although it can help in thinking about a telephone system or even about how a computer operates internally, it is more useful in thinking about a sales, finance, or production process that occurs over time. The limitation in regard to amorphous activities also raises a caution flag, however, since information systems directed at poorly defined activities are often ineffective because people aren't sure how to gain benefits from using them.

This chapter has described a method that any business professional can use for thinking about business processes and the information systems that support them. Unlike systems analysis methods for system builders, this method makes no attempt to create a rigorous specification of a desired system. Instead, it is designed to help business professionals think about different facets of a system so that their interactions with other business professionals and with system builders will be more effective. Unlike a dogmatic statement of exactly how systems must be analyzed, the WCA method is meant as a set of guidelines that encourage consideration of issues business professionals understand and care about. The rest of this book goes deeper into each element, presenting both ideas and examples that help business professionals understand information systems.

Chapter   Conclusion

SUMMARY

▶ *Why is it important to have a framework for analyzing information systems?*

A framework is a brief set of ideas for organizing a thought process about a particular type of thing or situation. A framework helps people make sense of the world's complexity by identifying topics that should be considered and showing how the topics are related.

▶ *In what sense are businesses and business processes systems?*

A system is a set of interacting components that operate together to accomplish a purpose. A system receives inputs from its environment and produces outputs that it sends back to its environment. Businesses and business processes are systems because they can be described in these terms.

▶ *What is the relationship between information systems and business processes?*

An information system is a system that uses information technology to capture, transmit, store, retrieve, manipulate, or display information used by one or more business processes. Information systems often play crucial roles in the business processes they support, but some aspects of those business processes are usually unrelated to information systems. The more information-intensive the business process is, the larger the role the information system plays.

▶ *What six elements can be used for thinking about the role of information systems within business processes?*

These six elements include the business process the information system supports, the product of the business process, the internal or external customers who receive value from the business process, information, process participants, and information and information technology used by the process.

▶ *What are the steps in systems analysis?*

Systems analysis and design is a process of defining a problem, gathering pertinent information, developing alternative solutions, and choosing among those solutions.

▶ *How can business professionals use the WCA framework for analyzing information systems?*

First the framework can be used to summarize the scope of the situation. The WCA (work-centered analysis) method can then be used to describe the system and identify potential improvements from five perspectives: architecture, performance, infrastructure, context, and risks. The WCA method is not a cookbook or straitjacket forcing use of a particular procedure. Its goal is to provide a way of thinking about systems that can be adapted to any practical situation. Anything unimportant for a particular situation should be deemphasized.

INTERNATIONAL VIGNETTES

Hong Kong's Hotline

Like Singapore, Hong Kong is a small nation that relies heavily on trading. Although its government sponsored a special council in 1983 to improve trade, it did not see its way to develop a system like Singapore's TradeNet, which was first used in 1989 (and is described in an International Vignette in Chapter 1). The council actually did propose supporting trade through the development of an EDI system called Hotline. But the Hong Kong government decided that the system would primarily benefit private business and therefore should be developed privately. A survey of trading companies by the council concluded that most trading companies would be uncomfortable with having sensitive trading data controlled by a private organization rather than the government, but the government remained unwilling to take the lead. The possibility of developing an EDI system was explored by several companies that had participated in the council, but they concluded that the system probably would not be profitable for them. When TradeNet went online in 1989, the potential benefits of this type of system became more clear, and the possibility of a partnership between government and private business was revived. The special project on EDI, SPEDI, was then started.

> Source: Konsynski, B. R. "Strategic Control in the Extended Enterprise." *IBM Systems Journal,* Vol. 32, No. 1, 1993, pp. 111–142.

- Use the WCA framework and the five perspectives to organize your understanding of this vignette and to identify important topics that are not mentioned.
- What issues (if any) make this case interesting from an international or intercultural viewpoint?
- Why didn't Hong Kong do the same thing Singapore did with TradeNet (see the International Vignette in Chapter 1)?

Ireland: CIGNA Processes Insurance Claims Across the Atlantic

Like many insurance companies, CIGNA faced the dual challenge of increasing claim volume and decreasing ability to attract the kinds of people who were willing and able to perform claim processing work. Claims processing is critical to an insurance company because it determines how much the company pays in claims and because speedy processing is a key customer service issue. The work itself requires mastery of insurance rules and the ability to work through many variations in the details of coverage, applicability, and pricing.

To find educated and literate claims processors, CIGNA looked across the Atlantic to Ireland. Except for the need to transmit claims and related information across the Atlantic, claim processing in Ireland operates similarly to claim processing in the United States. The claim adjuster reads the claim, gathers pertinent information, and enters the conclusion and supporting information into a computer system with a telecommunications link to the company's mainframe computers in the United States.

CIGNA's experience with claims processing in Ireland has been positive. Compared to operations in U.S. metropolitan areas, CIGNA is able to find better educated people willing to do the work at lower labor rates. The response time for customers is about the same. Even the phone inquiries can be answered from Ireland by simply directing toll-free calls to Ireland. The customers don't know where the call is answered.

> Source: Roche, Edward M. *Telecommunications and Business Strategy.* Chicago: The Dryden Press, 1991, pp. 356–358.

- Use the WCA framework and the five perspectives to organize your understanding of this vignette and to identify important topics that are not mentioned.
- What issues (if any) make this case interesting from an international or intercultural viewpoint?

     • What determines whether a company can perform important business processes overseas?

REAL-WORLD CASES

Soundscan: Obtaining Accurate Data About CD Sales

For decades, radio stations, purchasing agents for record stores, and consumers followed *Billboard* magazine's weekly phone surveys of store owners to chart the rise and fall of music albums. But the surveys were somewhat haphazard and were prone to distortion from record companys' attempts to influence the results by providing free recordings and other gifts.

Soundscan, a company set up in 1991 to monitor sales of music CDs at record stores, came up with a more accurate approach. They simply use the point-of-sale systems at 14,000 stores to identify exactly how many albums of each type were sold in a given week. Music executives were surprised to learn that country music was much more popular than previously believed. The data also proved there was unexpected demand for albums from small rap music labels.

> Source: Schiller, Zachary. "Making the Middleman an Endangered Species." Business Week, June 6, 1994, pp. 114–115.

     • Use the WCA framework and the five perspectives to organize your understanding of this case and to identify important topics that are not mentioned.

     • In the best of all possible worlds, would all purchases throughout the economy be performed through point-of-sale systems that send data to electronic databases? Why or why not?

Baxter International: Replacing a Famous Proprietary System with an Open System

American Hospital Supply (AHS), a distributor of a broad range of hospital supplies that merged with Baxter International in 1985, developed an order-entry system that helped it dominate its industry. Called ASAP (Analytical Systems Automated Purchasing), the system made it unnecessary for customers to endure delays and errors due to ordering supplies through the mail. Instead, the customers used an ASAP terminal linked directly to AHS's internal order processing system. Although this system is often cited as a classic example of a strategic information system, it was only a part of the AHS business strategy. The strategy had many elements, including a broad product line, aggressive salespeople, and a concerted effort to help customers manage their materials.

Although this system eventually had a great impact on AHS, its customers, and its competitors, it grew out of a series of smaller-scale systems. An early version allowed customers to enter orders using a touch-tone phone. The next version added a teletype at the hospital so that the customer could have a printed record of the orders. Next was a more computerized system that allowed customers to create files representing repetitive orders. By 1983, the system was a computer-to-computer link permitting automatic ordering with human overrides.

By 1994, however, the original concept of a proprietary system was no longer well accepted because hospitals disliked using different systems, often with different terminals, each time they ordered from a different vendor. Baxter decided to join with three other hospital supply firms in establishing a common data communications standard that hospitals and suppliers could use for processing orders, delivering price and product information, and making payments electronically.

> Sources: Gibson, Cyrus F., and Barbara Bund Jackson. *The Information Imperative.* Lexington, Mass.: Lexington Books, 1987.
> Winslow, Ron. "Four Hospital Suppliers Will Launch Common Electronic Ordering System." *Wall Street Journal,* Apr. 12, 1994, p. B7.

- Use the WCA framework and the five perspectives to organize your understanding of this case and to identify important topics that are not mentioned.
- Why should Baxter reverse its successful long-standing strategy of reliance on a proprietary system?

AT&T: Automating Operator Centers

In 1992, AT&T announced it would install computerized operator services throughout the country and close 31 offices, more than 25 percent of its operator centers nationwide. The move could eliminate over one-third of its 18,000 operators within two years although many people losing these jobs will be able to apply for other related jobs. The operators were to be replaced by voice recognition systems that prompt the long-distance caller to say "collect, third number, person-to-person, or calling card." When a collect call goes through, the system tells the person receiving the call "I have a collect call from...[and gives the caller's name]. Do you accept the call?" AT&T's action prompted an angry response from the Communication Workers of America, which had recently blamed service problems on overzealous cost-cutting. AT&T justified the cuts by saying that 90 percent of long distance calls are made without operator assistance, and assisted calls have been dropping 8 percent a year.

> Source: Keller, John J. "AT&T to Replace as Many as One-Third of its Operators with Computer Systems." *Wall Street Journal,* Mar. 4, 1992, p. A4.

- Use the WCA framework and the five perspectives to organize your understanding of this case and to identify important topics that are not mentioned.
- Are there any ethical issues about automating these operator jobs out of existence?

■ KEY TERMS

framework	outputs	information system	risks
model	business process	internal customers	external goals
system	scope	external customers	internal goals
subsystem	value added	systems analysis	critical mass
purpose	value chain	architecture	stakeholders
boundary	primary processes	performance	
environment	support processes	infrastructure	
inputs	functional areas of business	context	

■ REVIEW QUESTIONS

1. What is the difference between a framework and model?
2. What is the difference between a system and a subsystem?
3. What is a business process?
4. Distinguish between business processes that cross functional areas of business and those that are specific to functional areas.
5. Explain the concepts of scope and value added as they relate to business processes.
6. Provide examples of information systems that support aspects of a business process but not necessarily all of it.
7. Why is it important for the elements of the framework to be in balance?
8. In what situations would it be advantageous to transform customers of a business process into participants?
9. What characteristics do customers use to evaluate products?

10. How does the business process affect participants, and how do participants affect the business process?

11. What are the steps in a systems analysis process?

12. What five perspectives are necessary for understanding an existing or proposed system? Briefly describe each viewpoint.

13. How is the framework used to identify the scope of the analysis?

14. What is the difference between summarizing process operation and describing process architecture?

15. What are some of the performance characteristics associated with each element of the framework?

16. Explain why "more is better" is not always true for some performance characteristics.

17. What is meant by critical mass, and why is it an infrastructure issue?

18. What kinds of opportunities and issues should be explored when designing a new or revised business process?

DISCUSSION QUESTIONS

1. When anthropologists working in Xerox's Palo Alto Research Center asked clerks how they did their jobs, the descriptions corresponded to the formal procedures in the job manual. But when they observed clerks at work, they discovered that the clerks weren't really following the procedures at all. Instead, they relied on a rich variety of informal practices that weren't in any manual but were crucial to getting work done.[22] How is this finding related to the topics in this chapter?

2. Explain why you believe it is or is not important for managers and system participants to be able to analyze information systems.

3. Explain why you do or do not believe that the study of information systems is basically a study of how information technology operates.

4. Explain how the following passage from Machiavelli's *The Prince*, written in 1513, is related to the WCA method for analyzing information systems: "It must be remembered that there is nothing more difficult to plan, more doubtful of success, nor more dangerous to manage than the creation of a new system. For the initiator has the enmity of the old institution and merely lukewarm defenders in those who would gain by the new ones."[23]

HANDS-ON EXERCISES

1. This exercise involves using a drawing program to see how types of data other than text can be manipulated on a computer. It assumes a document is provided containing a drawing.

   a. Use a drawing program to modify the drawing provided. Make the following changes: Change the size of several objects in the picture. Change their shape. Change their shading. Change the thickness of their borders. Add additional objects to the drawing.

   b. Use the drawing program to create a template for the WCA framework (similar to Figure I.2 in the introduction to Part I).

   c. Make a copy of your template, and use it to summarize a system you are familiar with.

APPLICATION SCENARIOS

Palm Island Restaurant

Chris Ralston, owner of Palm Island Restaurant, listened to the sales proposal and wondered what to do. Chris had taken over Palm Island 12 years ago and had made it into one of the most popular restaurants in town. But profits were slipping, and the customers seemed drawn to some newer restaurants.

The proposal recommended using an information system to provide better control of all restaurant operations and to give better customer service at the same time. The new system would affect almost everyone who worked at the restaurant. Instead of writing down orders on a paper pad and bringing a copy to the kitchen, the waiters would use handheld terminals to key in the orders at the tables. When the order was complete, they would press a button and the order would be transmitted into the kitchen by radio waves. In the kitchen, the orders would be divided automatically into separate cooking tasks. The tasks for each order would be scheduled along with tasks for other orders to minimize delays. The tasks would also be sequenced so that the entire table's order would be finished around the same time. At the end of the meal, the bill would be computed and printed out automatically, including a complete, legible listing of every item ordered. By having these data on a computer, it would be easy to maintain sales statistics about which items were ordered when and about how well the waiters succeeded in encouraging guests to order high-profit items. The sales data would link directly to the inventory system used for ordering food, which should help in purchasing.

At first, Chris thought that most of the people affected by the system would like it. The waiters wouldn't have to run back and forth to the kitchen unnecessarily. The chefs wouldn't have to decipher messy handwriting. The customers would get the food more quickly and would never have to wonder about whether the bill was added up correctly. In addition, Chris would feel more in control and wouldn't have to worry as much about free meals and drinks served to waiters' friends.

When Chris told several staff members about the new system, their reaction was strange. They seemed very defensive, almost as though they were being accused of something. Chris wondered whether they would cooperate with the new system and wasn't sure what to do if they really resisted since they were important members of the team. Chris also wasn't so sure that the new system would significantly improve profits. After all, people came to the Palm Island for its food, not its computer system.

1. Summarize the Palm Island's value chain.

2. Use the WCA framework and the five perspectives to summarize the situation and identify issues that seem important to analyze.

DEBATE TOPIC   *Use ideas from the chapter to argue the pros and cons and practical implications of the following proposition: The proposed information system probably accomplishes little in solving Palm Island's problems.*

Luigi's Auto Sales

Luigi's Auto Sales is the leading East Coast dealership of Photon Motors. Although Luigi's gives relatively good prices for both new and used cars, it has always had a reputation for over aggressive salespeople. The original Luigi didn't mind this reputation and always believed that aggressive salespeople sold more. As long as the product was good and the customer was treated honestly, Luigi was happy.

One of the dealership's main drawing cards is its repair shop, which is recognized for both high-quality service and fair prices. To help maintain the shop's reputation and improve the efficiency of its internal operations, C.J. Martinez, the service department manager is thinking about changing the way some things are done. C.J. feels that too many things happen in a helter skelter way. For example, last week there was a major argument about who would go on vacation next month. Several mechanics thought they had reserved the same time, but no one had written it down. Even on a daily basis, there is often confusion about who should work on what cars, and lately several customers have been upset about repair jobs that were not finished on time or that were done sloppily and required a second visit for additional work at no charge. Some mechanics claim that C.J. tends to assign the easy jobs to certain mechanics although C.J. believes that most jobs are assigned based on who is both available and most able to do the work.

C.J. also wonders whether the way the mechanics are paid reduces their motivation to do a good job on a timely basis. Currently they are paid at a flat hourly rate with time and a half for overtime. C.J. thinks the overtime pay motivates some mechanics to slow down so that they will get the overtime pay. A possible new system would pay mechanics based on earned hours, a measure of the output they produce, rather than on clock hours worked. For example, if the Photon Motors repair manual estimates four hours as the standard labor time for a particular transmission job, the mechanic would be paid for four hours, regardless of whether the job took two hours or six. Consistent with the idea of earned hours, the mechanics would not be paid for rework done on cars returned by dissatisfied customers. If no work was available on a particular day, mechanics would be paid at an hourly rate.

C.J. wants to install computers to make it easier to do a number of things: scheduling for vacations, making service appointments with customers, assigning jobs to mechanics, and paying mechanics based on earned hours rather than hours worked. C.J. went to a computer store and selected a computer, but he isn't sure what to do next. The person in the computer store said a lot about how fast the computer operated but couldn't explain how it could improve scheduling or other things C.J. was concerned with.

1. Summarize the value chain for Luigi's Auto Sales.

2. Use the WCA framework and the five perspectives to summarize the situation and identify issues that seem important to analyze.

DEBATE TOPIC   *Use ideas from the chapter to argue the pros and cons and practical implications of the following proposition: There is little reason to believe a new computerized information system would help in this situation.*

■ Cumulative Case: Custom T-Shirts, Inc.

Note: This is a continuation of the case begun in Chapter 1.

To get started and learn the business first hand, Terry, Dale, and Pat rented a small storefront in a tourist area of San Diego. They bought an inventory of blank t-shirts of different sizes and colors and figured out how to print them quickly and sell them.

They soon learned that they might know how to print t-shirts but certainly didn't know how to run a business. In their second week of operation, they couldn't figure out why they had a discrepancy of $245 between their recorded sales and their total receipts for the week. In their third week, Dale accidentally paid a carpenter for a display rack that Terry had told Pat they should reject because it was poorly made.

They decided it would be a good idea to observe other businesses to learn more about the "business" side of the business. They visited cookie stores, stationery stores, one-hour photo stores, and other small businesses to get an idea of what it would take to run this type of business. They were concerned with things such as how to hire and manage people, how to handle money, how to keep track of inventory and not order too much or too little, how to work with suppliers, and how to decide whether the business was succeeding.

1. Look at the business processes in Figure 2.5. Identify the business processes you can visualize easily in this business and the ones that seem less clear or relevant to you.

2. Based on your general background, do your best to describe the value chain for this business.

3. Select one of the business processes that will probably use a computer, and use the WCA framework in Figure 2.8 to take a first shot at summarizing it as a system. (Remember that the rest of the book will help you understand each part of the framework more completely.)

REFERENCES

1. Slater, Robert. *The New GE*: *How Jack Welch Revived an American Institution*, Homewood, Ill.: Irwin, 1993, p. 261.

2. Coy, Peter. "The New Realism in Office Systems." *Business Week*, June 15, 1992, pp. 128–133.

3. Koselka, Rita. "Distribution Revolution," *Forbes*, May 25, 1992, pp. 54–61.

4. Bartholomew, Doug. "The Price is Wrong." *Information Week*, Sept. 14, 1992, pp. 26–36.

5. Sidey, Hugh. "The Two Sides of the Sam Walton Legacy." *Time*, Apr. 20, 1992, pp. 50–51.

6. Harrington, H. J. *Business Process Improvement*. New York: McGraw-Hill, 1991.

7. Davenport, Thomas H. *Process Improvement: Reengineering Work through Information Technology*, Boston: Harvard Business School Press, 1993.

8. Slater. op. cit., p. 216.

9. Porter, Michael E., and Victor E. Millar. "How Information Gives You Competitive Advantage." *Harvard Business Review*, Jul.–Aug. 1985, pp. 149–160.

10. Sherman, Stratford. "A Master Class in Radical Change." *Fortune*, Dec. 13, 1993, pp. 82–90.

11. Byrne, John A. "The Horizontal Corporation." *Business Week*, Dec. 20, 1993, pp. 76–81.

12. Sherman. *op. cit.*

13. Quinn, James Brian. *Intelligent Enterprise*: *A Knowledge and Service Based Paradigm for Industry*. New York: Free Press, 1992, p. 329.

14. Markus, M. Lynne, and Mark Keil. "If We Build It, They Will Come: Designing Information Systems That People Want to Use." *Sloan Management Review*, Summer 1994, pp. 11–25.

15. Bjerklie, David. "E-mail: The Boss Is Watching." *Technology Review*. Apr. 1993, p. 14.

16. Byrne, John A. "The Pain of Downsizing." *Business Week*, May 9, 1994, pp. 60–69.

17. Moad, Jeff. "The Second Wave." *Datamation*, Feb. 1, 1989, pp. 14–20.

18. Joyce, Ed. "Software Bugs: A Matter of Life and Liability." *Datamation*, May 15, 1987, pp. 88–92.

19. Hafner, Katie, and John Markoff, *Cyberpunk:*
    Outlaws and Hackers on the Electronic Frontier,
    New York: Simon & Schuster, 1991, p. 32.

20. National Research Council. *Computers at Risk: Safe*
    Computing in the Information Age. Washington,
    D.C.: National Academy Press, 1991.

21. Smith, Geoffrey. "The Computer System That
    Nearly Hospitalized an Insurer." *Business Week,*
    June 5, 1992, p. 133.

22. Brown, John Seeley. "Reinventing the
    Corporation." *Harvard Business Review,* Jan.–Feb.
    1991, p. 108.

23. Darnton, Geoffrey and Sergio Giacoletto.
    Information in the Enterprise. Maynard, Mass.:
    Digital Press, 1992, p. i.

3

Describing and Evaluating Business Processes

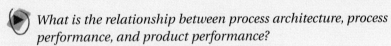
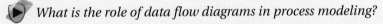

Study Questions

▶ *What is the relationship between process architecture, process performance, and product performance?*

▶ *What is the role of data flow diagrams in process modeling?*

▶ *What business process characteristics can be used to describe system design choices affecting business process success?*

▶ *What is the difference between structured, semistructured, and unstructured tasks?*

▶ *What are the five possible levels of integration of business processes?*

▶ *Why are planning and control important elements of many business processes?*

In the early 1980s, Ford Motor Company initiated a project to reduce its accounts payable staff from 500 to 400 people whose main function was to pay suppliers for products and services they provide. Before paying a supplier, the accounts payable staff had to verify that invoices from suppliers were consistent with what Ford's purchasing department ordered and with what Ford's receiving department actually received. Looking for fresh ideas, Ford representatives visited Mazda, a Japanese auto company affiliated with Ford. To say the least, the representatives were amazed to find that only five people performed Mazda's accounts payable function. Even though Mazda was a much smaller company, they had to be doing something totally different to account for the staffing difference.

The main difference was related to the business process Mazda used. When a shipment arrived at Mazda, the receiving department staff looked up the purchase order that had originally been sent to the supplier. If the material matched the purchase order completely, the receiving department would enter a receipt confirmation into the database. The accounts payable department now had a very simple job: Mazda had ordered the material, the supplier had delivered it, and Mazda should now pay. If the material received did not match the purchase order completely, the shipment was simply returned. Since Mazda would not accept an incorrect shipment, the accounts payable department never had to figure out how to reconcile inconsistencies between the purchase order, material delivered, and the invoice sent by the supplier.

Ford had used a very different method. The purchasing department would send a purchase order to the supplier. The receiving department would accept some orders even if they did not match the purchase order exactly. Later the arrival of an invoice triggered action by the accounts payable department, which verified that the material had been ordered and had arrived in the appropriate quantity. Much of the department's time was spent on cases where the material received didn't match the purchase order. These cases required looking in several places and possibly making phone calls to figure out what to do.

Comparing their version and Mazda's version of the same business process, Ford decided to change the logic of its process. In the new system, the purchasing department puts the purchase order on a database that the receiving department and accounts payable department can access. When material arrives, the receiving department finds the purchase order and verifies the quantity. If the purchase order and the material don't match, the material is returned. Now the accounts payable department can pay the bill immediately without ever receiving an invoice. Suppliers appreciate this because it reduces their paperwork and pays them sooner. Ford benefits because it can reduce overhead by eliminating work that does not contribute to producing automobiles efficiently. In 1986, Ford employed 500 people paying bills in the old way. By 1990, only 125 were needed.[1,2,3] Notice how the new information system was only part of the solution and succeeded only because of the reorganized work flow. Before changing its information systems, Ford fixed its business process by eliminating steps that did not add value.

DEBATE TOPIC   *Argue the pros and cons and practical implications of the following proposition:*
Based on the savings Ford enjoyed, we can conclude that a customer should accept material or work only if it fulfills the order precisely.

THE FORD CASE IS COMMONLY CITED as an example of **business process reengineering,** the complete overhaul and redesign of a business process using information technology. Regardless of what we call it, the important point is that Ford analyzed its business process before attempting to change its information system. An overhaul of the information system without changing the business process might have reduced staffing and provided benefits. Clearly, the benefits were multiplied by fixing the business process first.

This chapter explains a series of ideas that help you describe and analyze a business process. This is an essential step in developing an information system or evaluating it

Figure 3.1 Ford Motor Company: Linking Material, Purchase Orders, and Payments

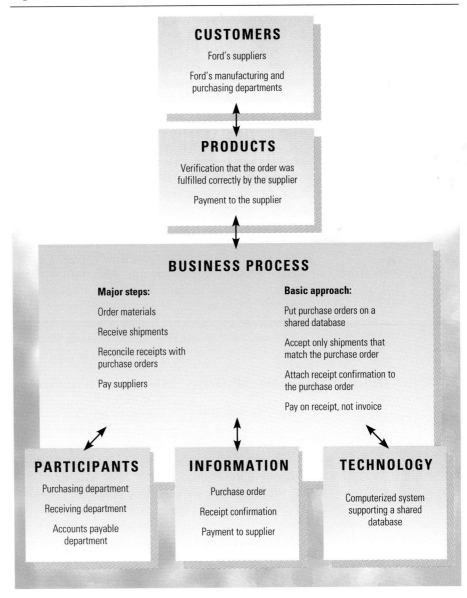

from a business professional's viewpoint. The chapter emphasizes two of the five perspectives in the systems analysis framework, architecture and performance. Key ideas in this chapter were identified in the parts of Figure 2.9 related to business process architecture and the parts of Figure 2.10 related to performance of business processes and products. Topics related to the other three perspectives, infrastructure, context and risks, are mentioned at various points in this chapter but are not highlighted because the first two perspectives are at the core of an understanding of business processes.

Figure 3.2 shows how the flow of the chapter reflects the relationship between process architecture and process performance. Process modeling is a method of defining business process architecture by identifying major processes and dividing them into linked subprocesses. **Architectural characteristics,** such as degree of structure, range of involvement, and level of integration, are business terms used to describe process architecture. Process architecture is a primary determinant of process performance, which can be viewed at two levels, internal performance of the process and the performance of the product of the process, as perceived by the customer. Performance is described in terms of **performance variables,** indicators describing how well the process is operating. Inward-looking process performance variables include capacity, consistency, productivity, cycle time, flexibility, and security. Outward-looking product performance variables include cost, quality, responsiveness, reliability, and conformance to standards and regulations. Each of these performance variables can be measured in terms of various **measures of performance.**

Since most of the architectural characteristics and performance variables are familiar from everyday life, you might wonder why they are discussed in a book on information systems. The reason is that these terms provide many ways to think about business processes and how the processes can be improved using information systems. In fact, most of these terms discussed are equally applicable when thinking about the application of information technology to the process of building information systems. For example, when you look at the trend away from mainframe computing toward client–server computing (discussed in Chapter 9), the technical vocabulary may sound arcane, but the rationale and pros and cons are stated in terms of the architectural characteristics and performance variables discussed here, such as cost, integration, flexibility, and security. Something similar happens when you look at alternative system development processes in Chapter 14. Consequently, ideas about business processes presented in this chapter are used throughout the book.

Process Modeling: Documenting Business Process Architecture

Process modeling is itself a business process. It is the business process of naming business processes and subdividing them into their basic elements so that they can be studied and improved. Process modeling is an essential part of information system development because it helps clarify the problem the system attempts to solve and the way it goes about solving that problem.

If this were a systems analysis text for systems professionals, we would cover a number of different process modeling techniques in some depth. Since this is an information systems text for business professionals, we will look carefully at one process modeling technique, the data flow diagram, and will mention flowcharts and structured English in less detail.

Figure 3.2 From Process Architecture to Customer Satisfaction

Process architecture is the prime determinant of process performance, in turn the prime determinant of product performance and customer satisfaction.

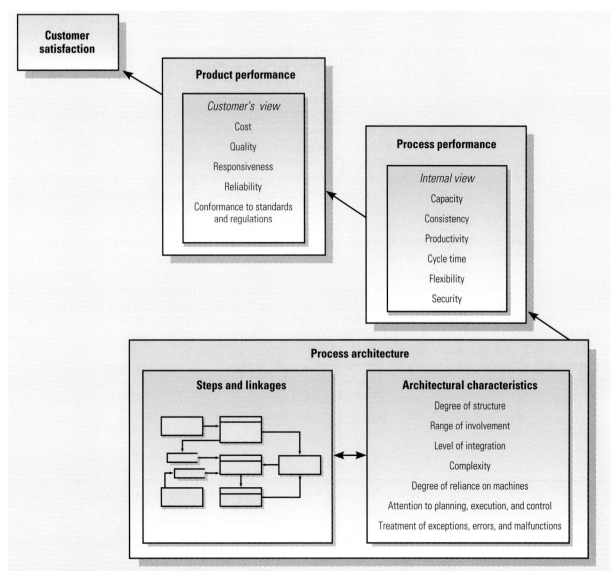

Data Flow Diagrams

Data flow diagrams (DFDs) represent the flows of data between different processes in a business. They provide a simple, intuitive method for describing business processes without focusing on the details of computer systems. Virtually anyone who works in a business can understand a carefully designed DFD and can point out errors or omissions. DFDs are an attractive technique because they describe what users do rather than what computers do and involve only four symbols: process, data flow, data store, and external entity (see Figure 3.3).

The four DFD symbols focus the analysis on flows of data between subprocesses rather than on the information technology used. This approach makes sense to business professionals, whose main concern is to make sure the information system supports or enforces a specific set of activities performed using specific methods.

An important limitation of DFDs is that they focus only on flows of information. There is no symbol for flows of material such as the physical things actually ordered by Ford using its purchasing system. In addition, DFDs do not include the symbols used in flowcharts for expressing decision points, sequences of operations, and other things that must be clarified before writing a computer program. The advantages of DFDs are actually tied to their limitations. The fact that so few symbols are included makes it easy for users to understand DFDs and helps them focus on the business process. Other techniques such as flowcharts are used later to document decision criteria, timing of subprocesses, and other details not handled by DFDs.

Figure 3.4 shows that the starting point in using DFDs is to create a **context diagram,** which verifies the scope of the system by showing the sources and destinations of data used and generated by the system being modeled. At the center of the context diagram, the purchasing system is represented as a single process. Surrounding that process are boxes representing the external entities that provide data for the purchasing system or receive data from it. The external entities in this case are the material planning department and the supplier. They are considered external to the business process because we are focusing on the flows of information related to ordering material, receiving it, and paying the supplier. System boundaries would be different for a different analysis.

Figure 3.3 Symbols Used in Data Flow Diagrams

Data flow diagrams use only four symbols but can be applied to aid in understanding almost any business process

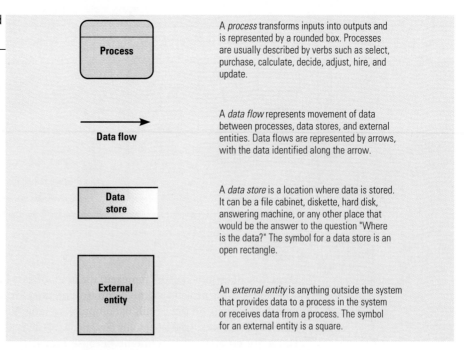

A *process* transforms inputs into outputs and is represented by a rounded box. Processes are usually described by verbs such as select, purchase, calculate, decide, adjust, hire, and update.

A *data flow* represents movement of data between processes, data stores, and external entities. Data flows are represented by arrows, with the data identified along the arrow.

A *data store* is a location where data is stored. It can be a file cabinet, diskette, hard disk, answering machine, or any other place that would be the answer to the question "Where is the data?" The symbol for a data store is an open rectangle.

An *external entity* is anything outside the system that provides data to a process in the system or receives data from a process. The symbol for an external entity is a square.

In addition to bounding the system and summarizing flows of data, Figure 3.4 might convey significant organizational issues and even surprises for some of the participants. For example, the context diagram says that the material requirement comes from only one source, the material planning department. People reviewing the context diagram might object that other groups should be able to submit orders to the purchasing system. This example shows how using data flow diagrams helps identify and resolve issues about responsibility and authority before the technical system design begins.

After using the context diagram to establish the scope of the system, the next step is to identify processes and break them down into subprocesses to describe exactly how work is done. DFDs make it possible to look at business processes at any level of detail by breaking them down into successively finer subprocesses. This type of analysis is needed to understand what an information system should do in this situation. Figure 3.5 shows what might have been the first step toward breaking down the original purchasing system into its constituent processes.

Figure 3.5 shows that the original purchasing system might be divided into three major processes: PCH 1, order the material; PCH 2, decide what to pay; and PCH 3, pay the supplier. Notice how the second process involves reconciling data generated from three different places at three different times. This might be a hint that a more effective process could be used. As is described in the Ford case, the new business process gave the receiving department access to the purchase order file. If the material received matched the purchase order precisely, they accepted it and added a receipt confirmation to the purchase order file. Otherwise, they simply returned it, and the complex reconciliation process disappeared.

Figure 3.4 Context Diagram for the Ford Purchasing System

This context diagram says that the system we are considering is the purchasing system and that external entities include the supplier and two internal departments.

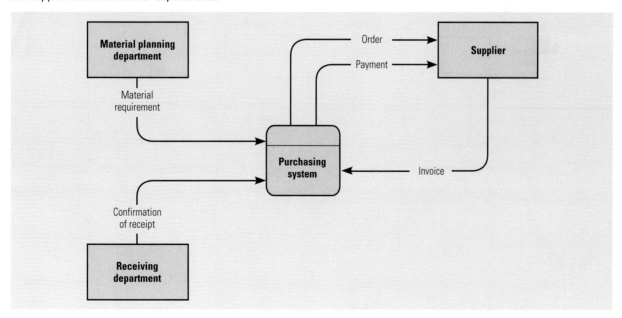

Compared to the context diagram, Figure 3.5 provides more information about how the business process operates but still doesn't give enough information to understand

it fully. Doing that would require breaking down each of the three processes into subprocesses. For example, depending on how Ford truly ordered material, the process PCH 1 might be broken down into the four subprocesses in Figure 3.6. Each of these subprocesses could be broken down further into smaller subprocesses. The completed analysis would cover many pages but would permit a person to look at the business process in whatever level of detail was important for thinking about a particular issue.

You might wonder whether all this detail is necessary, especially for a manager or end user. In fact, it is absolutely necessary because managers and users are the ones who understand how processes operate in the organization. For example, Ford's managers would certainly find fault with Figure 3.5 because much of Ford's purchasing is done through long-term agreements. But this is the point. Much of the value in developing DFDs results from resolving disagreements about how work is done currently or how it should be done in the future. If users and managers cannot or will not describe things at this level of detail, any attempt to build a new system will probably fail because no one will agree about what the new system should do.

The data flow diagram is only one of many process modeling techniques. This technique is easily understood by both system users and system developers, and is used widely during the initial phases of information system development to clarify the boundaries and internal operation of the business process being studied. It is also incorporated directly into most computer-aided software engineering (CASE) systems, described later in Chapter 10.

Figure 3.5 Data Flow Diagram Showing Main Processes in Ford's Original Purchasing System

This top-level data flow diagram breaks the business process into three separate processes: PCH 1, order the material; PCH 2, decide what to pay; and PCH 3, pay the supplier.

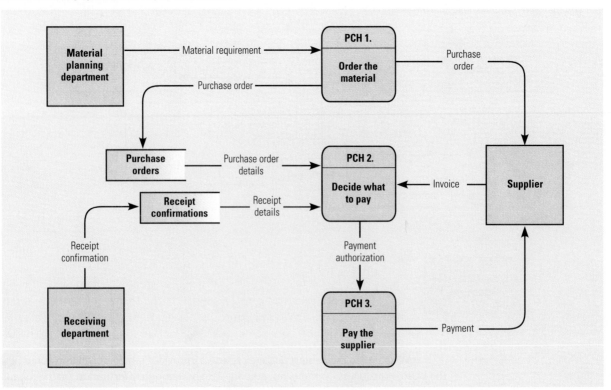

Figure 3.6 Data Flow Diagram Dividing PCH 1 into Four Subprocesses

This DFD divides business process PCH 1 into four possible subprocesses: PCH 1.1, identify qualified suppliers, PCH 1.2, negotiate prices and delivery terms, PCH 1.3, decide which supplier to use, and PCH 1.4, create the purchase order.

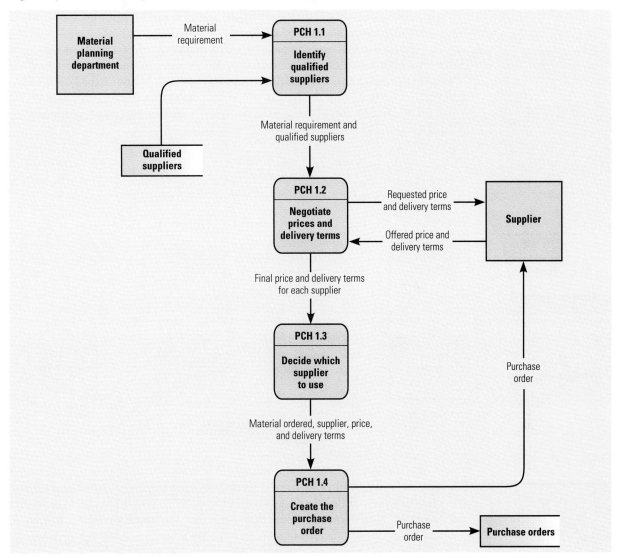

Flowcharts and Structured English

Even when DFDs are used extensively, other techniques are often used to fill in the details not adequately expressed by DFDs. For example, although they express data flows between processes, DFDs express neither the sequence and timing of processes nor the detailed logic of processes, such as the precise rules for selecting among alternative actions such as accept or reject. Furthermore, they do not represent the physical devices used by the data processing system. Flowcharts and structured English are two techniques used to document these essential details.

Flowcharts are diagrams expressing the sequence and logic of procedures using standardized symbols to represent different types of input and output, processing, and data storage. Figure 3.7 shows some of the many standard flowcharting symbols used to represent both the logical flow of a process and the physical devices that capture, store, and display the data. Flowcharts were once the primary diagramming tool used for documenting systems. They are still used in many ways but have been replaced by DFDs as tools for discussing overall system logic with users and for documenting the flow of data between business processes.

Figure 3.8 shows an example of the type of flowchart you might use directly to document business rules and calculations within a subprocess after the data flows between processes have been clarified using DFDs. The diamond-shaped decision box in Figure 3.8 exemplifies the type of procedural detail that DFDs do not capture but that flowcharts represent effectively. As with DFDs, flowcharts can be represented on many hierarchical levels and spread across many pages.

Figure 3.7 Standard Flowchart Symbols

These are some of the standard flowchart symbols. The punched card symbol is one of many that have become obsolete.

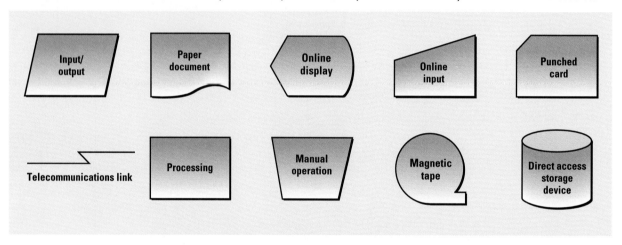

For specifying exactly how a procedure operates, pictures may not be as terse and precise as a carefully constructed set of declarative sentences. **Structured English** is a way to represent the precise logic of a procedure by writing out that logic using a few limited forms such as sequence, iteration, and selection using if–then or if–then–else formats. As an example, look at the following specification of how to decide whether the material received is equivalent to the material in an order:

Retrieve the purchase order.

For each item on the purchase order

If quantity received = quantity ordered

    then item code is "match"

If item code = "match" for all items in the purchase order

    then purchase order receipt code is "match"

If purchase order receipt is "match"

    then approve payment for order

    else return material received.

Figure 3.8 Flowchart Showing the Rules Governing a Procedure

This flowchart demonstrates something data flow diagrams cannot do, namely, show different paths depending on conditions such as whether the material received is equal to the material on order.

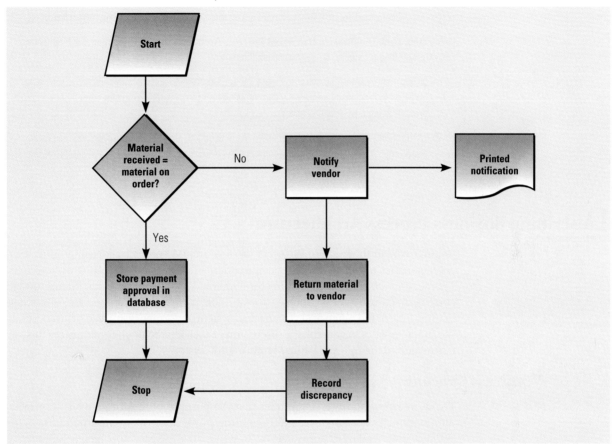

Structured English is sometimes called pseudocode because it resembles the code in a computer program except that it ignores the grammar or peculiarities of any particular programming language. This level of description is so detailed that it requires careful scrutiny. For example, many people might read these nine lines of structured English without realizing that it ignores the possibility of receiving merchandise that was not on the purchase order at all. If those lines were converted directly to a computer program, the program would contain a bug that would eventually cause problems.

This section has illustrated three techniques that are used to document business processes. DFDs are a primary tool for process modeling, which includes naming business process and subdividing them into their basic elements so that they can be studied and improved. Flowcharts and structured English are used to fill out the details that cannot be expressed well using DFDs.

You might be surprised that defining the architecture of an existing or proposed system is largely about giving names to subprocesses and data. The naming process is surprisingly difficult and often raises controversy. For example, an item on an invoice might be called an item, line item, stock item, or something else. Likewise, commitment date might refer to when a product will be completed, when it will be shipped, or when the customer will receive it. Such distinctions might seem like nitpicking but are absolutely essential for building systems whether or not computers are involved. Clarifying data definitions is especially important for avoiding confusion if the same term could be used in different ways by people working in different departments.

REALITY CHECK   **Using Data Flow Diagrams to Document Process Architecture**   In this section, we emphasized DFDs as a method for summarizing process architecture.

1. Write a one-level DFD (similar to Figure 3.5) for a process that you are familiar with, such as registering for classes, renting a video, or using an ATM to withdraw money from a bank account. Include at least two subprocesses.

2. Write a DFD for one of the subprocesses (as is done in Figure 3.6), and explain how you could keep track of everything if you needed to produce DFDs for subprocesses of the subprocesses.

Describing Business Process Architecture

Another way to think about business process architecture is by focusing on process characteristics rather than process components documented in a DFD or flowchart. This section looks at seven architectural characteristics that describe system design choices affecting business process success. Table 3.1 lists the characteristics and shows how too little or too much of each can affect system performance. Instead of just covering the characteristics in general, the discussion of each characteristic emphasizes the way it is related to the role and value of information systems.

Degree of Structure

The term *information system* implies that the purpose of these systems is to provide information. This is often true although the purpose of many information systems could be described more accurately as "to systematize and structure business processes through information."

The **degree of structure** of a task or a business process is the degree of predetermined correspondence between its inputs and its outputs. For example, an ATM system is highly structured because it is completely governed by rules stating how it will respond to each possible input. In contrast, the process of creating a perfume advertisement is quite unstructured. Since most tasks and decisions are neither totally structured nor totally unstructured, it is useful to compare structured, semistructured, and unstructured tasks.

Structured, semistructured, and unstructured tasks

A totally **structured task** is so well understood that it is possible to say exactly how to perform it and how to evaluate whether it has been performed well. For example, totaling the previous month's invoices is a typical structured task. Specific characteristics of a highly structured task include:

Information requirements are known precisely.

Methods for processing the information are known precisely.

Desired format of the information is known precisely.

- Decisions or steps within the task are clearly defined and repetitive.
- Criteria for making decisions are understood precisely.
- Success in executing the task can be measured precisely.

Table 3.1 Effects of Architectural Characteristics of Business Processes

Architectural Characteristic	Too Much	Too Little
Degree of structure	• People doing the work are prevented from using their judgment. • People doing the work feel like cogs in a machine because they have too little autonomy.	• Easily foreseeable errors occur because well-understood rules are not applied consistently. • Outputs are inconsistent.
Range of involvement	• Work is slowed down because too many people get involved before steps are completed.	• Work is performed based on narrow or personal considerations, resulting in decisions that may not be the best for the overall organization.
Level of integration	• Steps in the process are too intertwined. Participants in different business processes get in each other's way. To change one step, it is necessary to analyze too many other steps or processes.	• Steps in the processes are too independent. The process needs greater integration to produce better results.
Complexity	• Users, managers, and programmers have difficulty understanding how the system operates or what will happen if parts of it are changed.	• The system cannot handle the different cases that it should be able to handle.
Degree of reliance on machines	• People become disengaged from their work. • People's skills may decrease. • Mistakes occur because people overestimate what the computers are programmed to handle.	• Productivity and consistency decrease as people become bored performing repetitive work computers could do more efficiently.
Attention to planning, execution, and control	• Too much effort goes into planning and controlling within the process, and not enough goes into execution.	• Insufficient effort in planning and control leaves the business process inconsistent and unresponsive to customer requirements.
Treatment of exceptions, errors, and malfunctions	• The process focuses on exceptions and becomes inefficient and inconsistent.	• The process fails altogether or handles exceptions incorrectly, resulting in low productivity or poor quality and responsiveness perceived by customers.

In a **semistructured task,** the information requirements and procedures are generally known although some aspects of the task still rely on the judgment of the person doing the task. The way a doctor diagnoses an illness is often a semistructured task. It contains some structure because the physician understands common medical facts and diagnosis methods; on the other hand, it is not totally structured because many medical situations are ambiguous and require judgment and intuition.

An **unstructured task** is so poorly understood that the information to be used, the method of using the information, and the criteria for deciding whether the task is being done well cannot be specified. Unstructured decisions tend to be performed based on experience, intuition, trial and error, rules of thumb, and vague qualitative information. Examples include the selection of a company president or the choice of a picture for the cover of a fashion magazine. The decision about the president involves intangible factors such as how well the candidate gets along with people in the organization and the likelihood that the candidate would find the job challenging but not overwhelming. The magazine decision is based on artistic issues such as taste and intuition about what magazine readers would enjoy.

Using information systems to impose structure

Successful information systems impose the amount of structure that is appropriate for the activity being supported. Imposing too much structure stifles creativity and makes the participants in the process feel as though they have no responsibility for the outcome. Imposing too little structure results in inefficiencies and errors.

Table 3.2 shows that information systems can impose different degrees of structure on business processes. The extent to which a system structures a task can be divided into three broad categories, each of which has a number of gradations. Information systems that provide information and tools impose the least structure. This is consistent with the typical approach to personal computing, allowing people to do whatever computing they want to do, however they want to do it. Systems that enforce rules and guidelines impose more structure. This idea is consistent with parts of the TQM movement, which maintains that quality depends on using consistent methods and achieving consistent results. Systems that substitute technology for people automate tasks totally and impose the most structure. Substituting technology for people is a basic reason for using most machines.

Going in order from imposing the most structure to imposing the least structure, Table 3.2 lists the alternative approaches along with related examples. The table says nothing about whether imposing more structure is better or worse in general. Imposing a minimal amount of structure on well-understood tasks may permit excessive variability in results. Imposing too much structure on poorly understood tasks may prevent people from using their intelligence to produce good results and may generate problems when unanticipated circumstances occur.

The different degrees of structure apply in different situations. Automating tasks by substituting technology for people is pertinent for parts of business processes that handle information in a totally structured way. Enforcement of rules and procedures applies to process steps that are largely repetitive but involve some degree of judgment. Providing tools and information applies to process steps that are truly novel or unstructured. Providing tools and information in unstructured situations is a risky strategy, however, because most potential users often have no idea how to apply tools and information successfully in inherently unstructured situations. Despite the best efforts of software vendors, an information and tools strategy often fails unless it is reasonably apparent how the people will use the tools and information to perform aspects of their work.

The concept of structure can also be used to identify mismatches between an information system's goal and the way it tries to accomplish its goal. If its goal is to enforce consistency, providing access to information may not be powerful enough. If its purpose is to help people do their work, a system that enforces procedures may be overly restrictive or counterproductive. Looking at information systems this way also highlights a common problem in implementing systems. In some cases, the developer sees the system as a way to provide access to information, whereas the potential users see it as a personal threat because it may automate their work.

Finally, notice that it is often misleading to try to generalize about the degree of structure in a type of business process, such as granting automobile loans. Different businesses performing the same process may do it differently based on their business strategy or skills. One bank might use precise formulas and procedures to make automobile loan decisions and leave little discretion to the loan officer. Other banks might use formulas and procedures only as guidelines, leaving the task semistructured; yet other banks might leave the decision to the loan officer's discretion.

Table 3.2 Different Levels of Imposing Structure on Work

Degree to Which Structure Is Imposed	Approach for Imposing Structure	Example
Highest: Substitution of technology for people	Replace the person with technology.	An ATM performs work a teller would otherwise perform.
	Automate much of the work.	A construction company uses a program to generate bids for construction contracts. The computerized bids are usually changed only slightly.
High: Enforcement of rules or procedures	Control each step in the work.	A bank's loan approval system is based on a formula using data from a fill-in-the-blanks form.
	Provide active guidelines for work steps performed by people.	An interactive shop floor control system tells workers what machine settings to use and warns them when exceptions occur.
Low: Access to information or tools	Use a model to evaluate or optimize a potential decision.	A shipping company uses a model to help select the types of ships in its fleet. People make the decision.
	Provide specialized tools that help people do their work.	An architecture firm uses a computer-aided design system to help design buildings.
	Provide information that is filtered, formatted, and summarized to make it useful.	A management information system provides performance information for managers.
	Provide a general-purpose tool to help people do work.	Provide a telephone, spreadsheet, or word processor.

Range of Involvement

Range of involvement is the organizational span of people involved in a business process. When the range of involvement is too narrow, decisions are made from an excessively local viewpoint, often missing opportunities for the overall enterprise. When the range of involvement is too great, business processes seem to move at a glacial pace. For example, when IBM's laser printer and typewriter division was spun off as Lexmark Corporation, management pledged to avoid IBM's bureaucratic ways, such as the contention system that pitted line managers against corporate staff analysts whenever important decisions had to be made. They communicated the spirit of the new firm by encasing the old IBM operations manual in a transparent block of Lucite® in the middle of the plant floor. This allowed everyone to see the book that turned one-year projects into three-year projects, but no one could ever open it again.[4] Much smaller organizations can have the same problem. In one nursing home, new procedures aimed at controlling hiring more effectively raised the time to hire an employee by months because the personnel department had to place every ad and interview every applicant.

Range of involvement falls into five levels: individual-discretionary, individual-mandatory, work group, organizational, and interorganizational. Information systems operate differently depending on the range of involvement in an activity. Table 3.3 shows that the importance of an individual's unique abilities to carry out the activity usually diminishes as the range of involvement broadens.

The two lowest levels, individual-discretionary and individual-mandatory, are based on the individual's ability to exercise knowledge, skill, and responsibility. Information systems based on this type of assumption are more tailored to individual capabilities and preferences than at the other levels. The work group level focuses on teamwork in flexible situations and requires an ongoing process of adjusting usage patterns to the needs of the group. The organizational level focuses on consistency, coordination, and repetition across multiple users. It downplays the individual's unique contribution and treats the individual more like an anonymous agent of the business. The interorganizational level deemphasizes the user even further and views the organization as the user even though a person in the organization is responsible for the accuracy of the information in the system.

Table 3.3 Different Ranges of Involvement That May Be Required for System Effectiveness

Range of Involvement	Usage Pattern and Significance of User's Individuality
Interorganizational: The system promotes coordination across organizations. Inputs and outputs are owned by organizations rather than individuals within those organizations. Interorganizational coordination is required in systems for government reporting, paying taxes, and sharing information with investment industry organizations. Nonconformance by an organization would remove it from the system, with negative business or legal consequences.	Patterns: • Links separate enterprises • Usage patterns dictated by interorganizational agreements • Individuality of users largely irrelevant to users in other organizations Examples: • Use personal computer to make stock trades • Place orders by linking directly into supplier's inventory system
Organizational: The system promotes coordination within an organization, employing consistency and standardized usage patterns to maintain coordination and efficiency. Nonconformance to this system would undermine the organization's operation.	Patterns: • Usage across the organization required for system effectiveness • Usage patterns dictated by organizational standards • Individuality of use discouraged or eliminated Examples: • Financial accounting system consolidating monthly performance • Transaction processing system for tracking inventory in a factory
Work group: The system promotes coordination among a group of individuals who retain discretion about how and whether to use it.	Patterns: • Used with individual discretion as part of a work group or team • Usage patterns dictated by current needs of the work group Examples: • Online system for shared access to legal documents in a large lawsuit • Videoconferencing system to help dispersed work groups communicate
Individual-mandatory: An individual is performing individual managerial or professional work, but in a manner that is not discretionary. Information systems supporting this type of activity still deemphasize coordination because the work is individual in nature. However, the information system may enforce prespecified ideas about the best way to do this individual work.	Patterns: • Used for a task requiring individual skill or knowledge but in a manner dictated by organizational standards or requirements Examples: • Bank loan officer must use bank's standard loan analysis method • Programmer must use firm's standard programming style
Individual-discretionary: An individual user can decide how to perform the activity and hence whether and how to use the information system. Information systems that support this type of activity deemphasize coordinated effort since the participant has total freedom in deciding how and whether to use the information system.	Patterns: • Used for an individual task at the discretion of the individual • Usage patterns dictated by individual preference Examples: • Sales manager analyzes sales data to understand sales increase • Manager uses spreadsheet to test feasibility of possible plans

Information systems can be designed in ways that broaden or constrict the range of involvement in a business process. Information systems that provide upper management with daily access to detailed operational data give them the ability to examine data and ask questions they would not be able to ask if less information were available. Such systems broaden the range of involvement by allowing managers to get involved in the details of work their subordinates are managing. If done well, this may support the subordinates' performance. If done poorly, subordinates may feel intruded on and unable to manage their own work.

In contrast, information systems may reduce the range of involvement by supporting a **case manager approach** in which a single individual does different information-related tasks that many individuals might have done in the past. Pacific Bell moved in this direction when they redesigned their process of signing up business customers for Centrex telephone service. Previously, this involved 11 separate jobs and more than 5 business days. Service representatives had to switch back and forth between nine separate information systems involving things such as equipment inventory, customer requirements, and installation schedules. Frequent mistakes caused excessive rework and call-backs to customers. Now service coordinators handle all interfaces with customers and use workstations providing a consolidated view of the nine information systems. Service is installed on the day of the order 80 percent of the time, and within 2.3 days for more complicated situations.[5]

Level of Integration

It is often difficult to understand what people mean when they use the terms *integration* and *integrated system*. The confusion occurs in part because integration is not a single variable but rather exists on several conceptually distinct levels. Frame of reference is also a problem since these terms can be used to describe relationships between subprocesses within a business process or relationships between what might otherwise be considered separate processes. We will start with a single general definition but will then look at five separate levels of integration, each of which may provide a clue about the right level of integration in a system being analyzed.

Integration is the connection and mutual responsiveness and collaboration between distinct activities or processes. In general, the extent of integration between two processes or activities is related to the speed with which one responds to events in the other. This speed depends on both the immediacy of communication and the degree to which the processes respond to the information communicated. Information systems can play roles in both aspects of integration, first by supporting the communication and second by making it easier for each business process to use the information to respond effectively.

As an example, consider the way integration between the sales effort and the production effort has become a major competitive issue in many industries. The more integrated these processes are, the faster the production process responds to new orders from sales. Motorola saw this form of integration as an important issue, and cut the factory cycle time for building customized electronic pagers from two weeks to two hours. Highly automated production of the pager starts within 17 minutes of placing an order from the field.[6] Integration with suppliers has also become an important trend in manufacturing (see Figure 3.9 for a related example). For example, a computer in a Nissan factory in Great Britain looks at the cars currently on the assembly line and sends orders to Akeda-Hoover, which supplies its seats. Akeda-Hoover schedules its daily production for seats with the specific color and style ordered by Nissan. The seats move directly from Akeda-Hoover to an automobile on Nissan's assembly line.[7] Information systems play a crucial role in integration because they convey the information and process it.

Integration can even occur across several consecutive stages of a product's value chain, such as the way apparel and textile firms have used electronic data interchange (EDI) to speed reordering across the stages of the value chain. When the department store Dillard's finds its inventory of a pants style below a specified level, it notifies the apparel manufacturer Haggar electronically. If Haggar doesn't have the cloth to manufacture the needed pants, it notifies the textile manufacturer Burlington Industries electronically.[8]

Figure 3.9 McKesson Integrates Inventory Tracking and Ordering

McKesson has extended the scope of its value chain by permitting its customers to enter data directly into its computerized inventory system. On the other side of the integrated system, workers within McKesson's distribution warehouses use specially designed "strap-on" computers and bar-code readers to perform internal inventory tracking.

Five levels of integration

A basic question in business process redesign involves the desired level of integration between different business processes. Figure 3.10 summarizes five different levels of integration. The first two levels may not be as apparent as the types of integration mentioned in the examples but are worth mentioning as methods of maintaining both alignment and efficiency.

The difference between information sharing, coordination, and collaboration is especially important for thinking about potential benefits of information system investments. Although often touted as a major benefit of information technology investments, information sharing does not necessarily imply genuine coordination or collaboration will occur. Technology can provide access to information, but coordination and collaboration require action commitments by the participants. Therefore, system builders should be careful about finding the level of integration that people in the organization are willing to commit to.

On the other hand, many forms of information sharing provide significant benefits without requiring responsiveness between business processes. Consider two business processes in libraries, the cataloguing process that keeps track of what the library owns and the circulation process that keeps track of what has been checked out. If these are totally separate systems, you can find out that the library owns something but then find it is not on the shelves because it is checked out or missing. If the two systems are integrated using computers, the computer display that identifies catalogued items can also indicate whether they are checked out. This information sharing between the systems saves a lot of time for library users.

Problems with tight integration

Notice how some systems seem to be less integrated than they should be. For example, most current ATM systems have a delay between the time an ATM deposit is made and the time it is recognized as money available for use. This is especially apparent on weekends, when a Friday night deposit may not be recognized until Monday, the next working day. This time lag shows that the process of making deposits is not tightly integrated with the process of accounting for checking account balances.

Figure 3.10 Five Levels of Integration Between Business Processes

Business processes in a firm can be totally unrelated to one another or can be related at any of these five levels.

Common culture: Shared understandings and beliefs

People involved in two independent processes share the same general beliefs and expectations about how people communicate and work together. These shared beliefs make it easier to work together and resolve conflicts whenever necessary.

Common standards: Using consistent terminology and procedures to make business processes easier to maintain and interface

Two different business processes use the same standards but otherwise operate independently. For example, two different departments may use the same type of personal computer or the same word processing software. Operating with agreed on standards of this type may create economies of scale for the technical staff, who may be able to learn and service a smaller number of technical options. It also may enhance the possibility of other forms of integration in the future.

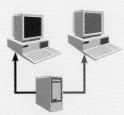

Information sharing: Mutual access to data by business processes that operate independently.

Two different business processes share some of the same information even though the information sharing does not directly involve mutual responsiveness. For example, a sales department and a manufacturing department might share the manufacturing database so that sales would know what capacity was still available for additional orders.

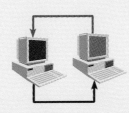

Coordination: Negotiation and exchange of messages permitting separate but interdependent processes to respond to each other's needs and limitations

Different business processes maintain their own unique function and identity but pass information back and forth to coordinate their efforts toward a common objective. For example, sales tells manufacturing what they can sell; manufacturing responds with a tentative output schedule; they negotiate to come up with a mutually feasible plan and go about their individual work.

Collaboration: Strong enough interdependence between processes that their unique identity begins to disappear

Two different business processes merge part or all of their identity to accomplish larger objectives of the firm. For example, based on the need to get more easily manufacturable products to market sooner, many firms have moved toward product development processes that involve close collaboration between marketing, engineering, and manufacturing.

Although the tight integration of processes might seem desirable, forcing processes to respond to each other too frequently may make it difficult for each process to get its work done. This is one of the reasons many factories that produce noncustomized products "freeze" their schedules a week or two at a time. Their managers believe that changing production schedules continually in response to daily events in the sales department causes too much chaos and inefficiency in production. The difficulty in responding rapidly while also maintaining high production quality and efficiency is one of the reasons responsiveness to customers is a genuine competitive issue.

Information system builders sometimes avoid highly integrated information systems for their own reasons. They often prefer to build two separate information systems plus an interface that operates on a schedule, such as daily or weekly. This approach is often far simpler than real-time integration assuring that any event recorded by either system is immediately reflected in the other. Thinking of the connection between two systems as an interface divides a large problem into two smaller problems that can be solved individually. Often this means that a usable information system will be available sooner. Building an interface is especially appropriate where the desired capabilities of a new system are open to debate or when the business situation is changing rapidly. The lower level of integration that results may have negative consequences, however. For example, there might be a long delay in the interface between a customer returns system and the inventory system used for customer orders. This delay could result in situations when material returned by one customer could be shipped for another order except that the inventory system does not yet recognize the return has occurred.

Another problem with tightly integrated (also called tightly coupled) systems is that they may be more prone to catastrophic failure than less integrated systems. Tightly coupled systems have little slack, require that things happen in a particular order, and depend on all components to operate within particular ranges. When one component fails, the others may also fail immediately. The most tightly coupled systems in our society include aircraft, nuclear power plants, power grids, and automated warfare systems.[9] In contrast, loosely coupled systems are decentralized, have slack resources and redundancies, permit delays and substitutions, and allow things to be done in different orders. Failures tend to be localized and therefore can be isolated, diagnosed, and fixed quickly. Thus, high levels of integration have both advantages and disadvantages that should be analyzed carefully.

Complexity

A system's **complexity** is a function of the number of differentiated components and the number and nature of their interactions. Differentiated components and additional interactions are added to systems to make the systems more powerful. But as complexity increases, systems are more difficult to develop and manage because more factors and interactions must be considered, evaluated, and tested. Complexity also makes it more difficult to understand what is going on and even more difficult to anticipate the consequences of changes throughout the system.

The U.S. federal income tax system demonstrates the problem of complexity. A simple system might just collect a sliding percentage of personal income and leave it at that. But such a system would not respond directly to additional social, political, and economic goals, such as making it easier to own a house, making it easier to send children to day care, recognizing the depletion on oil wells, and preventing high-income individuals from paying no taxes (through the dreaded "alternative minimum tax"). Each additional feature added to the tax code permits it to take another goal into account (for better or for worse) but also adds to the number of differentiated components and creates a wider range of interactions between components. The resulting complexity has become virtually unmanageable and has spawned a tax preparation industry. The audit of tax advice given by the Internal Revenue Service hotline in 1986 reveals a result of this problem. Around 39 percent of the advice given to taxpayers on tax law changes in 1986 was wrong.[10]

Although business systems may also be quite complex, there are a number of strategies for reducing that complexity. The first is to reduce the number of differentiated components. Manufacturers have used this strategy to simplify both products and manufacturing processes. In some of the most efficient manufacturing plants, even the number of specialized job classifications has been reduced significantly. The second strategy is to reduce the number of interacting components and simplify the nature of the interactions. This strategy has reduced some of the complexity of computer hardware. Much of the progress during the last 30 years results from combining multiple functions on the same semiconductor chip. Although the chip becomes more complex because it must absorb more functions, the design of systems becomes simpler because the individual building blocks are more powerful.

Degree of Reliance on Machines

This book focuses on business processes that use information technology. Such systems have a division of labor between people and machines. The general approach for this division of labor is to assign tasks in a way that emphasizes the strengths and deemphasizes the weaknesses of each. In general, tasks assigned to computers are totally structured, can be described completely, and may require a combination of great speed, accuracy, and endurance. Tasks with relatively little processing (such as keeping track of personal calendars) are also assigned to computers just to assure the tasks are handled in an organized and predictable way. In contrast, tasks people must perform are those requiring common sense, intelligence, judgment, or creativity. People handle these tasks better than computers because they are flexible and can identify and resolve previously unencountered situations.

Like other architectural characteristics, the degree of reliance on information technology is a design decision. As is apparent when shopping at retailers with totally manual inventory systems, doing things manually that could be done by computers is slow and inefficient and often makes it difficult to provide excellent service for customers. Furthermore, as illustrated throughout this book, computers enable business process capabilities that would be impossible without them.

Excessive reliance on computers can cause many problems, however. For example, although airline manufacturers and many pilots believe autopilot systems are usually safer and less error prone than human pilots, technical issues range from technical adequacy of autopilots to their impact on human pilots. An example of the technical adequacy problem occurred when a Lufthansa Airbus A320 landing in Warsaw received faulty wind-speed information and came in too fast, creating a lift that lightened the load on the landing gear. The flight control software concluded the plane was not on the ground and prevented the jets from braking the aircraft by reversing thrust. The resulting crash killed two people and injured 45.[11]

The human issues start with the "peripheralization" of the human pilots, the tendency for them to feel as though they are at the periphery of the action. Autopilots also generate complacency and inattention. And regardless of how much training pilots receive in realistic flight simulators on the ground, there is also the question whether pilots will get enough practice. For example, the survivors of a 1989 DC-10 crash in Sioux City, Iowa, owe their lives to an experienced crew that managed to guide the plane to an airport despite an engine explosion that destroyed all the plane's steering equipment.

Attention to Planning, Execution, and Control

Participants in a business process need to know what to do, when to do it, and how to make sure the work was done properly. We can think of this as a cycle of planning, execution, and control. **Planning** is the process of deciding what work to do and what outputs to produce when. **Executing** is the process of doing the work. **Controlling** is the process of using information about past work performance to assure that goals are attained and plans carried out.

Planning, execution, and control occur wherever people do work. For example, a carpenter making a bookcase plans the work, performs the work, and uses carpentry techniques to ensure that the work is being done correctly. A manager implementing an organizational change goes through the same three steps. The manager's plan outlines the process of explaining the change, training the people, and converting from the old method to the new method. The execution is the explanation, training, and conversion. The control is the collection and use of information to make sure that the change is occurring.

Figure 3.11 shows flows of information between planning, execution, and control. Planning determines both work standards and what work will be done when. As work is executed, it generates information that is used in control processes. A control system feeds information back to execution to keep the execution on track and also to the planning process to ensure that future plans use realistic assumptions. To keep execution on track, recent performance is compared with work standards or work schedules, and actions are taken to compensate for any deviations. Planning and control are information-intensive activities because a plan is information and because control involves the use of information to check how well the plan is being met and to take any necessary corrective action.

There are many ways to improve the cycle of planning, execution, and control. Planning for individual work can be supported by creating a standard planning format and then supplying information such as customer specifications or machine availability in a computerized form so that planning calculations can be automated. Organizational planning can be improved by creating standard formats and processing procedures for the structured parts of planning, such as transmitting and distributing plans, calculating planned results, and merging numbers from different organizations.

Execution can be improved by focusing information systems on execution per se rather than mostly on planning or control activities. The emergence of powerful interactive computing makes this much more feasible today than it was even ten years

Figure 3.11 Planning, Execution, and Control

Planning, execution, and control are separate activities. Execution receives the output of planning and provides information inputs into the control process.

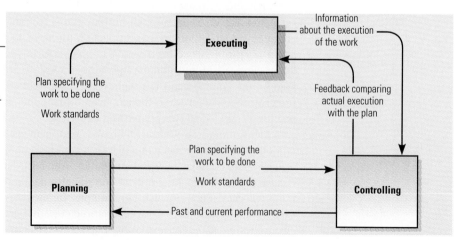

ago although its practicality depends on the nature of the work. Information-intensive processes such as designing a product or creating customer bills focus on information and require some type of information system. In contrast, information systems are less central for processes such as making a violin or helping employees work with peers.

Control processes can be improved in a number of ways using information systems, such as by making the collection of control data an automatic byproduct of doing the work. Beyond combining data collection with work tasks, it is also possible to integrate control activities into the work itself. For example, instead of having a historically oriented control system that tells what went wrong last week or last month, it is sometimes possible to use information systems to provide immediate feedback to the people doing the work.

Table 3.4 shows how information requirements for planning, execution, and control are different. Planning is about the future, whereas execution is about the present, and control is about learning from the past. The differences in information requirements for these activities explain why some information systems are not helpful for particular decisions. The information system supporting a business process may be useful for control decisions but ineffective for execution or planning decisions. For example, an information system for managers may summarize last month's sales performance effectively but still not address crucial questions about how to proceed into new markets.

Table 3.4 Comparison of Planning, Execution, and Control

Step in the Feedback Cycle	Time Focus	Important Issues Related to Information
Planning	Future	• Having reliable methods of projecting into the future by combining models, assumptions, and data about the past and present
Execution	Present	• Providing information that tells people what to do now to meet the plan and adjust for any problems that have occurred recently • Using current information to identify problems or errors in current work • Collecting information without getting in the way of doing the work
Control	Past	• Having reliable methods of using data about the past to develop or adjust plans and to motivate employees • Providing information current enough that it can be used to guide current actions

Treatment of Exceptions, Errors, and Malfunctions

Business processes and the information systems that support them may experience many types of exceptions, errors, and malfunctions. Consider **exceptions,** special cases not built into the formal operation of the system. For example, a system for taking customer orders may be built assuming no incomplete orders can be processed and that a complete order includes the customer's shipping address. But what if the customer wants to order a product that takes a long time to build but has not decided where it should be shipped? Should the order be accepted without the shipping address? Whatever the system builder's original intention, in many real-world cases the people taking the order would treat this as an exception. They would try to trick the information system by entering a "temporary" shipping address so that the system would accept the order.

A case like this is just the beginning. Issues that may arise include:

- Exceptions: The system does not handle special cases properly.
- Operational failures: the system fails to operate as intended.
- Bugs: The system does not correctly reflect the ideas of the system designers.
- Design errors: The system does what the designers intended, but they failed to consider certain significant factors.
- Capacity shortfall: The system cannot meet the current output requirements.
- Displacement of problems: The system creates problems that must be absorbed and fixed somewhere else.
- Computer crime: The system is used for theft, sabotage, or other illegal purposes; often based on fraudulent data inputs.

Table 3.5 shows how each type of problem could occur at three levels: information technology, information system, and business process. Although it is impossible to anticipate all problems that could occur, considering foreseeable problems helps users and managers understand these issues and take actions to mitigate them. Chapter 15 will discuss a number of strategies for avoiding these problems.

Table 3.5 Exceptions, Errors, and Malfunctions at Different Levels

Type of Problem	Level at Which Problem Appears		
	Information Technology	**Information System**	**Business Process That Uses the Information System**
Exception	• A different model of computer is used, making extra steps necessary for transferring files	• People trick the system by filling in bogus data to permit the transaction to complete immediately	• People delay an inspection step because the inspector is away temporarily
Operational failure	• Electrical failure causes shutdown • Machine malfunctions • Software crashes	• Incorrect data entered by data entry personnel • System technical staff installs database incorrectly	• People make errors by ignoring or bypassing procedures • User misinterprets data displayed by the system
Bug in system	• Machines installed incorrectly • Software bug causes computer to go down	• Incorrect application logic stores data incorrectly or skips data validation steps	• Incorrect work procedures • Workers do not understand what to do
Design error	• Machine design makes it hard to use	• Information system ignores important aspect of the business situation	• Design of business process ignores important variable or issue
Capacity shortfall	• Hardware/software combination insufficient to process required amount of data	• People lack the time needed to enter the amount of data required	• People are too overworked to pay attention to the information system
Displacement of problems	• Operating system upgrade requires extra work by users	• New information system requires data entry by sales staff, not central corporate staff	• Poor manufacturing quality increases work in customer service
Computer crime	• Computer virus wipes out data on hard disk • Theft of computer	• Programs changed to move money to unauthorized account • Fraudulent payment vouchers entered into accounts payable	• Collusion to steal proprietary data about customers • Use of computer to sabotage competitor's business

Architectural Characteristics   In this section, we discussed seven architectural characteristics of business processes and explained how these are related to choices about information systems.

1. Think about a business process you are familiar with, such as registering for classes, borrowing books from a library, or voting in an election. Based on your personal experience, describe that business process in terms of the seven characteristics.

2. Explain differences in the process if each characteristic were increased or decreased.

Linking Business Process Performance and Product Performance

The links in Figure 3.2 showed that process architecture is the main controllable determinant of process performance, which influences product performance and customer satisfaction in turn. Once we know how the business process operates, the next question is how well it operates currently or how well it might operate in a future form. Describing how well the process operates requires switching attention from architectural characteristics to performance variables.

Since the purpose of a business process is to produce a product (or service) for an internal or external customer, the evaluation of a business process can focus in two places. Focusing on the process itself, we can evaluate it using internal performance variables, such as capacity, consistency, productivity, cycle time, flexibility, and security. Improvements in each of these areas can be important whether or not they directly affect the product the customer receives. For example, increasing productivity or reducing cycle time may make it more profitable or less costly to produce and deliver exactly the same product that was produced previously. We can also evaluate the business process by focusing on its product using external performance variables the customer perceives, such as cost, quality, responsiveness, reliability, and conformance to standards and regulations. A change in business process architecture that generates benefits to customers in any of these areas may be worth pursuing whether or not internal costs decrease.

Figure 3.12 shows overlapping relationships between the inward-looking and outward-looking performance variables listed earlier in Figures 2.10 and 3.2. Each process performance variable affects at least two of the product performance variables. Furthermore, the variables within the group are related in some cases. For example, productivity is often related to capacity, consistency, and cycle time, and perceived quality is often related to responsiveness and reliability.

Despite these overlaps, the connotations and examples associated with each of the process and product performance variables in Figure 2.10 provide a starting point for evaluating current systems and thinking about improvements. If a potential architectural improvement would affect no aspect of process or product performance, it would not be worth pursuing because it would have no impact internally or externally. We conclude the chapter by discussing the performance variables of both types. The emphasis throughout is on ways information systems can improve process and product performance.

Evaluating Business Process Performance

Since the process performance variables in Figure 3.12 are common business terms, you might wonder why it is important to say anything more about them than just identifying them (as was done in Figure 2.10). We will look at each term individually because the different terms are associated with different ways to improve business processes using information systems.

Figure 3.12 Relation-
ship between Process
Performance, Product
Performance and
Customer Satisfaction

*Process performance
determines much of product
performance, which strongly
influences customer satisfaction.*

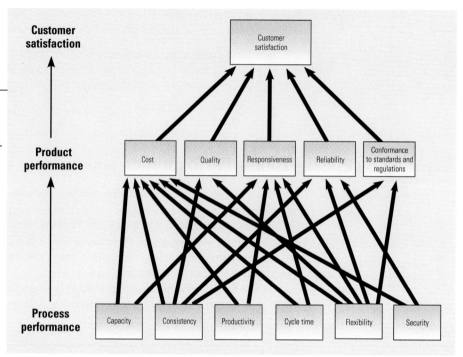

Tables 3.6 and 3.7 illustrate the need to look at each term. Table 3.6 shows that each performance variable involves genuine choices, with too much often as bad as too little along any of the dimensions. Users and managers should be involved in designing and evaluating information systems because of their insight into the advantages and disadvantages of different levels of process performance. Table 3.7 lists common performance measures for each process performance variable and identifies some of the ways information systems can be used to improve performance in regard to that variable. Looking at each variable in turn helps in understanding these information system applications.

Table 3.6 Finding the Right Level for Each Process Performance Variable

Process Performance Variable	Too Much	Too Little
Capacity	• Lower productivity due to the cost of unused capacity	• Insufficient capacity to satisfy the customer
Productivity	• Too much emphasis on cost per unit and too little emphasis on quality of the output	• Output is unnecessarily expensive to produce
Consistency	• Inflexibility, making it difficult to produce what the customer wants	• Too much variability in the output, reducing quality perceived by the customer
Cycle time	• Lack of responsiveness to customer • Excess costs and waste due to delays	• Product produced too soon is damaged or compromised before the customer needs it • Delivery before the customer is ready
Flexibility	• Too much variability in the output, reducing quality perceived by the customer	• Inflexibility, making it difficult to produce what the customer wants or difficult to modify the process over time
Security	• Excess attention to security gets in the way of doing work	• Insufficient attention permits security breaches

Table 3.7 Process Performance Variables and Related Roles of Information Systems

Process Performance Variable	Typical Measures	Common Information System Role
Capacity	• Average units per hour or week • Peak load units per hour or week	• Increase capacity by performing some of the work automatically • Increase effective capacity by systematizing the work
Productivity	• Output per labor hour or machine hour • Ratio of outputs to inputs (in dollars) • Scrap rate • Cost of rework	• Help people produce more output • Automate data processing functions people perform inefficiently • Systematize work to reduce waste • Schedule work to improve resource utilization
Consistency	• Defect rate • Percentage variation • Rework rate	• Systematize work to reduce variability of the product • Provide immediate feedback to identify and correct errors • Help process participants analyze the causes of defects
Cycle time	• Elapsed time from start to finish • Total work-in-process inventory divided by weekly output (a useful approximation in some situations)	• Perform data processing work more quickly • Make it possible to combine steps, thereby eliminating delays • Make it possible to perform steps in parallel, thereby eliminating delays • Systematize work to reduce waste
Flexibility	• Number of possible product variations • Ease of customizing to customer specifications	• Systematize the form and content of product specifications to make it easier to handle variations • Make it possible to control the process based on specifications that can be entered through a computer
Security	• Number of process breaches in a time interval • Seriousness of process breaches in a time interval	• Systematize record keeping about the business process • Systematize record keeping about computer access and usage • Track all nonstandard transactions such as changes to completed transactions

Capacity

The **capacity** of a system is the amount of work it can do. An information system's capacity can be measured relative to the organization's work. For example, an information system might process 50 transactions per hour or support 35 customers. At a more technology-oriented level, an information system's capacity can be measured relative to the amount or rate of work the system can do in capturing, transmitting, storing, retrieving, manipulating, and displaying data. An information system might, for example, store the equivalent of 700,000 pieces of paper or generate 25,000 dividend payments per hour.

The amount of work a system can support is usually measured either at average load or at peak load, the maximum load at which the system can operate. Anyone who has waited on line to pay a highway toll during a busy rush hour understands that peak loads are an important system issue, especially for systems that must operate without significant delays. When the stock market crashed on October 19, 1987, over 500,000,000 shares were traded on the New York Stock Exchange, more than twice the previous high volume. At this unprecedented information processing load, the online information about stock prices contributed to the panic during the crash because it lagged as much as two hours behind the trading on the floor of the stock market. Subsequent system investments through 1994 increased capacity to 1.4 billion shares per day, over twice the shares traded on the previous peak day.[12]

Establishing an appropriate capacity for a business process is a challenge because excess capacity is also a problem. Every unit of excess capacity typically has some monetary cost. In addition, excess capacity often permits sloppiness in the system, as was demonstrated repeatedly when downsized companies increased output and responsiveness to customers despite cutting layers of management and other staff. Similar effects apply when the excess capacity involves equipment or inventory. For example, a major advantage of minimizing the amount of the idle inventory sitting in warehouses or on factory floors is that nonexistent inventory cannot be broken, lost, stolen, or obsoleted. Minimizing inventory buffers also helps identify production problems, which become apparent quickly because they cannot hide behind excess inventory.

There are many ways to balance loads to satisfy peak capacity while minimizing costly underutilization. One approach is to purchase additional temporary capacity when needed, as is done by retail stores that hire additional staff during peak shopping periods. Another approach is to share capacity or shift work elsewhere. For example, to minimize the number of circuits required between New York City and Boston, some morning telephone calls between these cities are routed through circuits to and from the West Coast. These circuits would otherwise be underutilized because many morning calls on the East Coast occur before dawn on the West Coast. Yet another approach is to use peak load pricing to encourage customers to shift their usage to off-peak hours (mentioned further in the discussion of cost).

An important capacity-related characteristic of both business processes and the information systems that support them is **scalability,** the ability to significantly increase or decrease capacity without major disruption or excessive costs. The least scalable processes involve huge capital outlays for individual units of production, such as power plants or airports. Increased scalability is one of the important benefits of the technical advances in computing architectures discussed in Chapter 9.

Consistency

Consistency in a business process means applying the same techniques in the same way to obtain the same desired results. Since one of the TQM movement's main tenets is that unwarranted variation destroys quality, TQM calls for careful specification of exactly how a process should be performed and careful monitoring to ensure that it is being performed consistent with those specifications.

One of the main benefits of some information systems is that they force the organization to do things consistently. For example, companies in the air freight business such as Federal Express and United Parcel Service do very detailed tracking of each package as it passes each step. It is possible to say that the value of these systems is in keeping track of every package, but an equally plausible interpretation is that the value of the system comes from enforcing consistency in the way work is done. System participants know that if they deviate from the rules in their handling of a package, the information system will be able to show it was handled in a proper way until it got to them.[13]

Other information systems are designed to provide information that helps people perform business processes in a consistent manner. Figure 3.13 shows a control chart, a device used widely to monitor business process consistency. The control chart graphs a process measurement such as the average width of a sample of machined parts or the average length of time customers had to wait on hold. The process is considered "in control" if it stays within limits, has expected variability, and shows no trend toward going out of limits. The pattern of measurements over time helps in identifying problems before they have significant effects on quality or productivity.

Figure 3.13 Control Chart for Monitoring Consistency of a Business Process

This control chart shows data for a manufacturing process that is going out of control even though it has not yet exceeded a control limit. Machine operators looking at this control chart should stop the process and fix it before the output of their production step must be scrapped or reworked.

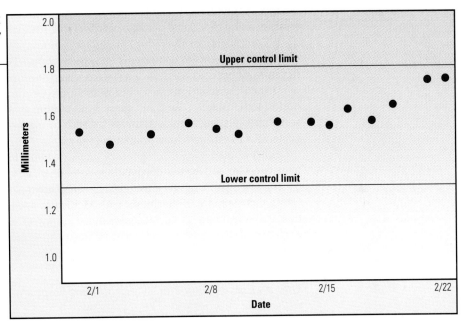

Productivity

Productivity is the relationship between the amount of output produced by a business process and the amount of money, time, and effort it consumes. Business process productivity can be improved by changing the process to produce more output from the same level of inputs or produce the same output from lower levels of inputs. One approach to improving productivity is to increase the rate of work, thereby reducing the labor time and inventory costs related to a particular level of output. Another approach is to eliminate waste and rework. This is especially important since quality experts often estimate that 20 to 30 percent of costs are actually just waste. As a firm's overall productivity improves, it can make a profit at lower selling prices.

Most early computerized information systems supported productivity improvement by collecting detailed information and summarizing what happened yesterday, last week, or last month. They collected data about business processes but rarely played a direct role in providing value for the internal or external customers of business processes (other than customers of data collection processes). More recently, information systems have attempted to increase productivity by supporting automation and providing interactive tools used directly by professionals in their work.

Perhaps surprisingly, there is often substantial question about whether information systems actually increase productivity. Looking at just computers, statistical studies relating computer investments to company performance have found little discernible impact on aggregate productivity although recent research has started to find more positive results.[14,15] Part of the question here is that a computer investment is not just the purchase price but all the other costs that are incurred. For example, think of the total price of a personal computer during the first year you own it. This includes the purchase price plus costs related to deciding what computer to buy, going to the store and buying the computer, installing it, buying software, and getting training about how to use it. The true price of a personal computer in most businesses far exceeds the purchase price. Hidden or unobserved costs related to support, training, facilities, maintenance, administration, and time spent by end users doing programming can push total spending to $20,000 per PC according to a 1992 study by Nolan, Norton & Co.[16]

Computers can also reduce productivity by tempting people to waste time making endless refinements in documents and spreadsheets. For example, a study of Internal Revenue Service examiners who were given laptop computers found that they performed examinations faster but didn't increase the number of examinations they performed. Instead, they spent more time writing aesthetically pleasing reports and sometimes playing games. A survey by accounting software maker SBT Corp. asked customers to estimate how much time they spent "futzing with your PC." They came up with 5.1 hours a week doing things such as waiting for computer runs, printouts, or help; checking and formatting documents; loading and learning new programs; helping co-workers; organizing and erasing old files; and other activities such as playing games.[17] Citing this estimate, a consultant with McKinsey, a leading consulting firm, quipped that if the estimate is correct, personal computers may have become the biggest destroyer of white-collar productivity since the management meeting was invented.[18]

Cycle Time

Time is a scarce resource for all organizations. Many authors have recognized the ability to use time effectively as a key competitive issue.[19,20,21] A powerful example comes from a book about the automobile industry published in 1990. From design to delivery, a typical Japanese car took 46 months and 1.7 million engineering hours versus 60 months and 3 million engineering hours in the United States and Europe.[22] Aside from the cost of extra engineering hours, bringing cars to market over a year earlier meant the Japanese companies could respond to changing consumer tastes more quickly. Similar advantages occur in the service sector, where some insurance companies and banks have significantly reduced cycle time for handling insurance and loan applications.

Self-imposed and legally imposed deadlines are another important aspect of time in business processes. Concerns about the freshness of packaged foods and pharmaceuticals led manufacturers to stamp expiration dates on packages and remove stale products. Time is also a regulatory issue, such as the way the Securities and Exchange Commission decreed that settlement time, the time between stock or bond purchases and payment, should be reduced from five days to three days by June 1, 1995. Some observers believed conformance to this deadline would reduce risks. Others believed the settlement deadline would simply be a bonanza for overnight delivery companies.[23]

The use of time in a business process can be summarized as **cycle time,** the length of time between the start of the process and its completion. Cycle time is determined by a combination of the processing time for performing each step in the process, the waiting time between completing one step and starting another, and the dependencies between steps. Waiting time when no value is being added is often a major problem. In factories with especially complicated manufacturing equipment and mixes of products, the amount of time actually spent adding value to the material is often less than 10 percent of total cycle time.

Bottlenecks are another important source of delays and excessive cycle times. A **bottleneck** is an essential work step where a temporary or long-term capacity shortage delays most of the items being produced or processed. In these situations, maximizing utilization of the bottleneck may be the key to reducing total cycle time. Information systems can help in these situations by helping people decide on the right order of work to improve flow through the bottleneck.

Just drawing a picture like Figure 3.14 can often help in identifying bottlenecks and unnecessary steps that expand total cycle times. In this example, steps 2 and 3 can overlap in time but cannot begin until step 1 completes. In turn, step 4 cannot start until steps 2 and 3 both complete. Part of the analysis for reducing delays in business processes involves drawing this type of diagram and examining the processing time, waiting time, and dependencies for each step. Sometimes the delays jump out at you. For example, if step 3 is a meeting involving people from different groups, there may be a two-week delay before any work on step 4 can begin. An attempt to reduce the process's cycle time would probably include an analysis of whether it is possible to eliminate the meeting, handle it by phone, or identify work that does not need to wait for the meeting to happen.

Figure 3.14 Identifying the Causes of Long Cycle Times

Five steps must occur before this process is complete. The total cycle time depends on several factors, including the elapsed time for each step, the amount of waiting time before each step begins, and the dependencies preventing one step from starting until several other steps are finished.

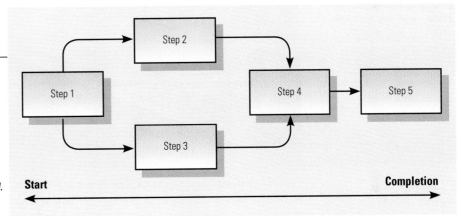

Flexibility

The **flexibility** of a business process is the ease with which it can be adjusted to meet immediate customer needs and adapted over the long term as business conditions change. The competitive advantages of flexibility are apparent: Customers prefer the product features they really want rather than the product features a supplier thinks they want. It is also possible to make business processes too flexible, however. Excessive flexibility in a business process leads to chaos because process participants need reference points for keeping themselves organized and productive. In addition, flexibility can be the enemy of consistency, a performance variable discussed earlier.

There are a number of approaches for using information systems to make business processes flexible. One general principle is to avoid restricting things about the process that can be left to the judgment of the process participants. For example, don't force the participants to fill out computerized forms in a particular order unless the sequence really matters. Another principle is to delay as long as possible those choices that convert information into a physical result that is hard to change. According to this principle, installation of physical customer options should be delayed as long as possible if those options would make a customized product hard to sell to another customer. A third principle is to create the business process using technical tools and methods that are flexible themselves. For example, use programming methods that generate programs that are comparatively easy to change. In an example of making processes flexible, Allen-Bradley built a highly automated factory that can produce 1,025 different electronic contractors and relays with zero defects in lot sizes as low as one.[24] The time from order placement to completion is one day. This type of flexibility relies on information systems to transmit orders to the factory and control the machines within the factory (see Figure 3.15).

Figure 3.15 Allen-Bradley Uses Information Systems for Flexibility in a Highly Automated Factory

Allen-Bradley's highly automated factory can produce over a thousand different items in lot sizes as small as one within one day of receiving an order.

Unfortunately, systems can be an obstacle to flexibility and innovation. They may force people to do things a particular way, thereby creating a straitjacket that prevents them from handling exceptions well or even doing their work effectively. Consider the description by a reform-minded undersecretary of defense about what happened when the Department of Defense (DOD) wanted to buy mobile radios during the Persian Gulf War. The best available radio was a commercial product from Motorola, but DOD rules required the contractor to have a DOD-approved system in place for justifying the selling price. Motorola did not have such a system, and DOD would not change its rules, even in time of war. The situation was resolved when Japan bought the radios and donated them to the United States.[25]

The time and effort required to change large information systems may also generate costs and delays that hinder process innovation. This problem is especially important when information systems related to production, sales, and finance are poorly designed and maintained. These systems do not age gracefully and often become very difficult to upgrade as business requirements change. Such systems are an obstacle to innovation because they make it much harder to implement innovative ideas.

Security

The **security** of a business process is the likelihood that it is not vulnerable to unauthorized uses, sabotage, or criminal activity. Although companies avoid discussing security issues publicly, a number of security problems are well known. One of these involves telephone fraud, in which someone steals another person's telephone credit card number and then uses it illegally. In another form of telephone fraud, the criminal penetrates a company's internal telephone system and then uses it to make outgoing calls. Telephone fraud costs at least several billion dollars per year.

The security of a business process depends on procedures that ensure accuracy and prevent unauthorized access (see Figure 3.16). Although preventing unauthorized access to computerized systems is obviously essential, even systems with adequate control over computer access may have insufficient controls over clerical procedures that surround the system. Accuracy is also obviously important, but many systems contain insufficient methods for checking the accuracy of input data, identifying errors in the data in the system, and correcting those errors.

Figure 3.16 Retina Scanner for Controlling Access

This retina scanner is used to control access to facilities requiring high security. It can store up to 1,200 "eye signatures," which are coded blood vessel patterns from the retina.

Information systems can improve security or can weaken it. They improve security when they contain effective safeguards against unauthorized access and use. They weaken security when they remove control from people and lead the people in the system to become complacent about security concerns and "trust the computer." Chapter 15 will discuss both the problems and the safeguards in some detail.

Vigilance of the participants is perhaps the most general characteristic leading to system security. Many system-and organization-related disasters prove the point. In 1987, a Pacific Southwest Airlines jet crashed because a recently fired employee brought a gun onto the airplane and shot the pilot and co-pilot. Unaware that he had been fired, airport security personnel had waved him past the security checkpoints even though regulations required that he show an ID card. Even security agencies can show insufficient vigilance. In 1994, the director of the U.S. Central Intelligence Agency (CIA) issued a scalding assessment of the failure to catch Aldrich Ames, a spy whose actions in exchange for more than $2 million between 1985 to 1994, had destroyed the CIA's network of spies inside the Soviet Union and caused the deaths of ten double agents. Though the CIA knew Ames was an alcoholic who repeatedly flouted its rules, it promoted him to run the counterintelligence branch within the Soviet division. The CIA director said the inattention of senior officials was almost universal and went on for years. "One could almost conclude not only that no one was watching, but that no one cared."[26]

We have now looked at six process performance variables, any one of which may hold the key to important insights into potential process improvements. All these performance variables focused inward and looked at the process without regard to what the customer sees. We will close the chapter by looking at product performance variables customers perceive directly.

REALITY CHECK   **Evaluating Process Performance**   In this section, we discussed a number of variables used to evaluate process performance.

1. Consider the business process you selected earlier. Identify the process performance variables that seem most important and least important in this situation. Explain how you might measure those variables.

2. Assume someone actually measured each variable. Estimate what the person would find currently and what the person might find if the business process were revamped to operate as well as is conceivable.

Evaluating Product Performance from a Customer's Viewpoint

Table 3.8 looks at five product performance variables internal and external customers commonly use to evaluate products, For each variable, it lists common performance measures and common ways information systems are used to improve the product. Other variables could have been mentioned, such as image and aesthetics, but those included in Table 3.8 are most directly affected by information systems. This section mentions several aspects of each variable along with some related information system applications. Many more such applications are covered in the discussion of competitive uses of information systems in Chapter 7.

Cost

Cost is a prime determinant of customer satisfaction. We will think of **cost** not in a strict accounting sense, but rather as whatever the internal or external customer must give up in order to obtain, use, and maintain the product of a business process. This includes money plus time, effort, and attention that might be used for other purposes. Seeing cost this way, the product of any business process involves cost to the internal or external customer even if no money is transferred.

Opportunities to use information systems to reduce the cost to an internal or external customer start with reducing the cost of acquiring or using the product, such as the way ATMs eliminate the time and effort of standing on line at a bank during bank hours or the way MCI provides special "friends and family" rates. Information systems can be incorporated into the product to make it more efficient, such as the way computers control combustion in car engines. Information systems can also provide more usable billing data to promote efficiency, such as by analyzing telephone bills and telling customers what service and pricing options would minimize their future bills if the same usage patterns continue. The discussion of competitive uses of information systems in Chapter 7 provides many related examples.

Information systems can also be used to increase costs to customers, such as by instituting pricing schemes that motivate customers to use resources efficiently. An example of this type is the decision to bill internal users or departments for telephone and copier usage. The process of billing departments inside the company absorbs time and effort, but this is usually a lower cost for the business to pay than the cost of excessive usage from treating telephones and copiers as free goods. Pricing can also be used to shift usage away from peak load periods, such as through higher internal pricing for use of networks and mainframe computers at busy times of the day. Electric power utilities can use similar peak load pricing strategies to reduce the need to purchase new power plants.

Table 3.8 Common Roles of Information Systems in Improving the Product of a Business Process

Process Performance Variable	Typical Measures	Common Information System Role
Cost	• Purchase price • Cost of ownership • Amount of time and attention required	• Reduce internal cost of business process or increase productivity, therefore making it easier to charge or allocate lower prices to customers • Improve product performance in ways that reduce the customer's internal costs
Quality	• Defect rate per time interval or per quantity of output • Rate of warranty returns • Perceived quality according to customer	• Ensure the product is produced more consistently • Make it easier to customize the product for the customer • Build information systems into the product to make it more usable or maintainable
Responsiveness	• Time to respond to customer request • Helpfulness of response	• Improve the speed of response • Systematize communication with customers • Increase flexibility to make it easier to respond to what the customer wants
Reliability	• Average time to failure • Failure rate per time interval • Compliance to customer commitment dates	• Make the business process more consistent • Make the business process more secure • Build features into the product that make it more reliable
Conformance to standards and regulations	• Existence of nonconformance • Rate of complaints about nonconformance	• Clarify the standards and regulations so that it is easier to know whether they are being adhered to • Systematize work to make the output more consistent

Quality

The concept of **quality** spans many dimensions. Some quality experts focus on the business process as the source of quality and say that quality is conformance to production specifications. Others focus on product features and performance and say customer satisfaction is the measure of quality because quality is evaluated by the customer. Expressing the breadth of the quality issue, Garvin identified the following dimensions of quality: performance, features, reliability, conformance, durability, serviceability, aesthetics, and perceived quality.[27] The concept of quality is complex in part because product quality is usually evaluated in comparison with expectations for the same type of product in the same price range. In other words, the criteria for evaluating a fast-food restaurant's quality are different from those for evaluating a fine French restaurant.

Information systems can be applied in many different ways to improve quality. Major approaches include increasing the consistency of internal business processes, providing product features that the customer associates with quality, providing excellent service, and providing information that increases the product's usefulness.

Responsiveness

Responsiveness means taking timely action based on what the customer wants. Here are four examples in which information systems increase responsiveness by making it easier to take action quickly to satisfy customer needs:

- Using a companywide inventory system to find and reserve the pair of shoes the customer wants even if they are at another store

- Making a customer phone call more effective by immediately finding an image copy of all correspondence about the customer's recent automobile accident, regardless of which branch office the letters came from

- Using a computer-aided design system to provide the customer a simulated walkthrough of a proposed building and to make immediate modifications based on customer feedback

- Designing production processes based on mass customization techniques that make it easier to respond to unique customer requirements

All four examples involve much more than answering the phone. The information systems made it easier to give the customer a useful response, not just an indication of presence. Figure 3.17 shows how Progressive, an auto insurance company, uses specially equipped vans to help its agents be responsive to customers by visiting the customer within several hours of an accident and sometimes printing a check on the spot. Cutting total settlement time from 18 days to 11 meant less paperwork, fewer hours spent by claim adjusters, and involvement of fewer lawyers.[28]

Figure 3.17 Progressive Provides Rapid Claim Adjustment for Insurance Customers

Progressive, an auto insurance company, uses this computer-equipped van as part of its effort to be responsive to its customers.

The fact that an information system is used does not mean that responsiveness will increase. In these two examples, responsiveness decreases:

- A doctor decides to perform an expensive diagnostic test but must receive approval first from the insurance company. The system reduces the doctor's responsiveness, which may or may not make sense economically and medically for this particular patient.

- A restaurant began using handheld terminals for taking orders. The terminals had many benefits but provided no way for waiters to record special customer requests, such as put the sauce on the side. Service was faster and more reliable but not as responsive to the customer.

In the first example, the information system helped the insurance company be less responsive to what the doctor wanted. In the second, a system reduced responsiveness as an unintended consequence of its features.

Reliability

The **reliability** of a product or service is its likelihood it will not experience significant operational failures. Information systems can increase reliability in some situations and decrease it in others. Grocery stores and department stores use information systems to make product availability more reliable for their customers. Companies providing individualized service processes such as tax preparation may use information systems to reduce dependence on the personal knowledge of specific individuals, thereby making the output more reliable. Likewise, systems (often called expert systems) that bring expert knowledge to help people make decisions may increase reliability by making the best knowledge available to whoever is making a decision.

On the other hand, extensive use of computer hardware and software rarely makes service 100 percent reliable and often introduces another potential source of error and malfunction. Consider two examples of information system failure based on infrastructure totally beyond the control of people relying on mission-critical systems:

> On January 15, 1990, a bug in new software used by AT&T's long distance-telephone network prevented completion of 44 percent of the 148 million long-distance calls on the network between 2:30 and 11:30 p.m. This disruption left national sales offices and other large-scale telephone users unable to operate and led many corporations to consider using MCI and Sprint as backup suppliers of telephone service. The new software had been tested carefully and installed in December, but the bug remained hidden until an unrelated event caused a malfunction in the network.[29,30]

> At 8:45 a.m. on September 14, 1994, a power failure occurred at an air traffic control center serving Chicago's O'Hare Airport, one of the world's busiest. At a time of peak load, thousands of airline passengers were delayed for hours because a contractor accidentally caused a short circuit while testing a system for preventing power failures. This was the second time in 1994 that installation of an "uninterruptible power system" interrupted power at an air traffic center.[31]

Both cases involved systems whose computerization provided many important benefits, including high reliability but certainly not 100 percent reliability.

Conformance to Standards and Regulations

Conformance to standards and regulations is the degree of adherence to standards and regulations imposed by external bodies such as major customers, industry groups, or the government. Unlike cost and quality, it does not fit well with return on investment and other common investment criteria, yet it is the driving force behind many information systems. The most obvious cases involve payment of taxes, where information systems gather the data, perform the calculations, and produce the tax returns (with substantial guidance and interpretation by the people who are part of the system).

Standards are precisely stated, widely publicized rules governing the size, shape, and operating characteristics of products or processes. The existence of an American standard for the size of copy paper (8 1/2 by 11 inches) means that any paper supplier can provide paper fitting any copy machine or laser printer built for the American market. Different standards can co-exist, as illustrated by the fact that Europe and Asia use different standard sizes for paper. Similarly, people in America and continental Europe drive on the right side of the road, whereas people in England and Japan drive on the left side. The chapters on information technology will explain why "competing standards" is a major competitive issue in the computer and telecommunications industries. The enormous growth and market power of Microsoft and Intel and the decline of IBM attest to the importance of controlling technical standards, in this case, the standards for personal computer operating systems and microprocessors.[32]

Where standards are either negotiated voluntarily or determined by the way things evolve in business or society, **regulations** are rules based on laws administered by federal, state, or local governments. International bodies such as the European Common Market also generate regulations. Regulations require businesses to operate in particular ways and to submit tax forms and tax payments consistent with specific rules. Depending on the size of the business, regulations may require much other information about hiring practices, energy utilization, waste disposal, and other topics.

As with the other evaluation characteristics, conformance may be important at any point in a customer's involvement with a product. Consider the way electronic data interchange (EDI) has become a requirement for suppliers selling to many firms. EDI is the electronic transmission of structured documents such as customer orders between companies. Before EDI, large companies like General Motors found they might spend $50 to process each invoice because of paperwork and inconsistent data formats. In many cases, these companies told their suppliers that reducing paperwork costs was so important that the use of EDI was a requirement for doing business. This forced changes in the smaller companies' internal information systems to permit linkage into the standardized EDI systems the large companies were establishing. In effect, EDI became an essential part of the product the large companies were buying.

We have now seen a number of ideas that help any user or manager describe and evaluate a business process and the information system that supports it. Architecture-related characteristics, such as degree of structure and range of involvement, affect process performance variables, such as consistency and cycle time, which eventually affect product performance variables customers perceive, such as quality and responsiveness. The ideas in this chapter cover a wealth of opportunities for improving business processes. There is no formula for deciding what to do, but documentation techniques, architectural characteristics, and process and product performance variables provide many starting points for identifying and evaluating alternatives.

REALITY CHECK   **Evaluating Product Performance**   This section discussed a number of product performance variables.

1. Consider the business process you selected earlier. Identify the product performance variables that seem most important and least important in this situation. Explain how you might measure those variables.

2. Assume someone actually measured each variable. Estimate what the person would find currently and what the person might find if the business process were revamped to operate as efficiently and effectively as is conceivable.

Chapter Conclusion

SUMMARY

 ► *What is the relationship between process architecture, process performance, and product performance?*

Process architecture is a key determinant of process performance, which in turn is a key determinant of product performance. Inward-looking process performance variables include capacity, consistency, productivity, cycle time, flexibility, and security. Outward-looking product performance variables perceived directly by customers include cost, quality, responsiveness, reliability, and conformance to standards and regulations.

 ► *What is the role of data flow diagrams in process modeling?*

Process modeling is a method of defining business process architecture by identifying major processes and dividing them into linked subprocesses. Data flow diagrams (DFDs) represent the flows of data between different processes in a business. They provide a simple, intuitive method for describing business processes without focusing on the details of computer systems. The four symbols used in DFDs are the process, data flow, data store, and external entity.

► *What business process characteristics can be used to describe system design choices affecting business process success?*

Seven characteristics determined by system design include degree of structure; range of involvement; level of integration; complexity; degree of reliance on machines; attention to planning, execution, and control; and the treatment of exceptions, errors, and malfunctions.

 ► *What is the difference between structured, semistructured, and unstructured tasks?*

The degree of structure of a task or a business process is the degree of predetermined correspondence between its inputs and its outputs. A totally structured task is so well understood that it is possible to say exactly how to perform it and how to evaluate whether it has been performed well. In a semistructured task, the information requirements and procedures are generally known although some aspects of the task still rely on judgment. An unstructured task is so poorly understood that the information to be used, the method of using the information, and the criteria for deciding whether the task is being done well cannot be specified.

 ► *What are the five possible levels of integration of business processes?*

Integration is the connection and mutual responsiveness and collaboration between distinct activities or processes. The five levels of integration include common culture, common standards, information sharing, coordination, and collaboration.

► *Why are planning and control important elements of many business processes?*

Participants in a business process need to know what to do, when to do it, and how to make sure the work was done properly. Planning is the process of deciding what work to do and what outputs to produce when. Executing is the process of doing the work. Controlling is the process of using information about past work performance to assure that goals are attained and plans carried out. Planning and control provide the direction and coordination needed to attain the objectives of an entire organization or any of its business processes.

INTERNATIONAL VIGNETTES

India: The Stock Market Encounters a Paperwork Obstacle

When an affiliate of Hongkong & Shanghai Banking Corp. bought shares worth $2 million in an Indian mutual fund, the transaction should have been simple. But completing this transaction required writing or stamping the new owner's name on 50,500 certificates, each representing 50 shares, and on another 50,500 share transfer forms. Other clerks counted hundreds of stamps on the certificates to make sure taxes had been paid. Yet other clerks performed other tasks in a settlement process that typically takes two to three months. Unlike Indian investors, foreign investors must take physical delivery of shares before being able to sell them. Without a computerized system, delivery of the shares takes months. Furthermore, between 2 and 10 percent of the documents are rejected at some point during the processing and have to be returned to brokers for reprocessing that sometimes takes 6 to 12 months.

Just as international interest in the Indian stock market heated up, major players in India's financial markets such as Citibank and Hongkong Bank have been hurt by the slow pace of this processing. Citibank has over ten million pieces of paper in its vaults representing investments by customers outside India. Hongkong Bank sent a letter to its customers asking them to slow down their investments.

> Source: Dubey, Suman. "India's Booming Stock Market Speeds Paper Chase, Running Banks Ragged." *Wall Street Journal,* Feb. 22, 1994, p. A13C.

- Use the WCA framework to organize your understanding of this vignette and to identify important topics that are not mentioned.
- What issues (if any) make this case interesting from an international or intercultural viewpoint?
- Use ideas related to process architecture, process performance, and product performance to describe the situation.

Canada: The Toronto Stock Exchange Delays Its Plans to Close Its Trading Floor

The Toronto Stock Exchange made the major strategic decision of closing its 115-year-old trading floor and moving to totally electronic trading. In other words, instead of going to human traders and specialists in a fixed location, orders to buy or sell stock would go to a computerized system that would execute those orders by matching buy offers to sell offers. Closure of the trading floor was originally planned for March 1993, but was delayed several times and was now planned for the end of 1994. Various factors had contributed to the delays, including a flood that damaged equipment in the Exchange's computer room and the time required to install a new generator needed for extra backup in the face of higher trading volumes.

A pilot test by 20 traders was a crucial part of the conversion plan. To reduce the risk of closing the stock floor and then being blind-sided by an unexpected problem, the pilot test would allow those traders to conduct live trades using the automated system. A spokesman for the Exchange described these tests as "where the rubber meets the road."

> Source: Buckler, Grant. "Toronto Stock Exchange Floor Closing Expected by Year-End." *America Online Newsbytes,* Apr. 1, 1994.

- Use the WCA framework to organize your understanding of this vignette and to identify important topics that are not mentioned.
- What issues (if any) make this case interesting from an international or intercultural viewpoint?
- Use ideas related to process architecture, process performance, and product performance to describe the possible effects of closing the trading floor.

REAL-WORLD CASES

Mutual Benefit Life: Using a Case Management Approach

Mutual Benefit Life (MBL) used a case management approach to convert an operational nightmare into a responsive process. Its previous process of deciding whether to issue a policy, setting the price, and issuing the policy involved 40 steps, 12 functions, and an average of 22 days. By assigning each policy application to a case team consisting of a case manager and two assistants, MBL reduced cycle time from 22 to 6 days or less, and reduced costs 40 percent. Aside from speeding the process, the case management approach provided the customer with a broader array of more responsive services. For this type of case management to work, the case managers require greater responsibility than employees working in an assembly line approach. MBL's case managers were responsible for dealing directly with customer issues instead of asking repeatedly for approval from senior managers or technical experts. Although MBL suffered major financial problems from unrelated problems with its real estate investments, many other insurance companies recognized its success in handling policy applications and adopted similar methods.

The human resource aspects of case management raised many difficult problems for MBL, however. Case managers felt great uncertainty about how the firm would measure their performance, how they would be compensated, and where their careers would lead. Initially, the personnel department wanted to classify the case manager job as clerical because it did not understand how difficult the case manager job was and because case managers had no subordinates and worked at a computer. There were also many issues related to skills since case management required not only intelligence and trained skills but also a customer-oriented personality. MBL had made a major commitment to hiring and training local, disadvantaged employees, many of whom could not master case management skills and felt betrayed. Some of these employees picketed the firm's headquarters to show their frustration.

Source: Davenport, Thomas H., and Nitin Nohria. "Case Management and the Integration of Labor." *Sloan Management Review,* Winter 1994, pp. 11–24.

- Use the WCA framework to organize your understanding of this case and to identify important topics that are not mentioned.

- Explain which of this chapter's ideas about process architecture, process performance, and product performance are most pertinent and least pertinent to this situation.

Incomnet: Helping Junkyards Find Auto Parts

Although auto repair shops, rebuilders, and the general public can usually buy auto replacement parts from car dealers and auto supply houses, they can often find cheaper prices at junkyards. Unlike other businesses, however, junkyards obtain their inventories through accidents and often don't have the specific part a customer needs. Since other junkyards might have that part, junkyards banded together in the 1950s using what they called a hotline, namely, a telephone network hooked to a speaker. A junkyard needing a part either called another junkyard directly or used the hotline to say what was needed, hoping someone would respond. But a voice hotline cannot handle more than about 100 active users.

In the 1970s, a small company called Incomnet created a computer network to accomplish the same purpose in a more systematic and less error-prone manner. By the early 1990s, 400 junkyards, mostly in Southern California, were using the network, which transmits 5,000 part requests per day. The person sending the request can select whether it goes to everyone or just to users in a local region. Of some 15,000 licensed auto dismantlers, about 2,000 use computer networks, and 8,000 use the less expensive voice hotlines.

Source: Tapscott, Don, and Art Caston. *Paradigm Shift: The New Promise of Information Technology.* New York: McGraw-Hill, 1993, pp. 113-114.

- Use the WCA framework to organize your understanding of this case and to identify important topics that are not mentioned.

- Explain which of this chapter's ideas about process architecture, process performance, and product performance are most pertinent and least pertinent to this situation.

- Explain why it does or does not make sense to extend this system to include suppliers of new replacement parts.

New York Stock Exchange: Possible Effects of Program Trading

Program trading is the use of computers to buy or sell securities automatically on detecting certain conditions in the stock market. To accomplish this, program trading requires an information system with real-time data about securities prices plus models that detect the triggering conditions and make the appropriate buy or sell decisions. Typically, program trading is done by pension funds and large financial institutions that can trade "baskets" of securities (such as the Standard & Poor's index of 500 stocks) rather than individual stocks. Most program trading relies on arbitrage, which is the process of detecting and exploiting discrepancies between prices in two different markets. Consider how arbitrage might be done using a stock index, such as the S&P index of 500 stocks. If the S&P 500 futures index rises above the S&P index itself, selling the futures contracts and buying an equivalent amount of S&P stocks guarantees a profit.

There is considerable controversy about whether program trading contributed to the drastic 508-point drop in the Dow Jones Industrial Average on October 19, 1987. Some analysts think it was a destabilizing factor, whereas others believe the market was simply overpriced and that a correction was inevitable. Although the controversy was never resolved, many firms stopped their own program trading activities, at least temporarily, in response to public outcry after a 190-point one-day plunge on October 13, 1989.

> Source: Kyle, Albert S., and Terry A. Marsh. "Computers and the Crash: Is Technology the Problem or the Solution?" *Institutional Investor,* June 1988, pp. 6-10.

- Use the WCA framework to organize your understanding of this case and to identify important topics that are not mentioned.

- Explain which of this chapter's ideas about process architecture, process performance, and product performance are most pertinent and least pertinent to this situation.

- Explain why there should or should not be limits on automated trading of stocks, bonds, options, and other financial instruments.

KEY TERMS

business process reengineering
architectural characteristics
performance variables
measures of performance
process modeling
data flow diagram (DFD)
context diagram
flowchart
structured English
degree of structure

structured task
semistructured task
unstructured task
range of involvement
case manager approach
integration
complexity
planning
executing
controlling

exceptions
capacity
scalability
consistency
productivity
cycle time
bottleneck
flexibility
security
cost

quality
responsiveness
reliability
conformance to standards
   and regulations
standards
regulations

REVIEW QUESTIONS

1. What is process modeling?

2. What are the four symbols comprise in a DFD, and what does each symbol represent?

3. What is a context diagram?

4. Why is it important to describe business processes at different levels of detail?

5. Why would a user of DFDs ever want to see information expressed in flowcharts or structured English?

6. Describe differences between structured, semistructured, and unstructured tasks.

7. Describe each of the five levels of range of involvement.

8. Define each of the five levels of integration.

9. What kinds of problems sometimes result from tight integration?

10. Will information sharing always result in coordination or collaboration between business processes?

11. In what ways can planning, execution, and control be improved?

12. Why is it important to discuss treatment of exceptions, errors, and malfunctions as part of the analysis of a business process?

13. Define each of the process performance variables. Describe how an information system can improve performance relative to each of them.

14. Define each of the product performance variables. Describe how an information system can improve performance relative to each of them.

15. Explain how information systems may increase responsiveness in some cases and decrease it in others.

16. Explain why conformance is or is not just a technical question.

DISCUSSION QUESTIONS

1. General Electric once had 34 different payroll systems but reduced that number to one by 1994. It went from five financial processing centers to one. These moves allowed it to cut finance operation payroll by 40 percent and from 1,000 to 600 people over a decade.[33] Explain whether these productivity-related changes could raise any ethical issues for General Electric.

2. Assume you are a manager in a company where a computerized calendar system has been installed. The system requires that you specify the times you are available for meetings, thereby making it possible for anyone you work with to set up a meeting without a lot of phone calls and delays. Explain why this productivity-motivated increase in integration may affect you personally in some positive ways and some negative ways.

3. Identify three business processes of which you are the customer. Based on what you have observed, evaluate each of them in terms of the five criteria customers often apply: cost, quality, responsiveness, reliability, and conformance to standards and regulations. Identify the criteria that seem most important and least important for each of the business processes.

4. Consider each of the three business processes in the previous question. Based on what you have observed, describe them in terms of architectural characteristics such as degree of structure, range of involvement, and level of integration.

5. Draw a data flow diagram identifying subprocesses within one of the business processes you identified in question 3.

HANDS-ON EXERCISES

1. This exercise involves creation and use of data flow diagrams. It assumes that a DFD program is available. If not, it can be adapted to some extent by using a drawing program.

   a. Use the data flow diagram program to inspect the example provided. What are the processes, data flows, data stores, and external entities? What does the system do?

   b. Use the data flow diagram software to enter a data flow diagram on two levels. (If DFD software is unavailable, do this using a drawing program.)

   c. Explain how the DFD program combines elements of a drawing program with elements of a database. In what sense does the DFD program have a greater "understanding" of data flow diagrams than a drawing program that can be used to draw a DFD?

   d. Use the process and product performance variables covered in this chapter to describe the impact of using a software tool for DFDs instead of doing the work by hand.

APPLICATION SCENARIOS

Granville Hospital

Janet Leong, medical director of Granville Hospital, felt pressured from all sides. The nurses were up in arms because of their work conditions, whereas the hospital's financial officers were concerned that the hospital was losing money and would have to cut costs somehow. The pressures from both sides seemed to lead toward lower-quality medical care.

Dr. Leong was generally sympathetic to the nurses' problems, which stemmed partially from the long-term nursing shortage. Aside from general overwork, many of the nurses had become more and more disgusted with administrative work. A survey in the hospital showed that the average nurse spent over 50 percent of work time filling out forms and doing other clerical work.

On the other side, the hospital's financial officers were concerned that the hospital would continue to lose money unless costs could be controlled. Lacking other ideas, and recognizing that nursing costs alone amounted to 30 percent of the hospital's budget, the hospital's financial officers were ready to suggest cutting staff even further.

Dr. Leong had just returned from a software firm's presentation about a hospital information system that might help. The system replaced much of the hospital's paperwork with an online computer system. When the patient checked in, all the information about the patient would be entered into the system, instead of filling out separate billing and admission forms. When anything happened concerning the patient, including doctors submitting orders for treatment, nurses taking vital signs, medical tests being run, or supplies being used, the information would be entered into a handheld computer at the bedside or a computer at a nursing station or office. Since these computers would be linked to a central database either through wires or by wireless transmissions, all data about patients would be consolidated and available for patient billing, hospital inventory, and management reporting.

Since the system would reduce the paperwork for nurses by making it unnecessary to write the same information repeatedly on different forms, Dr. Leong was certain that the nurses would see the system as beneficial to them. But she was not sure whether the other doctors would accept it. Some had already said that they would not be told by a computer how long their patients should be in a hospital. Others had said that although the new system might prevent nurses from repeatedly writing a patient's name and admission number, they would still spend a lot of their time entering data unless the entire billing system were changed. In fact, some doctors thought that the idea of billing a patient for every bandage and aspirin didn't make much sense at all. Dr. Leong thought the computerized system would help the nurses at least somewhat, but she was not sure how much and was not sure how to get the cooperation of the other doctors.

1. Based on the limited information in this case and on your general background knowledge, identify the major business processes in a hospital. Explain which of those business processes the information system would affect the most significantly and which it would affect the least.

2. Explain some of the information system's possible effects on business processes. Do this using some of the chapter's ideas for evaluating business process performance and describing business process operation.

DEBATE TOPIC *Use ideas from the chapter to argue the pros and cons and practical implications of the following proposition: Dr. Leong should explain to the doctors that a comprehensive hospital information system will not affect their decision-making processes.*

Photon Motors

The CEO has gone for a lot of ideas, but this one seems too far out, thought Terry Kim, strategic planning director of Photon Motors, a leading automobile manufacturer. The director of information systems had just proposed that Photon create a system for keeping track of all maintenance by Photon dealers on every Photon automobile starting with the next model year. The idea was to equip each car with a small, hidden microcomputer that could be hooked up to warn the owner when the car needed service, provide information to the mechanic, and give detailed information to Photon about exactly how the cars were driven and maintained.

The idea came up at a picnic, when some people from the marketing department complained about Photon's reputation for frequent repairs. Company officials had no adequate information to dispute that claim. Wouldn't it be nice if they could just keep track of who maintained the cars properly and who drove them into the ground?

One idea led to another, and a serious proposal emerged. The on-board computer would collect information from existing sensors that were already used to regulate the engine, fuel pump, brakes, alarm system, and other components. In addition to being used for automatic control of these components, the information would be displayed to the driver through warning indicators on the dashboard. The system would automatically store enough data to create a detailed history of how the car was driven. When the car came in for service, that data would be downloaded automatically into the maintenance computer used to diagnose many problems. That same data would also be forwarded automatically to the central marketing department, which would then know how every car was driven, where it was driven, when it was serviced, and what parts were needed. With that information linked to their automobile owner file, Photon could send letters to people warning them about maintenance needs as well as special promotional material targeted to different types of owners such as hot rodders or extra-cautious drivers. The database would be incomplete because some owners wouldn't get their service at dealers. Nonetheless, it would be extensive and would help the owners, mechanics, and marketing department.

1. What are the major business processes in this situation?

2. Explain how ideas in the chapter help you think about the operation and performance of these business processes.

DEBATE TOPIC *Use ideas from the chapter to argue the pros and cons and practical implications of the following proposition: The proposed system is likely to improve customer satisfaction substantially.*

▢ Cumulative Case: Custom T-Shirts, Inc.

After learning the details of the business while working in one store, the managers of Custom T-Shirts, Inc. have decided to expand. With the opening of other stores and the hiring of additional staff, it has become much more important to establish repeatable processes so that customers know what to expect whenever they go into a Custom T-Shirts store. Furthermore, permitting people in different stores to do things in fundamentally different ways will probably create confusion and waste time. Dale and Pat are currently trying to figure out what to do about the process of ordering blank t-shirts.

In the first store, ordering blank t-shirts seemed simple. The stores sold t-shirts in four colors, white, black, tan, and red, and in eight sizes, four children's sizes and four adult sizes. This gave a total of 32 types of blank t-shirts. The blank t-shirts sat on shelves in the rear of the store. When any size appeared to be running low, they reordered. Blank t-shirts cost around $2.50 each for adult t-shirts and $1.75 for children's t-shirts.

Dale and Pat are thinking about purchasing a computerized system for keeping track of inventory. That system will use a bar code to identify any shipment that arrives. The amount of the shipment will be added to the inventory on hand, and the inventory on hand will be adjusted automatically whenever a sale is logged by bar code reader. The shipments received will also be compared to purchase orders and returned if the material received does not match the material ordered.

This says something about how to keep track of what happens but does not say how the ordering decisions should be made. Dale and Pat think that these decisions should eventually be made based on a history of sales patterns in different cities during different parts of the year, plus monitoring current fads for wearing different types of t-shirts. But there is only minimal history now, and the decision must be made in some way. It typically takes one week for a t-shirt manufacturer to deliver an order after it is made. With many stores, allowing store managers to reorder whenever they want to could result in excess inventory or excess shortages. At the same time, having headquarters do the ordering might ignore local factors such as the convention that will come to town next week. One possibility is to have headquarters calculate a recommended order for each size and color and permit the store manager to modify that order.

1. Based on what you know and the limited amount of information presented here, use the WCA framework to summarize the scope of the situation. Be especially careful in defining the product and customer of the business process.

2. Explain how the customer of this business process should measure the product in terms of cost, quality, responsiveness, reliability, and conformance. Which of these characteristics seem more pertinent to this particular situation, and which seem less pertinent?

3. Using your own judgment and the limited information presented in the case, draw a data flow diagram identifying subprocesses and data flows within the business process. (Note: Different students will draw different data flow diagrams.)

4. Consider the architectural characteristics of business processes. Which seem more important or less important? How might your subprocesses change if you wanted to increase or decrease the degree of structure, range of involvement, or other architectural characteristics?

5. Explain how you might measure or evaluate the business process and its subprocesses in terms of capacity, consistency, productivity, cycle time, flexibility, and security. Which of these characteristics seem more important or less important in this situation?

REFERENCES

1. Harris, Catherine L. "Office Automation: Making It Pay Off." *Business Week*, Oct. 12, 1987, pp. 134–146.

2. Hammer, Michael. "Reengineering Work: Don't Automate, Obliterate." *Harvard Business Review*, Jul.–Aug. 1990, pp. 104–112.

3. Davenport, Thomas H., and Short, James E. "The New Industrial Engineering: Information Technology and Business Process Redesign." *Sloan Management Review*, Summer 1990, pp. 11–27.

4. Carroll, Paul B. "The Continuing Crisis at IBM." *Wall Street Journal*, Oct. 28, 1993, p. A18.

5. Davenport, Thomas H., and Nitin Nohria. "Case Management and the Integration of Labor." *Sloan Management Review*, Winter 1994, pp. 11–24.

6. Avishai, Bernard, and William Taylor. "Customers Drive a Technology-Driven Company: An Interview with George Fisher." *Harvard Business Review*, Nov.–Dec. 1989, pp. 107–114.

7. *The Economist*. "The Ubiquitous Machine." In an Information Technology insert, June 16, 1990, pp. 5–20.

8. Davenport, Thomas H., and James E. Short. "The New Industrial Engineering: Information Technology and Business Process Redesign." *Sloan Management Review*, Summer 1990, pp. 11–27.

9. Perrow, Charles. *Normal Accidents: Living with High-Risk Technologies*. New York: Basic Books, 1984.

10. Yang, Catherine, and Howard Gleck. "How to File: Even Accountants Don't Know for Sure." *Business Week*, Mar. 7, 1988, p. 88.

11. Ross, Philip E. "The Day the Software Crashed." *Forbes*, Apr. 25, 1994, pp. 142–156.

12. Pettit, Dave. "Technology Outruns Even the Runners on Wall Street." *Wall Street Journal*, Aug. 19, 1994, p. A7C.

13. Example supplied by John King.

14. Roach, Stephen S. "Services Under Siege—The Restructuring Imperative." *Harvard Business Review*, Sep.–Oct. 1991, pp. 82–90.

15. Brynjolfsson, Erik. "The Productivity Paradox of Information Technology." *Communications of the ACM*, Dec. 1993, pp. 67–77.

16. Betts, Mitch. "The Bite of Hidden Costs." *Computerworld*, July 26, 1993, p. 66.

17. Bulkeley, William M. "The Data Trap: How PC Users Waste Time." *Wall Street Journal*, Jan. 4, 1993, p. B2.

18. Heygate, Richard. "Technophobes, Don't Run Away Yet." *Wall Street Journal*, Aug. 15, 1994, p. A8.

19. Keen, Peter. *Competing in Time: Using Telecommunications for Competitive Advantage*. Cambridge, Mass.: Ballinger, 1988.

20. Stalk, George, Jr. "Time—the Next Source of Competitive Advantage." *Harvard Business Review*, Jul.–Aug. 1988, pp. 41–51.

21. Blackburn, Joseph D., ed. *Time-Based Competition: The Next Battleground in American Manufacturing*." Homewood, Ill.: Business One Irwin, 1991.

22. Womack, James P., Daniel T. Jones, and Daniel Roos. *The Machine That Changed the World*. New York: Rawson Associates, Macmillan, 1990, p. 111.

23. Peers, Alexandra. "'Paperless' Wall Street Is Due Next June." *Wall Street Journal*, June 7, 1994, p. C1.

24. Chase, Richard B., and David A. Garvin. "The Service Factory." *Harvard Business Review*, Jul.–Aug. 1989, pp. 61–69.

25. Brody, Herbert. "Reforming the Pentagon: An Inside Job." *Technology Review*, Apr. 1994, pp. 31–36.

26. Weiner, Tim. "No One Loses C.I.A. Job in Case of Double Agent." *New York Times*, Sept. 29, 1994, p. A1.

27. Garvin, David. *Managing Quality: The Strategic and Competitive Edge*. New York: Free Press, 1988.

28. Dumaine, Brian. "Times are Good? Create a Crisis." *Fortune*, June 28, 1993, pp. 123–130.

29. Sims, Calvin. "Disruption of Phone Service Laid to Computer Program." *New York Times*, Jan. 17, 1990, p. A1.

30. Thyfault, Mary E. "AT&T Lapse Teaches MIS to Diversify." *MIS Week*, Jan. 22, 1990, p. 1.

31. Pearl, Daniel. "A Power Outage Snarls Air Traffic In Chicago Region." *Wall Street Journal*, Sept. 15, 1994, p. A4.

32. Morris, Charles R., and Charles H. Ferguson. "How Architecture Wins Technology Wars." *Harvard Business Review*, Mar.–Apr. 1993, pp. 86–97.

33. Smart, Tim. "A Day of Reckoning for Bean Counters." *Business Week*, Mar. 14, 1994, pp. 75–76.

4

Information and Databases

Study Questions

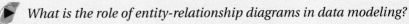

▶ *What is the role of entity-relationship diagrams in data modeling?*

▶ *What are the different types of data, and when is each type particularly useful?*

▶ *What is the difference between a database and a database management system?*

▶ *Why is a single file often insufficient for storing the data in an information system?*

▶ *What is a relational database?*

▶ *What are the purposes of a DBMS, and what functions does a DBMS perform?*

▶ *What are three methods for accessing data in a database?*

▶ *What characteristics determine the usefulness of information?*

▶ *What is the purpose of building and using mathematical models?*

The United States Internal Revenue Service (IRS) processes millions of individual and corporate income tax returns each year. Its goal is the prompt, accurate processing of this information to assure that every taxpayer pays the amount of tax dictated by the law. The IRS faces enormous challenges from many directions. The staggering amount of information it must handle includes one or more tax forms from tens of millions of taxpayers. It must check these forms for errors and for fraud, a nontrivial task to say the least because tax laws created by Congress are incredibly complex and are often open to different interpretations.

Identifying fraudulent submissions is a key challenge. By some estimates, tax evasion costs the United States $150 billion a year. Information on the basic federal income tax form, the 1040, can be cross-checked against salary and withholding information on W-2 forms submitted by employers. It is not so easy to verify tax forms from self-employed individuals, individuals whose income consists of tips, and individuals with complex investments. The IRS estimates that 500,000 self-employed individuals making more than $25,000 don't even file returns. The breadth of the tax evasion problem was publicized in the "Nanny-gate" scandal in which Clinton administration appointees withdrew from consideration after admitting they had failed to submit tax payments for their domestic help.

In the past, the ability of the IRS to merely collect the forms and key them into computerized files was questionable. By the 1990s, however, the IRS systems were much more efficient, and more tax forms were being submitted electronically by professional tax preparers, permitting the IRS to bypass the key entry stage entirely. Tax forms are received and entered into computerized systems that verify the arithmetic and identify inconsistencies with income and withholding information submitted by employers, and interest, dividend, and stock sale information submitted about individual account holders by financial institutions. Automatic screening also looks at common areas for finagling, such as excessive charitable contributions, questionable deductions for home offices, and major year-to-year swings in deductions.

The IRS sometimes cross-checks tax forms against information not originally generated for tax purposes. For example, in 1991, IRS investigators found 63 suspicious cash deposits of under $10,000 made by the John Long family, the nation's largest promoter of country folk art shows. They had deposited checks into corporate accounts and had skimmed off cash into personal accounts. The investigation resulted in prison sentences and $12 million in back taxes and penalties.

The IRS has many other sources for identifying leads. For example, the St. Louis district looks for prosperous nonfilers by matching its list of taxpayers against holders of Missouri drivers' licenses, owners of expensive cars, people who have professional licenses, and people who have made cash bank deposits of over $10,000 or who have suspicious patterns of deposits under $10,000. Matching of this type does not prove something is wrong, but it helps identify cases that should be studied further. For example, a house painter in El Paso, Texas, reported $13,925 of income from an employer who had submitted a form saying he had paid the painter $35,305. In that case, the employer apparently submitted an excessively high number to take a tax deduction himself.[1]

Database searching by government employees to scan through databases is not without risk, however. In the Social Security Administration (SSA), an 18-month investigation found a ring of "information brokers" who allegedly bribed SSA workers to steal personal information. The going rate to obtain a ten-year earnings history within three to five days was apparently $175, of which $25 went to the SSA worker. Buyers of the information apparently included private investigators, prospective employers, lawyers, and insurance companies. After pleading guilty, one set of information brokers cooperated with a sting operation using audit trail information to identify SSA workers who were data thieves.[2]

DEBATE TOPIC   *Argue the pros and cons and practical implications of the following proposition:*
The IRS should have guaranteed access to any computerized data related to a U.S. citizen or resident gathered by any government, business, medical, or educational organization in the United States. This information includes, but is not limited to, data involving state and local taxes, car registrations, checking accounts, credit card transactions, medical records, and telephone bills.

T HE **IRS** CASE REVEALS MANY IMPORTANT ISSUES about information in both computerized and noncomputerized systems, including accuracy, accessibility, and control of information to avoid misuse. A key point in this case is that tax forms can be checked for errors, but finding fraud often requires cross-checking with information generated for purposes other than taxation.

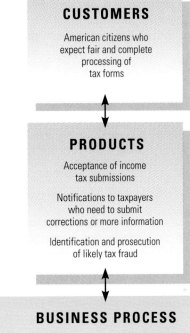

Figure 4.1 The Internal Revenue Service: Searching for Tax Cheats

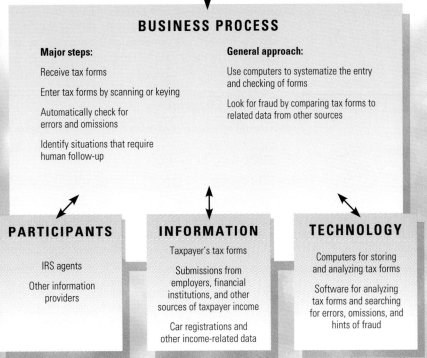

CUSTOMERS

American citizens who expect fair and complete processing of tax forms

PRODUCTS

Acceptance of income tax submissions

Notifications to taxpayers who need to submit corrections or more information

Identification and prosecution of likely tax fraud

BUSINESS PROCESS

Major steps:

Receive tax forms

Enter tax forms by scanning or keying

Automatically check for errors and omissions

Identify situations that require human follow-up

General approach:

Use computers to systematize the entry and checking of forms

Look for fraud by comparing tax forms to related data from other sources

PARTICIPANTS

IRS agents

Other information providers

INFORMATION

Taxpayer's tax forms

Submissions from employers, financial institutions, and other sources of taxpayer income

Car registrations and other income-related data

TECHNOLOGY

Computers for storing and analyzing tax forms

Software for analyzing tax forms and searching for errors, omissions, and hints of fraud

Given the essential role information plays in business processes, business professionals must know how to identify the information they want, decide whether it is adequate, and explain their suggestions for improvements to programmers and system designers. If you are unable to do these things, it is less likely that you will receive the information you need to do your job well.

This chapter presents ideas that will help you describe and analyze information in an information system. This chapter's ideas are directed at business professionals thinking about information and computerized databases. Focusing on the architecture perspective, the first section shows a method for summarizing the data in an information system. Databases and database management systems are covered next. The fourth section turns to the performance perspective by discussing the determinants of information usefulness. The last section looks at the role of models in turning data into information.

Data Modeling

From a user's viewpoint, most issues about organizing and accessing information in an information system boil down to just three questions:

- What information is in the information system?

- How is the information organized?

- How can users obtain whatever information they need?

In the IRS case, the information involved tax forms submitted by taxpayers and other information IRS agents could use to test the validity of the taxpayer submissions. The answer to these three questions would be very different for the Citibank, Wal-Mart, and Ford cases that opened the previous chapters.

Consistent with current system development ideas such as object-oriented analysis and design, the general discussion of these questions is introduced through **data modeling,** the process of identifying the types of entities in a situation, relationships between those entities, and the relevant attributes of those entities. Data modeling goes hand in hand with the process modeling introduced in Chapter 3. The basic tool for data modeling is called an entity-relationship diagram.

Entity-Relationship Diagrams

Assume you were designing a registration system for a university. What information should such a system contain? Consistent with current system development ideas, the question can be broken down into three parts:

- *What kinds of things does this system collect information about?* The specific things it collects information about are **entities.** The kinds of things it collects information about are called **entity types.** In a registration system, the entity types usually include courses, professors, students, course sections, classrooms, and perhaps many others. Specific entities of each type might include Economics 101, Professor Jones, Dana Watts, the Monday night section of Economics 101, and classroom E324.

- *What is the relationship between these entities?* The **relationship** between two entities is the way one of the entities is associated with the other. For example, a student can be enrolled in several courses, and a course section must meet in a particular classroom.

● *What specific information does the system collect about each of those things?* The specific information about the entities is called the **attributes** of the entity type. For example, attributes of the entity type "student" may include address, telephone number, and whether or not fees have been paid. The attributes of the entity type "classroom" may include its location and the number of seats it contains.

The first two questions are the basis of **entity-relationship diagrams (ERDs),** a technique for identifying the entity types in a situation and diagramming the relationships between them. ERDs help in identifying the information in a system and make sure it is represented properly. They help create a shared understanding of the basic ideas underlying the specific information in the system. This technique forces people involved in the analysis to focus on the business situation instead of just listing every relevant item they can think of.

Figure 4.2 contains an entity-relationship diagram for part of a registration system. Among several common notations for expressing the same ideas, it uses the one preferred by Andersen Consulting.[3] This diagram identifies six entity types and the relationships between those entity types. For example, it says that a course may have no sections or may have one or more, and that each section has a single professor and one or more students.

The relationships in Figure 4.2 apply at some universities, but they aren't true at others. Looking at the ERD raises questions such as:

Figure 4.2 Entity-Relationship Diagram for Part of a University Registration System

This entity-relationship diagram identifies six entity types and shows relationships among them. The different types of relationships in ERDs are explained in Figure 4.3

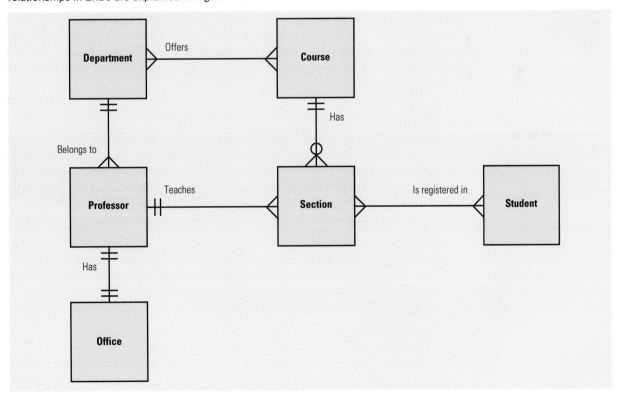

- Does each professor really belong to exactly one department? Is it possible for a professor to belong to several departments or none?

- Is it possible to have several professors assigned to the same section? This would be the case for a team-taught course.

- Does each section really have a professor, or is the more appropriate term "instructor" since people teaching some courses may not be professors?

- Is it permissible for a course to have no sections? This would be permissible if a course in the catalogue is not offered during a particular semester, but the rules of the school would determine whether that is allowed.

- Is it permissible for a section to have no students? This would certainly be true until the first student signed up for it, but a section that had no students would make no sense after the semester started.

Asking questions such as these is essential in building information systems. They help determine what information will be included and excluded, how the database will be structured, and some of the ways the system will eventually detect errors. In addition, they provide an excellent communication medium for system participants who often have trouble explaining the current and desired situation to the technical staff building the system. The term *entity-relationship diagram* sounds very technical, but these diagrams are actually used for the nontechnical purpose of identifying the types of things within the system's scope and the relationships among these types of things.

Identifying the Data in Information System

After identifying the entity types and their relationships, it is much easier to identify the information that should be in the system. For each entity type, this information is the attributes that are significant in the situation. Table 4.1 lists some possible attributes the registration system might include for each entity type in Figure 4.2. As the analysis continued, these attributes might be renamed or modified, and many other attributes would surely be added.

Believe it or not, the innocuous looking list in Table 4.1 could create a lot of debate among the users and designers analyzing the system. Here are some possible issues:

- Is any information missing about each entity type? For example, should the system include course prerequisites or the average grades given by this professor in this course in previous years? Including the prerequisites would be necessary if the system is supposed to check automatically that the student has taken all prerequisites. Including the average grades given by the professor might help students decide which section to attend but would also raise many contentious issues.

- Are some attributes unnecessary or inappropriate? For example, do we want to use the professor or student's social security number, birth date, gender, or ethnicity? Attributes such as these might be needed, might be extraneous, or might be improper or illegal to use or divulge.

- Is there any ambiguity in what the various attributes mean? For example, do the professor's name and address refer to their homes or their offices? To avoid mistakes, these attributes might be renamed office address and office telephone. Even seemingly obvious terms often have different meanings to different people. For example, the *Wall Street Journal* reported that EuroDollar, the European arm of Dollar Rent A Car, gives one-week specials but considers a week to be five days. A traveler who kept a car for seven days was surprised to receive a bill for one week plus two days.[4]

Figure 4.3 Types of Relationships in Entity-Relationship Diagrams

The ERD in Figure 4.2 includes four types of relationships: one-to-one, one-to-many, optional one-to-many, and many-to-many. Shown here are examples of each type from Figure 4.3 plus one additional type of relationship not included in that figure. Other types of relationships not shown include either-or relationships and relationships between entities and subentities.

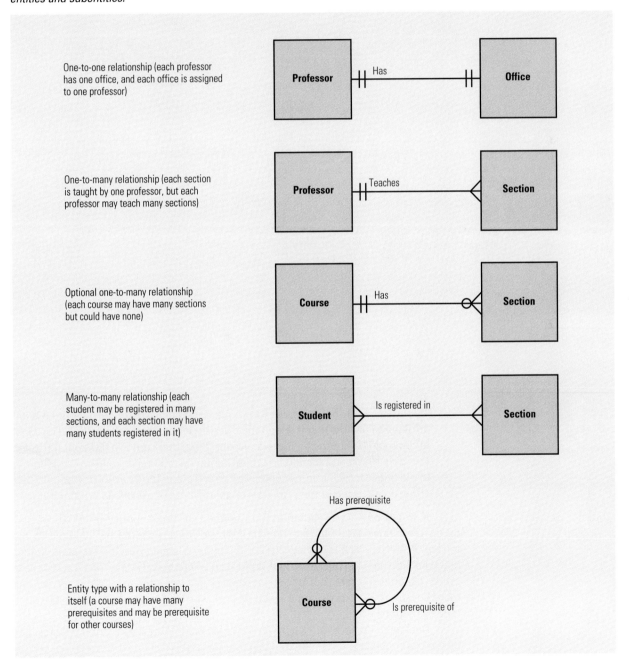

One-to-one relationship (each professor has one office, and each office is assigned to one professor)

One-to-many relationship (each section is taught by one professor, but each professor may teach many sections)

Optional one-to-many relationship (each course may have many sections but could have none)

Many-to-many relationship (each student may be registered in many sections, and each section may have many students registered in it)

Entity type with a relationship to itself (a course may have many prerequisites and may be prerequisite for other courses)

Table 4.1 Possible Attributes for the Entities in Figure 4.2

Entity Type	Possible Attributes of This Entity Type
Department	Department identifier College Department head Scheduling coordinator
Course	Course number Department Required of department major (y/n) Course description
Section	Section identification number Semester Year Classroom Start time End time Days of week for class meetings
Professor	Employee identification number Name Address Birth date Office telephone Social security number
Student	Student identification number Name Address Birth date Telephone Gender Ethnic group Social security number
Office	Office number Building Telephone extension

- Do the same attributes appear in two places? Notice how office telephone is an attribute of professor and telephone extension is an attribute of office. This kind of thing causes confusion for two reasons. First, there are two different terms for the same thing, and second, the information system needs to have each item in one place to make sure it updated correctly. Telephone extension should be either an attribute of the professor or an attribute of the office, but not both.

It would be easy to generate many more questions about the details of how things are named and what attributes of which entities should be included in the system. Work such as this can be tedious and requires great attention to detail. Notice, however, that the main questions at this point are about how the logic of the registration process should operate, not about the details of computer technology. Answering these questions incorrectly could result in work wasted developing a system ill-suited to the situation.

Data modeling is a comparatively new idea in building information systems. The first paper on the entity-relationship diagram was published in 1976,[5] but the need for this step is now widely accepted and has been incorporated in most current system development methods because it summarizes the business view of the information represented by the database.

REALITY CHECK   **Data Modeling**   This section introduced the idea of data modeling and explained how entity-relationship diagrams work.

1   Study Figure 4.2, and modify it to make it more consistent with your understanding of how your university's registration system operates. Add, remove, or modify entity types and relationships as is necessary.

2.   Study Table 4.1, and modify it to include other attributes you think might be important in the registration process. Include attributes of any entity types you added in question 1.

User's View of a Computerized Database

Data modeling helps identify the information that should be included in the system. The next step is deciding how to structure the information in the computerized information system. Although users are typically shielded from much of the internal complexity of computerized databases, they need to know about types of data, logical versus physical views of data, and other topics that help them understand what information the system contains and how they can access it.

Types of Data

The five types of data in today's information systems include formatted data, text, images, audio, and video. Traditional business information systems contained only formatted data and text, such as the price, quantity on order, and product description of each item in a supermarket. More recent advances in technology have made it practical to process pictures and sounds using techniques such as graphics, voice messaging, and videoconferencing.

Formatted data include numerical or alphabetical items arranged in a prespecified format in which the meaning of each item is defined in advance. This type of data is found in ATMs, accounting systems, order entry systems, and other transaction-oriented business systems that keep track of business operations. These systems are defined through the meaning and format of their data items. The examples in the discussion of data modeling involved this type of data.

Text is a series of letters, numbers, and other characters whose combined meaning does not depend on a prespecified format or definition of individual items. For example, word processing systems operate on text without relying on prespecified meanings or definitions of items in the text; rather, the meaning of text is determined by reading it and interpreting it.

Images are data in the form of pictures, which may be photographs, hand-drawn pictures, or graphs generated from formatted data. Images can be stored, modified, and transmitted in many of the same ways as text. Editing of images provides many other possibilities, however, such as changing the size of an object, changing its transparency or shading, changing its orientation on the page, and even moving it from one part of a picture to another. Figure 4.4 shows images that were produced by different types of information systems. Like text and unlike formatted data, the meaning of an image is determined by looking at the image and interpreting it.

Audio is data in the form of sounds. Voice messages are the kind of audio data encountered most frequently in business. Other examples include the sounds a doctor hears through a stethoscope and the sounds an expert mechanic hears when working on a machine. The meaning of audio data is determined by listening to the sounds and interpreting them.

Video combines pictures and sounds displayed over time. The term *video* is used here because it is becoming the catch phrase for multiple types of data display that involve both sound and pictures, such as a videoconference. The meaning of video data is determined by viewing and listening over time.

Although this book discusses these five types of data extensively, other types of data can be important in certain situations as well. For example, taste and smell are important in the restaurant and wine businesses, and the development of a fine sense of touch for robots is a key technical challenge in that area.

The five types of data serve different purposes and have different advantages and disadvantages. Formatted data provide a terse, coded description of an event or object but lack the richness of text, images, audio, or video. Suppose that you want to find out what happened when a car salesperson made a sale. Formatted data can convey pre-specified types of facts, such as the selling price, date, and purchaser's name. Text can convey more information about unique circumstances of the sale. If you could record the sales process on audiotape or videotape, you could get a much stronger overall impression of what happened, such as the sales techniques used.

Richer information is not necessarily better, however, and it can be worse. For example, the car dealer's accountants just want to know how much the car was sold for; they have no desire to read a story, listen to a tape, or watch a video. Formatted data suits them because it reduces the situation to the few limited items that they need to do their jobs. It might also be fine for a manager who needs to know whether weekly sales targets have been met. If the manager wants to understand why salespeople are having trouble meeting their goals, it might be more useful to observe their work.

What Is a Database?

The information in a computerized system is often called a database although the term is used in many ways. For our purposes, a **database** is a collection of data stored, controlled, and accessed through a computer based on the way the data are organized. (By this definition, paper memos in a file cabinet are not a database because they are not accessed through a computer.)

Databases come in different forms and are used in many different ways. Systems discussed thus far in this book use databases for storing and retrieving information needed for day-to-day operation of firms. The databases in these systems contain data about things such as inventory, orders, shipments, customers, and employees. Some of the everyday use focuses on retrieving and updating specific items of information, such as adjusting the units on hand of a product after each sale or recording an order from a customer. Other everyday uses of databases produce summaries of current status or recent performance. Examples include a listing showing the total units on hand for each product group, or a listing showing total sales last week broken out by state.

In some situations, the same database is used for both updating specific information and generating status and performance reports. In other situations, it is more practical to use one database (often called the production database) for real-time updating and to generate a copy of that database periodically for status and performance reports for management. If this is done, the copy will be up to one shift or one day out of date, depending on how frequently the downloads occur, but that is usually current enough for purposes related to reporting.

Notice the difference between the term *database* and **database management system (DBMS).** A DBMS is an integrated set of programs used to define, update, and control databases. We will look at databases first and then discuss the DBMS capabilities later.

Figure 4.4 Images Produced by Information Systems

These three photos show images produced by information systems. The pie chart represents numerical data in an easily understood format. The satellite photograph shows the extent of crop growth in a region. Estimates of crop growth are important in government and corporate planning. The MRI image of a patient's brain provides information for diagnosing a disease process. The MRI image combines multiple images into a form providing the best information for the doctor.

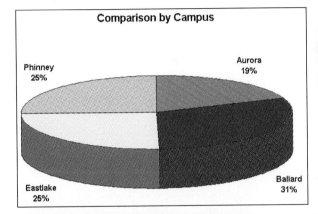

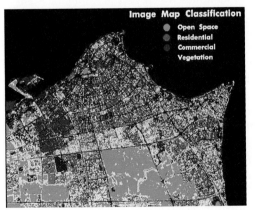

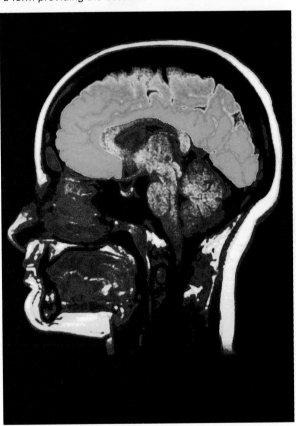

Logical versus Physical Views of Data

The basic idea about data organization in computerized information systems is that the person using the data does *not* need to know exactly where or how the data are stored in the computer. For example, a real estate agent wanting a list of all three-bedroom apartments rented in the last two weeks should ideally be able to say, "List all three-bedroom apartments rented in the last two weeks." Even if the system accepts only coded questions in special formats, the user should not have to know the computer-related details of data storage.

In fact, even most programmers do not need to know exactly where each item resides in the database. Instead, users and programmers need a model of how the database is stored. The technical workings of the information system then translate between the model of the database and the way the database is actually handled technically. Hiding unnecessary details in this way is totally consistent with the way many automated systems operate in everyday life. For example, people can drive a car without knowing exactly how its electrical system operates.

The terms *logical view of data* and *physical view of data* are often used to describe the difference between the way a user thinks about the data and the way computers actually handle the data. A **logical view of data** expresses the way the user or programmer thinks about the data. It is posed in terms of a **data model,** a sufficiently detailed description of the structure of the data to help the user or programmer think about the data. This data model may reveal little about exactly where each item of data is stored.

The technical aspects of the information system (the programming language, database management system, and operating system) then work together to convert this logical view into a **physical view of data,** that is, exactly where the data is stored what the machine has to do to find and retrieve the data. The physical view is stated in terms of specific locations in storage devices plus internal techniques used to find the data. Since this book is directed at business professionals rather than programmers, it emphasizes logical views of data.

Files

The file is the simplest form of data organization used in business data processing. A **file** is a set of related records. A **record** is a set of fields, each of which is related to the same thing, person, or event. A **field** is a group of characters that have a predefined meaning. A **key** is a field that uniquely identifies which person, thing, or event is described by the record.

Table 4.2 illustrates the meaning of these terms. It is an excerpt from a hypothetical student file that contains one record for each student. Each record contains a set of fields, such as social security number, last name, and birth date. Since two students might have the same name while each person has a unique social security number, that number is the key field.

These basic terms about files correspond to the entities, relationships, and attributes discussed in the previous section. The file contains data about a type of entity (student). Each record is the data for a particular entity (such as Alvin Bates). The key in the record identifies the entity. The other fields are attributes of that entity. Relationships in Figure 4.2 are not expressed in this file although they would be expressed if the student file included fields related to other entities in the registration system, such as sections, courses, departments, or professors.

This example shows that a file can be seen as a table. Each row of the table corresponds to a different record. Each column represents a different field. The importance of thinking of a file as a table will become clear when the relational data model is discussed. The representation of the data in Table 4.2 shows that the fields appear in the same order and format in each record in a file. This consistency is the fundamental characteristic of computerized files and databases that makes it possible to write programs that use the data.

The order of records in a file also matters. The four records in the table are sorted by last name. Their order would have been different if they had been sorted by social security number, which might be more appropriate for other applications, such as submitting payroll taxes.

Table 4.2 Excerpt from the Student File

Social Security Number	Last Name	First Name	Street Address	City	State	ZIP Code	Date of Birth
044-34-5542	Bates	Alvin	243 Third St.	Middleton	MA	02137	05/07/74
434-98-8832	Chang	Brenda	87 Palm Ave.	Oakdale	MA	02143	09/30/76
888-23-9038	Schmidt	Dieter	663 Cress Way	Cresston	MA	02184	12/17/75
334-59-3087	Toliver	Gail	743 First St.	Middleton	MA	02137	07/02/74

The general description of a file uses just a few terms (file, record, field, and key) that are widely applicable and easily understood. When data are in the form of a file, users or programmers can easily specify the subset of the data they need. They can select the records based on the values in individual fields. For example, they can say they want all the students who live in Oakdale or all students born before 1975. They can also identify the specific fields they want. For example, for a mailing list, they can select the names and addresses, but not date of birth.

Organizing data as an individual file works well when the information needed for the situation is limited to the attributes of a single type of entity. For example, if the business problem involved finding information about individual students, an expanded version of the student file in Table 4.2 might have been a good solution. The entity is the student (identified by social security number), and the attributes include name, address, and date of birth.

Unfortunately, organizing all the data in a situation as an individual file is often impractical. The registration system example in Figure 4.2 showed why. Many situations involve data about different types of entities and therefore require use of multiple files. The highly simplified registration example identified six different entity types. If you were using a paper-and-pencil system to keep track of this information, you would probably organize it into six separate file folders related to each of these types of entities. You would do this because it would be easier to keep track of the data that way.

But organizing the data as totally separate files for each of the six entity types has shortcomings because the entity types are related. Otherwise, there would be no reason to think of them as parts of the same system. The registration system requires combining data from different files and therefore needs to maintain links between entities of different types.

Relational Databases

Relational databases provide an easily understood way to combine and manipulate data in multiple files in a database. Relational databases provide users with a logical view of the data in terms of the relational data model. According to this data model, the database consists of a series of two-dimensional tables. (The term *relational* comes from the fact that relational databases use the term *relation* instead of *file*. A **relation** is a table consisting of records.) Although the internal structure of a relational database may be quite complicated, its straightforward appearance to users make it comparatively easy to work with by combining and manipulating tables to create new tables.

Box 4.1 demonstrates relational databases by showing several tables from a hypothetical registration system and how those tables might be combined to answer the following question: "Find all the business majors who are taking courses offered by professors in the economics department, and list these students along with the professor." The issue here is that the data needed to answer the question exists in different tables that must be combined somehow to produce the answer.

Although it does not name them, Box 4.1 illustrates three major relational operators: select, project, and join. *Selecting* means paring down a table by eliminating rows (records) according to a criterion. (This happens in steps 1 and 2.) *Projecting* refers to paring down a table by eliminating columns (fields) based on a criterion. (This also happens in steps 1 and 2.) *Joining* means creating a new table by combining two tables. This is done by identifying one or more fields they have in common and combining the records in each that have the same values for those fields. (This happens in steps 3, 4, and 5, each of which creates a new table by combining matching rows of other tables.)

Box 4.1 Answering a Question by Combining and Manipulating Tables in a Relational Database

---

This box assumes that a relational database exists for the registration example in Figure 4.2. That database contains the following separate tables:

PROFESSORS: name, department, and office for each professor

STUDENTS: name, major, and date of birth for each student

SECTION-PROFS: each section and the professor who teaches the section

SECTION-STUDENTS: each section and the students registered in it. Samples of each table are shown to demonstrate one of the ways these tables can be pared down and combined to answer the following question: "Find all the business majors who are taking courses offered by professors in the economics department, and list these students along with the professor and the course."

Step 1: Start with the table PROFESSORS. Eliminate unnecessary columns, and select just the economics professors. This creates a new table called ECON-PROFS, which contains just a single column.

Original Table
PROFESSORS

New Table
ECON-PROFS

Professor	Department	Office		Professor
Adams	Econ	UC 407		Adams
Baker	Bus	BUS 102		
Carter	French	HUM 325		
Daley	Econ	UC 421		Daley
Evans	Econ	UC 321		Evans
Frank	Bio	UC 410		

Step 2: Start with the table STUDENTS. Eliminate unnecessary columns, and select just the business majors. This creates a new table called B-STUDENTS, which contains just a single column.

Original Table
STUDENTS

Student	Major	Date of Birth
Unger	Bus	12/07/64
Villa	Econ	04/21/64
Wong	Bus	08/11/65
Xavier	Bus	02/09/64
Yarrow	Soc	11/05/63
Zellman	Econ	03/27/62

New Table
B-STUDENTS

Student
Unger
Wong
Xavier

Step 3: Start with two tables, ECON-PROFS from step 1 and SECTION-PROFS, which exists previously. Combine them to create a new table, ECON-PROF-SECTIONS. The new table is produced by matching the original tables on professor. Wherever there is a match, the section number and professor's name are retained.

Original Tables
ECON-PROFS   **SECTION-PROFS**

Professor
Adams
Daley
Evans

Section	Professor
ECON 101-02	Adams
ECON 325-01	Adams
BUS 337-01	Baker
BUS 521-02	Baker
FRENCH 113-01	Carter
FRENCH 113-02	Carter
ECON 101-01	Daley
ECON 101-03	Daley
ECON 207-01	Daley
ECON 202-01	Evans
ECON 202-03	Evans
ECON 202-05	Evans
ECON 202-06	Evans

New Table
ECON-PROF-SECTIONS

Section	Professor
ECON-101-02	Adams
ECON 325-01	Adams
ECON 101-01	Daley
ECON 101-03	Daley
ECON 207-01	Daley
ECON 202-01	Evans
ECON 202-03	Evans
ECON 202-05	Evans
ECON 202-06	Evans

Step 4: Start with the two tables, B-STUDENTS from step 2 and SECTION-STUDENTS, which exists previously and contains a row for each student in each section. Create a new table, B-STUDENTS-IN-ECON, each row of which contains a section of an ECON course and a business student in that section.

Original Tables:

B-STUDENTS

Student
Unger
Wong
Xavier

SECTION-STUDENTS

Section	Student
ECON 101-02	Unger
ECON 101-02	Villa
ECON 101-02	Wong
ECON 101-03	Xavier
ECON 101-03	Yarrow
ECON 101-03	Zellman
BIO 233-01	Villa
BIO 233-01	Wong
BIO 233-01	Yarrow

New Table:

B-STUDENTS-IN-ECON

Section	Student
ECON 101-02	Unger
ECON 101-02	Wong
ECON 101-03	Xavier

Step 5: Start with two tables, ECON-PROF-SECTIONS from step 3 and B-STUDENTS-IN-ECON from step 4. Matching on sections, create the table that gives the final answer. This table might be called ANSWER or SECTION-B-STUDENT-ECON-PROF. Each row would contain an economics section, a business student in that section, and the economics professor teaching that section.

Original Tables:

ECON-PROF-SECTIONS

Section	Professor
ECON 101-02	Adams
ECON 325-01	Adams
ECON 101-01	Daley
ECON 101-03	Daley
ECON 207-01	Daley
ECON 202-01	Evans
ECON 202-03	Evans
ECON 202-05	Evans
ECON 202-06	Evans

B-STUDENTS-IN ECON

Section	Student
ECON 101-02	Unger
ECON 101-02	Wong
ECON 101-03	Xavier

New Table:

SECTION-B-STUDENT-ECON-PROF

Section	Student	Professor
ECON 101-02	Unger	Adams
ECON 101-02	Wong	Adams
ECON 101-03	Xavier	Daley

Box 4.1 focuses on the process of answering the question but does not show how a user or programmer might instruct a computer to obtain this answer. This can be done a number of different ways, including using a programming language, a graphical user interface and mouse, or even a natural language in some cases. The industry standard programming language for expressing data access and manipulation in relational databases is called **SQL (Structured Query Language)**. Figure 4.5 gives an example of SQL and shows how queries in plain English can be translated automatically into SQL if the necessary background work has been done. In this case, a software product called Natural Language (because it permits queries in a limited form of natural language) analyzes the user's query, translates it into a query posed in SQL, transmits the SQL request to the DBMS, and displays the data to the user. Figure 4.5 also shows how the user's query is first converted into an equivalent English statement that the user can check to make sure Natural Language interpreted the request correctly. Customers buy the system if typical users are unwilling or unable to express queries in SQL, especially since a single incorrect comma or period could make the entire query meaningless to the computer.

Figure 4.5 Expressing a Query in Natural Language

This screen display shows how a user's English language query was restated by the Natural Language system and converted into a query in SQL, an industry standard language for relational database queries. The Natural Language system permits a user to obtain data from an information system without mastering a special query language.

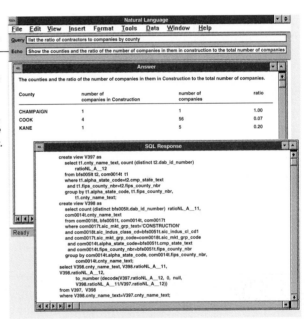

One of the advantages of relational databases is that they mesh with the data modeling techniques mentioned earlier. Entity-relationship diagrams provide a simple starting point for thinking about the tables in a relational database. The starting point includes a table for each entity (such as STUDENTS and PROFESSORS in Box 4.1) and for each relationship in the diagram (such as SECTION-PROFS or SECTION-STUDENTS in Box 4.1).

The next step is designing the actual database. Database theorists have developed the technique of **normalization,** which eliminates redundancies from the tables in the database and pares them down to their simplest form. Going beyond just normalization, database designers must also organize the database to achieve internal efficiency by reflecting the way the users will access the data. For a small database, this may be a simple question. For a large database with stringent response time requirements, this optimization process may stretch the knowledge of technical experts.

Relational databases have become popular because they are easier to understand and work with than other forms of database organization. Early implementations of relational databases were slow and inefficient, but faster computers and better software have reduced these shortcomings. For example, some relational systems contain optimization methods that determine the most efficient order for performing the steps in a particular query. Most new systems for processing transactions in business are developed using relational databases even though many existing systems still use older data models called the hierarchical data model and the network data model. Since system users are shielded from the details of these older data models even when they are used, we will treat them as specialized concerns of the technical system staff and will not discuss them here.

Nontraditional Databases and Multimedia

Without saying so explicitly, the previous section excluded several types of databases that are becoming more important because current computer technology makes them much more cost-effective than they once were, Although each of these approaches is introduced separately, aspects of image databases, text databases, and multimedia have already been used in conjunction with more typical databases in some applications.

Image databases

Most databases used in business contain only preformatted tabular data. Including images in early computerized databases was impractical because images took up too much space in storage. All the text paragraphs in this book can be stored on several pocket-sized diskettes, but a single high-resolution photograph could require a similar amount of storage. As the technology for handling image information improves, many applications of image databases are emerging.

Consider a business that owns a large collection of photographs and sells rights to use them in publications. You could think of their collection as an image database. Imagine the database capabilities that would be required to help an advertiser find a picture of a comfortable-looking rural house shaded by a large tree that could be used in an advertisement for their new country-style bread. Photographs would have to be indexed in a way that would help identify the most appropriate pictures quickly. Another example is a database of fingerprints used by law enforcement officials. Fingerprints are characterized in a way that allows locating a particular fingerprint in a database containing millions of fingerprints. The Automated Fingerprint Identification system developed by NEC of Japan uses pattern-matching techniques to identify a suspect within minutes (see Figure 4.6). Systems that use optical disks for storage are gradually beginning to solve the storage problem, but the problem of how to find images based on desired features remains very difficult.

Text databases

Commercial databases of legal decisions are important examples of text databases. Finding the information a user wants is a key issue in such databases. Unlike relational databases organized as predefined tables, records, and fields, text databases are organized as sets of documents. There are three basic ways to find data in text databases: indexes, keywords, and text search.

An **index** is a list organized to help a system user find specific information. Finding documents using indexes is familiar to anyone who has used a library. The books in a library are typically indexed by author, title, and subject. If the user knows the author or title, the index says where to look to find the book. **Keywords** are terms that describe a general area of information in which a book or magazine article may be classified. Keywords are used in subject indexes in libraries. Although they are often useful, they may be somewhat unreliable because the keyword in the index may not be stated in exactly the terms the user might express. For example, a book on information systems might be listed only under the traditional heading of management information systems.

Figure 4.6 Using a Fingerprint Database

The police officer is using an image database to identify a criminal suspect. The images are fingerprints.

The third method for finding information is **text search,** in which the computer looks at the text itself to verify that it meets search criteria, such as being about the dairy industry. Fortunately, text search can sometimes be combined with indexes and keywords to reduce the amount of computer resources needed to find information.

An innovative example of text search is performed by DowQuest, an information service that retrieves business information from hundreds of thousands of recent articles in 175 different publications. The user types a question such as "What are dairy industry reactions to farm subsidy legislation?" In response, the system lists articles that use the important words in the question most extensively. (The "importance" of a word is based on how infrequently it occurs in English. In the example, *what* and *are* are unimportant words, whereas *farm* and *subsidy* are important.) From this, the user identifies a few highly relevant articles. Using the important words in those articles, the system hones in on articles related to the topic the user wants to look at.

Multimedia

Combining different types of information in the same system is sometimes called **multimedia.** Advantages of multimedia are apparent in many computerized communication technologies. For example, the first computerized documents contained only text, whereas current word processing systems include images in documents. Some word processors (and spreadsheets) even make it possible to include voice comments when someone reviews the document and passes it on to others. A similar broadening has occurred for communication by telephone, which was traditionally a voice-only medium. Newer technology provides capabilities for transmitting computer screen images of spreadsheets or engineering drawings so that two people can work on the same image data at the same time. Incorporating full video capabilities into a telephone call is also possible with videoconferencing. Figure 4.7 shows a current example of a multimedia system.

Figure 4.7 Example of a Multimedia System

This workstation has been converted into a combination workstation and videoconferencing device. The tiny 1.5 inch color camera permits the user to turn a computer work session into a video conference. The camera can be pointed at an object or document, or at the user directly.

Hypertext

Hypertext is a term sometimes associated with certain forms of multimedia. **Hypertext** is an approach to data management in which data are stored in a network of nodes connected by links. The nodes are designed to be accessed through an interactive browsing system. The combination of nodes, links, and supporting indexes for any particular topic is often called a hypertext document. Hypertext is associated with some forms of multimedia because a hypertext document may contain text, images, and other types of information such as data files, audio, video, and executable computer programs.

To appreciate the difference between a hypertext document and a conventional paper document, consider their physical and logical structure. In most paper documents, physical and logical structure are closely related. The document is designed assuming that the user will proceed through it in the order prescribed by the author. Some paper documents such as encyclopedias and other reference works operate differently. They assume that the user will identify a topic of interest, read about that topic, and then use cross-references to find other information of interest. Hypertext documents are designed for this type of browsing but provide greater flexibility than paper encyclopedias because the users access information electronically and because the information can be presented using multiple media.

A key challenge in hypertext is in setting up and maintaining the links. In traditional databases, the structure is set up in advance, and all the data are stored to conform with the structure. In hypertext databases, the links are set up directly by people based on their understanding of the items in the database. The maintenance of hypertext databases requires this understanding.

As in other areas of computing, standards are an important issue. Efficient creation and use of flexible electronic documents requires standards for defining document formats and alternative paths through documents. With the support of most computer vendors, a standard from the International Organization for Standardization has been adopted for this purpose. The standard is called Standard Generic Markup Language (SGML). Its adoption speeds the preparation of technical documentation and facilitates classification and retrieval of complex technical and legal documents.[6]

REALITY CHECK **Computerized Databases** This section discussed computerized databases, emphasizing points such as logical versus physical views of data, files, relational databases, types of data, and non-traditional databases and multimedia.

1. Identify a database you are familiar with or have at least encountered in some way. If it is a relational database, identify the tables you think it contains. If it is a nontraditional database, describe its contents.

2. Based on what you have observed, describe how you think users of this database obtain the information they need. Possible answers might include queries in English, queries using a query language such as SQL, keyword search, or having data presented to users by programs that control data usage.

Database Management Systems

A database management system (DBMS) is an integrated set of programs used to define databases, perform transactions that update databases, retrieve data from databases, and establish database efficiency. Some DBMSs for personal computers can be used directly by end users to set up applications. Other DBMSs are much more complex and require programmers to set up applications. Most DBMSs include a query language that allows end users to retrieve data. DBMSs exist for two related purposes: to make data more of a resource and to make programming more efficient.

Making data more of a resource. DBMSs provide many capabilities that help in treating data as a resource. DBMSs improve data access by providing effective ways to organize data. They improve data accuracy by checking for identifiable errors during data collection and by discouraging data redundancy. They encourage efficiency by providing different ways to organize the computerized database. They encourage flexibility by providing ways to change the scope and organization of the database as business conditions change. They support data security by helping control access to data and by supporting recovery procedures when problems arise. They support data manageability by providing information needed to monitor the database.

Making programming more efficient. DBMSs also contain numerous capabilities that make programming more efficient. They provide consistent, centralized methods for defining the database. They also provide standard subroutines that programmers use within application programs for storing and retrieving data in the database. DBMSs free the programmer or end user from having to reinvent these complex capabilities.

DBMSs for different purposes provide vastly different features. A DBMS for a personal computer contains far fewer capabilities than a DBMS for a mainframe or complex network. For example, the simplest DBMSs for personal computers permit only one file within a database and are often called *file systems.* Although their capabilities are so limited they often are not called DBMSs, these systems are easy to use and broadly applicable when relationships between different files are unimportant.The following discussion focuses on the range of DBMS functions rather than on the capabilities in any one DBMS. Business professionals unaware of these issues do not appreciate what it takes to use a DBMS successfully.

Defining the Database and Access to Data

DBMS applications start with a **data definition,** the identification of all the fields in the database, how they are formatted, how they are combined into different types of records, and how the record types are interrelated.

The primary tool for defining data in a DBMS is a central repository called a **data dictionary.** For each data item, the data dictionary typically includes:

- Name of the data item

- Definition of the data item

- Name of the file the data item is stored in

- Abbreviation that can be used as a column heading for reports

- Typical format for output (for example, $X,XXX.XX or MM-DD-YY)

- Range of reasonable values (for example, the codes used for months)

- Identification of data flow diagrams where it appears in system documentation

- Identification of user input screens and output reports where it appears.

Data dictionaries can be used throughout the system development process. In the early stages, they serve as a repository of terms. This is especially useful for coordination when many people are working on the project at the same time. In the example in Table 4.1, the data dictionary might have helped resolve the confusion between office telephone as an attribute of the professor and telephone extension as an attribute of the office. During programming, data dictionaries make it unnecessary to write the same information multiple times and help check for errors and inconsistencies.

A data dictionary defines the data in the system and therefore, consists of **metadata,** data about the data in the information system. Although this term may sound like double-talk, metadata is actually an important idea because it facilitates linking computer equipment from different vendors. This can be done by using interfaces that include two types of data: the application data (such as the information about courses and sections) and metadata defining the meaning and format of the application data.

The data definition for a database is often called a **schema.** Since some users of a system may not be allowed access to part of the data in the database, many DBMSs support the use of subschemas. A **subschema** is a subset of a schema and therefore defines a particular portion of a database. Figure 4.8 shows how a system of schemas and subschemas can be used to identify the subset of a database that any particular group of users may access. The system of schemas and subschemas permits modifications of the format or content of part of a database without having to retest every program

Figure 4.8 Use of Schemas and Subschemas

Schema	Payroll department's subschema	Company telephone directory's subschema
Name	Name	Name
Home address	Home address	_____
Home telephone number	_____	_____
Office telephone ext.	_____	Office telephone extension
Office number	Office number	Office number
Department	Department	Department
Date hired	_____	_____
Employee grade	Employee grade	_____
Tax withholding information	Tax withholding information	_____
Pension plan information	Pension plan information	_____
Health information	_____	_____

in the system. This is a major convenience for programmers, especially in large systems with many programs that access the same database.

Although schemas and subschemas are logical views of how the database is organized, to store or retrieve data, DBMSs also need a physical definition of exactly where the files reside in the computer system. This physical definition can be quite complicated if the database contains many different files or is spread across multiple storage devices in multiple locations. A DBMS must also reserve the areas in physical storage where the data will reside. Since the number of records in any file in a database can grow or shrink over time, a DBMS must provide ways to change the amount of space reserved for each file in the database. After the database is defined, a DBMS plays a role in processing transactions that create or modify data in the database.

Methods for Accessing Data in a Computer System

A computer system finds stored data either by knowing the exact location or by searching for the data. Different DBMSs contain different internal methods for storing and retrieving data. This section looks at three such methods: sequential access, direct access, and indexed access. Programmers set up DBMSs to use whatever method is appropriate for the situation while also shielding users from technical details of data access.

Sequential access

The earliest computerized data processing used sequential access. In **sequential access,** individual records within a single file are processed in sequence until all records have been processed or until the processing is terminated for some other reason. Sequential access is the only method for data stored on tape, but it can also be used for data stored sequentially on a direct access device such as a disk. Sequential processing makes it unnecessary to know the exact location of each data item because data are processed according to the order in which they are sorted.

Although sequential processing is useful for many types of scheduled periodic processing, it has the same drawback as a tape cassette containing a number of songs. If you want to hear the song at the end of the tape, you have to pass through everything that comes before it. Imagine that a telephone directory were stored alphabetically on a tape. To find the phone number of a person named Adams, you would mount the tape and search until the name Adams was encountered or passed. If the name were Zwicky, you would need to search past almost every name in the directory before you could find the phone number you needed. On the average, you would have to read past half the names in the directory. As if this weren't bad enough, you would also need to rewind the tape. These characteristics of sequential access make it impractical to use when immediate processing of the data is required.

Direct access

Processing events as they occur requires **direct access,** the ability to find an individual item in a file immediately. Magnetic disk storage was developed to provide this capability. Optical storage is another physical implementation of the same logical approach for finding data. To understand how direct access works, imagine that the phone directory described earlier is stored on a hard disk. As illustrated in Figure 4.9, a user needing Sam Patterson's telephone number enters that name into the computer system. A program in the computer system uses a mathematical procedure to calculate the approximate location on the hard disk where Sam Patterson's phone number is stored. Another program instructs the read head to move to that location to find the data. Using the same logic to change George Butler's phone number, one program calculates a location for the phone number, and another program directs the read head to store the new data in that location.

Figure 4.9 Locating Data Using Direct Access

With direct access, a computer calculates the approximate location of specific data in a direct access device such as a hard disk.

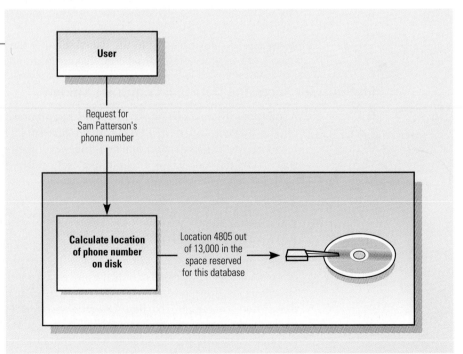

Finding data on disk is not as simple as this example implies because procedures for calculating the location of a specific data item on a disk sometimes calculate the same location for two different data items. This result is called a **collision.** For example, assume that the procedure calculates that the phone numbers for both Liz Parelli and Joe Ramirez should be stored in location 45521 on a disk. If neither phone number is on the disk and the user wishes to store Joe's number, it will be stored in location 45521. If Liz's number is stored later, the computer will attempt to store it in location 45521 but will find that this location is already occupied. It will then store Liz's phone number in location 45522 if that location is not occupied. If it is occupied, the computer will look at successive locations until it finds an empty one. When Liz's number is retrieved at some later time, the computer will look for it first in location 45521. Observing that the number in this location is not Liz's, it will then search through successive locations until it finds her number.

Since users just want to get a telephone number and don't care about how and where it is stored on a hard disk, the DBMS shields them from these details. Someone in the organization has to know about these details, however, because ignoring them can cause serious problems. When direct access databases are more than 60 to 70 percent full, the collisions start to compound, and response time degrades rapidly. To keep storage and retrieval times acceptable, the amount of disk space available for the database must be increased. Someone must unload the database onto another disk or a tape and then reload it so that it is more evenly distributed across the allocated disk space. Maintaining the performance of large databases with multiple users and frequent updating requires fine-tuning by experts.

Indexed access

A third method for finding data is to use **indexed access.** An index is a table used to find the location of data. The example in Figure 4.10 shows how indexed access to data operates. The index indicates where alphabetic groups of names are stored. For instance, according to the index, the names from Palla to Pearson are on track 43. The user enters the name Sam Patterson. The program uses the index to decide where to start searching for the phone number.

Figure 4.10 Locating Data Using Indexes

With indexed access, the computer uses an index that stores the location of ranges of data such as an alphabetical subset of a telephone directory.

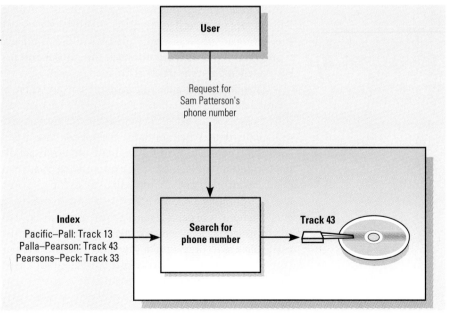

Using indexes makes it possible to perform both sequential processing and direct access efficiently. Therefore, access to data using such indexes is often called the **indexed sequential access method (ISAM).** To perform a sequential processing task, such as listing the phone directory in alphabetic order, a program reads each index entry in turn and then reads all the data pointed to by that index entry. If the index entries and the data pointed to by the index entries are in alphabetic order, the listing will also be in alphabetic order.

Although they solve many problems, using indexes also causes complications. Assume that all the space on a track of a disk is used up and that another telephone number needs to be stored that belongs on that track. This situation is called an overflow. ISAM will put the data in a special overflow area but then may have to look in two places when it wants to retrieve a telephone number. The system's performance degrades as more data goes into the overflow area. As a result, it is occasionally necessary to unload the data, store it again, and revise the indexes. Once again, these are the details the DBMS and technical staff take care of because most users have neither the desire nor the need to think about them.

Processing Transactions

When a DBMS stores or retrieves a particular item of data, it performs part of the translation from a query or program instruction into machine language instructions. A programmer using a DBMS uses its data manipulation language to write commands such as "Find the next inventory record." In this command, the term *next inventory record* is a logical reference to the data. A **logical reference** identifies the data the programmer wants but doesn't say exactly how to find the data. The DBMS converts the logical reference into a physical reference to the data, such as "retrieve the record at location 8452 on hard disk #5."

The DBMS also plays an important role in controlling access to data items when many transactions are occurring simultaneously, as happens in ATM systems and many other business systems. Suppose that two concurrent transactions need to use or update the same data item. What prevents one transaction from reading the data, checking some related data, and coming back to complete the transaction unaware that the other transaction has changed the data? To avoid problems of this type, multiuser DBMSs support **record locking,** the ability to lock a specific record temporarily, thereby preventing access by any other process until it is unlocked. In transaction processing, a programmer locks a record when the transaction first accesses it and unlocks the record when the transaction is finished.

Special synchronization problems occur when processing transactions in distributed databases, databases that are spread across more than one location. Consider a database in which sales offices maintain billing data and warehouses maintain product availability data. When an order is shipped, data in both places must be updated. If something goes wrong in the middle of the transaction, it is possible that the billing data would be updated, but not the product availability data. This would make the database inconsistent. To maintain consistency across distributed databases, DBMSs are incorporating a feature called **two-phase commit,** in which the DBMS first makes sure that both local parts of the database are ready for the transaction, and then performs the transaction. If a network failure occurs during the transaction, the database is rolled back to its previous state, and the transaction is attempted again. The two-phase commit remains a difficult technical problem for DBMS vendors because the double checking slows down transaction rates.

Backup and Recovery

Downtime in crucial transaction processing systems can virtually shut down a company. Therefore, the capability of a DBMS to recover rapidly and continue database operations after a computer or database goes down is essential. DBMSs contain backup and recovery capabilities for this purpose. **Backup** is storing one or more copies of data in case something goes wrong. For example, if mechanical failure in a disk destroys the data it contains, backup data stored elsewhere prevents data loss.

Figure 4.11 Backup and Recovery

The normal processing of transactions uses the database and updates it. The backup process creates a separate backup copy of the database as of a specific time. When the transaction processing system goes down, the recovery process reruns transactions to bring the database back to its status at the time when processing stopped.

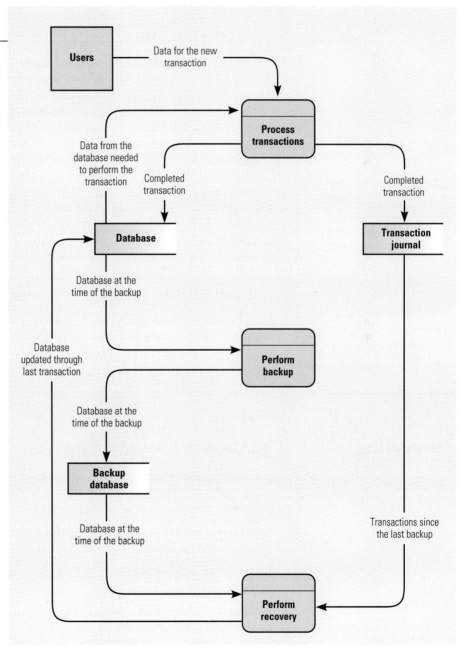

Recovery capabilities restore a database to the state it was in when a problem stopped further processing. As shown in Figure 4.11, the recovery process starts with the last complete backup plus a journal listing all the transactions since the last backup. The recovery process reruns all the transactions up to the one when the system crashed. That last transaction may be lost if it is not in the journal. Once the recovery is complete, processing of new transactions can continue. As with many other parts of a DBMS, backup and recovery are functions that a programmer would have to reinvent with each application system if a DBMS didn't provide them. DBMS capabilities for backup and recovery are successful only when they are used properly by people who administer the database.

Supporting Database Administration

Like an automobile, a database is a valuable resource that will break down if it is not monitored and maintained. The process of managing a database is often called **database administration.** The database administrator is responsible for planning for future database usage, enforcing database standards, controlling access to data, and maintaining efficient database operation. Planning for future usage starts with monitoring trends in database size and activity. Along with user comments, this data helps in deciding what resources are needed to support future database use. Enforcement of database standards includes procedures for ensuring data accuracy and proper backups. Control of database access is accomplished by defining subschemas and monitoring data access. An important issue here is the form of data sharing by users in different areas. Maintaining efficient database operation involves monitoring the database and making sure that response times and other key indicators are acceptable. The internal record keeping by the DBMS supplies much of the data needed for these functions.

REALITY CHECK   **Database Management Systems**   Roles of DBMSs include defining the database, methods for accessing data, and supporting transaction processing, backup and recovery, and database administration.

1. Think of a situation in which you have used a database or probably will use a database in the future. In what ways are these DBMS roles important in that situation?

2. The five roles are basically about formalizing rules and methods for handling data. Explain when this type of formalization is or is not advantageous.

Evaluating Information Used in Business Processes

We now turn from an architecture perspective to a performance perspective by looking at the usefulness of the information in the information system. In addition to the knowledge of the user, information usefulness is determined by three factors:

Information quality: How good the information is, based on its accuracy, precision, completeness, timeliness, and source

Information accessibility: How easy it is to obtain and manipulate the information, regardless of its quality

Information presentation: The level of summarization and format for presentation to the user, regardless of information quality and accessibility

Table 4.3 shows that each factor is related to a number of other more detailed characteristics. Some of these characteristics, such as accuracy, can be measured without regard to the way the information is used. Other characteristics, such as timeliness and completeness, depend on how the information is used and even on who the user is. For example, some managers feel comfortable making decisions with much less information than other managers might say they need. All these characteristics involve tradeoffs between cost and usefulness. For example, keeping data more current generally means increasing data costs.

Table 4.3 Determinants of Information Usefulness and Related Roles of Information Systems

Characteristic	Definition	Related Information System Role
Information Quality		
Accuracy	Extent to which the information represents what it is supposed to represent	Control data to ensure accuracy; identify likely errors
Precision	Fineness of detail in the portrayal	Provide information with adequate precision
Completeness	Extent to which the available information is adequate for the task	Provide information that is complete enough for the user and situation; avoid swamping users with excessive information
Age	Amount of time that has passed since the data were produced	Update information more frequently and transmit it to users more quickly
Timeliness	Extent to which the age of the data is appropriate for the task and user	Provide information quickly enough that it is useful
Source	The person or organization that produced the data	Verify source of information; provide information from preferred sources; analyze information for bias
Information Accessibility		
Availability	Extent to which the necessary information exists and can be accessed effectively by people who need it	Make information available with minimum effort
Access restrictions	Conditions under which specific items may be used	Prevent unauthorized users from accessing data or systems that process data
Information Presentation		
Level of summarization	Comparison between number of items in the original data and number of items displayed	Manipulate the data to the desired level of summarization
Format	Arrangement and appearance of information is displayed to the user	Manipulate the data to the desired format

Information Quality

Information quality is related to a combination of characteristics, including accuracy, precision, completeness, age, timeliness, and source.

■ **Accuracy and Precision**

Accuracy of information is the extent to which the information represents what it is supposed to represent. Increasing the accuracy of information is an important purpose of information systems. For example, the scanner systems used in supermarkets and department stores provide more accurate information about what has been received, what has been sold, and therefore what inventory is currently on hand. Accurate information of this type makes it possible to provide the same level of customer satisfaction with lower costs for inventory. Figure 4.12 shows that accuracy is an issue whenever information is used.

Figure 4.12 Data Accuracy: An Issue That Occurs Everywhere

Inscribed on the Vietnam War Monument in Washington, D.C., are the names of 58,513 soldiers who died in that war. At least 14 are the names of survivors who were included mistakenly because of clerical errors and other problems.[7] Many other collections of data have much higher error rates because they are not checked as carefully.

The related term *precision* is sometimes confused with accuracy. Whereas accuracy is the extent to which the information represents what it is supposed to represent, **precision** is the fineness of detail in the portrayal. Assume that you had $5,121.68 in the bank. A verbal statement that you had around $5,000 would be accurate but not as precise as the figure on your bank statement. On the other hand, a statement that you had $512,168.47 might appear to be very precise, but would actually be inaccurate, to say the least.

It is possible to measure both accuracy and precision although the measures depend on the type of data and the situation. The typical measure of accuracy is error rate, the number of errors compared to the number of items. The measure of precision for numerical data is the number of significant digits. Figure 4.13 shows how the precision of an image can be measured as the number of dots per inch. The more dots per inch, the more precise the picture. This measurement is commonly used to describe the precision of printers, computer screens, scanners, and other image and print-related devices.

Inaccuracy consists of two components: bias and random error. **Bias** is systematic inaccuracy due to methods used for collecting, processing, or presenting data. Bias is rarely an issue in the raw data from transaction processing systems (such as point-of-sale and purchasing) because they are built and documented carefully and scrutinized in many ways. However, data from these systems can be presented in a biased way using graphs and models. Bias pervades informal systems in many organizations, especially in the way verbal information and recommendations are repeatedly filtered and sanitized until their meaning changes. Extreme cases of bias are various forms of lying, such as distortions, misleading advertising, and fraud.

Figure 4.13 Illustration of the Precision of Images

The precision of images can be measured in dots per inch. The image on the left contains 72 dots per inch. The same image is presented on the right at 2470 dots per inch, the standard precision for reproducing photos in books. Laser printers typically produce images at 300 to 600 dots per inch.

Figure 4.14 uses different degrees of "intended truthfulness" to show the range of bias that may occur in business information. It implies that bias is expected, and in many cases even desired, in much important business information. For example, executives deciding which manager's proposal to adopt are not looking for impartiality. Rather, they are looking for a combination of integrity, persuasion, and the passion to follow through and implement the proposal. The implied challenge is to be clear about whether interpretations and suggestions are meant to be unbiased or whether they are meant to persuade and therefore stress some points and leave out others that might also be important.

The other component of inaccuracy, **random error,** also called noise, is inaccuracy due to inherent variability in whatever is being measured or the way it is being measured. The concept of random error is important for interpreting fluctuations in measures of performance reported by information systems. Consider a repair shop monitoring its work quality based on the percentage of customers who return with complaints. The average complaint percentage last year was 3 percent, but last week just 1 percent of the customers complained. This change may indicate that quality is going up or may just be part of the inherent variability in the percentage.

Part of the random error in the data in an information system may result from inadequate data entry controls and procedures for correcting mistakes. A well-known example is the commercial credit databases that sometimes contain errors preventing individuals from receiving loans or renting apartments.

Figure 4.14 Do Managers Expect the Truth?

The transaction data produced by formal information systems is only part of the important information people encounter in business. Raw data can be aggregated into key indicators. Data can be interpreted. Project proposals are produced based on personal goals and beliefs. Each of these cases involves a different form of expected bias in important information.

Intended degree of disclosure					
High	Transaction data	Detailed analysis / Model outputs	Legends	Detailed proposals	Stock fraud and other financial fraud
Low	Key indicators	Management reports / Management summaries / One-minute summaries	Water cooler gossip	Advertising / Slogans and exhortation	Misleading advertising / Evasions and misstatements
None	Secret data	Secret plans and recommendations			Relevant things purposefully left unsaid
	Raw and aggregated data	Interpreted data	Gossip and belief	Persuasion	Lies

Intended degree of distortion

■ *Completeness*

Completeness is the extent to which the available information seems adequate for the task. Except for totally structured tasks, it is often impossible to have totally complete information because some other factor might always be considered. In a practical sense, information is seen as complete if the user feels it is unnecessary to obtain more information before finishing the task or making a decision. Like it or not, people must often work with incomplete information. For example, doctors at a drop-in clinic often need to diagnose and treat seriously ill patients without having access to their patients' full medical history. Similarly, business professionals are often confronted with crises that need some kind of resolution immediately, even if more information might lead to a better or more comfortable decision.

Age and timeliness

Age and timeliness are data characteristics related to time. The **age** of data is the amount of time that has passed since the data were produced. The age of data produced daily, weekly, or monthly by a firm's information systems is easy to determine. The age of data from other sources may be less apparent. For example, population data used in creating the sample for a marketing survey might be based on the last census or on more recent data such as population changes since the census.

Timeliness is the extent to which the age of the data is appropriate for the task and user. Different tasks have different timeliness requirements. For example, up-to-the-second data is needed to control many chemical processes, whereas marketing departments tracking an advertising campaign are generally satisfied with week-old data. For other tasks such as long-range planning, data from months or even years ago may be satisfactory since some long-range trends change slowly and predictably.

The recall of 1,800 Saturn automobiles illustrates the importance of timely information. These cars were shipped containing defective cooling liquid. Information from Saturn's dealer information network revealed a sudden increase in water pump changes within three days of the initial occurrence. All affected cars were recalled within two weeks, avoiding a calamity in the field. Without the information system, the defect would not have been detected until warranty claims began to arrive.[8]

Source

The **source** of data is the person or organization that produced the data. The source is often a tip-off about bias—for example, when one economic forecaster tends to be more optimistic than another. Data sources may be internal or external to the firm. Most computerized information systems focus on internal data although external data is really needed for many purposes. For example, this is why market research firms gather and sell data related to supermarket sales and advertising by the major competitors in a local market. Combining and reconciling data from internal and external sources is crucial in analyzing the business environment.

Sources of data can also be formal or informal. Formal sources include information systems, progress reports, published documents, and official statements from company officers. Informal sources include personal communications such as meetings and conversations during and outside work; conversations with customers and competitors; and personal observations of work habits, work environments, and work relationships. Interpreting data from informal sources often involves more intuition and experience than interpreting data from well-defined formal sources. Even inaccurate data from formal sources is usually organized and reasonably clear. In contrast, data from informal sources is often disorganized. When a manager hears a tense confrontation between two employees, the data may be fragmented, incomplete, and hard to understand. Yet that data may be important if those two individuals need to work together to accomplish the organization's goals. In such situations, managers must use intuition and experience to fill in gaps and decide what to do.

Information Accessibility

Information systems affect information accessibility in opposite ways, namely, by making information available or by restricting access.

Availability

Availability of information is the extent to which the necessary information exists in an information system and can be accessed effectively by people who need it. Availability therefore has two parts: whether the information exists and whether the user can access it.

Accessibility is affected by factors such as the way data are stored, the user's options for displaying data, and the user's skill in finding whatever part of the data is needed. For example, data on a corporate mainframe computer but not on the user's personal computer may not be accessible in a timely fashion. This is why corporations provide data networks for downloading data from mainframe computers to local computers.

Using electronic storage rather than paper makes data much more accessible. For example, assume that the information needed is a summary of detailed data in a 300-page printout or in 7,000 paper invoices sitting in a file cabinet. In these cases, even information that can be derived from data in the user's own office may be inaccessible.

Access restrictions

Although information systems are typically considered a means of providing data, many of their important capabilities involve access restrictions. The most obvious access restriction method is using passwords and other schemes (explained in Chapter 15) for preventing unauthorized access to computers or specific data. As illustrated by the illegal actions of Social Security Administration employees mentioned in the opening case, access restrictions are often difficult to enforce, especially if systems are designed to allow users to analyze data.

Access restrictions apply for many types of data and for many purposes. Laws about access restrictions cover information ranging from employee marital status and medical history to insider information related to publicly traded stock. Laws and regulations restricting access to information are often controversial. For example, in 1993, MIT and the U.S. government settled an antitrust suit related to spring-time meetings when MIT and the Ivy League colleges exchanged information to equalize their financial aid offers to applicants accepted by more than one school. The U.S. government's antitrust division had maintained that the information exchange was a form of price fixing and was therefore illegal.[9]

Other access restrictions are related to management choices about how to run a business with maximum effectiveness and minimum friction. For example, many organizations consider salaries privileged information even though top management salaries are reported for publicly traded companies. Yet other access restrictions are attempts to conceal embarrassing information, such as the admission of Philip Morris's CEO before a congressional committee that Philip Morris had repressed publication of an addiction study showing that animals would press bars repeatedly to get nicotine.[10]

Information Presentation

Information may be difficult to absorb and understand if it is presented in the wrong format or if it contains too many details. This is why graphs are sometimes used instead of tables of numbers and why items of data are summarized into a smaller number of items. There are always alternative ways to present information to users, and the alternatives often have some advantages and some disadvantages. Graphs often make it easier to see general patterns, but they may hide particular items that are important exceptions. This also applies to summarized data presented in tables. For example, the fact that sales of a 600-product company increased 5 percent might be interpreted differently if you knew that sales of 10 new products had decreased. This is why it is important to look for exceptions and other unusual conditions.

Computerized tools for presenting information are much more powerful today than the voluminous paper listings generated by early computerized systems. Figure 4.15 shows a sample screen output of the type of system used by stock and bond traders in leading brokerage firms to give them a better feel for some of the choices they encounter. The geographical information system in Figure 4.15 uses colors on a map to summarize differences across a geographical area.

Figure 4.15 Presenting Information More Effectively Using Graphics

Terms used to describe data presentation include level of summarization and format. **Level of summarization** is a comparison between the number of individual items on which data are based and the number of items in the data presented. For example, a report combining 600 products into 4 product groups is more summarized (and less detailed) than a report combining the 600 products into 23 product groups. From a user's viewpoint, **format** is the way information is organized and expressed. Format involves things ranging from the number of decimal places displayed in numbers through the different ways to present the same material graphically.

Differences between individuals are also important to consider when thinking about summarization and format of information. For example, given the same information, some people will understand it more completely if it is presented graphically, whereas others will understand it better in tabular form. Fortunately, current information technology makes it much easier for users to look at information in whatever form is most valuable for them personally.

Information Usefulness

Information usefulness is the extent to which information can be used for a particular purpose. Information quality, accessibility, and presentation are all key determinants of usefulness although many other factors are important, such as the user's knowledge and the way processes are organized.

Perhaps surprisingly, information usefulness is much more difficult to measure than some of its components, such as accuracy, precision, and timeliness. For example, although it is easy to say that a particular fact, graph, or newspaper article seems useful, it is difficult to assign a value to most information.

Decision theorists have developed an elegant but not totally practical way of thinking about this. Their concept of the **value of information** assumes that reducing uncertainty about a particular decision is the purpose of acquiring information. If the decision would be the same with or without the information, it has no value for that decision because it does not reduce the uncertainty about what to do. It follows that the monetary value of information can be estimated by comparing the expected monetary value of the decision with the information and without it.

Although it is difficult to assess the value of information in these terms, the underlying idea is still helpful for thinking about information systems. Whether or not it can be measured easily, the usefulness of the information in a system is related to the extent to which it influences decisions.

REALITY CHECK   **Evaluating Information**   This section explained how various aspects of information quality, accessibility, and presentation are related to information usefulness.

1. Identify a systematic use of information that you have encountered, such as the use of standardized test grades to determine class placement, the use of medical records, or the use of teacher evaluations. Based on your experience, evaluate that information in terms of the various determinants of usefulness.

2. Considering the same information, explain how you might measure each of the characteristics discussed in this section.

Models as Components of Information Systems

Even accurate, timely, and complete data obtained through information systems and other sources may not provide the kind of coherent picture business professionals need to make decisions comfortably. They may also need models for converting the data into estimates or tentative conclusions directly related to the decision.

Recall from Chapter 2 that a model is a useful representation of something. Figure 2.2 showed examples of models. The dummy in the figure represents a person in a crash test. This example is an ideal use of a model because it permits testing that would otherwise be impractical or unsafe. The spreadsheet in the figure is a model that represents a situation mathematically rather than physically. Models stress some features of reality and downplay or ignore others. They are useful because they mimic reality without dealing with every detail of it.

Many information systems are actually models. Consider an information system that collects and reports sales results for a large company. Monitoring the company's sales by observing every sale would create an overwhelming amount of information. Instead, sales can be monitored by looking at a simple model such as the number of new customers and dollar volume for each salesperson. This model misses some of the richness of reality but contains enough information to support parts of an effective management process.

Mental Models and Mathematical Models

Two types of models are especially important in information systems: mental models and mathematical models. **Mental models** are the unwritten assumptions and beliefs that people use when they think about a topic. A sales manager's mental model might say that no salesperson with less than two years of experience can be trusted fully or that repeat customers are more important than new customers. Figure 4.16 uses a diagram to show some of the interrelated variables in a hypothetical manager's mental model of a marketing decision involving a new line of imported motorcycles. Since the motorcycle is produced elsewhere, the analysis focuses on advertising and hiring salespeople.

Figure 4.16 Diagram Representing a Mental Model

This influence diagram represents a manager's mental model of a new product marketing decision. Some aspects of this mental model might seem surprising, such as the belief that the number of units sold depends on the base market and additional units from marketing effort, but doesn't depend on price. To produce monetary estimates of revenues and profits, it would be necessary to describe each relationship precisely as part of a mathematical model.

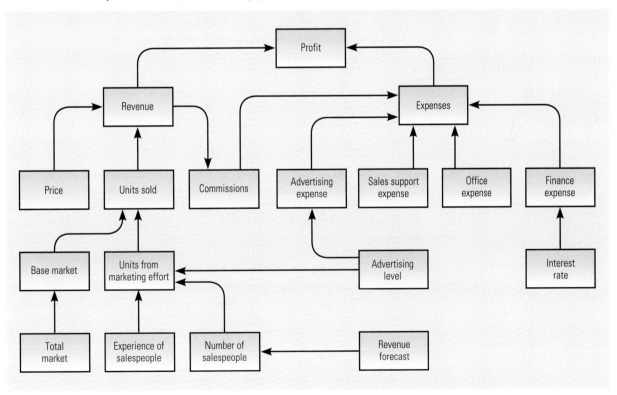

Mental models determine what information we use and how we interpret it. If our mental models don't include a particular type of information, we tend to ignore that information. Conversely, a sales manager who is very concerned about new prospects will find an information system inadequate unless it includes information about new prospects.

Although mental models are essential for organizing and interpreting information, they are often inconsistent. For example, a senator's mental models might include a series of ideas about the burden of excess debt plus a set of other ideas about the necessity of using debt to finance business growth. Such inconsistencies between vague mental models often make it difficult to assess the likely consequences of decisions. This is one of the advantages of mathematical models.

A **mathematical model** is a series of equations or graphs that describe precise relationships between variables. The explicit nature of a mathematical model forces people to say exactly what they mean, which clarifies and organizes various mental models that may be pertinent to a decision.

Both mental and mathematical models provide ways to distill the meaning of information for a particular situation. Mental models identify the factors that are important and the general way the factors interact. Mathematical models express these ideas precisely and produce more precise conclusions.

More important, mathematical models compensate for our inability to pay attention to hundreds of things at the same time. Putting a large number of tiny models into a single mathematical model helps organize an analysis and ensures that many factors have been considered, even if a person cannot think about all these factors at the same time. Keeping track of which factors have been considered, and in what way, is especially important when a group discusses a decision. Since individuals have different mental models, a mathematical model helps everyone focus on the same issues and visualize what has or has not been included.

What-If Questions

Mathematical models convert data into information by performing calculations that combine many elements, by evaluating tentative decisions, and by responding to what-if questions. Tentative decisions are possible decisions that users try out as part of a decision-making process. Users try these out by setting values of decision variables in the model. In a planning model for a bank, these decisions might include the number of people hired and the prices to be charged for services such as checking accounts. The model might start with tentative decisions and then calculate the value of other variables, such as expenses, profit, and estimated market share. These calculated variables could be used to think about whether the tentative decisions are wise.

Mathematical models also make it easy to ask **what-if questions** that explore the effect of alternative assumptions about key variables. For example, a bank's planning model may contain the assumption that it will be able to make loans next year at 9 percent interest. Bank managers might want to see whether the bank will still be profitable if the interest rate drops to 8 percent or if it takes six extra months to roll out a new service. Figure 4.17 shows how features of a spreadsheet program make it easy to ask what-if questions.

Using an organized sequence of what-if questions to study the model's outputs under different circumstances is called **sensitivity analysis.** A sensitivity analysis determines how much the results of the model change when a decision or important assumption changes by a small amount or a progression of amounts. If a large change in a variable generates a small change in the results, that variable probably doesn't affect the decision very much. If a small change in a variable generates a disproportionate change in the results, this indicates that something is wrong either with the model or with the user's understanding of the model.

Figure 4.17 What-If Questions in Lotus 1-2-3

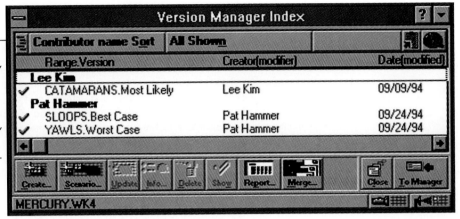

The Version Manager in Lotus 1-2-3, Release 4, makes it easy to organize the analysis of various what-ifs without disrupting the original model. It does this by permitting the user to name various "versions" of a model, such as the version in which a boat dealer emphasizes catamarans instead of sloops or yawls.

Virtual Reality: The Ultimate Interactive Model?

Virtual reality is a special type of model that is becoming important in entertainment and may become important in business. **Virtual reality** is a simulation of reality that engages the participant's senses and intellect, and may permit the participant to interact with the simulated environment. For example, virtual reality movie theaters that first appeared in Los Angeles and Las Vegas in 1993 use sight, sound, and motion to simulate a flight through an adventure environment. Instead of feeling like people sitting in a theater seat munching popcorn, audience members feel like participants because of the intense, coordinated sensations of movement, light, and sound.

Virtual reality models also have real-world applications. For example, they are used extensively in flight training for pilots. They can also be used to support telepresence, the ability to view and manipulate things in a distant, dangerous, or unreachable environment such as the surface of the moon, the part of a chemical plant where a dangerous spill has just occurred, or the interior of a blood vessel.

The idea of virtual reality clarifies the breadth and scope of information systems. Most systems covered in this book provide useful information because they model reality as a small number of specific types of data, such as orders, customers, and schedules. They purposely filter out huge amounts of extraneous information that might have been captured. Virtual reality does the opposite by bombarding the user with sensory information, sometimes to the point of overload. A challenge for future information systems is to enhance the scope and richness of information while remaining coherent and understandable.

REALITY CHECK   **Models as Components of Information Systems**   This section explained why models are often needed to convert data into information.

1. Think about the information needs of the president of a university or coach of a football team. In what ways might models be important to draw conclusions from information that is probably available from transaction databases, from external text databases, and from informal sources?

2. Assume you were helping the president or dean analyze the possible impact of a sequence of tuition increases over the next several years. What factors would you include in the model, and what potentially relevant factors do you think you would leave out?

Chapter Conclusion

SUMMARY

 What is the role of entity-relationship diagrams in data modeling?

Data modeling is the process of creating a graphical model identifying the types of entities in a situation, relationships between those entities, and the relevant attributes of those entities. It helps create a shared understanding of the information in the system and forces users to focus on the business situation instead of just listing data items. The entity-relationship diagram is a technique for identifying the entity types in a situation and diagramming the relationships between those entity types.

 What are the different types of data, and when is each type particularly useful?

The types of data include formatted data, text, images, audio, and video. Formatted data reduces reality to a manageable number of salient facts that can be recorded and retrieved for performing specific tasks. Text can convey more information about unique circumstances of a situation. Images, audio, and video add more richness.

▶ *What is the difference between a database and a database management system?*

The information in a computerized system is often called a database although the term is used in many ways. For our purposes, a database is a collection of data stored, controlled, and accessed through a computer. A database management system (DBMS) is an integrated set of programs used to define, update, and control databases.

 Why is a single file often insufficient for storing the data in an information system?

A file is a set of related records. In data modeling terms, a file contains data about entities of the same entity type. It is often impractical to identify all the data in a situation using a single file because many situations involve relationships between entities of different types.

  What is a relational database?

Relational databases provide users with a logical view of the data in terms of the relational data model, whereby the database consists of a series of two-dimensional tables. Relational databases have become popular because they are easier to understand and work with than other forms of database organization.

 What are the purposes of a DBMS, and what functions does a DBMS perform?

The two major purposes of a DBMS are making data more of a resource for an organization and making programming work more effective and efficient. A DBMS is used by programmers and end users to perform a variety of functions, including defining the database, performing the transactions that update the database, generating reports for users, performing backup and recovery, and supporting database administration.

▶ *What are three methods for accessing data in a database?*

The methods are sequential access, direct access, and indexed access. In sequential access, individual records are processed in sequence until all records in the file have been processed or until the processing is terminated for some other reason. Processing events as they occur requires direct access, the ability to find an individual item in a file immediately. In indexed access, the index indicates the approximate storage location of the data.

▶ *What characteristics determine the usefulness of information?*

Information quality is based on accuracy, precision, completeness, timeliness, and source. Information accessibility is related to how easy it is to obtain and manipulate the information, regardless of its quality. Information presentation is the level of summarization and format for presentation to the user, regardless of information quality and accessibility.

▶ *What is the purpose of building and using mathematical models?*

Models are useful because they mimic reality without dealing with every detail of it. Mathematical models are sets of equations or graphs that describe precise relationships between variables. They compensate for our inability to pay attention to hundreds of things at the same time and help organize an analysis. They also create information by evaluating tentative decisions and responding to what-ifs.

INTERNATIONAL VIGNETTE

Chile: A Futures Trader Loses Millions for His Country

At age 34, Juan Pablo Davila had an important job as chief of futures trading for Codelco, Chile's state-owned copper company. A key part of his job was engaging in futures contracts, the purchase or sale of copper at specific prices at future dates, in order to guarantee stable cash flow for the company. Over less than a year, he lost at least $207 million of the taxpayer's money, approximately 0.5 percent of the nation's gross national product. Editorial cartoonists portrayed him kicking up a mushroom cloud with his tasseled loafers and wielding a computer keyboard like a chain saw. The new verb coined based on his name, *davilar,* can be loosely translated as "to botch things up miserably."

According to his sworn testimony, the problems began when he accidentally recorded several sell contracts as buy contracts. He discovered the problems months later when he visited London on business. What he thought had been a profit turned out to be a $30 to $40 million loss. He tried to win back the money with over 5,000 speculative trades, hoping that prices would go down. But prices went up, and he lost another $180 to $210 million. He confessed in January 1994 and was fired. Apparently, he had received little supervision from his superiors and mostly kept them informed via oral reports. A subsequent audit showed that company controls on trading were ignored. After a management shakeup and during a criminal investigation, Codelco's new president said, "An error of that size can't be committed only by putting a finger on the wrong computer key. Davila will have to prove it was an error."

Source: Moffett, Matt. "A Typing Brush-Up Might Be in Order For a 'Mad Genius'," *Wall Street Journal,* Feb. 1994, p. A1.

• Use the WCA framework to organize your understanding of this vignette and to identify important topics that are not mentioned.

• What issues (if any) make this case interesting from an international or intercultural viewpoint?

- Explain how ideas in this chapter help you think about this situation.
- What could have prevented this problem?

REAL-WORLD CASES

Ocean Spray: Finding the News in Sales Results

Ocean Spray Cranberries is a $1 billion fruit processing cooperative. Working with Information Resources, Inc. (IRI), it developed an extensive marketing database plus analysis capabilities using a fourth-generation language called Express. The largest part of the database comes from grocery store scanner data and includes up to 100 measurements for 10,000 products in 50 geographical markets. Other data cover newspaper ads, flyers, in-store displays, and household purchase patterns. This is 10 to 100 times as much data as was available 10 years ago. Ocean Spray's mainframe computer with 10 gigabytes of secondary storage can process this detailed data, but users must figure out what to do with it. Looking at all the data is impossible, and creating giant printouts and reports is impractical.

IRI and Ocean Spray developed a number of ways to analyze the data and use models to support decision making by sales and marketing managers. One innovative tool is CoverStory, an expert system developed by IRI to generate automated news bulletins when the new data arrives. CoverStory grew out of a teaching exercise in marketing: "How would you summarize what is important in this data?" CoverStory uses a variety of models and analytical techniques to identify the important news in the latest scanner data. It reports the news as a brief memo containing data and graphs. Development is continuing as IRI and Ocean Spray gain experience with new situations.

> Source: Schmitz, John D., Gordon D. Armstrong, and John D. C. Little. "CoverStory—Automated News Finding in Marketing." *Interfaces,* Vol. 20, No. 6, Nov–Dec. 1990, pp. 29–38.

- Use the WCA framework to organize your understanding of this case and to identify important topics that are not mentioned.
- Explain how ideas in this chapter help you think about this situation.
- Explain what it would take to build an automated news finder like this in other business situations.

Kidder Peabody: Phantom Trades Cost $350 Million

Joseph Jett graduated from MIT in 1983, worked for General Electric until 1985, went to Harvard Business School until 1987, worked for Morgan Stanley until laid off in 1989, and was fired from CS First Boston Corp. in 1990 for poor performance. In July 1991, Kidder Peabody hired him as a bond trader. He worked long hours, and by year-end 1992 revenues from his zero-coupon bond trading nearly doubled to $30 million, compared to the previous record of $16 million in 1990. When the previous head of the firm's "government desk" switched to another job, Jett, the top performer in the group was chosen as head even though some colleagues questioned his knowledge of trading. In 1993, the government desk accounted for around 20 percent of the firm's operating profit of $439 million. He was paid a $9 million bonus for 1993, promoted to managing director (one of 135), and awarded Kidder's coveted Chairman's Award.

By 1993, Kidder's rivals on Wall Street were wondering how Jett could rack up $15 to $20 million per month in trading revenues doing legitimate bond trades that appeared to be unprofitable when tracked in the market. Managers within Kidder became suspicious in early 1994 when Jett's revenues soared to $100 million in the first quarter alone. By April, Kidder accountants concluded that Jett actually had $90 million in losses from legitimate trades and $350 million in fake profits from phantom trades. Jett was fired, and Kidder Peabody was forced to restate its earnings for 1993. A subsequent investigation by an outside law firm reported that questions about the unusual trading profits were "answered incorrectly, ignored, or evaded." As the inexperienced trader's apparent profitability increased, "skepticism about [his] activities was often dismissed or unspoken."

Kidder concluded that Jett had created phony profits by taking advantage of a flaw in Kidder's accounting system. Lawyers involved in the investigation say that Jett set up two custodial accounts for the Federal Reserve Bank and used these accounts for phony trades involving zero coupon bonds, government bonds in which future return of the capital and future interest stream are divided into two separate instruments that can also be recombined. Instead of performing typical trades that would settle in a day, he apparently set up a large number of "forward" trades that settle in up to 90 days, thereby generating a situation in which Kidder's accounting system would register a false profit. When settlement time came, he apparently rolled these contracts over into other forward contracts. There was much speculation about Jett's possible defense if Kidder took legal action against him. It seemed likely he would claim he was following orders because his direct boss and another top trader had access to daily reports about his trading positions and because part of their respective $10 and $12 million bonuses was determined by his performance.

> Sources: Freedman, Alix M., and Laurie P. Cohen. "How a Kidder Trader Stumbled Upward Before Scandal Struck." *Wall Street Journal,* June 3, 1994, p. A1.
> Spiro, Leah Nathans. "What Joseph Jett's Defense Will Look Like." *Business Week,* June 13, 1994, p. 70.
> Pare, Terence P. "Jack Welch's Nightmare on Wall Street." *Fortune,* Sept. 5, 1994, pp. 40–48.

- Use the WCA framework to organize your understanding of this case and to identify important topics that are not mentioned.

- Explain how information quality, accessibility, and presentation are pertinent to this situation.

- Explain how personal incentives might have been related to the use of information in this situation.

KEY TERMS

data modeling
entity
entity type
relationship
attribute
entity-relationship diagram (ERD)
formatted data
text
images
audio
video
database
database management system (DBMS)
logical view of data
data model
physical view of data

file
record
field
key
relational database
relation
SQL (Structured Query Language)
normalization
index
keywords
text search
multimedia
hypertext
data definition
data dictionary
metadata
schema

subschema
sequential access
direct access
collision
indexed access
indexed sequential access method (ISAM)
logical reference
record locking
two-phase commit
backup
recovery
database administration
information quality
information accessibility
information presentation
accuracy

precision
bias
random error
completeness
age
timeliness
source
availability
level of summarization
format
value of information
mental model
mathematical model
what-if questions
sensitivity analysis
virtual reality

REVIEW QUESTIONS

1. What is data modeling?

2. What is the difference between an entity and an entity type?

3. Describe some typical attributes of the entity type patient.

4. What is an entity-relationship diagram, and why is this technique important?

5. What is the difference between a database and a database management system?

6. Why does defining the data in a database sometimes generate a lot of debate?

7. What is the difference between a logical and physical view of data?

8. What is metadata?

9. Explain why it is impractical to organize all data in a given situation as an individual file.

10. What is a relational database?

11. Define the three relational operators: select, project, and join.

12. What five types of data are found in information systems?

13. What is the difference between a conventional paper document and a hypertext document?

14. Explain the difference between a schema and a subschema, and explain why this is important.

15. Define backup and recovery, and explain why these capabilities are needed in a DBMS.

16. Identify characteristics that constitute information quality, accessibility, and presentation.

17. Explain how bias is a component of inaccuracy, and explain whether total objectivity is always desired.

18. Describe the difference between mental and mathematical models.

19. What are the advantages of asking what-if questions?

DISCUSSION QUESTIONS

1. The chapter's discussion of accuracy raised the issue that people may intentionally shade or distort the truth. A survey published in the British medical journal *Lancet* asked doctors in Europe how they would break bad news about a cancer diagnosis. The survey found that doctors in Scandinavia, Great Britain, and the Netherlands would be the frankest with their patients, whereas doctors in southern and eastern Europe generally said they would be evasive even if asked directly by their patients.[11] Explain why this is or is not related to truthfulness of management explanations and recommendations.

2. Virginia Senator John Warner, ranking republican on the intelligence subcommittee said, "I was astonished at the magnitude of the site." The Clinton administration had just declassified information about a $310 million project to create a 70-acre office complex for the National Reconnaissance Office, which procures the nation's space-satellite systems. Senator Warner said that the full scope of the project, which had been approved and started during the Bush administration, hadn't been authorized or appropriated by Congress, as is required by law.[12] How are ideas in this chapter related to this situation? What does this situation imply about information systems in general?

3. Explain how models might be used in making the following decisions:

   a. Deciding how much to pay for an apartment building

   b. Deciding whether to build a nuclear or fossil fuel power plant

    c. Deciding which products to carry in a grocery store

    d. Deciding who to marry

    e. Deciding how to allocate a stock portfolio

    f. Deciding what to eat for lunch

4. Identify some of the important databases the following individuals might encounter in their work. Identify some of the files in these databases and the important fields in each file.

    a. Factory manager

    b. Owner of a construction company

    c. Mechanic working in a large automobile repair shop

    d. Loan officer in a bank

    e. Newspaper reporter

    f. Lawyer

    g. Marketing analyst in a frozen-foods company

5. A distributor of building supplies for contractors has a database involving three types of entities: suppliers, products, and customers. Identify some of the important attributes of each type of entity. Based on your own background and intuition, try to sketch out an entity-relationship diagram and a set of relations that might be applicable in this case.

6. A family uses a database to identify all its belongings. Assuming the database consists of a single file, identify ten fields that might appear in the database. Would there be any advantages to having different files for different types of belongings? Show the structure of a database that has different types of records for different types of belongings. Think about how you would include things such as the person in the family who owned the item, what room in the house it was in, and when it was purchased.

HANDS-ON EXERCISES

1. This exercise involves the use of entity-relationship diagrams. It assumes an ERD example is provided.

    a. Use the ERD program to inspect the example provided. What are the entities, relationships, and attributes? What do you think the related system does?

    b. Use the ERD software to enter the ERD presented in this chapter. (If ERD software is unavailable, do this using a drawing program.)

    c. Explain how the ERD program might be extended to generate data entry screens for data about particular types of entities.

2. This exercise involves the use of a relational DBMS. It assumes a sample database is provided.

    a. Examine the sample database and add several new records.

    b. Do several inquiries that require data residing in a single table.

    c. Do several inquiries that combine data across several tables.

    d. Describe what you need to know in order to define a query with the DBMS you are using.

3. This exercise is related to the operation of a DBMS. It uses the same sample database as the previous exercise.

    a. Look at the data dictionary, and identify the metadata maintained about each data item in the database.

    b. Find the metadata defining permissible values for the data items. Decide whether any of the permissible ranges of values seem questionable.

4. This exercise involves the use of graphically oriented modeling software. It assumes several models are provided along with appropriate software.

    a. Inspect the picture that represents the model. Look at some of the underlying equations. Run the model to try to understand the situation it is modeling.

    b. Identify some of the relationships in the model that appear to be assumptions (such as the rate at which increasing salary increases motivation) versus those that appear to be definitions (such as a statement that profit is revenue minus expenses).

    c. Do a what-if analysis by changing any assumption that is numerical in nature, such as that the annual growth rate will be 4 percent.

APPLICATION SCENARIOS

Megahit Feature Films

George McGinnis works for Megahit Feature Films and specializes in finding the supporting cast and extras after the director and producer have decided what film to make and have signed up several big-name stars for the lead roles. The script might call for a tall, skinny, freckled 15-year-old boy or a middle-aged woman who looks motherly and is a good story-teller. George's job is to find the right actors quickly and expeditiously. George has called you in as a consultant to help him think about a system he hopes his information systems group will build to help with his job. Since casting is a crucial activity throughout the entertainment industry, he hopes he will be able to sell or lease this system to other companies in the industry after proving the concept at Megahit.

    George has been thinking about the system as a database providing the information he needs to identify likely candidates for any role. Having a mile-high stack of resumes will not solve his problem. He wants to be able to use a computer to select a group of likely candidates so that he does not have to waste his time. The data in the database should go beyond just name, address, training, and performing credits. At minimum, it should contain a picture of the candidate. Ideally, it should contain a lot more. Given how ambitious most actors are, George thinks it should be easy to get most actors to submit almost any legitimate data about themselves if they know it will be used for this purpose. George wants you to help him create a description of the database so that he can go to his information system department with some clear ideas of his own.

    1. Use an entity-relationship diagram to help identify the specific data you think would go into a database to help George with casting. Be sure you consider the various types of data.

    2. What would be the major business processes in the system, and how would they operate? For example, how would the data get into the database? How would the users use it? What important aspects of the situation would be handled completely outside the information system?

DEBATE TOPIC   *Use ideas from the chapter to argue the pros and cons and practical implications of the following proposition: A computerized system would add very little to the process of selecting a supporting cast and extras.*

DistribuMart

DistribuMart was one of the largest distributors to corporations rather than consumers. The products they distributed ranged from paper supplies to furniture to uniforms. The company's strategy of providing a broad range of products had succeeded even in this age of specialization because they bought in huge quantities, had a unique network of warehouses and shipping facilities, and gave generous discounts to major customers.

In a brainstorming meeting to come up with new ideas, someone suggested that DistribuMart provide their catalogue to customers in some kind of computerized form rather than as an enormous paper catalogue. Ideally, customers should be able to use a computer to say what type of product they wanted, find out which products or close substitutes DistribuMart offered, and then choose based on any reasonable criteria, including price, features, service availability, warranties, compatibility with other products, product appearance, and anything else that might be pertinent.

Although many catalogue sales systems keep track of all past purchases by each customer, this online catalogue would also keep track of all inquiries by each customer. Since inquiries are related to customer interests, this information might be used to facilitate customer interactions. For example, if a customer had looked at paper supplies in the past, paper supplies might be displayed more prominently among the customer inquiry choices in the future, whereas product groups the customer had never looked at would appear less prominently. Furthermore, as the database grew, it might be possible to sell information about customer purchases and customer inquiries to other distributors who were not direct competitors.

One of the people in the meeting said the proposal was one of those ideas that sounded good in the abstract but also sounded impossibly difficult to implement. For example, what would the database be, and how would a customer really ask the questions needed to obtain product information?

1. Use an entity-relationship diagram to help identify the entity types you think would go into a database and the major attributes that would be collected for each entity type.

2. What would be the major business processes in the system, and how would they operate? For example, how would the data get into the database? How would the users use it? How would the orders be filled?

DEBATE TOPIC   *Use ideas from the chapter to argue the pros and cons and practical implications of the following proposition: As described, the system would be an invasion of the customer's privacy even though the data would be collected while the customer was using DistribuMart's information system.*

■ Cumulative Case: Custom T-Shirts, Inc.

After describing the process of ordering blank t-shirts and developing a data flow diagram (see the Cumulative Case in Chapter 3), Dale and Pat want to look in more detail at the information required in this business process.

The basic information about any order includes what was ordered, who ordered it, when it was ordered, and when the supplier committed to deliver it. Dale and Pat are especially concerned about timing. Given that there is a one-week delay between orders and receipts, any significant delays in collecting and handling information as part of the ordering process could result in missed sales because the material simply won't arrive on time or in excess inventory to compensate for a slow ordering process. Any participation in ordering by headquarters must not cause delays.

Dale and Pat are also starting to look at the entire cycle in more detail, and see that they may have to use different suppliers in different parts of the country and perhaps different suppliers for child versus adult sizes and colors. Because of the importance of delays, they may also have to use different shippers to transport the merchandise from the supplier to the retail stores. Ideally, it might be a good idea to see whether different store managers tend to maintain too much inventory. This might be done by tracking the inventory level versus sales level for different stores.

1. Draw an entity-relationship diagram identifying the important entities and relationships between those entities.

2. Identify what you think are the important attributes of these entities. Some of these attributes may be constant, such as their names or locations. Other attributes may be calculated periodically, such as the average lead time for shipping or the percentage of late shipments from a supplier.

3. Look at the characteristics of information, such as accuracy and precision. Explain what level of these characteristics you think would be necessary for the system to operate effectively. If any of the characteristics in the text seem unimportant in this situation, say why.

REFERENCES

1. Novack, Janet. "You Know Who You Are, and So Do We." *Forbes*, Apr. 11, 1994, pp. 88–92.

2. Betts, Michael. "Personal Data More Public Than You Think." *Computerworld*, Mar. 9, 1992. p. 1.

3. Flaatten, Per O., et al. *Foundations of Business Systems*, 2d ed. Fort Worth, Tex.: The Dryden Press, 1992.

4. Hirsch, James S. "Renting Cars Abroad Can Drive You Nuts." *Wall Street Journal*, Dec. 10, 1993, p. B1.

5. Chen, P. P. "The Entity-Relationship Model—Toward a Unified View of Data." *ACM Transactions on Database Systems*, Vol. 1, No. 1, Mar. 1976.

6. Konsynski, B. R. "Strategic Control in the Extended Enterprise." *IBM Systems Journal*, Vol. 32, No. 1, 1993, pp. 111–142.

7. "The Vietnam Undead." *New Yorker*, Nov. 30, 1992, p. 41.

8. LeFauve, Richard G., and Arnoldo Hax. "Saturn—The Making of the Modern Corporation." In Stephen P. Bradley, Jerry A. Hausman, and Richard L. Nolan, eds., *Globalization, Technology, and Competition*. Boston: Harvard Business School Press, 1993., pp. 257–281.

9. Stecklow, Steve, and William M. Bulkeley. "Antitrust Case Against MIT Is Dropped, Allowing Limited Exchange of Aid Data." *Wall Street Journal*, Dec. 23, 1993, p. A10.

10. Hilts, Philip J. "Cigarette Makers Dispute Reports on Addictiveness." *New York Times*, Apr. 15, 1994, p. A10.

11. Hudson, Richard L. "Frankness of European Doctors Differs From One Country to Next, Survey Shows." *Wall Street Journal*, Feb. 18, 1993, p. B7D.

12. Fialka, John J. "Supersecret Complex Outside Capital Is a $310 Million Surprise to Congress." *Wall Street Journal*, Aug. 9, 1994, p. B2.

PART II

Applications and Impacts of Information Systems

This introduction to Part II focuses on three ideas that permeate Chapters 5 through 8.

1. Information systems enable new forms of organization, new ways to work, and new ways to compete.

2. Information systems can give new meaning to everyday things such as money, books, offices, advertisements, and entertainment.

3. Impacts of information system innovations are often difficult to anticipate and may range far afield from the original idea of the innovation.

The next four chapters continue the discussion of these three ideas and introduce many others related to applications and impacts of information systems. Chapter 5 covers applications and impacts related to communication and decision making, two intertwined elements of every business process. It uses ideas about communication and decision making to explain roles of different types of information systems in both areas. Chapter 6 looks further at the role of information systems in business processes, focusing on ways information systems can be used to improve the efficiency and effectiveness of internal business operations within a firm. Chapter 7 focuses on the customer and discusses competitive uses of information systems. Chapter 8 looks at participants and covers human and ethical issues related to information systems.

Enabling New Forms of Organization, New Ways to Work, and New Ways to Compete

Advances in information systems have changed the way business operates, and they continue to spawn new changes. These changes affect most of us in terms of the content of the work we do, the way we do our work, and the way we are managed.

New Forms of Organization

Speculation about the potential impact on the management and organizational control has existed from the time the first commercial computer applications were developed.

Some believed organizations would become more centralized because middle managers would not be needed as much to filter and organize information.[1] Others believed computers would permit greater decentralization by helping local managers to control their own operations and be responsive to customers.

Both predictions turned out to be true. Managers found that computerized systems could support many different forms of centralization and decentralization depending on their goals and priorities. By the 1980s, managers and researchers began to see that organizations were changing in many other ways. By the late 1980s and early 1990s, many books were being written about the changing nature of organizations and work, including *Process Innovation,*[2] *The Virtual Corporation,*[3] *2020 Vision,*[4] *Business in a Post-Capitalist World,*[5] *Reengineering the Corporation,*[6] *The Age of Unreason,*[7] *Shaping the Future,*[8] *Liberation Management,*[9] *Mass Customization,*[10] *Intelligent Enterprise,*[11] *Paradigm Shift,*[12] and *In the Age of the Smart Machine.*[13]

Although these books disagree on many points, they generally do agree that information systems based on new information technology are enabling major changes in business operations. They are enabling new communication and decision-making patterns within organizations by facilitating information flows. They are permitting companies to operate with fewer layers of management. They are changing management by helping give responsibility directly to the people who do the work. They are supporting outsourcing of types of work that have little competitive significance and that other firms can do more effectively, ranging from running the cafeteria to running computer centers. They are creating changes that place more value in knowledge and less in organizational position. They are changing employment patterns by making it possible to reduce the number of workers and managers needed to produce more output than was formerly possible. They are helping companies be much more responsive to customer needs and perceptions.

New Ways to Work

Advances in information technology increased the feasibility of using information systems as tools for doing work rather than just tools for monitoring performance of yesterday and last week. Much previously manual record keeping was automated, often by capturing data as a byproduct of doing work rather than as a separate clerical step. Computerized systems helped monitor the work as it was being done, thereby warning workers about obvious or likely errors before those errors moved on to create problems elsewhere. Many previously manual processes were automated completely.

As anyone knows who has seen people using laptop computers on airplanes, information technology has changed the nature of the workplace. Where people once relied on the corporate office or factory as their workplace, much more of the work is being done wherever and whenever it is most convenient. Developments in networking strongly support the tendency to bring the work to the workers rather than the workers to the work. The ability to coordinate tasks in different geographical locations and time zones supports the trend toward time shifting. Taken to the extreme, this permits some companies to work around the clock on projects whose work can be passed between offices in North America, Asia, and Europe.

New Ways to Compete

Information systems are increasingly important as part of the way businesses compete. Their competitive impacts occur in a number of areas. First, they can help improve internal operations, thereby making it possible for firms to develop their products more quickly and reduce internal costs. Quicker time to market increases profits by making it possible to charge a higher price. Lower internal costs make profits possible even at lower selling prices.

Information systems support sales and marketing processes in many ways, such as by providing salespeople better information about prospects, by helping salespeople identify and demonstrate the right product choices, and by helping calculate individualized prices based on the needs and resources of specific customers. They can also make purchase transactions simpler and faster.

The role of information systems need not end once the customer has purchased the product. Information systems play important roles in customer service activities by keeping track of both general information about each customer and information related to specific customer interactions such as repairs or warranty claims. Information systems can also be built into products and services as an important component of what the customer is buying. For example, we may think of automobiles and airplanes as physical objects, but each is increasingly served and controlled using information systems.

Giving New Meaning to Everyday Things

By becoming intertwined with new forms of organization, new ways to work, and new ways to compete, information systems have started to give new meaning to everyday things. Consider what has happened to money and what is beginning to happen to books.

Money

The idea of money was certainly not obvious in nature. At some point in ancient history, people invented the first economic activity in the form of barter. But barter was inconvenient, so they created money as a way of exchanging value without needing to have the specific commodity the trading partner wanted.

Money had its own problems, however. What if you wanted to buy something but didn't have your cash at hand? Or what if you wanted to pay a bill without traveling to the merchant's place of business and handing over cash? These needs led to the invention of checking accounts, which are basically information systems that keep track of account balances and permit people to write checks if they have enough money in their accounts. But checking accounts operate using paper checks that take days to clear though a complex settlement process.

Credit cards were the next step, and they certainly required large-scale information systems for approving transactions as the customer waits, consolidating monthly customer statements, and paying vendors. Debit cards are the same idea in a different form. Instead of providing credit to be paid off later, they move money immediately from the card holder's account to the merchant's account. Useful as they are, credit and debit cards in their current form will also be replaced by something else in the future. That something else may provide absolute identification of the account owner, and it may not use cards at all. It may move money immediately or may grant credit or may do either at the user's discretion with fees determined accordingly. We know money will be different in the future, but we just don't know how different.

Books

Books are another aspect of life that we take for granted but that were invented and improved gradually. Ancient times saw the invention of written language. Later papyrus and paper created a moveable medium for information storage and access. Invented around 1453, the printing press made mass production of books possible, and along with it, mass literacy. Even though there have been many improvements, current books are still based on the same general model. This model consists of words, numbers, and pictures printed permanently on paper and read in any order the reader desires, even though most books are written to be read from front to back.

Information technology makes it possible to think of electronic books that differ from paper books in fundamental ways. Merely transcribing a book such as this one onto a CD-ROM would make it easier to carry but would not change its essential character. A version of the same information designed as an electronic book stored on a CD-ROM or other device would be much more like an information system than a current book. Interactive electronic textbooks or reference books would probably contain convenient ways to take detours, go into depth on a particular topic, and then return to the main flow. An interactive electronic text might contain quizzes for determining what the reader understands and therefore what should be the next material the reader sees. It might also present different information or examples depending on the reader's background and achievement level in the topic. But an electronic book would be impossible to read without a computer or other reading device. Furthermore, the production of an electronic book with many options would have to include a debugging phase much like the debugging of a spreadsheet or software application.

Money and books are only two of many everyday things that are changing rapidly with the incorporation of new capabilities based on information technology. Entertainment is another, with more choice and control over passive entertainment such as current television programs and new possibilities of interactive entertainment ranging from video games to interactive television. Newspapers, computers, advertising, offices, and many other aspects of everyday life are also changing rapidly, often in directions difficult to anticipate.

Difficulties Foreseeing the Impact of Innovations

A final theme is the unending stream of unanticipated uses of information technology. To balance the utopian view of technological progress that is common in our society, consider Jacques Ellul's pessimistic view:

- All technical progress exacts a price; while it adds something on the one hand, it subtracts something on the other.

- All technical progress raises more problems than it solves, tempts us to see the consequent problems as technical in nature, and prods us to seek technical solutions to them.

- The negative effects of technological innovation are inseparable from the positive. It is naive to say that technology is neutral, that it may be used for good or bad ends; the good and bad effects are, in fact, simultaneous and inseparable.

- All technological innovations have unforeseeable effects.[14]

For now, consider just the last statement, the claim that all technological innovations have unforeseeable effects. Here are several examples involving unanticipated uses of information systems.

When a British insurance company installed a system to speed claims processing, the clerks quickly discovered the rules in the system could weed out dubious claims.

They deluged the system with inquiries because asking the system about a dubious claim was much easier than asking a supervisor or looking up the rules.[15] In another case, a commercial media analysis system was used in a totally different way than intended. It contained models that an advertiser might use to decide which combination of magazine ads would reach its market most effectively. Instead, magazines used it to convince potential advertisers that placing ads with them would be part of an optimal advertising strategy.[16] An unrelated study of information systems in eight organizations in five countries concluded that virtually all the observed effects were accidental, rather than planned.[17]

Advances in telecommunications have yielded an especially large number of unanticipated uses. New and often unexpected communication patterns have resulted from introducing electronic mail. The adoption of fax machines for transmitting documents between businesses has led to a wide array of unexpected applications, such as sandwich shops taking customers' orders by fax instead of forcing them to stand in line or wait on hold on a telephone.

Some unanticipated uses have been unwelcome, however. For example, despite their numerous benefits, electronic mail and fax machines have also brought electronic junk mail and junk fax. Much more serious, international funds transfer systems developed by banks to support international commerce have also been used by drug traffickers to transfer billions of dollars. At a local level, cellular phones have provided dealers in illegal drugs and other criminals a method of communicating that is difficult for police to trace.

This book discusses many remarkable advances and some subsequent problems. Whether or not you are more optimistic than Ellul seems, the issues he raises about benefits, costs, and unforeseeable effects are useful in many situations because they make you wonder about what has been left unsaid.

REFERENCES

1. Leavitt, Harold, and Thomas Whisler. "Management in the 1980s." *Harvard Business Review,* Nov.–Dec. 1958.

2. Davenport, Thomas H. *Process Innovation: Reengineering Work through Information Technology.* Boston: Harvard Business School Press, 1993.

3. Davidow, William H., and Michael S. Malone. *The Virtual Corporation.* New York: Harper Business, 1992.

4. Davis, Stan, and Bill Davidson. *2020 Vision: Transform Your Business Today to Succeed in Tomorrow's Economy.* New York: Simon & Schuster, 1991.

5. Drucker, Peter. *Post-Capitalist Society.* New York: Harper, 1993.

6. Hammer, Michael, and James Champy. *Reengineering the Corporation: A Manifesto for Business Revolution.* New York: Harper Business, 1993.

7. Handy, Charles. *The Age of Unreason.* Boston: Harvard Business School Press. 1990.

8. Keen, Peter G. W. *Shaping the Future: Business Design through Information Technology.* Boston: Harvard Business School Press, 1991.

9. Peters, Tom. *Liberation Management: Necessary Disorganization for the Nanosecond Nineties.* New York: Alfred A. Knopf, 1992.

10. Pine, B. Joseph, II. *Mass Customization: The New Frontier in Business Competition.* Boston: Harvard Business School Press, 1993.

11. Quinn, James Bryant. *Intelligent Enterprise: A Knowledge and Service Based Paradigm for Industry.* New York: Free Press, 1992.

12. Tapscott, Don, and Art Caston. *Paradigm Shift: The New Promise of Information Technology.* New York: McGraw-Hill, 1993.

13. Zuboff, Shoshanna. *In the Age of the Smart Machine.* New York: Basic Books, 1988.

14. Ellul, Jacques. "The Technological Order." *Technology and Culture,* Fall 1962, p. 394. Quoted in Dizard, Wilson P., Jr. *The Coming Information Age.* New York: Longman, 1982.

15. "The Ubiquitous Machine." *The Economist,* June 16, 1990, pp. 5–20.

16. Alter, Steven L. "Interactive Market Systems." *Decision Support Systems.* Reading, Mass.: Addison-Wesley, 1980, pp. 225–246.

17. Robey, Daniel. "Implementation and the Organizational Impacts of Information Systems." *Interfaces,* Vol. 17, No. 3, May–June 1987, pp. 72–84.

5

Types of Information Systems: Different Ways to Support Communication and Decision Making

Study Questions

▶ *How are social context and nonverbal communication important when communication technologies are used?*

▶ *What are the phases of decision making?*

▶ *What are some of the common limitations and problems in decision making?*

▶ *What are the different approaches for improving decision making using information systems?*

▶ *What are the general differences between the types of information systems?*

Frito-Lay, Inc., a snack-food subsidiary of Pepsi-Cola, outfitted its 10,000-person direct store-delivery sales force with handheld terminals used while calling on the 400,000 stores that sell its 100 products. Salespeople use the terminals to enter replenishment orders and record the number of "stales" removed after their 35-day shelf life. Based on this data, a printer in the truck prints an invoice handed to the store manager as part of the day's deliveries. Salespeople hook the terminals to telephone lines to transfer each day's data to the company's mainframe computers in Dallas. This system saves salespeople four or five hours of paperwork per week.

The mainframes in Dallas consolidate the data each night as part of Frito-Lay's internal replenishment system. Requirements for that system changed drastically in the 1980s as Frito-Lay's regional competitors became stronger. Frito-Lay had to be able to respond quickly to a variety of competitive challenges, ranging from price changes to totally new products. Coordination between manufacturing and sales had to be much tighter because the company needed to be able to run local promotions on Thursday for a product that would have to be available on Monday.

The system also provided comprehensive, up-to-date data for studying sales by any combination of product, store, and time period. In South Texas, the data from these terminals showed an unexpected drop in the sales of Tostitos tortilla chips. Research into the cause of the drop indicated that a small competitor had launched a white corn tortilla chip. Frito-Lay developed a competitive white corn product within three months and regained market share.[1, 2,3]

DEBATE TOPIC   *Argue the pros and cons and practical implications of the following proposition:*
The ability of large firms to build information systems like the one in the case gives them unfair advantages over small firms that lack both the staff and money to build such systems.

THE FRITO-LAY INFORMATION SYSTEM supports a range of communication and decision-making functions typically associated with different types of information systems. It is a transaction processing system because it is used to enter orders from each retailer. It can be considered a management information system or executive information system because it provides information in a readily available form for their use. It is a decision support system because it supports decision making by helping route drivers, customers, and managers obtain needed information in a genuinely useful form.

This chapter serves two purposes. First, it explains basic ideas about communication and decision making, crucial aspects of almost all business processes. Table 5.1

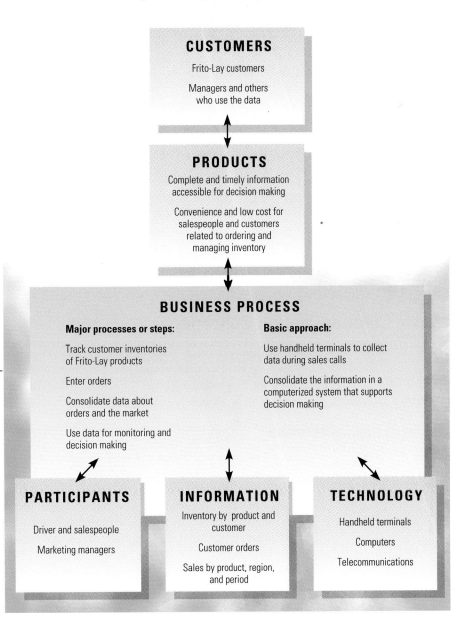

Figure 5.1 Frito Lay: Using Transaction Processing Information to Support Management Decision Making

shows that information systems can improve communication and decision making in terms of each of the internal business process performance variables identified by the WCA framework (see Figure 2.10). Second, the chapter summarizes eight types of information systems, each of which uses a different approach for supporting business processes. These two purposes are combined in a single chapter because the major differences between the types of information systems are related to the different ways they support communication and decision making.

Table 5.1 Ways Information Systems Can Improve Communication and Decision Making Performance Within Business Processes

Business Process Performance Variable	How Information Systems Can Improve Communication	How Information Systems Can Improve Decision Making
Capacity	Communicate more information or more types to more people	Make more decisions using better, more complete information
Consistency	Make sure different people receive the same communication	Make sure repetitive decisions are made in the same way
Productivity	Achieve more communication with less effort	Make better decisions with less effort
Cycle time	Eliminate undesirable delays in communication	Eliminate unnecessary delays in decision making
Flexibility	Permit communication in many different forms	Maintain decision quality across a wider range of situations
Security	Make sure communications go only to the intended recipients	Make sure decisions are controlled only by those authorized to make the decisions

Basic Communication Concepts

Basic concepts about communication are a necessary starting point for analyzing the uses and effects of many types of information technology. Where there is a mismatch between the technology and the situation's needs, communication technology may hinder rather than help communication.

Social Context

Social context, the situation and relationships within which communication takes place, includes social presence, organizational position, relationships, cultural norms, age, gender, and the topic being discussed. The first component, **social presence,** is the extent to which the recipient of communication perceives it as personal interaction with another person. We feel social presence strongly because we all learn how to communicate in face-to-face situations where social presence is powerful.

Much of what is communicated in face-to-face situations is communicated through **nonverbal communication,** such as facial expressions, eye contact, gestures, and body language. This is why two different people saying exactly the same words may communicate different thoughts and feelings.

This is also why different degrees of social presence are desirable in different communication situations. In some situations, getting the message across requires a strong feeling of social presence. In others, such as communication of orders and bills between companies, social presence is unimportant.

Different communication technologies filter out nonverbal information and decrease social context cues to varying extents. A face-to-face meeting provides richer communication than a telephone call because the telephone filters out body language, eye contact, and facial expressions. Similarly, a telephone call provides richer communication than a computerized text message because text filters out voice inflection and intensity.

Personal, Impersonal, and Anonymous Communication

The form and content of communication vary depending on whether communication is personal, impersonal, or anonymous. In **personal communication,** the personal relationship between the sender and recipient matters, affecting communication form and content even in business situations. For example, an employee's performance review is a personal communication between the manager and employee even though it occurs in a business setting. The review conveys factual information but also reinforces the personal relationship. In **impersonal communication,** the sender and recipeint act as agents implementing the policies and tactics of business organizations. Consequently, the specific identity and personality of the sender and recipient affects the communication less, if at all. Impersonal communication occurs when you pay a credit card bill because all that matters is receipt of the payment before the deadline. In **anonymous communication,** the sender's identity is purposely hidden from the recipient. Guarantees of anonymity are used in situations ranging from the suggestion box to crime tips for the police.

Information technology can be used to make communication more personal or more impersonal. For example, using an automated voice messaging system makes parts of communication more impersonal because the caller leaves a message without speaking to a person. On the other hand, customer service departments have used information technology to create the appearance of more personal service by making complete customer information readily available to customer service agents as soon as they answer a call.

Time, Place, and Direction of Communication

Communication can be described in terms of whether the sender and recipient are present at the same time, whether they are present at the same place, and whether the communication is inherently one way or two way. Communication between people in different places has roots as old as smoke signals, drums, and carrier pigeons. Today's communication technology can reach anywhere in the world, permitting people to communicate with each other virtually at any place and any time.

Same-time (also called synchronous) communication occurs when both sender and recipient are available simultaneously. *Different-time* (also called asynchronous) communication occurs when the participants are not available simultaneously and, therefore, requires recording of a message. As electronic communication technologies advanced, the first step was often same-time transmission, such as telephone, live radio, and live television. Different-time communication became possible as cost-effective recording technologies appeared, ranging from taping TV programs to recording phone messages.

Table 5.2 shows how common communication technologies can be categorized by the time and place of communication. Technologies under same time, different place and different time, different place are commonly thought of as communication technology. Some of the other technologies might seem surprising. As we describe later, presentation systems and group decision support systems help people in face-to-face meetings communicate more effectively. Even online databases from data processing systems, such as inventory and reservations systems, serve a role in communication. In situations where all that is needed is the data, these systems replace person-to-person communication with queries to a computer.

The direction of communication is also important because one-way and two-way communication are different. Typical radio and television broadcasting involves one-way communication. In contrast, videoconferencing systems support two-way communication needed for interactive business meetings. An important issue in planning for the future of a national information infrastructure for voice, computerized data, and video (sometimes called the Information Superhighway) is whether it will be one way or two way.

Table 5.2 Communication Technologies Classified by Time and Place of Communication

	Same Time	Different Time
Same Place	• Presentation systems • Group decision support systems (GDSS)	• Transaction databases • Electronic mail • Voice mail
Different Place	• Typical telephones • Computer conferencing • Video telephones and videoconferencing • Nonrecorded radio or TV broadcast	• Transaction databases • Electronic data interchange (EDI) • Electronic mail • Voice mail • Fax • Prerecorded radio or TV broadcast

Approaches for Improving Communication

Information systems provide many ways to improve communication, thereby improving a firm's internal operation, its contact with customers, and ultimately its success. This section looks at several areas of opportunity.

Making face-to-face communication more effective

Face-to-face communication is a starting point for thinking about using technology to improve communication. **Presentation technologies** are devices and techniques used to help present ideas more effectively in same-time, same-place meetings. Here are some presentation technologies used today:

- Blackboard

- Prepared paper handouts

- Overhead projector or slide projector with transparencies or slides

- Electronic blackboard that produces paper copies for the listeners at the end of the presentation

- Projector for displaying a screen image from a computer

- Computer that summarizes data or performs what-if analysis to answer questions from the audience

- Computer-controlled multimedia, including slides and video

- Computerized multimedia used interactively to permit the presenter to change sequence or content during a presentation

The list purposely starts with unsophisticated, noncomputerized techniques and moves toward complex techniques using computers. These different approaches can be compared in terms of cost-effectiveness, degree of preparation required, availability, and other characteristics. Although least expensive, the blackboard is probably the least effective because people have trouble writing clearly while saying something interesting and because the audience must split its attention between listening and taking notes. However, blackboards are readily available and can be used with little preparation. Computer-controlled multimedia presentations require more preparation but can communicate more effectively than a speaker with a blackboard. Similar advantages and disadvantages should be considered when comparing any computerized or noncomputerized techniques for improving communication or decision making.

Eliminating unnecessary person-to-person communication

Substituting online data access for person-to-person communication has been essential for keeping costs under control while firms expand. For example, this permits a salesperson at a customer site to find out about product availability without disturbing someone else's work. In this and similar situations, communication to obtain data is important, but personal communication is not.

This same approach has been used to improve links with both suppliers and customers. After negotiating long-term commitments with suppliers, some firms transmit their daily production schedules to the suppliers, who then time their shipments so that components arrive when needed. Similarly, firms ranging from airlines to stock brokerages improve customer service by permitting purchases using computerized systems to bypass unnecessary person-to-person communication.

Whether or not person-to-person communication is necessary is especially important when external customers are involved. Bank customers seem to accept "talking to" ATMs instead of bank clerks but sometimes wish a person would answer the telephone instead of an automated attendant with the message "Hello, this is Intergalactic Savings. Press 1 to obtain account information. Press 2 for customer service. Press 3 for the personnel department." Firms such as McDonald's might be able to replace their order takers with an automated system, but this might make them appear less personal and more machinelike to their customers.

Making communication systematic

Communication between people tends to be poorly structured. Usually, there is little or no effort to make the individual messages conform to a preconceived format, such as saying this is a formal request from a specific *sender* to a specific *recipient* about doing a specific *task* by a specific *date*. Instead of using this type of formal structure in their communications, people tend to say things in whatever way makes the most sense at the time, consistent with the social context. In contrast, record-keeping practices long before computers showed that structuring information is essential for handling it systematically. At minimum, having structure reduces the effort required to figure out what the information means.

As communication systems became more automated, users found more advantages in structuring parts of these systems. The greatest structuring goes into impersonal or anonymous communications between departments in a business or between separate businesses. For example, systems using computers to communicate orders between suppliers and customers must conform to strict data formats and definitions; otherwise, people on both sides of the transaction would have to communicate directly to clarify what it meant. Even with communication between groups of people rather than computers, it is often more efficient to systematize the repetitive aspects of communication. For example, repetitive approval cycles for expenses or projects typically use a prescribed format so that the people involved don't have to waste time figuring out what communication format to use each time a similar situation arises.

Combining and extending electronic communication functions

Early electronic communications came from several different directions. The telegraph transmitted a coded text message across a wire. The telephone supported a same-time/different-place voice conversation between two people using wired telephones connected by a human telephone operator. Radio and television broadcasting transmitted audio and video signals through space. These original ideas have been combined and expanded to create more powerful communication tools.

Figure 5.2 illustrates some of these possibilities, all of which are related to the idea that a telephone call is not necessarily a two-person conversation over a wire. Seeing things this way, the caller or receiver could be a person or computer, any type of data might be transmitted, the data might be stored when received, the device used for sending or receiving might be portable, and the addressing information for locating the receiver might be used in many ways.

REALITY CHECK   **Effects of Communication Situations**   This section differentiated between different degrees of social presence in communication (personal, impersonal, and anonymous) and between different combinations of time, place, and direction of communication (same time versus different time, same place versus different place, and one way versus two way).

1.   Considering about things you have done personally, give examples of communication illustrating each variation on these two aspects of a communication situation.

2.   For each example, identify ways it might have been possible to improve the communication by changing these aspects of the communication situation in some way.

Basic Decision-Making Concepts

An understanding of decision making is essential because most information systems are designed to support decision making in one way or another.

Phases in a Decision Process

Researchers have proposed many descriptions of decision processes. This book uses a model combining ideas from several different sources. Figure 5.3 shows decision making as a problem-solving process preceded by a separate problem-finding process. **Problem finding** is the process of identifying and formulating problems that should be solved.[4] Although often overlooked, problem finding is the key to effective decision making because a seemingly good solution to the wrong problem may miss the point.

Figure 5.2 Extending Telephone Functions and Features

These photos show three different extensions of the original idea of the telephone as a same-time/different-place voice conversation between two people using wired telephones connected by a human telephone operator.
(a) This electronic mail message is being composed at a personal computer using WordPerfect GroupWise. The message is direct to two individuals. This type of mail system can be used to transmit anything from telephone messages to lengthy reports.
(b) This financial analyst is working out the financial details of a large investment with another financial analyst 2,000 miles away. To aid in their discussion, they are both looking at the same spreadsheet model displayed on both their screens.
(c) These managers are having a face-to-face meeting even though they are hundreds of miles apart. Although not as real-istic as being in the same room, the videoconference provides more social presence than a regular telephone call and costs much less than getting on an airplane.

(a)

(b)

(c)

For example, we might come up with many solutions to the problem of how to expand our airports, but it might be better to formulate the problem as "How can we avoid expanding our airports by using transportation substitutes such as videoconferencing?"

Information systems can play important roles in problem finding by helping identify problems that might not otherwise be recognized. For example, Proctor & Gamble, a consumer-products giant took a pretax $157 million write-off in 1994 to cover the cost of two leveraged interest rate swaps. These transactions were originally designed to protect P&G from interest rate fluctuations but went sour when interest rates rose rapidly. Some observers believed that unlike banks who specialize in this area, many companies such as P&G lack the information systems needed for keeping track of exposure to possible losses if interest rates change dramatically.[5]

This chapter will discuss many ways information systems are used for both problem finding and problem solving. **Problem solving** is the process of using information, knowledge, and intuition to solve a problem that has been defined previously. The problem-solving portion of Figure 5.3 says that most decision processes can be divided into four phases: intelligence, design, choice, and implementation.

- **Intelligence** includes the collection and analysis of data related to the problem identified in the problem-finding stage. Key challenges in the intelligence phase include obtaining complete and accurate data and figuring out what the data imply for the decision at hand.

- **Design** includes systematic study of the problem, creation of alternatives, and evaluation of outcomes. Key challenges in this phase include bounding the problem to make it manageable, creating real alternatives, and developing criteria and models for evaluating the alternatives.

- **Choice** is the selection of the preferred alternative. Key challenges here include reconciling conflicting objectives and interests, incorporating uncertainty, and managing group decision processes.

- **Implementation** is the process of putting the decision into effect. This includes explaining the decision to the appropriate people, building consensus that the decision makes sense, and creating the commitment to follow through. Key challenges involve ensuring that the decision and its implications are understood and that others in the organization will follow through, whether or not their preferred alternative is chosen.

The first three phases of the problem-solving process are Simon's classic model of decision making.[6] Since the problem is not solved until the decision is put into operation, implementation is the fourth phase. Perhaps surprisingly, many systems designed to support decision making have their greatest impact not in making decisions, but in implementation activities such as explaining and justifying decisions.

Although the model separates problem finding from problem solving and then divides problem solving into four separate phases, real decision processes are iterative and return to previous phases. The intelligence phase of problem solving may show that the problem-finding phase didn't identify the right problem. For example, the intelligence phase for solving a problem about communication with customers might raise questions about whether the real problem is inadequate product documentation. This question would require gathering more data about documentation effectiveness. Questions arising in the design phase may require returning to the intelligence phase to collect more data. For example, if Frito-Lay identified the alternative of countering a competitor with a new ad campaign, it might have to obtain more information about what that campaign might cost. Similarly, the choice or implementation phase might identify criteria and issues requiring the return to previous phases.

Figure 5.3 Steps in Decision Making

The diagram shows decision making as a four-phase problem-solving process preceded by a problem-finding process.

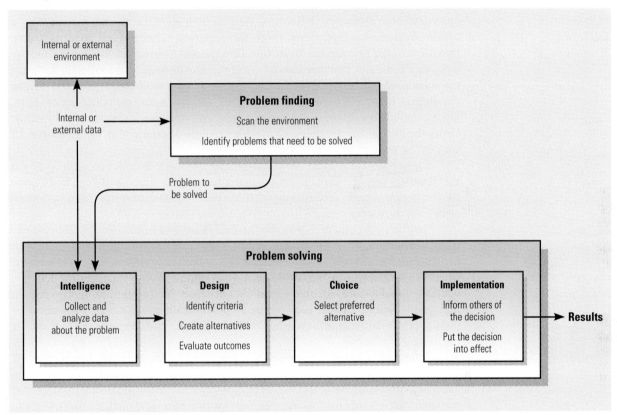

Rationality and Satisficing

Describing the phases in decision making is a starting point for explaining how people make decisions, but it raises questions as well, such as whether people are rational decision makers and what that means.

Rationality is a common model for explaining how people should make decisions. Classical economic theory says that rational decision makers maximize their welfare by performing the first three phases of problem solving thoroughly. First, they gather all pertinent information and interpret it. Second, they identify all feasible alternatives and evaluate them based on criteria that maximize the good of the individual or organization. Third, they choose among the alternatives based on consistent and explicit tradeoffs between the criteria.

For centuries, economists have argued about whether people show rationality by making economic decisions that maximize their own welfare and whether the sum of these decisions ultimately maximizes society's welfare. Consider two situations. In the first, Pat is an unmarried employee who has decided to move to a new apartment in the same city. Pat has plenty of time to look for a good apartment. In the second situation,

Pat has volunteered to move temporarily to another city to work on an important project that will last eight months. Pat can stay in a hotel for a few weeks but needs to find an apartment for the remainder of the time. The project has been underway for over a year, and there is a lot of work to catch up on.

Although the process of renting an apartment involves the phases of intelligence, design, and choice in both situations, the phases would proceed differently. In the first situation, Pat would have more time to look around, identify what he wants in an apartment, and choose the best one within his budget. In the second, Pat would have to make a decision quickly, even if the available apartments weren't very good. As is often the case, it would be necessary to identify a few feasible alternatives and choose one. The fact that Pat did not optimize doesn't mean that the decision was irrational. Rather, it means that this situation called for finding several acceptable apartments and renting one of them. In another sense, the problem being solved was not just finding an apartment, but a combination of which apartment to rent and how much time to spend looking. Under the circumstances, spending much more time to get a slightly better apartment wouldn't be feasible.

Choosing a satisfactory alternative rather than searching for an optimal one is called **satisficing.** The concept of satisficing came from Simon's attempt to describe the way people actually behave rather than the way they should behave if they optimized all or even most decisions.

Satisficing is consistent with the theory of **bounded rationality,** whereby people make decisions in a limited amount of time, based on limited information, and with limited ability to process that information. Think about any decision you made recently: where to live or what to do next weekend. As you examine the way you made the decision, you will probably conclude that you could not obtain all the relevant information. In fact, you probably couldn't even define all possible alternatives, much less consider them seriously. You may also have had difficulty defining the criteria to use in choosing the desired alternative.

Information systems have value in decision making because they reduce the boundedness of rationality. Information systems may provide more information than you would otherwise have; they may help you generate and evaluate alternatives; and they may help you choose. Nonetheless, except in extremely structured decisions, you might still feel that you don't have all the information you would like to have and that you aren't totally sure how to create and evaluate the alternatives.

Common Flaws in Decision Making

Both business professionals and psychologists have observed common flaws in the way people make decisions. To supplement the examples that follow, Table 5.3 defines each problem and mentions some of the ways information systems might be used to avoid the related errors. Although few information systems are designed specifically to counter these flaws in decision making, recognizing these common problems helps in understanding what information systems can and cannot do for us.

> *Poor framing:* Decision makers often allow a decision to be "framed" by the language or context in which it is presented. In one experiment, two groups of students were given identical information about a business strategy. One group was told that the strategy had an 80 percent probability of success; the other was told that it had a 20 percent probability of failure. The majority of the "80 percent success" group gave the go-ahead, whereas the majority of the "20 percent failure" group did not. Given exactly the same information, the group majorities had different conclusions because the words were stated differently.[7]

- *Recency effects*: People frequently make decisions based on the information they have seen most recently. This explains why an indecisive executive's advisors sometimes jockey to be the last person to give advice. This effect is sometimes called availability bias, meaning that the most easily visualized or most readily available information has the greatest weight in the decision.

- *Primacy effects*: Once people develop an opinion about something or a frame of reference for analyzing an issue, it is often difficult for them to move from that position. Since they are stuck on that spot, this effect is sometimes called anchoring. Recognizing the significance of this effect, negotiators often establish a bargaining position and then give in somewhat.

- *Poor probability estimation*: People tend to overestimate the probability of events that are familiar or dramatic, are under their control, or are beneficial to them, and greatly underestimate the probability of negative events. This is why people overestimate the frequency of deaths from causes such as accidents, homicides, and cancer and underestimate the frequency of deaths from unspectacular causes and diseases that are common in nonfatal form such as diabetes, stroke, tuberculosis, and asthma.[8]

- *Overconfidence*: Both experts and the general public tend to be overconfident about the accuracy of what they know. As they think about an issue and reach preliminary conclusions, they tend to remember the supporting facts and ignore the contrary ones. This may be one reason why one year before the space shuttle Challenger disaster, NASA estimated the probability of such an accident as 1 in 100,000 even though the historical proportion of booster rockets blowing up is 1 in 57[9] (see Figure 5.4).

Figure 5.4 How Likely Was This Tragedy?

NASA demonstrated over-confidence by ignoring history when estimating the probability of this type of accident.

- *Escalation phenomena*: Decision makers often find it difficult to abandon courses of action that have already been adopted and therefore ignore feedback indicating the course of action is failing. Instead of throwing good money after bad, decision makers who are not caught in escalation phenomena are more likely to cut their losses by changing strategies.

- *Association bias*: Decision makers trying to repeat their past successes may choose strategies more related to a past situation than the current one.

- *Groupthink*: Groups have a strong desire to maintain consensus and cohesiveness. Groupthink describes what happens when the need to maintain cohesiveness overpowers the group's desire to make the best decision. A famous example is the acceptance of faulty assumptions by President Kennedy and his advisors during the disastrous decision to support the Bay of Pigs invasion of Cuba. They assumed a force outnumbered 140 to 1 could prevail because the Cuban people would immediately join invaders trying to overthrow the government.[10]

Although Table 5.3 lists some possible ways information systems could be used to counteract these flaws, few information systems are designed specifically for this purpose. A much more general way to think about the role of information systems is to look at different approaches information systems use for improving decision making.

Approaches for Improving Decision Making

There are many ways to use information technology to improve decision making. Since communication and decision making are tightly intertwined, any of the approaches mentioned earlier for improving communication can have an impact in improving decision making. Since those ideas have already been covered, this section focuses on ideas specifically related to decision making.

Much of an information system's impact is determined by the extent to which it imposes structure on decisions or other tasks. Table 3.2 showed that the extent of decision structuring can be divided into three broad categories, each of which has a number of gradations. An information system imposes a small degree of structure if it provides tools or information a person can use but does not dictate how the tools or information should be used in making the decision. It imparts more structure if it enforces rules and procedures but still permits the decision maker some leeway. It imposes the most structure when it automates the decision.

The categories in Table 3.2 and their gradations constitute basic design choices in using information systems to improve the way decisions are made and work is done. Structuring decisions appropriately is important because imposing too little structure or too much can reduce decision quality. Each category will be discussed, starting with the lower degrees of structure.

Providing access to tools and information

Access to tools or information means they are available but their use does not force the user to perform the task or make the decision in a particular way. The gradations within this category start with the availability of general-purpose tools such as telephones, word processors, and spreadsheets, which benefit individual professionals but have little or no impact on the content of the information being communicated or analyzed. The raw data in a marketing database is the basis of part of a brand manager's analysis but doesn't determine exactly how the analysis will be done. The filtered and summarized information in a management report provides structure by focusing on pertinent performance measures and leaving out irrelevant detail; again, it doesn't tell the manager what to do.

Specialized tools such as computer-aided design (CAD) systems for architects add more structure because they determine parts of the architect's design and problem-solving process. Nonetheless, they determine neither the function nor the features of the building being designed. Finally, simulation or optimization models may structure parts of an investment analysis even though the planner's recommendations will be based on other factors as well, including organizational history, politics, and personal ambitions. This shows that even use of an optimization model doesn't guarantee that the information system greatly restricts the final decision.

Table 5.3 How Information Systems Might Help Counteract Common Flaws in Decision Making

Common Flaw	Description	How an Information System Might Help
Poor framing	Allowing a decision to be influenced excessively by the language used for describing the decision	Provide information encouraging different ways to think about the definition of the issue
Recency effects	Giving undue weight to the most recent information	Provide information showing how the most recent information might not be representative
Primacy effects	Giving undue weight to the first information received	Show information inconsistent with the first information received
Poor probability estimation	Overestimating the probability of familiar or dramatic events; underestimating the probability of negative events	Make it easier to estimate probabilities based on pertinent data
Overconfidence	Believing too strongly in one's own knowledge	Provide counter examples or models showing that other conclusions might also make sense
Escalation phenomena	Unwillingness to abandon courses of action that have been decided on previously	Provide information or models showing how the current approach might give poor results
Association bias	Reusing strategies that were successful in the past, whether or not they fit the current situation	Provide information showing how the recent situation differs from past situations
Groupthink	Overemphasizing group consensus and cohesiveness instead of bringing out unpopular ideas	Provide information inconsistent with the current group conclusion and show why that information might be pertinent

Enforcing rules and procedures

Many business situations contain structured repetitive decisions for which the information requirements are known along with the rules or methods for making the decisions most of the time. In such cases, major parts of the decision process can be structured to improve the consistency and quality of the outcome. Structured repetitive decisions occur often in everyday tasks such as authorizing, assigning, scheduling, pricing, buying, and diagnosing.

An information system that enforces rules and procedures exerts more control over the process and substance of work than a system that just provides tools or information. A minimal level of enforcement occurs when an information system identifies exceptions or provides warnings, indicating the possible need for corrective action. An information system that provides active guidelines for each step, such as a system for processing automobile loan applications, imposes more structure by dictating what information will be used and how it will be combined in making the decision. Finally, a system that controls work, such as a short-order chef's system that beeps when a hamburger should be done, monitors a work process and tells someone what to do.

An example of structuring repetitive decisions is the use of standardized procedures by banks to authorize car loans and other types of credit. The basic approach is to obtain particular data about the loan applicant, assign a weight or number of points for each item, and then calculate a total score (see Figure 5.5). The data include things such as salary, available collateral, and length of time at the current address and job. In such situations, the system tries to ensure consistent decision making based on consideration of all key factors.

Typical of information systems that structure repetitive work, this example uses an explicit model for making or evaluating a decision. Models in such systems may be as simple as rules and formulas on paper and pencil worksheets. They may also be computerized simulation or optimization models.

Although adding up the numbers is helpful, using a computer provides other benefits. Using a computer allows storage of data for later analysis and use of more complex rules and procedures than might be possible on a paper and pencil worksheet. Computerized systems also store data that regulators can use to decide whether loans have been allocated fairly among different ethnic and income groups.

Automating decisions

Information systems that impose the most structure automate most or all of a task and therefore dictate how it is done. Automating a decision means using a set of rules or procedures to make the decision instead of relying on human judgment. Decisions are automated to improve the results by replacing the person who would otherwise make the decision.

Automating decisions can have important advantages if a great deal of information must be processed or if small time delays affect the outcome. For example, automatic collision avoidance systems in airplanes perform high-speed evasive actions more reliably than human pilots. In the very different realm of finance, brokerage firms use computerized program trading systems to find short-term discrepancies between prices of large groups of stocks and options to buy or sell these groups of stocks in the

Figure 5.5 Structuring Loan Authorizations

One way to structure loan authorizations is to assign a certain number of points for each response on a loan application. If the application scores more than a high cutoff amount, the loan is automatically granted. Applications with less than a low cutoff are automatically rejected. Applications between the high and low cutoffs are in a gray area, and the loan officer makes the decision based on judgment.

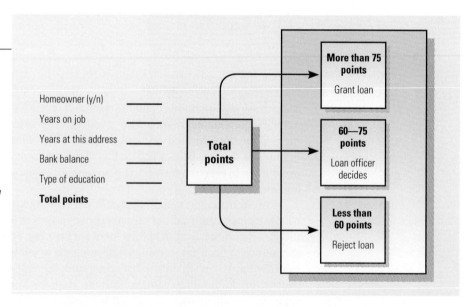

future. Upon finding such discrepancies, the system can lock in a guaranteed profit by buying stocks in one market and selling options in the other.

Another reason to automate decisions is to improve consistency or efficiency and make errors less likely. Systems for automating inventory reordering are of this type. Some automated systems such as ATMs are simply cheaper and more convenient than having a person perform similar work.

Automating a decision can be seen as a two-step process. First, decide exactly how the decision is to be made. Second, create an automatic system for making the decision that way. A computer may play an important role in this second step or may simply automate exactly what a person might do. Consider a college admissions office deciding whom to admit. The dean has decided to divide applicants into two groups: those whose college board scores exceed a cutoff and those whose scores are lower. Anyone below the cutoff will receive a rejection letter. Whether this process is carried out by a computer or by a clerk, the dean has made the decision automatic. The dean's decision rule has replaced any discretion that a person might have in considering a candidate whose score is below the cutoff.

A person receiving a computer-generated rejection letter from this college might complain that a computer made the decision. In fact, the computer was only carrying out a decision the dean made. The real decision was whether to use a fixed rule as part of the admissions process and exactly what rule to use.

This example shows that key issues in automating decisions are often not about computers but about advantages and disadvantages of delegating a decision to an automatic process instead of human judgment. In some cases, decisions should be automated because using a rule or computerized procedure will give better results. In others, decisions shouldn't be automated because human judgment applied to each case will yield better results.

Totally automatic decision making is risky unless every aspect of the decision is so well understood that any mistakes will be minor. For example, an automatic inspection machine on a canning line in a food-processing factory may incorrectly designate some good fruit as bad. As long as the percentage of error is tolerably small, this automated system may be cheaper and just as reliable as a system using human inspectors.

In contrast, even repetitive business decisions may be difficult to automate without risking too many mistakes. Consider the automated reordering of inventory based on recent usage. If a store sells 1,000 different items, think of the time saved if a computer could automatically reorder an item whenever its inventory goes below a cutoff. But this automatic method would make poor decisions for many fad or fashion items. A totally automated approach might also have difficulty with factors such as quantity discounts, the need to supply an entire product line, and the importance of cooperating with suppliers to maintain business relationships. Except where occasional mistakes are unimportant, human judgment and intuition should be part of any decision process.

REALITY CHECK   **Decision-Making Concepts**   This section named the phases of decision making, discussed the idea of rationality, identified common flaws in decision making, and explained different ways to improve decision making.

1. Identify several decisions you have made recently, and explain how well or poorly these ideas fit with what happened.

2. Identify aspects of these decisions that seemed easier or more difficult, and explain how the ideas in this section are related to what was easy and what was difficult.

Roles of Different Types of Information Systems in Communication and Decision Making

This section identifies the different types of information systems and summarizes the way each type supports communication and decision making. Any discussion of types of information systems faces a difficult problem because the categories simply won't hold still. This section will look at eight types of information systems used in all the functional areas of business. In 1992, the first edition of this book identified six categories, several of which have now been combined into new categories. If that edition had been written in 1982, it probably would have identified only three or four types.

The categories can't hold still because real-world applications have expanded into many new areas. The first computerized systems were used to collect and summarize data about financial transactions or work that had been done in the past. The advent of real-time computing made it possible to integrate computers into the process of doing the work itself. The advent of personal computers made it possible to provide personal tools individuals could use to keep track of their own information, independent of what the rest of the organization was doing. And the vast expansion of communication capabilities and computer networks made new types of team-oriented systems possible.

Perhaps more problematic from a purist's viewpoint, system categories are not mutually exclusive. Information system categories differ in this regard from categories used in the natural sciences, where there is often detailed agreement about minute differences between biological species or chemical compounds. In contrast, information system categories often overlap and change as applications combine new capabilities with old ones.

Despite this classification problem, general categories must be discussed because the terms are used frequently in business and because each category supports communication and decision making from a different and important viewpoint. Table 5.4 summarizes the basic idea of each type of system along with the ways each type supports communication and decision making. Table 5.5 gives a brief example of each in the functional areas of sales, manufacturing, and finance.

Office Automation Systems: Supporting General Office Work

An **office automation system (OAS)** facilitates everyday information processing tasks in offices and business organizations. These systems include a wide range of tools, including spreadsheets, word processors, and presentation packages. Although telephones, e-mail, v-mail, and fax can be included in this category, we will treat communication systems as a separate category. We will also treat groupware separately because it is an important current extension of both OAS and communication systems.

OASs help people perform personal record keeping, writing, and calculation chores efficiently. Of all the system types, OASs and communication systems are the most familiar to students. Tools generally grouped within the OAS category include:

Spreadsheets are an efficient method for performing calculations that can be visualized in terms of the cells of a spreadsheet. Although spreadsheet programs seem second nature today, the first spreadsheet program was VisiCalc, which helped create the demand for the first personal computers in the late 1970s.

Table 5.4 Typical Ways Each Type of Information System Supports Communication and Decision Making

System Type	Typical User	Impact on Communication	Impact on Decision Making
Office automation system: Provides individuals effective ways to process personal and organizational business data, perform calculations, and create documents	Anyone who stores personal data, creates documents, or performs calculations	• Provides tools for creating documents and presentations, such as word processors and presentation systems	• Provides spreadsheets and other tools for analyzing information • Communication tools also help in implementing decisions
Communication system: Helps people work together by sharing information in many different forms	Anyone who communicates with others, including office workers, managers, and professionals	• Telephones and teleconferencing for interactive communication • E-mail, v-mail, and fax, for communicating using messages and documents	• Telephones and teleconferencing for decision making • E-mail, v-mail, fax, and other tools for obtaining information
Transaction processing system (TPS): Collects and stores information about transactions; controls some aspects of transactions	People whose work involves performing transactions	• Creates a database that can be accessed directly, thereby making some person-to-person communication unnecessary	• Gives immediate feedback on decisions made while processing transactions • Provides information for planning and management decisions
Management information system (MIS): Converts TPS data into information for monitoring performance and managing an organization	Managers and people who receive feedback about their work	• Provides a basis of facts rather than opinions for explaining problems and their solutions	• Provides summary information and measures of performance for monitoring results
Executive information system (EIS): Provides executives information in a readily accessible interactive format	Executives and high-level managers	• Same as MIS but also incorporates e-mail and other communication methods	• Provides easy ways to analyze the types of information provided in less flexible form by MIS
Decision support system (DSS): Helps people make decisions by providing information, models, or analysis tools	Analysts, managers, and other professionals	• Analysis using DSS helps provide a clear rationale for explaining a decision	• Provides tools for analyzing data and building models • Analysis using a DSS helps define and evaluate alternatives
Execution system: Directly supports the organization's value-added work. (for example, helps salespeople sell, doctors practice medicine, or architects design buildings)	People who do an organization's value-added work, especially if that work involves special skills or knowledge	• May support communication or information sharing between people doing different parts of the task • May help explain the result of the task to customers	• May provide tools, information, or structured methods for making decisions • May store and provide expert knowledge to support decisions in specific areas
Groupware system: helps teams work together by providing access to team data, structuring work flows, structuring communication, and making it easier to schedule meetings	Anyone who is a member of a business team or department that uses this type of system	• Provides access to memos and other shared information • Scheduling meetings • Controlling flow of work • Structuring group meetings and making some communication anonymous	• Supports sharing information related to making joint decisions • Helping groups identify problems, suggest solutions, and vote

Text and image processing systems store, revise, and print documents containing text or image data. These systems started with simple word processors but have evolved to include desktop publishing systems for creating complex documents ranging from brochures to book chapters.

Presentation packages help managers develop presentations independently instead of working with typists and technical artists. These products automatically convert outlines into printed pages containing appropriately spaced titles and

Table 5.5 Examples of Each Type of Information System in Three Functional Areas of Business

System Type	Sales Examples	Manufacturing Examples	Finance Examples
Office automation systems	• Spreadsheet to analyze different possible prices • Word processor to create sales contract	• Spreadsheet to analyze a production schedule • Word processor to write a memo about how to fix a machine	• Spreadsheet to compare several loan arrangements • Word processor to write a memo about new financial procedures
Communication systems	• E-mail and fax used to contact customer • Videoconference to present new sales materials to sales force	• E-mail and v-mail used to discuss a problem with a new machine • Videoconference to coordinate manufacturing and sales efforts	• V-mail and fax to communicate with bank about loan arrangements • Videoconference to explain effect of financing on factory investments
Transaction processing system (TPS)	• Point-of-sale system for sales transactions • Keeping track of customer contacts during a sales cycle	• Tracking movement of work in process in a factory • Tracking receipts of materials from suppliers	• Processing of credit card payments • Payment of stock dividends and bond interest
Management information system (MIS)	• Weekly sales report by product and region • Consolidation of sales projections by product and region	• Weekly production report by production and operation • Determination of planned purchases based on a production schedule	• Receivables report showing invoices and payments • Monthly financial plan consolidation
Executive information system (EIS)	• Flexible access to sales data by product and region	• Flexible access to production data by product and operation	• Flexible access to corporate financial plan by line item
Decision support system (DSS)	• System helping insurance salespeople test alternatives • Marketing data and models to analyze sales	• System displaying current priorities of machine operator • Production data and models to analyze production results	• System analyzing characteristics of customers who pay bills promptly • Stock database and models to help in selecting stocks to buy or sell
Execution system	• System to generate competitive bids • System to help salespeople suggest the best choice for the customer	• System to diagnose machine failures • System to transfer customer requirements to an automated machine cell	• System to support a loan approval process • System to find price inconsistencies between different equity markets
Groupware system	• Work flow system to make sure all sales steps are completed • System to coordinate all work on a complex sales contract	• Work flow system to make sure engineering changes are approved • Use of a GDSS to identify production problems	• Work flow system to make sure invoices approval precedes payment • System for exchanging the latest information related to a lawsuit

subtitles. These pages can be copied directly onto transparencies or slides used in presentations.

Personal database systems and *note-taking systems* help people keep track of their own personal data (rather than the organization's shared data). Typical applications include an appointment book and calendar, a to-do list, and a notepad.

When used for personal productivity purposes, OASs are typically applied when work is unstructured and the users can use the tools however they like. In these situations, some individuals use them extensively and enjoy major efficiency benefits, whereas others do not use them at all. The same tools can also be used for broader purposes, however, in which they are parts of larger systems that organizations use to structure and routinize tasks.

Originally, the various tools within an OAS were marketed as separate products with list prices around $500. More recently, these products have been bundled together in the form of "office suites" including a spreadsheet, word processor, presentation package, electronic mail, and possibly a personal organizer or database management system for a combined price of $300 to $500 (see Figure 5.6). The ability of Microsoft, Novell, and Lotus to sell these office suites for such low prices made it difficult or impossible for smaller firms with standalone spreadsheets or word processors to compete in this market.

Communication Systems: Making Communication Effective and Efficient

Electronic **communication systems** have changed the way many businesses operate. This section looks at two groups of communication systems: teleconferencing systems and systems for transmitting individual messages and documents.

Teleconferencing

Teleconferencing is the use of electronic transmission to permit two or more people to "meet" and discuss an idea or issue. We can think of a traditional telephone call as a minimal teleconference, but the term is normally applied to other options, including audioconferencing, computer conferencing, audiographic conferencing, and video-conferencing.

Audioconferencing is a single telephone call involving three or more people participating from at least two locations. If several people on the call are in the same office, they can all participate using a speakerphone, which includes a high-sensitivity microphone and a loudspeaker that can be heard by anyone in a room. Although audioconferencing allows people in several locations to share information, it can be awkward when the groups are too large or are in so many locations that it is hard to know who is talking.

Computer conferencing is the exchange of text messages typed into computers from various locations to discuss a particular issue. A computer conference permits people in dispersed locations to combine their ideas in useful ways even though they cannot speak to each other face to face. Any conference participant may be able to add new ideas, attach comments to existing messages, or direct comments to specific individuals or groups. Proponents of computer conferencing recognize some disadvantages of working through computers but emphasize major advantages, such as preventing a single forceful individual from dominating a meeting. Further, because everything is done through a computer, a record of how ideas developed is automatically generated.

Figure 5.6 Competition in the OAS Market

Microsoft and Lotus both used the strategy of competing in the OAS market by selling office suites combining spreadsheets, word processors, and other frequently used office products.

Audiographic conferencing is an extension of audioconferencing permitting dispersed participants to see pictures or graphical material at the same time. This is especially useful when the purpose of the meeting is to share information that is difficult to describe, organize, or visualize. Since visual aids are important in face-to-face meetings, it is no wonder that visual aids are useful when the participants are far away. Tools used for audiographic conferences include electronic blackboards or writing pads that display the same information on a similar device at a remote site.

Videoconferencing is a form of teleconferencing in which the participants can see the distant participants. The least expensive forms of videoconferencing use tiny cameras and 4-inch screens added to telephones or separate videoconferencing windows displayed on computer screens. In typical business videoconferencing, remote participants appear on a television screen, as was shown in Figure 5.2. Videoconferencing simulates a face-to-face meeting without requiring unnecessary travel, which absorbs a lot of time and energy, not to speak of the cost of airplane and hotel bills. However, the effectiveness of videoconferences decreases if the participants don't have a prior social bond. For example, doing sales calls via videoconference might seem tempting but might not foster the personal relationship needed to succeed in many sales situations.

Electronic mail, voice mail, and fax for documents and messages

Different-time/different-place communication has been used for centuries in the form of books and letters. Electronic technologies, including electronic mail, voice mail, and fax, became popular in the 1980s to make different-time/different-place communication more effective. Each of these technologies sends documents or messages from one location to another.

Electronic mail (e-mail) is the use of computers to send and retrieve text messages or documents addressed to individual people or locations. The basic idea is as follows: Each user is identified by an individual account entered upon logging onto the computer. That account number is usually based on the person's name and also serves as the person's e-mail address. For example, according to a book of e-mail addresses published in 1994,[11] President Clinton's e-mail address was President@whitehouse.gov, whereas Bill Gates' address was billg@microsoft.com. (The general format is *[person's name]@[business establishment].[type of establishment]*.) Many public figures no longer give out their e-mail addresses freely because it is so easy to send e-mail. When Bill Gates's e-mail address appeared in an article in *New Yorker* magazine, over 5,000 messages poured in.[12]

The sender uses a word processor to create a message and then addresses it to a distribution list. The distribution list might be an individual account number or a group of numbers, such as those for the sales department or everyone working on a particular project. Figure 5.2 showed a typical e-mail message. The recipient can read the message immediately or wait until it is convenient. The recipient of an e-mail message can save it, print it, erase it, or forward it to someone else. The recipient can also edit the message to extract just parts to be saved, printed, or passed on.

E-mail is effective in many situations, such as permitting you to leave a message without going through an additional person who might garble it. With e-mail, you can send a message to a person traveling away from the office who can log onto a network using a laptop computer. If you are working on a memo or other document and want to get feedback from someone before you distribute it, you can use e-mail to get a quick response. E-mail also allows you to send the same message to many individuals without having to contact them individually. For example, a product designer can send a request for product ideas to 100 salespeople simultaneously. If even one of them responds with a good idea, the minimal effort of distributing the request is worth it. In addition, sending the messages electronically eliminates distribution of 100 sheets of paper that people glance at and throw away.

There have been many innovative uses of e-mail to improve communication. People in large organizations have used it to bypass bureaucratic structures. For example, top managers have used e-mail to bypass intermediate management levels by obtaining specific information directly from people throughout the organization. Some organizations have eliminated many formal memos by using e-mail and getting directly to the point. As happened at IBM's Europe headquarters in Paris, e-mail has also been used as a communication tool for people who are not fluent in the language in which business is conducted. E-mail removes accents and permits nonfluent speakers to read a message several times that otherwise might be misunderstood in a phone conversation. It also helps them express their ideas more effectively than they might using a telephone.[13]

Although e-mail has many advantages and potential uses, it does have the major disadvantage of being a computerized text (or text plus image) file. Messages in this form are useful, but the most natural form of communication for most people remains the human voice, not electronic files.

Voice mail (v-mail) is a computerized method for storing and forwarding messages that are spoken rather than typed. V-mail systems combine the voice recording feature of telephone answering machines with the editing and forwarding concepts of e-mail systems. V-mail systems record voice messages on a direct access device. This makes it possible to access, edit, and forward the messages in ways that are impossible on an answering machine that uses a sequential tape.

V-mail is typically used to automate message taking by telephone attendants. Instead of transferring an unanswered call to a person who would write out a message, the v-mail system records the voice message. The recipient retrieves messages by calling in to the v-mail system and entering an identification code using a touch-tone telephone. This telephone can be anywhere, making v-mail more practical than e-mail for sending and receiving brief messages in most situations. Once the recipient learns that a v-mail message is waiting, v-mail operates much like e-mail. The recipient can listen to the message, erase it, save it, or forward it. As with an e-mail system, a message can be sent to an individual or to a distribution list.

Voice mail has been used in many innovative ways. Instead of sending notes home with students, teachers in a Connecticut school use voice mail to record messages for parents. The parents call a special telephone number, key in their identification number, and receive the messages. They also use the system to leave messages for the teachers. One teacher who formerly talked to parents once a year at parents' night now receives up to ten messages every day.[14] In another innovation, some pharmacies use v-mail for prescription refill orders. Instead of having to talk to a pharmacist, a person with a prescription on file can just call a special v-mail number and leave a message indicating the patient's name, prescription number, and doctor.

V-mail has several advantages over e-mail. The most important is that telephones are much more commonly available than computers linked to networks. V-mail can be installed in an organization that makes minimal use of computers. Another advantage is that v-mail can convey more emotion and social context than e-mail. However, e-mail has advantages over v-mail in certain areas. For example, e-mail is much better than v-mail for conveying details and complex technical information, whereas v-mail is effective for short, nontechnical messages.

Fax is a third electronic form of different-time/different-place communication. A fax machine scans a piece of paper, digitizes its image, and then transmits this image to another location, where it is printed or stored on a computer for later use. With the technical advances commercialized in the early 1980s, digital fax went from a decades-old but impractically slow technology to an everyday tool used in millions of offices. It is possible to send a fax on the day a contract or engineering drawing is due and still have it arrive on time, even if the sender is in Minneapolis and the recipient is in Hong Kong. Fax also generates an immediate confirmation of receipt. A fax sent late at night (when transmission costs are lowest), can cost less to send than a first-class letter. Thus, fax reduces the impact of geographical separation and helps in working with customers at any location with modern communications systems. By 1994, 36 percent of total telephone spending in large American companies was fax related,[15] and over 60 percent of trans-Pacific calls were faxes.

E-mail, v-mail, and fax are all used to send electronic messages from one address to another. They have been seen as separate technologies but have started to merge in some ways. The first e-mail systems transmitted text only, but some current systems allow images within e-mail messages. In this way, e-mail has added a capability of fax. Likewise, some e-mail systems make it possible to add voice annotations to documents by pointing at a spot on a document and speaking into a microphone. The document then contains a visible mark at that spot to indicate the presence of the voice annotation. By selecting the mark and instructing the computer to play back the message, the reader can play back the voice annotation. Some products have even begun to combine e-mail, v-mail, and fax features under a single umbrella.

Issues related to e-mail, v-mail, and fax

As with any technology, e-mail, v-mail, and fax all have both strengths and weaknesses, some of which limit their effectiveness and generate unanticipated consequences.

Social context: E-mail, v-mail, and fax all filter out some of the social context. Ideas communicated using these tools may seem less forceful or caring than the same thoughts communicated personally. These tools should be used only when social presence is unimportant for understanding the message.

Danger of misinterpretation: The meaning of speech is conveyed partly in the inflection of a voice. Consider the sentences, "That really helped" and "I think you made a mistake." Depending on the context and inflection of the speaker's voice, the first comment could be complimentary or sarcastic. The second could be anything from a mild observation to a reason for firing someone. E-mail and fax provide no clue about inflection, and v-mail filters out body language. People using these tools need to be especially careful not to say things that could be misconstrued, such as jokes.

Power relationships: Use of e-mail and v-mail may create new communication patterns, sometimes involving people who have never communicated previously. With these tools, high-level managers find it easy to obtain information directly from people lower in the organization without going through intermediate managers and chains of command. People in the middle may find themselves out of the loop, as happens with assistants who formerly served as conduits to their bosses.

Privacy and confidentiality: Confidentiality problems may arise because fax outputs can be read by whoever is near the machine, which is often in a clerical work area. The issue of privacy took a bizarre turn in the Iran-gate investigation of secret arms sales to Iran. Government officials who sold the arms had communicated with each other using e-mail but carefully covered their tracks by erasing the messages. Investigators found backup tapes that had been produced before many of the messages were erased. In this way, the use of e-mail left a trail that eventually aided the investigation.

Electronic junk mail: All three technologies can distribute messages that waste the recipient's time. Users may find that half their e-mail messages are something like "Has anyone seen a green sweater left in room 10-250?" This might seem trivial except that many people receive 20 or more mail messages daily. Junk fax may tie up fax machines when important faxes should be arriving or use up all the paper in the machine. Some states have considered legislation against it. Companies sending these faxes argue that prohibiting this practice would violate their right to free speech.

Information overload: Common use of e-mail, v-mail, and fax means that people receive more information faster than they ever did before. Sometimes there is an expectation that people will respond quickly and thoroughly, even from home. For managers and professionals already overloaded with information and work, this is not always a welcome development. Some complain that e-mail, v-mail, and fax have generated higher workloads, more stress, and an inability to get away from work.

Transaction Processing Systems: Structuring Repetitive Communication and Decision Processes

A **transaction processing system (TPS)** collects and stores data about transactions and sometimes controls decisions made as part of a transaction. A transaction is a business event that generates or modifies data stored in an information system. TPSs were the first computerized information systems. We encounter computerized TPSs frequently, including every time we write a check, use a credit card, or pay a bill sent by a large company. A TPS used to record a sale and generate a receipt is primarily concerned with collecting and storing data. If the TPS validates a credit card or helps a clerk determine whether to accept a personal check, it also controls decisions made within the transaction. Figure 5.7 contains a TPS data entry screen.

Figure 5.7 Data Entry Screen for a Transaction Processing System

This is a data entry screen from a TPS used to enter customer orders. A well-designed TPS can minimize data entry effort and reduce errors by automatically filling in data such as customer address or unit price once the user has entered the customer number or product indentification.

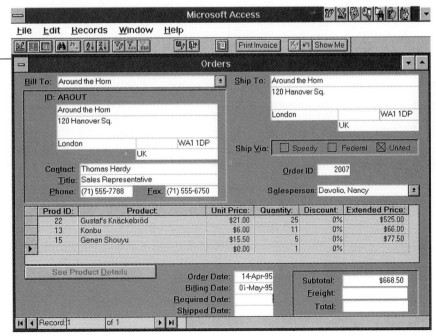

TPSs are based on detailed models of how the transaction should be processed. Most contain enough structure to enforce rules and procedures for work done by clerks or customer service agents. Some TPSs bypass clerks entirely and totally automate transactions, such as the way ATMs automate deposits and cash withdrawals.

TPSs control the collection of specific data in specific formats and in accordance with rules, policies, and goals of the organization. A well-designed TPS checks each transaction for easily detectable errors such as missing data, data values that are obviously too high or too low, data values that are inconsistent with other data in the database, and data in the wrong format. It may check for required authorizations for the transaction. Certain TPSs such as airline reservation systems may automate decision- making functions such as finding the flight that best meets the customer's needs. Finally, when all the data for the transaction have been collected and validated, the TPS stores the data in a standard format for later access by others.

As anyone knows who has tried to make a reservation when a computerized reservation system is down, organizations rely heavily on their TPSs. Breakdowns disrupt operations and may even bring business to a complete halt. As a result, a well-designed TPS also has backup procedures that allow business to continue even when the computerized system is down.

Batch versus real-time processing

The two main types of transaction processing are batch processing and real-time processing. With **batch processing,** data for individual transactions are gathered and stored but aren't entered into the system immediately. Later, either on a schedule or when a sufficient number of transactions have accumulated, the transactions are sorted and processed to update the database. With **real-time processing,** each transaction is processed immediately. The person providing the data is typically available to help with error correction and receives confirmation of transaction completion. Batch processing was the only feasible form of transaction processing when data were stored only on punched cards or tapes. Real-time transaction processing requires immediate access to an online database.

Batch processing is currently used in some situations where the transaction data comes in on paper, such as in processing checks and airline ticket stubs. A batch approach is also used for generating paychecks and other forms of paper output that will be distributed after a delay. Unfortunately, time delays inherent in batch processing may cause significant disadvantages. The central database may never be completely current because of transactions received while the batch was being processed. Worse yet, the batching of transactions builds delays into the system, with transactions not completed until the next day in some cases. Even systems with interactive user interfaces may include lengthy delays before transactions are completed. For example, weekend deposits into many ATMs are not posted to the depositor's account until Monday. Even though the ATM's user interface is interactive, the system in a larger sense doesn't perform real-time processing due to built-in delays.

Compared to batch processing, real-time processing has more stringent requirements for computer response and computer uptime. As is obvious when a travel agent says "Sorry, the computer is down," the jobs and work methods of the people in the real-time TPS are designed under the assumption that the system will be up and available.

Management and Executive Information Systems: Providing Management Information

A **management information system (MIS)** provides information for managing an organization. The idea of MIS predates the computer age. For example, as long ago as the mid-1500s, the Fugger family in Augsberg, Germany, had business interests throughout Europe and even into China and Peru. To keep in touch, they set up a worldwide news reporting service through which their agents wrote letters about critical political and economic events in their areas of responsibility. These letters were collected, interpreted, analyzed, and summarized in Augsberg and answered through instructions sent to the family's agents. This paper-based system encompassing planning, execution, and control helped the family move more rapidly in the mercantile world than their rivals.[16]

Computerized MISs generate information for monitoring performance, maintaining coordination, and providing background information about the organization's operation. Users include both managers and the employees who receive feedback about performance indicators such as productivity. Figure 5.8 shows a sample report generated by an MIS. Notice how it provides summary information rather than the details of individual transactions.

The concept of MIS emerged partly as a response to the shortcomings of the first computerized TPSs, which often improved transaction processing but provided little information for management. Computerized MISs typically extract and summarize data from TPSs to allow managers to monitor and direct the organization and to provide employees accurate feedback about easily measured aspects of their work. For example, a list of every sale that occurred during a day or week would be extremely difficult for a manager to use in monitoring a hardware store's performance. However, the same data could be summarized in measures of performance, such as total sales for each type of item, for each salesperson, and for each hour of the day. In this example the transaction data remain essential, and the MIS focuses it for management.

As part of an organization's formal control mechanisms, an MIS provides some structure for the comparatively unstructured task of management by identifying important measures of performance. The fact that everyone knows how performance is measured helps them decide what to do and helps managers motivate workers. For example, in a sales group expecting $1,000 per day of evenly distributed sales, the MIS might report that a salesperson met weekly and monthly sales targets but usually did poorly on one group of products. In this typical situation, the MIS reports information but leaves it to the people to decide how to improve performance.

From MIS to EIS

An **executive information system (EIS)** is a highly interactive MIS system providing managers and executives flexible access to information for monitoring operating results and general business conditions. Sometimes called executive support systems (ESS), these systems attempt to take over where the traditional MIS approach falls short. Although sometimes acceptable for monitoring the same indicators over time, the traditional MIS approach of providing prespecified reports on a scheduled basis is too inflexible for many questions executives really care about, such as understanding problems and new situations.

Figure 5.8

A Management Report
from an MIS

*This figure represents a
management report showing
last month's sales results for
an office supplies company
that is expanding out of its
major Midwest markets into
the Southeast and Far West.*

Division/ Branch	Sales	Plan	Perf vs. Plan	Sales Per Rep.	% Repeat Sales
Southeast					
Atlanta	1217	1189	1.02	112	.51
Miami	1643	1734	0.95	137	.34
New Orleans	1373	1399	0.98	108	.44
Tampa	2300	2106	1.09	145	.53
	....	....	....	....	....
Total	6533	6428	1.02	129	.46
Midwest					
Chicago	6323	6523	0.97	144	.66
Detroit	6845	6448	1.06	137	.53
Minneapolis	5783	6300	0.92	150	.71
St. Louis	5345	5318	1.01	129	.55
	....	....	....	....	....
Total	24296	24589	0.99	140	.61
Far West					
Phoenix	2337	2445	0.96	104	.44
Portland	3426	3276	1.05	120	.52

An EIS provides executives with internal and competitive information through user-friendly interfaces that can be used by someone with almost no computer-related knowledge. The EIS is designed to help executives find the information they need whenever they need it and in whatever form is most useful. Typically, users can choose among numerous tabular or graphical formats. They can also control the level of detail, the triggers for exception conditions, and other aspects of the information displayed. Most EISs focus on providing executives with the status and performance information they need, as well as helping them understand the causes of exceptions and surprises. This leaves executives better prepared to discuss issues with their subordinates.

A typical sequence of EIS use is shown in Figure 5.9. The EIS user starts with a menu listing available types of information, such as sales results, manufacturing results, competitive performance, and e-mail messages. The categories are customized for individual executives. The user selects a category from the menu and receives an additional menu identifying available subcategories plus the specific online reports that can be obtained. Often, the executive can customize these reports by choosing options such as selecting a subset of the data, sorting, or providing more detail. For example, while looking at last month's sales results, a user might select the products with less than 2 percent improvement in volume, sort these sales branches from highest to lowest percentage improvement, and obtain more detail for these branches by looking at results for individual departments within these branches. In addition, users can generate graphical displays such as trend charts and pie charts to make it easier to visualize what is happening.

Figure 5.9 Use of an Executive Information System

An EIS allows the user to isolate and model information from a standard financial report interactively. As shown in these examples, the user can employ a variety of tools to investigate and model business activity according to geographical region, volume and revenue, product line or cost center. The process of breaking out specific items and information is sometimes called a drill down.

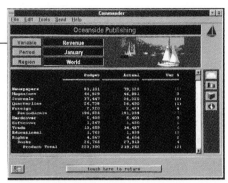

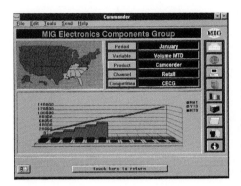

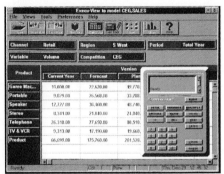

For an EIS to operate, technical staff members must ensure that the right data are available and are downloaded to the EIS from other systems in a timely manner. The data in EISs are usually replenished periodically from internal company databases and external databases. Although technical advances in data display and networking capabilities have made EISs much easier to maintain, EISs continually modified to keep up with current business issues still require major efforts and substantial technical maintenance. An extensive EIS at Lockheed-Georgia had a staff of nine people: a manager, six information analysts, and two computer analysts.[17]

Although current EIS users are executives and managers, ideally anyone in a business should be able to get the right information in the right format. Even when commercial EIS software is used, the time and effort to customize and maintain an EIS limits use to high-level managers. Ideally, the flexibility and ease of access built into EISs should also be built into other systems. Ten years ago, it was much more expensive to provide EIS capabilities to executives. Ten years from now, the interfaces in systems at all organizational levels may mimic or exceed those in today's EISs. This can be seen in the way some EIS consultants are starting to replace the word *executive* with the word *enterprise*, saying that EIS now stands for enterprise information system.

Decision Support Systems: Providing Information and Tools for Analytical Work

A **decision support system (DSS)** is an interactive system that helps people make decisions, use judgment, and work in areas where no one knows exactly how the task should be done in all cases. DSSs support decision making in semistructured and unstructured situations, and they provide information, models, or tools for manipulating data. DSSs solve part of the problem and help isolate places where judgment and experience are required.

DSSs may support repetitive or nonrepetitive decision making. They support repetitive decision making by defining procedures and formats but still permit the users to decide how and when to use the system's capabilities. They support nonrepetitive decision making by providing data, models, and interface methods that can be used however the user wants. The spectrum of different systems called DSS is wide, ranging from general tools such as spreadsheets, graphics packages, and DBMSs to highly customized simulation or optimization models focusing on a specific business situation. Figure 5.10 shows an output of one particular DSS.

Figure 5.10 Graphical Output from a Decision Support System

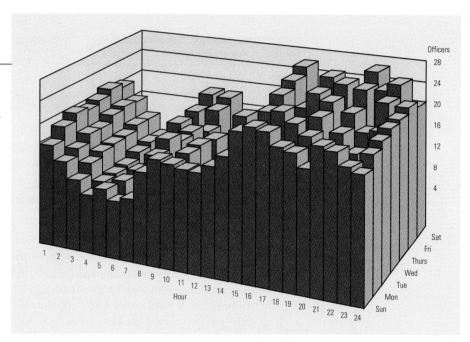

This is the output from a decision support system used by the San Francisco Police Department to schedule police officers. This three-dimensional graph shows the average requirement for police officers for each hour in each day of the week.

Basic DSS concepts, such as interactive problem solving, availability of online tools, and direct use of models, grew out of dissatisfaction with the limitations of TPSs and MISs. TPSs focused on record keeping and control of repetitive clerical processes. MISs provided reports for management but were often inflexible and unable to produce the information managers needed in a form in which it could be used. In contrast, DSS was intended to support managers and professionals doing largely analytical work in less structured, nonroutine situations with unclear criteria for success.

The common thread through the wide range of DSS applications is that the situation emphasizes analytical work rather than general office work, transaction processing, or general management work. DSS supports this work by providing flexible, user-controllable methods for displaying and analyzing data and formulating and evaluating alternative decisions. DSS originally relied on improved user interfaces, graphical and statistical methods, and simulation and optimization models to support better decision making.

Many of the originally innovative DSS concepts are now common across many types of information systems. Nonetheless, there are still many applications with a distinct

DSS flavor. Consider two examples reflecting common approaches for using DSS today: helping people make a repetitive decision by structuring that decision to some extent and helping analysts by providing information, models, and analytical tools.

In an example of repetitive use, many insurance agents apply a structured DSS to help customers choose the insurance policy options that they would prefer. The DSS operates on a portable laptop computer the insurance agent brings to the customer's business or home. Insurance agents are trained to use this flexible tool to structure sales situations. After surveying the available options, the insurance agent and customer identify a few possible choices. The agent enters the appropriate data, and the DSS responds with a report showing costs and benefits. After reviewing this report, the agent and customer try other options. Using this system, the insurance agent can do a better job of selling insurance.

In an example of nonrepetitive use, marketing managers in a consumer products company use DSS as an analytical tool. Their DSS consists of a set of models and databases. The data in the system include internal sales results and databases purchased from market research firms. These external databases cover sales of all brands in the industry, advertising in various media, and supermarket shelf space devoted to various brands. The models focus on issues such as advertising effectiveness, consumer perceptions of product features, and strategies of competitors. The DSS helps marketing managers evaluate alternative marketing plans and then helps them track the results and recalibrate if the results deviate from their expectations.

The second example shows how DSSs may overlap with EISs to some extent even though they support a different type of usage. Most DSS users do a lot of analytical work and feel comfortable working with models, data analysis, and statistics. Executives who use EISs often receive the results of analyses done by others but rarely spend time doing analytical work themselves. Consequently, EISs are much more concerned with providing information in an easy-to-use format than with providing sophisticated analytical capabilities such as statistical tests or model building.

Execution Systems: Helping People Do the Work That Provides Value for Customers

Figure 5.11 shows that the system categories discussed so far are primarily oriented toward planning and control activities or toward general office and communication activities. What about systems designed to directly support people doing the value-added work that customers care about, such as practicing medicine, designing buildings, or selling investments? Some people call these systems functional area systems, but Table 5.5 showed that name is not very helpful because the same types of systems (OAS, TPS, MIS, DSS) are used in every functional area.

Since there is no generally accepted name for such systems, we will call them **execution systems.** These systems have become much more important in the last decade as advances in computer speed, memory capacity, and portability made it increasingly possible to use computerized systems directly while doing value-added work. Such systems help plastic surgeons design operations and show the likely results to their patients, help lawyers find precedents relevant to lawsuits, and help maintenance engineers keep machines running (see Figure 5.12). Some of these systems focus on retrieving information from external databases, some focus on storing and displaying design data, and yet others focus on using transaction data to help people do their work instead of just looking back at how well they performed in the past.

Since Chapter 6 will discuss many examples of execution systems, this section will discuss just one type of execution system that receives a lot of attention, the expert system. An **expert system** supports the intellectual work of professionals engaged in design, diagnosis, or evaluation of complex situations requiring expert knowledge in a well-defined area. Expert systems have been used to diagnose diseases, configure computers, analyze chemicals, interpret geological data, and support many other problem-solving processes. This type of work requires expert knowledge of the process of performing particular tasks. Although these tasks may have some repetitive elements, many situations have unique characteristics that must be considered based on expert knowledge. Intellectual work even in narrowly defined areas is typically much less repetitive than transaction processing or general office work.

Despite the designation "expert system," these systems are not true experts because they lack common sense and contain only some of the knowledge of a human expert. Instead, these systems use techniques developed in artificial intelligence research to capture some of the special knowledge of experts and make it available to others who have less knowledge or experience. The knowledge is captured not only as facts but also in the form of reasoning processes that the expert would go through in solving a problem. Some expert systems use these reasoning processes to guide a problem-solving dialogue with the user. In such a dialogue, the user provides information that the expert system uses as it mimics an expert's reasoning process.

The common reasons for developing expert systems include preserving an expert's knowledge, improving the performance of less experienced people doing similar tasks, and enforcing some consistency in the way people do particular types of work. These were among the reasons Campbell's Soup developed an expert system to capture the knowledge of Aldo Cimino, a long-time plant engineer who was about to retire. He was the company's best expert on soup sterilizers. The system preserved

Figure 5.11 Relationship Between Different Types of Information Systems and the Cycle of Planning, Execution, and Control

This diagram recalls the links between planning, execution, and control in Figure 3.11. It shows that four of the common system categories are primarily directed toward planning or control activities. Three (in the middle) are equally applicable to planning, execution, and control. Just one category, execution systems, is directed primarily at performing the value-added work that affects customers most directly.

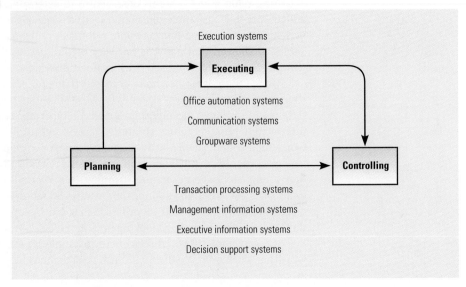

some of his knowledge in the form of 151 rules built into an interactive system used by other engineers to diagnose problems with the sterilizers.

Groupware Systems: Supporting Work in Groups

Groupware is a new and somewhat unshaped category of commercial products that help groups and teams work together by sharing information and by controlling work flows within a group. Coined in the late 1980s,[18] the term *groupware* has attained wide recognition because of a combination of the need for groups to work together more effectively and technical progress in networks and group support products. Products considered groupware are still new enough that their long-term direction is unclear. What is clear, however, is that the downsizing and rapid organizational change of the 1990s make the effective operation of work groups an even more important competitive issue.

Many groupware products are related to specific group-related tasks such as project management, scheduling meetings ("calendaring"), and retrieving data from shared databases. Lotus Notes, a prominent product in this category, is designed as a system for sharing text and images, and contains a data structure that is a cross between a table-oriented database and an outline. For example, a law firm in Seattle uses Lotus Notes to permit everyone working on a particular case to have access to the most current memos and other information about that case, even if they are traveling. Other companies use Lotus Notes to store and revise product information for salespeople selling industrial products, thereby replacing the massive three-ring binders they formerly lugged around. Figure 5.13a shows a sample screen identifying the user options for a Lotus Notes installation in a particular organization.

Figure 5.12 Execution System That Helps a Surgeon Plan an Operation

The photo shows how a surgeon can use an interactive simulation to plan the steps in an operation before lifting a scalpel.

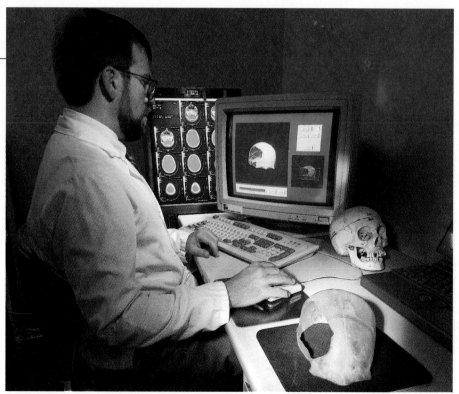

Other groupware products focus primarily on the flow of work in office settings. These products provide tools for structuring the process by which information for a particular multistep task is managed, transferred, and routed. For example, Figure 5.13b shows a work flow application involving the approval of a travel expenditure. In this case, one person must propose the expenditure and someone else must approve it. The workflow application is set up to make the approval process simple and complete. In effect, groupware is being used as a small transaction processing system for multistep transactions.

Yet other groupware systems are basically e-mail systems extended by classifying messages and using those classifications to control the way messages are handled. For example, a message classified "urgent" would appear first on the recipient's screen, and the system might highlight all unanswered messages classified "please respond" to make sure the responses occurred.

Group decision support systems

A special type of groupware called a **group decision support system (GDSS)** existed in experimental forms before the term *groupware* was coined, but is now becoming a special type of groupware. In its original concept, a GDSS is a specially outfitted conference room containing hardware and software that facilitates meetings. This technology may include advanced presentation devices, computer access to databases, and capabilities for the participants in a meeting to communicate electronically. These rooms improve same-time/same-place communication by a group of people working together in a meeting. The meeting's purpose could be anything from brainstorming about possible new product features to reviewing business operations or responding to an emergency.

To date, GDSS has been more of a research topic than common practice in business. Figure 5.14 shows the layout of a GDSS developed at the University of Arizona. This decision room contains the following computer-based capabilities, plus many others:[19]

- *Display.* A workstation screen or previously prepared presentation material is displayed to the entire group.

- *Electronic brainstorming.* Participants enter and share comments anonymously through their computer screens.

- *Topic commenting.* Participants add comments to ideas previously generated by themselves or others.

- *Issue analysis.* Participants identify and consolidate key items generated during electronic brainstorming.

- *Voting.* Participants use the computer to vote on topics, with a choice of prioritization methods.

- *Alternative evaluation.* The computer ranks alternative decisions based on preferences entered by users.

Experience to date suggests that GDSS has significant potential for improving certain types of decision making. Typical meetings in a pilot study of GDSS for internal problem solving at IBM generated a large number of high-quality ideas. The meetings took about half as long as participants' estimates of the length of regular meetings on the same topics.[20]

Photo 5.13 Two Groupware Examples

(a) This top-level Lotus Notes screen shows the options available to a Lotus Notes user in a particular organization.
(b) This process definition screen in the groupware product Edify shows how the work flow for approving travel vouchers might be defined.

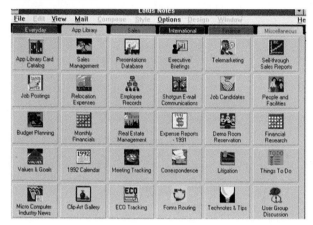
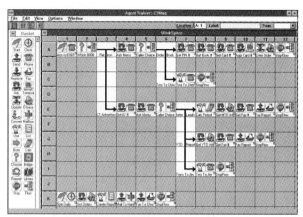

An important GDSS phenomenon is the impact of entering and transmitting ideas anonymously. Unlike typical meetings, very little crosstalk occurs during anonymous brainstorming sessions, and participants tend to comment on the topic at hand. Anonymity encourages participation by all members of the group, independent of their status. It tends to reduce groupthink, pressures for conformity, and dominance of forceful individuals. It also tends to heighten conflict because people's comments in this context may be more assertive and less polite than spoken comments. In a GDSS experiment in Singapore, this anonymity allowed dominant members of groups to openly express negative opinions about other group members' contributions. Such behavior would otherwise be culturally unacceptable and, in this case, led to dissatisfaction and lower consensus among group members. This result differs from results of a similar experiment in the United States.[21]

Although the work to date has shown potential areas of benefit, GDSSs haven't been integrated into everyday business operations. Still in question is whether or not electronically supported same-time/same-place meetings will become commonplace. Not in question, however, is the potential usefulness of computerized systems that perform GDSS functions such as collecting ideas and providing an organized forum for sharing information on a topic, even among people who may be anywhere in the world. Products such as Lotus Notes that support these activities have been used widely and are becoming more powerful all the time. Whether or not GDSS will retain an identity distinct from other groupware systems remains to be seen.

REALITY CHECK   **Types of Information Systems**   This section identified eight different types of information systems, each of which can have an impact on both communication and decision making.

1. For each type of information system, either identify an example that you have encountered or explain when you think you will first encounter an example (if ever).

2. In each of the situations, explain how the system affects communication and decision making.

Figure 5.14 GDSS Developed at the University of Arizona

This computerized conference room has been used for research and pilot studies of group decision making. It combines carefully designed physical space with extensive software capabilities for recording and processing ideas, votes, and other data generated by meeting participants.

Going Beyond the System Categories

The field of information systems and information technology moves so rapidly that terminology often fails to keep pace with innovation. Consider why the stiff 3.5-inch diskettes used with personal computers today are still called floppy disks. The 5.25-inch diskettes from an earlier generation were called floppies because they were flexible. The physical characteristic changed, but the name stuck. Similarly, strange examples include "recordable CD-ROMs" (ROM means read-only memory) and "wireless cable" (which means using wireless transmission to accomplish the function previously performed by cable television).

The same problem occurs with system classifications. People identify a new type of system, such as DSS, EIS, or ESS, and describe its characteristics. Ten years later, the name still exists but some of the original characteristics are no longer as important or have become commonplace.

In addition, many information systems contain characteristics from several system categories. Furthermore, a system that fits in a category today may not fit once new features are added. Information systems that contain characteristics of several different categories can be called **hybrid information systems.**

The Frito-Lay system in the chapter opening case is a hybrid. At one level, it is a TPS that collects and uses information about individual sales transactions with Frito-Lay customers. At another level, it is a DSS that provides information for analyzing the market. At yet another level, it is an EIS providing information for executives.

Despite the shortcomings of information system classification schemes, they still do have a practical use. Even though there is overlap, each system category emphasizes certain features that may be relevant in any particular situation. The practical use of system classifications is in identifying a number of widely usable features that are typically associated with particular system types.

Table 5.6 identifies some of these features and suggests questions about any information system. For example, in a TPS, the absence of DSS and expert system features might indicate a direction for future improvement. Likewise, while analyzing an MIS, one might wonder why it doesn't look more like an EIS to its users. As technology improves, the interface will probably look more like an EIS. As the trend toward hybrid information systems continues, it will be more difficult to classify real information systems using current categories—a small price to pay for more powerful and usable systems.

Table 5.6 Transferable Features of Particular Types of Systems

Type of System	Transferable Features
Office automation system	• Multiple forms of information, sometimes used in combination • Immediacy and interactivity of communication • Avoidance of unproductive work
Communication system	• Emphasis on communication in addition to data processing • Consideration of social presence and other communication characteristics when building systems • Recognition of need to handle different combinations of same or different time or place
Transaction processing system	• Control • Procedures and rules • Repetition
Management information system	• Emphasis on measures of performance • Use of standard formats and measures by people in different departments
Executive information system	• User-friendly interface • User-friendly methods for analyzing data
Decision support system	• User-controlled interaction with computers • Use of models and data • Information systems applied to semistructured tasks
Execution system	• Integrating computerized systems into doing the organization's value-added work • Bringing knowledge in active form to people doing the work
Groupware system	• Sharing information between different people working on different parts of a task • Controlling work flows and approval loops within a group • Incorporating efficient methods of scheduling meetings

Chapter Conclusion

SUMMARY

▶ *How are social context and nonverbal communication important when communication technologies are used?*

Social context is the situation and relationships within which communication takes place. Much of what is communicated in face-to-face situations is communicated through nonverbal communication, such as facial expressions, eye contact, gestures, and body language. Technologies that filter out nonverbal information decrease social context cues and, therefore, limit communication.

▶ *What are the phases of decision making?*

Decision making is a problem-solving process preceded by a problem-finding process. The phases of decision making are intelligence, design, choice, and implementation.

▶ *What are some of the common limitations and problems in decision making?*

In the real world, rationality is always bounded by the amount of time available to make the decision and the limited ability of people to process information. Additionally, many common flaws in decision making have been observed, such as poor framing, recency and primacy effects, poor probability estimation, overconfidence, and groupthink.

▶ *What are the different approaches for improving decision making using information systems?*

Since communication and decision making are intertwined, different ways to improve communication often improve decision making in turn. Much of an information system's direct impact on decision making is determined by the extent to which it imposes structure on decisions or other tasks. This can be divided into three broad categories. An information system imposes a small degree of structure if it provides tools or information a person can use but does not dictate how the tools or information should be used in making the decision. It imparts more structure if it enforces rules and procedures but still permits the decision maker some leeway. It imposes the most structure when it automates the decision.

▶ *What are the general differences between the types of information systems?*

Office automation systems (OASs) provide tools that support general office work such as performing calculations, creating documents, scheduling meetings, and controlling the flow of office work. Communication systems include telephone and teleconferencing systems that permit two or more people in different locations to "meet" and discuss an idea or issue, and systems such as e-mail, v-mail, and fax used for transmitting individual messages and documents. Transaction processing systems (TPSs) collect and store data about transactions and control aspects of transaction processing and related decision making. Management information systems (MISs) summarize data from transaction processing systems to convert it into information useful for managing an organization and monitoring performance. Executive information systems (EISs) provide information for executives in a readily accessible, interactive format. Decision support systems (DSSs) help people make decisions by providing information, models, or tools for analyzing information. Execution systems directly support people doing the value-added work such as practicing medicine, designing buildings, or selling investments. Groupware systems help groups and teams work together by sharing information and controlling work flows within a group.

INTERNATIONAL VIGNETTE

Russia: Using Electronic Mail Instead of Phone or Fax

Most Americans expect to be able to pick up a telephone and immediately call anyone they need to talk to. The recipient may not be there, but the call will almost always go through immediately. In Moscow and in the rest of the former Soviet Union, sending a fax or placing a long-distance telephone call often involves delays of several hours. Consequently, many businesspeople and private individuals are beginning to use e-mail extensively because computers are very patient and will keep trying to get through. Russia has over 20 networks that may have as many as 300,000 users. According to Anatoly Voronov, a director of the non-profit network Glasnet, "E-mail succeeds here in part because everything else fails so badly."

Some people in Russia see e-mail as their life-line to the world. For seven decades, so free an exchange of information was forbidden. Sometimes Russian scientists even had to ask Western colleagues to smuggle physics and math journals into Russia for them. Yet during the 1991 coup in which Mikhail Gorbachev was ousted briefly, the Soviet authorities did not disconnect the phone lines, and Glasnet never stopped sending urgent messages to the outside world. E-mail is currently being used for activities ranging from arranging business transactions and doing research to sending personal messages.

One of the advantages of e-mail is that a private mailbox provides more privacy than is often available with fax or even telephone calls. Although some see e-mail and networking as a springboard toward democracy, the networks in the former Soviet Union ultimately require some degree of participation by the governments and telecommunications industry. The networks could turn out to be tools for individual expression or tools for government surveillance.

> Sources: Charlton, Angela. "E-Mail Beats Phone, Fax in Russia." *San Francisco Examiner,* Apr. 17, 1994, p. C5.
> Specter, Michael. "Russians Newest Space Adventure: Cyberspace." *New York Times,* Mar. 9, 1994, p. C1.

- Use the WCA framework to organize your understanding of this vignette and to identify important topics that are not mentioned.

- What issues (if any) make this case interesting from an international or intercultural viewpoint?

- Which, if any, of the eight types of information systems is represented here?

- Explain whether there is any important difference between using e-mail in personal or business settings.

REAL-WORLD CASES

Cypress Semiconductor: No-Excuses Management

T. J. Rodgers, founder and CEO of Cypress Semiconductor, established a highly structured management system to monitor the organization. All 1,400 employees commit to accomplishing particular goals by particular due dates and enter these commitments into a central database organized by project and task. In Monday project meetings, employees set short-term goals and prioritize them. These goals take between one and six weeks, and different employees have different numbers of goals. In any week, around 6,000 of those goals come due. On Tuesday morning, all managers receive a listing of their subordinates' new and pending goals. These reports are used on Tuesday afternoon to work out overloads and conflicts and to organize the work. A revised schedule is fed into the computer.

This system is designed to maximize accountability and minimize surprises. Rodgers believes this is competitively significant in the fast-moving, highly uncertain semiconductor marketplace. He sees the computerized management information system as just an electronic version of what he had done previously using a blackboard to keep track of projects. The computer record for each goal includes a description of the task, a priority code, the date the commitment was made, the due date, the employee's manager, and the vice president the manager works for. With just a few keystrokes, Rodgers can use the system to find out not only about projects, but about whether managers and vice presidents are keeping their organizations on track. The detailed information Rodgers can call on whenever anything goes wrong helps make sure people do not try to hide the truth about difficulties they are having.

Source: Rodgers, T. J. "No Excuses Management." *Harvard Business Review,* Jul.–Aug. 1990, pp. 84–98.

- Use the WCA framework to organize your understanding of this case and to identify important topics that are not mentioned.

- Which, if any, of the eight types of information systems is represented here?

- Explain why you think this system is or is not exceedingly intrusive on employees. If it is exceedingly intrusive, explain the system you would replace it with. If it is not exceedingly intrusive, explain why few companies use this type of system.

Chemical Bank: Using Technology to Support Cooperative Work

Chemical Bank's use of Lotus Notes began as an experimental addition to a major infrastructure upgrade. The original purpose included providing programmer productivity tools to facilitate system development activities. Management believed the investment in better communication and coordination tools would enable system developers to spend around 15 percent more time doing programming work. The use of Lotus Notes was also to be a testbed for further applications of computer-supported communications throughout the bank.

Within 17 months of the initial implementation in November 1990, over 500 Corporate Systems Division (CSD) employees and contractors were using Lotus Notes from six New York locations and other locations in New Jersey and Texas. More than 92 specific Notes applications had been developed in areas such as broadcasting bulletins, discussing projects, supporting projects, providing technical support (such as answering questions about computer software), and testing systems. A survey of CSD employees revealed a wide range of usage, with some individuals accessing the system more than 100 times per week and 17 not using it at all.

The Lotus Notes implementation occurred at a time of major reorganization, including a merger with Manufacturers Hanover, another large bank. The uncertainty surrounding the massive changes was the impetus for one of the most popular and widely used Lotus Notes applications, the Rumor Mill. This application permitted anyone to submit an anonymous comment or rumor and expect a quick, public response from CSD management. The head of CSD saw this application as a catalyst for promoting open communication but believed it could cause more harm than good if the management at all levels failed to take actions consistent with a philosophy of openness.

Source: Applegate, Lynda M., and Donna B. Stoddard. "Chemical Bank: Technology Support for Cooperative Work." Harvard Business School case 9-193-131, Sept. 1993.

- Use the WCA framework to organize your understanding of this case and to identify important topics that are not mentioned.

- Which, if any, of the eight types of information systems is represented here?

- Explain why you do or do not believe that Lotus Notes applications could have an important impact on what it felt like to be an employee in a large organization.

KEY TERMS

social context	design	computer conferencing	management information system
social presence	choice	audiographic conferencing	(MIS)
nonverbal communication	implementation	videoconferencing	executive information system (EIS)
personal communication	rationality	electronic mail (e-mail)	decision support system (DSS)
impersonal communication	satisficing	voice mail (v-mail)	execution system
anonymous communication	bounded rationality	fax	expert system
presentation technologies	office automation system (OAS)	transaction processing system	groupware
problem finding	communication systems	(TPS)	group decision support system
problem solving	teleconferencing	batch processing	(GDSS)
intelligence	audioconferencing	real-time processing	hybrid information system

REVIEW QUESTIONS

1. What are some of the ways information systems can improve the capacity, consistency, productivity, cycle time, flexibility, and security of communication and decision making?

2. Why is it important to differentiate between personal, impersonal, and anonymous communication?

3. Why is the distinction between same or different time or place important when discussing communication technology?

4. Why is it sometimes important to make communication systematic?

5. How is problem finding related to problem solving?

6. What is the relationship between rationality and satisficing?

7. What are the different degrees of structuring decisions?

8. What are examples of tools typically grouped with office automation systems?

9. What are the forms of teleconferencing?

10. What are the similarities and differences between e-mail, v-mail, and fax?

11. What is the difference between batch processing and real-time processing?

12. What is the difference between MIS, DSS, and EIS?

13. Why is it difficult to keep EISs current?

14. Where are the different types of systems typically used in the cycle of planning, execution, and control?

15. What is an expert system?

16. What kinds of functions do group decision support systems (GDSS) contain?

17. Why are many information systems hybrids?

18. What typical features of particular types of information systems are often transferable?

DISCUSSION QUESTIONS

1. Alana Shoars, the e-mail administrator for Epson computer company in Torrance, California, trained 700 employees to create and send e-mail messages to fellow workers. She assured them that e-mail communications would be totally private but later discovered that her boss was copying and reading employees' e-mail. When she was fired after complaining, she sued her former employer on behalf of the employees whose e-mail had been opened. Epson argued that state privacy statutes

make no mention of e-mail. The judge agreed and dismissed the case.[22] What ethical issues does this case and the legal finding raise?

2. Although executives are typically described as people who work on long-term, strategic issues, the discussion of EIS emphasizes the use of these systems to monitor recent organizational performance. Assuming you were an executive concerned with long-term issues, explain why you would or would not find this type of EIS useful. Explain some of the things an EIS would have to do if it were to focus specifically on long term strategic issues.

3. Some people believe that e-mail, v-mail, and fax have reduced the quality of work life for many professionals by making it difficult to escape work for an evening or weekend. These observers believe anytime, anyplace may be a fine goal for serving customers, but may not be appropriate as an expectation of company employees. Discuss the pros and cons of this issue.

4. You are a manager looking for a secretary. You place an ad in a newspaper and receive 500 resumes. Use ideas about decision making to describe the process of deciding whom to hire. Assume that 400 of the 500 applicants meet all objective criteria you can think of, such as typing speed, business experience, and education.

5. Why is there a distinction between management information systems and decision support systems? After all, one of the basic purposes of management information systems is to provide information that is used for decision making.

6. Assume that all current telephones were replaced with picture phones that could transmit both audio and video, and could operate as video extensions of v-mail. Explain whether this would have any important impact on you personally.

HANDS-ON EXERCISES

1. This exercise illustrates uses of e-mail and v-mail and assumes that these capabilities are available.

   a. Send an e-mail message to yourself. After inserting a brief explanatory note, forward it to a small distribution list, and then delete it.

   b. Leave a v-mail message for yourself. After adding a brief explanatory comment, forward it to a small distribution list, and then delete it.

2. This exercise illustrates uses of transaction processing systems, and assumes that a small transaction processing system has been provided.

   a. Identify the types of transactions in the transaction processing system provided, and enter one transaction of each type.

   b. Generate several different management reports based on data in the system.

   c. After identifying which reports are affected by which transactions, perform several additional transactions, generate management reports that should be affected by those transactions, and explain whether the information on the management reports changed in ways you would have predicted.

APPLICATION SCENARIOS

Transcontinental Movers

Bob Trumbull, president of Transcontinental Movers, has been criticized over the last few years for allowing profits to slip even as revenues and tonnage increase. The long-haul moving industry is becoming more competitive, and differentiating any mover's capabilities from those of its competitors is difficult. Bob wants to increase profit by improving internal efficiency.

Based on problems that occurred when cooperating with other moving companies in the past, Transcontinental will accept only internal solutions and will not subcontract work to other firms.

Bob believes that dispatching is an area where better information systems might help. (Dispatching is the decision of which truck to assign to which load. This decision is often made long after signing a contract with a customer.) Each week, the 12 dispatchers at Transcontinental's central headquarters dispatch hundreds of trucks from customer origins to customer destinations. For example, the response to a customer needing a shipment from Chicago to Dallas might be to dispatch a van that is currently in St. Louis, knowing that it has no preassigned job after the delivery in Dallas and that it will eventually return home to New Orleans. Ideally, the dispatcher should send the truck that can provide the best service for the customer without unnecessary deadheading, that is, unpaid driving miles.

The information system must keep track of van locations and must help in the dispatching decision. Several factors might be considered in developing an information system:

- Only full truckloads are being considered. After a system is developed for full truckloads, it may be expanded to include multiple pickups for the same truck on the same trip.

- Transcontinental's national dispatching center operates 24 hours a day, 7 days a week. When customers call, they prefer an immediate commitment correct to within four hours for the time the van will arrive for the pickup and the time the van will arrive for the delivery. Transcontinental meets its schedule commitments 90 percent of the time.

- Transcontinental has stored years' worth of data about every delivery and every request for delivery that could not be handled.

- Transcontinental divides the United States into 60 geographical regions to simplify the decision process. Based on historical data plus informed guessing, it develops and maintains load forecasts by week for each region for six months into the future.

1. Explain possible roles of OAS, communication systems, TPS, MIS, DSS, EIS, execution systems, and groupware in this situation. If any type of system is not relevant, explain why not.

2. Identify specific information that might be included in systems of each type. Sketch some possible outputs.

3. Explain how the entire system might work.

DEBATE TOPIC   *Use ideas from the chapter to argue the pros and cons and practical implications of the following proposition: When one digs into a situation like this, one soon finds that it involves so many details and procedures that typical managers and business professionals will not be able to contribute to the solution.*

Brinkley Bank

Catherine O'Malley was not convinced that the proposed system was the best system for the job. She headed Brinkley Bank's Trust Department, which managed the stock and bond portfolios of wealthy clients. The money managers in her department were hired by their customers to buy and sell the stocks and bonds in their portfolios subject to individualized arrangements. Some clients authorized the managers to use their own judgment, but others said they did not want to own particular types of securities such as tobacco stocks, or wanted to be consulted whenever trades occurred. The bank's fee for managing the portfolios was 1 percent of the first $1 million in assets and 0.5 percent beyond the first million.

At least once a year, the money managers talked with their clients and revised a written agreement specifying the client's type of preferred investment strategy. Some clients wanted to be aggressive and were willing to go into riskier securities in the hope of getting higher returns. Others were more conservative and preferred lower risk, greater safety, and lower expected returns. Money managers usually allocated portfolio assets between stocks, bonds, and cash, based on the client's preferred risk profile. Aggressive portfolios had a higher proportion of stocks, whereas conservative portfolios had a higher proportion of government bonds. Once a portfolio was established, money managers typically bought or sold mostly when the current prices of individual securities seemed out of line or when the client needed additional cash. They were careful about not trading too often since each trade cost the client a commission that was paid to an outside broker.

The proposed system would automate much of the money manager's decision making. It would use mathematical procedures to examine each portfolio every night to try to find more advantageous ways to deploy the assets, consistent with the client's goals. Since individual money managers were often tied up in meetings with clients, and sometimes out of town, the system would be able to trade up to 10 percent of any portfolio automatically to take advantage of short-term anomalies in the market. For the remaining 90 percent, however, the portfolio manager would have to submit any trades that occurred.

1. Explain possible roles of OAS, communication systems, TPS, MIS, DSS, EIS, execution systems, and groupware in this situation. If any type of system is not relevant, explain why not.

2. Consider different approaches for improving decision making. Which approach or approaches does the proposal use? How could it be expanded to include aspects of other approaches?

3. Describe an information system you would recommend in this situation. Be as specific as possible in identifying the business process and how the information system would be used. Explain your recommendation.

DEBATE TOPIC   *Use ideas from the chapter to argue the pros and cons and practical implications of the following proposition:* The proposed system will improve performance without increasing risk.

Cumulative Case: Custom T-Shirts, Inc.

Opening new stores has been exhilarating, but has left Terry, Dale, and Pat exhausted. They are each working 80-hour weeks, and there is no end in sight. They just can't keep up with all the details and worry that the business is going out of control. Instead of going to work on Saturday morning, as they usually do, they decide to take that time off to think about where things stand and what they can do to make things more manageable.

Terry thinks the main problem is communication and they are swamped with too many communications from too many places in too many forms. They need to communicate with each other; they need to communicate with the stores to monitor what is happening, to make sure plans and budgets are met, and to deal with problems and exceptions. Between meetings, phone calls, e-mail, v-mail, and fax, maybe there are just too many options. Perhaps it would be useful to come up with some guidelines about what form of communication to use under what circumstances and how to make each form of communication more efficient.

Dale thinks the heart of the problem is in their style of decision making. Decisions about everyday operations include things such as how much to reorder for each store, what hours particular employees should work, and how to resolve disputes with employees and customers; longer range decisions include things such as employment policies and expansion plans. Even though they have set up some basic systems for keeping track of cash and ordering inventory, they seem to be swamped with everyday decisions. Perhaps it would be a good idea to look at their decision-making processes to identify some general strengths and weaknesses.

Pat thinks the problem is that they haven't thought adequately about the different ways different types of information systems could help with their decisions and communication. Perhaps they should start with different types of information systems and look for ways these systems might be applied. Just finding opportunities wouldn't solve the problems, but it would be a first step toward deciding what to do.

1. Follow Terry's line of reasoning. Assume the issue is too much communication from too many places in too many forms. Propose guidelines about what forms of communication should be used when and how to make each form of communication more efficient.

2. Follow Dale's line of reasoning. Try to apply concepts such as the steps in decision making, rationality, and the common flaws in decision making to propose guidelines they might try to use for some of the decisions in some important business processes.

3. Follow Pat's line of reasoning. Think about the different types of information systems. Propose one or two places each type of information system might be used in their business.

REFERENCES

1. Rothfeder, Jeffrey, and Jim Bartim. "How Software Is Making Food Sales a Piece of Cake." *Business Week*, July 2, 1990, pp. 54–55.

2. Main, Jeremy. "Computers of the World, Unite." *Fortune*, Sept. 24, 1990. pp. 115–118.

3. Feld, Charles S. "Directed Decentralization: The Frito-Lay Story." *Financial Executive*, Nov.–Dec. 1990, pp. 22–24.

4. Pounds, William. "The Process of Problem Finding." *Industrial Management Review*, Vol. 11, No. 1, 1969, pp. 1–20.

5. Hansell, Saul. "For P.&G., A Bet That Backfired." *New York Times*, Apr. 14, 1994, p. C4.

6. Simon, Herbert. *The New Science of Management Decision.* New York: Harper & Row, 1960.

7. Tversky, Amos, and Daniel Kahneman. "The Framing of Decisions and the Psychology of Choice." *Science*, Vol. 211, Jan. 30, 1981, pp. 453–458.

8. Slovic, Paul, Baruch Fischhoff, and Sarah Lichtenstein. "Risky Assumptions." *Psychology Today*, June 1990, pp. 44–48.

9. Rubin, John. "The Dangers of Overconfidence." *Technology Review*, July 1989, pp. 11–12.

10. Janis, Irving L. *Groupthink: Psychological Studies of Policy Decisions and Fiascoes*. Boston: Houghton Mifflin, 1983.

11. Godin, Seth. *E-Mail Addresses of the Rich and Famous*. Reading, Mass.: Addison-Wesley, 1994.

12. Zachary, G. Pascal. "It's a Mail Thing: Electronic Messaging Gets a Rating—Ex." *Wall Street Journal*, June 22, 1994, p. A1.

13. Goldstein, David K. "IBM Europe Headquarters." In James J. Cash, et al. *Corporate Information Systems Management: Text and Cases*. 2d ed. Homewood, Ill.: Irwin, 1988, pp. 515–534.

14. Perry, Nancy J. "Computers Come of Age in Class." *Fortune,* Vol. 121, No. 2, Spring, 1990, pp. 72–78.

15. *Business Week*. "Up Front: Ignorant of the Fax." May 9, 1994, p. 8.

16. Mason, Richard. "Information Systems Technology and Corporate Strategy: A Historical Overview." In F. Warren McFarlan, ed., *The Information Systems Research Challenge Proceedings*. Boston: Harvard Business School Press, 1984, pp. 261–278.

17. Houdeshel, George, and Hugh J. Watson. "The Management Information and Decision Support (MIDS) System at Lockheed-Georgia." *MIS Quarterly*, Vol. 11, No. 1, Mar. 1987, pp. 127–140.

18. Johansen, Robert. *Groupware: Computer Support for Teams*. New York: Free Press, 1988.

19. Dennis, Alan R., et al. "Information Technology to Support Meetings." *MIS Quarterly,* Dec. 1988, pp. 591–624.

20. Nunamaker, Jay, et al. "Experiences at IBM with Group Support Systems: A Field Study." *Decision Support Systems*, Vol. 5, No. 2, June 1989, pp. 183–196.

21. Ho, T. H., K. S. Raman, and Richard T. Watson. "Group Decision Support Systems: The Cultural Factor." In Janice I. Gross, John C. Henderson, and Benn R. Konsynski, eds., *Proceedings of the Tenth International Conference on Information Systems*. Boston, Dec. 4–6, 1989, pp. 119–129.

22. Bjerklie, David. "E-mail: The Boss Is Watching." *Technology Review*. Apr. 1993, p. 14.

6

Increasing Efficiency and Effectiveness of Internal Operations

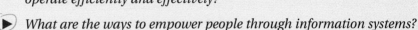

Study Questions

 What are six general ways to use information systems to help firms operate efficiently and effectively?

 What are the ways to empower people through information systems?

▶ *What are the ways information systems support the various management roles?*

 What are the ways to eliminate waste using information systems?

▶ *What are the advantages of eliminating paper?*

▶ *How can information systems help structure work to promote best practices?*

 What important areas of work have been automated?

▶ *What can current robots do?*

 How is it possible to integrate suppliers and customers?

▶ *Why is computer-integrated manufacturing (CIM) necessary for highly automated factories?*

Mrs. Fields Cookies was founded in 1977 as a single cookie store and grew to 600 stores within a decade. The company appealed to customers through warm cookies, friendly service, and reasonable prices. As it grew, Mrs. Fields Cookies faced the problem of training and motivating relatively inexperienced store managers to use the standards and procedures Mrs. Debbi Fields developed when she operated her first store in California. Furthermore, as part of its business strategy, it needed to make sure store personnel spent more time pleasing customers and less time doing paperwork.

Mrs. Fields Cookies used information systems as part of its approach to these issues. Years of experimentation and development work created a unique information system that minimizes paperwork and permits headquarters to monitor and control day-to-day operations at each store. Each store manager starts the day using a computer program called a Day Planner, which uses the store's history for similar days to suggest how many batches of what type of cookies to bake at what times during the day. At the end of each hour, the cash register automatically transmits to the central computer the details of every sale that has occurred. A computer program uses this information to revise earlier projections. If sales are unexpectedly slow, the system might suggest that someone stand outside the store and give away samples. When common problems occur such as cash registers jamming, a program in the system provides guidance by asking typical troubleshooting questions.

Although this part of the system makes data collection and repetitive decision making as routine and automatic as possible, another part provides a more human touch. It permits Debbi Fields to send voice or text messages to store managers to discuss problems or pass on news. It also permits store managers to request help from headquarters. They know the computerized part of the system will help with repetitive decisions and paperwork and that even Debbi Fields herself is readily available for issues requiring personal help.

After many years of gradual evolution, the software in the system has been generalized and is being sold under the name Paperless Management to other businesses that need to manage numerous retail outlets. The system's 25 mix-and-match modules cover diverse areas such as messaging, sales forecasting, time and attendance, executive information, and auditing. Disney Stores uses it to distribute customized personnel and reporting forms, as well as electronic mail. The major benefits are in clarity and consistency since everyone receives similar information in similar formats. Randy Fields, Debbi's husband, who founded a separate software company to sell this software, explains in a promotional video that in any group of store managers, some will simply be better at tasks such as employee scheduling. Therefore, it makes sense for all store managers to use the methods these individuals would use.[1, 2]

Unfortunately, the strategy of maintaining consistency across the stores was not sufficient to maintain the company's rapid growth in the face of a recession in the late 1980s. In March 1993, Mrs. Fields Cookies was forced to exchange 80 percent of the company's stock for a write-off of 80 percent of its $94 million debt. Debbi Fields relinquished her posts as CEO and president and took a $150,000 salary cut. Industry experts attributed the company's problems to a range of factors, including customers' unwillingness to pay nearly a dollar for a cookie, the limited product line, the excessive growth that was attempted, and the fact that Debbi Fields tried to maintain too much control over the local stores and probably should have started selling franchises earlier.[3]

DEBATE TOPIC   *Argue the pros and cons and practical implications of the following proposition:*
Use of information systems to automate management decisions is appropriate only if managers are not competent to make these decisions themselves.

D ESPITE THE COMPANY'S OVEREXPANSION PROBLEMS, the Mrs. Fields Cookies case illustrates how information systems can be integrated into a company's approach for performing and controlling its internal operations. Although its product is a low-technology item you can make at home, information systems play a key role in running the stores efficiently. The company's strategy of using standardized methods for repetitive operational decisions allows employees to focus on customers. This exemplifies the point that data processing related to repetitive decisions often absorbs energy best applied elsewhere.

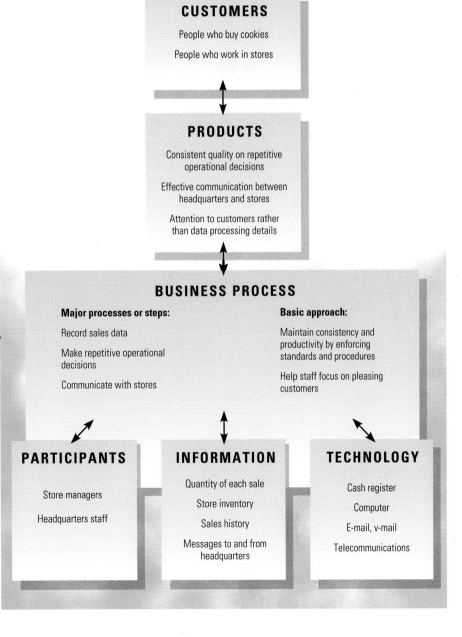

Figure 6.1 Mrs. Fields Cookies: Standardizing Repetitive Decision Making at Retail Outlets

Executing business processes is at the heart of a firm's ability to compete. When competitors have similar resources, the competitor with better execution has the advantage. It is possible to improve execution by improving efficiency or effectiveness or both. Improving **efficiency** means doing less work or incurring less expense to produce the same outputs. Improving **effectiveness** means producing different outputs that are more appropriate. Figure 6.2 shows that efficiency is related to internal process performance, whereas effectiveness is related to the internal or external customer's evaluation of the product of the business process. In this chapter, you will see some examples that focus on efficiency, some that focus on effectiveness, and many that improve both.

Figure 6.2 Efficiency and Effectiveness

Efficiency is related to internal process performance, whereas effectiveness is related to the internal or external customer's evaluation of the product of the business process.

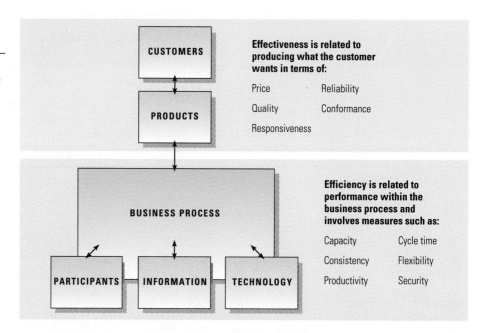

This chapter's purpose is to help you identify potential uses of information systems and possible ways to enhance existing systems. It is organized in terms of six approaches for using information systems to improve execution: empowering people, supporting management work, eliminating waste, structuring work to promote best practices, automating work, and integrating across functions and organizations. Although there is some overlap between these approaches, each provides a useful way of thinking about applying information systems to improve execution.

Empowering People

All general management courses discuss ways to empower people. **Empowerment** means giving people the ability to do their work: the right information, the right tools, the right training, the right environment, and the authority they need. Information systems help empower people by providing information, tools, and training.

Providing Information

Providing information to help people perform their work is a primary purpose of most information systems although they provide information in many different ways. Some systems provide information that is essential in performing a business process, such as the prices used to create a customer's bill at a restaurant. Other systems provide information that is potentially useful but can be used in a discretionary manner, such as medical history information that different doctors might use in different ways.

Other information systems such as MISs provide feedback concerning the productivity, consistency, and speed of work. Feedback about results yesterday, last week, or last month helps employees and their managers identify problems and decide how to solve them. The feedback is in terms of measurements that summarize the work for a time interval. Typical measurements for productivity include units produced, units per hour, and units reworked. Measurements for consistency include total defects and average defects per unit.

Depending on how it is handled, feedback can have important direct effects. During the 1970s and 1980s, Japanese air-conditioner firms made large competitive gains against U.S. firms, due in part to differences in quality. In 1981 and 1982, the U.S. companies with the worst quality collected minimal data about factory defects and failures in the field. The best U.S. companies collected defect rates at each inspection point in the factory and failure rates in the field for each model. Japanese firms with better quality collected even more detailed data about specific types of defects and failures so that their workers could use it to improve quality.[4]

Interactive information systems used directly as part of a work process create the possibility of another type of feedback. These systems can provide immediate feedback to help people identify possible errors or problems while they are still doing the work. Systems of this type are used in clerical work such as word processing or taking reservations. They are also used in sophisticated professional work such as designing buildings or evaluating investments. The feedback in a transaction processing system is relatively simple, such as notification of missing data or data outside a permissible range. Immediate feedback in sophisticated professional work may be similar, or it may be the result of a complex model running in the background to check the results on many criteria.

Providing Tools

In addition to providing the right information, empowering people means giving them the right tools. Consider the way planning analysts produce consolidated corporate plans based on plans of individual divisions and departments. If the plans are submitted on paper, it is a major task to add up the numbers to determine the projected corporate bottom line. When the plan is changed during a negotiation process, the planning analyst has to recalculate the projected results. With the right tools, the numerical parts of the plans arrive in a consistent, electronic format permitting consolidation by a computer. This leaves the analyst free to do the more productive work of analyzing the quality of the plan.

Information systems provide many types of tools. Tools directed toward clerical tasks and general office tasks include telephone systems, word processors, spreadsheets, and DBMSs for personal computers. Tools directed toward analysis work range from spreadsheets to programming tools for data analysis and model building. As information systems become more interactive, tools play a more important role. For example, the evolution from paper-based MIS to interactive DSS and interactive EIS is largely about providing better tools that make the information in the system more useful.

Interactive tools have strongly affected the way professionals and managers do their general office work such as gathering and analyzing information, drafting and responding to memos, placing and receiving telephone calls, and creating reports. The thinning of corporate staffs means that fewer assistants are available to help with these tasks, which makes it all the more important that managers and professionals have efficient tools to minimize time wasted with general office work. These personal productivity tools include note-taking systems, presentation graphics systems, word processors, spreadsheets, e-mail, v-mail, and meeting schedulers.

Most personal productivity tools can be used virtually anywhere. Thanks to electronic technologies, office work can be done in an airplane, hotel, car, or home. This has popularized the concept of the **logical office,** that is, any place where office work is done.

Providing Training

Since information systems are designed to provide the information needed to support desired work practices, they are often used for training and learning. As shown by an expert system and a decision simulator, they sometimes provide new and unique training methods.

IBM developed an expert system for fixing computer disk drives. The expert system was an organized collection of the best knowledge about fixing these disk drives, and it fostered rapid and efficient training. Before the system was developed, technicians typically took between 14 and 16 months to become certified, but with the expert system, training time dropped to 3 to 5 months. Novice technicians using this system could ask the same question again and again without being embarrassed. Personal control over their learning experience facilitated their learning.[5]

Weyerhauser developed a decision simulator much like an early video game to train lumberjacks to make better decisions about cutting felled trees into logs. The value of a tree can vary by 50 percent, depending on how the lumberjack allocates different parts of it to foreign or domestic use, plywood, and other uses. The training system shows the user the size and shape of a tree stem. The user decides how to cut it and allocate the logs. The system then displays the revenue generated by the user's solution and by the optimal solution created by an optimization model. Eventually, the simulator was used to develop log-cutting guidelines that could be printed on a pocket-sized card.[6]

In one case, an operational system was used for training. In the other, a special information system was developed to train people to make an important repetitive decision correctly. In both situations, people used an information system as a way to learn how to do their jobs better.

REALITY CHECK   **Empowering People**   Three ways to empower people by using information systems include: providing information, providing tools, and providing training.

1. Identify situations you have encountered when you lacked the information, tools, or training needed to do what you should have done.

2. Describe whether and how it might have been possible to get the information, tools, or training if the circumstances had been different.

Supporting Management Work

Even though management is often performed in idiosyncratic ways, trying to look at management as a business process is a good starting point for finding opportunities to support management work. This section discusses managers' activities and links them to both formal information systems and other information sources that managers use.

What Do Managers Do?

Different managers have very different types of responsibilities. First-line managers are deeply involved in the technical details of how work is done. Higher-level managers are more concerned with making an entire organization operate effectively. Top managers are also concerned with developing and instilling a long-range vision of where the organization is going. Most introductory management texts start discussing what managers do by identifying the classical management functions, such as planning, organizing, leading, and controlling. After identifying these functions, many texts point out that these functions do not adequately describe what managers actually do.

In an attempt to answer this question, Mintzberg spent a week observing each of five CEOs. Although CEOs have broader jobs than most managers and although this research was done over 20 years ago, the resulting characterization of managerial work[7] is still used frequently.

Figure 6.3 identifies Mintzberg's list of managerial roles along with the types of formal information systems that support these roles. The roles are grouped into three categories: interpersonal, informational, and decisional. Even though the mix of roles would differ greatly between the CEO of General Motors and a branch accounting manager, most managers perform most of these roles to some extent. For example, as part of organizing a department, a manager could play interpersonal roles such as figurehead for the organizational effort, leader for meetings, and liaison to other departments. Informational roles in the process could include monitoring activities, disseminating the principles behind the new organization, and serving as organizational spokesperson. Decisional roles could include the entrepreneur defining the new goals, the negotiator resolving conflicts, and the disturbance handler.

As indicated in Figure 6.3, different types of information systems may support the different roles. The relevance of communication systems to all the management roles illustrates an important point about the nature of management. Management is a highly interactive job. As Mintzberg learned, typical managers spend little time doing detailed analytical work. To the contrary, managerial work is characterized by brevity, variety, and fragmentation. Many managers prefer verbal media rather than written media and work through their network of personal contacts.

If brevity, variety, fragmentation, verbal media, and working through personal contacts characterize managerial work, the information managers use must be consistent with this work style. Therefore, it is not surprising that much of the information managers use does *not* come from formalized information processing systems. Rather, managers get their information from their network of contacts inside and outside the organization and gather information related to particular issues or problems of current importance. They also get information from being present in an organization and observing what is happening, or from "management by walking around."[8] The discussion of information in Chapter 4 summarized some of these ideas by pointing out that management information includes not only "objective" data generated by formal systems, but also information meant to be persuasive, such as suggestions, warnings, and detailed proposals (see Figure 4.10).

Figure 6.3 Information Systems Related to Mintzberg's Management Roles

Different types of information systems support different types of management roles.

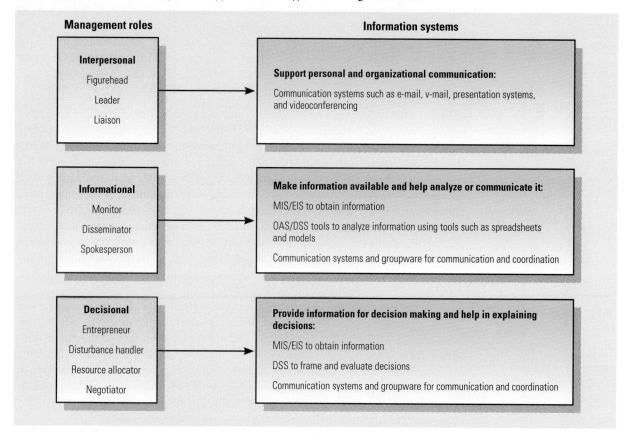

What Types of Information Do Managers Need?

Table 6.1 extends this idea by summarizing common sources of management information and categorizing them as formal or informal and internal or external. Formal information may come from computer-based data processing systems, written documents, or scheduled meetings. Informal information comes from a range of sources such as lunchtime gossip, trade shows, and what managers learn while walking around.

Recognizing this range of information sources helps clarify the managerial uses of formal information systems. Formal information systems contain much essential management information and much more information that could be very useful if it could be accessed effectively. However, these systems can provide managers with only part of the information they need. The high degree of variety and action in managerial work implies that systems used by managers should be flexible and easy to use. Since managers often deal with exceptions and nonroutine situations, the particular information they need tomorrow may not be the same as the information they need today. If a formal information system does not readily support tomorrow's needs, an action-oriented manager will simply bypass it and find some other source of information.

Table 6.1 Common Sources of Management Information

Character of the Information	Internal Sources	External Sources
Formal, computer based	Key indicators generated by internal tracking systems	Public databases
Formal, document based	Planning reports, internal audits	Industry reports, books, magazines
Formal, verbal	Scheduled meetings	Industry forums
Informal	Lunch conversations, gossip, management by walking around	Trade shows, personal contacts

Is Management Really a Process?

The discussion so far has focused on the nature of management work and on management information requirements. But it certainly has not described management as a process with a beginning and end and with repeatable methods for using specific resources to create specific outcomes.

The extent to which ideas about processes can be used to describe management activities in any particular situation depends on what the organization and its managers want. Informal management styles often succeed if the organization is small and personalized enough that it is easy to see what is happening just by being present and talking to people. Even with informal systems for managing people, however, these organizations still need formal systems to keep track of essential business information, such as what has been ordered and how much customers owe.

In contrast, as organizations get larger and become geographically dispersed, formal management processes become more important. This is part of the rationale behind the Mrs. Fields Cookies system, which created carefully defined methods for performing management tasks such as scheduling employees and deciding what to produce on a given day. A company that has taken formal management methods to an extreme is Cypress Semiconductor. Under the controversial leadership of T. J. Rodgers, it uses a highly formalized system to keep track of each employee's work commitments on a weekly basis. This system is designed to make sure everyone is coordinated and nothing falls through the cracks, even for a single week. Rodgers calls this method "no excuses management."[9]

REALITY CHECK   **Supporting Management**   In this section, we identified different roles of managers and how different types of information systems can support management work; we also explained that management can be done with varying degrees of formality.

1. Identify several situations you have encountered personally in which management was important, such as in jobs, clubs, or group projects. What types of information were used to support management in these situations?

2. For each situation, explain the extent to which that information was used in a formal management process and the alternatives for making the process more or less formal.

Eliminating Waste

TQM experts have estimated that 20 to 30 percent of the effort in many business processes is simply waste. Waste occurs when people do work that adds no value. It also occurs when they do work that is faulty and must be redone. Information systems can help eliminate waste in many ways.

Eliminating Unproductive Uses of Time

Information systems can reduce the amount of time people waste doing unproductive work. A study of how professionals and managers at 15 leading U.S. corporations spent their time concluded that many professionals spent less than half of their work time on activities directly related to their functions.[10] Although the primary function of salespeople is selling, the time breakdown for salespeople averaged 36 percent spent on prospecting and selling, 39 percent on servicing accounts, 19 percent on doing administrative chores, and 6 percent on training. Better use of information systems could save much of their unproductive time performing chores such as collecting product or pricing information, determining order status for a customer, resolving invoice discrepancies, and reporting of time and expenses.

The leverage in avoiding unproductive uses of time is enormous. Consider a salesperson who is making $50,000 per year but who really spends only 50 percent of work time doing sales work. If this could be increased to 60 percent, the salesperson might be 20 percent more productive. This same phenomenon applies in many professions. For example, nurses typically spend 50 percent of their time doing paperwork. Although much of the data is needed, better use of technology could allow nurses to spend more time providing care for patients (see Figure 6.4).

Figure 6.4 Reducing Data Processing by Nurses

Providing better data processing methods is one way to help nurses spend their time with patients rather than paperwork.

Consider the way a voice messaging system helped salespeople at Gordon Food Service eliminate wasted time in their communications with headquarters. Gordon

Food Service distributes food to retailers. Before the introduction of voice messaging, its 160 sales reps took an average of 10 minutes per call to get through to the company's 15 product managers about prices and availability of produce. With v-mail, they phoned in questions and called back at their convenience to get the answers. Conversely, sales managers no longer needed to spend hours each day tracking down reps in the field. Instead, they sent and retrieved messages using v-mail. Gordon's communications manager estimates the system paid for itself in one year by increasing time available for selling and by reducing inefficiencies.[11]

Although many examples show how information systems can eliminate unproductive uses of time, the use of information systems and information technology certainly doesn't guarantee time will be spent well. For example, consider the way current word processors make it possible to format documents using multiple fonts and styles. In at least some cases, much of the formatting is unnecessary window-dressing, and the message can be conveyed about as well with less work. The same criticism sometimes applies to multiple iterations of spreadsheet models. The multiple runs eat up time but may not contribute much to the decision being made.

Eliminating Unnecessary Paper

One common way to improve data processing is to eliminate unnecessary paper. Although paper is familiar and convenient for many purposes, it has major disadvantages. It is bulky, difficult to move from place to place, and extremely difficult to use for analyzing large amounts of data (see Figure 6.5) Every F-18 fighter produced by Northrup in the late 1980s was accompanied by 8,000 pounds of paper drawings and approvals.[12] More recently, Aetna Life & Casualty has saved at least $6 million a year by creating insurance manuals and other texts only on computers, thereby avoiding distributing 100 million pages of updates at 4.5 cents a sheet.[13]

Figure 6.5 Connecticut Mutual and Its Sea of Paper

In 1990, Connecticut Mutual Life Insurance used this warehouse, which is the size of a football field, to store paper files. Vans stuffed with paper shuttled between the office and warehouse hourly. Simple changes in an insurance policy could take a week.

Since users want the information on the paper, rather than the paper itself, removing unnecessary paper is a way to improve efficiency and effectiveness, often cutting cycle times by 50 percent or more. Storing data in computerized form takes much less physical space and destroys fewer forests, but that is only the beginning. It makes data easier to analyze, easier to copy or transmit, and easier to display in a flexible format. Compare paper telephone bills with computerized bills for a large company. The paper bills identify calls but are virtually impossible to analyze for patterns of inefficient or excessive usage. Paper has other problems as well. By one set of estimates, 7.5 percent of paper documents get lost completely, 3 percent of the remainder are misfiled, and it may cost $120 in labor just to find a misfiled document.[14]

Management information no longer requires as much paper as it once did. Firms can now provide online access to transaction data, standard summary reports, and analysis tools for selecting and formatting what the manager needs. Earlier generations of MIS provided weekly deliveries of immense printouts just in case some of the data might be needed. Each week the old printout was thrown away and replaced by a new one. This kept the paper industry busy but was ineffective in providing information summarized and formatted in the most useful way.

Although it is easy to see how computerized systems can eliminate a great deal of paper, most of the information in most companies remains on paper. Ironically, some observers believe computerized systems are generating more paper outputs than ever before.

Reusing Work

At a time when there is much talk about recycling, an obvious place to look for better execution is **reusing work**. This is the basic advantage of word processors, which make it unnecessary to retype the correct portions of a document that needs changes. It is possible to take the idea of reusing work in many other directions, such as the use of prewritten letters and spreadsheet templates.

Imagine you were writing a letter to a customer whose payments were delinquent. Wouldn't you think that such a letter had been written before by someone? Collections of common business letters are available on diskettes. Instead of composing the entire letter, you can modify an existing letter to make it suit your purpose. Lawyers have used this approach effectively in writing wills, deeds, pension plans, and other documents that are repetitive but must be comprehensive and must comply with laws. Beyond this, some law firms have created expert systems that automatically insert paragraphs based on a lawyer's responses to standard questions.

The approach of reusing work has been used in spreadsheets and other software. Why should you develop a new spreadsheet application for planning your wheat farm or for determining the breakeven point on your apartment building? Instead, you can buy a spreadsheet **template** and modify it for your business situation. This type of template is a spreadsheet set up to solve a particular problem in a particular type of business. Instead of starting from scratch, the user installs the template and modifies it.

On a much larger scale, reusing work is the idea behind all purchased application software, such as a general ledger system or payroll system sold by a software firm. A company buying such a system can reuse the developer's work in several ways. It can use the system without changing it and can adapt its own business processes to those prescribed by the purchased system. It can also modify the purchased system to fit its business processes.

Eliminating Unnecessary Work Steps and Delays

A common warning applies when people introduce computers into business situations: Adding computers to a mess creates a computerized mess. Before building a new information system, it is always advisable to rethink what the organization is trying to do and how it is trying to do it. In many cases, reorganizing the work flow without computerizing yields many of the intended benefits of the computerized system. Introducing a computer after reorganizing may provide even greater benefits.

Reorganizing work flows using information systems typically involves eliminating unnecessary steps and delays. A sales example involves the use of laptop computers by insurance salespeople while working directly with clients. Instead of discussing alternative insurance policies with a client and then going back to the office to calculate the cost and potential benefits, they use the laptops to present and evaluate alternatives as part of their sales pitch. The use of laptops removes unnecessary steps because the alternatives are evaluated immediately instead of waiting for separate data processing activities later in the week.

Wrangler Womenswear found a similar way to remove unnecessary delays for its salespeople and their customers. Previously, the salespeople visited clothing retailers, received orders, and mailed them to headquarters. By the time the orders were entered into the corporate mainframe (often a two-week delay), many orders were lost because the merchandise was now out of stock. By using laptops, the salesperson and retailer check the sizes, styles, colors, and quantities and enter the order directly to reserve what is needed. The salesperson can suggest alternatives to unavailable items on the spot. Some salespeople using this system increased their sales 10 to 20 percent.[15]

Eliminating Unnecessary Variations in Procedures and Systems

In many companies, separate departments use different systems and procedures to perform essentially similar repetitive processes, such as paying employees, purchasing supplies, and keeping track of inventories. Although these procedures may seem adequate from a totally local viewpoint, doing the same work in different ways is often inefficient in a global sense. Whenever the systems must change with new technology, new regulations, or new business issues, each separate system must be analyzed separately, often by someone starting from scratch.

Du Pont, one of the world's largest chemical companies, saw this type of problem in the way it printed paychecks no fewer than 3,300 times a year. Some plants and divisions paid on the 1st and 15th of the month, others in the middle and end of the month, and yet others every other Monday. Seeing little advantage in this way of doing things, Du Pont converted most of its payroll to the same bimonthly cycle and consolidated to 36 payrolls. This eliminated over 100 jobs and saved $12 million annually.[16]

Eliminating Counterproductive Incentives

Putting time and effort into doing the wrong thing is a form of waste, however efficiently the work might be done. The centralized planning in the old Soviet Union generated legendary examples. These included the ball bearing plant that produced huge ball bearings because its was paid by the total weight of its output, and the shoe factory that produced all left shoes because it was paid based on the total number of shoes produced.

In both cases, group or personal incentives were inconsistent with what should have been the true goals of the enterprise. Companies in market economies cannot survive doing things like that, but a close look at many companies would reveal situations with group or individual incentives contrary to the firm's professed goals.

Incentive issues doomed a production planning system built for an electronics division of RCA, a conglomerate with many unrelated business units before its acquisition by General Electric. The system calculated how to use factory resources to best meet projected customer demand for over 50 products. It had little impact, however, because RCA management measured the factory not on meeting projected demand, but rather, on attaining labor and material cost standards set earlier in the year. In other words, by the incentives under which the factory operated, keeping people and machines busy was more important than meeting customer demand. The emphasis on "cost absorption" came from a desire for an equitable way to compare performance across RCA business units ranging from Hertz Rent-A-Car to electronics. This led to incentives focused on RCA's internal management problems rather than on what customers wanted.

Information systems can help with some aspects of this type of problem. Merely by capturing data about different aspects of a process, they can generate multiple measures of performance (such as productivity, consistency, and cycle time) that can be used to make sure important outcomes are not ignored. They can also inform workers of short-term priorities such as rush orders. However, the system will probably be ignored if the real measures of performance are unrelated to the system's data.

REALITY CHECK   **Eliminating Waste**   In this section, we cited a number of different ways to eliminate waste inherent in business processes.

1. Identify several situations you have encountered in which a business process operated in a way that appeared to be wasteful.

2. For each of these situations, explain why this section's various approaches for eliminating waste are or aren't applicable.

Structuring Work to Promote Best Practices

A basic idea of TQM is that business processes should be performed using **best practices,** the best known ways to do the work. Although individual virtuosos may be able to perform tasks better than anyone else, companies trying to use best practices are not looking for virtuoso performance. Rather, they are looking for repeatable, structured business processes that reliably generate excellent productivity, quality, and responsiveness. Information technology often plays a key role in best practices even though the idea of best practices by no means implies that computers must be used.

As part of their search for best practices, many leading companies do benchmarking studies of business processes at other companies that are not direct competitors. The **benchmark** is the measurable results, such as productivity and responsiveness attained by the company performing the process in the best way. In a typical benchmarking study, Xerox sent its representatives to L.L. Bean, the mail-order clothing distributor, to analyze their process of filling customer orders, involving products that differ so much in size and shape that the work must be done by hand. L.L. Bean was able to "pick" orders three times as fast as Xerox, which later cut its warehousing costs 10 percent by applying lessons it learned about organizing warehouses and generating pick lists for warehouse workers.[17] The secret combined warehouse layout and software. Items in Bean's warehouse are stored not according to category, but according to velocity. The items that sell fastest are shelved closest to the desk where the pickers receive their order sheets. Orders come in randomly, but the software sorts them so that the pickers can combine what would otherwise be separate trips for the same item.[18]

Whether work is highly repetitive, such as transaction processing, or largely non-repetitive, such as writing books, the role of information technology is to perform specific tasks that are highly structured. For example, in transaction processing, information technology can control data collection and validate the parts of the transaction that can be checked automatically, such as whether the customer is on the customer list. For largely unstructured work such as writing books, information technology helps structure parts of storing, changing, and publishing the manuscript but may play no role whatsoever in the creative work of deciding what to say. Whether or not the overall process is repetitive, people doing repetitive tasks never have to guess about how to do them. Instead, they do them according to best practices and devote more of their time and effort to the novel parts of their work.

The value of structuring the repetitive parts of work is apparent in the use of a Contract Drafting System at Nynex, which provides local telephone service in the Northeast. To place one of dozens of multimillion-dollar orders for cable and other supplies, an internal buyer sits at a computer and answers a set of questions involving things such as the supplier's name, contract duration, and contract extension options. A half hour and 25 to 35 questions later, the system prints out a comprehensive 14-page agreement tailored to the transaction. This bypasses four hours of the buyer's time, two hours of attorney time, and four hours of word processing. Such systems promise to slash corporate legal costs on routine legal documents.[19]

Minimizing the Burden of Record Keeping, Data Handling, and General Office Work

Since processing data is included in most jobs, improving the way people process data is an obvious place to look for information system applications. This section mentions several approaches for thinking about minimizing the burden of record keeping, data handling, and general office work.

Focus on basic data processing tasks: Reducing the burden of record keeping means being more efficient and effective with the six components of data processing. Those components are capturing, transmitting, storing, retrieving, manipulating, and displaying data. Table 6.2 presents common ideas for identifying opportunities in each of these areas.

Capture data automatically when generated: Capturing data automatically at the time of data generation is especially important in minimizing the burden of record keeping. The alternative is to generate the data and later perform recording or transcription steps that handle the same data again and often introduce errors. Some factories capture data automatically by placing bar codes on individual items that are being manufactured. Whether the item is a car or a computer terminal, a bar-code reader records changes in the item's status automatically when the item moves past particular points in the production line.

Capture data as a byproduct of other tasks: A related way to minimize the burden of record keeping is to make it a byproduct of other parts of the business process. Consider the use of bar coding as part of customer checkout. Instead of having two separate subprocesses, creating a customer bill and collecting inventory data about what was sold, use of bar codes to generate the bill permits both to happen at the same time. In addition to eliminating a separate step in the inventory replenishment process, efficient entry of transaction data also affects the customer's perception of service quality. Toys 'R' Us spent $30 million to install bar-code scanners in its stores, thereby cutting the average time to ring up a sale to two minutes.[20]

Structure general office tasks: Although a lot of nonrepetitive work occurs in offices, many work steps in handling documents and messages are repetitive and can be performed by structuring them in terms of best practices. Prior to current OAS and communication systems, huge amounts of time were wasted on activities such as retyping or reformatting the same letter or document, setting up meetings involving many people, converting notes and ideas into finished documents, recording messages and transmitting them to the recipient, storing and retrieving personal documents, and performing calculations. Just having the tools doesn't solve anything, however, unless the tools are integrated into the way people perform general office work.

Table 6.2 Efficiency and Effectiveness Guidelines for Data Processing.

Data Processing Activity	Guideline	Description or Example of the Problem the Guideline Addresses
Capturing data	• Capture a given item of data only once. • Capture data automatically rather than by keying it in or using other inefficient and error-prone methods. • Include in data capture techniques the identification of obvious or likely errors in the data.	• Many firms capture the same items of personnel and customer data in multiple systems. • Reduce the burden of capturing data for tracking work, inventory levels, and other business activities. • Accepting erroneous data and correcting it later is much less efficient.
Transmitting data	• Transmit data in the least expensive way. • Transmit whatever type of data is really needed, including tabular data, text, pictures, sounds, and video. • Require immediate, automatic confirmation of receipt of transmitted data.	• Failure to select the cheapest carrier for a phone call can cause unnecessary expenses. • Long-distance meetings are difficult using only telephones. • Without confirmation, there is no way to know the message was actually received.
Storing and retrieving data	• Store a given item of data only once. • Make the form of the storage and retrieval details invisible to the user. • Make it easy for users to retrieve data they need from the database. • Store data using data structures that facilitate the types of retrieval that will be needed.	• Avoid maintaining redundant copies of data unless this is necessary for efficient report generation or transaction processing. • Many users do not understand exactly how data are stored inside systems and do not want to know. • Many systems are inflexible and give the user limited control beyond a choice of preformatted reports. • Data structures inappropriate for the end-use consume computing resources inefficiently.
Manipulating data	• Enable users to control the manipulation of data. • Warn users when the way the data are being manipulated will likely produce bad or misleading results. • Help the users by providing data, manipulation capabilities, and models to the extent needed.	• Many existing systems provide the users only preformatted reports. • For example, extrapolations beyond the range of the original data are often misleading. • Many systems provide data but not analytical capabilities or models.
Displaying data	• Make the display of data independent of the way the data are stored. • Make the display of data controllable by users. • Display only the information the user needs.	• Data should be stored to maximize the efficiency of storage and retrieval but displayed in the way most helpful to the user. • Users' information needs change. If they cannot control the display of data, they cannot get what they want. • Many existing systems fail to filter out unneeded data, overload users with inappropriate data, and produce unnecessary paper.

Supporting Appropriate Work Flows

A basic choice in designing a business process involves the size of the tasks within the process and the way those tasks are distributed among the people doing the work. At one time, most manufactured items were produced by craft specialists who did the entire job. But craft production is slow, and the results are not standardized.

Henry Ford invented the assembly line to attain mass production by engineering the entire process to tight specifications. With an assembly line, each worker specializes in a small task performed repeatedly in a standard way. This approach gives the benefits of mass production but has many disadvantages. Workers in many assembly lines lose interest in their work because their tasks are so small. They feel like cogs in a machine rather than people using their intelligence. To differing degrees, automobile assembly plants and other factories have modified their assembly lines to permit more work by teams performing larger tasks and controlling distribution of work among their members.

Assembly line processes have been adopted for many repetitive business processes that occur in offices, such as approving loan requests and checking insurance claims. Before redesigning its processing of equipment loans, IBM Credit used an assembly line method starting with logging a salesperson's loan request on a slip of paper. The next steps included entering the request into a computerized system, checking for creditworthiness, modifying the standard loan document based on customer requests, determining the interest rate for the loan, and producing a quotation letter sent to the sales representative by Federal Express. These steps were done by different people in different groups, in a process averaging six days, but sometimes taking up to two weeks. When two managers took a financing request and walked it through the steps while asking people to do the work immediately, they were amazed to find the actual work took only 90 minutes. During most of the six days, the requests simply sat on people's desks waiting for action. Salespeople hated the delays because this gave the customers six extra days to change their minds.[21]

IBM Credit and others with similar processes have moved to a case manager approach (introduced in Chapter 3's discussion of range of involvement) in which a single individual, the **case manager,** is in charge of the entire processing of a case. Instead of specializing in a small aspect of the task, the case manager is more of a generalist. With the new process, the case manager has direct access to all the standard information required and uses discretion to call on specialists in other departments whenever necessary. The new system cut turnaround to four hours with no staffing increase.

An important insight in all types of work flows is that different types of cases can be treated differently even though the business process is structured. Consider a hospital emergency room. Even with standard procedures for checking in patients before treatment, the procedure applied to an emergency room case should depend on whether the patient's problem is life threatening, such as respiratory failure or severe bleeding. At IBM Credit, the new process had three versions. Simple cases were processed entirely by computer, intermediate cases were processed by a case manager, and complex cases were processed by a case manager aided by specialist advisors.

Permitting Work to Occur Wherever and Whenever It Should Be Done

Traditional work occurred in a factory or office during business hours. Today, there is a clear trend toward structuring business processes so that the work occurs wherever and whenever it should be done. Many customer service operations are even moving toward the goal of 24 × 7, shorthand for the ability to provide service any time of any day of the week.

We will look at three of many possible ways to permit work to occur wherever and whenever it should be done. One approach is transferring work to customers that would otherwise be done by company personnel. Another is providing ways for employees to do work wherever they happen to be, whether at the office, at home, or on the road. Some global companies even pass work around the world to improve response time.

Transferring work to customers

Companies traditionally have done work that customers might have been willing and able to do themselves if business processes were structured differently. For example, the traditional process of entering orders involved receiving an order from a customer, entering the order into a computer system, and eventually sending the material and an invoice back to the customer. But the customer order was often already on a computer. Reentering the order caused delays, provided no additional value for the customer, and sometimes introduced errors.

Using information technology to change the process, many companies now permit direct transfers of orders from a customer's information system into their information systems. This is one of many forms of electronic data interchange (which we will discuss later under the topic of automating the customer interface).

Remote work and telecommuting

Remote work is work done somewhere other than the organization's office or work-place. Although few jobs can be done effectively without occasionally meeting with co-workers, managers, and subordinates, the work in many businesses can be done without being on the premises. Common reasons for doing remote work include time wasted in commuting, availability of trained workers at remote locations, and responsibilities at home.

An important example of remote work is telemedicine, transmission of medical images such as x-rays to make them available to specialists at remote locations (see Figure 6.6). Telemedicine has started slowly in part because high-resolution images require high capacity data transmission. Rural areas are the biggest potential beneficiaries because they lack specialists who can read subtle x-rays and diagnose unusual symptoms.

Figure 6.6 Telemedicine

This doctor is "reading" a color x-ray taken in a different city.

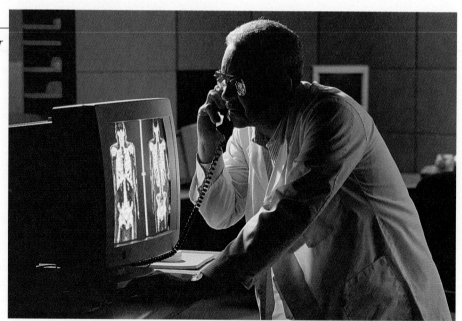

The combination of computer and communication technology allows sales-people, field service representatives, managers, and others to do some information-related work wherever they happen to be. Laptop computers can be used on airplanes for sales summaries and expense reports. Cellular phones can be used for phone calls while driving to the morning's first appointment. These tools for remote work almost make it possible to define one's office as wherever one happens to be.

Computer and communications technologies have also made it more effective for people to do at least some of their work at home, thereby avoiding the wasted time and effort in traffic. Using telecommunications to permit working at home and avoiding travel to an office even has a name, **telecommuting.** The ability to transmit computerized data, send documents by fax, and work collaboratively at a distance is increasing rapidly. Figure 6.7 shows equipment in a home office designed for remote work. As we move toward global communications, the ability of educated people throughout the world to do knowledge work either at home or wherever they happen to be will increase. Correspondingly, the competitive advantage of living near the customer or employer may decrease.

Figure 6.7 A Home Office

Having a personal computer, fax machine, modem, copier, and laser printer at home permits many people to work productively without commuting to an office every day.

Time shifting

Time shifting means doing something whenever it is most convenient, not on a schedule set by someone else. VCRs permit an everyday example of time shifting by permitting television viewers to record a program and watch it whenever they want to.

Global companies have started exploiting time shifting by creating around the clock business processes thay pass work around the world. When Texas Instruments had to generate a price quote for a new hand held electronic device, a design team in Dallas began the work. At the end of their workday, they transmitted their work to Tokyo. The designers in Japan later transmitted their work to a design team in Nice, France. A price quote and a computer-generated sketch of the product were ready in Dallas the next day.[22]

Structuring Work to Promote Best Practices   Methods for structuring work to promote best practices range from reducing the burden of record keeping and general office work through restructuring work flows and permitting work to be done wherever and whenever it should be done.

1. Think about the different types of work you or your family or friends do, and identify instances of this work that might be done better if some of these ideas could be applied.

2. Explain why you do or do not think information technology will have an important effect on where and when you do your professional work in the future.

Automating Work

Another way to change the nature of business processes is to automate a substantial part of the work, the mere mention of which raises fears in many people. Sometimes the fears are based on misunderstandings, but in other cases jobs are threatened directly, even if the people displaced might find other jobs elsewhere. For example, between 1994 and 1997, Ohio's Huntington Bancshares plans to close up to 40 percent of its 350 traditional branches, leaving only ATMs and specialized video phone devices in their place.[23]

Such situations remind us that changing business processes through automation or any other process improvement approach has implications for both participants and customers and raises many ethical questions in addition to typical efficiency versus effectiveness tradeoffs. Since human and ethical issues related to systems will be the main topic of Chapter 8, we will focus here on basic ideas about the types of processes that can be automated using information systems.

In general, structured work involving a lot of data processing is often a good candidate for automation. Automation starts with automating record keeping but can also include automating the value-added steps that directly create value for customers.

In **automating record keeping,** the real work is still done by people, whereas the record keeping is electronic. For example, the real work might be performing an operation in a hospital; the record keeping is collection of data about what was done and what the results were. Wherever practical, data generated by the real work should be entered into a computer automatically on being created. Doing this avoids errors and minimizes delays in making data available to the people doing the real work.

The distinction between real work and record keeping is not so clear for jobs such as supermarket checkout and inventory clerk. Bar-code scanners have reduced the need to enter item codes and prices into cash registers and have eliminated many data entry errors. Bar-code data entry has also reduced the importance of many job skills, such as remembering product codes and prices.

Automating value-added work means substituting machines for the people whose work formerly added value for customers. In factories, the automated steps might involve moving material, drilling holes, or assembling devices. In sales, the automated work might involve demonstrating a customer option or calculating a price bid.

To present the various sides of automation, we will look at three types of automation in more detail: automating customer interfaces, automating design work, and automating manufacturing.

Automating Customer Interfaces

Firms have many interfaces with customers, including advertising, direct selling methods, product distribution methods, and service after the sale. ATMs, telephone answering systems, and autodialing will be used to illustrate a trend toward automating customer interfaces.

The opening case in Chapter 1 explained that ATMs are an important customer interface for many banks. ATMs automate work a human teller would have done for certain simple transactions, such as making deposits or withdrawing cash. As with much automation, the purpose of ATMs is not just to do what people would do, but to do it better. ATMs can be spread across a city economically, can be open any time of day or night, and don't need the training and management human tellers require. Since ATMs tie into networks, a customer from Kansas can use an ATM system to deposit or withdraw money not only at home, but across the United States and even in some cities in Europe. ATMs did more than replace tellers because they transformed the way some customers interact with their banks. Participation in ATM networks has become a competitive necessity for most large banks because customers appreciate the convenience of these automated interfaces.

Telephone answering systems are another form of automated customer interface. These systems answer incoming phone calls by greeting the customer and offering several options, such as "Please press 1 for store hours and locations, 2 for recorded information about our big September sale, and 3 to speak to a customer service representative." Each of these options may bring up additional choices, such as "Please press 1 for exchanges and returns, 2 for deferred payment plans, and 3 for anything else our associates can help with." Although these automated dialogues can be tedious, customers have begun to accept them as part of normal business practice.

Automated systems that automatically dial customers and leave prerecorded messages are not so well accepted. In fact, they were banned by the Federal Consumer Protection Act of 1991. This law was disputed by owners of small companies such as the A-Aa-1-Lucky Leprechaun chimney sweeping company in Keizer, Oregon. It had purchased a $1,800 system that dials telephone numbers, delivers a recorded sales pitch, and lets potential customers leave messages. For many people, such calls are an intrusion, but the company owners maintained this type of system is the key to survival for many small businesses. In 1993, a court granted a preliminary injunction preventing the Federal Communications Commission from enforcing the 1991 ban. The judge wrote that the law might not make much of a dent in the volume of unsolicited telemarketing calls, and it could wipe out Lucky Leprechaun.[24]

Automating Design Work

Interactive systems have become essential in designing buildings, machines, electrical circuits, consumer products, and even chemical or biological structures. Although they do not automate many of the creative aspects of design work, they have automated some of the labor-intensive parts of design work so thoroughly that even early systems yielded 5-to-1 reductions in labor and 2-to-1 reductions in lead time for some design work.

Using a computer to support a design process is called **computer-aided design (CAD).** CAD requires special software that can accept descriptions of components or processes and can display graphical representations of design data. CAD starts with the ability to draw the shape of an object but extends it much further. It includes the ability to create photorealistic representations that allow a designer to see exactly what an object will look like without ever producing a physical model. Many types of CAD also include the ability to evaluate an object, such as by testing a circuit or verifying that a building is strong enough before it is built.

Table 6.3 shows that CAD systems perform for a designer the same types of functions that word processors perform for a writer. Word processors can be used to create, modify, and evaluate and test a document; CAD systems can be used to do the same things for the design of a physical object. The basis of CAD is the ability to represent design data in electronic form. Whether or not it is later printed out on paper, representing and storing design data in an electronic form means that it can be manipulated and extended much more easily than if it were stored on paper.

Table 6.3 A Word Processor versus a CAD System

Word Processor	CAD System
Create Document	**Create Design**
• Duplicate and use all or part of another document as a starting point (if desired). • Type text at any point in the document.	• Duplicate and use all or part of another design as a starting point (if desired). • Insert objects or links at any location in the design.
Modify Document	**Modify Design**
• Cut and paste. • Change type font, margins, and other physical characteristics of a document.	• Translation (move an object from one place to another). • Scaling (change the size or proportions of an object). • Rotation (rotate an object in two or three dimensions).
Evaluate and Test Document	**Evaluate and Test Design**
• Print document to see what it looks like. • Use computer to evaluate difficulty via words per sentence, grammatical complexity, and other factors. • Use automatic spell checking. • Use automatic grammar checking.	• Display the design in various ways such as wire frame diagrams or photorealistic renderings. • Use computer to evaluate via simulation, mathematical formulas, or comparison to design criteria.

Screen images in Figure 6.8 show how various CAD capabilities improve the efficiency and effectiveness of a business process. If the two-dimensional floor plan were on paper, moving some of the walls would require erasing existing walls and adding new walls. After a few erasures of this type, the floor plan would be a mess. Walls simulated on a computer could be moved repeatedly. But the two-dimensional picture is only a starting point.

The second screen image demonstrates the capability of some CAD systems to generate a photorealistic picture of any part of the building from any vantage point with simulated light sources, shading, and realistic color. Some CAD systems can show the lighting in rooms and corridors at various times of day as well as how rooms will look with furniture in place. The third screen image shows how an industrial CAD system inserted a simulated robot into the picture to see whether the planned welding would be practical. An architect, builder, or designer can use such capabilities to show a customer what the product will look like and how it will be used and maintained before it is built. CAD systems therefore affect not only the product of design work but also the ability to interact with customers.

Having the data in electronic form also creates opportunities to evaluate designs and perform tests without building physical models. It is possible to perform calculations such as the area of the rooms and the amount of paint required. By automating both drawings and calculations, it is easy to evaluate the cost and acceptability of design alternatives. Going further, systems for designing mechanical objects can use the laws of geometry and physics to check for design flaws such as two objects occupying the same space, moving parts that will interfere with each other, or excessive physical stresses that may cause structural failure. Systems for designing electrical circuits and semiconductor chips can run exhaustive simulations to determine whether correct outputs will be produced under all foreseeable conditions.

Aside from the technology, one of the most fascinating things about CAD is the wide range of applications for which it has been used. Although most CAD applications are for electronic, mechanical, and architectural design, CAD has also moved into a broad range of activities that use two-or three-dimensional representations. Orthopedic surgeons and plastic surgeons use CAD to design operations; clothes designers use CAD to design clothes; even hairdressers can use a form of CAD to try out alternative hair styles before they cut hair (see Figure 6.9).

Figure 6.8 From Two Dimensions to Photorealism and Virtual Reality

The most basic type of architectural CAD permits manipulation of two-dimensional floor plans. Powerful CAD systems can produce photorealistic representations, including light sources, shading, and color, plus inclusion of simulated people or robots.

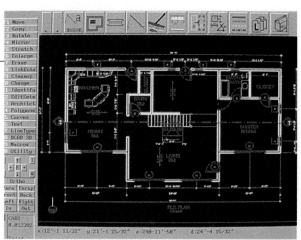

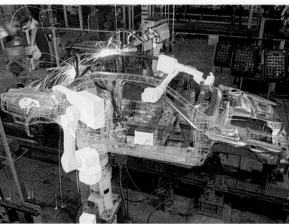

Automating Manufacturing

Mechanization that started with the Industrial Revolution has evolved into today's highly automated factories. Some of these factories operate under conditions that once seemed like science fiction. For example, as early as 1983, a Fanuc factory in Japan producing 10,000 electric motors a month operated with people doing maintenance during the day and only robots working at night. The factory contains 60 machining cells and 101 robots and produced 900 types and sizes of motor parts in lots ranging from 20 to 1,000.[25]

Automated manufacturing works only if the product is designed to be manufactured automatically. Consider the IBM ProPrinter for personal computers. In their study of competitive printers, the development team found around 150 separate parts. They reduced that number to 62; designed it in layers so that robots could assemble it from the bottom up; and eliminated screws, springs, pulleys, and other items requiring human adjustment.[26] If these design changes had not been made, the printers could not have been produced using automated manufacturing. In fact, the design simplifications made the product easy to assemble manually, and it was moved back to a largely manual plant after being started in an automated plant.

This and many other examples show that adoption of automated factories has been much slower than many proponents had hoped. Demonstrating how little agreement there is about the desired degree of automation in some type of manufacturing, Toyota and Nissan adopted different approaches for their new luxury models, the Lexus and Infiniti. Toyota built one of the most automated assembly lines in the world for the Lexus, whereas Nissan decided to make the Infiniti virtually by hand. The purpose of Toyota's approach was to take people out of the assembly process—not to reduce the number of workers, but to ensure consistent quality. At Nissan, workers did some welding by hand, and white-gloved workers later examined the entire exterior of the car for defects.[27]

Automated machinery is actually only one type of component of an automated factory. In totally automated factories, all production is scheduled and performed automatically. This requires automatic material movement, automatic scheduling of all work steps, automatic execution of work steps, and automatic sensing of quality. Information systems play a crucial role in integrating the various components and in the operation of individual components. We will discuss this integration role later.

Figure 6.9 CAD in Unexpected Places

CAD has been used for a wide range of applications, some of which might seem surprising.

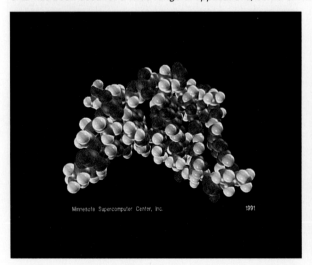

Robots and automation

Just as automation is often associated with automated factories, automated factories are often associated with robots. The term *robot* was invented in the 1920s by the Czech playwright Karel Capek. Today, **robot** is commonly defined as a reprogrammable multifunctional manipulator that can move material, parts, or tools through variable programmed motions. The key terms in the definition are "programmed" and "reprogrammable" since the definition says that a robot is not just a machine that does a repetitive task, but rather one that can do different kinds of things and can be reprogrammed.

Current industrial robots used for highly repetitive tasks look nothing like the humanlike robots in science fiction movies. Most consist of three parts: a controller, a manipulator, and an end-effector. The controller is the hardware and software guiding the robot; the manipulator is usually a device with a movable arm; and the end-effector is a gripper, welding gun, or other device the robot uses.

Since industrial robots are not meant to be like people, they don't do things the same way a person would do them. For example, manual sewing machines and totally automated sewing machines handle simple things differently. A person handling the needle lets go and regrasps it repeatedly while changing orientation 180 degrees. The machine never lets go and uses two threads, one going in each direction.

Robots can be programmed in several different ways, including numerical control programming and training-by-example. In numerical control programming, a program is written that tells the robot arm exactly which movements to make and what to do at the end of each movement. This technique is often used for cutting or forming metal to the desired dimensions of a part. In training-by-example, a person "trains" the robot by guiding it through the path it must take. This path is automatically recorded and can be repeated later by the robot. The recording of the path is expressed using programming symbols and commands that can be modified later somewhat like the way a document can be edited using a word processor (see Figure 6.10).

Most current robots are used in dirty, dangerous, or repetitive applications, such as spray painting, spot welding, and loading or unloading of materials. Robots are also used in automated assembly of printed circuit boards, which can be done much more rapidly and accurately by a machine. Current robots have important limitations in areas such as accuracy of sensing (both vision and touch), degree of programmability, and control of physical movement. With the current state of the art, each robot application tends to be unique and requires customization. Software development and support are critical for further progress. Sensor development leading to much greater visual and tactile feedback is needed for progress in assembly applications.

The discussion of automating work has covered automating the customer interface, automating design work, and automating manufacturing. In each area, some aspects of automation are related to machine capabilities whereas others are related to information systems that control the machines. In all three areas, automation achieves the greatest benefits when it is integrated with other functions in the organization.

REALITY CHECK   **Automation** This section described automation in three areas: customer interfaces, design work, and manufacturing.

1. Explain why you do or do not believe that automation will have a major personal impact on your career.

2. Explain some of the things you think you might do in your career that could eventually be automated and other things that could never be automated.

Figure 6.10
Choreographing Partly
Automated Work

*This man is wearing sensors
to demonstrate software that
helps engineers maximize
efficiency on a production line
where humans work side by
side with robots.*

Integrating Across Functions and Organizations

Separating business functions, such as sales, finance, and production, encourages focused effort and specialized knowledge. However, this separation leads to an inward focus within each function and requires effort to integrate activities across the entire organization. The more integrated an organization is, the more quickly events in one area generate responses in other areas.

We will now look at examples showing some of the different levels of integration introduced in Chapter 3. Linking suppliers and customers through electronic data interchange (EDI) is an example of coordination of groups that do their work separately. Organizational planning processes and integrated product design are examples of business processes in which people from different disciplines work together to accomplish joint aims. Computer-integrated manufacturing (CIM) uses various levels of integration ranging from shared access to information and through tight coordination and collaboration.

Linking Suppliers and Customers Through EDI

The 1990s have seen a strong trend toward integration of suppliers and their customers. The more integrated they are, the quicker suppliers respond to customer requests and the quicker customers respond to schedule changes at the supplier. These effects apply whether the supplier and customer are separate firms or departments within a single firm.

Electronic data interchange (EDI) is the electronic transmission of business data, such as purchase orders and invoices, from one firm's computerized information system to that of another firm. Since EDI transmission is virtually instantaneous, the supplier's computer system can check for availability and respond quickly with a confirmation.

Some of the advantages of EDI are apparent when you look at the traditional way of transmitting data such as purchase orders between firms that use computers. Traditionally, the firm uses a computer to generate a printed purchase order, puts the purchase order in an envelope, and mails the envelope to the supplier. The supplier receives the envelope, sends it to the order processing department, and enters the data on the purchase order into an internal computer system. Thus, data from one computerized system are printed on paper, mailed, and reentered into another computer. An analyst for Sears estimates that 70 percent of one business computer's input is another business computer's output[28] (see Figure 6.11).

Figure 6.11 Customers Link to Suppliers Using EDI

Before EDI, purchase orders and many other communications between customers and suppliers were generated by computer, mailed, and then manually reentered into another computer. EDI eliminates delays and increases accuracy by providing electronic transmission of data from the customer's computer to the supplier's computer.

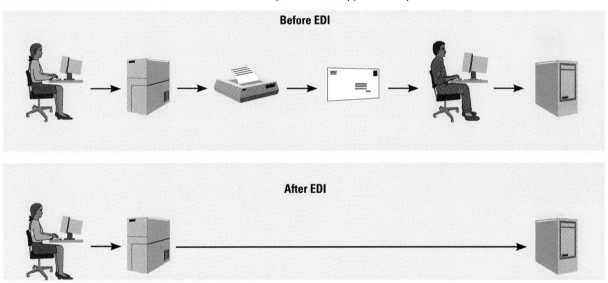

Speed and reliability are major advantages of EDI. It eliminates the delay and uncertainty of regular mail and generates an automatic receipt confirmation. Since both the sending and receiving firm have the same electronic message, EDI eliminates transcription errors that might have occurred when the other firm's clerks entered the data into their own computer.

One of the major EDI successes to date is a national EDI system developed in Singapore. The TradeNet EDI system replaced 40 percent of Singapore's paper transactions for imports and exports in less than one year. It saves an estimated $1 billion annually in reduced paperwork and increased productivity. According to a director of Singapore's National Computer Board, the technology was less of a challenge than the organizational and business issues. The most difficult issue was the cultural change of having traders use electronic documents they couldn't see and feel.[29]

EDI links between suppliers and customers improve responsiveness and coordination while permitting each party to continue doing its own work. The next two examples involve collaborative work done by people in different departments of a single firm.

Supporting Organizational Planning Processes

Organizational planning processes are essential for maintaining coordination in departments and firms. Planning systems help organizations establish mutually consistent financial plans, work schedules, and commitments to produce results. This consistency permits individuals to do their work with a reasonable expectation that it will mesh with the work of others and that the necessary human and material resources will be available. Without these planning processes, different parts of a department or firm would not know their individual plans are consistent with plans of other groups. At best, the firm would be a bit disorganized. At worst, different departments would be working at cross-purposes.

Xerox provides an example of how to use a computerized information system to improve an organizational planning process. Previously, the company's 20 strategic business units each generated plans in different formats, with different levels of detail and different terminology. People came to the annual planning meeting overwhelmed by information. Much time was wasted in the meetings just agreeing on facts. With the new method, each business unit had to submit a five-page plan electronically in a specific format five days before the meeting. The same approach was pushed downward in the organization. In addition, the system fostered more consistent reporting of results and trends across international marketing units.[30]

As an example of how organizational planning processes operate, consider Abbey Appliances. Each month, the finance, sales, and production departments develop a consistent plan for the next six months. They start with the last six-month plan. They look at the results for the month just ending, consider additional information from the market, and create a monthly plan for the next six months. For the plans to be consistent, the sales department must be able to sell what the production department plans to produce, and the plan for the finance department must include the sales revenues and all expenses.

Figure 6.12 shows that the monthly planning process begins with an estimate of demand from the sales department and an estimate of capacity from the production department. The demand is what sales could sell if production could produce it; the capacity is the output production could produce assuming that sales would commit to sell it. A negotiation process begins by converting demand into a rough schedule of product starts in the factory or shipments out of the factory. A model uses lead times and capacities of factory operations and component purchasing to calculate how

Figure 6.12 Developing Sales and Production Plans at Abbey Appliances

The planning process starts with initial estimates of demand and capacity. The sales and production departments negotiate to produce a mutually acceptable plan.

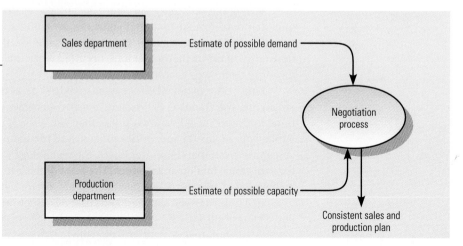

much work would occur at each operation, when it would occur, and what resources would be required. From a sales viewpoint, an ideal plan would meet demand without building excess inventory. From a production viewpoint, the ideal plan would utilize capacity fully, not exceed capacity, maintain steady production levels, and provide enough time for factory maintenance.

Table 6.4 illustrates one of many ways the initial sales plan could be inconsistent with production capabilities. Sales wants to start shipping the new T213 toaster in March and also wants to phase in a new mini-oven starting in February while phasing out an older style. The sales and production plans are inconsistent because unused capacity goes negative; in other words, the proposed schedule would use up more capacity than is available.

Table 6.4 Inconsistency Between a Sales Plan and Production Capacity

	Jan	Feb	Mar	Apr	May	June
Toasters*						
T104	400	490	420	500	550	550
T109	150	150	150	150	150	150
T213 (new)	0	0	100	140	180	180
Total	550	640	670	790	880	880
Mini-ovens						
M123	220	220	200	160	120	80
M124 (new)	0	40	80	120	160	200
Total	220	260	280	280	280	280
Total capacity*	3000	3000	3000	3500	3900	4300
Capacity used	2750	3220	3410	3770	4040	4040
Unused capacity	250	<220>	<410>	<270>	<140>	260

*Note that production is in 100s of units, whereas capacity is stated in machine hours. Assume each month's sales come from the same month's production.

Something has to change. Perhaps the sales department can delay commitments for the new products while obtaining additional sales of an older product. Perhaps the production department can use overtime or change its maintenance or training schedules. Sales and production must negotiate to produce a consistent plan that recognizes their departmental needs. This negotiation starts with the inconsistent plan in Table 6.4 and is revised until a mutually acceptable plan is agreed on. Only when this plan is in place can the finance department prepare a financial plan. It may turn out that the cash flow or other financial results from the previously negotiated plan are insufficient. In this case, finance must negotiate with both sales and production to create a feasible combined plan.

To emphasize the nature of planning, these descriptions stressed the planning process rather than the role of the information system. Information systems can support planning processes in many ways, such as providing background data, performing calculations, and providing models for developing and evaluating proposed plans. They can also provide a structure for combining and manipulating data and for the process of negotiating and distributing a plan. The main role of the computerized part of the planning system was to structure a repetitive process by enforcing requirements for what data people must submit, when they must submit it, how the data will be processed, what the output will look like, and when it must be distributed. This type of system standardizes the planning process but does not automate the decisions. Although it usually leads to better plans than a less structured system, the essence of planning is still negotiation and evaluation.

Collaborating in Product Design

The development of new products is an area where collaboration across functions has generated important benefits. In the past, new product development was frequently a sequential process involving handoffs between marketing, engineering, and manufacturing departments. This relationship between the departments was seen as an interface, with each department doing its own work and passing the result to the other departments. This approach emphasized the unique contributions of each department but has serious shortcomings. Frequently, marketing defined a need unnecessarily difficult to meet, engineering produced a design unnecessarily difficult to manufacture, and manufacturing produced a product that missed some of what the market wanted.

Figure 6.13 compares the traditional approach with **concurrent manufacturing,** a more integrated product development system that has cut product development times in half and reduced the need for expensive redesign work. The basic idea is to use a cross-functional team to define the product. Representing all functions from the outset means that tradeoffs between marketing needs and manufacturability are considered much earlier in the process. Engineering and manufacturing ensure that marketing requirements are feasible and that the product can be produced reliably at reasonable cost; marketing makes sure that engineering compromises don't hurt the product's appeal in the market. This collaborative effort reduces rework as well as delays.

Although concurrent manufacturing can succeed only with great cooperation across the organization, information systems play a crucial role. They provide much of the data used in the marketing and manufacturability analysis. CAD systems store, transmit, and display the design data at each stage. When the design is complete, the CAD data links to manufacturing systems for the production startup.

Concurrent manufacturing is a technique for developing a product. A much more complex form of integration occurs when a firm integrates its ongoing sales, product customization, and manufacturing activities. Systems that support this form of integration are called computer-integrated manufacturing systems.

Computer-Integrated Manufacturing

Computer-integrated manufacturing (CIM) is one of the most extensive examples of integration in industry today. CIM is the use of computers and communication technology to integrate design, manufacturing, planning, and other business functions. It is a manufacturing strategy that tightly links the systems supporting the various organizations involved in design and manufacturing. When people in one department complete their tasks, the data produced are immediately available and usable by people in other departments. Reasons to adopt CIM include reduced cost, better quality, better customer service, greater flexibility in responding to customer requirements, and quicker time to market with new products.

CIM tries to improve business operations through the integration and tight coupling of work in different departments. Computer technology needed to link departments cost-effectively makes CIM possible although a great deal of organizational work is needed before it can succeed. Technical advances in the last decade that have made CIM a reality include increased computer power at much lower cost, better data management, and distributed computing and telecommunications. CIM is one of the prerequisites for advanced factory automation even though it can be used advantageously even if manufacturing is not totally automated.

Figure 6.13 Integration Through Concurrent Manufacturing

In the traditional method for developing a new product, marketing develops the requirements and passes them to engineering, which produces the design and passes it on to manufacturing. With concurrent manufacturing, the three departments collaborate through a sequence of iterations.

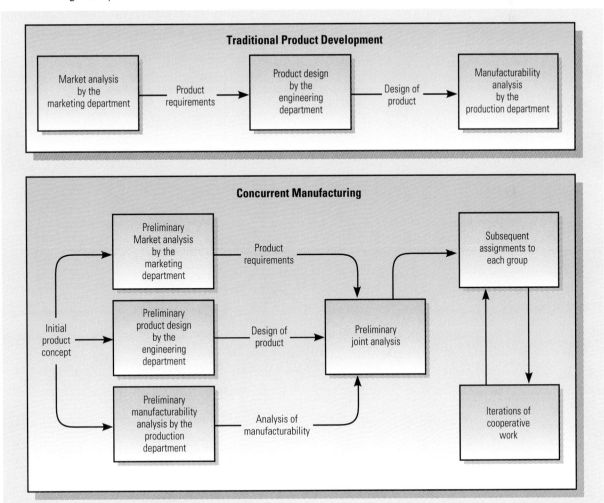

CIM has been applied in a number of ways. Ford Motor Company's electronic components plant in Lansdale, Pennsylvania, focuses its CIM efforts on "agile manufacturing," the ability to respond quickly to customers even with a wide range of product variations. Between 1991 and 1993, the time between receiving an order and shipping the finished product dropped from 7.8 days to 1.2 days. The plant's daily production includes 124,000 engine controllers, antilock brake sensors, and speed-control units, each containing up to 500 parts. The heart of these units is a circuit board. Each circuit board's unique serial number is printed on a bar-code label, which can then be used to track the board throughout the manufacturing process. The plant's information system provides workers with information about product changes and helps them trace defects and production problems to their source. According to an engineer in the plant, "We are more of a software business than hardware. ... When we get changes, the software allows us to accommodate it."[31]

The production of the B-2 Stealth bomber is an example of what has been accomplished using CIM for huge production projects. With around 30,000 parts (many of them requiring state-of-the-art technology), this was one of the most complex products ever produced. Yet it was conceived, engineered, and produced using little paper. The computer model of the plane was so precise that Northrop did not have to build a mockup. Nonetheless, all but 3 percent of the plane's parts fit perfectly the first

Figure 6.14 Components of CIM

CIM is much more than automation. Its core is an integrated systems architecture that supports three major groups of processes.

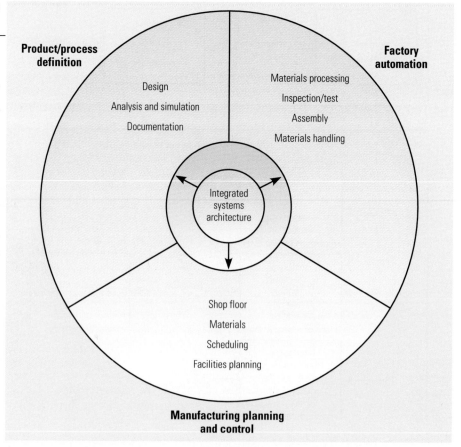

time, compared to the previous Northrup record of 50 percent. Engineering changes occurred at one-sixth the typical rate and were implemented five times as fast.[32]

Figure 6.14 identifies the components of CIM by showing that CIM is a way to improve the total manufacturing enterprise, not just a way to implement automation. The central core is the integrated systems architecture that provides the data and telecommunications needed to support CIM. CIM directly supports three families of processes: factory automation, product and process definition, and manufacturing planning and control. Each of these is subdivided into major subprocesses. Not shown are the surrounding general business processes that CIM may support indirectly, such as finance, human resources, marketing, and strategic planning.

Just looking at Figure 6.14 tells you that CIM is a complex undertaking that encompasses much more than just robots. It calls for planning and long-term cooperation across the entire organization. Implementing CIM in existing manufacturing environments is so complicated that it takes many years. The implementation is typically done in an incremental way so that useful results are obtained while moving toward a long-term goal.

Implementing CIM is a technical and human challenge. CIM technology is expensive and often difficult to introduce into existing factories. Compatibility is a key technical issue because integrating incompatible types of equipment is excessively expensive. Even with the movement toward standards, every competitor is aware that the ability to define the standard gives a significant competitive advantage, at least in the short run.

The human challenge of CIM and automation involves changing the way people work. At minimum, automation requires developing new job skills such as calibrating and fixing machines instead of performing manual production tasks. Many job skills become obsolete, and the new job skills required do not suit all current factory workers. The new jobs may require higher levels of literacy, knowledge, and technical skill, and may rely less on strength and repetition. There is no question that many individual careers will be affected, either through opportunity or obsolescence.

CIM also brings major challenges to management. Merely buying the latest equipment doesn't guarantee competitiveness. For example, a study of the use of flexible manufacturing systems in the mid-1980s showed great differences in the way these systems were used. Flexible manufacturing systems are designed to produce many different products in small production runs using the same equipment. The average U.S. plant in the study produced 10 parts with annual volume per part averaging 1,727. The Japanese plants in the study produced 93 parts with annual volume per part averaging 258. At the time of the study, U.S. manufacturers weren't taking as much advantage of flexible manufacturing as their Japanese competitors.[33]

REALITY CHECK   **Integrating Across Functions and Organizations**   This section explained a number of ways information systems can be used to support integration across functions and organizations.

1. Identify the different functional areas in any business, educational, or social organization you are familiar with, and describe some of the reasons these functions should be integrated at least to some extent.

2. For the organization you have chosen, describe ways information systems currently support integration of functions or might do so in the future.

Chapter Conclusion

SUMMARY

▶ **What are six general ways to use information systems to help firms operate efficiently and effectively?**

The six general approaches address different aspects of how work gets done. These include empowering people, supporting management work, eliminating waste, structuring work to promote best practices, automating work, and integrating across functions and organizations.

▶ **What are the ways to empower people through information systems?**

Empowerment means giving people the ability to do their work: the right information, the right tools, the right training, the right environment, and the authority they need to do their work. Information systems help empower people by providing information, tools, and training although management commitment is also required to provide the work environment and authority people need to do their work.

▶ **What are the ways information systems support the various management roles?**

Management roles can be grouped into three categories: interpersonal, informational, and decisional. For interpersonal roles, information systems support personal and interpersonal communication. For informational roles, information systems make information available and help in analyzing it or communicating it. For decisional roles, information systems provide information for decision making and help in explaining decisions.

▶ **What are the ways to eliminate waste using information systems?**

Ways to use information systems to eliminate waste include eliminating unproductive uses of time, eliminating unnecessary paper, reusing work, eliminating unnecessary work steps and delays, eliminating unnecessary variations in procedures and systems, and eliminating counterproductive incentives.

▶ **What are the advantages of eliminating paper?**

Paper is convenient for many purposes, but it has many major disadvantages. It is bulky, difficult to move from one place to another, and awkward to use for analyzing data rather than just looking up individual facts. Paper is a poor medium for storing data because changing data stored on paper is inefficient.

▶ **How can information systems help structure work to promote best practices?**

Information systems can help promote best practices in three ways: minimizing the burden of record keeping, supporting appropriate work flows, and permitting work to occur wherever and whenever it should be done. Approaches for minimizing the burden of record keeping include capturing data automatically when generated, capturing data as a byproduct of other tasks, and structuring general office tasks. Supporting appropriate work flows involves combining features of two ways to organize work, assembly line work and case management. Permitting work to occur wherever and whenever it should be done is accomplished by transferring work to customers and supporting remote work.

▶ *What important areas of work have been automated?*

Automation starts with automating record keeping but can also include automating entire processes or even entire factories. In automating record keeping, the value-added work is still done by people, but the record keeping is electronic. Automating a process means substituting machines for the people who formerly performed that process.

▶ *What can current robots do?*

A robot is a reprogrammable multifunctional manipulator designed to move material, parts, or tools through variable programmed motions. Most current robots are used in applications that are dirty, dangerous, or totally repetitive such as spray painting, spot welding, loading or unloading of materials, and assembly of circuit boards.

▶ *How is it possible to integrate suppliers and customers?*

The more integrated suppliers and customers are, the quicker suppliers respond to customer requests and the quicker customers respond to schedule changes at the supplier. Retailing and distribution are areas where high degrees of integration have been achieved using electronic access and electronic handoffs between marketing, production, and distribution. Electronic data interchange (EDI) has also served an important integrating role between suppliers and customers.

▶ *Why is computer-integrated manufacturing (CIM) necessary for highly automated factories?*

CIM is the use of computers and communication technology to integrate design, manufacturing, planning, and other business functions. Robots and other components of factory automation are just part of CIM. CIM supports three families of processes: factory automation, product and process definition, and manufacturing planning and control. In turn, all these require an integrated systems architecture that permits machines and systems to communicate.

INTERNATIONAL VIGNETTE

Germany: Siemens Nixdorf Service Redesigns Its Basic Processes

Siemens Nixdorf Service is a $2.1 billion firm that installs, services, and maintains computer hardware and software sold by recently merged Siemens and Nixdorf. In 1991, a business redesign team projected losses by 1995 as competition increased. Before the redesign, Siemens Nixdorf Service operated through 30 support centers, 20 of which were in Germany. Although these centers were fully staffed with technical specialists who were available to answer customer's calls, only 10 to 12 percent of the service issues could be resolved by phone, and service technicians were often dispatched to the customer's location. Although most repairs were completed within several days, two customer visits were often required: the first to diagnose the problem and decide what should be done and the second to install parts after picking them up at a customer service office.

The process was revised to solve the customer's problem as quickly as possible. The number of support centers was reduced from 30 to 5, each of which had a higher level of technical knowledge. In about 80 percent of the cases, the technical expert could diagnose the problem over the phone. Either the parts would be sent to the customer by air freight or the service technician would bring them on the first visit. To support these and other changes, the management structure was simplified, and measurements and incentives were changed to focus on quick problem resolution and customer satisfaction. A pilot study of the new methods produced an increase in technician productivity from two to four customer calls per day. Return trips to the customer were largely eliminated, and the percentage of calls solved remotely increased to 25 percent.

> Source: Hall, Gene, Jim Rosenthal, and Judy Wade. "How to Make Reengineering Really Work." *Harvard Business Review,* Nov.–Dec. 1993, pp. 119–131.

- Use the WCA framework to organize your understanding of this vignette and to identify important topics that are not mentioned.

- What issues (if any) make this case interesting from an international or intercultural viewpoint?

- If such large improvements were possible, why do you think they weren't undertaken in the past?

REAL-WORLD CASES

City of Chicago: Improving Parking Enforcement

The ineffectiveness of Chicago traffic court was painfully obvious. It took an average of two years before a parking ticket appeared in the city's microfilmed files. Most cases that reached traffic court were dismissed because the ticketing officer failed to appear. During the 1980s, 19 million tickets went unpaid.

With a new system built by EDS, the city's 46-member parking enforcement staff writes tickets using handheld computers that include small printers. The 14,000 parking tickets a day written by police officers are delivered to the traffic court building and stored. Anyone who doesn't pay promptly receives a computer-generated letter. Replacing the thick paper printouts the parking staff previously used to identify cars with overdue tickets, the handheld computers permit the enforcement staff to punch in a license plate and receive an immediate response showing whether the car has outstanding tickets. After five unpaid tickets, the city immobilizes the car with a wheel-clamp. Parking ticket revenues nearly doubled after the system was implemented.

> Sources: Henkoff, Ronald. "Some Hope for Troubled Cities." *Fortune,* Sept. 9, 1991, pp. 121-128. Weber, Thomas E. "Portable Pioneers." *Wall Street Journal,* Nov. 16, 1992, p. R24.

- Use the WCA framework to organize your understanding of this case and to identify important topics that are not mentioned.

- Explain how this system would affect a typical automobile owner in Chicago.

Entergy Enterprises: Installing "Smart" Electric Meters

Entergy Enterprises, an electric utility based in New Orleans, plans to install "smart" meters in up to 10,000 homes in its four-state service area. These new meters will be built around 386-level microprocessors and will measure the exact amount of electricity each major appliance consumes. They will relay that information over a wide area network to a mainframe computer. The new meters will replace previous systems for collecting data about home usage of electricity. The old systems required periodic visits by meter readers who record current meter readings. This was once done on paper although handheld terminals can now reduce delays and transcription errors by permitting direct data entry into a computer.

In addition to providing more precise data for adjusting to second-by-second power demand, this system could provide better information to customers. For instance, customers' monthly bills could show them how they could save money by running their dryers at different times when the electricity rates are lower. In the future, linking this type of meter to a household control system could permit the system to switch off appliances at times of peak demand or cut power when the home is vacant. Aside from questions about economic feasibility, moving in this direction raises questions about privacy because an intelligent meter linked to appliances would sense every time someone opened a refrigerator or turned on a microwave oven.

> Source: Morrison, David. "With Middleware, Maybe You Can Get There From Here." *Beyond Computing,* May–June 1994, pp. 18–21.

Use the WCA framework to organize your understanding of this case and to identify important topics that are not mentioned.

Explain why this system does or does not raise serious issues about privacy.

KEY TERMS

efficiency	template	telecommuting	robot
effectiveness	best practices	time shifting	electronic data interchange (EDI)
empowerment	benchmark	automating record keeping	concurrent manufacturing
logical office	case manager	automating value-added work	computer-integrated manufacturing
reusing work	remote work	computer-aided design (CAD)	(CIM)

REVIEW QUESTIONS

246 **1.** What does empowerment mean, and how can information systems help empower people?

2. How can providing data to factory workers affect the factory's results?

3. What are the characteristics of managerial work?

249 **4.** How do information systems affect the various management roles? *Info, Interpers, Decision*

252 **5.** Why does management information no longer require as much paper as it once did?

254 **6.** How is it possible to reuse work?

7. How can information systems help eliminate counterproductive incentives?

256 **8.** How is benchmarking related to best practices?

9. What are some ways to minimize the burden of record keeping and data handling?

10. What are some examples of permitting work to occur wherever and whenever it should be done?

262 **11.** What is the difference between automating record keeping and automating value-added work?

263 **12.** How is it possible to automate customer interfaces?

13. How is it possible to automate design work?

269 **14.** What are the advantages of electronic data interchange (EDI)?

15. How can information systems support organizational planning processes?

16. What is concurrent manufacturing?

17. What are the primary challenges of CIM?

DISCUSSION QUESTIONS

1. Great Western Bank in Chatsworth, California, started using a computerized 20-minute job interview in which the interviewee performs tasks ranging from making change to responding via microphone to video clips involving tense customer service situations. Bank managers say the system helps weed out the four of ten candidates who would be a waste of time to interview in person. Some weary job hunters find being interviewed by a computer even more depersonalizing than a normal job interview.[34] Explain your view of the tradeoff, if any, between productivity issues and ethical issues in this situation.

2. In 1973, an official of the United Auto Workers (UAW) asked that the following notice be posted on the union's in-plant bulletin boards in General Motors plants: "Quality products are our concern too." A General Motors executive called him to complain that quality is solely management's responsibility and demanded that the notices be taken down.[35] Explain why this story is consistent or inconsistent with ideas in this chapter.

3. Federal Express charges incurred by the New York office of a financial services firm soared during a three-month period. People in the firm had discovered that sending a memo or file from the 13th floor to the 5th was slower using the company's interoffice mail system than using Federal Express. With the faster option, Federal Express picked up the package, transported it to Memphis, Tennessee, sorted it, and sent it back to the same building for delivery.[36] How is this example related to ideas in this chapter?

4. Assume you were a manager of a factory and had just seen a demonstration of a new robotic machine that seemed to be about twice as productive as a person doing the same repetitive task. What competitive, ethical, and practical issues would you consider in deciding whether to acquire this device for your factory?

5. How are the ideas about CIM applicable in a business that distributes products to a dispersed group of retailers, such as clothing retailers or supermarkets?

HANDS-ON EXERCISES

1. The following questions pertain to the use of presentation software and assume that a sample presentation is provided.

   a. Use a presentation software package to page through the example provided.

   b. Switch to outline mode to look at the example in an outline format.

   c. Change the presentation in several ways. Use the outline mode to change the order of the foils. Go into an individual page in presentation mode, and add a picture to the page.

2. The following questions pertain to the use of CAD software and assume that an example using the software is provided.

   a. Identify and try out the various icons used for placing symbols in the drawing.

   b. Using the example provided, move existing elements to a different location, and add several new elements.

   c. Try out any capabilities the CAD software may contain for measuring or evaluating the thing that is being designed. Identify capabilities of this type that might be added to make the software more useful.

APPLICATION SCENARIOS

Global Containers

Global Containers leases shipping containers to companies that want to ship goods by sea. Each container is approximately the size of a railroad boxcar. To lease containers, customers call up 1 of 15 local offices and request what they want. Because the record keeping is done using large, paper journals, it is often difficult to provide a quick answer about whether the desired containers will be available when the customer wants them. Furthermore, it is often difficult to even locate the containers because the 20 local container depots at various U.S. ports use similar paper journals for tracking the location, condition, and availability of containers.

Hank Peterson, sales vice president of Global, has discussed this situation with you and wants you to help prepare him for a meeting with a software firm that has proposed building a system. The system must help in making availability commitments to customers, negotiating container rental prices (which sometimes include discounts), tracking the containers, telling customers when containers may not be available at the committed time, and billing the customers when the containers are returned.

1. Describe the potential applicability of each of the six general ways to increase the efficiency and effectiveness of internal operations.

2. Propose a system that might help. Identify the important business processes, and summarize the database that might be needed. Explain how the introduction of new technology might help provide better service to customers.

DEBATE TOPIC *Use ideas from the chapter to argue the pros and cons and practical implications of the following proposition: Developing a better information system for tracking containers is largely an internal problem that has little effect on customers.*

Wellsby & Wellsby

Wellsby & Wellsby was one of the leading architectural firms in England. Roy Wellsby, son of the founder and currently director of marketing and planning, looked out at the room full of architects working on drawings and wondered how many of them would still be there five or ten years from now. Wellsby had always been a traditional firm, proud of its excellent reputation and staff. In the last few years, however, it had started to feel new types of competition. Small companies had sprung up that used CAD systems to do many simple drafting jobs much faster. Often, these firms could get the same work done in half the time using less-experienced architects with lower salaries. Although Wellsby's prestigious name and reputation have helped maintain its business, Roy wonders how long this can go on without major changes in the firm.

Wellsby's attempts to experiment with CAD had been only partly successful. Some architects loved the new tools and wanted to switch to them immediately. Roy was especially surprised at the dazzling creativity several 60-year-old architects showed after using traditional methods for almost 40 years. On the other hand, a number of important old-timers hated the new system. Godfrey, who had won the national design prize in 1983 for his post-modern "city hall of the future," refused to even try the new system, saying that playing with keyboards at work offended him. Two talented younger architects had also responded in an unfortunate way. Believing that Wellsby & Wellsby was impossibly behind the times, they left to form their own firm.

Roy Wellsby was troubled as he tried to identify the practical alternatives. How could they continue to employ the number of people they now had when it seemed that some of their CAD-using competitors were clearly much more efficient? Even if they moved to CAD, they would still have downsizing problems.

1. Describe whether each of the six general approaches for improving execution using information systems might be applicable.

2. Roy Wellsby seems to think of CAD mostly as a threat. Is there any way he could think of it as an opportunity?

DEBATE TOPIC *Use ideas from the chapter to argue the pros and cons and practical implications of the following proposition: The primary ethical issue Wellsby needs to deal with here is the survival of the firm and its continued ability to compete.*

Cumulative Case: Custom T-Shirts, Inc.

During a freewheeling discussion of how the business was operating and how much pressure they were under, Terry, Dale, and Pat focused previously on communication and decision making. Now they have decided to use another approach. They are thinking about how to improve business processes by identifying and sharing "best practices" for specific types of processes.

They start by looking at some of the general guidelines for business processes, such as empowering employees, reducing the burden of record keeping, eliminating unnecessary paper, and bypassing unnecessary human communication when all that must be conveyed is a formatted message. They also look at the choice between automating a task, structuring it, or just supporting the work with tools and information.

To have something specific to look at, they decide to think about two business processes that might be done more effectively: creating the artwork on a t-shirt and making sure that each store stays within its monthly budget and meets its profit goals. Currently, the artwork is produced in individual stores in one of three ways: the pattern already exists in computer storage, an existing pattern stored by a computer is modified by a store employee while the customer waits, or the store employee uses a scanner to capture a picture or sketch provided by the customer and then modifies that image to make it fit what the customer wants.

The current budget and profit management process begins with an annual negotiation that sets a store's monthly budget and profit goals. Pat thinks the store managers typically try to set the expense budget high and the profit goals low to make it more likely they will end the year below budgeted expenses and above their profit expectation. Either Pat or Dale compares the store to other stores and then negotiates what is usually a 5 to 10 percent increase in the profit goal. At the end of each month, the system produces a report comparing the budgeted amount to the actual results for each budget category, such as wages, utilities, and inventory holding costs. Since sales are somewhat seasonal, with a peak in the summer and spikes around certain holidays, the monthly reports are not totally informative about how the year is progressing.

1. Making any assumptions needed because of the limited information provided, apply the WCA method and the chapter's ideas about best practices and organizational integration to suggest modifications to the process of creating the artwork for t-shirts. Discuss the advantages and disadvantages of your recommendations.

2. Do the same thing for the process of managing budgets and profitability.

REFERENCES

1. Schember, Jack. "Mrs. Fields' Secret Weapon." *Personnel Journal*, Sept. 1991, pp. 56–58.

2. Gillin, Paul. "Mrs. Fields Spin-off Cooks Up Paperless Retail Product Line." *Computerworld*, 1993.

3. Pogrebin, Robin. "What Went Wrong with Mrs. Fields?" *Working Woman*. July 1993, p. 9.

4. Garvin, Donald. "Quality in the Line." *Harvard Business Review,* Sept.–Oct. 1983, pp. 65–75.

5. Feigenbaum, Edward, Pamela McCorduck, and H. Penny Nii. *The Rise of the Expert Company.* New York: Times Books, 1988.

6. Lembersky, Mark R., and Uli H. Chi. "Weyerhauser Decision Simulator Improves Timber Profits." *Interfaces*, Jan.–Feb. 1986, pp. 6–15.

7. Mintzberg, Henry. *The Nature of Managerial Work.* New York: Harper & Row, 1973.

8. Peters, T. J., and R. H. Waterman, Jr. *In Search of Excellence.* New York: Harper & Row, 1982.

9. Rodgers, T. J. "No Excuses Management." *Harvard Business Review,* Jul.–Aug. 1990, pp. 84–103.

10. Poppel, Harvey. "Who Needs the Office of the Future?" *Harvard Business Review,* Nov.–Dec. 1982, pp. 146–155.

11. Kovac, Carl. "Voice Messaging Frees Sales Reps from Phone Booths." *Communications News,* Oct. 1988, pp. 80–81.

12. Rohan, Thomas M. "Factories of the Future." *Industry Week,* Mar. 21, 1988, pp. 33–66.

13. Bulkeley, William M. "Advances in Networking and Software Push Firms Closer to Paperless Office." *Wall Street Journal*, Aug. 5, 1993, p. B1.

14. Mamis, Robert A. "The Optical Disk: Big Files on Small Budgets." *Inc.*, May 1993.

15. Honan, Patrick. "Computers as Traveling Sales Aids." *Personal Computing,* Aug. 1985, p. 21.

16. Tully, Shawn. "A Boom Ahead in Company Profits." *Fortune*, Apr. 6, 1992, pp. 76–84.

17. Port, Otis. "Beg, Borrow—and Benchmark." *Business Week*, Nov. 30, 1992, pp. 74–75.

18. Main, Jeremy. "How to Steal the Best Ideas Around." *Fortune*, Oct. 19, 1992, pp. 102–106.

19. France, Mike. "Smart Contracts." *Forbes ASAP*, Aug. 29, 1994, pp. 117–118.

20. Dunkin, Amy. "Power Retailers." *Business Week*. Dec. 21, 1987, pp. 86–92.

21. Hammer, Michael, and James Champy. *Reengineering the Corporation: A Manifesto for Business Revolution*. New York: Harper Business, 1993.

22. Magnet, Myron. "Who's Winning the Information Revolution?" *Fortune*, Nov. 30, 1992, pp. 110–117.

23. Hansell, Saul. "Ohio Bank's Strategy Relies on Electronics, Not People." *New York Times*, Mar. 31, 1994, p. A1.

24. Carnevale, Mary Lu. "Telemarketers Fight Banning of Autodialers." *Wall Street Journal*, Jan. 20, 1993. p. B1.

25. Bylinsky, Gene. "The Race to the Automatic Factory." *Fortune,* Feb. 21, 1983, pp. 53–64.

26. Gomory, Ralph E. "From the 'Ladder of Science' to the Product Development Cycle." *Harvard Business Review,* Nov.–Dec. 1989, pp. 99–105.

27. Sanger, David E. "Japan's Luxury-Car Gains Pose New Threats to Rivals." *New York Times,* Jan. 3, 1990, p. 1.

28. Brandel, William. "EFT: If Money Could Talk." *Computerworld*, Mar. 26, 1990, p. 92.

29. Wilder, Clinton. "Singapore, K-Mart Wear SIM Laurels." *Computerworld*, Oct. 2, 1989, p. 2.

30. Rockart, John F. and David W. DeLong. *Executive Support Systems: The Emergence of Top Management Computer Use*. Homewood, Ill.: Dow-Jones Irwin, 1988.

31. Holusha, John. "Industry Is Learning to Love Agility." *New York Times*. May 25, 1994, p. C1.

32. Port, Otis. "Smart Factories: America's Turn?" *Business Week,* May 8, 1989, pp. 142–150.

33. Ramchandran, Jaikumar. "Postindustrial Manufacturing." *Harvard Business Review,* Nov.–Dec. 1986, pp. 69–76.

34. Bulkeley, William M. "Replaced by Technology: Job Interviews." *Wall Street Journal*, Aug. 22, 1994, p. B1.

35. Pfeffer, Jeffrey. *Competitive Advantage through People: Unleashing the Power of the Work Force*. Boston: Harvard Business School Press, 1994, p. 177.

36. Keen, P. G. W. "Information Technology and the Management Difference: A Fusion Map." *IBM Systems Journal*, Vol. 32, No. 1, 1993, pp. 17–39.

7

Helping Firms Compete Through Selling, Pricing, and Product Differentiation

Study Questions

▶ What are the basic competitive strategies?

▶ How can the value chain be used to identify opportunities to use information systems competitively?

▶ How can information systems change the scope and nature of products?

▶ How can information systems be used to improve sales and distribution processes?

▶ How can information systems be used to compete on cost?

▶ How can information systems be used to assure that the product fits customer needs?

▶ How can information systems be used to make products easier to use and maintain?

Otis Elevator uses Otisline to achieve the responsiveness and quality essential to compete in the elevator service business. Otisline is a centralized system for dispatching mechanics to elevators requiring service. It uses a centralized database containing complete service records for each elevator installed. Prior to Otisline, the local Otis field office dispatched mechanics during normal working hours, whereas answering services used a duty roster to dispatch them after hours and on weekends and holidays. These answering services often handled multiple elevator service companies and rarely displayed great interest or ingenuity in ensuring that elevator service calls were answered promptly. Record keeping related to service calls was haphazard.

Otisline improved service by handling all calls for service at a centralized service center that handles 9,000 calls per day. Highly trained, often multilingual operators use complete information about each elevator to make sure that the right mechanic gets to the scene promptly. The system maintains detailed records and reports exception situations such as elevators with high levels of maintenance.[1]

The use of information technology also extends to the service technicians and to the elevators. Using handheld computers linked to Motorola's nationwide wireless network ARDIS, Otis field service technicians across the country can communicate instantly with a central office in Connecticut for technical assistance and job dispatching. Communication can be initiated from a location as remote as the inside of an elevator shaft. Before this wireless network was available, field workers needing to contact the office were forced to secure the elevator, leave the work site, search for a phone, call, and sometimes wait on hold while the elevator was out of order.

Additional enhancements include remote elevator monitoring, direct communication with trapped passengers, and monthly reports on each elevator for subsequent analysis of performance patterns. Customers purchase the remote monitoring function for an additional monthly charge. It uses a microprocessor to report elevator malfunctions to the dispatching office via modem.[2] In some cases, this information can be used to fix problems before they cause elevator failure.

Beyond supporting the dispatching function, Otisline serves as a central conduit for exchanging crucial information among field service mechanics, salespeople, design and manufacturing engineers, and managers. For example, salespeople use Otisline to access an integrated database used for providing immediate quotes to customers.

DEBATE TOPIC   *Argue the pros and cons and practical implications of the following proposition:*
The type of centralized dispatching and remote monitoring used by Otis is impractical with most products and services.

O TIS ELEVATOR IS IN THE ELEVATOR BUSINESS, not the information system business, yet its information systems are an important part of the products and services it offers customers. By centralizing dispatching and attaining better control of the maintenance process, Otis Elevator succeeded in giving customers better service than would otherwise be available. Aside from supporting better maintenance, the infrastructure that supports Otisline is used to provide information to salespeople and as the basis of additional revenue from remote monitoring.

Figure 7.1 Using Information Technology to Make Elevator Repair Service More Responsive and Reliable

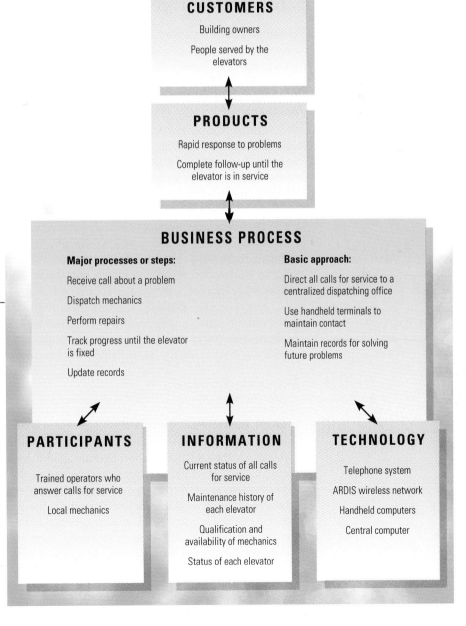

CUSTOMERS

Building owners

People served by the elevators

PRODUCTS

Rapid response to problems

Complete follow-up until the elevator is in service

BUSINESS PROCESS

Major processes or steps:

Receive call about a problem

Dispatch mechanics

Perform repairs

Track progress until the elevator is fixed

Update records

Basic approach:

Direct all calls for service to a centralized dispatching office

Use handheld terminals to maintain contact

Maintain records for solving future problems

PARTICIPANTS

Trained operators who answer calls for service

Local mechanics

INFORMATION

Current status of all calls for service

Maintenance history of each elevator

Qualification and availability of mechanics

Status of each elevator

TECHNOLOGY

Telephone system

ARDIS wireless network

Handheld computers

Central computer

This chapter focuses on information systems that have a significant impact on business competition. The previous two chapters focused inward and looked at how companies use information systems to improve internal communication, decision making, and business operations. This chapter focuses on ways to use information systems to improve a company's product and service offerings. It begins by surveying aspects of competition, such as strategic information systems, competitive strategy, ways of extending product and service features, competing on time, and linking suppliers and customers more tightly in the value chain. The bulk of the chapter is organized around ways to use information systems for competing on sales and distribution processes, price, and product differentiation.

Striving for Competitive Advantage

Organizations compete based on their products' **value chains,** the series of activities that create the value customers pay for (see Chapter 2). Products enjoy **competitive advantage** when their value chains outperform those of rival products by providing more value to customers or the same value at a lower cost. Products can compete on many aspects of value, such as better features, higher quality, better service, or greater availability.

Competitive advantage comes from many sources. Some companies have a natural competitive advantage (for example, a steel mill that has lower transportation costs because it is near a good source of iron ore and coal). Others must create competitive advantage through superior product design, marketing, customer service, or distribution channels. Information systems are one of many ways in which a company can either create competitive advantage or counteract competitors' advantages.

The first computerized information systems focused primarily on support functions such as accounting, record keeping, and providing information for management. Although these tasks supported the primary activities on a product's value chain, they affected a product's competitive stance only indirectly. Even if these systems reduced the organization's costs, the customer rarely perceived their impact directly.

More recently, organizations have used information systems that directly affect their products' value chains. Some of these systems eliminate unnecessary activities or combine the work of different departments to improve quality and responsiveness; in other cases, they extend or improve the product itself.

Strategic Information Systems

Information systems that play a major role in a product's value chain are often called **strategic information systems.** Although there is no clear-cut separation between strategic information systems and other systems, a number of characteristics indicate whether an information system should be considered strategic. Systems should be seen as strategic if they help differentiate the product from its competitors; if the customers directly perceive the value of the information system to them; or if the product's production, sales, and service require the system. Typically, strategic information systems increase the customer's perceived value by providing information and services with products, customizing products, eliminating delays, improving reliability, making products easier to use, bypassing intermediaries, or reducing transaction times.

We will look briefly at strategic information systems used by Merrill Lynch, McKesson, and USAA. Although these systems differ in many ways, they all play an essential role in providing products and services for customers.

The oldest example involves Merrill Lynch's Cash Management Account, introduced in 1977 as a way to combine three previously distinct investment services: credit using a margin account, cash withdrawal using a check or Visa card, and automatic investment of cash in a money market. The Cash Management Account was aimed at customers who were tired of the confusion and inefficiency of having too many different accounts in too many different places. Combining these services required a state-of-the-art transaction processing system. Building such a system along with developing the other business activities required for a product of this type was so complex that Merrill Lynch enjoyed a monopoly for four years. It had gained over 450,000 new customers by the time its competitors could respond with a me-too product of a type that is now commonplace.

McKesson, a distributor of pharmaceuticals, used an innovative system to help its customers simultaneously achieve two seemingly contradictory goals: reducing inventory costs and avoiding stock-outs. The traditional system pharmacies used for ordering inventory from distributors was inefficient and prone to error. A pharmacy employee checked the pharmacy's inventory, recorded amounts needed, and mailed orders to distributors, who responded days later. Delays in all the steps and errors in transcribing information several times forced pharmacies to tie up money in large inventories. To minimize these problems, McKesson's system allows pharmacies to record their orders using a handheld calculatorlike terminal. Bar-code labels on shelves make it unnecessary to even write product names. Orders recorded on the terminal are transmitted over phone lines to McKesson's computer system and entered automatically. McKesson attained a competitive edge by reducing its internal costs, reducing customers' internal costs, and providing better customer service. The benefits for McKesson included a reduction in order entry clerks from 700 to 15. From 1975 to 1987, McKesson's sales increased 424 percent whereas its operating expenses increased only 86 percent.[3, 4]

Like most of its competitors, USAA, a major insurance company based in San Antonio, Texas, once stored most of its customer contact information on paper in a warehouse. Finding a particular document such as a letter from a customer often took a day or more. Working with IBM on one of the first systems of its type, USAA developed a system that eliminates the paper altogether. All incoming mail containing more than a check is scanned and stored on an optical disk. Now customer service agents enter a customer account number at their terminal and receive all the recent correspondence with that customer. This improves customer service because the customer does not have to wait until the files can be located.[5]

These three systems are representative examples of strategic systems that affect customers directly, but many of the systems mentioned in the previous chapter could be seen as strategic systems because they significantly improved the firm's internal operations. With the many reasons for believing a system is strategic, describing a system as "strategic" adds little to our understanding of how it works or how to analyze the competitive significance of information systems in general. Understanding the competitive use of information systems requires looking at the nature of competition.

Competitive Strategy

Consider companies you are familiar with, and think about how they compete. Table 7.1 compares the basic strategies of two competitors in each of four industries. These examples show that organizations compete on a wide range of product and service features. Thinking more generally about competition requires looking at several fundamental ways companies compete.

Although competitive situations vary widely, most companies adopt some variation on one of three strategies described by Porter.[6] A firm using a **cost leadership strategy** competes on lower costs. A firm using this strategy can reduce its own costs, its supplier's costs, or its customer's costs, or it can raise its competitor's costs. A firm using a **product differentiation strategy** provides more value than competitors or eliminates the competitor's differentiation. A firm using a **focus strategy** sells its product or service into a restricted market niche with limited competition.

Table 7.1 Competing on Product and Service Features in Different Industries

Automobile A	Automobile B
Solid car at reasonable price	Flashy foreign car
Good for families	Excellent power and handling
Good service	Image associated with youth and wealth
Long warranty	Reasonably good repair record
	Reputation for the newest features

Hospital A	Hospital B
Best service and best doctors	Lowest cost for the patient
Excellent food	High-volume general care
High ratio of nurses to patients	Few complex cases
Pleasant rooms	Cooperation with local ambulance companies
Ability to treat complex cases	

Cereal A	Cereal B
Product image aimed at children	Product image aimed at parents
Prizes in cereal boxes	Emphasis on nutritional values without sacrificing good taste
Product features aimed at children	Good product features for the entire family

University A	University B
Large university	Small private university
All major specialties	Substantial attention to individual students
Large faculty, including famous researchers	Participatory athletic programs for students
Major intercollegiate sports programs	Strong ties to alumni
Substantial work–study opportunities	

For thinking about possible information system roles, these three strategies can be reduced to two factors: cost and value. If two products provide the same value, they must compete on cost to the buyer. If two products have the same cost to the buyer, they must compete on value. Information systems can reduce cost or increase value. Think about value you receive and cost you incur when buying a car. To most people, a car's value involves more than transportation. Buying a car also means buying a source of enjoyment and an image. The true cost is much more than the purchase price because it includes maintenance, gasoline, parking, and insurance. Expenses after the purchase therefore are an important part of the cost of many purchased items.

The WCA framework distinguishes carefully between the product and the process that produces it. Figure 7.2 illustrates how product-related costs borne by the internal or external customer differ from costs related to producing the product. This distinction is reflected in the performance variables shown in Figure 2.10 in the overview of the WCA method. The term *cost* is used as a performance variable perceived by the customer, whereas *productivity* is the cost-related term for measuring business process operations. Since both cost and value result from what happens on the value chain, we will look at that area next.

Figure 7.2 Internal Business Process Costs versus Costs Borne by the Customer

The analysis of a system should look at two types of costs: product-related costs borne by the internal or external customer and process-related costs of producing the product.

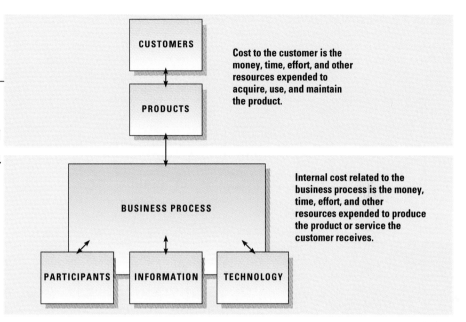

Cost to the customer is the money, time, effort, and other resources expended to acquire, use, and maintain the product.

Internal cost related to the business process is the money, time, effort, and other resources expended to produce the product or service the customer receives.

Competitive Advantage Through the Value Chain

Looking at the value chain reveals a number of different approaches for using information systems competitively. These include competing on internal business processes, viewing suppliers and customers as part of the value chain, and competing on time.

Competing on internal business processes

Although it might seem obvious that better business process performance should lead to greater customer satisfaction, Figure 3.2 made this point in detail. It showed that process performance variables, such as productivity, consistency, and cycle time, have the potential to affect product performance in areas such as cost, quality, and responsiveness. The relationship between process performance and product performance perceived by customers is far from automatic, however. Even internal customers may never know or care about the way information systems helped reduce internal costs or other aspects of process performance.

The previous two chapters looked extensively at the way information systems can improve internal business process performance. To complete the picture, this chapter will emphasize competitive system uses that extend outside the firm by affecting suppliers or customers directly.

Viewing suppliers and customers as part of the value chain

Figure 7.3 shows how to extend the value chain concept to identify different ways information systems can affect the cost incurred and value received directly by the customer.[7,8] It shows a product's value chain extending from the firm's suppliers to the firm itself and to the firm's customers. Steps inside the firm and its suppliers include developing, producing, selling, delivering, and servicing the product's components or the product itself. Steps involving the customer directly include purchasing the product, assuring that the product fits, using the product, and maintaining it.

Figure 7.3 Extended Value Chain for a Manufactured Product

This extended value chain starts with business processes at suppliers and includes business processes within the firm and business processes at the customer.

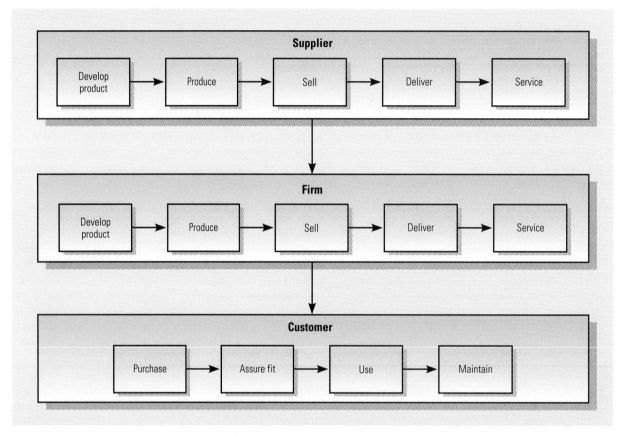

Each step in Figure 7.3 is an opportunity to increase value or decrease costs or prices, whether the improvement occurs within the firm's internal operation or for a supplier's or customer's direct benefit. For example, coordinating schedules between the supplier and the firm can help the firm manufacture its product with less waste and using less inventory. This helps the firm price its products competitively. Within the firm, systems can improve sales processes by providing better information for salespeople and customers. They can improve service processes by maintaining customer records and hastening response. In the customer's part of the value chain, information systems can help fit the product to the customer's requirements and can make the product easier to use and maintain.

Competing on time

Time has become a key corporate resource. **Competing on time** is a business strategy of providing more value by doing things faster, including bringing new products to market more quickly, responding more quickly to customer demand, and providing faster service.

Many companies have slashed both time to design a product and time to manufacture it by more than 50 percent. They have done this by reorganizing work flows, removing unnecessary bureaucracy, and using information technology to eliminate redundant work and speed up necessary work. For example, CAD systems allow the use of computerized drawings and parts lists for the previous version of a product as the starting point for designing the next version. These systems also speed up the process of designing new components from scratch. Designs may be tested using simulation to avoid delay and expense of building unnecessary physical models or prototypes. On completion, some designs can be transmitted to the factory in a form that can immediately drive numerically controlled machine tools.

Thanks to information systems that track and coordinate sales, inventory, and orders, inventories have been slashed 50 percent or more in both manufacturing and distribution. The enabling technology includes bar coding to identify individual items and prevent data errors; data communications to consolidate the information from multiple locations; and rapid computing to convert the raw data into new orders, scheduled receipts, projected shortfalls, and other information needed to support customer demand with minimal inventory levels. Retailing and distribution are also areas where high degrees of integration have been achieved by integrating marketing, production, and distribution. The system is sometimes called *quick response.* At its core are bar-code scanners that identify individual items and provide complete visibility when each item is moved or sold. The benefits include not only inventory control but also increased profitability by avoiding out-of-stock situations that sometimes cut sales by 25 to 40 percent.[9]

Competing on internal business processes, viewing suppliers and customers as part of the value chain, and competing on time are three somewhat overlapping approaches mentioned often in discussions of the competitive impact of information systems. Although they emphasize different points, each of these ideas is related to the way business processes are performed. A contrasting idea is to use information systems competitively by extending product and service features of the offering sold to customers.

Extending Product and Service Features

To describe how information systems can improve products directly, this section uses the marketing concept of positioning. Figure 7.4 shows how a firm's product can be positioned as a combination of features along two dimensions: product versus service and physical object versus information. Following common usage, the term *product* is used in two different senses in this discussion, depending on the context. One sense of product is "whatever a firm sells," as in "a railroad's product is transportation." The other sense of product is "a thing that a firm sells, as opposed to a service it provides," as in "Otis Elevator sells elevators (products) and elevator maintenance (a service)."

One dimension for positioning extends from product-oriented features to service-oriented features. **Product** features are objects or information the customer receives. **Service** features are actions the seller performs for specific customers. In automobiles, product features are more prominent than service features. However, service features determine part of an automobile's value and may be the deciding factor in choosing one automobile over another.

The other dimension for positioning an offering is the way it combines features of a physical product with features of an information product. **Physical products** derive most of their value from their physical form and operation, whereas **information products** derive most of their value from information they contain. Notice that few products are purely physical things or purely information. For example, although the physical features of an automobile are more prominent than its information features, part of its value involves information features, such as the dashboard displays and service manuals. Likewise, the value of information products such as encyclopedias has been enhanced by removing some of their physical trappings. This became clear when sales of encyclopedias sold in the form of CD-ROMs exceeded sales of encyclopedias in the form of a shelf full of hardbound volumes.

Figure 7.4 positions various products along the two dimensions based on their primary value. For example, the primary value in legal advice involves service and information even though a physical piece of paper is often produced. Likewise, the primary value of a pharmaceutical is as a product and physical object even though services and information can be included.

Figure 7.4 Positioning Products

Conceptualizing a product along the dimensions of product versus service and physical object versus information provides a way to position products. and think about possible directions for improvement

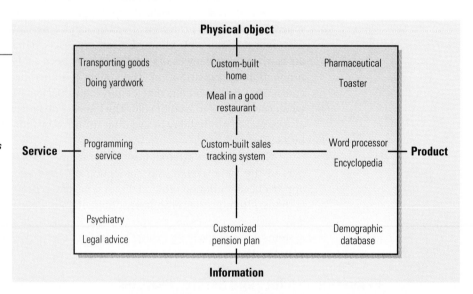

Information systems provide many opportunities to expand a product's nature and scope, such as by enhancing either product or service features. They can improve product features by providing information that makes the product more usable or reliable. They can also improve service features by enhancing responsiveness to customer problems, delivery speed, customization to the customer's needs, and speed and ease of purchasing. Service components can be especially important where a product might otherwise appear to be an undifferentiated commodity.

Figure 7.5 uses examples from opposite corners of the positioning map to show possible directions for using information systems competitively. Pharmaceuticals are products used as physical objects. Their value might be increased by providing additional service and information. Legal advice is information and service whose value might be increased by packaging it differently and giving it productlike features. Any of the products from Figure 7.5 can be enhanced in similar ways.

Figure 7.5 Using the Positioning Map to Identify Product Enhancements

The figure shows possible directions for change in two of the products in Figure 7.4. (a) The pharmaceutical is a product and a physical object whose value to the customer might be increased by moving in the direction of more service and information. (b) Legal advice is information provided as a service. Possible changes in its positioning might move it in the direction of product and physical object.

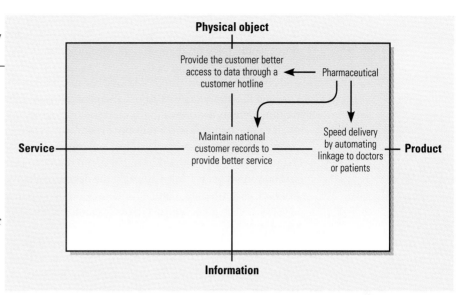

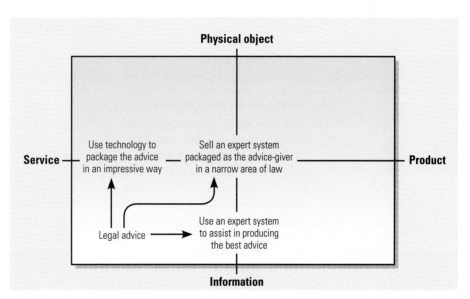

Avoiding Hype: Being Realistic About What Information Systems Can Do

Before we look at specific ways to use information systems competitively, it is important to recognize that competitive uses of information systems have some limits. This is especially important because of the common tendency to exaggerate the importance and impact of information technology.

One of many aspects of business

Since information systems are one of many components of business, attributing business success to this one component is often an exaggeration. "When the Dallas Cowboys were consistently winning football championships, their success was attributed to the fact that computers were used to evaluate and select team members." But when Dallas did poorly, "not much was said about the computers, perhaps because people realized that computers have nothing to do with winning football games, and never did."[10]

The author of this quote disagrees to some extent with the Dallas coaches. If they thought computerized systems have nothing to do with winning football games, they never would have used computers. On the other hand, attributing football success to computers does seem an exaggeration because other factors such as having top players and coaches are more directly related to success.

As illustrated by Figure 7.6, the general point behind the example is that information systems are one of many components of business. The figure shows a business as an engine that contains a number of connected elements: strategy, leadership, culture, people, physical resources, systems, and information. Although it might seem obvious that these elements should be aligned, top managers often reflect on how difficult it is and how many years it takes to attain the degree of alignment that maintains competitive product performance. Figure 7.6 shows that competition is based on firms' relative success in each area. Improving performance in these areas is a key use of information systems.

This book emphasizes the part of Figure 7.6 involving information and systems, but it always recognizes that information systems are one of many components of business success. Figure 7.6 also highlights issues about context, one of the five perspectives in the WCA method. Information systems have to operate within the context of the other components of business. Information systems that are inconsistent with a firm's strategy, culture, or staff capabilities may do more harm than good. For example, an information system that permits different divisions to track inventory using incompatible brand codes and incompatible computers may become an obstacle if the firm's strategy requires close coordination between divisions.

Often a competitive necessity

Some strategic information systems are built not to achieve competitive advantage but because these systems have become a **competitive necessity.** This happens when providing the same capabilities competitors already have or are working on becomes a de facto requirement to succeed in a market. For example, Merrill Lynch's competitors found it necessary to build systems with capabilities similar to those of the Cash Management Account mentioned earlier. Even though this previously unavailable capability was now a competitive necessity, it took competitors four years to catch up.

The typical cycle of competitive advantage followed by competitive necessity starts with an innovation that achieves temporary advantage through information systems. Competitors recognize their disadvantage and try to catch up. Eventually, the competitive innovation becomes a requirement for doing business.

Even when a system requires an enormous investment, competitors can still catch up by sharing development and operational costs. Companies can band together directly in a consortium, as eight major New York banks did when they saw Citibank's consumer banking market share rise. They can also work with a software firm interested in developing and selling such a system.

The history of EDI contains many examples of early adoption for competitive advantage and later adoption as a competitive necessity. Many firms adopt EDI because it provides benefits for their large customers, who need it to make their own data processing more efficient. The impact on large firms is substantial. For example, Service Merchandise Co. estimates that EDI has reduced its cost of writing of purchase orders from $50 to around $13.[11] Firms such as General Motors, Wal-Mart, and Sears have even told their suppliers that they would place their orders electronically or not at all. This motivated small suppliers to move to EDI whether or not EDI reduces their internal costs.

Figure 7.6 How Elements of a Business Combine to Determine Competitive Outcomes

Information, systems, and many other elements combine to generate the controllable results that are the basis of competition.

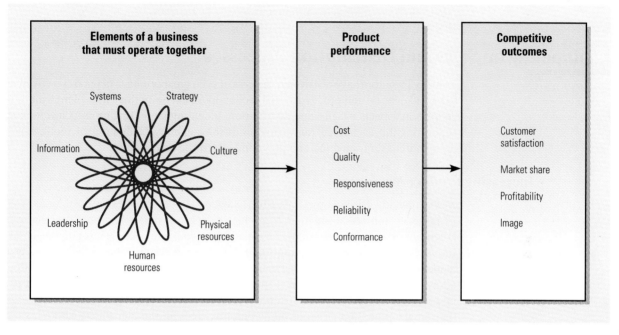

Not a silver bullet

Although examples of the competitive use of information systems abound, there is no guarantee that an attempt to use information systems competitively will succeed. Some strategic systems absorb huge amounts of effort and then fail before they are put into operation. This happened when the London Stock Exchange tried to build Taurus, a paperless system for settling stock purchases and sales more rapidly than their existing system's two-to four-week settlement cycle. This was crucial for the LSE because its two main competitors, the Paris and Frankfurt exchanges, could settle trades within four days.

But the project was canceled in 1993 after ten years of work, $106 million spent by the LSE, and over $600 million spent by other financial institutions rebuilding their systems to make them compatible with Taurus. A project review had revealed that the 1989 system design was too complex because it tried to reconcile too many different interests. Completing it would have taken three more years and would have doubled its costs. Canceling Taurus left the future of the LSE in doubt, with some LSE board members wondering whether London, Europe's leading financial center, really needs a stock exchange.[12, 13]

Even an initial success does not guarantee that a system will provide **sustainable competitive advantage,** advantage that other firms cannot counter effectively. If one firm can build a system, others can often build a similar system. Therefore, the main issue about sustainability is how long any single system or capability will provide advantage before its is copied, equaled, or even surpassed by competitors. This is the nature of competition since most product features or capabilities can eventually be copied or equaled in some way. The most sustainable sources of competitive advantage are the firm's human resources, its major business processes, and its special resources such as patents or land that cannot be copied.

The remainder of this chapter will look at competitive uses of information systems in different parts of the value chain related to customers. First it will look at competitive uses of information systems in sales and distribution processes, then in pricing, and finally in differentiating the product or service being sold.

Competing on Sales and Distribution Processes

As many inventors have discovered, success of even great products depends on effective sales and distribution processes. This section looks at competitive uses of information systems in aspects of sales and distribution, including increasing product awareness, supporting the sales force, improving product availability, facilitating payment, expediting purchasing activities, and providing electronic markets.

Increasing Product Awareness

Newspaper advertising, broadcast advertising, and paper catalogs are traditional ways to make customers aware that a product exists and might be worth purchasing. Traditionally, all three approaches have had a low yield rate because most of the people who see the message are not interested. Information systems that establish and use marketing databases have created many new ways to reduce this problem by exploiting **addressability,** the ability to direct specific messages to specific individuals or groups. By providing information such as purchase patterns, affiliations, and age, these databases make it possible to focus marketing resources on the individuals with a higher probability of making a purchase.

Addressability is the basis of **direct marketing,** the process of selling through mail or other forms of communication addressed to specific individuals. External sources of mailing lists include organizations that sell their membership lists, magazines that sell their subscription lists, and public record information such as births and home sales. Extensive transaction databases provide even more targeted mailing lists by permitting companies such as American Express to send mailers to specific groups of customers, such as those who made purchases from golf pro-shops, those who charged symphony tickets, or those who traveled more than once to Europe. Before these databases existed, direct marketing response rates of as little as 2 percent were considered acceptable. In contrast, Canon Computers used a 1.3 million customer database to achieve an extraordinary 50 percent response rate to a direct-mail solicitation asking printer owners if they would like information on a new color scanner for desktop publishing.[14]

Combining customization techniques with addressability creates possibilities of directing different messages to different customers. For example, *American Baby* uses selective binding to adapt the mix of editorial and advertising pages to the age of the baby in each subscriber's household. *Farm Journal* produces a different edition for each of 5,000 different subclassifications of farm type and geographic region.[15]

Even small companies can use direct marketing techniques based on addressability. Some small clothes retailers maintain a customer list and record the color and size of each item sold to each customer. This enables them to send out pre-Christmas mailings to their customers' spouses mentioning Christmas gifts that might go well with "the tan slacks Terry purchased last month."

A form of direct marketing, **telemarketing** is the process of selling products and services by telephone. Although it requires nothing more than a telephone and a list of telephone numbers, important aspects of telemarketing can be automated. Having the telephone numbers on a computer makes it possible to dial phone numbers automatically and even redial automatically if the line is busy. Once the telephone connection is established, the computer can display a script outlining the main points to be covered in the call. The script can branch depending on responses to particular questions. If any follow-up action is required, the system can record that data in the database. If a product or service is sold, the sales transaction can be processed immediately. Any data gathered during the phone call can remain in the database to improve the targeting of future telemarketing efforts toward this account.

Techniques used for direct marketing and telemarketing have raised controversy about privacy and confidentiality. An example is the public uproar that ended a joint venture between Lotus Development Corporation and Equifax. They had intended to sell Marketplace, a $695 CD-ROM product containing name, address, estimated income, and buying habit data for 120 million households in the United States. This product would have been a valuable source for direct marketing and telemarketing efforts of small businesses with a personal computer. Although large companies could already obtain the same data through Equifax, publishing the data on a CD-ROM made it much more accessible to anyone. Over 30,000 people cited violation of their privacy and demanded to be removed from the database.[16] Similar privacy concerns are felt strongly in Europe as well. In Finland and Sweden, laws require direct marketers to indicate the source of the addressee's name and address.[17]

Supporting the Sales Force

People often have the image of sales work as a matter of charming the customer based on the salesperson's charisma and guile. Sometimes this may be part of the equation, but it is far more general to view successful selling as a business process involving many separate tasks, each of which must be performed well.

For example, salespeople at AutoZone, an auto parts distributor with 822 stores, are expected to ask customers if they need help within 30 seconds after they enter the store. Whether the customer wants windshield wipers or hubcaps, the salesperson can back this service attitude by entering the make and year of the customer's car into a computerized system that responds immediately with the appropriate options.[18]

Table 7.2 shows some of the ways information systems can support various steps in the sales process for industrial products such as copiers, earth movers, or computers. Its left-hand column shows that the process starts with designing the sales program and identifying prospects, and includes steps such as negotiating prices, taking the order, and follow-up to maintain the relationship. Some of these tasks are unstructured, but most of them have enough structure to be supported using information systems, as is shown in the column on the right.

Improving Product Availability

Often people are willing to pay more for a product if they won't have to wait to get it or know they can get it soon. This is one of the reasons people buy clothes at full retail price instead of waiting for sales at the end of the season. Computerized inventory systems provide an effective way for some businesses to maximize merchandise availability without excessive inventory levels. Many large retail chains have developed extensive systems for tracking the quantity on hand of every item in each store. These systems can assure availability in several ways. First, they ensure inventory is replenished quickly after items are sold. In addition, they make it possible to treat inventory at other stores as backup. For example, sales associates at the New York-based retailer Saks Fifth Avenue can use their regular point-of-sale terminals to order direct home delivery for an item located at another Saks store.[19]

Table 7.2 Supporting the Sales Process for an Industrial Product

Steps in the Sales Process	Ways to Use Information Systems
Design the sales program and supporting materials	• Provide information and tools for analyzing strengths and weaknesses of past and current sales processes • Customize sales materials for specific groups of customers
Identify, prioritize, and contact prospects (potential customers)	• Create lists of prospects from commercially available mailing lists or from internal customer lists • Obtain information about individual prospects prior to sales calls
Meet with prospects to qualify their interest, explain the product, and counter objections	• Use communication technology to set up meetings • Use computers to demonstrate product options or simulate product operation • Use databases to provide information for justifying the purchase or countering objections
Negotiate pricing and delivery options	• Perform pricing calculations while exploring the customer's options • Link to corporate databases to find current product availability and delivery options
Take the order	• Perform the recordkeeping related to taking the order and conveying it to the delivery department
Follow-up to maintain the customer relationship	• Maintain customer database • Perform customer surveys • Store and analyze warranty and repair data

One chain of stores that uses a computerized inventory system to the utmost is Japan's 7-Eleven. Its 5,000 convenience stores have limited shelf space but stock over 3,000 items. A network of point-of-sale terminals captures every sale and supports paperless inventory ordering for each store. 7-Eleven plots the sales of individual products by hour of the day and day of the week. This is essential for compact stores that can receive three deliveries a day within eight hours of ordering. Average daily sales per 7-Eleven store are 30 percent more than at Family Mart, its most direct rival. 7-Eleven analyzes the sales statistics to help the stores decide what products to sell and what products to eliminate.[20]

The Walgreen drugstore chain uses telecommunications to ensure the availability of prescription refills for its customers, even when they are out of town. Details of each prescription Walgreen fills are stored in a corporate database accessible from any Walgreen store. This means that the same customer can get a refill at over 1,700 stores across the country. As Figure 7.7 shows, other companies have begun using commercial computer networks to promote and sell their products.

Facilitating Payment

Facilitating payment is another way to help the customer purchase the product. The first use of money was a breakthrough in this direction because it permitted people to buy and sell things without bartering. More recently, checking accounts and credit cards made it possible to perform money transactions without carrying cash. All three of these innovations (the use of money, checking accounts, and credit cards) benefited customers by making it easier to purchase things.

Figure 7.7

800 Flowers uses America Online, an interactive computer network, to explain its products and attract customers.

Credit cards, debit cards, and smart cards all use information systems to facilitate payment for consumers by making cash or checks unnecessary. Credit cards create a temporary loan due within a month after the credit card statement arrives. In contrast, **debit cards** transfer money from a buyer's bank account into a seller's bank account. Some gasoline stations and other retailers have formed alliances with banks that permit customers to buy gasoline using their ATM cards as debit cards. The cost of credit and debit card transactions has dropped dramatically as computer and telecommunications systems have become more efficient. For example, a typical credit authorization from an electronic terminal cost $0.35 in 1981 but costs less than $0.03 now.[21] This is far less than the cost of processing a check.

Smart cards are the size of credit cards but contain magnetically or optically coded data that can be changed. They may even contain an embedded semiconductor chip. Simple versions are used to pay for copies in libraries, for telephone calls at pay phones in Europe and Japan, and for bus rides in New Zealand. These cards contain data indicating how many copies, calls, or rides the user has paid for. The system automatically reduces the amount left on the card each time it is used. Future credit cards may be smart cards that store identification information such as fingerprints and the motions by which people sign their name. This same technology can be used for many applications unrelated to transferring funds, such as replacements for keys and storage of medical records. The near future will probably see a proliferation of smart cards as a replacement for cash and for many other uses.

Although businesses still use checks for the majority of their payments to suppliers, moving toward electronic transfers between businesses has many potential advantages. A number of electronic alternatives are cheaper and less error prone than processing paper checks, which involves, among other things, rushing bundles of checks from one location to another so that they can get to a bank before an 8 a.m. cutoff. Some electronic payment systems create linkages between specific suppliers and customers, whereas others simply replace checks or transfer funds electronically from one account to another (see Figure 7.8).

Figure 7.8 Using Information Systems to Facilitate Payment

(a) The credit card reader built into this gasoline pump facilitates payment by making it unnecessary for the driver to wait for a human attendant. (b) Smart cards like this one are used at some pay phones in New Zealand. Other phones there take cash or credit cards.

A system directed at linkages to specific suppliers is an extension of McKesson's ordering system for its drug store customers. As described earlier, the ordering system provided an online link from these drug stores to McKesson, thereby improving the efficiency and accuracy in the reordering process. Seeing that insurance companies paid for the pharmaceuticals many drug store customers purchased, McKesson built a system that collected funds from the insurance companies, thereby freeing the drug stores from involvement in this process. This system established linkages to insurance companies in addition to drug stores and opened new strategic possibilities for McKesson.[22]

Where the McKesson system is specialized to a particular application, **electronic funds transfer (EFT)** systems serve more general purposes. EFT is the use of computerized systems to transfer funds from one person or organization to another. The use of an ATM is a step toward EFT because the user withdraws or deposits money using a telecommunications network. In a complete EFT link, the entire transaction occurs by balancing accounts on a computer without using cash or checks. EFT between organizations is widespread. Many EDI systems include both transfer of transaction data and electronic transfer of funds. Large-scale transfer of funds is often handled by consortiums of financial institutions that create and maintain the electronic network. These consortiums include CHIPS (Clearing House Interbank Payment System) and SWIFT (Society for Worldwide International Financial Telecommunication). Since these networks transfer billions of dollars every day, security is a critical issue. These systems contain elaborate security schemes to ensure that each message is received intact.

Expediting Purchasing Activities

Any purchasing function in business includes recording data about the purchase transactions. Recording transaction data is essential for keeping track of inventories. Since most businesses would rather devote their scarce human resources to their core business activities rather than processing transactions, effective processing of purchase transactions is another way a supplier can provide value for a customer.

Levi Strauss & Co., a leading apparel manufacturer, used this strategy in developing the LeviLink system, an extensive transaction processing add-on to their usual product offerings. Figure 7.9 shows the system was designed to help Levi's customers, the retail clothing stores, at every stage in the retailing cycle. LeviLink uses bar-code labels affixed on goods at the factory as the basis for material and sales tracking. This system has reduced the time between the order and receipt of shipment from 40 days to as few as 3. By 1990, electronic purchase orders through LeviLink represented 35 percent of domestic sales. Sales increased 20 to 30 percent in accounts using LeviLink because fewer customers left without finding the size or style they wanted. This sales increase was accomplished with lower inventory levels because ordering is tightly linked to sales and because the orders arrive quickly.[23]

Yet by 1994, Levi Strauss was back to the drawing board trying to reengineer its basic replenishment processes because too many customers still believed they carried too much inventory. A 2-year, $400 million project was initiated to be able to replenish all standard stock within 3 days (versus up to 2 weeks) and to change existing stock to a new fabric or finish in 30 days (versus up to 6 months). Although information system improvements were essential, other changes were also required, such as changing the organization of distribution centers and the location of sewing and finishing facilities.[24]

Distributors in many areas such as hospital supplies and pharmaceuticals have moved even further toward expediting purchasing activities by literally taking over the management of inventory for their customers. Working with its hospital supply customers, Baxter International has negotiated risk-sharing arrangements based on setting a cost target and sharing the savings or additional costs if expenses overshoot targets. Hospitals participating in the ValueLink inventory management program cede ownership and management of inventory to Baxter, which will even deliver supplies to hospital floors. At some hospitals, Baxter employees are on site 24 hours.[25]

The "manage my inventory" approach has been tried and abandoned by other companies, however. J.C. Penney dabbled with some pilot projects in this area but prefers to rely on its own experience and systems in inventory management. In general, suppliers who try to manage their customers' inventories have to start worrying about any special discounts their customers are offering and about local conditions such as road construction in front of a particular store. These issues are hard enough for the customer to manage, no less a supplier lacking complete information.[26]

Providing Electronic Markets

Instead of looking for merchandise at a store or in a paper catalogue, shoppers for many types of goods can learn about them and order them using telecommunications. Use of computers and telecommunications to create direct electronic links between multiple buyers and sellers is called an **electronic market.** The trend toward electronic markets provides many intriguing possibilities for making the purchasing process more convenient and less expensive for customers. It also provides suppliers opportunities to reach customers in new ways and to reduce internal costs.

Moving toward electronic markets can have several types of effects on the purchasing process.[27] Compared to a paper catalogue, an electronic market can provide more usable information about a particular product. For airline reservations, an electronic market can list flights in order based on any combination of criteria such as cost, convenience, and airline preference. For other products, the electronic market might be able to show product comparisons, installation procedures, and other information indicating the product's effectiveness. An electronic market can also serve brokerage

Figure 7.9 LeviLink Services in the Retailing Cycle

This diagram identifies a subset of the services provided by LeviLink as part of a retailer's cycle of selling and replenishing inventory.

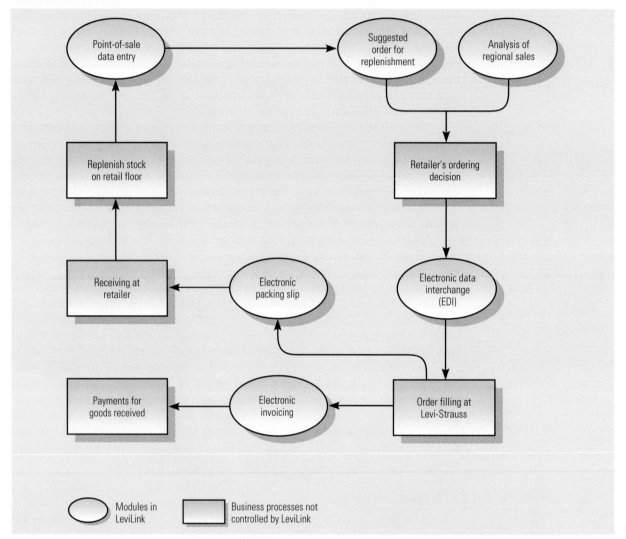

roles by connecting many buyers and sellers through a centralized database. Brokerage effects can increase the number of alternatives considered and can decrease the cost of the selection process. Electronic markets can also integrate within the same system different activities, such as airline, hotel, and car rental reservations.

Changes in the process of making airline reservations show how much is at stake in the way people purchase things. Figure 7.10 shows three of many possible processes for reserving airline seats. In the first method, the customer works through a travel agent who uses a published airline guide but needs to call individual airlines to determine seat availability and make reservations. In the second, the travel agent uses a computerized database of flight availability information. In the third, the customer uses a personal computer to make the reservation directly, bypassing both the travel agent and airline personnel. In the first and second airline reservation methods in Figure 7.10, the travel agent plays the role of broker; in the third method, the computer system plays this role, and the travel agent loses a commission. One of the effects of some electronic markets is to eliminate brokers and other intermediaries involved in purchase transactions.

Electronic markets can create either threats or opportunities for brokers of all kinds, including travel agents, insurance brokers, stockbrokers, and brokers of food and mechanical parts. The threat is that brokers will be bypassed because the customer will be able to obtain information directly. At the same time, a broker has the opportunity to use the electronic market to provide better service than a customer could otherwise obtain. This opportunity is exemplified by the use of electronic markets by Charles Schwab & Co., a discount financial products brokerage. Schwab was built based on the idea of eliminating the investment advisory role of stockbrokers and providing only transaction processing services. As part of this strategy, it introduced an inexpensive software package allowing investors to use personal computers to call up research reports from independent firms such as Standard & Poor's, get current price quotes, and execute trades at a 10 percent discount from their regular low price. Schwab offered the software (see Figure 7.11) free to anyone who transferred $15,000 into a Schwab account. Schwab's Telebroker service also lets customers place stock orders and obtain quotes from a touch-tone phone.

Figure 7.10 Three Ways to Make Airline Reservations

The first method is largely obsolete, the second is the most common today, and the third became possible with the widespread availability of personal computers.

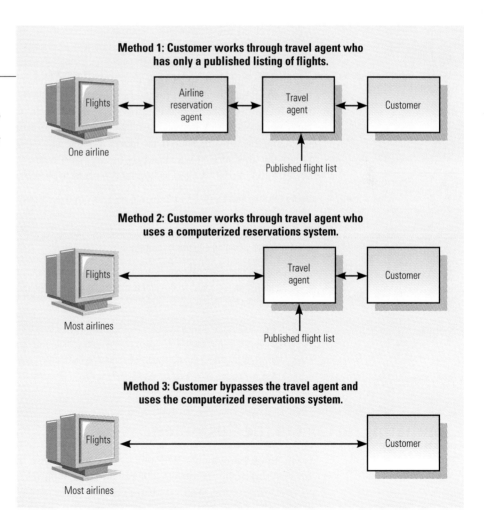

Figure 7.11 Providing Online Access to Lure Brokerage Customers

This screen shot shows how Charles Schwab's Street Smart software provides online portfolio information that helps customers make investment decisions.

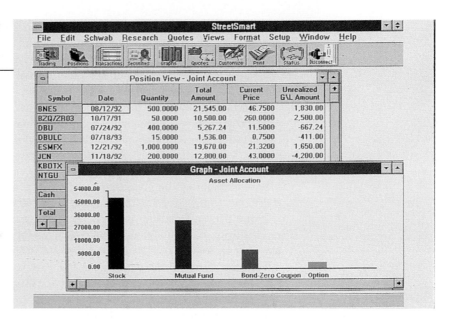

An electronic market for airplane parts illustrates how such markets can turn from an opportunity into a threat. Inventory Locator Service, Inc. is used to find and purchase replacement parts for airplanes. Before this service existed, obtaining replacement parts required multiple calls to parts dealers and brokers. The search was slow and relied heavily on personal relationships. Pressed for time, the caller often purchased the first available part. Inventory Locator Service provides an online database listing the suppliers who carry particular stock items, as well as their phone numbers and other information. By reducing the time to search for parts, planes can be back in the air much sooner. Originally, this service was used by brokers and dealers rather than by airlines themselves. Later, airlines began to bypass the brokers by subscribing themselves.[28]

REALITY CHECK   **Using Information Systems to Compete on Sales and Distribution Processes**   This section explained how information systems have been applied competitively in sales and distribution processes for supporting the sales force, improving product availability, facilitating payment, expediting purchasing activities, and providing electronic markets.

1. Assume that store catalogues and price lists were readily accessible through a personal computer and that stores could accept orders placed through the computer. Identify some of the products you might buy this way.

2. Assume that the next generation of personal computers is much more powerful than current computers. Explain why this might or might not make electronic markets more desirable and how it might affect other aspects of sales and distribution processes.

Competing on Cost to the Customer

Companies using a cost leadership strategy often use information systems to reduce the costs borne by customers. The previous two chapters discussed many opportunities to use information systems to reduce internal costs, thereby making it possible to charge customers lower prices. This section will discuss other information system uses related to cost competition, including providing information needed for better pricing decisions, providing a means to adjust prices and segment the market, and providing cost control information reducing the customer's internal costs related to the product.

Using Information for Better Pricing Decisions

One of the basic ideas of economics is that people use market information to set the selling price of their products. Farmers in Sri Lankan villages learned the value of that information when telephones were installed recently. Until then, farmers had sold their produce to wholesalers for but a fraction of its market value in the capital city of Colombo. After telephones were installed, the farmers always knew the prices in the city market and increased their income by 50 percent.[29]

Information systems support pricing decisions in many different ways. The most direct is simply to provide immediate results about the relationship between price and sales, as happened early in the 1990 Christmas season when K-mart realized its porcelain dolls were not selling as expected. Sales skyrocketed when the manager of toy merchandising cut the price from $29.88 to $24.99, but plummeted again when the price was reset near the original price. This process helped K-mart find a good selling price slightly above $25, and the dolls sold out for the season. With 2,400 stores, monitoring price response this way was possible only because K-mart had an integrated information system that could consolidate sales by product on a timely basis.[30]

Adjusting Prices and Segmenting the Market

Maintaining price lists and product catalogues in computerized form provides a convenient way to change prices rapidly. For example, stores using bar-code scanners for customer checkout can implement price increases or reductions by changing prices in the computer without remarking each item in stock.

An important way to maximize profits is **market segmentation,** dividing the market into different customer groups willing to pay different amounts for different types or levels of service. For example, MCI Communications developed a billing system that makes possible its Friends & Family service, which gives residential customers 20 percent discounts on calls to a dozen preselected locations. The information systems supporting this service helped MCI win market share and increase profits by maintaining its basic prices and giving a reduced price to a specific set of customers, many of whom switched to MCI only because of the special discount. Within several years, ten million customers signed up, taking at least 4 percent of the consumer long-distance market away from AT&T and helping reposition MCI as a powerful $10 billion firm.[31]

Airline yield management systems are the heavy-weight champions of market segmentation. Unlike products that retain their value from day to day, a seat on a specific flight has value until flight time and has no value thereafter. **Yield management** systems try to maximize revenue by selling the same product (a seat on a flight) to different customers at different prices. Since vacation travelers can usually plan their trips longer in advance than the business travelers, there is a natural segmentation in the market. Exploiting this segmentation, these systems charge higher prices for tickets purchased at the last minute and try to fill the planes by giving lower prices to vacationers who can reserve weeks in advance but wouldn't fly at higher prices. The economic challenge for these systems is to avoid two types of errors: selling too many cheap seats that last-minute travelers would have purchased at high prices and having too few cheap seats, resulting in empty seats on flights. These systems also have other challenges, however, such as maintaining customer satisfaction when people sitting next to each other on a flight have paid vastly different amounts for what they see as the same thing.

Providing Cost Control Information

Many business relationships generate a large amount of data, such as customer orders, telephone bills, and insurance claims. Suppliers in many situations have started providing customer-related information that helps their customers control costs.

Telephone companies have extended their product by providing billing information in a useful form. Previously, businesses received paper telephone bills that were hundreds of pages long. This information was adequate for justifying the total bill but useless for analyzing how telephones could be used more efficiently. Recently, telephone companies have begun sending bills in computerized form to help their customers analyze telephone usage and reduce their costs. Other companies have developed software products for analyzing this billing data to uncover excessive telephone use.

Insurance is an area where transaction data has become especially valuable in controlling costs. For example, instead of treating its claims data as a secret, Travelers Insurance analyzes the data for its customers. When Allied-Signal noticed a rise in some of its self-insured workman's compensation claims, data from Travelers pinpointed a large number of hand injuries by maintenance workers. Allied-Signal halved these injuries by providing better training and using gloves.[32]

Competing on Product Differentiation

Information systems are becoming an important tool for differentiating products. This is done a number of ways, including customizing the product and providing information systems as part of the product.

Customizing the Product

An important part of purchasing is ensuring that the product actually fits the customer's needs. There are two stages in assuring fit. The first is to use product information and customer requirements to find the specific product that fits customer needs. The second stage, customization, is often necessary even if the product generally fits the customer's needs. **Customization** is the creation or modification of a product based on a specific customer's needs, thereby increasing the product's value for that customer. A tailor's adjustment of the length of a pair of pants is a form of customization. The result is not as customized as it would be if the tailor simply made the pants for you but is more customized than if you bought the pants and skipped the alterations.

This section covers the use of information systems for matching to customer requirements and then looks at customization of information products and customization of physical products. In many cases, information products are ideal candidates for customization since information is often easier to manipulate than physical things.

Matching to customer requirements

Information systems have been used in many ways to find products that match a customer's requirements. Airline reservation systems exemplify the way an information system can help with product matching. If a traveler wants to fly from Phoenix to

Cleveland around 4:00 p.m. Thursday, the reservation system can identify the most likely alternatives. A system with additional information about the customer's relative preference for price and convenience might even list the alternatives in order of preference. Similar systems are used by real estate agents to identify homes or apartments that meet a client's needs and ability to pay.

The fashion and cosmetics industries have seen innovative uses of information systems for matching products to customer needs. Cosmetics companies such as Elizabeth Arden and Shiseido have used computers to augment their sales techniques. One system allows a cosmetologist to use a computer to try out a number of different make-up combinations electronically. Another determines the best product for an individual's skin type. These systems have generated dramatic sales increases at cosmetics counters.[33] An electronic dressing room called a Magic Mirror has boosted clothing sales by projecting a woman's face, hands, and feet onto a clothed image that replicates her size and shape. This system makes it possible to "try on" a large number of outfits in a few minutes. After identifying the best choices, the shopper actually tries the clothes on. Sales increased 700 percent in an early use of this system.[34]

Customizing information products

Many techniques for customizing information products grew out of innovations for internal efficiency. Consider the impact of electronic technology on publishing. Information in electronic form is easier to edit and possible to review using automatic checking of spelling and some aspects of grammar and writing style. Pictures in electronic form can be edited in far less time than is required by manual techniques such as airbrushing. Information in electronic form also makes it possible to compose a publication in one location and transmit it to local printing presses, thereby avoiding the cost and delays of transporting paper long distances.

These techniques enable both new types of electronic publications and highly customized paper publications. The information in electronic publications is in computer-readable form and, therefore, more effective for retrieving specific facts or manipulating the information. This is one reason bibliographic references and law cases are available online. Electronic publications can be personalized in two ways: by selecting the information transmitted to the individual or by transmitting all the information and then permitting the individual to select and view only the subset purchased. Customized magazines were mentioned earlier as an example of the first approach. Figure 7.12 shows how the customer can participate directly in customizing an information product. Whether or not the second approach becomes popular in some type of "pay for use" for parts of databases remains to be seen.

Financial instruments such as futures contracts and options are also information products and can be combined in many ways to match a firm's financial needs. Virtually any cash flow stream from a combination of securities can be swapped for another cash flow stream as long as a willing counterpart can be found.[35] For example, a firm that sells soybeans around the world can purchase a combination of commodity and currency options that meet its particular needs for protection against changes in soybean prices and currency exchange rates.

Customizing physical products

Customization is becoming an important competitive issue for many physical products. With the ability to link CAD systems to computer-aided manufacturing (CAM) systems, it is becoming more practical to tailor anything from clothes to machines based on the customer's requirements or wishes. This approach has been used extensively by the prefabricated housing industry in Japan. These businesses are set up to standardize production even though the product is customized. This technique is called **mass customization.** Customers meet with salespeople to design their homes on a computer screen using representations of thousands of standardized parts. The completed designs are transmitted to a factory that produces the building's structural components on an assembly line. It takes one day for a crane and seven workers to put up the walls and roof of a two-story house. Finishing the job takes another 30 to 60 days.[36]

Figure 7.12 Direct Customer Participation in Customizing an Information Product

Hallmark Cards has installed over 1,200 computerized kiosks that customers can use to create customized greeting cards via touch-screen inputs.

An attempt at mass customization in the clothing industry is being researched by the Textile/Clothing Technology Consortium, which is sponsored by over 100 retail and fashion companies, including J.C. Penney, Levi Strauss, and L.L. Bean. The research is trying to build a "body scanner" that allows people to buy clothes that fit precisely. Shoppers would slip into a bodysuit and be measured three dimensionally from head to toe. The shopper would select a garment such as a shirt, pants, or a dress, and the system would superimpose an image of it onto an image of the shopper's body, thereby showing how the garment would look. The shopper could then order a custom-cut version of the garment. The body scan (which is done with mirrors and cameras rather than lasers to alleviate health concerns) could be stored and reused for future purchases.[37]

Information systems supporting customization are based on the ability to describe individual customer requirements and feed them directly into otherwise repetitive production processes. Mass customization is a growing trend in many areas of business that produce products based on specifications. The next section discusses another trend, the movement toward applying information systems to make products easier to use.

Making It Easier to Use the Product

Another direct way to apply information systems for competitive advantage is to make products easier to use. This can be done in three ways: incorporate information systems into the product, provide better service, and provide information or knowledge about the product. In the first case, the information system is built into the product; in the others, it is provided in addition to the basic product.

Incorporating information systems into the product

Advances in semiconductor technology have made it possible to build computerized systems into manufactured products that traditionally existed without those systems. A simple example is a coffee maker. Although it is still possible to make coffee manually by dripping boiling water through ground coffee, some current coffee makers contain programmable features that control start times and fineness of the grind. In this case, the computerized system adds convenience but is not essential for the product's primary function. In contrast, some current jet fighters simply can't be flown by an unaided human being. The pilot determines the direction and speed of these jets, while a real-time information system in the background performs adjustments that make sure that the jet remains stable enough to be controllable.

Automobiles are an everyday product in which information systems are playing an increasingly important role. So many electronically controlled systems are being included in planned automobile models that electronics could account for 30 percent of the cost of building a car by the year 2000.[38] Automotive electronic systems that either exist now or are anticipated will improve driving performance and safety and may even reduce driving times (see Figure 7.13). Systems that improve driving performance include computer-controlled gear shifts and fuel injection systems that attain high fuel economy, active suspensions that sense and automatically adjust to bumps and potholes, and traction control systems that prevent brakes from locking. Safety systems include adaptive headlights that turn on and dim automatically, collision avoidance systems that warn of impending crashes, heads-up displays that make instrument readings appear in front of the hood, and antitheft systems that prevent the car from being hot-wired. In Germany, BMW has worked on a safety system that uses a camera to track the center stripe and the line on the side of the road. A future version of this system may be able to tug at the steering wheel when a driver is driving in the wrong part of a lane.[39]

Current automotive navigation systems can track the location of a car and display it on a map. Future navigation gear may receive real-time information from large-scale systems that monitor traffic flows and congestion. By combining this information with map information, a navigation system could potentially suggest the route to any location that takes the least time. Such systems would maximize the utilization and safety of existing highways in congested areas.[40] However, like adding any new product feature, making cars "intelligent" has its risks. Chrysler's Neon auto had three recalls in its first year, one of which was to fix the computer.[41]

Figure 7.13 Information Systems Built into Automobiles

Information systems play an increasingly important role in automobiles since many basic driving functions are controlled or supported using computers.

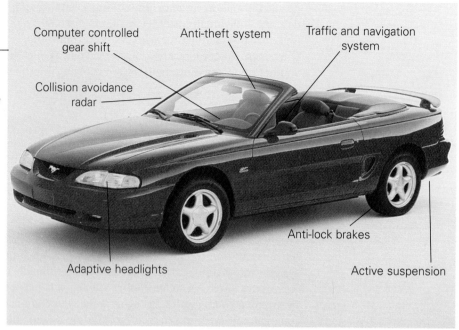

Information systems are also being built into buildings. So-called **intelligent buildings** contain features that reduce the need for building maintenance and security personnel. Computer-controlled systems check the temperature of each floor, the location of every elevator, and the status of all doors (locked or unlocked). They turn the lights on when people enter offices and off 12 minutes after they leave. They maintain security by recording the electronic ID card used whenever someone enters a secured area. In the home market, control systems are being sold that allow homeowners to change light settings or set burglar alarms by phone. Electric utilities such as Detroit Edison are trying to encourage use of home control systems to automatically turn on loaded dishwashers late at night when electricity usage and prices are low.[42]

Providing better service

Leading companies in many industries attempt to differentiate themselves by providing an extra measure of service for their customers. Service through excellent attention to customers is one of the ways Nordstrom's department stores have differentiated themselves from their competition.

Consider the way Avis uses information systems competitively in the car rental business. From a busy traveler's viewpoint, every minute spent in the process of renting or returning a car is a total waste. In the early days of car rentals, the rental and return processes involved waiting in line and filling out paper forms. Today, Avis and some of its competitors have minimized the waiting and paperwork in these business processes. Figure 7.14 shows the handheld terminal a service representative uses to record a car's mileage reading and gas-tank level. The handheld terminal uses a radio link to a computer network to transmit the check-in information and receive the billing information in return. For customers who presented a credit card when they rented the car, it can then print out a final receipt without requiring the customer to set foot in an office again. This process enhances Avis's productivity at the same time it ensures the quality and responsiveness the customer wants.

Providing product information or knowledge

Another way to enhance a product is to provide better information or knowledge about the product itself. For example, consider the frequently misplaced owner manuals for household items. Even when they can be found, these manuals are often difficult to use because they can't adjust to the user's knowledge or to the situation the user faces. Some manufacturers recognize these shortcomings by providing telephone hotlines staffed by human operators, although explaining anything but the simplest problem over the phone is usually quite difficult.

A somewhat different approach is to provide information and knowledge add-ons in the form of information systems. For manufactured products, the information may provide a complete life history of the item, including the quality, ownership, and processing performed during manufacturing. The knowledge may focus on how to use the product effectively under different circumstances or how to solve common operational problems.

Information and knowledge products show some of the possible ways information systems can help customers use products effectively. Many templates, models, and expert systems are available commercially that make knowledge available to users in an active form. Interactive templates ask a series of questions or enforce a data collection format based on an expert's understanding of what is important in a particular type of situation. Models evaluate a decision mathematically or calculate an optimal solution by combining information about the important factors in a situation. Expert systems support a decision process that imitates what an expert might do.

An example that demonstrates what is possible is the Mudman system developed by N. L. Baroid, a supplier of drilling muds used in oil wells. These muds are pumped into oil wells to lubricate the drilling process and carry away rock shavings. The engineers at the well collect and analyze up to 20 types of data, such as viscosity and silt content. Mistakes can cause serious problems with the well. To help differentiate its commodity product, N. L. Baroid built an expert system that helps with the analysis and recommends adjustments in the mud. At one site, Mudman diagnosed a contamination problem that people had misdiagnosed for a decade.[43]

Figure 7.14 Handheld Terminal Used to Speed the Process of Returning Rental Cars

The system Avis uses for checking in returned cars has competitive significance because user convenience is one of the ways Avis differentiates itself from its competition.

Making It Easier to Maintain the Product

Although sometimes overlooked, product maintenance is an important determinant of whether a customer's experience with a product is favorable. Products prone to excessive downtime or catastrophic failure simply don't provide the value the customer expects. We will look at several ways to use information systems to support product maintenance.

Supporting service and repair processes

Good information systems are an essential part of an effective field service operation. The Otis Elevator case at the beginning of the chapter described a system that supported field service through communication, storage, and analysis of data. The communication role of the system was to ensure that technicians were contacted immediately whenever an elevator problem occurred. The informational role was to store a complete history of service calls for each elevator. This information could be used to identify long-term service problems and to monitor the emergency response process.

Pitney Bowes has used a similar strategy successfully for maintaining fax machines. Its National Diagnostic Center in Florida has 22 engineers on duty around the clock and receives 30,000 calls a month from customers. The Pitney Bowes system creates a phone link to the fax machine and copies its operating instructions to a similar machine at the center. The technicians at the center analyze the problem and often fix the operating instructions and send them back electronically to make the machine operate correctly. This system can correct 75 percent of the situations without an on-site service call. The average time for a repair is 20 minutes instead of hours for an on-site service call. Around 30 percent of the calls are related to operator error.[44]

Field service systems also serve many other functions. Some provide direct linkages to computerized parts inventories. These systems help field technicians find the parts they need and help them estimate when repairs will be completed; other systems provide

Figure 7.16 Ford's Service Bay Diagnostic System

Ford Motor Company's Service Bay Diagnostic System is designed to help mechanics with two of the most frustrating service department occurrences: intermittent problems and hard-to-find problems.

direct guidance for repair people. Figure 7.15 shows a picture of a mechanic using one of these systems developed for Ford to analyze electrical problems. The system surveys computer chips built into the car. If the mechanic doesn't find the problem, the customer can borrow a five-pound recorder and turn it on when the problem reappears.

Using remote monitoring

Remote monitoring is the use of information technology to observe a building, business operation, or person from a distance. An everyday example of remote monitoring is the service burglar alarm companies provide. They place sensors in a building that detect events such as a door opening, a motion, and a sudden impact such as breaking glass. On detecting any of these events, the automatic system notifies operators in a central location, who then try to decide whether it is a false alarm by phoning the premises or studying the signals from the sensors.

Many manufacturers of equipment such as PBXs and computers provide remote monitoring services as an add-on following the purchase of equipment. Typically, these remote monitoring systems poll each machine nightly to try to identify electronic components that have failed or are going bad. Doing this frequently minimizes emergency calls when the customer's operations are disrupted by a hardware failure. This also makes it less likely that the customer will even notice equipment failures. In addition, these systems make it possible to perform some repairs by entering machine instructions over the phone, thereby reducing the cost of service calls.

REALITY CHECK   **Using Information Systems to Compete on Product Differentiation**   Information systems can be used to differentiate products by customizing them and by including information systems as part of the product.

1. Identify examples of these types of competitive use of information systems that you have encountered.

2. Identify other products that are not considered information systems but that might be customized using information systems in the future or might contain information systems in the future.

Chapter Conclusion

SUMMARY

▶   *What are the basic competitive strategies?*

There are three basic competitive strategies. A firm using a cost leadership strategy competes on lower costs, a firm using this strategy can reduce its own costs, its supplier's costs, or its customer's costs; or it can raise its competitor's costs. A firm using a product differentiation strategy provides value competitors don't provide or eliminates the competitor's differentiation. A firm using a focus strategy sells its product or service into a restricted market niche where the competition is limited.

▶   *How can the value chain be used to identify opportunities to use information systems competitively?*

A value chain is the series of activities performed to create the value customers pay for. It is possible to extend the value chain to identify activities in which the customer incurs cost or receives value related to the product. The steps involving the customer directly include purchasing the product, assuring that the product fits, using the product, and maintaining it. Each of these steps is an opportunity to increase value or decrease cost.

▶ *How can information systems change the scope and nature of products?*

Customers buy a combination of product and service as well as physical features and information. Information systems can add service and information components to physical products, add product characteristics to services, and improve the usefulness of information products and services.

▶ *How can information systems be used to improve sales and distribution processes?*

Information systems can be used to increase product awareness, support the sales force, improve product availability, facilitate payment, expedite purchasing activities, and provide electronic markets.

▶ *How can information systems be used to compete on cost?*

Information systems make price reductions possible by improving internal business processes, but they can also support price competition in many other ways, such as providing information needed for better pricing decisions, providing a means to adjust prices and segment the market, and providing cost control information reducing the customer's cost of ownership.

▶ *How can information systems be used to assure that the product fits customer needs?*

Information systems can compare product characteristics and the customer's requirements to identify likely alternatives that meet the customer's needs. They can also be used to customize products.

▶ *How can information systems be used to make products easier to use and maintain?*

Information systems can be built into products, as happens with automobiles, buildings, and airplanes. In service industries, such as car rental, they can make service more effective. They also can help maintain the product by supporting field service operations and by remote monitoring.

INTERNATIONAL VIGNETTE

United Kingdom: Reuters Comes Close to Competing with Its Customers

Reuters is a large financial information service headquartered in London. Until the world's fixed exchange rate system broke up in 1973, it was primarily a provider of domestic news. But with the new exchange rate system, currency traders needed real-time data about currency exchange rates. In the last ten years, its financial information business soared as its newspapers, magazines, and broadcasting dropped to less than 10 percent of its revenues. Its main customers are now banks, brokerage firms, and stock exchanges needing financial information such as stock and bond prices and currency exchange rates. In 1994, it agreed to buy Citicorp's Quotron unit, which could boost its marketshare in the United States from 3 to around 30 percent.

Reuters has also used its information system expertise to move from gathering information to performing the transactions as well. It built Instinet, an electronic network that can be used to buy and sell stock. In a letter to the U.S. Securities and Exchange Commission, Reuters said that electronic brokers such as Instinet could "render stock exchanges obsolete." Moving in this direction leaves a delicate question for Reuter's customers, who are increasingly concerned about whether their information supplier is trying to take their business. For example, a group of mostly American banks decided to stop using Reuters' foreign exchange system and build their own.

> Source: Helliker, Kevin, and Glenn Whitney. "Reuters Pursues Trading Areas, Raising Conflict Issues," *Wall Street Journal*, Feb. 28, 1994, p. B4.

- Use the WCA framework to organize your understanding of this vignette and to identify important topics that are not mentioned.

- What issues (if any) make this case interesting from an international or intercultural viewpoint?

- If Reuters is a potential competitor, why would companies in the financial services industry create partnerships with it to build systems?

REAL-WORLD CASES

Globe Glass & Mirror Co.: An Alliance with Allstate

In 1990, Globe Glass & Mirror Co. entered into a business agreement with Allstate Insurance Company that eventually had an important impact on many small auto glass suppliers. Globe Glass and Allstate agreed that when Allstate received insurance claims involving broken windshields, it would direct those claims to Globe and other glass installers linked to Allstate through a computer network. Instead of dealing with many different glass companies using different forms and different business practices, Allstate would deal with just a few who would do things in a consistent manner. Instead of paying for each windshield claim separately, it would send a single check for a large group of claims. This approach would reduce Allstate's internal processing costs and provide rapid service for customers. It would also permit Allstate to use its buying power to drive down prevailing prices.

Although beneficial for Allstate and its partners, this arrangement was disastrous for small independent glass installers who were excluded from such systems or chose not to participate. An association of these glass installers banded together to push legislation outlawing compulsory use of preferred providers. Although some states have laws protecting independents, most of the laws are ineffectual. The same types of preferred providers are in the forefront of discussions about how to manage health care costs.

> Source: Schiller, Zachary. "Making the Middleman an Endangered Species." *Business Week*, June 6, 1994, pp. 114–115.

- Use the WCA framework to organize your understanding of this case and to identify important topics that are not mentioned.

- Explain why you believe the preferred provider concept is or is not unfair.

IBM and Blockbuster: Proposing a New Way to Distribute Music CDs

IBM and Blockbuster Entertainment announced a partnership to develop a new way to distribute music CDs. Instead of buying prepackaged CDs, the customer would use a touch screen to select the desired album. After the customer slipped a credit card through a reader, the system would retrieve the content of the CD using a high-speed data link to a regional computer. The selection would then be recorded on a blank CD while labels and packaging were printed by a color printer. The printing process would take six minutes, during which the customer might purchase other items such as concert tickets. Unlike an earlier system tried at Tower Records, this venture planned to offer only the same CDs that could be shipped from a factory, with shipping eating up $3 to $4 of the $15 purchase price. Consumers would not have the option of creating their own album by picking and choosing from other CDs. Record companies were notably unenthusiastic because the system raised many current and future issues about their control over their own product.

Source: Lohr, Steve. "Record Store of Near Future: Computers Replace the Racks." *New York Times,* May 12, 1993. p. A1.

- Use the WCA framework to organize your understanding of this case and to identify important topics that are not mentioned.

- Explain whether this method of distributing CDs could be used to create customized CDs and why this should or should not be done.

- Explain how similar ideas might be used in distributing other products.

KEY TERMS

value chain	product	direct marketing	yield management
competitive advantage	service	telemarketing	customization
strategic information system	physical product	debit card	mass customization
cost leadership strategy	information product	smart card	intelligent buildings
product differentiation strategy	competitive necessity	electronic funds transfer (EFT)	remote monitoring
focus strategy	sustainable competitive advantage	electronic market	
competing on time	addressability	market segmentation	

REVIEW QUESTIONS

1. What are the sources of competitive advantage?
2. What are strategic information systems?
3. What are Porter's three basic competitive strategies?
4. What steps on the value chain occur at the supplier? At the customer?
5. What is the meaning of "competing on time?"
6. How can a positioning map be used to identify ways to improve products?
7. How can an information system become a competitive necessity?
8. Why is it difficult to sustain competitive advantage from information systems?
9. Why is addressability important in direct marketing?
10. What is the difference between credit cards, debit cards, and smart cards?
11. What is electronic funds transfer, and why is it important?
12. Why are electronic markets both a threat and an opportunity for brokers?
13. How can information systems be used to help exploit market segmentation?
14. How are information systems used in mass customization?
15. What are some examples of information systems built into automobiles?
16. How can information systems bring information or knowledge as part of a product?
17. What is remote monitoring?

DISCUSSION QUESTIONS

1. Marui Department Store in Tokyo has over seven years of purchase history for eight million customers. By integrating data from its customer and credit files, it can target offers to individual customers, such as a designer watch offered to males who are 30 to 40 years old, own a house, have purchased (or whose wife has purchased) a diamond

or fur coat in the last two years, and currently have enough credit available.[45] Explain why this situation does or does not raise ethical issues.

2. One response to the privacy concerns raised by database marketing is the proposal that individuals should own all data about themselves and should be able to sell that data to others. This leads to the idea of a consensual database, in which a consumer might receive coupons, samples, or even money in exchange for yielding the rights to a personal transaction history. Identify some of the practical and ethical issues related to consensual databases and explain whether you believe that this form of marketing database could become widespread.

3. A university is considering automating parts of its course advising and enrollment process. One possibility is to automatically analyze a student's record and make a list of courses or groups of courses needed to graduate on time. Another possibility is to perform the registration process through a computer to avoid long registration lines. Explain why you do or do not believe these capabilities could have competitive significance for the university. Identify any other capabilities related to information systems that might have competitive significance.

4. Use the customer's parts of the value chain to identify a number of ways an automobile manufacturer's information systems could provide extra value for its customers.

5. Why do you think it is or is not difficult to attain sustainable competitive advantage through the use of information systems?

HANDS-ON EXERCISES

1. This exercise involves a spreadsheet model related to the pricing of a product.

a. Calculate total demand and total profit for five different price levels using the spreadsheet model provided.

b. By trying different alternatives, estimate the price level that gives the highest profit.

c. Look at the model, and identify the relationships that are definitions and the relationships that are assumptions. Identify any important assumptions that you believe may be questionable. Do some what-ifs to determine whether plausible changes in those assumptions have a major impact on the results.

APPLICATION SCENARIOS

Elton's Markets

Elton's Markets is a large chain of supermarkets serving a ten-state region in the Midwest. Since the first store opened 35 years ago, the chain has tried to differentiate itself on excellent service for customers. Elton's is one of few supermarket chains in its region where someone still helps shoppers load groceries into their cars. Its internal efficiency, selection of foods, and prices to customers are about average, as are its profits.

Brenda McKay, the recently appointed CEO of Elton's Markets, felt that the strategies of the past might not be as effective in the future. Giant warehouse stores had opened that provided very poor service but much lower prices. Their parking lots were always full. New competition had also emerged on the upscale side of the market. Several competitors had refurbished stores in affluent areas and now provided a wide range of ethnic specialties, fresh vegetables packaged in servings for one or two, and other targeted products.

Ms. McKay was intrigued by an idea that had come up in a brainstorming meeting with her executive staff. Perhaps Elton's could differentiate itself to some extent based on new uses of information systems. Catching up with other major supermarket chains, it had recently installed an up-to-date inventory system, including scanners at the checkout counters. With the success of this project, perhaps Elton's was ready to be an innovator.

A number of ideas from the brainstorming session seemed worth considering, including issuing special debit cards, providing a frequent shopper program that would give special discounts, sending targeted advertisements to individuals, providing a delivery service for phone-in orders, using targeted electronic coupons for special discounts, and providing some kind of chef's hotline that could be activated using the frequent shopper number. Ms. McKay wants your thoughts about how these ideas would operate in practice and whether they would attract customers.

1. Consider each of the new ideas in turn. What would the customer have to do to obtain value if each idea were adopted? What information would Elton's need to maintain to put these ideas into operation? Could these new applications be linked to the existing inventory system?

2. Describe a typical customer's value chain, and explain where each of the ideas from the brainstorming fits into the value chain. Can you suggest any other ideas that might help differentiate Elton's?

DEBATE TOPIC   *Use ideas from the chapter to argue the pros and cons and practical implications of the following proposition: Elton's should not bother to try to use information systems to differentiate itself because its competitors could probably copy almost any innovation they tried.*

Eden Travel

The idea struck Suresh Hindawi like a flash. Although he had founded Eden Travel 16 years ago, he suddenly had a better understanding of his business, but now he was worried. He had recently heard someone say that travel agents are basically information brokers. He had never thought about it this way but believed this might help in thinking through the long-term directions for the travel agency. Thinking of his company as an information broker led him to wonder what would happen when computers made travel information readily available to anyone.

Looking back at the history of his firm, Hindawi remembered when his agents had to call the airlines directly to make any reservation. Later, computerized reservation systems allowed them to make reservations through a terminal without making a phone call. Recently, several agents mentioned that some customers seemed to be using the Official Airline Guide themselves and requesting specific flights instead of waiting for suggestions from the agents. Yesterday, an agent told him that one long-time customer had started to make airline reservations using a personal computer hooked up to a public information service that included airline reservations.

Hindawi didn't see this trend as an emergency situation since it was happening slowly. However, in the long term, he thought that there would be some growth in the number of individuals making their own reservations. He saw big trouble for travel agents if the airlines started giving these individuals small rebates instead of paying 10 percent commissions to travel agents. He wondered if that would happen. Meanwhile, he decided to analyze the different segments of the business. His agency's business was currently 70 percent business travel and 30 percent holiday travel. About 80 percent of the business was linked to major corporate accounts, with about 65 percent of revenues coming from airline reservations. The rest came from other reservations, such as hotels, cruises, and car rentals. Suresh wants your help in developing a long-term strategy.

1. Who are the travel agency's customers? Describe the customer's value chain in this industry. If different customers have different types of value chains, describe the differences.

2. Use the positioning map to characterize the travel agency's offering as a product versus service, and as information versus physical objects. Use the positioning map to identify some possible strategic directions.

DEBATE TOPIC   *Use ideas from the chapter to argue the pros and cons and practical implications of the following proposition: A small travel agency like Eden Travel doesn't have a chance against larger agencies. Suresh should try to sell his business and go into something else.*

Cumulative Case: Custom T-Shirt, Inc.

While Terry focused on improving the existing business processes, Dale and Pat worked more on looking at current and future competition. They knew the four layer screening patent would soon afford them less differentiation from their competitors, some of whom had developed other techniques for achieving roughly the same results. To maintain the company's competitive edge, they wanted to find new product and service offerings for customers and better ways to provide whatever products and services they produce.

First they think about adding new dimensions to their product and service offerings and ask themselves what their business is really about:

* Is the business really about t-shirts? If so, they should stick with t-shirts. If not, perhaps they could branch out into other items. Perhaps the business is really about providing rapid service for inexpensive customized clothing.

* Is the business really about providing service for individual walk-in customers? If so, they should continue focusing on small retail outlets. If not, perhaps they could augment the small retail outlets with one or several centralized facilities in low-cost locations where they could produce larger production runs and possibly provide better art service. Perhaps they could do some form of catalogue sales.

* Is the business really about artwork? If so, perhaps they can do a better job of providing artwork customers would want.

The other side of the question is cost, and they might handle that in the following ways:

* They might simply reduce prices across the board.

* They might make their costs more closely reflect the order size, the amount of custom work it entails, and the speed the customer wants.

1. Flesh out some of their lines of thought about adding new dimensions to the business. Be more specific about what the new directions might be, and explain how the new directions might require different business processes and new or different uses of information technology.

2. Explain some of the ways they might be able to use information systems to segment their market in terms of price.

3. Explain some of the alliances they might try to establish with complementary companies and how these alliances might involve different business processes and new uses of information technology.

REFERENCES

1. Ives, Blake, and Michael P. Vitale. "After the Sale: Leveraging Maintenance with Information Technology." *MIS Quarterly,* Mar. 1988, pp. 7–21.

2. Venkatraman, N. "IT-Enabled Business Transformation: From Automation to Business Scope Redefinition." *Sloan Management Review*, Winter 1994, pp. 73–87.

3. Clemons, Eric K., and Michael Row. "A Strategic Information System: McKesson Drug Company's Economost." *Planning Review*, Sept.–Oct. 1988, pp. 14–19.

4. Johnston, H. Russell, and Michael R. Vitale. "Creating Competitive Advantage with Interorganizational Information Systems." *MIS Quarterly*, June 1988, pp. 153–165.

5. Magnet, Myron. "Who's Winning the Information Revolution?" *Fortune,* Nov. 30, 1992, pp. 110–117.

6. Porter, Michael. *Competitive Advantage: Creating and Sustaining Superior Performance.* London: The Free Press, 1985.

7. Porter, Michael E., and Victor E. Millar. "How Information Gives You Competitive Advantage." *Harvard Business Review,* Jul.–Aug. 1985, pp. 149–160.

8. Ives, Blake, and Gerard P. Learmonth. "The Information System as a Competitive Weapon." *Communications of the ACM,* Vol. 27, No. 12, Dec. 1984, pp. 1193–1201.

9. Brownstein, Vivian. "Business Exuberance Fades as the Economy Slows." *Fortune,* May 22, 1989, p. 22.

10. Postman, Neil. *Technopoly: The Surrender of Culture to Technology.* New York: Alfred A. Knopf, 1992, p. 120.

11. Canright, Collin. "Seizing the Electronic Information Advantage." *Business Marketing,* Jan. 1988, pp. 81–86.

12. Waters, Richard. "Stock Exchange Head Quits Over Taurus." *Financial Times*, Mar. 12, 1993.

13. Whitney, Glenn. "Giant London Bourse Seeks New Identity and Focus After Costly Project Fails." *Wall Street Journal*, Apr. 22, 1993, p. A11.

14. Jacob, Rahul. "Why Some Customers Are More Equal Than Others." *Fortune*, Sept. 19, 1994, pp. 215–224.

15. Blattberg, Robert C., and John Deighton. "Interactive Marketing: Exploiting the Age of Addressability." *Sloan Management Review,* Fall 1991, pp. 5–14.

16. Deighton, John, Don Peppers, and Martha Rogers. "Consumer Transaction Databases: Present Status and Prospects." (In Robert C. Blattberg, Rashi Glazer, and John D. C. Little, eds., *The Marketing Information Revolution.* Boston: Harvard Business School Press, 1994, pp. 58–79.

17. Cespedes, Frank V., and H. Jeff Smith. "Database Marketing: New Rules for Policy and Practice." *Sloan Management Review*, Summer 1993, pp. 7–22.

18. Stern, William. "Trading Celery for Oil Filters." *Forbes*, Jan. 17, 1994, p. 69.

19. Wilson, Linda. "The Big Stores Fight Back." *Information Week*, Apr. 26, 1994, pp. 25–32.

20. Eisenstodt, Gale. "Information Power." *Forbes*, June 21, 1993, pp. 44–45.

21. Violino, Bob. "The Cashless Society." *Information Week*, Oct. 11, 1993, pp. 30–40.

22. Rockart, J. F., and M. S. Scott Morton. "Implications of Changes in Information Technology for Corporate Strategy." *Interfaces,* Vol. 14, No. 1, Jan.–Feb. 1984, pp. 84–95.

23. Schendler, Brenton R. "How Levi Strauss Did an LBO Right." *Fortune*, May 7, 1990, pp. 105–107.

24. Wilson, Linda. "One Leg at a Time." *Information Week*, Apr. 18, 1994, p. 52.

25. Jacob, *op. cit.*

26. Betts, Mitch. "Manage My Inventory—Or Else." *Computerworld*, Jan. 31, 1994, pp. 93–96.

27. Malone, Thomas W., Joanne Yates, and Robert I. Benjamin. "Electronic Markets and Electronic Hierarchies." *Communications of the ACM,* Vol. 30, No. 6, June 1987, pp. 484–497.

28. "The Logic of Electronic Markets." *Harvard Business Review,* May–June 1989, pp. 166–172.

29. Walter Wriston. *The Twilight of Sovereignty: How the Information Revolution Is Transforming Our World.* New York: Charles Scribner's Sons, 1992.

30. LaPlante, Alice. "Shared Destinies: CEOs and CIOs." *Forbes ASAP*, Dec. 7, 1992, pp. 32–42.

31. Keen, Peter G. W., and J. Michael Cummings. *Networks in Action.* Belmont, Calif.: Wadsworth Publishing Company, 1994, p. 389.

32. Driscoll, Lisa. "Think of It as Insurance for Insurers." *Business Week,* Jan. 8, 1990, p. 44E.

33. Wiseman, Charles. "Attack & Counterattack: The New Game in Information Technology." *Planning Review,* Vol. 16, No. 15, Sept.–Oct. 1988, p. 6.

34. Davis, Stanley M. "From 'Future Perfect': Mass Customizing." *Planning Review,* Mar.–Apr. 1989, pp. 16–21.

35. Lenzner, Robert, and Heuslein, William. "The Age of Digital Capitalism." *Forbes*, Mar. 29, 1993, pp. 62–72.

36. Davis, *op. cit.,* pp. 16–21.

37. Lee, Louise. "Garment Scanner Could Be Perfect Fit." *Wall Street Journal*, Sept. 20, 1994, p. B1.

38. Hampton, William J. "Smart Cars." *Business Week,* June 13, 1988, pp. 68–74.

39. Buderi, Robert. "BMW Puts a Backseat Driver on a Chip." *Business Week,* July 30, 1990, p. 70.

40. French, Robert L. "Cars That Know Where They're Going." *The Futurist,* May–June 1989, pp. 29–36.

41. Lavin, Douglas. "Chrysler's Neon Had Third Defect, U. S. Agency Says." *Wall Street Journal*, Apr. 8, 1994, p. A4.

42. Clark, Don. "High-Tech Gurus Develop Cheap Networks of Chips to Control Array of Tasks." *Wall Street Journal*, May 20, 1994.

43. Leonard-Barton, Dorothy, and John J. Sviokla. "Putting Expert Systems to Work." *Harvard Business Review,* Mar.–Apr. 1988, pp. 91–98.

44. Feder, Barnaby J. "Repairing Machinery from Afar." *New York Times,* Jan. 30, 1991, p. C7.

45. Haeckel, Stephan H. "Managing the Information-Intensive Firm of 2001." In Blattberg, Glazer, and Little, *op. cit.,* pp. 328–354.

8

Human and Ethical Issues

Study Questions

▶ *What kinds of dilemmas do the impacts of information systems on people pose?*

▶ *What is the difference between machine-centered design and human-centered design?*

▶ *What are the characteristics of healthy work, and how do information systems affect these characteristics?*

▶ *How is computer-mediated work different from other types of work?*

▶ *What are the different ways to explain resistance to change?*

▶ *What are ethical theories, and how are they related to information systems?*

▶ *What are the major ethical issues related to information systems?*

At a cost of several hundred million dollars, American Airlines developed the Sabre reservation system used by its own ticketing agents and by travel agents in booking flights. Other major airlines developed similar systems. When a customer calls to book a flight, the agent enters information concerning the date and time of the flights required. The system displays the flights that meet these criteria, and the agent presents the choices to the customer.

Sabre is widely viewed as part of American Airlines' competitive advantage, so much so that several competitors sued American Airlines (and United Airlines) in 1984. These competitors claimed that American and United used their systems unfairly by charging excessive fees for listing other airlines' flights and by giving unfair priority to their own flights on the screen displays used by travel agents. Not surprisingly, busy travel agents were more likely to book these flights instead of looking further for flights on other airlines. American and United countered that their use of these systems was not unfair. They had invested in these systems many years earlier and were now enjoying the fruit of these investments. Although American and United agreed to discontinue preferential display of their own flights, some observers claim this practice has not been eliminated totally.[1,2] A similar issue arose again in 1994 when Southwest Airlines refused to pay $2.50 per ticket for every ticket booked through the Apollo system owned by United Airlines, with Southwest claiming that they could not maintain their low prices and pay this amount at the same time.[3]

There have been times when these systems did not provide competitive advantage. A faulty enhancement to Sabre in 1988 cost about $50 million in lost revenue by causing the system to close out discount seats prematurely during 60 days of the summer peak travel season. Customers bought discount seats from other airlines. The bug was found while analyzing the summer's disappointing results.[4]

The right to use company property competitively is one of many controversial issues related to reservation systems. In a situation involving access to data, a large travel agency created a system that searched the Sabre database to find lower fares for customers with existing reservations. American changed the pricing for database access to make this type of search impractical. In a situation involving privacy, a 1993 lawsuit by Virgin Atlantic Airways accused British Airways of stealing data by tapping into the confidential segment of the British Airways reservation system that Virgin Atlantic rented. A former British Airways employee was ready to testify about being shown how to tap into the Virgin Airways data to obtain telephone numbers and departure times of first-class passengers to ask them to switch their bookings. British Airways settled the case by agreeing to pay $935,000 in damages and $3 million in court costs.[5]

DEBATE TOPIC   *Argue the pros and cons and practical implications of the following proposition:* In today's world, ownership of airline reservation systems by particular airlines is inherently unfair. Regardless of the history of the systems, they should be spun off to completely separate companies.

HE INTRODUCTION OF NEW TECHNOLOGIES often has both positive and negative effects far beyond the immediate problem they were supposed to solve. Technological change is not neutral because it can be used for good or bad ends, because the positive and negative effects are often intertwined, and because many of the impacts are not anticipated.[6]

The Sabre system illustrates these generalizations. Initially, it was built to solve the internal problem of tracking seat availability efficiently. Eventually, it evolved and generated consequences far beyond its original purpose. It became a fundamental tool for travel agents by permitting them to book flights more efficiently through online terminals than through telephones. In addition to changing the way travel agents worked, it helped American Airlines influence their decisions and gather information essential for its pricing policy. Although many uses of reservation systems have been successful, there have also been errors and even misuse.

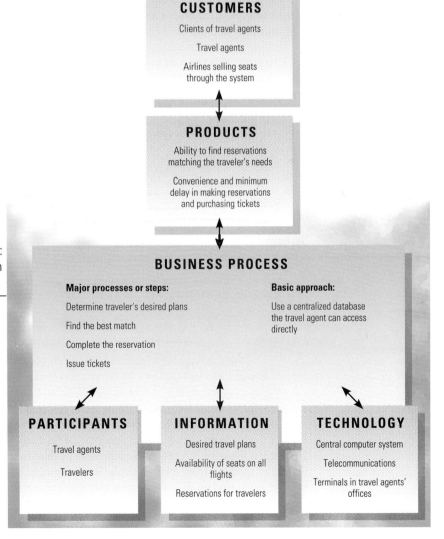

Figure 8.1 American Airlines: Competing through Reservation Systems

CUSTOMERS

Clients of travel agents

Travel agents

Airlines selling seats through the system

PRODUCTS

Ability to find reservations matching the traveler's needs

Convenience and minimum delay in making reservations and purchasing tickets

BUSINESS PROCESS

Major processes or steps:

Determine traveler's desired plans

Find the best match

Complete the reservation

Issue tickets

Basic approach:

Use a centralized database the travel agent can access directly

PARTICIPANTS

Travel agents

Travelers

INFORMATION

Desired travel plans

Availability of seats on all flights

Reservations for travelers

TECHNOLOGY

Central computer system

Telecommunications

Terminals in travel agents' offices

As information systems become more pervasive in today's businesses, managers need to think about the way systems depend on people and the way they affect people. Dependence on people starts with the process of developing and implementing systems and extends to reliance on the knowledge and skills needed to use the system effectively. Impacts on people occur in many areas. In some cases, the people affected are participants in the system; in others, they are served by the system; in yet others, they are monitored by the system.

This chapter explores these issues and emphasizes the management dilemmas posed by today's technical capabilities. A theme throughout is that the technology itself does not cause the social and psychological impacts on people; rather, the way the technology is used causes the effects.

Technology and People

Information systems are much more than information technology applied to a business process. This is why the framework for analyzing information systems contains a link between participants and the business process. Using a two-headed arrow for this link also says that the business process affects the participants and that their abilities, interests, and skills determine whether the business process is practical.

Machine-Centered Design versus Human-Centered Design

For a business process to operate well, the division of labor between people and machines should take into account the particular strengths and weakness of both people and machines. Table 8.1 summarizes these strengths and weaknesses. It shows that people are especially good at tasks involving understanding, imagination, and the ability to see a situation as a whole. Machines are especially good at repetitive tasks involving endurance, consistency, speed, and execution of unambiguous instructions.

The challenge in the division of labor between people and machines is to give each the tasks they are best suited for and to design business processes that exploit their respective strengths and weaknesses. This is easier said than done. This chapter includes a number of examples of problems that occurred when business processes treated people somewhat like machines.

The contrast between machine-centered design and human-centered design is useful in thinking about the design of technologies and business processes. In **machine-centered design,** the technology or process is designed to simplify what the machine must do, and people are expected to adjust to the machine's weaknesses and limitations. In **human-centered design,** the technology or business process is designed to make participants' work as effective and satisfying as possible.

Machine-centered design has been the tradition in many computerized systems although there has been much progress in the last decade. An assumption within this tradition is that system users will read and understand system manuals, regardless of how arbitrary and illogical systems seem. Another assumption is that people will follow procedures, regardless of how confusing or contradictory they are.

When accidents occur, this type of thinking leads people to conclude that the user is the problem rather than the system. Perrow's study of major accidents in power plants, aircraft, and other complex systems found that 60 to 80 percent of the accidents were blamed on **operator error,** mistaken or incorrect action by people who operate equipment or systems.[7] For example, the commission investigating the partial melt-down at the Three Mile Island nuclear plant concluded that operator error caused the problem. Given the nature of human limitations, much of the blame might have gone to poor system design that created a high likelihood of operator error. The same issue was mentioned earlier in the discussion of the Iranian airliner shot down by an American ship over the Persian Gulf in 1988.

As an everyday example of machine-centered versus human-centered design, consider the way typical telephone calls are completed.[8] One person dials a number, a telephone rings in another location, and someone picks up the phone. This method is comparatively simple for the machine because it rings the same way whether the caller is a spouse, an acquaintance, a colleague from work, or someone trying to sell magazine subscriptions. From the user's viewpoint, there might be better ways to announce calls, such as by including with the ring a five-second message identifying the caller and purpose of the call. Perhaps simpler, the system might ring differently for emergencies, family matters, calls by acquaintances, or uninvited sales calls. Although each alternative system has both advantages and disadvantages, the point is that the simplest system for the machine might not be best for the participants, customers, and stakeholders.

Table 8.1 Human versus Machine Strengths and Weaknesses

Characteristic	People	Machines
Endurance	• Get tired and bored • Need variety • Need to stop to rest and eat	• Never get tired or bored • Don't need variety • Need to stop for servicing
Consistency	• Often somewhat inconsistent even when doing highly structured tasks	• Operate totally consistent with their programmed instructions
Speed	• Comparatively slow in storing, retrieving, and manipulating data	• Enormously fast in storing, retrieving, and manipulating data
Memory	• Often forget things • Time required for remembering can be unpredictable • Are able to retrieve information based on associations not programmed in advance	• Storage and retrieval times are predictable • In most cases, can retrieve data based only on associations programmed in advance
Ability to perform programmed tasks	• Can perform highly structured work, but may find it boring and unsatisfying	• Can perform only totally structured tasks (which may be parts of larger tasks that are not totally structured)
Understanding	• Capable of understanding the meaning of work • Want to understand the meaning of work	• Incapable of understanding the meaning of work • Only capable of following instructions
Imagination	• Can invent new ideas and associations • Can draw conclusions from data without using formulas	• Basically unable to invent ideas • In a few limited areas, can draw conclusions by combining specific facts in preprogrammed ways
Ability to see the whole	• Can recognize things as wholes in addition to recognizing details	• Recognize details and combine them into recognizable wholes only if programmed to do so

User Friendliness

Although often no more than a slogan, genuine user friendliness is an important outcome of human-centered design. Anything a person uses, ranging from everyday objects such as utensils and vacuum cleaners to technically advanced products such as computers and copiers, should be user friendly. User friendliness involves more than just cosmetic issues. Something is **user friendly** if most users can use it easily with minimal startup time and training, and if it contains features most users find useful. User-friendly technologies are more productive because users waste less time and effort struggling with features that get in the way of doing work.

Unfortunately, computers and computerized systems have often been more user hostile than user friendly. A technology is **user hostile** when it is difficult to use or makes many users feel inept. Early computers were truly user hostile because they were noninteractive and could be programmed only in languages appropriate for professional programmers. Advances in computer languages, interactive computing, and graphical interfaces were driven in part by the desire for user-friendly computing.

Demonstrating the nature of user hostility in a simple example, Figure 8.2 shows what users saw on computers running under MS-DOS, the predominant operating system for personal computers in the 1980s. Although the user manual explains its meaning, and although this cryptic interface doesn't trouble frequent users, first-time users probably wonder what the system designers were thinking about when they designed a system that interacts with people this way. (In the early 1990s, the enormously successful Windows 3.1 was sold as an overlay on top MS-DOS that made the interface friendlier.)

Figure 8.2 An Example of Machine-Centered Design

The original MS-DOS operating system uses cryptic commands to sort files within a directory. Though these commands are straight forward for the experienced, they can easily confuse the first-time user.

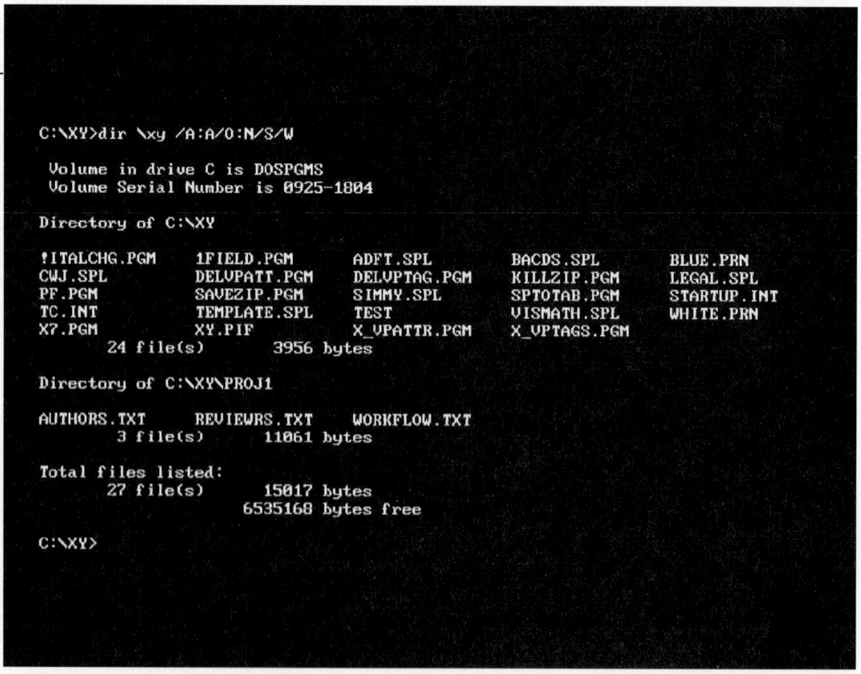

```
C:\XY>dir \xy /A:A/O:N/S/W

    Volume in drive C is DOSPGMS
    Volume Serial Number is 0925-1804

 Directory of C:\XY

!ITALCHG.PGM    1FIELD.PGM      ADFT.SPL       BACDS.SPL      BLUE.PRN
CWJ.SPL         DELUPATT.PGM    DELUPTAG.PGM   KILLZIP.PGM    LEGAL.SPL
PF.PGM          SAVEZIP.PGM     SIMMY.SPL      SPTOTAB.PGM    STARTUP.INT
TC.INT          TEMPLATE.SPL    TEST           VISMATH.SPL    WHITE.PRN
X7.PGM          XY.PIF          X_VPATTR.PGM   X_VPTAGS.PGM
       24 file(s)         3956 bytes

 Directory of C:\XY\PROJ1

AUTHORS.TXT     REVIEWRS.TXT    WORKFLOW.TXT
        3 file(s)        11061 bytes

Total files listed:
       27 file(s)        15017 bytes
                       6535168 bytes free

C:\XY>
```

Box 8.1 identifies some of the features and characteristics that make computerized systems more user friendly or more user hostile. It shows that user friendliness goes far beyond details such as the command language and the naming of files. Genuinely user-friendly systems help the user focus on the business problem rather than on the computerized tool being used to help solve the problem. In contrast, user-hostile systems force the user to use codes and procedures that seem arbitrary and absorb effort that should go into doing useful work.

Box 8.1 User Friendly System Features and Characteristics

A system's features and characteristics can be designed to make the system more user friendly or less user friendly. In general, systems are more user friendly when their features help the user focus on the business problem rather than the computerized tool being used to help solve the problem. Aspects of user friendliness are related to the nature of what the user must learn and remember, the nature of applications, the nature of application programs, and the nature of the user interface.

Nature of what the user must learn and remember. A user-friendly system interacts with the user in readily understood terms, never forcing the user to learn or pay attention to seemingly arbitrary or irrelevant details. Consequently, the user must understand basic principles but does not have to remember the precise spelling or grammar for commands. Multiple applications have similar organization and appearance, and are therefore easier to learn. If the system operates this way, the user manual is basically a reference. The users can figure out how the system works mostly by playing with and modifying an example.

Nature of the applications. A user-friendly system provides easy ways to access and reuse work done earlier by the user or by others who built templates as starting points for users. System flexibility fits task flexibility, making it possible to do the task in whatever way the user finds easiest. The system is designed to minimize errors by users and to make it easy to fix any user errors that occur.

Nature of the interface. In a user-friendly system, input methods are tailored to the task at hand. Different methods are combined to make the work efficient. The menu system is well structured, easy to understand, and consistent with menu systems in other applications. Ideally, the system adjusts to what the user knows. Novices see and use only basic features. Experts are not forced to interact in the same way as novices. The user can name files or other objects in the system with whatever names make sense instead of being constrained by computer limitations such as the requirement that file names use a format such as xxxxx.com.

Technology as a Metaphor and Influence

Combining the ancient Greek roots for man (anthropo) and form (morpho), the word **anthropomorphize** means to ascribe human attributes to an animal or object. One often hears statements such as the computer *knows* the client's age, the computer *chooses* the best move in a chess game, or the computer *understands* the difference between discount prices and regular prices. Although basically a way to say the computer has stored certain data or performs certain preprogrammed processing, taken literally terms such as *knows* and *understands* are extreme exaggerations of what computers can currently do. (See more on this in Chapter 12.)

"The computer *knows*" may seem a trivial concern but what about "the computer *made a mistake*?" People who say that seem to experience computers as autonomous entities that can act on their own behalf and are therefore blamable. When things go wrong, these individuals might blame the computer instead of their company's policies or their fellow workers.[9]

Although there may not be a fancy word for it, the reverse of anthropomorphizing is using computer functions and attributes to describe people. Some psychiatrists have observed patients who work with computers all day and end up describing themselves and their relationships using computer terminology. These patients sometimes prefer computers to human company. Computers provide immediate, unambiguous responses and provide a tiny world a user can control. The world of people, with its slow responses, ambiguous messages, and disagreements is messier, more difficult to control, and in some ways less safe for these patients.

Extensive use of certain computerized systems may even affect the way people perceive the world. Noting that over 30 million American homes had Nintendo, a book about Nintendo[10] cited 1990 surveys showing that the Nintendo character Super Mario was more recognized by American children than Mickey Mouse. Childhood entertainment had once been imbued with Mickey's message, "We play fair and we work hard and we're in harmony." Mario's message imparts different values: "Kill or be killed. Time is running out. You are on your own."

The chapter has opened by identifying some of the relationships between technology and people. It is clear so far that computerized systems have meaning and impact far beyond basic functions such as storing and retrieving information. The next section goes into more depth by looking at positive and negative impacts on people at work.

REALITY CHECK   **Technology and people**   In this section we discussed the relationship between technology and people in terms of machine-centered versus human-centered design, user friendliness, and technology as a metaphor and influence.

1. Considering technologies you use or have seen used, identify several features you see as especially human-centered or user friendly, and compare these to features that are machine-centered or user hostile.

2. Considering computers, cars, or other machines, give examples of anthropomorphizing that you have encountered. and explain why you do or do not believe this is a problem.

Positive and Negative Impacts on People at Work

The effects of information systems on individuals vary widely. For some, new technology has brought professional and personal gains. For others, it has meant obsolescence and frustration. For some, work has become easier or more enjoyable. For others, it has become more difficult and sometimes intolerable. We will explore personal impacts by identifying characteristics of a healthy job and then looking at related effects of information systems.

Table 8.2 summarizes the characteristics of a healthy job. People in healthy jobs use their skills in meaningful work, enjoy autonomy and social relations with others, have personal rights including some control over the demands of the job, and can have enough time and energy to participate in family and community life.[11] Based on these characteristics, the least healthy types of work are those with continual pressure to perform but little personal control. Examples include assembly-line workers, clerks who process business transactions, and telephone operators. These are jobs with rigid hours and procedures, threats of layoff, little learning of new skills, and difficulty in taking a break or time off for personal needs. Stereotypical high-stress jobs such as manager, electrical engineer, and architect are healthier because professionals have more control over their work.

Table 8.2 Characteristics of a Healthy Job

Job Characteristic	Meaning to You as an Employee
Skills	You can use and increase your skills.
Meaningfulness	You understand and respect the importance of your work and see how it fits into the work of the organization.
Autonomy	You can control your work. You are not made to feel childish by the methods of supervision.
Social relations	Your job includes collaboration and communication with others.
Psychological demands	Your job includes a mix of routine demands and new but reasonable demands. You have some control over what demands to accept.
Personal rights	You feel that you have appropriate personal rights at work and have reasonable ways to settle grievances.
Integration with life outside work	The job does not interfere excessively with your ability to participate in family and community life.

Health and Safety

Researchers have found relationships between psychological well-being at work and physical health. People with active jobs involving initiative, discretion, and advancement have the lowest heart attack rates even though these jobs often involve stress. People in high-strain jobs at the bottom of the job ladder have the highest rate of heart attacks. Even when such risk factors as age, race, education, and smoking are considered, those in the bottom 10 percent of the job ladder are in the top 10 percent for illness. These workers have four to five times greater risk of heart attack than those at the top, whose jobs give them a high sense of control.[12]

Information systems can have an impact on health because they are part of the job environment. The impact is positive if the system contributes to a person's feelings of initiative, discretion, advancement, and control. It is negative if the system reduces these feelings by diminishing skills, meaningfulness of work, autonomy, and social relations. We will see examples in both directions.

Even though they may have generally healthier jobs, some professionals and managers believe their stress level has increased because of information overload. They believe information technology has contributed to this overload and that routine use of v-mail, e-mail, fax, and personal computers has not been liberating at all. To the contrary, they feel unremitting work pressure because the technology brings work faster, and people expect immediate responses.

Using video display terminals at work

An additional aspect of information systems that has come into question is the effect personal computers have on intensive users. These individuals often suffer higher stress levels and more physical problems than other workers in the same businesses. This stress has been attributed to a combination of lack of control, feelings of being monitored, lack of social contact, and physical discomforts such as eyestrain and physical tension. A study comparing clericals who worked on video display terminals (VDTs), clericals who did not work on VDTs, and professionals who worked on VDTs revealed that clericals working on VDTs had the highest stress. They had to follow rigid work procedures and had little control over what they did. They felt they were being controlled by a machine. In contrast, the professionals who used VDTs experienced the least stress. They were newspaper reporters who found satisfaction in their work and had flexibility in meeting deadlines.[13]

Figure 8.3 Guidelines for VDT Users

This figure shows a person sitting at a VDT practicing habits that help minimize eyestrain, reduce radiation, avoid carpal tunnel syndrome, reduce lower back pain, and reduce backaches.

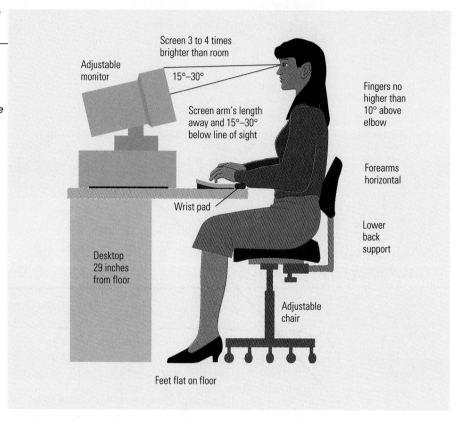

Effects of the physical work environment on people are studied in the field of **ergonomics.** Many VDT operators suffer eyestrain, backache, and muscle tension (see Figure 8.3). Some also suffer repetitive-use injuries such as carpal tunnel syndrome, which causes severe pain due to nerve irritation in the wrist. Figure 8.4 shows one of the new keyboards that attempts to reduce these risks.

A number of studies have raised concerns about the effects of electromagnetic emissions from VDTs. In one with a sample size too small for statistical significance, pregnant women who spent 20 or more hours per week working at VDTs were twice as likely as non-VDT users to suffer a miscarriage during the first trimester of pregnancy. Reviewing these findings and many others, a World Health Organization report concluded that "psychosocial factors are at least as important as the physical ergonomics of workstations and the work environment in influencing health and well-being of workers."[14]

Autonomy and Power

Autonomy in a job is the degree of discretion individuals or groups have in planning, regulating, and controlling their own work. **Power** is the ability to get other people to do things. Information systems can cause increases or decreases in either area.

Information systems may increase autonomy whenever the individual can control the use of the tools. For example, a data analysis system might permit totally independent

Figure 8.4 Adapting the Keyboard to the Person

This is one of several ergonomically designed keyboards that try to reduce repetitive-use injuries by permitting the typist's hands to remain in a more natural position.

analysis work by a manager who previously had to ask for assistance to analyze data. Likewise, professionals such as engineers and lawyers can use information systems to do work themselves that previously would have required more collaboration and negotiation with others (see Figure 8.5).

Figure 8.5 Increasing Autonomy Through Tools

A presentation software package automatically converts this chapter's outline into the format and appearance of a professional-looking presentation. Using convenient tools like this makes business professionals more independent.

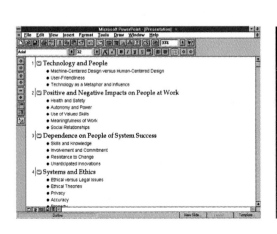

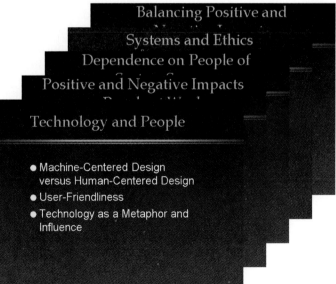

In contrast, many systems are designed to reduce autonomy. The need for limited autonomy is widely accepted in transaction processing and record keeping. Systems in these areas are designed to assure that everyone involved in a repetitive process, such as taking orders or producing paychecks, uses the same rules for processing the same data in the same format. If individuals could process transactions however they wanted to, tracking systems and accounting systems would quickly degenerate into chaos.

Systems that decrease autonomy are often experienced as threats. Systems that help supervisors monitor their subordinates generate this response if the monitoring seems excessive. Introducing systems that increase employee monitoring may lead to resistance and may result in turnover of personnel, especially if autonomy is traditional in the work setting. Consider the example of a truck driver who loved his job because he was on his own and had no one looking over his shoulder. After the company installed a computer in his truck's dashboard, he wanted to retire early. The computer tracked speed, shifting, excessive idling, and when and how long he stopped for coffee breaks. He felt spied on and untrusted.[15]

Driven by competitive pressures to cut costs, there is a general trend toward more on-the-job monitoring of individuals in many jobs. Electronic surveillance is especially common in situations where computerized systems are used continually as part of work. With the wide range of methods for employers to monitor employees, customers, and competitors, over six million Americans are monitored electronically at work.[16] For data entry jobs, every keystroke may be monitored and statistics taken for speed and accuracy of work, and even time spent on breaks. For jobs using telephones intensively, this means someone may be listening in. For jobs involving sales transactions or anything else that can be tracked, every completion of a unit of work may be recorded and available for analysis by someone at a remote location.

Capabilities to monitor minute details of work may create the temptation to misuse the available information, but the way the information is used determines whether system participants feel as though "big brother" is watching. For example, recording of conversations by telemarketers can help resolve disputes with customers even if it is never used for day-to-day monitoring of individuals. Similarly, random samples of calls can be used for training rather than for punishment. Given the natural tendency to wonder whether systems are being misused, it is especially important for managers to explain whether such systems will be used for monitoring work and, if so, how they will be used.

Just as information systems can affect autonomy, they can also affect power by redistributing information, changing responsibilities, and shifting the balance of power in an organization. Across the entire organizational spectrum, information systems have increased the power of people who operate largely on facts and technical competence, and have reduced the ability of people to give orders based on the power of their position. The availability of information across business functions has also made it easier to resolve conflicts based on facts rather than on opinions and power.

Information systems have had an important impact in reducing the power of many middle managers. Higher-level executives can often use their MIS or EIS directly to get some of the information they once received from middle managers. In addition, they can use communication systems such as e-mail and v-mail to bypass middle managers and go directly to the individuals who know the most about a particular situation or issue. Middle managers therefore may see information systems squeezing them from below and above.

Use of Valued Skills

Information systems may have either positive or negative effects on people's skills. As a simple example, consider what happens when you rely on a pocket calculator to do arithmetic. Although you usually get the right answer more quickly, your ability to compute without the calculator deteriorates through disuse. The calculator has the positive effect of helping you calculate more quickly and the negative effect of allowing your skills to decline.

New information systems have enhanced the skills in a wide range of jobs. MIS and EIS have provided information to managers that helps them learn how to manage based on analyzing facts rather than just on intuition. DSS and execution systems such as CAD have helped professionals analyze data, define alternatives, and solve problems in new ways.

Introducing systems has had the opposite effect in some cases, especially when the system automated the judgment and discretion in the work. Such systems redefined jobs by replacing the individual's autonomy and authority with computer-enforced consistency and control. Now a less-skilled person could do the same task, and previous skills had less value. Reducing the value of skills previously needed to do specific types of work is called **de-skilling.**

Tasks most susceptible to de-skilling call for repetition, endurance, and speed rather than flexibility, creativity, and judgment. Such tasks are highly structured and can be described in terms of procedures. They could involve the processing of data, or they could involve physical actions such as spray painting a new car or cooking. In some cases, de-skilling has occurred with the partial automation of decision processes once thought of as requiring years of experience. For example, managers of an insurance company once believed it took five years to become a reasonably good group health insurance underwriter. (An underwriter determines rates for insurance premiums.) The mystery in training new underwriters disappeared when a new system automated standard underwriting calculations. Although the system's purpose was to provide better customer service and reduce the stress of year end peak loads, it also de-skilled the job. New underwriters could be productive on simple cases within months, and the knowledge of the more experienced underwriters was less valued.[17]

Automating significant job components also tends to reduce people's skills by encouraging mental disengagement. Consider the way automatic flight control systems built into airliners (see Figure 8.6) allow pilots to almost become spectators. Many aviation experts wonder whether pilots of highly automated planes will be able to react quickly enough in emergencies. The quandary of how much control to put into automatic systems came up when an airliner with highly automatic systems crashed at an air show in June 1988, killing 3 people and injuring 50. Although the automatic system was suspect, it is now believed that a dangerous maneuver caused the crash and that the automatic system prevented a worse crash by keeping the wings level after the plane hit a group of trees.[18]

Information systems may require that workers learn new skills. For professionals, the skills may involve new analytical methods or new ways to obtain information. For nonprofessional workers, the necessary skill may simply be literacy. Many companies installing flexible manufacturing systems found that their workers were not literate enough to read the instructions for product changes or new machine setups. In some cases, the employees were foreigners who couldn't read English. In others, the employees were long-time workers who had not learned to read in school. In response to this problem, many companies now provide literacy training for employees.[19]

Figure 8.6 Cockpit of a 747 Airliner

Flying a modern jet requires a great deal of skill and experience even though some aspects of a pilot's job have been automated.

Meaningfulness of Work

Information systems can be set up to either expand or limit the scope, variety, and significance in the user's job. In addition, the mere fact that work takes place through the medium of a computer may affect the way people experience their work.

Variety and scope of work

Task variety is the range of different types of things people do at work. Most people desire variety in their work environments and get bored if the work becomes too routine and repetitive. **Task scope** is the size of the task relative to the overall purpose of the organization. Installing a single door lock on an automobile assembly line is a task with minimal scope. Assembling the entire door is a task of larger scope. Information systems can either increase or decrease the variety and scope of work.

Systems reduce variety if they force the worker to focus on a small aspect of work. Consider what happened with the implementation of a computer-based dental claims system at an insurance company. With the previous paper-oriented system, the benefits analyst pulled information about each account from a set of paper files, checked contract limitations, completed the necessary paperwork, and returned the account information to the files. Analysts were often hired based on their prior knowledge of dental procedures and frequently discussed cases with their supervisors and other analysts. With the new computerized system, much of the information was on the computer, which also ran programs that assured claims were processed in a standard way. The analysts now spent more time entering claim data into computers and less time using their knowledge and judgment. Claims analysts who previously knew a lot about each account started saying things like "I don't know half the things I used to. I feel that I have lost it—the computer knows more. I am pushing buttons. I'm not on top of things as I used to be."[20] Within a year, the system had increased productivity 30 to 40 percent, but at the cost of job satisfaction for the analysts.

The nature of computer-mediated work

The fact that work is done through a computer may affect its meaningfulness to participants. Work done using computers, rather than through direct physical contact with the object of the task, is often called **computer-mediated work.** Box 8.2 identifies different types of computer-mediated work and emphasizes the relationship between how work is done and how people experience their work.

There are many situations in which working through a computer affects the way workers experience their work. The **abstractness of work** is a related issue because computer-mediated work doesn't involve direct physical contact with the object of the task. This work is designed to focus on symbols on a computer screen rather than a more tangible reality.

Consider the example of a bank auditor. With a new system, he had less need to travel to the branches, talk with people, and examine financial paperwork. Although some tasks were quicker, he felt it was more difficult to define what information he needed. With nothing in front of him except numbers, he had a limited basis for figuring out what the numbers meant. The job had become abstract and for better or worse didn't feel like the kind of auditing he had done before.[21]

Social Relationships

Social interaction at work is an important part of many people's lives that work systems can affect. In some cases, computerized systems may create new possibilities for interaction by automating repetitive paperwork and calculations, thereby giving people more time to work on the issues that require interaction with others. Furthermore, communication systems such as e-mail and v-mail support additional contact between people separated geographically or organizationally.

Effects of computerized systems on social relationships may also be negative, however. Jobs that require sitting at VDTs all day doing repetitive work tend to reduce social interaction. The people in Figure 8.7 are performing work that makes workstations their primary information source and work tool, and minimizes interaction with their peers. People working in this type of environment may feel the lack of social contact and become alienated. Trends toward downsizing and telecommuting amplify isolation and alienation because they reduce the number of people working in organizations and permit these people to work from their homes.

The chapter started by discussing human interface issues such as human-centered design and user friendliness, and then described five areas in which information systems can have positive or negative effects on people at work. The next section reverses the viewpoint and looks at the impact of people on system success.

REALITY CHECK   **Positive and Negative Impacts on People at Work**   Positive and negative impacts on people occur in areas such as health and safety, autonomy and power, use of valued skills, meaningfulness of work, and social relationships.

1. Explain whether you or others you know have ever felt positive or negative impacts of information systems in any of these areas.

2. For the examples you identify, describe the extent to which you think the impact was the type of issue managers should be concerned with.

Box 8.2 Different Types of Computer-Mediated Work

The fact that work is done through a computer affects the way people experience their work and exercise their skills. The meaning of working through a computer is somewhat different in different types of computer-mediated work.

Computer-mediated production work. The worker enters instructions into a terminal attached to a robot or numerically controlled machine. Instead of the person holding tools and doing the work, the machine does the work based on instructions the person enters. The person becomes more like a programmer and less like a machinist.

Computer-mediated office work or record keeping. The worker uses a terminal to record and retrieve data instead of writing on paper. The work takes place through a keyboard that puts data on a screen. Since so much of the work goes through the keyboard, there is less reason to get up, walk over to a file cabinet, or even open a drawer. The computer terminal may become the only important physical object.

Computer-mediated intellectual work. The worker uses a computer as a tool for creating ideas, performing analysis, or doing other intellectual work. Computers allow analysis and manipulation of information in new and different ways. But computerized systems may also constrain both the form of the work and the ability to change to a different method after a major investment in one way of doing things.

Computer-mediated control or supervision. The worker receives instructions through a computer or is monitored based on the rate or accuracy of inputs into a computer. The nature of interactions with supervisors changes. The instructions come from the computer, and it is less necessary to interact with other people to find out what to do. The feedback is based more on data the computer recorded and less on the supervisor's direct observation.

Figure 8.7 Impacts on the Social Side of Work

The nature of the work forces the employees to sit at their terminals while having little interaction with their peers.

Dependence on People for System Success

The most brilliant state-of-the-art system is a waste of time and effort unless people in the organization accept it and use it. Many information systems never succeed in the organization even though the software operates correctly on the computer. This section looks at several areas in which information system success depends on people.

Skills and Knowledge

Anyone who has learned how to use a computer recognizes that information systems operate successfully only if participants have the necessary skills and knowledge. These start with literacy and include knowledge about how to use computers for specific tasks and how to interpret information in the system.

Some companies have addressed skill and knowledge issues by designing systems requiring minimal skills from employees. To attain consistent results with a labor force of 500,000 teenagers, McDonald's reduces work to procedures requiring little or no judgment. For example, the system for producing French fries in consistent portions monitors the boiling grease and beeps to tell the worker to remove the fries. The worker then uses a special fry scoop designed to produce 400 to 420 servings per 100-pound bag of potatoes and make the fries fall into the package attractively. A former employee said he quit because he felt like a robot. Timers controlled every step of his work on the hamburger grill to produce consistent burgers in 90 seconds. He said, "You don't need a face, you don't need a brain. You need to have two hands and two legs and move them as fast as you can. That's the whole system. I wouldn't go back there again for anything."[22]

The McDonald's system represents an extreme, but it helps in seeing the range of system design choices. Many transaction processing systems are highly structured but still call on employees to exercise judgment. MIS, EIS, and DSS all call for knowledge in interpreting the data. Specialized execution systems for professional work such as designing buildings or analyzing financial statements require a high level of knowledge because the work process is much less structured.

System design is clearly important to system participants, ranging from the teenagers working at McDonald's to professionals and managers doing highly skilled work. Because participants care about the ways systems affect them, their acceptance of a system or resistance to it is a key determinant of its success. This acceptance or resistance is often tied to involvement and commitment while the system is being designed and implemented.

Involvement and Commitment

Improving a business process using an information system means changing that business process and overcoming the inertia of current ways of doing things. **Social inertia** is the tendency of organizations to continue doing things in the same way and, therefore, to resist change. Unless a business problem is both evident and painful, overcoming inertia often takes a lot of work. For some projects, more time and effort is spent in overcoming inertia than in the computer-related parts of system development.

The main force against social inertia is involvement and commitment by participants and their managers. Low levels of involvement and commitment make it more likely that the system will never reach its full potential or will fail altogether. If commitment is low, even a system that has been implemented somewhat successfully may be used for a while and then gradually abandoned, soon making it seem as if the project never happened.

Table 8.3 shows some of the possible levels of **user involvement** in a system development project, ranging from noninvolvement to active ongoing participation in the project team. Noninvolvement occurs if the users are unable to participate or if the system is to be imposed on them and they are not invited to participate. It is possible for systems to succeed even with noninvolvement by the users. For example, software packages developed elsewhere may be the most practical solution to the users' problems even though some users' ideas are not included.

Table 8.3 Alternative Levels of User Involvement in System Development

Level of Involvement [23]	Description of Involvement at This Level
Noninvolvement	Users are unwilling to participate, unable to contribute, or are not invited to participate.
Involvement by advice	User advice is solicited but others decide which features are included.
Involvement by signoff	Users approve the analysis and design produced by the project team.
Involvement by design team membership	Users participate actively in design activities, such as interviews and creation of system specifications.
Involvement by project team membership, management, and project ownership	Users participate throughout the entire project, including initiation, development, implementation, and operation; a user representative manages the project; the user organization owns the project.

Involvement through advice or signoff obtains users' inputs through interviews, questionnaires, or participation in review meetings. Using a small amount of users' time, this approach influences priorities, helps determine system features, and reduces political problems. Unfortunately, limited involvement often leads to overlooking system shortcomings and organizational issues that fuller participation would catch.

The highest levels of involvement require ongoing participation by users in the project team. One common suggestion is that a user representative should manage the project to make sure that it genuinely solves the problem. Another suggestion is that the information system should be owned by the users rather than by the information systems group. User ownership makes it more likely that the system will be changed as user problems change.

Higher levels of involvement often improve the negotiations involving the system's scope and features. Issues negotiated include mutually inconsistent requests from different users, different needs that cannot all be supported because of resource constraints, and requested features or capabilities that the analysts believe are too difficult or expensive to provide.

The importance of involvement and commitment are clear from attempts to implement the same system in four unrelated life insurance firms, Sun Alliance Insurance Group in the United Kingdom, National Mutual in Australia, and Prudential and Lutheran Brotherhood in the United States. All sold a full line of life insurance products and had a geographically diverse field sales force with a central home office. All attempted to implement a system developed by Applied Expert Systems to perform comprehensive financial planning in areas such as cash management, risk management, income protection, general insurance, education funding, and retirement planning. The system used an extensive questionnaire to obtain data and produced a professional-looking personal financial profile and agent's report. It was designed to create a better client relationship based on a thorough understanding of client needs but had the disadvantage of requiring an extra sales call to obtain the client data. Early use of the system in all four organizations showed that profiling might increase the total premium per sales call between 10 and 30 percent.

Figure 8.8 shows the number of profiles done per month in the four organizations. The pilot project peaked and then died out at National Mutual and Lutheran Brotherhood, both of which were, and continued to be, successful companies. In contrast, system usage increased steadily at Sun Alliance and Prudential. In the two firms that abandoned profiling, the system was presented to the sales force much like a new insurance product that they could sell if they so desired. The initiative was championed by someone from headquarters who tried to persuade the sales force about how the technology could help them. In the two firms where profiling succeeded, it became a central concept in training of new agents and in the way the organization intended to operate. The implementation was done on a focused, office-by-office basis, with a senior manager taking an intimate role in training and implementation. In these cases, the involvement and commitment of both managers and agents contributed strongly to the system's growing use.[24]

The differing results at these four companies show that a system's success is determined partly by its features and partly by the development and implementation process itself. The likelihood of success drops if this process cannot overcome the inertia of current business processes or if the implementation itself causes resistance.

Figure 8.8 The Importance of Involvement and Commitment During Implementation

These are the results of similar expert systems installed at four unrelated insurance companies. The system was used widely by two companies, even though its use was discontinued at two others.

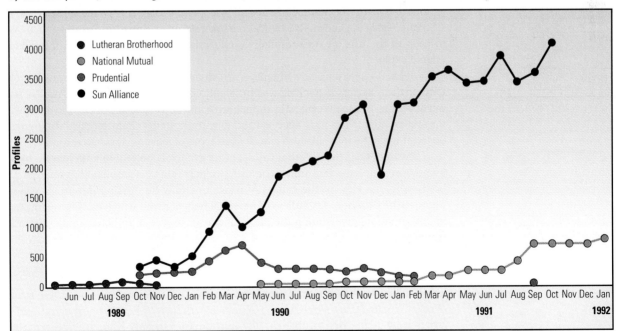

Source: Sviokla, John J. "Managing a Transformational Technology: A Field Study of the Introduction of Profiling." Harvard Business School Working Paper #93-059. Reprinted by permission.

Resistance to Change

Even with a lot of effort to make the change process successful, many systems encounter significant resistance from potential users and others. **Resistance to change** is any action or inaction that obstructs a change process.

Resistance may come in many forms ranging from public debate about the merits of the system to outright sabotage. Public debate can be expressed through direct statements about system shortcomings or reasons the system is unnecessary or undesirable. Sabotage can occur through submission of incorrect data or other forms of conscious misuse of the system. Between the extremes of public debate and sabotage are many less overt forms of resistance, including benign neglect, resource diversion, inappropriate staffing, and problem expansion.[25]

A person resisting the system through *benign neglect* would say nothing against the system but would take no positive action to improve its chances of success. A person resisting through *resource diversion* would say nothing against the system but would divert to other projects the resources it needs. Resistance through *inappropriate staffing* involves assigning people to the project who lack the background and authority to do a good job. A final form of resistance is *problem expansion.* This is done by trying to delay and confuse the project effort by claiming that other departments need to be involved in the analysis because the system addresses problems related to their work.

Resistance is a complex phenomenon because it often comes from a combination of motives. It can be a highly rational response motivated by a desire to help the organization. For example, a manager might believe a new system is useless and might try to get others to come to agree. In contrast, resistance can have selfish or vindictive motives. For example, a manager might feel that the system will undermine personal ambitions or improve the prospects of personal rivals.

It is useful to think about resistance by looking for multiple causes. One approach is to say that resistance can be caused by people or by the system or by interactions between the characteristics of the people and the characteristics of the system.[26] Table 8.4 shows five typical person-related explanations of resistance. Next to each of these is a corresponding system-related explanation and an interaction-related explanation.

Table 8.4 illustrates how different individuals might cite different reasons for resistance to the salesperson tracking system. Highly committed members of the project team might view resistance as caused by the action or inaction of people. Users who didn't want the system might view resistance as caused by the system's characteristics. An unbiased observer might be more likely to cite all three types of reasons shown in the table.

Awareness of the different causes of resistance is helpful in anticipating implementation problems that may arise in a project. Table 8.4 implies that anyone who holds only one view of the causes of resistance may be missing important ways to improve the situation. Regardless of personal beliefs about which causes are foremost in any situation, considering the range of causes may lead to better implementation strategies.

Unanticipated Innovations

A final aspect of the impact of people on information systems is the unending stream of unanticipated uses. Some may be beneficial, others may just be unexpected, and yet others may create new problems. The introduction to Part II mentioned examples, including an insurance claims processing system, an advertising decision system, and uses of e-mail and fax machines, all of which were unexpected and some of which were

Table 8.4 Corresponding Explanations of Resistance to Systems

Caused by People	Caused by the System	Caused by Interactions
Perhaps the resisting users are not smart enough to understand the system's advantages.	Perhaps the system is too difficult to learn in a reasonable amount of time or too difficult to use effectively.	Perhaps the system is wrong for these particular users.
Perhaps users are involved in a political fight unrelated to the system.	Perhaps the system is causing a political problem for some of the users	Perhaps the system will change the political distribution of power in the organization.
Perhaps users are lazy and want to continue doing things the outmoded way they have always worked.	Perhaps the system doesn't solve enough of the problem to make the change worthwhile.	Perhaps the system will help some users but harm others by increasing their workloads or devaluing their skills.
Perhaps users' complaints about missing or poorly designed features are an excuse for not plunging in.	Perhaps the system is poorly designed.	Perhaps the system needs to be enhanced to make it more effective for these users.
Perhaps users are overly perfectionistic in their expectations.	Perhaps the system doesn't solve the problem well.	Perhaps the system doesn't meet expectations and needs to be improved.

unwelcome. Since this chapter is full of other examples of surprising uses and impacts, we will not discuss the topic further at this point.

REALITY CHECK   **Dependence on People for System Success**   People-related determinants of system success include skills and knowledge, involvement and commitment, resistance to change, and unanticipated innovations.

1. Identify situations you know about in which involvement and commitment had important impacts on the success or failure of a project or activity.

2. Think of an example of resistance to change in which you were the person resisting the change. Explain how you resisted the change and how you justified your position.

Systems and Ethics

Ethics is a branch of philosophy dealing with principles of right and wrong behavior related to other people. Ethics is a key concern for everyone involved with information and systems because of the many ways one's actions in this area can affect other people.

Ethical versus Legal Issues

Table 8.5 summarizes important distinctions between ethical issues and legal issues. Laws are a society's official statements defining proper behavior and governmental actions in response to improper behavior. Laws typically grow out of the society's ethical sense of right and wrong in dealing with people but never cover all ethical issues. Laws typically cover only ethical issues that can be described clearly, have an impact on society, and are governed by commonly accepted ethical principles.

Ethical dilemmas are difficult choices related to ethical issues that may or may not be covered by laws. Here are examples of ethical dilemmas that occur every day in business and society:

* The supervisor of five telephone attendants has received numerous complaints lately and is considering secretly listening in on the attendants' phone conversations to monitor their service. Is this right or wrong?

* A software engineer working for a city government lists a file while debugging a computer program and notices that a large number of unpaid parking tickets have been canceled for several individuals, one of whom is an elected official. Is it right or wrong to publicize this?

* A manager under severe competitive pressure is thinking about installing a new computerized system that will eliminate the jobs of five people who will probably be unable to get equally good jobs anywhere else. Is this right or wrong?

* A programmer in a software firm is dissatisfied with the way a new system has been tested and is considering telling his manager's boss that the system should not be distributed to customers even though it has no obvious bugs.

These situations all pose ethical dilemmas related to the impact of one person's actions on others, whether or not laws could be used to decide what to do. None of these dilemmas involves either conscious lawbreaking or malicious acts such as trying to hurt someone, steal something, or damage something mischievously. If malicious acts were involved, the perpetrator would be less likely to think about ethical dilemmas and more likely to think about the chances of being caught and the nature of punishment. In each case, the person faced with the dilemma is trying to figure out what principles and values to apply in deciding what to do.

Table 8.5 Distinctions Between Ethical Issues and Legal Issues

	Ethics	Laws and Regulations
What is the basis?	Customs and beliefs about how people should treat each other	A combination of: • Society's consensus about ethics • Practical issues about what can be enforced • Historical precedents from existing laws
Who is the judge?	Individuals	Judges appointed or elected through a governmental process
What is the price of nonconformance?	Criticism or ostracism	Legal penalties such as fines or jail sentences
How universal is the ethical or legal principle?	May differ from society to society or region to region	May differ from society to society or region to region

Ethical Theories

Over thousands of years, philosophers have proposed a range of **ethical theories,** principles that can be used as the basis for deciding what to do in ethical dilemmas. Some of these theories are based on the potential consequences of the action, whereas others are based on the way people should be treated. Here are simplified statements of three common ethical theories:

* *Maximize the overall good.* This theory says that people should choose to act in ways that maximize the overall good of society. As the examples in the preceding

section illustrate, it is often difficult to decide what will maximize the overall good. Consider the manager who is trying to decide whether to install a system that will displace five people. That action may be part of the only practical strategy for keeping the company in business. On the other hand, there may be alternative approaches such as changing people's jobs but maintaining their salaries and working conditions.

- *Maximize personal good.* This theory says people should make choices that maximize their own personal outcomes. In industrial situations, this theory can be translated into a theory of employer rights whereby an employer has the right to treat any employee at the job site in any way the employer wants, limited only by the law. In the phone switchboard example, the supervisor might use this theory to justify listening in on the phone conversations even though other methods of supervision might work equally well.

- *Treat others well.* This theory resembles the biblical rule of acting toward others as you would have them act toward you. It differs from the other two theories because it focuses on the actions one might take rather than the consequences of those actions. For example, someone following this theory might feel it is never appropriate to lie, whereas someone trying to maximize the overall good might feel that lying could be justified depending on the likely consequences. In business situations, the ethical theory of treating others well is translated into theories of employee rights based on personal respect, healthy working conditions, fair wages, and employment continuity.

However the ethical principles are stated, ethical dilemmas such as those described are difficult to resolve. Over time, societies and organizations gradually develop negotiated guidelines for what constitutes ethical behavior in that environment and what happens when these guidelines are broken. With technology changing so rapidly in today's world, people frequently face ethical choices with minimal precedent. This is one of the reasons major professional societies involved in information systems have issued codes of ethics for their members.

Now that we have seen typical ethical dilemmas and introduced several ethical theories, it is important that we identify some of the major ethical issues that face people working in information systems. These ethical issues are organized under the headings of privacy, accuracy, property, and access (summarized by the acronym PAPA[27]).

Privacy

Information systems can have effects on two types of privacy: physical privacy and information privacy. **Physical privacy** is the ability of individuals to avoid unwanted intrusions into personal time, space, and property. **Information privacy** is the ability of individuals to determine when, how, and to what extent information about them is communicated to others.[28]

Physical privacy

Information technologies provide numerous opportunities to intrude on others.[29] Computer-generated phone calls interrupt dinner to invite you to buy things you don't want or to give to a charity you may not support. Your fax machine runs out of paper because of a long, unsolicited fax. You receive junk mail you don't want. Your phone calls are interrupted three times for call waiting. Computer-generated "personalized" letters have no person at the other end. High-decibel loudspeaker systems force you to listen to sounds so loud that they have damaged the hearing of many rock stars.

A variety of state and federal laws and regulations protect physical privacy. For example, the Telephone Consumers Protection Act of 1991 prohibits "any telephone call to any residential telephone line using an artificial or prerecorded voice to deliver a message without the prior express consent of the called party, unless the call is initiated for emergency purposes."

Taking a different approach, Private Citizens, Inc. was founded in Illinois in 1985 to fight against what it calls "telenoyers." For a $20 annual fee, it puts your name on a list it distributes to thousands of telemarketing companies with a notice saying, "I am unwilling to allow your free use of my time and telephone for such calls.... I will accept junk calls, placed by or on your behalf for a $100 fee, due within 30 days of such use." When the retailer J.C. Penney either didn't receive the warning or ignored it, an attorney on the list sent a bill for $100 and later sued for more. J.C. Penney eventually settled the suit in a closed decision not permitting the terms to be revealed.[30]

Information privacy

Most Americans feel that they should not be monitored without consent, that they should not have to divulge personal information, and that personal information they provide should be treated confidentially. Whereas most Americans think of privacy as a right, no specific provision in the United States Constitution guarantees the right to privacy. A century ago, innovations in technology motivated the publication of an influential article raising issues about privacy.[31] The technologies of concern at the time were "instantaneous photographs" and newspapers, and the issue was the right to be free from unwarranted publicizing of one's private affairs.

Even today concepts about privacy are by no means universal. For example, the idea of privacy is so much less prominent in Japan that a word equivalent to privacy doesn't exist in the Japanese language.[32] This difference in emphasis stems from a cultural emphasis on the group rather than the individual. On the other extreme, Article 18 of Spain's 1978 Constitution codifies a concept of privacy exceeding what one expects from American newspapers and television, especially in regard to public figures. It establishes a right to privacy, saying, "Rights to honor, personal and family privacy, and one's own image are guaranteed. ... The law shall limit the use of known information for the sake of guaranteeing honor and personal and family privacy of citizens and the full exercise of their rights."[33]

Widespread use of computers and computerized databases makes privacy a much broader issue than in the past. Each of us leaves a trail of computerized data every time we use a credit card, write a check, use medical insurance, or subscribe to a magazine. Data from various sources can be combined to create a very detailed picture of how you live, who you associate with, what your interests are, and how you handle money.

The top five credit-rating companies have information on more than 150 million Americans. A summary fact sheet about any one of these individuals can be obtained in several seconds by merchants all over the United States. Many other publicly accessible databases contain information about financial transactions, media preferences, political affiliations, insurance claims, and much more. These databases are used for many different purposes and are very valuable to people who need to make business decisions such as granting credit, renting apartments, or hiring employees.

There is considerable question about how much and which information about an individual should be available through a computerized information service. It is hard to know what personal information exists in these databases, whether it is correct, or who is actually using that information. It is also not clear what information is held in government databases and whether that information is more or less threatening than information in private databases. Finally, regardless of the true purpose of the system, there is no way to guarantee the system will not be breached by someone wanting to steal the information for an inappropriate or illegal purpose.

To demonstrate how easy it is to obtain private information about individuals, Jeffrey Rothfeder obtained fiscal histories, phone numbers, and consumer preferences of Dan Rather, Arsenio Hall, Dan Quayle, and others. Before publishing this information in his book *Privacy for Sale,* he wrote a letter to Rather, who hit the roof, saying Rothfeder's actions were akin to breaking into his home, stealing his diary, and publishing it. Publication of the book was delayed two months, and Rothfeder said that Rather's angry response reinforced the book's point that privacy really matters.[34]

Many other examples show how trails of computerized data have jeopardized common expectations of privacy. For example, as revenge against a magazine columnist who had written an article critical of computer hackers, a computer hacker broke into a national credit database and posted the columnist's credit card number on a national bulletin board. During the confirmation hearing of Supreme Court nominee Robert Bork, a list of the videotapes that he or his household had rented from a video store was printed in a Washington newspaper. When he rented those videotapes as a private citizen, he probably did not believe that the record of the rentals would become public information. Congress reacted swiftly with the Video Privacy Protection Act of 1988, but this involved only one of many types of transaction data that could be used to breach personal privacy.

Code of Fair Information Practices

Many aspects of physical privacy and information privacy have generated a discussion and debate. The following are five principles proposed within the U.S. government in 1973 as the beginnings of a Code of Fair Information Practices related primarily to databases:

1. There must be no personal record-keeping systems whose very existence is secret.

2. There must be a way for an individual to find out what information about him or her is on record and how it is being used.

3. There must be a way for an individual to correct or amend a record of identifiable information about him or her.

4. There must be a way for an individual to prevent information about him or her that was obtained for one purpose from being used or made available for other purposes without his or her consent.

5. Any organization creating, maintaining, using, or disseminating records of identifiable personal data must assure the reliability of the data for their intended use and must take reasonable precaution to prevent misuse of the data.

These principles are equally applicable to personal information record-keeping systems in the government and in the private sector. With the collection of data by computerized systems whenever anyone uses a credit card, gets on an airplane, or even rents a videotape, implementing and enforcing this code would be an enormous undertaking. And in many ways, governments are no more sensitive to privacy issues than other organizations. For example, 34 states sell driver's license information, including name, address, height, weight, age, vision, social security number, and type of car. Buyers include private investigators, who pay a few dollars for an individual lookup, and direct marketers, who receive complete databases to build targeted mailing lists based on personal characteristics.[35] Most people who apply for a driver's license wouldn't imagine their personal information is made available this way. Nor would most people who submit a change of address card to the U.S. Post Office dream that this information is sold to organizations that use lists of recent movers for targeted marketing.

REALITY CHECK   **Privacy**   This section discussed various aspects of privacy and the way computerized information systems may compromise your privacy. Explain what you think is acceptable in the following questions related to privacy:

1. To what extent should your medical records be available to your boss?

2. To what extent should your financial records such as credit card and car payments be available to anyone who pays for them?

3. To what extent should your conversations at work be monitored by your employer?

4. To what extent should you be able to avoid unwanted intrusions such as phone solicitations during dinner, junk mail, and loud music?

5. To what extent should there be limits on the types of information others can collect about you without telling you they are doing so?

Accuracy

Chapter 4 introduced the issue of information accuracy and indicated that it involved much more than questions about data errors. Figure 4.10 showed why managers should expect some degree of bias in analysis, proposals, and suggestions. Although some bias exists in any explanation from a personal viewpoint, bias becomes an ethical issue when relevant information is knowingly suppressed or misrepresented. This is a recurring ethical issue throughout business, government, and society. Here are several health-related examples reported in the news within one month:

Suppression of information. Executives of Philip Morris admitted before a congressional committee that publication of a company study of the addictiveness of cigarettes had been suppressed.[36]

Misrepresentation of information. The Agriculture Department gave the milk industry a dispensation allowing them to use the "low fat" label for milk with 2 percent fat even though all other products with the same percentage of fat do not qualify.[37]

Acceptance of misleading information because it fits the rules. A watchdog agency demonstrated that the "smoking machines" used by the government to identify cigarettes as "low in tar and nicotine" actually "puff" the cigarettes in a way that absorbs much less tar and nicotine than an average smoker would absorb. This discrepancy, which exaggerates the benefits of smoking low-tar cigarettes, was known for years, but no one did anything about it.[38]

One case involves suppression of information whereas the other two involve varying degrees of misrepresentation. At the heart of all three is a set of ethical issues about accuracy regardless of whether computerized systems are involved.

As business and society rely more on information in computerized databases and control systems, people are more likely to be harmed by inaccuracies in these systems. Every year, people come forward with horror stories about not being able to rent an apartment because of a past dispute with an unfair landlord or because a data entry error became a virtually indelible mark against them in a database. For example, after surprising difficulty finding a job, a former employee of a large retail store in New York received a dishonorable discharge notice from the army. Since he had never served in the army, he checked into the situation and found that a former roommate was using his social security number. That former roommate's jail record and bad credit rating had been recorded under his name. Unable to persuade the credit agencies to change his records, he applied for a new social security number and driver's license.[39]

In another example, a clerical error at the U.S. Treasury Department deleted the social security number of Mrs. Edna Rissmiller, a 79-year-old widow. Soon thereafter, her pharmacy refused to honor her insurance card, and the government recollected a $672 pension check from her bank account. Her son William found it difficult to reestablish that she was alive. Her bank told him that as far as they were concerned she was dead until he could prove otherwise.[40]

Accuracy is a significant issue for all computerized databases. Databases developed to record business transactions such as credit card purchases tend to be accurate because of the large number of validations and procedural controls they contain. However, systems designed to collect personal information often lack the follow-up required to ensure high levels of accuracy. Even if these databases are carefully maintained, they often contain errors due to factors ranging from transposed numbers to mistaken identities. When the Congress's Office of Technology Assessment investigated criminal history records maintained and operated by state governments and the FBI, a random sample of these records found less than 20 percent of the summaries for California and North Carolina were complete, accurate, and unambiguous.[41]

Lest you believe that incorrect personal information in databases is a problem only for people accused of crimes, consider the "credit doctors" who access credit bureau files without authorization, searching for a person with a good credit rating who has the same name as the person with a bad credit rating. They give the person with the bad credit rating the social security number of the person with the good credit rating. Months or years later, the person with the previously good rating discovers it has slipped because part of the information in the file is from the other person's subsequent actions.[42]

REALITY CHECK **Accuracy** Many computerized databases contain inaccurate information about individuals that may cause them inconvenience and harm.

1. Explain why you do or do not think there should be a legal requirement for accuracy in public databases containing information about individuals. If the requirement existed, what do you think it should be?

2. If you were in charge of a database of financial and medical information about individuals, what do you think you might do to assess the accuracy of the data?

Property

Imagine that you were in a video rental store and saw someone steal a blank videotape. Imagine that the same person rented a videotape of a film and copied it. Both situations involve theft, but the nature of the theft seems different to many people. In the first case, the person stole a physical object. In the second case, the person stole the information recorded on the physical object. Although the information is more valuable than the physical object, many people act as though copying the information is not theft.

As children, we come to understand the concept of property and ownership by recognizing our own bodies, our own clothes, and our own toys. This concept of ownership involves physical things. If someone takes a child's toy, the child no longer has it.

If the child has one toy and would like another like it, there is no instantaneous way to duplicate it. The world of computerized information products does not follow these common-sense features of the physical world. Someone can copy a movie, a piece of music, a computer program, or a database without changing it. The original owner still has the original even if a million copies were made. However, if copies are made, the original may lose value.

The widespread existence of electronic information on different electronic media has made property rights for information a difficult legal and ethical question. Databases, music, and video can all be stored, transmitted, and reformatted in a variety of ways. Techniques such as desktop publishing are making it increasingly easy to produce information by modifying other information, thereby leaving issues about rights to intellectual property even blurrier. Legal issues concerning property rights to information arise in many areas, such as the departure of employees to start new companies, the copying and modification of creative work, and the look and feel of software. Consider some examples:

> *Departure of employees to start new companies.* Even though high-technology industries such as semiconductors produce physical products, much of the value of those products exists in the ideas and understanding that went into the products. Employees who leave high-technology companies to start or join competitors are often accused of stealing intellectual property developed over many years by their former employers.

> *Look and feel of software.* Lotus Development Corporation sued other companies for violating the copyright on its Lotus 1-2-3 spreadsheet because their products looked very much like Lotus 1-2-3. Lotus argued that the essence of their program was its "look and feel" rather than the computer code. The dispute centered on what Lotus actually owned.

> *Copying and modification of creative work.* Digital sampling is a technology that can be used to record any sound and reproduce it at any pitch, in any combination, and in any tempo. An attorney was hired by the American Federation of Musicians Local 802 to look into the use of a sampled conga drum sound for the "Miami Vice" sound track. David Earl Jones, the drummer whose original sounds had allegedly been transformed into this sound track wanted compensation for this use of some of his best work.

Intellectual property is different from other forms of property and has therefore become a specialty in the legal profession. In general, property is usually defined as an exclusive right to own and dispose of a thing. When the thing is an automobile, the ideas of ownership and disposal are reasonably clear. When it comes to information or knowledge, neither ownership nor disposal is as straightforward as with other forms of property. The preceding examples illustrate the issue: Who owns the appearance of a product or the knowledge in the mind of the engineer or the musical sounds produced by the drummer? How would anyone know if the information in these cases were stolen? If a car is stolen and then found, it is usually possible to verify that it is the same car. What about the knowledge or the sounds, especially if they are used in a slightly different context and therefore modified or extended in some way?

Ownership rights for intellectual property have traditionally been protected in the United States by copyright, patent, and trade secret laws. Copyright laws protect the literary expression of an idea, not the idea itself, for the life of the author plus 50 years. Patent laws protect for 17 years inventions or discoveries having distinguishing features that are innovative, useful, and not obvious. Both copyrights and patents require public disclosure of the intellectual property that is being protected. Trade secrets are protected by contracts designed to ensure confidentiality. All these tools have serious practical shortcomings at a time when new intellectual property products can be developed in months rather than years.

About 14,000 software patents have been awarded, and several patented information systems were mentioned earlier in this book, including Merrill-Lynch's cash management account (U.S. Patent #4,346,442 dated Aug. 24, 1982) and Mrs. Fields Cookies' staff scheduling system (U.S. Patent #5,111,391, dated May 5, 1992). The latter was titled "system and method for making staff schedules as a function of available resources as well as employee skill level, availability, and priority."[43] Scheduling employees is a common problem in most businesses and is used commonly as an example in operations research textbooks. Even if Mrs. Fields uses a unique technique, there are important practical questions about how anyone trying to develop a method for scheduling employees would know about this patent and how Mrs. Fields would enforce it. Although the U.S. Patent and Trademark Office had made it more difficult to patent software-related inventions, a July 29, 1994, ruling by the U.S Court of Appeals for the Federal Circuit seemed to open the floodgates for new patents. That ruling declared that a general-purpose computer run by software can be patented because the program essentially creates a new machine.

REALITY CHECK   **Property**   The special characteristics of information raise a number of issues about property. Explain what you think is acceptable in these questions related to information as property:

1. To what extent should an engineer be allowed to take any of his or her original work for a company on leaving for another job?

2. To what extent should an executive who moves to another company be prevented from discussing the affairs of the company he or she left? Is there any practical way of doing this?

3. Under what circumstances should you be allowed to store or copy a magazine article, a book, a computer program, a taped rendition of a song, a football game broadcast on television, a video-taped movie?

Access

A citizen in an information society needs at least three things: intellectual skills to deal with information, access to information technology, and access to information. Although access to information and information technology has exploded in recent decades, the explosion has not been uniform. Some people have much greater access and others have much less, with effects involving power in organizations, employment opportunities, job satisfaction, and many other issues.

Consider the workers in a factory under great competitive pressure to automate using numerically controlled machines. The workers may be skilled machinists with relatively little formal education but 20 years of experience working effectively using the tools that are available now. To run the new machines, these people would have to do a form of programming, and they may lack the necessary literacy.

Access is also important for handicapped workers (see Figure 8.9). Using specially adapted technology, people with vision, hearing, or mobility impairments can do a wide range of jobs that might have been unattainable for them.[44] Cost-effective technologies that compensate for visual limitations include Braille printers and high-speed voice synthesizers. Although these new technologies have increased access for the visually handicapped, graphical interfaces provide another challenge because tactile displays for graphical information are not generally available.

Finally, consider access to information. What kind of access should individuals have to information about themselves? One large credit bureau provides a free listing of personal data once a year, but others charge for personal credit information, including notification of recent requests for that information. But why should you need to pay to obtain information about yourself? Why should it sometimes be necessary to pay companies to intervene with credit bureaus to correct inaccurate information in credit reports?

Figure 8.9 Extending Technology to Increase Access

(a)

These are photos of the many ways information technology can be used to aid people who have problems with muscular control, vision, or hearing. (a) This computer is outfitted with a voice input device that permits a user to speak commands such as "print" and "copy" instead of typing them or pointing with a mouse. This device allows a person with physical limitations to use a computer productively without touching it.
(b) The Kurzweil reading machine uses synthesized speech to read texts to people with visual impairments. After working with a Kurzweil music synthesizer, the rock star Stevie Wonder encouraged Ray Kurzweil to build a reading machine. Years later, Stevie Wonder stayed up all night listening when he received the first release of the product. (c) This photo shows an engineer who is still able to work despite an advanced case of Lou Gehrig's disease, or ALS, which causes muscular degeneration. Technology used to help the engineer includes a special camera that determines what part of the screen his eyes are focused on, plus software to convert eye focus into computer system commands.

(b)

(c)

REALITY CHECK   **Access**   This section explained that access to information and information technology is an ethical issue in an information age. Explain the degree to which you agree with the following:

1. Businesses should not build internal systems that might exclude potential participants because of deficits in mobility, vision, or hearing.

2. Universities should not use educational materials that might exclude potential participants because of deficits in mobility, vision, or hearing or because of lack of access to technology such as personal computers and networks.

Balancing Positive and Negative Impacts

Many readers probably came to this book thinking that technology was the main topic when one thinks about information systems. The framework introduced in Chapters 1 and 2 emphasized that people play key roles as participants and customers. This chapter goes further by showing that information systems have impacts on people and raise human issues and ethical dilemmas.

As in many business situations, decisions about information systems often involve conflicts between positive effects in some areas and negative effects in others. Table 8.6 shows how many of the systems mentioned in this chapter had effects of both types. You and your business colleagues may well decide that a system is appropriate, even if it will have negative impacts on some people. This issue should be understood and dealt with rather than ignored.

The examples in this chapter concerning negative impacts on people inside or outside an organization should also remind you to be skeptical in evaluating claims about the success and benefits of a system. A new system that ostensibly improves quality or responsiveness perceived by business process customers may nonetheless have negative effects on job satisfaction, loyalty, and length of service of people within the organization. It may also raise ethical concerns related to privacy, accuracy, property, or access. Decisions about information systems clearly involve many factors other than technology.

Table 8.6 Positive and Negative Impacts of Innovations Mentioned in This Chapter

Innovation	Positive Impacts	Negative Impacts
Airline reservation systems	Efficient reservation process; ability to charge other airlines for reservations placed using the system	Competitive disadvantage for other airlines
Computerized systems for monitoring truck usage	Increased efficiency through better use of equipment and time	Reduced feeling of autonomy; feeling of being spied on and distrusted
Computerized systems for insurance underwriters	Better service to customers; shorter training time; better work conditions	De-skilling of experienced underwriters
Use of autopilots in airplanes	Greater safety and consistency in many situations	Mental disengagement of pilots; de-skilling
Data processing automation of insurance claims	Greater productivity in claim processing	Decreased social interaction at work; feelings of alienation
Auditing through a computer system	Less need to travel to branches because the computer provides information	Increasing abstractness of work; difficulty relating numbers to reality
Highly structured work in fast food-restaurants	Making it likely that somewhat unskilled workers will produce consistent results	Feeling that the work requires participants to act like machines
Development of national credit-rating services	Better information for decisions related to granting credit, renting apartments, and hiring employees	Possibility of incorrect decisions based on incorrect information in the database; possibility that information will be retrieved and used illegally
Proliferation of electronic information on various media	Ability to disseminate and use that information more effectively	New opportunities to steal that information and use it illegally

Chapter Conclusion

SUMMARY

▶ *What kinds of dilemmas do the impacts of information systems on people pose?*

Information systems can have positive or negative effects on people inside and outside the organization. Positive impacts involve empowering people to do their work well by making work more enjoyable and by helping people grow professionally. Negative impacts involve eliminating jobs, de-skilling jobs, making jobs less satisfying, creating greater job stress, or reducing personal privacy.

▶ *What is the difference between machine-centered design and human-centered design?*

In machine-centered design, the technology or process is designed to simplify what the machine must do, and people are expected to adjust to the machine's weaknesses and limitations. In human-centered design, the technology or business process is designed to make participants' work as effective and satisfying as possible.

▶ *What are the characteristics of healthy work, and how do information systems affect these characteristics?*

People in healthy jobs use their skills in meaningful work, enjoy autonomy and social relations with others, have personal rights including some control over the demands of the job, and have enough time and energy to participate in family and community life. Especially unhealthy jobs are those with continual pressure to perform but little personal control. Information systems can provide tools and information that make jobs healthy, or they can contribute to work patterns and control methods that make work unhealthy.

▶ *How is computer-mediated work different from other types of work?*

Computer-mediated work is work done through computers. This kind of work is more abstract than most other types of work because it does not involve direct physical contact with the object of the task. At least part of a worker's reality is of symbols on a computer screen rather than the more tangible physical world.

▶ *What are the different ways to explain resistance to change ?*

Resistance to change is any action or inaction that obstructs a change process. Resistance can be a highly rational response motivated by a desire to help the organization, or it can have selfish or vindictive motives. Resistance to change can be explained as determined by people, by the system, or by interactions between people and the system.

▶ *What are ethical theories, and how are they related to information systems?*

Ethics is a branch of philosophy dealing with principles of right and wrong behavior related to other people. Ethics is related to information systems because of the many ways one's actions in this area can affect other people. Ethical theories are principles that can be used as the basis for deciding what to do in ethical dilemmas. Stated simply, three ethical theories maximize the overall good, maximize personal good, and treat others well.

▶   *What are the major ethical issues related to information systems?*

The major ethical issues related to information systems can be broken down under the topics of privacy, accuracy, property, and access.

INTERNATIONAL VIGNETTE

Thailand: Trying to Reduce Software Piracy

Although laws concerning copying of music cassettes, movie videos, and software are reasonably well enforced in the United States and some other countries, many countries either lack these laws altogether or barely enforce them. Thailand had long been seen as one of the most flagrant violators of intellectual property rights. In 1991, the United States listed Thailand as one of the biggest havens for intellectual property theft. Under pressure from the United States and other intellectual property exporters, a major government crackdown started in 1993 and reduced the illegally copied music cassettes from 95 percent in 1992 to around 50 percent in 1994 according to industry trade organizations.

Copying of software was another matter because current laws don't provide clear protection for software. It is generally believed that virtually all business software used in Thailand is pirated, theoretically costing software manufacturers around $135 million per year. (In contrast, the cost of software piracy within the United States is estimated at around $2.25 billion.) Under pressure from the United States, the Thai government is trying to pass a stronger law that would include penalties for copying software, thereby bringing Thailand into compliance with international trade accords it has signed. At a debate in the lower house of the Thai legislature, opposition politicians fought against the law, saying that since few Thai companies produce software, the only effect of a copyright law for software would be to help foreign software developers.

> Source: Sherer, Paul M. "Piracy Crackdown by Thailand Reduces Copying of Music, Films." *Wall Street Journal,* June 3, 1994, p. A5C.

°   Use the WCA framework to organize your understanding of this vignette and to identify important topics that are not mentioned.

°   What issues (if any) make this case interesting from an international or intercultural viewpoint?

°   What kinds of countermeasures might software vendors adopt to reduce software piracy?

REAL-WORLD CASES

Sterling Winthrop: Using Patient Comparisons to Cut Mental Health Costs

The effectiveness of therapy and counseling treatments for mental illness and substance abuse is difficult to assess. Often it is difficult to decide whether the patient is progressing and when the treatment should end. Since mental health and substance abuse care make up around 10 percent of health costs and have increased 57 percent in five years, companies with these coverages in their health plans are concerned about controlling these costs. A number of companies have gone to structured methods for assessing patient progress and deciding on the therapy plan.

Sterling Winthrop, a chemical company owned by Eastman Kodak, went to this type of approach when they expanded their health care coverage in a new contract for their 4,200 employees. At Sterling Winthrop, this system led to a reduction in average patient visits per episode from 5.5 to 3.5. Expenses that had increased 15 percent in 1990 and 17 percent in 1992 dropped 47 percent in 1993 after introducing a managed care model of the following type.

In a typical situation, a new patient feeling depressed or extremely anxious fills out a questionnaire covering symptoms, family relationships, and ability to function. These answers and a therapist's initial appraisal are fed into a computer system that compares the patient's behavior and feelings with those of hundreds of other patients and people functioning normally. This information is used to set up a plan that may include a combination of therapy and medication. The plan is based on achieving outcomes that can be related to those achieved by other patients. An external case reviewer may confer with the therapist before the plan is approved. If a therapist disagrees with a model under some circumstances, such as when the powerful antidepressant drug Prozac is recommended, the health care organization may ask for another therapist's opinion. Continuing to disagree may reduce the likelihood the initial therapist will be retained by the health care network. Progress relative to the outcome measures is reviewed periodically in a similar way.

This type of system generates emotional debates among members of the medical community. On the one hand, there is the need to control spiraling medical costs. On the other, many therapists say this approach relies more on a mathematical model than on the judgment of professionals assessing the situations they confront.

> Source: Freudenheim, Milt. "Business Using Therapy Data to Lower Costs." *New York Times,* Apr. 12, 1994, p. A1.

- Use the WCA framework to organize your understanding of this case and to identify important topics that are not mentioned.

- What ethical issues does this system raise?

- Explain why you believe this type of system is or is not appropriate.

The Internet: Breaching Netiquette in an Electronic Community

The Internet is an international network of computer networks. Originally developed for use by the military, it now has millions of users and many types of use, including electronic mail and discussion groups. Differentiating it from Prodigy, Compuserve, and other commercial networks, its unwritten rules, often called netiquette, emphasize severe limits on posting commercial messages or advertisements.

Laurence Canter, a Phoenix lawyer, violated netiquette by posting an ad explaining how he could help noncitizens participate in the government's immigration lottery for green cards. With just 90 minutes of work, he posted the ad to over 5,000 news groups with a potential audience of millions. People logging to discussion groups such as "talk.politics" saw a listing starting "Re: green card lottery."

The response was immediate and passionate. The Internet Direct, Inc., the service company he used for access to the Internet, was overwhelmed with over 30,000 e-mail messages, so many that it crashed their computer over 15 times. Most of the messages were hate mail harangues about his breach of netiquette, but there were also numerous inquiries from potential clients. Internet Direct cut off access for Canter, who countered by threatening to sue for $250,000 unless he was reconnected. Canter had previously been disconnected by other Internet service organizations, but this time he vowed not to be unplugged again,

> Source: Lewis, Peter H. "An Ad (Gasp!) in Cyberspace." *New York Times,* Apr. 19, 1994, p. C1.

- Use the WCA framework to organize your understanding of this case and to identify important topics that are not mentioned.

- Explain why you do or do not believe Canter's breaches of netiquette are unethical.

- Explain what you think should happen if Canter continues posting ads in thousands of news groups ads on the Internet.

KEY TERMS

machine-centered design	ergonomics	computer-mediated work	ethical theories
human-centered design	autonomy	abstractness of work	physical privacy
operator error	power	social inertia	information privacy
user friendly	de-skilling	user involvement	
user hostile	task variety	resistance to change	
anthropomorphize	task scope	ethics	

REVIEW QUESTIONS

1. What is the difference between machine-centered design and human-centered design?
2. Compare the strengths and weakness of people versus machines.
3. What characteristics make computerized systems user friendly or user hostile?
4. What are the characteristics of a healthy job, and how are information systems related to these characteristics?
5. What characteristics of work determine whether people who use VDTs find their work stressful?
6. How can information systems affect a person's autonomy?
7. What is de-skilling? Explain whether information systems necessarily lead to de-skilling of their users.
8. What are some of the impacts of information systems on the meaningfulness of work?
9. Explain why user involvement in system development is related to implementation success.
10. What are the different forms of resistance to systems?
11. What is the difference between ethical issues and legal issues?
12. Compare three common ethical theories.
13. What is the difference between physical privacy and information privacy?
14. What are some of the issues related to the storage of personal information in databases?
15. Why would it be difficult to enforce a national code of fair information practices?
16. Why is the accuracy of information in publicly available databases an important problem?
17. How is intellectual property different from other types of property in terms of the ethical issues it raises?
18. In what ways is access an ethical issue?

DISCUSSION QUESTIONS

1. Recognizing that two-thirds of all trucking accidents are caused by fatigue, alcohol, and drugs, the Federal Highway Administration funded Evaluation Systems, Inc., to develop a computerized driver-monitor system. At a set time, the driver pulls off the road and takes a simulated driving test, giving the driver orders to turn left or turn on the lights. The result is transmitted via satellite to a central computer that compares them to the driver's baseline results. If the driver fails, a retest is given. If the driver fails again, the computer orders a rest and can prevent the truck from restarting until the driver passes the test.[45] Identify any human and ethical issues in this situation. Explain whether you do or do not believe this system should be used.

2. When Dr. Donald Miller closed his family practice in Taylors, South Carolina, in 1991, he auctioned off the patient records for his 10,000 patients to the highest bidder, an auto junk dealer who paid $4,000. The dealer sold photocopies to some former patients for $25 each and eventually resold the records for $6,000 when a new doctor moved into town.[46] Explain why ethical, economic, and practical considerations should or shouldn't have called for different actions.

3. A Georgia furniture store targeted residents of upscale neighborhoods in Atlanta suburbs with offers of free credit and a 25 percent discount on initial purchases but did not offer the same rates to residents of less prosperous adjoining suburbs.[47] Explain why this use of database marketing does or does not raise ethical issues. Would your answer be different if you knew that the targeted neighborhoods were primarily white and the nontargeted neighborhoods were primarily black?

4. The legal scholars Arthur Miller and Alan Westin have suggested that information privacy problems could be solved by giving individuals property rights in all personal information about themselves.[48] They, and not the credit bureaus, private firms, and government organizations, would own all information related to themselves. Identify legal, ethical, and practical issues that this approach raises.

5. *Fortune* quoted a senior vice president of IBM as saying, "The laptop is becoming a personal badge like a Lexus or Piaget watch. It can be sold not only because it does something rationally, but because it has an emotional content to it."[49] Explain whether you think it is ethical to sell computers as "personal badges" or status symbols. Would your answer be different if the product were automobiles or watches?

6. The chapter emphasized the abstractness of computer-mediated work. Have you ever noticed this either in work or in play, such as when using a video game? If so, has it made your activity either more or less enjoyable, and in what ways?

HANDS-ON EXERCISES

1. This example looks at user-friendliness issues related to operating systems and application software. It assumes a document or spreadsheet is provided.

   a. Starting from the top level of the operating system, open the document or spreadsheet, make a change, and save the revised document or spreadsheet. If possible, repeat the exercise using a different operating system.

   b. Identify things that are especially user friendly or unfriendly for each operating system you used.

   c. Look at application software you use in your lab. What is user friendly about it? What is user hostile about it?

APPLICATION SCENARIOS

Investments Ltd.

Investments Ltd. is in the highly competitive retail brokerage and mutual funds industry. Customers call an 800 phone number to obtain information, set up accounts, and make initial investments. Calls are automatically transferred to the available agent who has waited the longest since the end of a previous call. Agents are expected to answer customer questions quickly and expeditiously and to maintain departmental productivity by completing calls within several minutes.

A supervisory information system monitors the productivity of the sales agents. An agent logs on in the morning by entering a password, thereby signaling availability to receive calls. Agents are deemed unavailable while they are on the phone, while they are doing paperwork after completing a call, or while they are away from the desk. The system records the length of all calls, tracks each agent's availability, and translates these data into productivity statistics such as completed calls per day, productive time per day, and average length of incoming and outgoing calls. The system records all calls so that supervisors and managers can listen in to monitor the quality of the interaction. This is important because agents might otherwise increase their productivity measures by simply talking faster and getting the customers off the phone. Reviewing past calls with an agent also helps the agent improve.

The overall operation is monitored using both real-time displays and management reports. The real-time display consists of a large board with large red, yellow, and green lights at the top and smaller lights laid out below to represent the desk location of the individual agents. The red, yellow, and green lights indicate whether the incoming calls are experiencing excessive delays. When the red or yellow lights are on, the average delay on incoming calls is unacceptably high, and agents are expected to speed up all calls except those for large accounts or certain types of new accounts. Average length and quality of calls during red and yellow conditions is an important measure of an agent's effort and cooperation. The lights for individual agents also have different color codes, indicating whether the agent is available, on the phone, or on a call lasting more than four minutes.

Supervisors are measured for maintaining agents' productivity and quality. They provide on-the-job training to supplement the three weeks of training agents receive in a separate training group before answering their first customer call. Supervisors use both direct observation and the information system to monitor agents' work. Supervisors can stagger agents' work schedules to minimize the amount of unused time.

As the new vice president of operations for Investments Ltd., you have scheduled a meeting with several agents who have some complaints about the personal impact of the way work is performed and monitored. You have just left a meeting in which you have been instructed to increase productivity 20 percent in the coming year or start looking for a new job.

1. Use the WCA framework to describe the situation.

2. Use the ideas in this chapter to identify human and ethical issues here.

3. Think about three alternatives: loosen up the system, leave it as is, or make it tighter. What factors would you consider, and what would you do?

DEBATE TOPIC *Use ideas from the chapter to argue the pros and cons and practical implications of the following proposition: There should be a law preventing companies from creating working environments like this.*

Envirotrust

Alice Rivers gulped and tried to think fast. In front of 200 people at the New Technologies Forum, someone had just stood up and asked why her company felt it had the right to disturb the dinners of 500 people every night and, furthermore, why she seemed to be proud of what they were doing.

Ms. Rivers was director of telemarketing for Envirotrust, an investment company devoted to environmentally appropriate land, water, and mineral development. Among other methods, Envirotrust used telemarketing to contact potential investors. If a potential investor showed genuine interest during an initial conversation, printed marketing materials and sign-up forms would be sent, and follow-up calls would be made to complete the arrangement.

The telemarketing system worked as follows: Envirotrust had purchased mailing lists and customer lists from various magazines and retailers whose upscale customers might be interested in the environment and financially able to invest in Envirotrust. The phone solicitors all had computer terminals that displayed information about the person they were calling and showed an outline of the script for the call, including branches depending on the person's interests and enthusiasm level. When one call was completed, the computer would choose the next person the solicitor would call, display the information about that person, and automatically dial the call. If the line was busy, the computer would automatically call back later. As the conversation unfolded, the solicitor would enter key responses into the computer, such as the potential investor's comments about other investments, political beliefs, or willingness to invest in something like Envirotrust. Based on what the solicitor entered, the computer would display different branches in the script. This had proved an effective way to keep the conversations more or less on track and to ensure that as much information as possible could be gained.

This use of telemarketing had proved 50 percent more effective than the previous, less organized methods of calling potential clients. Although it was true that some people's dinners were disturbed, calling during dinner time had generated the highest response rate and generated the most interest in Envirotrust.

1. Use the WCA framework to describe the situation.

2. Use the ideas in the chapter to explain why this case is or is not an indictment of telemarketing technology.

3. What do you think Ms. Rivers should say?

DEBATE TOPIC   *Use ideas from the chapter to argue the pros and cons and practical implications of the following proposition: This form of telemarketing will probably become ineffective because companies will invent smart answering machines that can eliminate unwanted calls.*

▦ Cumulative Case: Custom T-Shirts, Inc.

Pat called Terry out of a meeting with Lynn Ballard, a writer for a business magazine. "Sorry to interrupt you this way, but Ballard may be setting you up for a curve ball. I just heard about a 200 t-shirt order we produced yesterday in store 48. Remember about how I was worried about that new store manager in store 48? Anyway, he wasn't paying attention, and the shirts had a neo-Nazi slogan on them. The mayor of the town is going berserk. He wants to shut us down. If Ballard asks you about this, you'd better say we just found out about it and that we were blindsided by this one and plan to review the situation pronto."

Terry was relieved that Ballard hadn't heard about the problem and kept the interview on predictable business topics such as growing the business and the pressures of being an entrepreneur. When Terry, Dale, and Pat got together that evening, Pat started with the results of some quick research done using the company's newly improved voice-mail system. A voice-mail message broadcast to all the stores had asked whether anything like the neo-Nazi situation had occurred before. The result was disturbing.

The stores responded with many examples that raised difficult problems. Most stores responding had one or two examples of distasteful or close-to-obscene slogans on otherwise innocent-looking t-shirts. Three stores also had recent examples of customers trying to get store employees to make t-shirts by scanning drawings or photos that were clearly pornographic. The employees in each case had refused to make the t-shirts but felt uncomfortable because they weren't sure about the limits of what was acceptable. In another case, just two weeks ago the artist Frudelli's attorney had called a store and demanded to know who had given permission to make 150 t-shirts using that artist's famous caricature of England's Prince Charles. Fortunately, they worked out an arrangement allowing Frudelli to sell some artwork at the event the t-shirts were made for. But the lawyer was adamant that his client's work was never to be used again without prior permission.

This kind of thing certainly wasn't what Terry, Dale, and Pat had bargained for when they set out to start a business. They were stumped. Their whole business strategy was designed around giving customers and store employees the greatest possible flexibility in producing the t-shirt artwork the customer really wanted. But what if the customer wanted something that was socially unacceptable or illegal? Who was to decide? Would they have to have a resident lawyer in each t-shirt store?

1. Based on the ideas in the chapter and on your own personal background, suggest some guidelines that might be sent to store employees to help them make decisions about whether t-shirt inscriptions and artwork are acceptable.

2. Propose some ways that information technology (possibly including computer hardware, software, and telecommunications) might be used to deal with problems raised in these situations.

▦ *REFERENCES*

1. Copeland, Duncan G., and James L. McKenney. "Airline Reservations Systems: Lessons from History." *MIS Quarterly*, Sept. 1988, pp. 353–370.

2. Keen, Peter. *Competing in Time: Using Telecommunications for Competitive Advantage.* Cambridge, Mass.: Ballinger Publishing Company, 1988.

3. O'Brian, Bridget. "Giant Reservation System to Dump Southwest." *Wall Street Journal*, Apr. 22, 1994, p. B1.

4. Bozman, Jean S. "Airline Hurt by Faulty Fare Estimations." *Computerworld*, Sept. 19, 1988, p. 2.

5. Heichler, Elizabeth. "Airline Hacking Case Reveals CRS' Security Shortcomings." *Computerworld*, Jan. 18, 1993, p. 2.

6. Ellul, Jacques. *The Technological Bluff.* Grand Rapids, Mich.: William B. Eerdmans Publishing Company, 1990, p. 39.

7. Perrow, Charles. *Normal Accidents: Living with High-Risk Technologies.* New York: Basic Books, 1984.

8. Norman, Donald A. *Things that Make Us Smart: Defending Human Attributes in the Age of the Machine.* Reading, Mass.: Addison-Wesley Publishing Company, 1993, pp. 233–236.

9. Turkle, Sherry. *The Second Self: Computers and the Human Spirit.* New York: Simon & Schuster, 1984, p. 271.

10. Sheff, David. *Game Over: How Nintendo Zapped an American Industry, Captured Your Dollars, and Enslaved Your Children.* New York: Random House, 1993, p. 10.

11. Karasek, Robert, and Tores Theorell. *Healthy Work.* New York: Basic Books, 1990.

12. "Healthy Lives: A New View of Stress." *University of California, Berkeley Wellness Letter,* June 1990, pp. 4–5.

13. Schlefer, Jonathan. "Office Automation and Bureaucracy." *Technology Review,* July 1983, pp. 32–40.

14. McKay, Colin J. "Work with Visual Display Terminals: Psychosocial Aspects and Health." *Journal of Occupational Medicine,* Vol. 31, No. 12, Dec. 1989, pp. 957–966.

15. Marx, Gary, and Sanford Sherizen. "Monitoring on the Job." *Technology Review,* Nov. 1986, pp. 63–72.

16. Office of Technology Assessment. *The Electronic Supervisor: New Technology, New Tensions.* Washington, D.C.: U.S. Congress, Office of Technology Assessment, 1987.

17. Alter, Steven L. "Equitable Life: A Computer-Assisted Underwriting System." *Decision Support Systems.* Reading, Mass.: Addison-Wesley, 1980.

18. Stockton, William. "New Airliners Make Experts Ask: How Advanced Is Too Advanced?" *New York Times,* Dec. 12, 1988.

19. Dreyfus, Joel. "The Three R's on the Shop Floor." *Fortune,* Vol. 121, No. 2, Spring 1990, pp. 86–89.

20. Zuboff, Shoshana. *In the Age of the Smart Machine.* New York: Basic Books, 1988, p. 135

21. "Problems of Symbolic Toil." *Dissent,* Winter 1982, pp. 51–61.

22. Garson, Barbara. *The Electronic Sweatshop.* New York: Penguin Books, 1989.

23. Ives, Blake, and Margrethe H. Olson. "User Involvement and MIS Success: A Review of Research." *Management Science,* Vol. 30, No. 5, May 1984, pp. 586–603.

24. Sviokla, John J. "Managing a Transformational Technology: A Field Study of the Introduction of Profiling." Harvard Business School Working Paper #93-059.

25. Keen, Peter G. W. "Information Systems and Organizational Change." *Communications of the ACM,* Vol. 24, No. 1, Jan. 1981, pp. 24–33.

26. Markus, M. Lynne. "Power, Politics, and MIS Implementation." *Communications of the ACM,* Vol. 26, No. 6, June 1983, pp. 430–444.

27. Mason, Richard. "Four Ethical Issues of the Information Age." *MIS Quarterly,* Vol. 10, No. 1, Jan. 1986.

28. Westin, Alan. *Privacy and Freedom.* New York: Atheneum, 1967.

29. Marx, Gary T. "Taming Rude Technologies." *Technology Review,* Jan. 1994, pp. 66–67.

30. Branscomb, Anne Wells. *Who Owns Information: From Privacy to Public Access.* New York: Basic Books, 1994, pp. 30–31.

31. Warren, Samuel D., and Louis D. Brandeis. "The Right to Privacy." *Harvard Law Review,* Vol. 4, Dec. 15, 1890.

32. Ito, Youichi, and Takaaki Hattori. "Mass Media Ethics in Japan." In Thomas W. Cooper, *Communications Ethics and Global Change*, White Plains, N.Y.: Longman, 1989, pp. 168-180.

33. Asenjo, Porfirio Barroso. "Spanish Media Ethics." In Thomas W. Cooper, *Communications Ethics and Global Change*, White Plains, N.Y.: Longman, 1989, pp. 69–84.

34. Calandra, Thom. "'Privacy for Sale': Tales of Data Rape." *San Francisco Chronicle*, Sept. 12, 1992, p. E1.

35. Betts, Mitch. "Driver Privacy on the Way?" *Computerworld*, Feb. 28, 1994, p. 29.

36. Hilts, Philip J. "Cigarette Makers Dispute Reports on Addictiveness." *New York Times,* Apr. 15, 1994, p. A1.

37. McGinley, Laurie. "New Labeling Doesn't Tell All About Nutrition." *Wall Street Journal,* May 6, 1994, p. B1.

38. Hilts, Philip J. "Big Flaw Cited in Federal Test on Cigarettes." *New York Times*, May 2, 1994, p. A1.

39. Field, Anne R. "'Big Brother Inc.' May Be Closer Than You Thought." *Business Week*, Feb. 9, 1987, pp. 84–86.

40. Knecht, G. Bruce. "Reports of Mrs. Rissmiller's Death Have Been Greatly Exaggerated." *Wall Street Journal*, Apr. 20, 1994, p. B1.

41. Burnham, David. *The Rise of the Computer State.* New York: Random House, 1983.

42. Reibstein, Larry. "Clean Credit for Sale—A Growing Illegal Racket." *Newsweek*, Sept. 12, 1988, p. 49.

43. Betts, Mitch. "Ruling Opens Door to Software Patents." *Computerworld*, Sept. 5, 1994, p. 73.

44. Lazzaro, Joseph J. "Computers for the Disabled." *Byte*, June 1993, pp. 59–64.

45. Coxeter, Ruth. "A Computerized Overseer for the Truck Drivin' Man." *Business Week*, Sept. 19, 1994, p. 90.

46. Betts, Mitch "Computerized Records: An Open Book?" *Computerworld*, Aug. 9, 1993, p. 1.

47. Cespedes, Frank V., and H. Jeff Smith. "Database Marketing: New Rules for Policy and Practice." *Sloan Management Review*, Summer 1993, pp. 7–22.

48. Branscomb, *op. cit.*, p. 180.

49. Kirkpatrick, David. "What's Driving the New PC Shakeout." *Fortune*, Sept. 19, 1994, pp. 109–122.

PART III

Understanding the Role of Information Technology

The first eight chapters have provided a business professional's viewpoint for thinking about information systems and for understanding their applications and impacts. These chapters were written under the assumption that most readers are familiar with information technology from their everyday experience with televisions, VCRs, CD players, portable telephones, computers, and video games. Therefore it was possible to focus on systems, business processes, information, competition, and human impacts before discussing information technology.

Now that you have studied the application and impacts of information systems, the next four chapters on information technology should be more meaningful than they would have been earlier. This part introduction focuses on three thoughts underlying many specific points in Chapters 9 through 12:

1. It is important to identify basic ideas for understanding information technology because technology takes many forms, changes rapidly, and sometimes introduces difficult jargon and acronyms.

2. Improvements in technology performance have an impact only if they can be used to improve the product of a business process or its internal operation.

3. It is so difficult to foresee the progress of information technology that even experts often misread the possibilities for the future.

The next four chapters explain aspects of information technology users and managers need to understand to appreciate the relationship between technical advances and the changing nature of business processes. Chapter 9 explains computers and peripherals, with substantial emphasis on underlying ideas rather than merely cataloguing different technologies. Chapter 10 takes a similar approach in explaining software and programming. Chapter 11 looks at networks and telecommunications. Chapter 12 discusses the types of applications usually included under the heading of artificial intelligence; it also describes major limitations of today's "intelligent" systems.

Behind the Magic: Basic Ideas Underlying Information Technology

"Any sufficiently advanced technology is indistinguishable from magic."[1] This famous quote from Arthur Clark certainly applies to information technology. Although we may eventually take personal computers for granted, the things they do probably should seem like magic to people who don't understand exactly how they operate. (This is just about everybody.) Four technology chapters in this book cannot explain the internal workings of technology in enough detail to make the feeling of magic disappear, but the chapters can demonstrate ideas for thinking about functions served by information technology. Basic ideas crossing all types of computer and telecommunications hardware and software include:

- Six functions performed by information technology

- Representation of data and instructions

- Translating from human intentions to machine instructions

- Attaining efficiency and effectiveness through modularity, compatibility, and reusability

- Optimizing performance based on current hardware and software capabilities

- Trends and limitations related to "intelligent" technology

Six Basic Functions Performed by Information Technology

Everything computer systems do can be boiled down to six basic functions of information technology: capturing, transmitting, storing, retrieving, manipulating, and displaying data. For example, think about what a grocery store's customer checkout system does:

- It *captures* data using the bar code.

- It *transmits* data to a computer that looks up the item's price and description.

- It *stores* information about the item for calculating the bill.

- It *retrieves* price and description information.

- It *manipulates* the information when it adds up the bill.

- It *displays* information when it shows each price and prints the receipt.

Table III.1 defines the six functions and shows some of the devices or technologies used to perform each of them.

Representation of Data and Instructions

To perform any of these six data processing functions, information technology needs a way to represent data. Chapter 9 will explain how any type of data, even pictures and sounds, can be represented for processing by a computer. Visualizing the representation of data is important to users because it helps them understand things such as:

- How to specify a system's data storage or data transmission requirements

- Why the representation of a photograph is actually an approximation that may not have as much clarity as the original

- Why a picture may be worth a thousand words but may require as much data storage or data transmission resources as a million words

- Why videoconferencing and sharing of graphical data may require much greater data transmission capabilities than electronic mail designed to transmit text messages

- Why the likely standard for high definition television (HDTV) changed from analog representation of data to digital representation, effectively negating a billion-dollar effort by Japanese manufacturers attempting to create the new HDTV standard

Since computers execute instructions that have been stored in advance, there must also be a way to represent those instructions. Chapter 10 will show how the internal representation within computers is unsuitable for direct use by most people. This is why software capabilities have been developed that translate from computer languages such as COBOL, FORTRAN, C, and SMALLTALK into the internal machine language used within the computer.

Table III.1 Six Basic Functions of Information Technology

Function	Definition	Example of Devices or Technologies Used to Perform This Function
Capture	Obtain a representation of information in a form permitting it to be transmitted or stored	Keyboard, bar-code scanner, sound recorder, video camera
Transmit	Move information from one place to another	Telephone network, local area network, cable television network, wireless broadcast network
Store	Move information to a specific place for later retrieval	Paper, magnetic tape, floppy disk, hard disk, optical disk, CD-ROM, flash memory
Retrieve	Find the specific information that is currently needed	Paper, magnetic tape, floppy disk, hard disk, optical disk, CD-ROM, flash memory
Manipulate	Create new information from existing information through summarizing, sorting, rearranging, reformatting, or various types of calculations	Computer (plus software)
Display	Show information to a person	Laser printer, computer screen, loudspeaker

Translating from Human Intentions to Machine Instructions

People can use many different methods for conveying their intentions to machines. Examples include turning the steering wheel of a car, pushing the controls of a video game, or pressing keys on a computer keyboard. In all these cases, there must be an automatic way to convert the user's instructions into an internal form of instruction the machine can execute.

The principle guiding progress in software is that people should be able to express themselves in a form that is easy and natural for them and that can be translated automatically into a form of instructions the computer can execute directly. Ideally, people should be able to concern themselves only with the details of the problem they are thinking about, not with the details of how the computer operates or how to represent the problem for the computer. Progress through various generations of programming languages has permitted people to apply relatively more of their effort thinking about their problem and relatively less of their effort figuring out how to express themselves to the computer. Although great progress has occurred, many people are still scared to use computers because current methods of expressing instructions to computers remain somewhat unfriendly and forbidding.

Attaining Efficiency and Effectiveness Through Modularity, Compatibility, and Reusability

Modularity, compatibility, and reusability are basic ideas at the heart of most progress in both hardware and software. These three characteristics are virtually essential for information technology that is efficient and effective.

Modularity involves the separation of a system or device into a set of subsystems each of which can be developed, tested, and understood independently. Dividing systems into modules makes them easier to build and understand because solving many small problems is usually easier than solving one big problem. The modules work together based on the way the outputs of one become the inputs of others.

Compatibility is the extent to which the characteristics and features of a particular technology fits with those of other technologies relevant to the situation. Compatibility permits modules to work together. You understand why compatibility requirements accentuate the need for conformance to standards if you have ever wanted to plug an American hair dryer into a typical wall socket in Europe or Asia. The plug's shape is not compatible with the outlet's shape, and the hair dryer won't operate unless you have a special adapter. In information technology, compatibility issues range from "technical" details, such as internal machine languages and data coding methods, to mundane issues such as the size of paper in copy machines and the shape of plugs.

Reusability is the idea that software modules should be designed so that they can be used in many different situations instead of forcing programmers to create modules from scratch for each situation. For example, if an information system contains eight different places in which a person's name and address are printed at the top of a form, the instructions for printing should be written once and reused seven times. Doing things this way makes systems simpler and eliminates a lot of unnecessary work although it also requires greater care in planning the work and creating libraries of reusable modules.

Chapters 9 through 12 will mention these ideas in several ways because they serve as the basis for creating systems out of hardware and software components. They are highlighted here to emphasize their significance to topics including programming methods, network architecture, and open systems.

Optimizing Performance Based on Current Hardware and Software Capabilities

Many people who are not directly involved with the information technology industry find the onslaught of product announcements and technical jargon overwhelming. What are they to make of all these announcements and all the new technical terminology? For example, how should they decide whether they really want client–server computing, object-oriented programming, ISDN telephone systems, or expert system shells?

From a user's viewpoint, it is important to separate two things: first, what does the user want to accomplish, and second, what combination of currently available hardware and software provides the necessary capabilities and at what cost? Each of the technical advances mentioned in the previous paragraph may support business capabilities that would otherwise be impractical or impossible. Alternatively, they may simply reduce costs compared to other methods for performing similar functions. As you read the chapters, look for ways each successive improvement adds new capabilities users perceive directly or performs the same functions at lower costs.

Sometimes missed in the discussions of hardware or software advances is the point that having a faster computer or more powerful software may not matter at all if some other part of the system is a limiting factor in overall performance. For example, assume someone is concerned with how slowly a computer system produces printed outputs and is considering buying a computer that runs three times faster. A faster computer may help if the current computer is limiting the speed of printing, but if the laser printer itself is the limiting factor, making another part of the system faster will have no effect. From a user's viewpoint, upgrading any individual part of a system's hardware or software without looking at how the overall system will operate may have no effect at all.

Trends and Limitations Related to "Intelligent" Technology

The introduction to Part I mentioned the hype often associated with information technology and the way people tend to exaggerate what computers can do. An important purpose of the technology chapters is to help you recognize the current limitations in the "intelligence" of computerized systems. Chapters 10 and 12 emphasize both the great progress that has occurred and the immense challenges that remain.

Part of the hype problem is that the terms *intelligent* and *intelligence* are used so many ways. Consider the following titles of books from the late 1980s and early 1990s: *Artificial Intelligence,*[2] *The Age of Intelligent Machines,*[3] *Intelligent Enterprise,*[4] *The Intelligent Corporation,*[5] and *Intelligent Systems for Business.*[6] Some of these books focus on artificial intelligence research and practical business techniques partially derived from that research. Others focus on ways organizations are changing or could change based on the availability of computers and networks unrelated to artificial intelligence.

Even though these books go in many different directions, the common thread throughout them is the idea that intelligence is related to the ability to receive and use information. In these terms, a drip coffee maker has no intelligence, whereas an electronic coffee maker has a little. A database that stores whatever data is entered has no intelligence whereas a database that checks the data for likely errors has a little. In this sense, a business that ignores what the customers and employees think applies less intelligence than a business that pays attention to them. None of these three examples involve artificial intelligence, but all involve different degrees of capturing and using information. Chapters 10 and 12 carry on from this point in explaining the meaning, applications, and limitations of artificial intelligence. In general, we will see how progress has made machines more intelligent in terms of being able to capture and use information but has not yet made them intelligent in terms of being able to understand situations well enough to use information reliably in unanticipated situations.

Thinking About Information Technology Performance

As we embark on four chapters discussing various aspects of information technology, it is useful to remember why information technology exists and how it should be evaluated. In terms of the WCA framework from Chapter 2, information technology succeeds only if its use improves the product of the business process or the internal operation of the business process. In some cases, technical advances improve the process or its products by reducing the cost or increasing the reliability of fundamentally similar capabilities such as performing calculations or accessing data. Other advances have an impact by creating previously unavailable capabilities, such as voice recognition or handwritten input to computers.

The coverage of information technology in these chapters is generally organized around architectural issues, such as different types of devices and how they operate together as systems, but the coverage often mentions the other four WCA perspectives. The chapters discuss performance by asking how well the technical components operate individually and how well the technical system operates as a whole. They note some of the ways human and technical infrastructure present opportunities and obstacles. They stress the technical context by discussing trends, opportunities, and obstacles related to technical advances. And they cover risks by mentioning some of the things that go wrong with technology.

Although all five WCA perspectives are important, the performance perspective brings special problems because of continual announcements about ever greater computer and telecommunications capabilities. Back in Chapter 2, Figure 2.10 implied that technology performance could be summarized in terms of just four performance characteristics: functional capabilities and limitations, ease of use, compatibility, and maintainability. Table III.2 shows that each of these general performance variables for information technology is tied to a set of more specific performance variables. Notice how some of the terms used to talk about information technology performance are also used at other times to talk about process or product performance.

The **functional capabilities** of a particular type of information technology identify the types of processing it is supposed to perform and the degree of capability it has. Depending on the type of information technology, functional capabilities are often measured as capacity or speed using terms such as number of instructions executed per second, amount of data that can be stored, and rate of data transfer. Another aspect of technology performance is reliability, the likelihood that the technology will continue operating without errors or unplanned interruptions. A final aspect of functional capabilities is operating conditions, issues such as how much a device weighs, how much space it takes, and how much electricity it uses. These questions may not seem very high-tech but often determine whether a particular technology, such as the laptop computer, is practical in a particular situation.

Since the productivity of a business process depends partially on the cost of the technology and other resources it uses, it is always important to think of performance in terms of **price-performance,** the relationship between the price of technology and the performance it provides. (The more general term is cost-effectiveness, the relationship between what something costs and how much it accomplishes.) For example, competition among personal computer manufacturers in the early 1990s generated major improvements in both performance and price-performance. Computers became faster and more powerful (performance) while the price for any given level of processing power plummeted (price-performance).

Although ease of use is often associated with the user interface, the discussion of user-friendliness in Chapter 8 implied that **ease of use** is actually a broader idea including ease of learning how to use the technology, ease of setting it up, and ease of using it directly. Everyday experience with audio equipment such as a Walkman shows that ease of use includes features ranging from size, portability, user interface, and the compatibility with technology standards such as the dimensions of the tape cassette. These same aspects of ease of use apply for business technology such as telephones and computers.

Table III.2 Information Technology Performance Variables

Group of Performance Variables	Typical Issue Raised When Using This Term to Describe a Particular Technology
Functional Capabilities and Limitations	What types of processing is it supposed to perform, and what degree of capability does it have?
• Capacity	How much information can it store or process?
• Speed	How fast can it process data or instructions?
• Price-performance	How many dollars does it cost per amount of information stored or number of instructions executed?
• Reliability	How long will it likely continue operating without errors or unplanned interruptions?
• Operating conditions	How much space does it take up? How much does it weigh? What temperature does it require? How much electricity does it use?
Ease of use	How easy is it to use this technology?
• Quality of user interface	How intuitive and easy to learn and use is the method for instructing the technology to perform its task?
• Portability	How easy is it for the user to move the technology in the course of doing work?
Compatibility	How easy is it to get this technology to work with other complementary technologies?
• Conformance to standards	To what extent does the technology conform to known industry standards?
• Interoperability	To what extent does the technology use the same internal coding and external interfaces as other technology it must operate with or substitute for?
Maintainability	How easy is it to keep the technology operating over time?
• Modularity	Is it divided into modules that can be snapped in place to construct a system and replaced by equivalent modules if necessary?
• Scalability	Is it possible to significantly increase or decrease capacity without major disruptions?
• Flexibility	Is it possible to change important aspects of system operation without major disruptions?

Earlier we mentioned compatibility, along with modularity and reusability, as the basic ideas at the heart of most progress in information technology. Compatibility is also important when we think about technology at any point in time because most information technology is genuinely useful only in combination with other information technology. Aspects of compatibility include the methods for coding the data; the specific way the technology processes the data; and physical attributes of the technology such as size, speed, and even shape.

Just as there were different levels of integration (Chapter 3), compatibility issues arise at several different levels. At one level, the question is whether two devices or programs that do not have to work together both operate consistent with the same standards. Questions of this type range from whether they use the same voltage or type of electric plugs to whether they use the same operating system, such as Windows 95 or UNIX. At another level, the question is whether the two devices or programs can be used together, even if they use different brands of hardware or are written using different computer languages. This type of compatibility is called **interoperability** and was mentioned in the discussion of connectivity and open systems in Chapter 1. (Recall that open systems use clearly described, nonproprietary industry standards anyone can use.)

The last general characteristic is **maintainability,** the ease with which users or technical specialists can keep the technology running and upgrade it to suit the changing needs of the situation. In general, it is easier to maintain technology if the parts are simpler and are designed as modular components meant to be plugged into other components operating consistent with accepted industry standards. Scalability is an important part of maintainability because upgrading capacity beyond certain limits often requires a complete change in the system. For example, it is possible to hitch a trailer behind most cars, but if the trailer is too big the car can't drive safely, and it is necessary to switch to a truck.

Recall these characteristics each time the four chapters on technology bring up a new technical topic such as parallel processing, optical disks, local area networks, or object-oriented programming. In each case, technical advances improve some aspect of these technology characteristics, thereby creating the potential to improve business process performance.

Table III.3 Technology Predictions or Business Assessments That Missed the Mark

Expert and Topic	Prediction or Comment
Alexander Graham Bell, inventor of the telephone, around 1876	He thought the telephone network would be primarily an entertainment instrument, transmitting concerts and operas to homes.[7]
Chairman of Western Union when offered exclusive patent rights to the telephone in 1876	"What use would this company have for an electrical toy?"[8]
Mercedes Benz, around 1900 on the future demand for cars	"In 1900 Mercedes Benz did a study that estimated that the worldwide demand for cars would not exceed one million, primarily because of the limitation of available chauffeurs."[9]
General Electric, RCA, IBM, Remington Rand, refusing chance to develop the basic patent for copy machines	Chester Carlson invented xerography in 1938 but spent years trying to find a corporate sponsor for his invention. Only after a long series of refusals did he persuade Battelle Memorial Institute in Ohio to continue the research.[10]
Thomas Watson, Sr., CEO of IBM, in the early 1950s	The worldwide demand for data-processing computers is less than 50 machines.[11]
Xerox Corporation, on funding early development work on the laser printer	Garry Starkweather of Xerox invented the laser printer in 1971 by modifying existing copier technology. Before he built a prototype, he was instructed to stop working on the project. He might have had to leave the company to pursue the project if he had not learned of the new Xerox research lab in California where other researchers were interested in being able to print computer screen images.[12]
Herbert Simon and Allen Newell, early AI researchers, in 1958	Within ten years, a digital computer will be the world's chess champion unless the rules bar it from competition.[13]
Ken Olson, CEO of Digital Equipment Corporation, 1977	"There is no reason for any individual to have a computer in their home" (attributed to Ken Olson, at a convention of the World Future Society in Boston, 1977).[14]
IBM's view of the MS-DOS operating system in the early 1980s	The DOS operating system was first purchased by Microsoft for $50,000. IBM did not realize the significance of the operating system and did not insist on owning it. Eventually, ownership and future development of the operating system became more important and profitable than the hardware it ran on.
Microsoft's view of Lotus Notes in the mid-1980s	Lotus Development Corporation started developing this system in 1984. Later it tried to sell it to Microsoft for $12 million, but Microsoft would go no higher than $4 million. In 1993, Lotus Notes generated $100 million in revenue and was central to Lotus Development Corporation's strategy.

Difficulty Foreseeing the Progress of Technology

Even inventors, business leaders, and major researchers often have great difficulty foreseeing the development and potential application of their inventions. Table III.3 shows several commonly cited examples of this phenomenon.

Keep this table in the back of your mind as you read Chapters 9 through 12. Use it to remember that what might seem like an inevitable unfolding of technical advances was not at all obvious before the fact. Many alternative technologies might have succeeded but failed for various business and technical reasons. Many currently commonplace technologies such as fax machines and the use of a mouse in computing languished for years before becoming commercially important. Today's researchers and business managers know some of the technical capabilities that will come out of the lab three to five years from now, but even in that short time frame there will probably be surprises, especially in the ways the new technical capabilities are combined into usable products. This uncertainty is one of the reasons to stay focused on the basic ideas underlying information technology.

KEY TERMS

modularity	reusability	price-performance	interoperability
compatibility	functional capabilities	ease of use	maintainability

REFERENCES

1. Yourdon, Edward. *Decline & Fall of the American Programmer.* Englewood Cliffs, N.J.: Yourdon Press, 1993, p. 267.

2. Crevier, Daniel. *AI: The Tumultuous History of the Search for Artificial Intelligence.* New York: Basic Books, 1993.

3. Kurzweil, Raymond. *The Age of Intelligent Machines.* Cambridge, Mass.: MIT Press, 1990.

4. Quinn, James Bryant. *Intelligent Enterprise: A Knowledge and Service Based Paradigm for Industry.* New York: Free Press, 1992.

5. Stanat, Ruth. *The Intelligent Corporation: Creating a Shared Network for Information and Profit.* New York: AMACOM, 1990.

6. Zahedi, Fatemeh. *Intelligent Systems for Business: Expert Systems with Neural Networks.* Belmont, Calif.: Wadsworth, 1993.

7. de Sola Pool, Ithiel, ed. "Bell's Electrical Toy: What's the Use." In *The Social Impact of the Telephone,* Cambridge, Mass.: MIT Press, 1977, pp. 19–22.

8. Ofiesh, Gabriel. "The Seamless Carpet of Knowledge and Learning," in Lambert, Steve, and Suzanne Ropiequet. *CD ROM: The New Papyrus,* Redmond Wash.: Microsoft Press, 1986, pp. 299–319.

9. Brand, Stewart. *The Media Lab.* New York: Viking Penguin, 1987, p. 256.

10. Smith, Douglas K., and Robert C. Alexander. *Fumbling the Future. How Xerox Invented, then Ignored the First Personal Computer.* New York: William Morrow and Company, 1988, pp. 35–36.

11. Hammer, Michael, and James Champy. *Reengineering the Corporation: A Manifesto for Business Revolution.* New York: Harper Business, 1993, p. 85.

12. Johnstone, Bob. "Case Study: Inventing the Laser Printer." *Wired,* October 1994, p. 99.

13. Simon, H. A., and Allen Newell. "Heuristic Problem Solving: The Next Advance in Operations Research." *Operations Research,* Jan.–Feb. 1958, pp. 7–8, cited in Crevier, *op. cit.*

14. Armstrong, J. Scott. *Long Range Forecasting.* New York: John Wiley & Sons, 1985.

9

Computer Hardware

Study Questions

▶ *What are the basic components of a computer system?*

▶ *What are the different types of computers?*

▶ *What are the organizational approaches to computing?*

▶ *How is client–server computing different from centralized computing?*

▶ *How is it possible for computers to process any type of data?*

▶ *What are the different approaches for increasing data manipulation speeds?*

▶ *What are the different forms of data input?*

▶ *What are the different forms of data storage?*

▶ *What are the different forms of data output?*

VoiceEM is a voice-to-computer system used by doctors in over 200 emergency rooms to replace handwritten medical charts. A similar system is used in over 175 radiology departments. Emergency room physicians at Mercy Hospital see 30 to 50 patients a day and compile a report on each case. Instead of writing out emergency room medical histories by hand or dictating them for typing the next day, physicians dictate their reports into VoiceEm and see a typed version on a computer screen in a minute.

VoiceEM provides the doctor with a menu of over 110 emergency room situations, ranging from stab wounds to heart attacks. The system prompts the doctor with a set of questions; the doctor then answers into a microphone. This prompting helps assure that the doctor has not left out important observations or tests. In less than a minute, VoiceEM produces signature-ready reports that can be edited on a keyboard. Because reports produced this way don't require separate transcribing, medical charting is equally effective any time of day or night. An unexpected benefit of using VoiceEM is that physicians have been able to save about $4,000 per doctor on annual malpractice premiums. Previously some malpractice cases were lost because the documentation was poor even if the care met medical standards.[1]

An earlier version of VoiceEM had to be "trained" to understand a user's voice inputs before it could be used. A typical vocabulary for producing medical charts is 1,000 words, and the user trained the system by speaking each word into a microphone three times. Then the system combined these samples to create a stored pattern it could use later for matching to each word the doctor dictates. Since the system was trained for each individual doctor, different accents were not a factor. A subsequent version of VoiceEM is not as restricted because it recognizes voices well enough to be used initially without training. What's more, it keeps a running record of each user's voice profile to improve its performance over time.

DEBATE TOPIC   *Argue the pros and cons and practical implications of the following proposition:* VoiceEM demonstrates that keyboards will soon become a relic, much like the punched cards that were once used for data storage.

THE FEATURED CASE ILLUSTRATES a recent technological development with future implications. Early computers required totally unambiguous inputs using punched cards or tapes. Current systems are starting to be able to decipher certain types of speech, handwriting, and even gestures. Voice recognition methods also illustrate that the distinction between hardware and software is becoming more blurred all the time. Doctors using VoiceEm see it as a machine (hardware), yet the greatest challenge in building the system was in writing the programs (software) for recognizing speech.

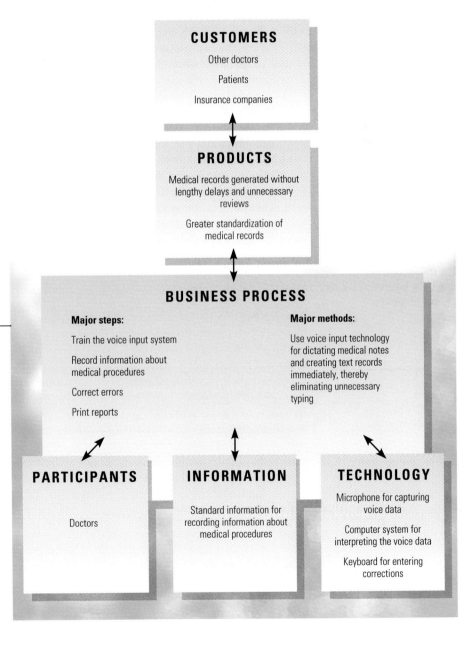

Figure 9.1 Mercy Hospital: Using Voice Recognition

CUSTOMERS

Other doctors

Patients

Insurance companies

PRODUCTS

Medical records generated without lengthy delays and unnecessary reviews

Greater standardization of medical records

BUSINESS PROCESS

Major steps:

Train the voice input system

Record information about medical procedures

Correct errors

Print reports

Major methods:

Use voice input technology for dictating medical notes and creating text records immediately, thereby eliminating unnecessary typing

PARTICIPANTS

Doctors

INFORMATION

Standard information for recording information about medical procedures

TECHNOLOGY

Microphone for capturing voice data

Computer system for interpreting the voice data

Keyboard for entering corrections

Computer systems are changing in many other directions simultaneously. At one time, the computer was a centralized piece of equipment that could operate only if run by highly skilled technicians. Today, millions of people use personal computers (PCs) routinely. Furthermore, with computer functions becoming distributed across networks, computer users in many firms may not know or even care about the physical location of the computer. New ways of thinking about computers are required as the traditional definitions of different types of computers become less meaningful.

The first eight chapters of this book focused on basic ideas about the use and impacts of information systems. They were written under the assumption that your familiarity with information technology in everyday life is sufficient for getting started in understanding information systems. Now that you appreciate these systems, you are in a better position to think about the significance of ideas about information technology discussed in this chapter and the three that follow it.

As a business professional, it is unnecessary for you to be an expert on computer system technology. However, you do need to recognize and appreciate computer system technology on several levels:

1. You need to understand basic terminology and concepts, which are part of basic literacy for business professionals in an information age.
2. You need some historical perspective; otherwise, you will focus too much on the details of today's technology and not appreciate future trends in technology.
3. You need to be able to think about computer technology in relation to the way people work; otherwise, you cannot participate effectively in discussions of how computer systems will affect you and your organization.

The combination of these needs dictates this chapter's approach, especially the way it refers to user and management concerns wherever these concerns are intertwined with the computer system topics.

Overview of Computer Systems

A **computer** is a device that can execute previously stored instructions. Since the instructions for performing a particular task are called a **program,** computers are programmable devices. A **computer system** consists of computers and computer-controlled devices that process data by executing programs. The physical devices in a computer system are its **hardware.** The programs are its **software.**

The introduction to Part III mentioned that everything computer systems do can be boiled down to six functions: capturing, transmitting, storing, retrieving, manipulating, and displaying data. Table III.1 defined these functions and showed some of the devices or technologies used to perform each of them. Later in this chapter, we will look in more detail at devices for capturing, storing and retrieving, and displaying information. Chapter 11, Telecommuinications and Networks, will discuss data transmission.

Basic Model of a Computer System

The first step in understanding computer systems is to identify their basic components. In the late 1940s, John von Neumann and his colleagues published a description of the internal architecture of an idealized electronic computer. The components included:

- An arithmetic-logic unit to perform calculations

- A central control unit to control the sequence of operations

- A memory to hold both data and programs so that programs could be executed efficiently

- Input and output units

Most computers dating from 1945 until today are based on this architecture. Unlike parallel processing (an innovation described later), the von Neumann architecture dictates that instructions be executed one at a time under the control of the central control unit. The PC in Figure 9.2 exemplifies the processing, input, storage, and output capabilities called for by the von Neumann architecture.

Figure 9.2 Hardware Components of a Personal Computer System

From a user's viewpoint, the hardware components of a personal computer system include the computer, keyboard, monitor, diskettes, hard disk, and printer.

The **central processing unit (CPU)** controls computer system operation by decoding and executing programs. Decoding and execution are carried out by a microprocessor chip made of silicon. The CPU uses other silicon chips called **random access memory (RAM)** to store instructions and data it is currently using. The term *random access* implies that the CPU can directly address and access any data location in the RAM. A related term encountered frequently in discussions of PCs is **read only memory (ROM).** Programs stored in this permanent memory control the operation of the computer and cannot be changed by the user's programs.

An **input device** is used for entering instructions and data. Input devices for the PC in Figure 9.2 include a keyboard and mouse. Other input devices (not shown in the figure) include light pens, touch screens, scanners, and even voice input devices.

An **output device** is used for displaying data to people. The output devices for the PC in Figure 9.2 include a monitor and laser printer. A monitor of this type is often called a video display terminal (VDT). Other output devices (not shown) include various types of printers and plotters for paper output, flat panel screens (rather than VDT screens), and speakers for audio output.

Storage devices hold programs and data for future processing. Storage for the PC in Figure 9.2 includes a hard disk. Other storage devices (not shown) include various types of magnetic storage such as magnetic tapes and disks, optical storage such as erasable optical disks, and micrographic storage such as microfilm. Since input, output, and storage devices are usually considered to be options separate from the computer, they are often called **peripherals.**

Types of Computers

The original concept of computation, storage, input, and output has developed into many types of computers. This section focuses on computers whose users see them as computers rather than as components of other machines. A computer that is an internal component of another machine is called an **embedded computer.** Machines ranging from airplanes to television sets and automatic coffee makers contain embedded computers. Embedded computers used for controlling chemical and mechanical processes in industry are essential components of information systems for factory automation.

Nonembedded computers are classified based on a combination of power, speed, and ability to control or link to other computers or terminals. In 1990, a reasonable first cut at computer categories included personal computer, workstation, minicomputer, mainframe, and supercomputer. After looking at these categories, which are still part of everyday terminology, we will see that the advent of networked computer systems is creating many new possibilities.

A **personal computer (PC)** is a single-user computer that sits on a desktop or can be carried around by the user. The entire PC in Figure 9.2 fits on a desktop. Laptop computers, and even smaller notebook and subnotebook computers, are PCs that fit into a briefcase but contain enough computing power and disk storage to support a business professional's personal requirements for word processing, spreadsheets, and storage of documents. Pen computers that lack a keyboard and use an electronic pen for writing input on the screen have been adopted in specific types of applications where keyboards are inconvenient and handwritten input is adequate (see Figure 9.3). A **workstation** is a powerful single-user computer used for complex data analysis and engineering design work. Workstations often come with large screens needed to work with complex images. Although the first PCs could run only simple word processors, spreadsheets, and specialized applications, technical advances in hardware and software have made current PCs much more able to perform tasks previously reserved for workstations.

Specialized single-user computers are also becoming more common that fall somewhere between general-purpose PCs and task-specific machines. For example, Digital Biometrics has developed a 3-pound portable computer for police work. It contains a camera for snapping mug shots, a small lens for capturing the print of a finger pressed against it, and a radio transmitter for two-way communication with a nearby patrol car. The patrol car can transmit the picture and fingerprints to a police station and can receive criminal database data in return.[2] The more mundane world of office work has a variety of portable computers that include hard disks for storing data, small printers, and connections to telephones or networks for transmitting data or faxes.

Minicomputers and mainframes typically perform all the processing for a large number of users working at terminals. **Minicomputers** are centralized computers typically shared by a department in a company for processing transactions, accessing corporate databases, and generating reports. **Mainframe** computers are even more powerful; they are typically linked to hundreds or even thousands of terminals for processing high volumes of online transactions and generating reports from large databases. Mainframe systems contain extensive data storage capabilities. The tape library might

Figure 9.3 Portable Computers

(a) This Canon Notejet computer includes a small inkjet printer whose cartridge holds enough ink for about 80 pages, enough f or occasional needs of travelers. (b) This pen computer is used for data input where a keyboard would not work.

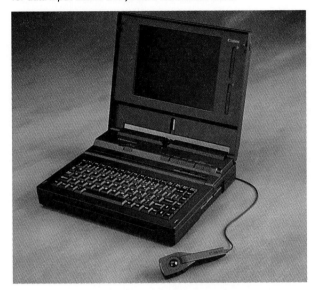

contain thousands of tapes, and the computer center could include dozens of free-standing hard disk units containing enormous databases. Printed outputs could be produced on high-speed printers at centralized locations or on low-speed printers at end-user locations. Mainframes are usually housed in environmentally controlled and physically secure computer rooms (see Figure 9.4). **Supercomputers** were initially thought of as computers designed for exceptionally high-volume, high-speed calculation rather than transaction processing. Such computers have been used for complex analysis problems such as simulations of the weather or the flow of air around a wing. More recently, supercomputers have also been used for applications in banking, manufacturing, and data retrieval.

Figure 9.4 Comparison of a Mainframe Computer and a Notebook Computer

The IBM mainframe computer requires a large, environmentally controlled computer room. The IBM ThinkPad is the size of a book and can be used virtually anywhere.

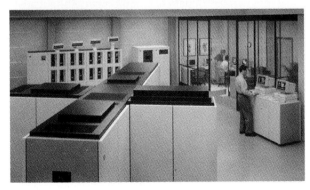

Twenty years ago, mainframe computers contained CPUs that operated at a much higher **MIPS** (millions of instructions per second) rate than minicomputers, which were much faster than the early PCs. By the 1990s, however, CPUs of both mainframes and advanced PCs started using the same types of microprocessors. This is one of the reasons computer categories are breaking down, and the breakdown is hastened by the fact that the cost per MIPS for PCs may be one hundred times lower than for mainframes.

Improvements in raw computing power do not mean that PCs can replace centralized computers, however. Minicomputers and mainframes are designed to accept inputs from many simultaneous users. PCs cannot support this type of application, regardless of whether they can perform an individual user's numerical calculations at the speed of a larger computer. Using PCs for applications that formerly ran on mainframes requires that they be linked in a network.

The trend toward computer networks has spawned an additional category of computers. **Servers** are specialized computers linked to other computers on a network in order to perform specific types of tasks requested through those computers. Low-end servers are basically powerful PCs configured to perform specific tasks, such as finding data in a database, controlling printing, or controlling electronic mail. High-end servers perform similar functions for larger networks or larger databases. Many observers believe that mainframe computers will gradually evolve into database servers capable of handling large databases.

Computer System Architectures

Computer systems should be deployed in a way that mirrors business processes. If people work individually and rarely share their work products, computer systems should provide effective tools for individual work. If people work as a group, computer systems should make it easier to share work. If the organization relies on a central database for orders, reservations, or inventory, computer systems should provide access to the database.

Figure 9.5 shows three ways to deploy computer systems: centralized computing, personal computing, and distributed computing. In centralized computing, all the processing for multiple users is done by a large central computer. In personal computing, users have their own machines and rarely share data or resources. In distributed computing, users may have their own computers, and the organization uses a network to share data and resources. These alternative forms of computing are tied to how the organization operates. The discussion here follows a progression from a totally centralized approach to a totally decentralized approach and arrives at a partially decentralized approach that requires central controls. Each approach raises its own management issues concerning the effective and efficient use of data and equipment. Although we introduce the three approaches separately, they may be combined in many ways. Figure 9.5 summarizes and compares the approaches.

Centralized computing

In **centralized computing,** a single centralized computer performs the processing for multiple users. (The computer that performs the work might be a mainframe or a minicomputer.) The first computerized systems for business transaction processing operated in batch mode and used punched cards for data input and storage. Later, online transaction processing permitted multiple users at terminals to perform transactions simultaneously. In this original form of online transaction processing, every input went directly from the terminals to the central computer, and all outputs to the

Figure 9.5 Three Approaches to Computing in Organizations

With the first computer systems, centralized computing was the only option. Personal computing arose as an alternative providing more flexibility to individual users. Distributed computing attempts to combine the best of the other two approaches.

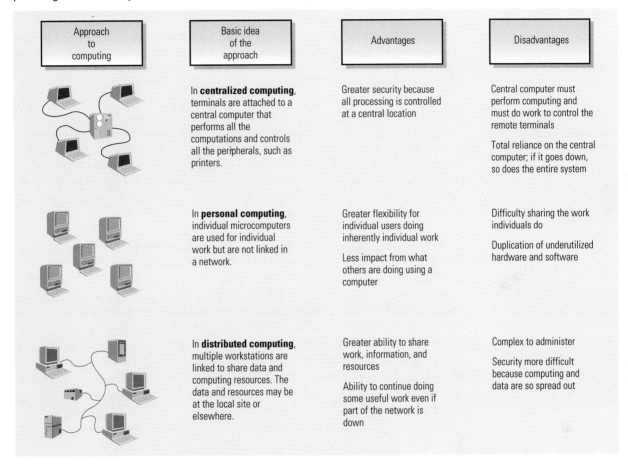

Approach to computing	Basic idea of the approach	Advantages	Disadvantages
	In **centralized computing**, terminals are attached to a central computer that performs all the computations and controls all the peripherals, such as printers.	Greater security because all processing is controlled at a central location	Central computer must perform computing and must do work to control the remote terminals Total reliance on the central computer; if it goes down, so does the entire system
	In **personal computing**, individual microcomputers are used for individual work but are not linked in a network.	Greater flexibility for individual users doing inherently individual work Less impact from what others are doing using a computer	Difficulty sharing the work individuals do Duplication of underutilized hardware and software
	In **distributed computing**, multiple workstations are linked to share data and computing resources. The data and resources may be at the local site or elsewhere.	Greater ability to share work, information, and resources Ability to continue doing some useful work even if part of the network is down	Complex to administer Security more difficult because computing and data are so spread out

users came from the central computer. The terminals in these systems were eventually called **dumb terminals** because they could perform no processing and served only as an input/output mechanism linking users with the central computer.

Centralized computing to service multiple users has many shortcomings. First, the computer has to perform two types of work: It has to do the computing for the users, and it has to manage the status and progress of work being done for each online user. The operating system software that keeps track of the jobs uses a lot of the CPU's processing power. As a result, a substantial percentage of the available computing resources go toward controlling the job stream rather than accomplishing the work the users want. A second shortcoming is total reliance on the central computer. If either the telecommunications line to the computer or the computer itself goes down, no work can be done using the dumb terminal. A third shortcoming is the necessity to balance the computer's workload to avoid peak-load problems when people across the organization want to use it simultaneously. This necessitates tight schedules and controls on the corporate (or departmental) computer to ensure that it can provide reliable service. Centralized controls, procedures, and schedules support the scheduled processing but limit users' flexibility in doing their own work.

Despite these problems of mainframe computing, centralized functions are needed for many business operations. For example, order entry functions in many businesses such as airlines, distributors, and large manufacturers require online access to central databases by geographically dispersed users. Mainframe computing has evolved in many ways to perform these functions while reducing the problems of totally centralized processing. For example, the dumb terminals in many systems have been replaced by **intelligent workstations** that can perform some of the processing. In addition, various forms of redundancy have been built in to improve overall system reliability.

Personal computing

Computer system deployment changed dramatically following the introduction of personal computers in the late 1970s. For the first time, these systems provided powerful computing to individuals and small businesses at an affordable price. In the 1980s, worldwide shipments of personal computers exceeded the shipments of the large-scale systems that had previously dominated the market. The basic idea of **personal computing** is that a computer should be available as a tool for individual work at any time. This approach is particularly effective for inherently individual work such as word processing, spreadsheets, presentations, personal calendars, and simple design work. It also succeeds for small companies whose limited record keeping fits on a PC.

The first PCs had awkward user interfaces, software with limited capabilities, and stored both data and software only on diskettes. Major advances have occurred in all these areas. Use of a **graphical user interface (GUI)** permits the user to express commands by using a mouse in conjunction with icons and flexible menus. This reduces the need to memorize command languages, filenames, and other details that previously made personal computing difficult for nonprogrammers. They can store data and programs on hard disks, making it easier to start programs, access data, and work with several programs at the same time. With the increasing power of microprocessors, software such as spreadsheets and word processes provide many more capabilities and operate much faster. The most powerful PCs can run several jobs at the same time, for example, permitting a user to print out a large document while doing other work on the computer. Portable computers such as laptops and notebook computers provide additional convenience because they can be used virtually anywhere, even if an electric plug is unavailable for several hours. Overall, personal computing made computer usage practical and affordable on a much wider scale.

Distributed computing

Despite all these advances, personal computing is a limited organizational approach because people in organizations work together. Even departments that enthusiastically embraced PCs soon felt the need for individuals to share information and computing resources. The information included databases, phone messages, memos, and work in progress such as drafts of documents. The resources included printers, fax machines, and external databases.

In **distributed computing,** individuals do their own work on PCs or workstations and use a telecommunications network to link to other devices. The need for the network as part of the computing system is one of the reasons for the great attention to the convergence of computing and communication.

Distributed computing improves coordination; helps in sharing data, messages, and work products; and permits sharing of resources such as printers. Data, messages, and work products are shared in two ways. First, an individual may send a message or file to other computers on the network. Second, an individual may access data residing on a hard disk attached to a different computer on the network. For example, an insurance adjuster using a portable computer can download the day's data to a central database. Later, an insurance pricing analyst might access the claims database through another part of the network. The sharing of printers is accomplished by creating a list of documents to be printed and controlling the printing independently of what individual users are doing on their own computers.

The degree to which computing should be distributed depends on tradeoffs between the cost of transmitting data over telecommunications lines and other factors such as user convenience, maintainability, and security. For infrequently changed data, such as product specifications, it is usually better to send a copy of the data to each site periodically. For data that changes frequently, such as sales orders, it is usually better to maintain the data in fewer sites and use telecommunications more extensively for access to the most current data.

Unfortunately, the advantages of distributed computing come with a price: the need for controls and administration that make it more complex than personal computing. The need for greater controls is apparent from the fact that two users on the same network may not want to share all of their files. For example, a supervisor may wish to share work-related files with subordinates but keep employee salary review files private. This makes it necessary to state explicitly who can access what files. It is also critical to enforce standards to facilitate access to data controlled by someone else. The result is a more restricted environment than personal computing but one in which a group of people can work more effectively.

Much current research is moving toward highly distributed systems, in which the users (and programmers) will not need to know in advance exactly where specific processing will take place. Instead, a network management system will decide where the processing should occur, much as a regional electric power grid can shift generating capacity depending on the current relationship between needs and resources. Topics related to networks will be discussed further in Chapter 11.

This section has introduced three different ways to deploy computers: centralized computing, personal computing, and distributed computing. Comparing these approaches shows that computer systems in organizations involve not only performing calculations, but also making sure that computer deployment reflects the way the organization operates. Since there is a strong trend toward a particular type of distributed computing, we will discuss this in more detail.

The Trend Toward Client–Server Computing

Distributed computing has been accomplished using several new ways to deploy computers. In **client–server architecture,** different devices on the network are treated as clients or servers. The client devices send requests for service, such as printing or retrieval of data, to specific server devices that perform the requested processing. For example, the client devices might consist of ten workstations within a department, and server devices might be a laser printer and a specialized computer (called a **file server**) dedicated to retrieving data from a database. In many networks, the file server is a powerful computer containing special data retrieval and network management capabilities. Some networks use other types of specialized servers such as print servers that execute requests for printing, mail servers that handle electronic mail, and communication servers that link the network to other external networks.

In effect, client–server computing is a way to modularize the work performed by computers. Figure 9.6 shows the difference between client–server and centralized mainframe computing in terms of the division of labor in handling the user interface, application program logic, and database access. Instead of having a mainframe computer control everything from the displays on user terminals through the application logic and the updating of the database, client–server divides these functions between specialized client and server components.

The advantages of client–server computing include user convenience, technical scalability, and greater ability to accommodate and maintain hardware and software from different vendors. User convenience starts with having a powerful PC that can serve personal computing needs but can also link into a network. Attaching a PC to a network instead of using a dumb terminal also means that user interaction functions, such as the graphical user interface and the validation of data inputs at the user's workstation, no longer have to be controlled by an overworked central computer. Scalability is improved because it is easier and less disruptive to add or enhance individual client or server devices instead of modifying a centralized system.

Figure 9.6 Client–Server versus Centralized Mainframe Computing

With the centralized mainframe approach, the central computer controls the user interface, the application logic, and database access. Permitting the same program to control aspects of all three elements makes it much more difficult to change the software over time. With the version of client–server shown, the application programs and user interface are controlled by the client workstation, whereas database access is controlled by the server. With other variations of client-server, control of application logic can be split between the client and the server.

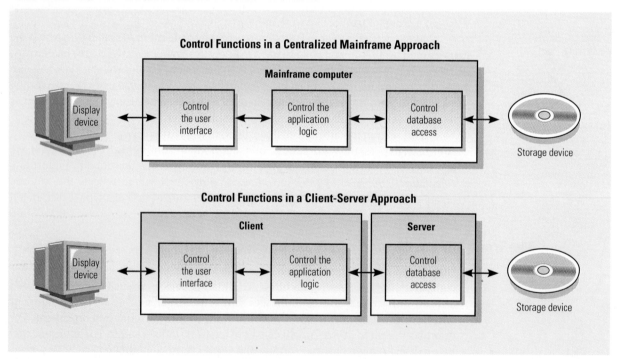

A client–server approach may accommodate hardware and software from different vendors with reasonable ease because the interfaces between each vendor's products and the other parts of the network are becoming more like off-the-shelf products. For example, a client device might request particular customer data from a network without "knowing" the type of database management system used to store the data. The query simply goes to the right server, which contains off-the-shelf software that can interpret the query for the type of database it contains.

The common requirement for using different types of hardware and software on the same network generated a need for new programming methods. These methods divide programming tools between client tools such as methods for creating graphical user interfaces and validating data inputs, and server tools, such as database management systems. Between the client tools and server tools is another category of tool sometimes called middleware. **Middleware** controls communication between clients and servers and performs whatever translation is necessary to make a client's request understandable to a server device. There are several types of middleware. Distributed database middleware provides a common, high-level programming interface, such as structured query language (SQL) that packages information so that it can be used by multiple applications. In contrast, message-oriented middleware facilitates interaction with other applications and operating systems by sending data or requests in the form of messages.[3]

Despite its advantages, client–server computing also has disadvantages, and it is not a panacea. Many early adopters of client–server computing have found that it increases data and system administration efforts. In addition, since the interfaces and middleware translations between modular components take a certain amount of computing time, networks can be slow. The separation between clients and servers also requires using rapidly changing programming methods that are unfamiliar to many programmers.

Peer-to-peer architecture is an important alternative to client–server for small computer networks. In **peer-to-peer**, each workstation can communicate directly with each other workstation on the network without going through a specialized server. Peer-to-peer is appropriate when the network users mostly do their own work but occasionally need to exchange data. In these cases, it may be more efficient to keep data and copies of the software at each workstation to avoid the delays of downloading data and software each time a user gets started. Peer-to-peer also has potential problems in security and consistency. For example, with data at someone else's workstation, the data may be difficult to retrieve when that person is out of the office and the workstation is shut off.

Although client–server and peer-to-peer are very different from mainframe computing in the way they divide the labor for computers and networks, they still require human infrastructure responsible for many of the centralized chores in mainframe computing. Someone must set up the network and maintain it. Someone must make sure that the data files are defined properly, that the network provides adequate performance, and that it is secure from misuse. If the network delivers the software to the workstations, someone must make sure that the software is updated appropriately and that users know when it is updated. The combination of new administrative burdens and unfamiliar and sometimes incomplete programming technology has led many industry observers to question exaggerated claims about the benefits of client–server even though it puts a high-MIPS computer close to the user.

Progress in distributed computing has raised questions about the future role of both minicomputers and mainframes. One industry analyst estimates that the percentage of new, multiuser applications using client–server architecture will grow to 75 percent by 1996 and 90 percent by the year 2000.[4] Some experts believe that centralized computing using mainframe computers will gradually give way to an expanded form of distributed computing, which will provide both sharing of data and immediate availability of computing power. Others think that mainframe computers will operate primarily as servers linked to large databases, whereas most data manipulation will occur at workstations. Still others predict that there will always be a place for centralized computing in large corporate applications.

REALITY CHECK   **Computer System Architectures**   This section identified three computer system architectures: centralized computing, personal computing, and distributed computing.

1. Identify times (if any) when you have used a computer system of each type.

2. Referring to the characteristics in Table III.2, explain how the architectures felt different from a user's viewpoint. If you have used only one, explain how you think the others might feel different to a user.

Looking Inside the Black Box

With this background on types of computers and organizational approaches to computing, we can now take a deeper look at what actually happens inside a computer system. We will introduce a series of computer-oriented topics, each of which helps you appreciate something about the way computers are used in business. Understanding the coding of data will help you understand why a single picture may be worth a thousand words, but may use 100 times as much storage in a computer system. Visualizing machine language is the beginning of understanding the advances in software that led to user-programmable tools such as spreadsheets. The discussion of the semiconductors inside the computer helps you understand why it has been possible to shrink computer sizes and make them portable.

Box 9.1 lists some of the technical terms used in this section and elsewhere in the book for measuring the performance of computers and peripherals. These terms involve things such as the amount of information (number of bits and bytes), time (milliseconds and microseconds), speed of processing (MIPS, FLOPS, bits per second), and frequencies. Familiarity with these technical terms is useful because people use them to talk about computer and telecommunications devices just as they talk about cars using number of passengers, gas tank capacity, number of cylinders, miles per hour, and miles per gallon.

Coding Data for Processing by a Computer

To understand how computers operate, it is essential to understand the way any type of data, including numbers, text, pictures, and sounds, can be coded for processing by machines. This is not just a technical detail because it helps in understanding the capabilities and limits of current computers.

Binary representation of numbers

Before a computer can process data, the data must be converted into a form the computer can process. This section will show how any type of data (numbers, text, images, and sounds) can be represented in the form of 0's and 1's. Each 0 or 1 is called a **bit,** or binary digit. Representing data as a series of bits is especially efficient because digital computers are built from components that switch between off–on (0–1) states.

Consistent with their off–on internal components, computers perform calculations using the base-2, or binary, number system. Figure 9.7 shows binary addition and multiplication tables to illustrate the advantage of using binary representation for the internal operations within a computer. The addition and multiplication tables involve only 4 entries instead of 100 entries that would be required for base-10 tables. This implies that the internal circuitry inside the computer is much simpler because binary representation is used.

Box 9.1 Technical Terms for Describing and Measuring Computer Performance

Much of the progress that has occurred in computing can be described in terms of measurements related to the amount of data processed or stored, the amount of time required, the amount of time needed to execute instructions, and other similar factors.

Measuring amounts of data: *bit, byte, kilobyte, megabyte, gigabyte, terabyte*

bit: a binary digit, a 0 or 1
byte: 8 bits, whose 256 different possible combinations are sufficient to represent 256 different characters, including all 10 digits (0, 1, 2, 3,...), all 26 uppercase and 26 lowercase letters (a, b, c,...), and all the common special characters (:,;,@,#,$,...).

kilobyte (KB):	10^3	(one thousand) bytes
megabyte (MB):	10^6	(one million) bytes
gigabyte (GB):	10^9	(one billion) bytes
terabyte:	10^{12}	(one trillion) bytes

The term *kilobyte* is slightly inaccurate since it usually refers to 1,024 bytes. RAM in the first PCs was stated in kilobytes, such as 16KB or 64KB. Now it is usually measured in megabytes, such as 8MB or 12MB. Computer diskettes come in sizes such as 640KB, 800KB, and 1.44MB. Typical capacities for hard disks in new personal computers exceed 200MB of data. The capacity of hard disks for mainframe computers can be much greater. Optical disks go from 500MB to several GB.

Measuring time: *millisecond, microsecond, nanosecond, picosecond*

millisecond	10^{-3}	(one thousandth of a) second
microsecond	10^{-6}	(one millionth of a) second
nanosecond	10^{-9}	(one billionth of a) second
picosecond	10^{-12}	(one trillionth of a) second

Hard disks for PCs can access data in 12 to 18 milliseconds. Computers can execute machine language instructions in fractions of a microsecond. The switching speed of a semiconductor circuit might be 200 picoseconds, although switching speeds of 2 picoseconds have been produced in research labs.

Measuring the data path of a chip: *16-bit, 32-bit, 64-bit*
Chips are often classified as 16-bit, 32-bit, or 64-bit chips. This refers to their data path, the number of bits of information that the chip can receive, process, or send at one time. Due to the way machine languages work, the data path also gives the number of internal memory locations the computer can access directly.

Measuring the speed of executing instructions: *MIPS, FLOPS, megaflops, gigaflops*

MIPS: This term describes the speed of computation and is an abbreviation for one million instructions per second. It is typically used in a context such as, "This microprocessor can operate at 25 MIPS." Although an indicator of a computer's speed, MIPS tells only part of the story because the effective speed of a computer also depends on other factors. For example, different computers have different data paths (16-bit, 32-bit, or 64-bit), use different internal machine languages, and divide work between the computer and peripherals in different ways. This means that different computers may accomplish different amounts of work while operating at the same speed.

FLOPS: This term stands for floating point operations per second. Floating point operations are the addition, subtraction, multiplication, and division of decimal numbers. FLOPS are a better measure than MIPS for talking about the computing power of computers used to do complex scientific calculations. Millions, billions, and trillions of FLOPS are called megaflops, gigaflops, and teraflops, respectively.

Measuring internal clock speed of computers or transmission frequency for telecommunications devices: *hertz, kilohertz, megahertz, gigahertz* (Hertz is a measure of frequency)

Hertz (Hz): one cycle per second.
kilohertz (KHz): one thousand cycles per second.
megahertz (MHz): one million cycles per second.
gigahertz (GHz): one billion cycles per second.

The internal clocks in current microprocessors operate between from 33 to over 200 MHz. Data transmissions are broadcast at different frequencies. For example, AM radio is broadcast in the range around 1 MHz, FM radio is around 100 MHz, and satellite transmissions are around 10 GHz.

Measuring the rate of data transfer: *bits per second, baud*
Data transmission is measured in bits per second. Data travel over copper telephone lines between 300 bits per second and 64,000 bits per second depending on the physical connections and switching system. Devices that transmit and receive data from PCs often operate at 9600, 14400 or 28800 bits per second. Data travel over fiber optic cable at 100 million bits per second or more. The engineering term *baud* is sometimes used instead of bits per second. Baud refers to the rate of signal changes per second. If a device can send only off–on signals, its bits per second rate equals its baud rate. Higher speed devices that transmit individual signals with gradations finer than just 0 versus 1 can send messages whose bits per second rate is higher than their baud rate.

Figure 9.7 Addition and Multiplication Tables for Binary Numbers

Addition and multiplication tables for binary numbers have only four entries, each of which is either a 0 or a 1. Implementing these tables within a computer's circuitry is much simpler than implementing base-10 tables that would have to include 100 situations.

+	0	1
0	0	1
1	1	10

Addition table

*	0	1
0	0	0
1	0	1

Multiplication table

Figure 9.8 Expressing Numbers in Base-2

It is possible to convert any base-10 number to binary. The opposite transformation is always possible.

The location of each digit in a base-10 number determines that digit's value. For example, the base-10 number 3,597 can be expressed in powers of 10 as follows:

$$
\begin{aligned}
3{,}597 = \quad & 3 \ * \ 1{,}000 \ = \ 3 \ * \ 10^3 \\
+ \ & 5 \ * \ 100 \ \ \ \ \ \ + \ 5 \ * \ 10^2 \\
+ \ & 9 \ * \ 10 \ \ \ \ \ \ \ \ + \ 9 \ * \ 10^1 \\
+ \ & 7 \ * \ 1 \ \ \ \ \ \ \ \ \ \ + \ 7 \ * \ 10^0
\end{aligned}
$$

Base 10 uses the ten digits 0 through 9. In contrast, base 2 uses only two digits, 0 and 1. The location of digits in base 2 has the same effect as the location of digits in base 10, except that each position represents powers of 2 rather than 10. For example, the base-2 number 10111 (which is equivalent to the base-10 number 23) represents the following combination of powers of 2:

$$
\begin{aligned}
10111 = \quad & 1 \ * \ 2^4 \ = \ 1 \ * \ 16 \quad\quad 16 \ \text{(in base-10)} \\
+ \ & 0 \ * \ 2^3 \ \ \ \ + \ 0 \ * \ 8 \quad\quad + \ 0 \\
+ \ & 1 \ * \ 2^2 \ \ \ \ + \ 1 \ * \ 4 \quad\quad + \ 4 \\
+ \ & 1 \ * \ 2^1 \ \ \ \ + \ 1 \ * \ 2 \quad\quad + \ 2 \\
+ \ & 1 \ * \ 2^0 \ \ \ \ + \ 1 \ * \ 1 \quad\quad + \ 1 \\
& \quad\quad\quad\quad\quad\quad\quad\quad\quad\quad\quad\quad 23 \ \text{(in base-10)}
\end{aligned}
$$

It is possible to express any base-10 number as an equivalent base-2 number by breaking it up into successive powers of 2. The base-10 example (3,597) is equivalent to the base-2 number 111000001101.

Since people work with base-10 numbers, computers automatically convert these numbers into binary form before they perform calculations. They then convert the results back into base-10 for use by people. Figure 9.8 explains how to convert a number from our everyday base-10 number system into binary.

Numerical representation of text

The electronics inside most computers are organized in groups of 8 bits. Eight bits, or 1 **byte,** is enough to uniquely identify 256 different characters (digits, uppercase and lowercase letters, punctuation marks, and special characters such as $ and @). The 256 possible configurations of a single byte can represent all characters used in English and most other languages that have alphabets. However, 256 different characters are not sufficient for coding the thousands of different Chinese characters, or kanji. This is one reason computers were adopted slowly in the Far East.

The terms *bit* and *byte* are basic terms for describing computer memory and processing power. Box 9.1 defines related terms such as **kilobyte, megabyte,** and **gigabyte** and identifies other terms used to describe computers and computerized devices.

The industry requirement for standard ways of coding data comes from the frequent need to move data between different brands of computers even if their internal operation is inconsistent. **ASCII** is one of several standard codes for representing letters, digits, and special characters on computer systems. ASCII stands for American Standard Code for Information Interchange. Table 9.1 shows how ASCII-8 represents letters and digits as sequences of 0's and 1's.

Table 9.1 ASCII-8 Code for Data

Digit	ASCII Representation	Letter	ASCII Representation
0	0101 0000		
1	0101 0001	A	1010 0001
2	0101 0010	B	1010 0010
3	0101 0011	C	1010 0011
4	0101 0100	D	1010 0100
5	0101 0101	E	1010 0101
6	0101 0110	F	1010 0110
7	0101 0111	G	1010 0111
8	0101 1000	H	1010 1000
9	0101 1001	I	1010 1001

Numerical representation of sounds and pictures

Images and sounds can also be represented as a series of numbers and therefore as a series of 0's and 1's. The process of generating these numbers is called **digitizing,** and the result is called a digital representation of the image or sound. Figure 9.9 shows how an image can be digitized by dividing it into tiny squares and assigning a number to each square representing the shade in the square. Imagine that a 1-by-1-inch image is covered with a 200-by-200 grid that isolates tiny picture elements, or **pixels.** Each pixel is coded on a scale ranging from absolutely white to absolutely dark. With the 200-by-200 grid, the 1-inch square image would be represented by 40,000 numbers, which could then be stored in a computer or transmitted.

Figure 9.9 Digitizing Images and Spoken Sounds

(a) A black and white image can be digitized by subdividing it using a fine grid and then assigning a number to each point on the grid. The number for each point represents its value on a scale from absolutely white to absolutely black. The fineness of the grid (in lines per inch) determines the precision of the digitized image. (b) Spoken sounds can be digitized by dividing their waveforms into tiny increments and coding each increment. The picture shows how voice waveforms can be represented.

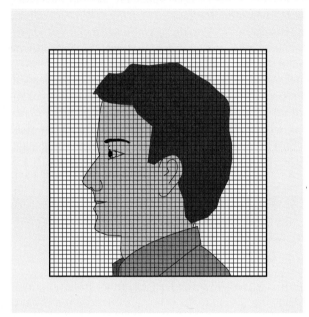
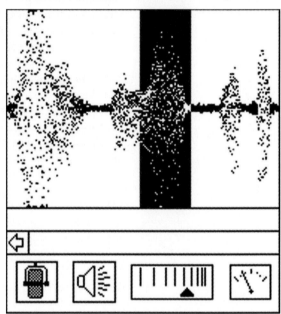

Representations of this type are actually approximations. The denser the grid, the more precise the representation, as was demonstrated by Figure 4.13. Four times as many numbers would be required to represent a color image which can be represented as a combination of four colors such as red, blue, yellow, and black. Sounds can also be digitized by a process of dividing their waveforms into tiny increments, each of which is coded numerically (see Figure 9.9).

The fact that any type of data can be represented as a series of bits means that a computer can process any type of data. For example, it can add two numbers using a base-2 addition table built into its circuitry. The details of how electronic circuits perform such operations are found in computer science texts. Likewise, it can change the shade of part of an image by changing the related bit pattern.

Until the 1980s, computer systems processed numbers and text almost exclusively. They rarely processed images and sounds because insufficient price-performance made it too expensive to handle the amount of data required for useful applications. Although most of the data processed by business computers today are still numbers and text, important applications involving images and sounds have become widespread. Image applications include creating engineering drawings, storing correspondence from customers, and displaying graphical information for decision makers. Audio applications are increasing because they fit into the way people do work. Current applications include voice mail systems, systems for inserting voice annotations into documents, systems for controlling computers by voice commands, and even some systems (see the chapter's opening case) for voice entry of numbers or text.

Data compression

Digitizing images and video generates an enormous number of numbers. Consider a black-and-white 8-by-10 photograph digitized at the resolution of 200 dots per inch. Since each square inch contains 40,000 dots and the photograph contains 80 square inches, the digitized image would contain 3,200,000 numbers, more than enough numbers to represent every letter in every word in this book. A picture may be worth a thousand words but may require the same computer resources for storage and transmission as a million words.

Data compression is one of the ways to increase the storage and transmission capability of computer and communication hardware without upgrading the hardware. **Data compression** is the coding of data to remove types of redundancies that can be detected easily. The basic idea is to use mathematical techniques to compress data whenever it is stored or transmitted and to decompress it whenever it is used. Data compression software for PCs can shrink programs and word processing documents to roughly half their normal size, permitting you to squeeze more data into the same floppy disk or hard disk. This is often accomplished by overriding the computer's directory system to eliminate blank spaces in the internal storage. Data compression of 90 percent or more for video signals helps make videoconferencing possible. The sources of the reduction include taking fewer frames per second, transmitting only the parts of the picture that change from frame to frame, and identifying and coding special patterns within individual frames, such as areas of uniform color.

Data encryption

A special type of coding is sometimes used to prevent unauthorized or illegal use of data that can be stolen or intercepted while being stored or transmitted. **Encryption** is the process of coding data to make it meaningless to any unauthorized user. The encrypted data is meaningful only to someone who can use a special decoding process for converting the data back to the original form. Encrypting data is essential for networks that transfer money between accounts in different financial institutions. It is also important to pay television operators who don't want their signals used for free. Some people encrypt data on their own PCs to prevent unwarranted access.

An example of a simple encryption scheme is to replace each letter in a word by the letter five positions after it in the alphabet. With this scheme, the word *encryption* would appear as *jshwduynts*. Since a scheme like this would be easy to figure out, real encryption schemes are much more complicated, often requiring that some part of the encryption rule change frequently. A number of encryption products have been built based on complex manipulations of bit patterns. The manipulations in one method include scrambling bit order, dividing a bit string into two halves, and applying 16 additional transformations to each half. Recent attempts to adopt an encryption standard for telecommunications generated a storm of controversy involving privacy, law enforcement, commercial, and computer science issues. (See the Bell Labs real-world case at the end of this chapter.)

We have now seen how any type of data can be coded for processing by a computer. Next we will look at the way computers execute instructions to do useful things with the coded data.

Machine Language

Computers are devices that can execute previously stored instructions: Although the details of computer circuitry are immensely complicated, the basic idea of executing previously stored instructions is quite simple. We will use a hypothetical example to illustrate the internal machine language in which machine instructions are expressed and will then look at the developments that gave current laptop computers more processing power than room-size computers once had.

Instructions a computer can execute directly are expressed in **machine language,** the computer's internal programming language. Different brands of computers may use different machine languages because their CPUs contain different microprocessors. For example, a Macintosh computer from Apple might use a Motorola PowerPC chip, whereas IBM-style PCs from both IBM and Dell might use a Pentium microprocessor. The difference in machine languages implies that software written for one PC brand may not run on a different brand.

Figure 9.10 shows a hypothetical example of a highly simplified machine language (for example, a real machine language would not have a multiply instruction of this type). In this example, the instructions are performing the calculation

$$A = (B - C) * D + (E * F)$$

The machine language instructions in the figure look nothing like the formula. Instructions in this hypothetical machine language consist of a numerical operation code and the location of the data item that is being added, subtracted, or multiplied. For example, the second instruction in the program is 37−202, which says, "Add contents of location 202 to contents of accumulator." Each instruction is in a physical location inside the computer; each data item is in a physical location that must be referenced explicitly by the program.

This last point about referencing specific locations has important implications for the effective speed of the processor that executes machine language instructions. Microprocessors such as the Intel 486 or Pentium use **32-bit addressing,** meaning that they can address over 16 million (2^{32}) locations directly. Previous 8-bit or 16-bit processors could address only 64 (2^8) or 4,096 (2^{16}) locations directly. Since machine language programs are often much larger than this, computers with 8-or 16-bit addressing had to do extra work to keep track of data in memory locations that they could not address directly. In addition to making it even harder to program these computers, limited address spaces therefore slowed these computers down compared to what they might otherwise do. In 1993, Digital Equipment Corporation released the Alpha Chip, a 64-bit microprocessor that can address 2^{64} locations directly.

Writing instructions in machine language is extremely difficult for people because it forces them to make a large number of explicit choices they do not care about. For instance, the physical location of the data and machine instructions are of little interest to someone who merely wants to use the formula to calculate the value of *A.* Another problem is that the code itself is inexpressive, making it difficult to understand what another person's machine language program is trying to do. In fact, after a few months, even the original programmer would find a complex program difficult to understand.

Early programmers developed an ingenious solution to this problem. As illustrated in Figure 9.11, the solution was to have the person write the program using an appropriate tool such as a higher-level language or spreadsheet program and then have the computer automatically translate that program into machine language instructions. We will discuss the idea of higher-level languages in depth in Chapter 10.

Figure 9.10 Hypothetical Example of a Simplified Machine Language

As in real machine languages, instructions in this hypothetical machine language are stated in terms of a numerical operation code and the location of (one or more) operands. The instructions themselves must also reside at some location within the machine in order to be executed. Requiring people to break things down to this level of detail makes machine language an extremely unfriendly and inefficient tool for human programmers. Chapter 10 will explain how programs written in typical programming languages are translated into machine languages.

| Location of instruction | Instruction | | Meaning of instruction |
	Operation code	Location of operand	
101	19	–	Clear accumulator
102	37	202	Add contents of location 202 to contents of accumulator
103	46	203	Subtract contents of location 203 from contents of accumulator
104	52	204	Multiply contents of accumulator by contents of location 204
105	24	207	Store contents of accumulator in location 207
106	19	–	Clear accumulator
107	37	205	Add contents of location 205 to contents of accumulator
108	52	206	Multiply contents of accumulator by contents of location 206
109	37	207	Add contents of location 207 to contents of accumulator
110	24	201	Store contents of accumulator in location 201

Figure 9.11 Automatically Translating a Formula into Machine Language

Instead of forcing the programmer to convert a formula into machine language, it is possible to use a translating program called a compiler to perform the translation.

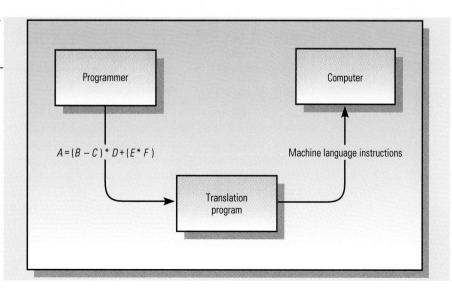

Programmer

$A = (B - C) * D + (E * F)$

Translation program

Machine language instructions

Computer

Approaches for Increasing Computer Performance

We will look at three approaches for improving computer performance: making processors faster and more powerful, making specialized processors, and programming computers so that the processors operate in parallel. A fourth approach, converting the computer into a network, has already been introduced.

Faster and more powerful processors

Developments in miniaturization and speed of computing devices have changed computers from room-sized machines to machines the size of a notepad. The first computers represented data using off–on switches that were wired together. Today's computers would not be possible without the **integrated circuit** that was first developed in 1958. The concept of the integrated circuit was that an entire electronic circuit could be embedded into a single piece of silicon called a **chip.** The **microprocessor** was another key development because it integrated control logic and memory on a single chip (see Figure 9.12). Extensions of this 1971 invention led to the development of personal computers and are the heart of current computers.

Figure 9.12 An Intel Main Circuit Board

The Intel Pentium microprocessor contains complex logical circuitry along with the equivalent of 3.2 million transistors.

In general, advances in computers have been related to advances in the miniaturization and integration of semiconductor chips. This miniaturization is accomplished through a complex manufacturing process that etches circuits on thin slices of silicon called wafers. Later, these wafers are cut into individual chips and put into small plastic packages. It is possible to increase the speed and reduce the power consumption of circuits by making the individual devices smaller, putting more devices on one chip, and packing them more tightly. Improvements in performance occur because the electrons travel a much shorter path and because off–on switching times decrease.

Existing 4-megabit memory chips contain over 4 million miniaturized transistors separated by etched lines around 0.8 micron wide. A **micron** is one-millionth of a meter, equal to around .000039 inch or one-hundredth of the width of a hair. Existing production methods are used to produce 16-megabit chips with .5-micron line widths. Chips of more than 64, 256, and 1,024 megabits require line widths around .35, .25, and .18 micron, respectively. At one of these points, a switch to a new type of manufacturing equipment using ultraviolet light or x-rays instead of visible light may be necessary.

Miniaturization and integration have led to vast increases in the power of the software that computers can execute. The first spreadsheet program, VisiCalc, was released in 1980 and occupied 29 kilobytes of memory on an Apple II computer. Current spreadsheet programs and their add-ons occupy several megabytes. Similar differences apply for word processors and other commonly used programs. The additional memory capacity in current personal computers makes it possible to include numerous capabilities that simply wouldn't fit in smaller memories.

Miniaturization and integration have also led directly to major improvements in the cost-effectiveness of computing equipment. Consider the way these developments powered the microcomputer revolution of the 1980s. An IBM PC/AT built in 1984 using an Intel 286 microprocessor contained around 100 chips. One of the first chip sets built by the firm Chips and Technologies for clones of the PC/AT consisted of only six chips and cost $65. A much more powerful single-chip version cost $25 in 1990.[5] Table 9.2 looks at the successive generations of microprocessor chips produced by Intel corporation to date, showing advances in memory and speed, as well as what those advances meant for PC users.

Table 9.2 Advances in Intel's Microprocessors

Processor Number	Release Date	Number of Transistors	Addressing	MIPS	What This Meant to a PC User
8086	1978	29,000	16 bit	.33–.75	Ran MS-DOS, once the most common operating system for PCs
286	1982	134,000	16 bit	1.2–2.7	Runs MS-DOS with Windows but with poor performance
386	1985	275,000	32 bit	5–11.4	Runs Microsoft Windows with adequate performance
486	1989	1.3 million	32 bit	20–54	Runs Microsoft Windows with good performance
Pentium	1993	3.2 million	32 bit	112 (initial release)	Runs Microsoft Windows NT, an operating system for more complex environments, and can support computing-intensive desktop publishing and transaction processing

Another approach to increasing speed is to change the types of instructions the individual processors perform. The **RISC** (reduced instruction set computer) microprocessor was developed to increase speed by using a simpler processor that operated faster. The concept of RISC was originally developed by IBM but was not commercialized at first for fear it would compete with IBM's existing technologies. Instead, RISC was first exploited in the 1980s by other manufacturers. By 1989, RISC chips were helping increase computer speeds at an annual rate of 70 percent. In 1993, Digital Equipment Corporation used RISC technology in its 64-bit Alpha chip that can operate up to 300 MIPS.[6] As the

RISC advances were occurring, CISC (complex instruction set computer) microprocessors were also attaining performance improvements such as those shown in Table 9.2. Intel's 386, 486, and Pentium are all CISC microprocessors, whereas the PowerPC microprocessor developed by Motorola, IBM, and Apple uses a RISC design. It remains to be seen whether the distinction between RISC and CISC will be important in the future or whether the best aspects of each approach will be combined.

Specialized processors

The chips recognized most widely by the general public are microprocessors that control workstations and dynamic RAMs that serve as memory. A second way to increase speed is to use specialized chips designed to perform a particular type of processing very efficiently. Chips tailored to a particular application such as controlling a machine or a videogame are called **ASICs** (application-specific integrated circuits). A type of specialized chip devoted to processing voice or video signals is the **digital signal processor** (DSP). DSPs are used in electronic musical equipment, voice mail systems, and video applications. DSPs make it much more efficient to manipulate voice or video data as it arrives or is generated. General-purpose microprocessors would be slower and wouldn't provide the level of performance needed.

Parallel processing

As if progress due to miniaturization were not enough, many advances have also occurred by rethinking basic methods computers use in their internal processing. In **parallel processing,** a larger computation or query is divided into smaller computations or queries performed simultaneously. This idea is inconsistent with the traditional von Neumann architecture of general-purpose computers, which dictates that the computer fetches and performs one instruction at a time. Parallel processing works only if programmers can figure out how to decompose the problems they are solving into subproblems that can be solved in parallel.

Parallel processing has been used in a number of ways. Its first use was for complex scientific and engineering calculations, predictions of weather patterns, studies of fluid mechanics, and detailed simulations of physical systems. An important current use is in engineering workstations that generate photorealistic images from detailed engineering specifications. Some of these systems simultaneously create an outline of the drawing, color it, shade it, and rotate it. Performing these tasks simultaneously allows speed and picture quality that would be impossible if everything were done in sequence.

Business applications of parallel processing are typically based on querying and analyzing different parts of a huge database simultaneously. For example, in the first general business application of parallel processing was DowQuest, an information service that retrieves business information from hundreds of thousands of recent articles in 175 different publications (mentioned in Chapter 4). DowQuest originally used a computer with 32,000 processors that operate in parallel on different parts of the database. Dividing the problem this way permits a machine built of comparatively slow, inexpensive processors to operate at 4,000 MIPS and respond to the user in one second. To match this performance, the processor of an equally fast single processor machine would have to be 32,000 times faster than these slow processors.

A number of large companies have started using parallel processing for "data mining," finding and understanding otherwise obscure patterns in their own operational data. For example, Kmart noticed that some stores were selling large amounts of confetti around Easter. Analysis of their detailed sales data showed that the confetti was being sold primarily in areas with large Hispanic populations who used confetti as part of their holiday celebrations.[7]

Parallel processing may also have important applications in attempts to get computers to mimic intelligent behavior. Some artificial intelligence researchers see the human mind as a complex network of parallel processes. Although human consciousness focuses on one train of thought at a time, many other processes are going on in parallel in the background. These range from maintaining proper heart rate to filtering out background stimuli so that we don't get overloaded by all the things happening around us. This area will be discussed further in Chapter 12.

REALITY CHECK   **Increasing Computer Performance**   This section discussed several approaches for increasing computer performance.

1. At a time when PCs can operate as fast as mainframes of the past, explain why you do or do not think computer performance is an important issue for users and managers.

2. Identify several situations in which inadequate computer system performance or improved computer system performance affected you directly.

Data Input: Capturing Data

Input devices are used to enter data into computer systems. Although the keyboard is the primary tool for inputting data into PCs, many other input devices are used in other situations. Before looking at specific devices, it is worthwhile to ask what characteristics an ideal input device should have. Like any other device, it should be inexpensive, reliable, accurate, and convenient to use. An ideal input device would also have characteristics unique to input devices. It should capture data automatically at its source and shouldn't require human intervention that might cause delays and might introduce errors. For example, it should be unnecessary for people to record data in one form (such as handwriting) and then transcribe it into another form (by typing it). In addition, an ideal input device should do whatever is possible to ensure accuracy of the data. This section looks at several forms of data input involving keyboards and related devices, character recognition, and inputting images and sounds.

Keyboards

Although many Americans take keyboards for granted, even this familiar technology raises many issues, starting with the shape and layout of current keyboards. People who designed the first typewriters experimented with many different layouts before standardizing on what is called the "qwerty" keyboard because of the order of letters in the third row. Ironically, this layout of keys was developed to force people to type more slowly, thereby reducing the incidence of jammed keys in the mechanical typewriters of the time. Typewriters are no longer mechanical, but the qwerty keyboard has remained the standard. Figure 8.4 shows another attempt to improve on the keyboard, in this case by adapting its shape to the shape of the hands.

Whether or not the qwerty keyboard is ideal for English, it simply doesn't fit many other languages, which have different alphabets or writing systems. Consider, for example, the problem faced by a consultant doing a training session in Belgium for Digital Equipment Corporation. The training center had three types of keyboards: Flemish, French, and U.S. English. Trainees switching between exercises sometimes had to use different computers that had different keyboards. Needless to say, the resulting confusion did not speed the training.

The whole idea of a keyboard containing a limited number of alphabetical symbols breaks down for Asian languages whose ancient writing system uses thousands of symbols called kanji, each representing an idea rather than an alphabetic character. Since it takes a long time to learn thousands of symbols, Japanese is written in 2 ways. Within the first few years at school, children learn approximately 100 kana, phonetic characters in two alphabets called hirigana and katakana. But since kana are rarely used by adults in business settings, computer usage in business requires a way to deal with kanji.[8] Figure 9.13a shows an early Japanese word processor that took input using a pointing device and an electronic tablet. Difficulty dealing with kanji is a key reason Japanese offices have not used PCs as much as U.S. offices. PCs are becoming more widespread in Japan as direct input of handwritten kanji becomes easier.

The basic idea of the keyboard has also been adapted to make it more effective for particular situations. Modified cash registers such as those used in McDonald's make it unnecessary for the cashier to remember the price of an item (see Figure 9.13b). Instead, the cashier presses a key that represents a particular type of hamburger or drink. The handheld terminal and touch-tone phone made it possible to enter data from work locations without being anchored to a bulky VDT. Since the touch-tone phone has no visual display, data input through a touch-tone phone occurs in response to audio prompts from the computer system.

The last adaptation of the keyboard is to eliminate the keys altogether. The touch screen made it possible to enter data by pointing to a spot on a screen (see Figure 9.14c). Pointing on a touch screen is less precise than pointing with a mouse and is therefore limited to applications where pointing to areas of the screen suffices.

The PC mouse (shown in Figure 9.2) made it possible to point with more precision. The mouse was an important breakthrough for a particular type of input, namely, expressing commands to a computer. Before it was developed, users had to type commands such as Print Cust_File. Users had to know the commands, syntax, and filenames, and had to spell everything correctly, which made it difficult for users to control computers. With the mouse, touch screen, or screen designed for input using an electronic pen, a user can simply point to select the command and the file. Pointing is an excellent way to make computers easier to use, but it is not a way to enter large amounts of data. This is where the keyboard remains the most effective device.

Optical Character Recognition

Several types of input technology are based on recognizing characters or special markings. **Magnetic ink character recognition (MICR)** was developed by banks as an early technology of this type. With MICR, account numbers are written on checks and deposit slips in a standard location and format using magnetic ink that can be recognized by special input devices. This technology expedites the clearing of checks and deposits.

Optical character recognition (OCR) applies a similar idea to capture machine-generated or hand-printed numbers or text. OCR involves two steps: capturing an image and then deciphering it. The deciphering step is a software function that consists of finding the individual characters, subdividing them into pixels, and identifying the input character by comparison with previously stored patterns.

Although early OCR systems collected data from forms filled in carefully by hand, bar coding to identify objects is the most important current application of the general idea. As you can see by looking at the bar-code label on a grocery product, bar coding represents characters using bars in a standard format. Bar code readers come in several forms. Some are stationary and scan the bar code as the object moves by. Others are more like pens that scan across a stationary object. Bar codes are often integrated

Figure 9.13 Data Input Examples

(a) Even with successors to this technology, using a keyboard to enter Japanese kanji characters is awkward. The first step is to type a word or sentence phonetically using either the English alphabet or a combination of two alphabetic forms of Japanese writing called hiragana and katakana. The computer uses a dictionary to find the equivalent kanji. Since two different kanji characters can sound the same (like "red" and "read" in English), the user must occasionally stop to select among such alternatives.
(b) This specialized cash register permits the cashier to ring up a restaurant purchase without having to enter or even remember the price of each item.
(c) This touch screen is used for taking orders in a coffee store. This form of input is effective in applications involving user choices rather than extensive data entry.

(a)

(b)

(c)

into point-of-sale terminals used in department stores to record sales and track inventory. Bar coding makes it unnecessary for people to read the data and then copy it. Barcoding applications typically decrease the effort required to input data and increase accuracy substantially.

OCR for hand printing can be used with paper input forms or electronic tablets. For OCR to work with hand printing, either the person must be trained to write letters in a prespecified format or the computer must be trained to recognize an individual's printing. OCR is used with portable computers for applications such as checking

Figure 9.14 Optical Character Recognition

This handheld scanner can be used to capture images and text in the form of a static picture. Converting the text back into a word processing document requires OCR software. This example shows a fax, which is scanned information, being converted, saved and edited into another document.

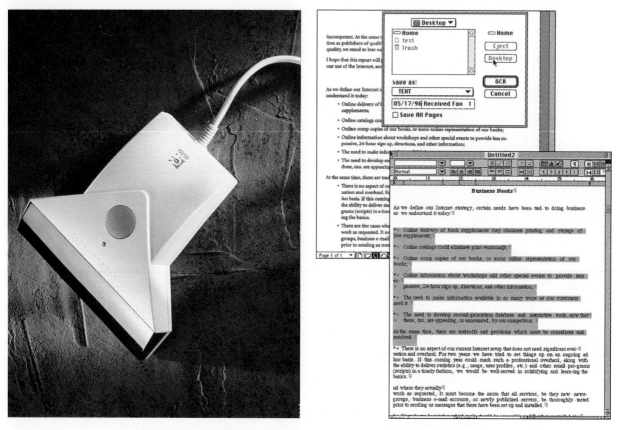

inventory and writing parking tickets. New OCR capabilities in notebook computers are powerful enough for filling out forms. However, existing OCR systems are not efficient for inputting large amounts of text and cannot decipher cursive handwriting reliably. Moreover, OCR can be used for inputting previously typed or typeset characters. For less than $500, a combined handheld scanner and OCR program can input previously typed text at 500 words per minute with 98 percent accuracy (see Figure 9.14).

Capturing Pictures, Sounds, and Video

Earlier in this chapter, we showed how every type of data can be digitized and can therefore be handled by a computer. Two approaches are used for inputting image and audio data into computer systems. One approach consists of simply recording or copying the data in a computer-readable form. This is what happens when a scanner captures an image and stores it in a computer system. Electronic cameras can perform a similar function (see Figure 9.15). The other approach is to capture image or audio data and then, as part of the input process, do something to interpret what it means. This approach is used with voice recognition systems.

Figure 9.15 An Electronic Camera for Input to a Computer System

The Apple Quick Take 100 takes electronic pictures that can be downloaded to a Macintosh computer. The camera holds between 8 and 32 color pictures depending on the resolution. The higher resolution is not as good as the resolution from a camera that uses film but is still adequate for many purposes.

Voice recognition matches the sound patterns of spoken words with sound patterns previously stored in the system. Work situations in which voice input is important include input while the speaker's hands are busy, input while mobility is required, and input while the user's eyes are occupied. A typical user is an aircraft engine inspector, who can use a wireless microphone and a limited vocabulary to issue orders, read serial numbers, or retrieve maintenance records.

Voice recognition also has potential advantages for workers who lack reading or writing skills. At a Raytheon plant that produces circuit boards for Patriot missiles, inspectors gazing through microscopes dictate defect reports instead of writing them by hand. One special beneficiary is a Vietnamese refugee who has trouble reading and writing English but has "trained" the system to understand his pronunciation as long as he says the words the same way each time.[9]

Since deciphering spoken words is harder than identifying letters or numbers printed by hand, current voice recognition systems work effectively only when there is a brief pause between each word. In contrast to the continuous speech that occurs in typical conversations, this type of speech with pauses is called discrete speech. The first voice recognition systems were speaker dependent since each user had to train it separately by reading a list of words. Such systems have a simpler problem than speaker independent systems and can therefore operate more quickly or use cheaper machines. However, the cost of a PC add-on with a 30,000 word vocabulary that takes reasonably good dictation from voices it has never heard before has dropped to $1,000.[10]

There has been some speculation about whether keyboards will be bypassed in favor of direct voice input or handwritten input in many applications over the next several decades. Although it is not known what will happen, this type of development would have major effects on managerial, professional, and clerical work. Bypassing keyboards may also be crucial for expanding computer use in China and Japan, whose use of kanji was mentioned earlier. Surprisingly, the complexity of these characters may help computers recognize them. Since the strokes in kanji characters are typically written in a particular order, handwriting-recognition notepads have been developed that use the order of the strokes as information for deciphering the characters.

REALITY CHECK **Data Input** In this section, we identified a number of data input technologies.

1. Identify times (if any) when you have entered data into a computer system. Explain why the process seemed as efficient as possible or, alternatively, why it could probably have been improved.

2. Explain the most advanced ways you think you will input data or interact with computers in your career.

Storing and Retrieving Data

As with other types of devices, storage devices ideally should be inexpensive, fast, accurate, and reliable. An ideal storage device should also have several characteristics specifically related to storage. It should be possible to store and retrieve any data in any form immediately and in a minimum amount of space. Space used and storage and retrieval times are useful indicators for comparing storage technologies. This section looks at several forms of data storage: paper, micrographics, magnetic storage, optical storage, and flash disks.

Paper and Micrographics

Paper is a 2,000-year-old medium for storing data. Punched cards were the primary medium for storing data in the first computerized business systems (see Figure 9.16a). Although paper is easy for people to use when they are reading or annotating a document, it has many shortcomings. For one thing, it is so bulky that many large businesses have rooms full of paper records and documents. Finding specific data in a personal file cabinet can take seconds or minutes. Finding it in a firm's paper archives can take hours, days, or weeks, if it can be found at all. Another shortcoming is that paper is not conveniently computer readable even though OCR scanners can input text from paper documents.

Micrographics, an early solution to the bulkiness of paper, uses photographic techniques to reduce the paper into miniature-sized pictures on microfilm. Microfilm is used for archival storage rather than transaction processing. **Computer output microfilm** is a form of computer output that bypasses paper and reduces pages of output to tiny images stored on film. A hand-sized card called a microfiche can store the equivalent of hundreds of pages of computer output. Although microfilm greatly reduces the amount of physical space required to store data, it is not conveniently computer readable, which makes it useful only for rarely accessed data. Finding a particular item of information on a microfilm takes several minutes at best. Furthermore, microfilm cannot be changed once it is produced.

Magnetic Tapes and Disks

The shortcomings of paper media led to the development of media based on the magnetization or demagnetization of tiny locations on an iron oxide surface. The first of these was **magnetic tape,** a plastic tape on which character-oriented (number and text) data could be stored using numerical codes. Since it is possible to magnetize and demagnetize the same region of a magnetic tape without punching a hole, the data on the tape can be altered by writing over it in a process similar to recording over an audiotape or videotape.

Data can be stored densely on tapes. For example, a single digital audiotape can store over 1 gigabyte of data. Like entertainment audiotapes and videotapes, tapes for storing computer data are sequential devices whose data are read in their order of location on the tape. The fact that tapes must be read sequentially greatly limits the types of processing they can be used for.

Data can also be stored magnetically on a **hard disk,** which is a rotating device that stores data using magnetization and demagnetization methods like those for magnetic tapes. Like diskettes, hard disks store data in concentric circles called tracks. While in use, a hard disk rotates continually. Chapter 4 explained how a program determines the location of required data on the disk and instructs a disk arm to move a read head into position over the correct track and perform the read. Hard disks are also called DASDs, which stands for direct access storage devices. The special advantage of hard disks over tapes is their ability to access data directly instead of having to read sequentially through all previous data on the device.

Rotating disks come in a variety of sizes. Pocket-sized 3.5-inch diskettes commonly hold around a megabyte of data (see Figure 9.16b). Hard disks for new PCs typically held 10 to 40 megabytes in 1991, 210 megabytes in 1994, and should reach 1.2 gigabytes by 1997 according to Dataquest.[11] This represents up to a 100-fold increase in 6 years. (see Figure 9.16c). The combination of vastly increased RAM and hard disk capacities has made it practical to use PC software with capabilities vastly more powerful than were available with early PCs, whose software had to reside entirely on a single diskette or within limited hard disk storage.

Hard disks have a number of shortcomings. For one thing, they rely on continuous rotation at thousands of revolutions per minute with a read head just 15-millionths of an inch above the disk. Occasionally, the read head crashes into the disk, destroying both the data and the disk. In addition, unless they are installed in a portable computer, they are not very portable. Although diskettes are more portable, they don't contain enough data to permit managers or other users to carry around most of the data they use frequently.

Optical Disks

Optical disk technology involves the use of a laser beam to store or retrieve data as microscopic spots on a disk. A single optical disk weighs only ounces, fits into a small briefcase, and can store the equivalent of over 400 diskettes or the text in hundreds of books. The first optical disks came out in 1978 and competed with videotapes in the home entertainment market. Audio compact disks came out in 1982 and revolutionized the record business in the late 1980s. The **CD-ROM** was the first application of optical storage for business processing. CD-ROMs are compact disks that can be read but not modified. They emerged in 1985 for publishing databases, directories, and encyclopedias. CD-ROMs make huge amounts of data readily transportable but are limited because the user cannot change the data. By 1988, the read-only limitation was solved using a different type of recording technology, and the **erasable optical disk** hit the market.

Optical disks provide random access to an enormous amount of data stored in a comparatively small space. In one of the first commercial versions, a FileNet "jukebox" containing up to 288 12-inch optical disks could find the required optical disk and retrieve data within 20 seconds. This device provided enough storage for the images of 14.4 million pages that might otherwise pack a warehouse. Optical disks are also more reliable than magnetic disks because they are not susceptible to head crashes.

Optical disks are used for two types of applications, based on whether the data can change. CD-ROMs are excellent for distributing large files of computer-readable data ranging from software programs to technical manuals. They cost about $1 to produce and therefore deliver large amounts of data more cheaply than diskettes, which cost around $0.75 to produce. Erasable optical disks are used mostly for backup and long-term data storage of image data. Insurance companies and other paper-intensive businesses find optical storage especially attractive for this purpose. However, current erasable disk technology is too slow for high-volume online transaction processing. Optical disks provide so much storage in such a small space that most managers and professionals could use them to carry around most of the computerized information they need on a pocket-sized 3.5-inch optical disk holding 128 megabytes (see Figure 9.16d). However, readers for small erasable optical disks still cost $1,000 in 1994 and were not cost-effective compared to hard disk storage for most applications.

Figure 9.16 Data Storage Examples

a) Early business data processing was based on punched cards. The pattern of holes punched in each column represents the letter or number at the top of the column. The card reader senses the holes. The typed line at the top of the page is for the convenience of a person looking at the card.

(b) Early 5.25-inch diskettes were superceded by 3.5-inch diskettes that held more data. The circular object in the photo is the "floppy" recording surface inside the plastic shell.

(c) The first magnetic disks for PCs contained 10 to 40 megabytes of data. This hard disk is only 3.5 inches in diameter but can hold a 2 gigabyte database and costs less than $2,000.

(d) This removable optical disk combines the high storage capacity of current hard disks with the portability of diskettes. This 3.5-inch optical disk holds 128 megabytes of data.

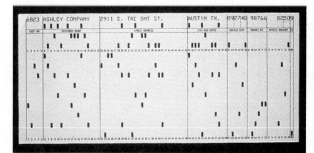

(a)

(b)

(c)

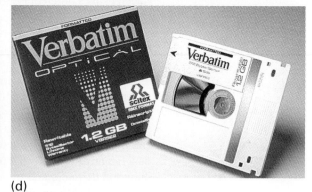

(d)

Flash Memory

Although hard disks and optical disks can store an enormous amount of information, they are both mechanical devices with moving parts. They therefore have two problems: breakage of the moving parts and energy usage necessary to spin the disk and move the read/write mechanism. In contrast, the RAMs within the computer itself are semiconductor devices without moving parts. But they have the problem of losing information when the computer is turned off.

A **flash memory** is a semiconductor device that stores and modifies information while the computer is operating but that also retains information when the computer is turned off. An early demonstration of the potential of flash memory came in 1993 with the Hewlett-Packard Omnibook 300, a 2.9-pound portable computer that can run on 4 AA batteries. The 10-megabyte flash memory chips (effectively doubled with data compression) are packaged in a card the size of a thick credit card inserted into one of four slots in the computer. But the flash memory costs $400 more than a tiny 40-megabyte hard disk that fits in the same slot. How the price-performance of flash memories versus hard disks will evolve remains to be seen.

REALITY CHECK   **Data Storage and Retrieval**   This section mentioned that most managers and professionals could carry around much of the computerized information they need on a single 3.5-inch optical disk.

1. Explain why you do or do not believe you could store everything you have ever written and every test you have ever taken on a single portable optical disk.

2. Assume that someone develops a cheap electronic camera that can capture an entire page in one second and can store it on a 3.5-inch optical disk. Explain how this would or would not affect you at school or work.

Data Output: Displaying Data

Output devices display data for users. Aside from being inexpensive and reliable, an ideal output device would make it easy to convert data into the most useful information for the users. Early printers and terminals were limited because they were anchored to fixed locations and because they could not produce good graphical output. Recent advances have incorporated graphics, images, voice, other sounds, and video. The capabilities that started becoming technologically feasible in the 1980s make it possible to go far beyond the forms of data output that are common even today. We will look at output devices in the following categories: screen outputs, paper outputs, and audio outputs.

Screen Outputs

The most common device for interactive output on screens is the VDT monitor, such as those used with most PCs. Improvements in monitors over the years include higher resolution (more dots per inch), larger screen size, graphical outputs rather than just numbers and text, and color outputs rather than just black and white. All these improvements have made monitors easier to use and have permitted them to display better information to users.

VDTs have shortcomings, however, such as being bulky and taking up a lot of space on a desk. Extensive use often leads to eyestrain. In addition, they give off electromagnetic radiation that may be a health hazard, at least for people whose desks are behind the monitors where the emissions are strongest.

A great deal of work has been done to produce flat screens such as those used with laptop computers (see Figure 9.17a). By the early 1990s, it was even possible to produce these screens with color displays although they remain much smaller than screens for comparable PCs and are difficult to see under some lighting conditions. Flat screens are also used in some factories, where a wall-mounted screen is more convenient than a desktop device. Screen display technology is important not only for the future of computer displays but also for television, where flat screens would have obvious advantages.

Specialized displays of many other types have also been used. "Heads-up" displays originally developed for military applications have been used in some automobiles to project auto control panel information in front of the driver instead of forcing the driver to look down. In a more advanced version of this idea, Figure 9.17b shows a prototype of a head-mounted display developed by Boeing to help workers perform complex wiring tasks in airplane manufacturing. This display uses semireflective lenses that permit the worker to see a wiring diagram transmitted from a computer superimposed on top of the circuit board he or she is wiring.

Paper Outputs

Many different types of printers are available for paper outputs from computer systems (see Figure 9.17c). The first computer systems used impact printers, which create marks on paper by hitting a print head against a ribbon. Nonimpact printers include inkjet printers and laser printers. Inkjet printers "spit" ink onto the paper. Laser printers create marks on paper by focusing laser beams on black particles of toner. It is now possible to buy a small laser printer for less than $400, whereas other types of personal printers may cost less than $200. Color also became a practical feature of printers in the early 1990s, with inexpensive color printers costing less than $500, but taking a minute to print a full page of text and up to 15 minutes to print a full-page picture at top resolution.

Audio Outputs

Audio outputs are starting to appear more prominently in many business computer systems. In voice-mail systems and many systems for obtaining standardized data such as bank balances, prerecorded prompting messages help the user specify what information is needed. In applications such as voice annotation of spreadsheets and documents, users can hear a comment recorded earlier by someone else. In other computer audio applications, the voice sounds are synthesized. For example, Bell Canada uses voice synthesis to read locations of broken phone equipment to field technicians and to tell them how to fix the equipment. Gradual refinements in speech synthesis have resulted in more natural-sounding synthesized speech, making future applications more likely.

Figure 9.17 Data Output Examples

(a) This laptop computer's flat panel display is one of the features that allows portability.
(b) Boeing developed this head mounted display to help the production worker by projecting a wiring diagram into the visual field of the circuit board the worker is wiring. (You can see the projected wiring diagram in the lenses.) The image changes when the worker turns or proceeds to a new task.
(c) Unlike the small printers found in most offices, this plotter can print complex engineering drawings on large sheets of paper.

(a)

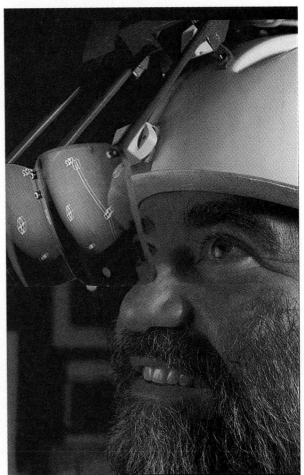

(c)

(b)

Chapter Conclusion

SUMMARY

▶ *What are the basic components of a computer system?*

A computer system consists of computers and computer-controlled devices that process data by executing programs. The physical devices in a computer system are its hardware, and the programs are its software.

▶ *What are the different types of computers?*

Embedded computers are internal components of other machines. Nonembedded computers are classified based on their power and speed as personal computers, workstations, mini-computers, mainframe computers, or supercomputers. The newer category of servers crosses many of the older classifications.

▶ *What are the organizational approaches to computing?*

The organizational approaches to computing are centralized computing, personal computing, and distributed computing. In centralized computing, all the processing for multiple users is done by a large central computer. In personal computing, users have their own machines and rarely share data or resources. In distributed computing, users have their own computers and use a network to share data and resources.

▶ *How is client–server computing different from centralized computing?*

In client–server computing, different devices on a network are treated as clients or servers. The client devices send requests for service, such as printing or retrieval of data, to specific server devices that perform the requested processing. Client–Server computing differs from centralized computing in terms of the division of labor in handling the user inter-face, application program logic, and database access. Instead of having a central computer control everything from the displays on user terminals through the application logic and the updating of the database, client–server divides these functions between specialized client and server components.

▶ *How is it possible for computers to process any type of data?*

Digital computers are built from components that switch between off–on (0–1) states. Since 8 bits, or 1 byte, is enough to uniquely identify 256 different characters, numerical data and text can be represented as a series of 0's and 1's. Pictures and sounds can be represented as 0's and 1's by breaking them into tiny elements and assigning a numerical value to each element.

▶ *What are the different approaches for increasing data manipulation speeds?*

The approaches include miniaturization, simplifying the instruction set, using special-purpose processors, and using parallel processing. Miniaturization has been accomplished by changing the manufacturing processes to pack more individual devices into more highly integrated circuits. RISC microprocessors increase speed by using fewer instructions that a microprocessor can execute faster. Special-purpose processors are tailored to specific tasks. In parallel processing, a large computation is divided into smaller computations that are per-formed simultaneously.

▶ *What are the different forms of data input?*

Keyboards are the dominant input device for business data processing but are used when a person has already captured (or just created) the data and is now entering the data into the computer as a separate step. Character recognition techniques such as optical character recognition and bar coding reduce the handling of data being entered into a computer system. Scanners capture images. Voice recognition systems bypass keyboard input but operate with limited vocabularies.

▶ *What are the different forms of data storage?*

The principal forms of data storage include paper, micrographics, magnetic storage, and optical storage. Micrographic devices reduce paper into miniature pictures on microfilm. Magnetic tapes and disks store data through the magnetization and demagnetization of tiny regions on an iron oxide surface. Magnetic tapes must be used sequentially, whereas disks can be used for direct access. Optical disks use laser beams to store or retrieve data as microscopic spots on a disk. Optical disks can store more data than comparably sized magnetic disks, but they operate more slowly. Flash memories use chips that retain data when the computer is turned off.

▶ *What are the different forms of data output?*

The most common device for interactive output on screens is the VDT monitor although flat screens have been used for portable computers and factory applications. Many types of printers and plotters are used for paper outputs. Audio outputs are used both for prerecorded messages and for synthesized interaction with computer system users.

INTERNATIONAL VIGNETTE

New Zealand: Using Client–Server to Improve the Tax System

In 1988, New Zealand's Inland Revenue Department (like the IRS in the United States) decided to rethink its business processes from the ground up. The goal was to increase efficiency, improve tax collection, and reduce staff. After a 12-month study, the information technology group decided to replace an inflexible, 20-year-old host-based system with a distributed network of UNIX servers. Among other reasons, an open, UNIX-based architecture was chosen to reduce reliance on any single hardware platform.

Implementation of the new system began in 1990. Client–server applications were deployed at each of 40 district offices and 4 regional offices. All transactions would be processed on local PCs rather than through mainframes although mainframes would still be used for large reporting and analysis applications. Overall, the network included 160 Sparcservers and Sparcstations from Sun Microsystems and a wide area network linked to 1,700 terminals and 570 PCs. The pace of implementation was gauged to minimize organizational disruption and assure complete training.

By the time the project is completed in 1997, it is expected to cost more than $300 million. But it has already saved 90 percent of its annual implementation costs and has permitted a 26 percent staff reduction from 7,000 to 5,200. Currently, tax payers can submit returns by mail or electronically. Tax return processing that used to take 3 or 4 months to process by hand now takes 14 days.

Source: McMullen, John. "Taxation without Vexation." *Information Week,* Mar. 22, 1993, p. 20.

* Use the WCA framework to organize your understanding of this vignette and to identify important topics that are not mentioned.

> • What issues (if any) make this case interesting from an international or intercultural viewpoint?
>
> • What is the advantage of client–server in this situation?

REAL-WORLD CASES

Chicago Board of Trade: Stomp-Proof Handheld Terminals for Use in the Pits

For over a century, traders at the Chicago Board of Trade (CBOT) and Chicago Mercantile Exchange had used an open outcry bidding system to make trades and paper cards to record those trades. Every day 100,000 of these cards moved from the trading area, called the pits, to keypunchers who entered the data into computers over night. But the U.S. Congress demanded that the system be changed after an FBI sting operation led to indictments of dozens of traders for cheating customers by writing false entries on the paper cards. Congress didn't care about open outcry but demanded an audit trail requiring the use of computers.

The design of a computerized system that could be practical amid the screaming and human gyrations in the pits was not obvious, however. Each trader needed a way to record trades, ideally a way that shared some of the advantages of paper, such as being light and very simple to use. Desktop computers and laptops just wouldn't do. Handheld terminals seemed promising, but needed to bear up to the frenetic trading environment while being light enough and comfortable enough to hold for hours.

Synerdyne, a small California design firm, bested over 100 competitors by designing a handheld terminal whose specially designed contours maximize its "holdability." To retain the simplicity of old paper cards, the handheld terminals take handwritten input using a cordless, and therefore easily dropped, stylus made stomp-proof by encasing it in steel tubing. The terminal uses radio waves to beam each trade directly to the exchange's computers. If the data from the buyer and seller don't match for some reason, the terminal gives a warning using a vibrating pad under the fingertip grip. At the end of the day, each trader puts the terminal in an electronic safe deposit box that checks the hardware and software and recharges the eight-hour battery. Equipping the exchanges with these devices would eventually cost $40 million, but could reduce errors, cut back office costs, and make fraud much more difficult.

After sinking $12 million into replacing paper trading cards with tamper-proof computers, both exchanges announced in June 1994 that they would not complete the project by October 1995 as required by law. Instead, they sought to postpone meeting tougher trade-monitoring standards until late 1999. The staff of the Commodity Futures Trading Commission (CFTC), which oversees commodity exchanges, was angered by the Board of Trade's attempt to use its influence with the House Appropriations Committee to push through the extension, especially after the printed proceedings of the Appropriations Committee linked funding of the CFTC operating budget to the extension.

Sources: Burns, Greg. "A Handheld Computer That's Combat-Hardened." *Business Week*, Apr. 18, 1994, pp. 94–95.
Taylor, Jeffrey. "Plans to Boost Fraud Detection Hit Snags." *Wall Street Journal*, June 13, 1994, p. C1.

• Use the WCA framework to organize your understanding of this case and to identify important topics that are not mentioned.

• Explain how the ideas of infrastructure and context from the WCA method are relevant to this situation.

• Identify the ethical issues raised by this situation.

• Explain why you do or do not believe this product will be used for only a few years until the pits are replaced with computer screens in private offices.

Taco Bell: Using Information Technology to Support Value-Based Pricing

Taco Bell, a $3.3 billion fast-food chain owned by Pepsico, tripled its profits between 1988 and 1993 by reengineering itself to focus everything about the business on providing good value to customers. Instead of thinking of itself as a manufacturing company that produced customer meals in stores, it changed to thinking of itself as a service company emphasizing good value, speed, and efficiency. Since the customers really didn't care where the food is cooked, Taco Bell virtually removed the kitchens from the stores. Doing as much food preparation as possible in consolidated facilities reduces labor and production costs while permitting store personnel to focus more on customers.

Providing an information system that could support value-based pricing was essential to the reengineering effort. Initially installed in 1990, and used in 70 percent of Taco Bell's 3,000 company-owned restaurants by 1993, the TACO (Total Automation of Company Operations) system covers functions such as point-of-sale data collection, inventory control, labor scheduling, sales forecasting, product ordering, and management analysis. The system runs on industry-standard IBM 486-based PCs. Every night, each store downloads data to corporate headquarters in Irvine, California. Regional managers who manage 30 stores, instead of the 8 stores that is the norm in the fast-food industry, use this information to analyze sales trends, staffing levels, and the success or failure of product promotions such as tie-ins to popular movies. At 15-minute increments, they know how many customers came in, what they ordered, and how fast they were served. Since similar systems that could be purchased from outside vendors typically required use of the vendor's proprietary hardware, the company decided to build its own system based on readily available PCs but using software developed for Taco Bell.

Source: Wilder, Clinton. "Breaking Out of Its Shell." *Information Week,* Oct. 25, 1993, pp. 28–32.

- Use the WCA framework to organize your understanding of this case and to identify important topics that are not mentioned.

- Explain how Taco Bell uses distributed processing and whether there are any alternatives to what they do.

- Explain the importance of computer hardware to Taco Bell.

Bell Laboratories: Finding a Way to Break a Proposed Encryption Standard

Data encryption presented a difficult problem to the U.S. government. It wanted private individuals and industry to have enough encryption capabilities to maintain telecommunications privacy but also wanted to limit these capabilities so that the government could intercept information while investigating spies, terrorists, and other criminals. In early 1994, the government proposed that a special chip called the Clipper chip be embedded into all workstations that send and receive telecommunications messages. The Clipper chip in each workstation would contain a unique serial number identifying that workstation, plus a unique encryption key. Lists of chip serial numbers and associated encryption keys would be held separately by the National Bureau of Standards and by the U.S. Treasury Department. Government law enforcement agencies could monitor and store encrypted messages, but these would be meaningless until they were decoded using the two keys, which could be obtained only by a court order.

A passionate debate about adopting the Clipper chip pitted the government's law enforcement priorities against individual concerns for absolute privacy plus industry concerns that the government's design would be cumbersome because it required using a special chip rather than just software. The Clipper chip would also be unacceptable to foreign governments, which could not access the keys.

Some of these concerns lost steam, at least temporarily, when Matthew Blaze, a researcher at AT&T's Bell Laboratory discovered a way for two people to set up communication using the Clipper chip without exchanging the special law enforcement access fields that are the gateway to decoding. He did this by creating an invalid, but valid-looking law enforcement code using a typical computer workstation. Since this process took the computer 28 minutes, the technique probably is not effective for use in scrambling telephone calls. AT&T, a producer of the Clipper chip, stated that this frailty did not affect its ability to encrypt secure voice, fax, and low-speed data transmissions. A cryptographer who was on the five-person consulting team that had reviewed the Clipper chip for the government said he felt embarrassed they had not asked the question in the form Blaze had discovered.

> Sources: Thyfault, Mary E. "The Data Security Furor," *Information Week,* Feb. 14, 1994, pp. 12–14.
> Markoff, John. "At AT&T, No Joy on Clipper Flaw." *New York Times,* June 3, 1994, p. C1.

- Use the WCA framework to organize your understanding of this case and to identify important topics that are not mentioned.

- What ethical and practical issues does this case raise?

- What implications does this example have for system development in general?

KEY TERMS

computer	minicomputer	bit	micron
program	mainframe	byte	RISC
computer system	supercomputer	kilobyte	ASIC
hardware	MIPS	megabyte	digital signal processor (DSP)
software	server	gigabyte	parallel processing
central processing unit (CPU)	centralized computing	ASCII	magnetic ink character recognition (MICR)
random access memory (RAM)	dumb terminals	digitizing	
read only memory (ROM)	intelligent workstations	pixel	optical character recognition (OCR)
input device	personal computing	data compression	voice recognition
output device	graphical user interface (GUI)	encryption	computer output microfilm
storage device	distributed computing	machine language	magnetic tape
peripherals	client–server architecture	32-bit addressing	hard disk
embedded computer	file server	integrated circuit	CD-ROM
personal computer (PC)	middleware	chip	erasable optical disk
workstation	peer-to-peer	microprocessor	flash memory

REVIEW QUESTIONS

1. What is the von Neumann architecture, and why is it important?

2. Identify the difference between an embedded computer and a nonembedded computer.

3. What is a server?

4. Describe the difference between centralized computing, personal computing, and distributed computing.

5. Why does distributed computing require more controls and administration than personal computing?

6. What is client–server architecture, and what does it accomplish?

7. Explain the role of middleware in client–server architecture.

8. How is peer-to-peer architecture different from client–server?

9. Why are base-2 numbers important in computing, and how is it possible to convert a base-10 number to base 2?

10. Define digitizing, and explain what determines how closely a digitized picture resembles the original.

11. Why does high-resolution storage of a one-page picture involve more data than storing several hundred pages of text?

12. What are data compression and data encryption, and why are they important?

13. Describe the difference between 8-bit, 16-bit, 32-bit, and 64-bit addressing and why this is important.

14. Explain the difference between RISC and CISC microprocessors and why this is important.

15. What is parallel processing, and why is it potentially useful for studying artificial intelligence?

16. Describe optical character recognition and how it operates.

17. How does voice recognition operate?

18. What are the advantages and disadvantages of optical disks?

DISCUSSION QUESTIONS

1. Responding to Japan's 95 percent market share in flat panel displays, the U.S. government announced a nearly $1 billion "flat panel display initiative" providing incentives for American manufacturers to achieve full-scale manufacturing. According to the president of the U.S. Display Consortium, flat panel screens will be used in everything from autos to fighter planes and on "every exit ramp on the Information Highway."[12] Explain why you agree or disagree that it is important for the United States (or any other leading industrial power) to have a significant share of this market.

2. The introduction to Part III mentioned information technology performance variables in four areas: functional capabilities and limitations, ease of use, compatibility, and maintainability. Assume you have a five-year-old PC and are considering buying a new one. Explain how each group of performance variables is or is not pertinent to your purchase decision.

3. Assume that computerized voice recognition is widespread. Identify some of the possible applications of this technology. How do you think it might affect you personally? How would it affect people you know?

4. Assume that a hand-printing pad and hand-drawing pad became standard components of both desktop and portable PCs. Would this have any effect on you? Identify some ways it might affect work practices in specific jobs.

5. Assume that you had an erasable optical disk that could carry all the text data you have generated in your life. This includes your medical records, finances, homework assignments, papers, and so on. It also has enough room to store data you need for your current work, such as papers you have written and the syllabus for all of your courses. How would this technology affect you? What would you be able to do differently if it were readily available?

6. Estimate how many megabytes would be required to store this entire book. (Your answer will depend on your assumptions.) In making your estimate, consider the fact that the book contains both text and graphics. Based on your results for this book, estimate the number of bytes required to store all the books in a 600,000-volume college library. How many optical disks would this require?

HANDS-ON EXERCISES

1. This example is related to the amount of storage used by different types of data. It assumes you have access to three text examples, a drawing program, and a paint program.

a. Look at the directory listing of the three text examples provided, which are approximately one, two, and three pages long. Explain the difference in the amount of storage they use.

b. Using a drawing program and then a paint program, draw a large face or sketch a person. Be sure the sketch is fully shaded in some way. (In other words, it is not just a stick figure.) Save both drawings. Compare the amount of storage needed for each. Use the ideas in the chapter to explain why the amount of storage is different and why the paint program uses more storage than the drawing program.

APPLICATION SCENARIOS

Omnitel: The does-it-all

"That's amazing," thought R. J. Lin, director of R&D for Omnitel. "Here I am, in charge of R&D, and I can barely believe what we are producing."

Lin had just seen a demonstration of a new prototype product temporarily code-named the "does-it-all." Although it looks like a half-inch thick writing tablet, it is an advanced 3-pound portable computer, including an 8-x-10-inch screen and a keyboard. It contains 32 megabytes of RAM and a 9.3 gigabyte hard disk based on a new superminiaturized storage technology. But that is only the beginning. The does-it-all accepts printed or cursive written input using a special built-in light pen. The computer contains special tracking capabilities that permit the user to "write" directly on the screen. This creates the illusion of writing on paper, except that the computer reads the handwritten inputs and converts them to printed characters in any of 20 fonts. The screen also serves as a television monitor or as a picture phone. A lever releases a small handheld electronic scanner that can scan an entire page of a book in two passes of five seconds each. Flipping a different switch while holding the laptop on its side uncovers the lens of a camera. This camera can take acceptable electronic photographs that are stored in electronic form and can be displayed immediately on the screen. It also contains a tiny microphone that can store comments electronically and link them to documents such as reports. Even more valuable for some people, the does-it-all contains voice recognition software. It also includes an optional cellular telephone attachment and a modem through which it can be plugged into a telephone line for transmitting data anywhere.

The system still doesn't work perfectly, and Lin is concerned about its marketability. The screen is still somewhat grainy and neither the voice recognition nor hand-writing recognition system works perfectly although both function well enough to be useful after two hours of training. During the training session for cursive writing, the user writes a large number of words three times so that the computer can recognize how individual letters are formed, how they are linked, and how the user writes common words such as I, a, an, and the. The batteries still aren't up to snuff even though they run the machine for 15 hours or more.

"We still have a way to go on perfecting some of the technology," Lin thought, but she believed the system was reliable enough to take to the market. She wondered who the marketing people would sell it to, however, and where to go next when everyone else had an equivalent product in a year or two.

1. Explain how the does-it-all captures, transmits, stores, retrieves, displays, and manipulates data.

2. An early prototype of the does-it-all lacked a keyboard. Explain how that feature might have been beneficial to some users and detrimental to others.

3. Without evaluating the does-it-all's technical feasibility, identify five possible uses of the does-it-all that take advantage of the simultaneous availability of so many functions in a small package.

DEBATE TOPIC   *Use ideas from the chapter to argue the pros and cons and practical implications of the following proposition: Although the does-it-all provides impressive capabilities, it probably will do little to change the way managers and business professionals do their work.*

Mainframes, Inc.: The Threat of Client–Server

George Tomkins left the meeting at Ridgeway Foods and set up a meeting with his boss, Fred Kowalik, the Regional Sales Manager for Mainframes, Inc. George had been a mainframe salesman for 15 years, and he was starting to encounter a new type of sales resistance. Customers used to quibble on the price and say that the other mainframe systems had better features or better service. Now Ridgeway and a number of customers were saying they just didn't want mainframes. Instead, they wanted client–server computing because that was the wave of the future.

Kowalik was not surprised by Tomkins's visit. Several other salespeople had voiced the same concerns lately. The marketing department was working on a better sales approach as a temporary measure until the product development group could provide a genuinely different set of products. The stopgap marketing message was based on three premises: (1) Businesspeople don't really want client-server. They want cost-effective solutions to business problems, and client-server is just a technical computing approach that may cost more money than centralized computing. (2) Client-server often doesn't live up to its promise because it involves new types of software, because the programming tools for this type of system are not nearly as developed as those for mainframe systems, because the technical staff will require new knowledge, and because there will be new risks and uncertainties. (3) The mainframe can play the role of a server in a client–server network. Instead of abandoning their existing mainframes, they should maintain their centralized mainframe databases while gradually migrating from a centralized mainframe computing approach to a more decentralized approach in which more of the processing is done by workstations.

Kowalik saw this as a chance to drive home the importance of keeping up with current developments in both business and technology. He reminded Tomkins that the world was changing and that a certain salesperson had not paid much attention to recent sales training programs. Kowalik said he doubted whether Tomkins understood Ridgeway's business well enough to tell them why they should keep the mainframe instead of moving toward a client–server option now. Tomkins countered that his job was to sell computers, not to study the customer's business.

1. How plausible does the interim marketing idea sound? Can you suggest any better approaches?

2. Explain why it is or is not important for a computer salesperson such as Tomkins to understand a customer's business.

DEBATE TOPIC   *Use ideas from the chapter to argue the pros and cons and practical implications of the following proposition: With the obvious advantages of client–server computing, any forward-looking company should migrate in that direction as quickly as possible.*

■ Cumulative Case: Custom T-Shirts, Inc.

Custom T-Shirts, Inc. is now 3 years old and has over 50 stores in 14 states. With this many branches, the information system linking the stores to corporate headquarters is unable to handle the volume of information required to run the business. That system is based on a specialized software package designed for running a small retail business that buys and sells merchandise but does not do manufacturing. The system includes modules for estimating future sales, ordering and receiving materials, recording sales and adjusting inventory levels, recording hourly work for payroll, keeping track of cash, and generating financial statements. This system was selected by the company's first programmer, who was one of Dale's college friends.

This system seemed fine for one store, but it contained no effective way of consolidating the results for the entire corporation. This was not a big problem when there were 2 stores, or even 10, but with 50 stores, the burden of coordination had become intolerable. Running the business efficiently meant that it was necessary to purchase t-shirts in a coordinated way to attain volume discounts. It also meant automatically combining results from the different stores instead of having to go through time-wasting manual processing to understand how the corporation was doing and to generate financial statements and pay tax.

The programmer wanted to hire a staff to reprogram the entire system over the course of two years, but Terry and Dale were so skeptical they decided it was time to bring in more experience. They hired Lee Tanner as Director of Information Systems. Lee had 15 years of experience in the clothing industry. Although Lee wanted to keep Dale's friend on the staff, that arrangement lasted only 2 weeks until Dale's friend found another job.

During the interviews, Lee had asked some probing questions about both the overall corporate computing needs and those of the individual stores. If the company needed to consolidate financial information and needed to coordinate purchasing and other functions, why was its information system architecture designed around PCs in each of the stores? How did they make sure each store was following normal data processing procedures, such as keeping backup copies of the data in case of computer failure, human error, or other problems causing lost data? (Dale immediately thought of the time a store manager spilled a large soft drink on the computer and lost all of his purchase order data.)

Furthermore, Lee wondered about whether the in-store computers and their peripherals could do everything they should. Next year, Terry wanted each store to have 2,000 different images that could be printed on a t-shirt. Unless they could be compressed substantially, these 10-by-12-inch images at 200 dots per inch would overwhelm the hard disks in the existing computers. If the hard disks were insufficient, Terry wondered whether the input and output devices would have similar problems.

1. Use the ideas of personal, centralized, and distributed computing to describe the current situation and what you think should be the direction for a new system. Does client–server seem pertinent to this situation? If so, where would the clients and servers be, and what would they do?

2. Estimate the amount of storage needed at each store just for the images if they are stored uncompressed. Explain why you do or do not think the images could be compressed.

3. Identify all the input, storage, and output devices you think the stores should have, and explain why and how those devices would probably be used.

4. The introduction to Part III mentioned information technology performance variables in four areas: functional capabilities and limitations, ease of use, compatibility, and maintainability. Explain whether or not each group of performance variables is important in this situation and whether or not each is being considered.

◼ *REFERENCES*

1. Alexander, Michael. "Doctors Save Time Writing Without Pens." *Computerworld*, Jan. 28, 1991.

2. Yamada, Ken. "Identifying Criminals with a Portable Device," *Wall Street Journal*, Apr. 27, 1993, p. B1.

3. Morrison, David. "With Middleware, Maybe You Can Get There From Here." *Beyond Computing*, May–June 1994, pp. 18–21.

4. Rin, Adam. "CASE and Application Development Technologies." In Wang, Richard Y., ed., *Information Technology in Action: Trends and Perspectives*. Englewood Cliffs, N.J.: PTR Prentice Hall, 1993 pp. 83–115.

5. Pitta, Julia. "Victim of Success." *Forbes*, Dec. 10, 1990, p. 278–280.

6. Rifkin, Glenn. "Fastest PC Is Poised to Enter a Market in Flux," *New York Times*, May 19, 1993, p. C5.

7. Gardner, George O. "The Evolution of Parallel Processing." *Beyond Computing*, May–June 1994, p. 22.

8. Straub, Detmar. "The Effect of Culture on IT Diffusion: E-Mail and FAX in Japan and the U.S." *Information System Research,* Vol. 5, No. 1, Mar. 1994, pp. 23–47.

9. Bulkeley, William M. "Computer Use by Illiterates Grows at Work." *Wall Street Journal*, June 9, 1992, p B1.

10. Schaeffer, Richard D. "Computers with Ears." *Forbes*, Sept. 12, 1994, p. 238.

11. Hof, Robert D. "The Keys to the Future." *Business Week Special Bonus Issue/The Information Revolution,* 1994, pp. 60–63.

12. Carey, John. "Thinking Flat in Washington." *Business Week*, May 9, 1994, p. 36.

10

Software and Programming

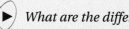

Study Questions

► *What are the different types of software?*

► *How is programming like a translation process?*

► *What aspects of programming do not depend on the programming language used?*

► *What are the four generations of programming languages?*

► *What are some of the other important developments in programming?*

► *What are operating systems, and why should managers and users care about them?*

What is more basic for a gas company than sending out bills? Yet Brooklyn Union Gas Company could not produce bills in the required form. The Public Service Commission had ruled that certain types of customers such as elderly and disabled persons should be offered additional forms of service. In addition, new system capabilities were required to accommodate the highly focused micromarketing necessary for sales growth. But in 1986, the company's 13-year-old customer information system was so inflexible it could not be updated to meet these requirements. It couldn't even be updated to accommodate gas bills over $99,999.99 per month.

Looking at this problem as a long-term issue rather than a requirement for a quick fix, Brooklyn Union decided to reprogram their entire information system. The new system would keep 70 to 80 percent of the functions in the existing system but would have a technical structure that could be maintained and extended over 20 years. The software would encompass over 10,000 program modules, 400 online programs, and 1,000 business functions. Among other things, the system would have to handle up to 10 messages a second and generate 40,000 bills every night.

To meet this goal, Brooklyn Union decided to use object-oriented programming even though no previous projects of this size had used it. With this programming method (described later in more detail), systems are divided into objects, such as customers, billing accounts, and gas meters. Each object is a member of a class of objects, such as groups of customers or gas meters, and automatically "inherits" data handling and business rules from the object class it belongs to. Similarly, system users, data entry screens, and data files are objects that inherit methods from their own object classes. Objects communicate with each other using "messages," such as the way a customer object such as Mr. Jones might send a repair request message to the repair department object.

The upgrade project lasted from 1986 to 1990. Even though Brooklyn Union chose not to change its programming language (PL/1), analyzing the entire system as a set of objects with inherited methods greatly simplified the programming process because the analysis preceding programming was much cleaner. The old system's 1.5 million lines of code shrank to 900,000 lines because important code modules could be reused. The system has proved easier to maintain because its design was much clearer.[1,2]

DEBATE TOPIC   *Argue the pros and cons and practical implications of the following proposition:* The success of this project demonstrated why object-oriented programming will become the primary programming method within a decade.

T HE BROOKLYN UNION GAS CASE describes an application of object-oriented programming, a technique that many industry experts believe is the wave of the future. Noting that programming methods changed even though the programming language stayed the same, the case shows that programming and system development involve much more than simply writing programs using a programming language. The link between the analysis and the programming effort is an essential element of whether the system will be efficient and easy to maintain over time.

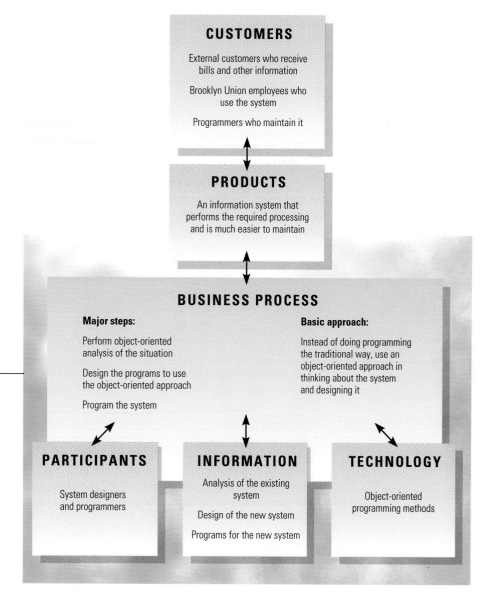

Figure 10.1 Brooklyn Union Gas: Upgrading Crucial Systems

CUSTOMERS

External customers who receive bills and other information

Brooklyn Union employees who use the system

Programmers who maintain it

PRODUCTS

An information system that performs the required processing and is much easier to maintain

BUSINESS PROCESS

Major steps:

Perform object-oriented analysis of the situation

Design the programs to use the object-oriented approach

Program the system

Basic approach:

Instead of doing programming the traditional way, use an object-oriented approach in thinking about the system and designing it

PARTICIPANTS

System designers and programmers

INFORMATION

Analysis of the existing system

Design of the new system

Programs for the new system

TECHNOLOGY

Object-oriented programming methods

This chapter surveys software and programming methods, and emphasizes the changing nature of both programming tools and programming as a business process. The heart of the programming process is translating a person's ideas into maintainable instructions that a computer can execute. Improvements in programming tools and techniques expedite this translation.

Most of this chapter is written as though an information system were being programmed from scratch. This approach is a good starting point for introducing basic ideas about programming even though it is increasingly inconsistent with the trend toward programming by snapping together previously programmed modules instead of reinventing the wheel. Accordingly, topics such as modularity, compatibility, and reusability (defined in the introduction to Part III) appear in various forms throughout the chapter.

Types of Software

The software in a computer system is the coded instructions, or programs, created by programmers and users to tell the computer system what to do. As summarized in Table 10.1, managers and users are affected directly or indirectly by four types of software: application software, end-user software, system development software, and system software. Although these four categories overlap in practice, the categories help in visualizing the different functions of software.

Application software processes data to structure or automate specific business processes. For example, application software in a sales department might include programs for forecasting sales, controlling purchase transactions, maintaining customer data, and sending bills to customers. This software may be built by a firm's programmers or may be purchased from an application software vendor. In either case, it is developed by analyzing specific work practices, deciding how they might be improved, and writing programs that structure or automate some part of the desired process.

Of all the types of software, application software has the greatest potential for competitive impact. This software is more tightly linked to business processes that the organization hopes will differentiate it from its competitors. Effective use of the other types of software is still important, however, because they support the organization's internal effectiveness and efficiency.

End-user software includes general purpose tools such as spreadsheet programs, word processors, file or database systems for personal computers, and graphics packages. These general-purpose tools are designed for use by end users without programming assistance. They are used in two ways: (1) simply to get work done, such as writing a memo or performing a calculation and (2) to create personal systems for accomplishing particular business tasks. When used to build systems, end-user software is typically applied to systems that are comparatively small and don't require a professional level of programming knowledge and expertise. It often permits end users to access and analyze data generated by large, complex systems developed by programmers. Although end-user software does not control business processes as much as application software, firms that adopt it especially effectively may enjoy some competitive advantage in internal efficiency.

Programmers and analysts use **system development software** in the process of building and enhancing information systems. Examples of system development software emphasized in this chapter include compilers and computer-aided software engineering (CASE) systems. (Chapter 4 covered DBMS.) Compilers translate programs written

Table 10.1 Four Types of Software

	Application Software	End-User Software	System Development Software	System Software
What It Accomplishes	Tells the computer how to perform tasks that structure or automate specific steps in business processes that apply only in specific settings	Tells the computer how to perform tasks that support general business processes that apply in many settings, such as writing memos or performing calculations	Helps analysts and programmers build information systems	Controls or supports the operation of the computer system so that it can execute application software or end-user software
Example	Billing system, inventory system	Word processor, spreadsheet	Compiler, DBMS, CASE system	Operating system, utility program
Effect on End User	Automates or structures specific steps in business processes	Hands-on tools for the end user; may be used to develop small systems	No direct effect; helps technical staff produce better systems	Controls computer system operations so that the end user can use it
Generality	Used for a specific type of business process in a specific business or group of similar businesses	Concerned with a general business process that could apply in many firms	Used to build a general class of systems, such as business applications	Concerned with how a computer operates, regardless of what business problem it is solving

in languages such as COBOL or FORTRAN into instructions that can be executed by computers. System development software affects managers and users in an important, but indirect, way because they can help programmers produce more benefits for an organization with the same level of effort. The ultimate effect is a combination of better systems and lower costs.

System software controls the internal operation of a computer system and is produced by programmers who are technical experts. Examples of system software include operating systems and data communication software. An operating system controls the way programs are executed and the way computer system resources, such as disk space, are used. Examples for personal computers include Windows 95 and the Macintosh operating system. Data communication software controls the transmission of data among devices and computer systems. Other system software includes utilities for sorting and merging files and performing background functions related to maintaining computer systems.

Decisions about operating system software affect managers and users in several ways. Since programs are written to run under a particular operating system on a particular type of computer, the choice of an operating system affects the portability of programs and the ability to use purchased software. The need to move systems from one type of computer to another has led to the growing demand for the UNIX operating system and for languages such as C. Operating systems also control the interface between users and computers. The popularity of graphical interfaces for personal computers demonstrates the importance of this aspect of operating systems.

So far, four types of software have been introduced, each of which plays a different role. Application software and end-user software have the most direct impact on the firm's business operations. Some forms of system software, such as operating systems, have a direct impact on ease of use, but other forms of system software along with system development software are oriented toward the technical staff.

Types of Software   This section identified four types of software: application software, end-user software, system development software, and system software.

1. Think about the ways you have used computers. Give specific examples of each type of software that you have used, and explain why it was useful to you.

2. Software in every category is improving continually. For each example in the previous question, identify ways you think the software should be improved.

Programming Viewed as a Business Process

Programming is the process of creating instructions that a machine will execute later. This is done by organizing and communicating ideas in a form a machine can recognize. Setting a telephone to forward calls to another extension is a simplistic form of programming. Setting up a spreadsheet to calculate budget alternatives is a more complex form. Building large transaction processing systems is a much more complex form. These instances all involve generating instructions that a machine will execute.

Since programming is a business process, programming performance can be evaluated using the terms in the WCA method (see Figure 2.10). For example, the programs that are the product of the programming process can be evaluated in terms of cost to the customer (including learning time), quality, responsiveness, reliability, and conformance. The programming process itself can be evaluated in terms of capacity, consistency, productivity, cycle time, flexibility, and security.

Infrastructure and context issues are important to consider for programming because it is part of the larger process of building and maintaining information systems (introduced in Chapter 1). Steps that precede programming include analyzing the problem, getting agreement on how the system should operate, and designing the computer system. Steps after programming include training users, implementing the information system in the organization, and maintaining the system over time. Part IV of this book discusses these steps in depth. For now, we focus on programming to help in understanding tools such as programming languages.

Programming as a Translation Process

Programming is an important type of work done in most organizations. Tools and methods used for programming affect the firm's costs and its ability to create systems needed to compete.

Unfortunately, people often find it difficult to communicate ideas in the form of instructions for machines. Consider the programming of a VCR to record television programs. Although 70 percent of U.S. homes owned VCRs in 1990, a vice president of Panasonic, a major VCR producer, estimated that less than half of VCR owners even tried to use this capability.[3] Although user interfaces for many VCRs are awkward to use, programming a VCR is vastly simpler than programming a computer. The failure of so many people to program VCRs highlights a basic programming problem. Even in simple situations, programming requires people to express instructions in a form that is not natural for them but that a machine can execute.

Computers are programmed by writing computer programs. A **computer program** is a set of instructions in a programming language that describes data processing to be performed by a computer. Figure 10.2 shows that writing programs is part of a process of translating from what a user wants to accomplish into instructions that can be executed by a computer. Writing the programs expresses the user's ideas in a programming language. In most cases, these computer programs cannot be executed directly by the computer; instead, they must be translated into machine language. This additional step is performed automatically by other programs written by experts in the programming language.

Figure 10.2
Programming: A
Translation Process

Programming is a process of translating a user's idea of what a system should do into a set of instructions that a computer can execute.

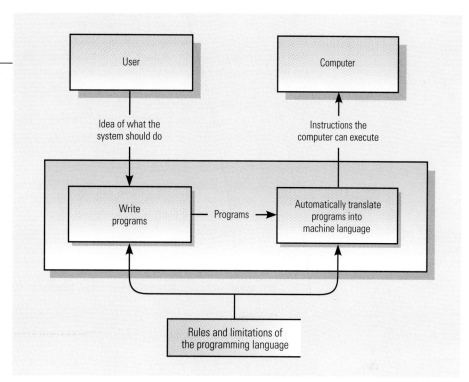

The rules and limitations of the programming language affect both the programs expressing the user's ideas and the automatic translation process. The rules determine what kinds of statements and commands can be used in the programs, as well as the exact grammar for using them. Programs that perform the same processing but are written in different languages use different commands and different grammar. The automatic translation step uses the rules of the language as a guide in deciphering the programs. One reason programming languages contain so many seemingly arbitrary rules is to make this automatic translation practical.

The discussion so far has assumed that the programmer knows exactly what is to be accomplished and that these ideas are well organized. In fact, organizing the ideas is a key issue that programmers face every day.

Organizing Ideas

Regardless of the programming language used, programming involves careful organization of ideas. The traditional technique programmers use for organizing ideas is **successive decomposition.** This "divide and conquer" strategy is consistent with the way process modeling with data flow diagrams divides business processes into successively smaller subprocesses (see Chapter 3). This strategy is an essential skill for programmers, who need to keep track of the various parts of complex problems. When successive decomposition is applied to programming, programs are divided into small, independent subprograms typically called **modules.** Modules are self-contained subsystems that produce predictable outputs from known inputs. Figure 10.3 illustrates how a program can be divided into a set of subprograms, which can be divided further. Decomposition into modules makes the logic of a program more apparent by separating the details of the modules from the overall logical flow.

Successive decomposition allows programmers to solve a problem with a module and then reuse that solution in new situations. This avoids reinventing program logic that has already been developed. For example, suppose that you want a computer to list every customer whose payments are delinquent. The same module that finds the next customer might also be used in a different program that sends a promotional mailing to specific categories of customers.

Even though most programming languages contain methods for successive decomposition, undisciplined programming still produces poorly organized programs that are difficult to test and to maintain. These problems led to the development of **structured programming,** a disciplined style of programming based on the successive decomposition. Structured programming has achieved wide acceptance because it results in programs that are much easier to create, understand, test, and maintain. Such programs have the following characteristics:

- The program code is divided into functional constituent parts called modules.

- The modules can be executed as independent programs.

- The modules are related to each other hierarchically.

- A main module at the top of the hierarchy controls program execution.

- Each module should have only one entry point and only one exit point.

- Each module should operate depending only on the input data and not on any information remembered from the last time it was used.

- The logical flow within any module should be specified using only three basic control structures shown in Figure 10.4: sequence, selection, and iteration. The use of GO TO statements that jump forward or backward in a program should be minimized or eliminated.

- Each module should be small enough to be understood easily.

Organization of ideas and structured programming are not just issues for professional programmers. Programs written by business professionals without programming training are often poorly structured. One reason spreadsheet models often contain errors is that spreadsheet software does little to encourage or enforce structured programming.

An error of this type occurred when the Florida construction firm James A. Cummings, Inc., used a spreadsheet to prepare a bid for an office building complex. After the bid was accepted, the firm realized that $254,000 for general costs had not been included in its bid. The spreadsheet user blamed the spreadsheet software he had used. He stated that while preparing the bid, he had entered the general cost amount into the correct column, but when the calculation was performed, the formula did not pick up the right amount. He assumed the program was correct and sent out the bid without checking the calculations. This error cost the firm $254,000. Cummings tried

Figure 10.3
Decomposition into
Modules

*The calculation of gross and
net pay in a payroll system
can be decomposed into several
levels of subprograms. On the
first level, the calculation is
expressed as three smaller
subprograms. Each of these is
then divided into several
modules, each of which could
be specified in more detail to
show the precise logic. (Note
that the data flows between
modules are not included in
the diagram.)*

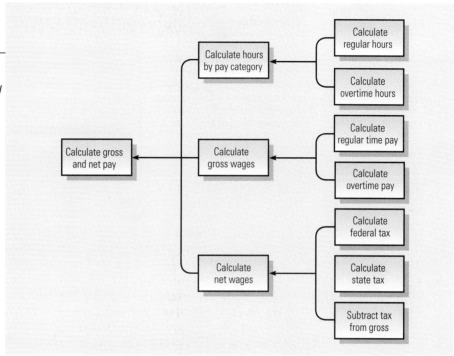

to sue Lotus Development Corporation, which responded that the problem was human error since the person using the spreadsheet didn't understand how it operated. The lawsuit was dropped.[4]

Although few spreadsheet mistakes cost $254,000, vigilance about possible spreadsheet errors is important for any user or manager. The simplest expression of that vigilance is to ensure that spreadsheets and other programs are tested.

Testing Programs

Testing is the process of determining whether a program or system performs the desired processing. A flaw in a program that causes it to produce incorrect or inappropriate results is called a **bug.** The process of finding and correcting bugs is called **debugging.** The two types of bugs are syntax errors and logic errors.

Syntax errors involve incorrect use of the programming language. The SQL translation of the user's query in Figure 10.4 demonstrates the meaning of syntax. Each verb in the translation is a command with a specific meaning in SQL. Conceivable English alternatives for these verbs would be syntax errors unless these terms were valid commands in SQL. Since syntax errors are inconsistent with programming language rules, the automatic translation process that converts programming language into executable machine language can identify syntax errors and warn the programmer.

The syntax of programming languages is a traditional stumbling block for nonprogrammers developing their own systems or using databases in nonrepetitive ways. Where possible, current user interfaces eliminate many aspects of this problem. For example, they may let the user select from a list of commands instead of asking the user to remember command names. Figure 10.4 shows how it is even possible to express queries in plain English if the necessary background work is done to set up the system.

Figure 10.4 A SQL Translation

Terms such as create, select, from and where in the SQL translation of the query in figure 10.4 demonstrate the concept of syntax. Conceivable English alternatives to those terms are not part of SQL and would not be acceptable.

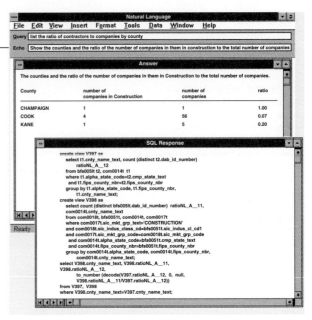

Logic errors are bugs that cause a program to perform incorrect processing even though the program is syntactically correct. The program may simply do the wrong thing. For example, it may add $x + y$ when it should add $x + z$. Programs that operate correctly individually may also fail because of mutual inconsistencies when they are combined with other components of a system. Another possible logic error is that the program performs the intended processing, but the initial intention was incorrect or too limited. In software firms, this problem has become a standing joke: Customer service people explain to customers that the way a particular program operates is a "feature," not a "bug." This means that the program operates the way it was supposed to operate, and the way the manual says it should operate, whether or not the user believes this is what it should do.

Most programs initially contain bugs and inappropriate features no matter how carefully they are first written. Business programs rarely work correctly the first time. The larger the program and the larger the number of interactions with other programs, the higher the likelihood of bugs. Furthermore, some bugs will probably go undetected until after the program has been used in practice for weeks or months. Box 10.1 describes an example of this type.

Good practice in real-world programming includes the development of a test plan for debugging the program and the system it is part of. The debugging of an individual program is sometimes called **unit testing,** which is usually done by testing a program under a wide range of conditions. For example, inputs that are transformed or that participate in program logic are set to typical values and to their high and low values in different tests. Tests using the high and low values often reveal bugs because they generate results that are often more obviously erroneous than erroneous results calculated from typical values. In contrast to unit testing, **system testing** determines whether the entire system operates as intended. System testing is more complicated than unit testing because the number of possible combinations of conditions is much larger. Since it is extremely difficult to prove that even a simple program is correct, testing of programs and systems is a key area of computer science research.

Figure 10.5 Three Control Structures Used in Structured Programming

To make sure that computer programs are understandable and easy to maintain, structured programming calls for consistent use of only three control structures within programs. These are sequence, selection, and iteration. The two types of iteration are "do until" and "do while".

Sequence: Steps or processes are performed in turn.

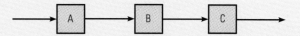

Selection: The next step depends on the results of a test at a previous step. For example, the test at step D might be to ask whether the applicant is at least 18 years old. Depending on whether the results is true or false, either E or F is performed next.

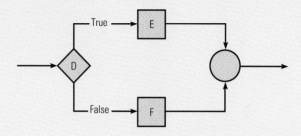

Iteration: A set of steps are performed repetitively until a particular condition occurs. There are two versions of iteration. With *do until*, process G is performed and then process H asks a question (such as whether the last applicant is in this group.) If the result is true, continue; if not , perform G again. *Do while* works in a similar way except that the test is performed before rather than after the repeated process.

Do until

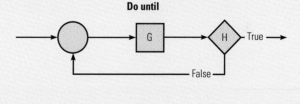

Do while

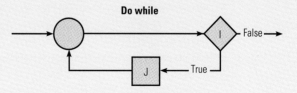

Surprisingly, it is often difficult to debug your own work because you are too familiar with the program's intent. Programmers testing their own work often test for what they think it is supposed to accomplish and decide that the program is correct, but they never test for situations or conditions they have overlooked. To avoid such omissions, many programming groups have someone else test a program after a round of unit testing by the programmer.

Box 10.1 The $5 Million Bug

Software bugs have caused significant financial losses even in large, well-run businesses. On November 21, 1985, a software bug terminated the processing of transactions involving $23 billion of securities at the Bank of New York. Since the transactions couldn't be completed, the bank was $23 billion out of balance when it needed to close its books for the day. It had to borrow this amount from the Federal Reserve Bank for one day, at a price of $5 million, all for a single bug in a large system. The bug was a simple error in defining a single field. A program for processing securities transactions contained a field that assigned a sequence number to each transaction in a batch of tranactions. The system was used as part of the legally mandated process of closing the bank's books for the day. The programmer could have programmed this counter in a number of ways but happened to make it a field with a length of 2 bytes. Two bytes is 16 binary digits (0's or 1's). Because the maximum numerical value that can be stored in 2 bytes is 65,535, the counter went back to 0 on the 65,536th transaction causing subsequent transactions to write-over, or erase, previous transactions stored in an internal list. The incorrect value of a single counter in a program prevented the bank from closing its books.

Transaction Number	Binary Value of the Counter
1	00000000 00000001
2	00000000 00000010
3....	00000000 00000011
65,534	11111111 11111110
65,535	11111111 11111111
65,536	00000000 00000000
65,537	00000000 00000001

The Changing Nature of Programming

The last 40 years have seen enormous improvements in programming techniques. The first programming languages required programmers to keep track of minute details about how programs operated. The history of programming technology since then has been a series of improvements making programming less procedural. Figure 10.5 identifies some of the major advances in this direction. It illustrates how these advances have changed the balance of responsibilities between humans and computers over the last 40 years. With the first machine languages, programmers performed 100 percent of the translation from the idea of what users wanted to accomplish into machine-executable code. With the development of assembly language, people performed a smaller part of the overall translation because they could program in a language that could then be translated automatically into machine language.

Each of the advances in Figure 10.6 has more of the translation done automatically and less done by people. These advances in programming technology couldn't have happened without the advances in hardware speed and storage discussed in Chapter 9. Figure 10.6 illustrates that we don't know whether programming methods will ever advance to the point where people can just say what they want and have it programmed automatically. The natural language that we use in everyday speech will remain ineffective for this purpose for the foreseeable future because everyday speech is so unstructured.

Figure 10.6 From User Requirements to Executable Machine Code

This figure summarizes the history of programming as a set of milestones in translating from what a user wants into instructions that can be executed by a computer. With each step, more of the translation is done automatically and less is done by a person. Where object-oriented programming belongs in this progression remains to be seen. The question marks at the bottom of the figure indicate future developments whose form and content are unknown.

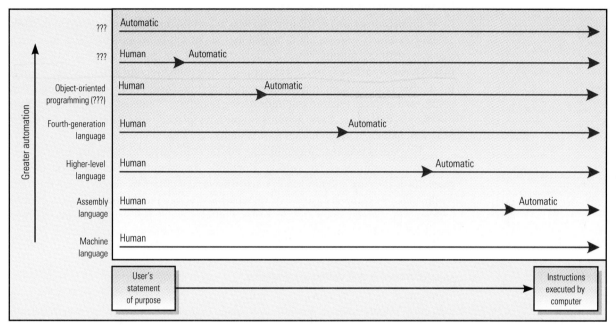

Before discussing specific developments in programming languages and operating systems, it is useful to recognize some of the major trends supporting the automation summarized in Figure 10.6. These trends are moving in four related directions: greater nonprocedurality, greater modularity and reusability, greater machine and data independence, and tighter links between analysis and programming. In combination, these trends are changing the nature of programming by reducing the number of steps between specifying how the system should help users and getting it to operate correctly on the computer.

Greater nonprocedurality

People can increasingly express *what* should be accomplished instead of *how* it should be done by a computer. A program that specifies the procedures for how something should be done is described as **procedural.** One that specifies what should be accomplished, but not the procedures for doing it, is termed **nonprocedural.** The user query in Figure 10.4 is nonprocedural because it explains what the user wants, but not how the computer should answer the question. Although the SQL translation was more procedural, SQL itself is somewhat nonprocedural because it does not tell the computer exactly how to find the data in storage.

With the trend toward nonprocedurality, people can increasingly specify the required processing in the terms in which they think about the problem. Programming is more directly linked to the analysis, which is often done with diagrams such as data flow diagrams for process modeling (Chapter 3) and entitiy-relationship diagrams for data modeling (Chapter 4). This means that less programming effort is needed to express the user's ideas in a programming language. It is less necessary for people to make choices about computer-related details that are unrelated to the business problem being solved. People can focus more on the business problem and less on the process of translating into a format the computer can use.

Greater modularity and reusability

As we initially described in the introduction to Part III, **modularity** is a form of division of labor in which systems are designed as a set of self-contained modules that work together, with the output of one module serving as the input of another. Modularity makes it easier to design and test systems because each function is defined in isolation from other functions. An important example of modularity is the separation between graphical interfaces that present information to users and database programs that find the data in databases. Early systems might have placed both functions in the same program, making it much harder to maintain.

As systems become more modular, it is more practical for IS departments to discourage programmers from writing programs from scratch. With the trend toward **reusability,** they are encouraged to reuse the work of others by cobbling together and modifying pre-existing modules. Typical reusable modules include programs that control windows on a screen, open and close files, find data in databases, or perform repetitive calculations. For reusability to be practical, programs must be created as carefully chosen modules and stored in a module library that makes reuse easy.

Greater machine and data independence

Trends toward open systems (discussed in Chapter 1) and modularity have reinforced long-term trends toward machine and data independence. With greater **machine independence,** programs are increasingly written in ways that permit them to be executed on a variety of machines from different vendors. This is accomplished by using industry standard programming languages and operating systems. With greater **data independence,** programs are increasingly written in ways that make it possible to change the physical storage of the data without changing the program. Chapter 4 explained that this is typically accomplished using DBMS features that separate the application program from the details of data definition and access.

Tighter links between analysis and programming

Although students often see programming as an end in itself, businesses see programming as part of a larger process of building and maintaining information systems (summarized in Figure 1.15). That larger process includes analyzing the problem, comparing alternatives, designing the new business process, designing the technical system, coding the system, testing it, implementing it in the organization, and maintaining it over time. For this reason, businesses often choose not to use a new language or technique until it is integrated into an overall approach for building and maintaining information systems.

Each of the advances in Figure 10.6 moves toward linking analysis and programming by eliminating steps between the expression of what people want (analysis) and the instructions for the computer (programming). Tools for process and data modeling generate information for defining the system being built. There is a strong trend toward linking these types of analysis directly into the programming process using **computer-aided software engineering (CASE)** systems. Although these systems differ in detail and scope, they typically include process and data modeling, a comprehensive data dictionary, methods for designing the technical structure of programs and databases, and modules for creating user interfaces and reports.

Taken in combination, the trends create new programming environments that are more effective than those used by programmers just a decade ago. The entire technical system becomes more self-explanatory because the programs are less procedural, more modular, more machine and data independent, and more tightly linked to the analysis. This makes it easier for people other than the original programmers to understand what the information system and the individual programs accomplish. The original programmers or other programmers also find it easier to return to the system later to modify it as is necessary.

These trends may seem very abstract at first blush, but they are basic ideas underlying much of the progress that has occurred in programming languages and techniques. As we look at programming in more depth, many specific advances can be seen as examples of these trends in action.

REALITY CHECK **Programming Viewed as a Business Process** As part of this section's overview of basic programming ideas, we discussed the necessity to test programs and mentioned several costly programming errors.

1. What techniques do you use to test spreadsheets or other programs you write? Explain why you believe those techniques would or would not be adequate if the problem you were solving involved 20 times as many variables and relationships.

2. Explain how you feel about this statement: "I don't know whether my bank programmed its systems correctly, but I just have to trust those systems and assume that my checking account is being handled correctly."

Four Generations of Programming Languages

The succession from machine language to fourth-generation languages and beyond is often called the **generations of programming languages.** We will summarize this progression to explain the directions in which progress is continuing to occur. Although business professionals do not work with machine language directly, starting from this point provides useful background for understanding the advances that are continuing today.

Machine Languages

As part of its introduction to computers, Chapter 9 introduced the basic idea of **machine language,** the internal programming language for a particular computer. Although the first programmers had to write programs in machine language, today's programmers no longer have to do so. The machine language example from Chapter 9 is shown in Box 10.2 along with the equivalent assembly language.

Machine languages have serious drawbacks as tools for the business process of programming. Programmers using this type of language must specify the desired processing in terms of minute operations involving specific physical locations inside the computer. This means that programmers must make a large number of explicit choices they do not really care about. Another problem is that the code itself is inexpressive, making it difficult to understand what another person's machine language program is trying to do. In fact, after a few months, even the original programmer would find a complex program difficult to understand. Moreover, programs written in a machine language are extremely difficult to modify or expand in any substantial way. Changes as seemingly simple as inserting several lines of code may require many corrections in location references. In machine language, major changes in data configurations or program flows are a programming nightmare. In addition, programs written in the machine language of a computer usually do not work on other computers with different machine languages, which means that it would be necessary to rewrite a program for it to accomplish the same processing on a different type of machine. Thus, machine language is essential for the internal operation of the machine but is an inordinately difficult medium for business programmers to use.

Assembly Languages

The disadvantages of machine language led to the development of assembly language, the second generation of programming languages. Box 10.2 compares a hypothetical assembly language program with an equivalent machine language program. **Assembly language** allows the programmer to write the program using the names of the variables (such as *A, B, C*) rather than the location of the data in the computer (201, 202, 203 in the machine language example). Working with the names of variables avoids the problems of physical references required in machine language programming and makes programs easier to write and maintain.

Programs called assemblers and loaders were developed to work together in translating the programmer's assembly language program into a machine language program. Translation includes a number of things. It converts all mnemonic operation codes (such as *add* and *sub* in Box 10.2) into the equivalent machine language codes (such as *37* and *46*). More important to programmers, the translation identifies all variables in the program and assigns a machine location to each of them. When the program runs on the computer, a machine location is assigned for each translated instruction. Assemblers also perform other important functions such as identifying syntax errors and certain logical errors. For example, if a program statement says ADD *X*, but *X* does not yet have a value, the assembler identifies *X* as an "undefined variable."

Despite the improvements embodied in assembly language, programming in assembly language retained many of the major drawbacks of programming in machine language. It remained a laborious, highly detailed, and error-prone activity. In addition, since assembly language is so directly related to the machine it runs on, transferring a program to a different computer with a different set of internal instruction codes remained tedious and error-prone. The next step was to provide a better tool than assembly language.

Higher-Level Languages

In response to the problems related to assembly language programming, the first **higher-level languages** were developed in the late 1950s. Also called third-generation languages (3GLs), their purpose was to permit people to program at a higher level. In the assembly language example, the programmer is thinking about how to calculate *A* from the variables *B, C, D, E,* and *F.* Ideally, the programmer should be able to give the formula instead of having to break the calculation into ten tiny steps. Higher-level languages permit concise statements of this type.

A program called a **compiler** translates higher-level language programs into machine language. For example, a compiler allows a programmer to simply write the equation in the example and translates the equation into machine language. In this type of translation process, the original program is called the **source code,** and the equivalent machine language program is called the **object code.** The object code is used each time the application is executed. When it is necessary to change the program, the

Box 10.2 Comparison of Machine Language and Assembly Language

A programmer wants the computer to calculate the value of **A** using the formula

A = (B - C) * D + (E * F)

On the left is a set of instructions expressing this calculation in a hypothetical machine language discussed earlier in Figure 9.10. On the right is an equivalent set of instructions in a hypothetical assembly language. For example, the operation code *sub* in the third assembly language instruction is equivalent to the operation code *46* in the third machine language instruction. Although programming in assembly language is easier than programming in machine language, it is still much harder than just stating the formula.

Machine Language	Assembly Language
To program in this machine language, one must specify the location of each instruction, the numerical operation code, and the location of the operand (the data item the instruction uses).	To program in this assembly language, one must specify the operation code and the name of the variable. Notice how the programmer had to make up a temporary variable that was not part of the business problem.
LI = location of instruction OC= operation code LO = location of operand	OC = operation code VAR= variable name

MACHINE LANGUAGE INSTRUCTION			MEANING OF INSTRUCTION	ASSEMBLY LANGUAGE INSTRUCTION		MEANING OF INSTRUCTION
LI	OC	LO		OC	VAR	
101	19	—	Clear accumulator	cle	—	Clear accumulator
102	37	202	Add contents of location 202 to contents of accumulator	add	B	Add B to contents of accumulator
103	46	203	Subtract contents of location 203 from contents of accumulator	sub	C	Subtract C from contents of accumulator
104	52	204	Multiply contents of accumulator by contents of location 204	mpy	D	Multiply contents of accumulator by D
105	24	207	Store contents of accumulator in location 207	sto	T	Store contents of accumulator as a temporary variable T
106	19	—	Clear accumulator	cle	—	Clear accumulator
107	37	205	Add contents of location 205 to contents of accumulator	add	E	Add E to contents of accumulator
108	52	206	Multiply contents of accumulator by contents of location 206	mpy	F	Multiply contents of accumulator by F
109	37	207	Add contents of location 207 to contents of accumulator	add	T	Add T to contents of accumulator
110	24	201	Store contents of accumulator in location 201	sto	A	Store contents of accumulator in A

changes are made in the source code, which is then translated into new object code. These procedures make it unnecessary to translate the source code each time an application is executed. In addition to allowing programmers to express arithmetic statements directly, compilers (along with system software) provide automatic mechanisms for handling input, output, and data formatting. These mechanisms permit the programmer to use a command such as PRINT, which is automatically translated into hundreds of machine language instructions that take care of all the details required for the computer to retrieve the data. These details are related to the internal operation of the computer and its interface with the printer and are of no interest to the programmer, who simply wants certain data printed.

Computers with different types of CPUs have different internal instruction codes. Consequently, the same higher-level language needs a different compiler for different computers. This is an important issue related to the portability of programs between different types of computers. Ideally, most application programs should be machine independent and therefore able to operate on any computer with sufficient capacity. Although many higher-level languages were designed with machine independence in mind, compilers for the same language on different machines often have some inconsistencies. Consequently, programs written in a higher-level language on one type of computer may not run properly on another type of computer. Such programs must be retested on the second computer and may have to be modified before they can be used.

Many higher-level languages have been developed, but only a few have attained widespread use, including COBOL, FORTRAN, PL/1, BASIC, Pascal, C, and ADA. All these were initially developed with a particular set of capabilities but have been modified and expanded through subsequent versions on different computers. They are sometimes called problem-oriented languages because they were designed for different types of work, such as business data processing or scientific calculations. Box 10.3 explains more about these languages.

Figures 10.7 and 10.8 show extracts of programs written in COBOL and in C. COBOL is the traditional language for most business data processing. C is a newer language used frequently for developing new software. To a nonprogrammer, the differences between these languages may appear superficial, but each important language has certain features that make it especially useful for a particular purpose. For example, the COBOL program contains a mandatory data division for defining the format of the data in the program. Capabilities related to data definition and the formatting of inputs and outputs are one of the major reasons COBOL has been the leading programming language for business data processing.

Third generation languages made it practical to produce the business data processing systems in common use today. However, they still required programs to describe in detail exactly how the data were to be processed. The next step was to make programs less procedural.

Fourth-Generation Languages

Other than programming languages for teaching, third-generation languages are basically tools for professional programmers. The high level of programming skill needed to use these languages for business applications makes their direct use by business professionals impractical. Using these languages is arduous and time consuming even for professional programmers, and the amount of work for professional programmers has always exceeded programmer availability. These factors encouraged the development of new ways to make programmers more productive and to permit nonprogrammers to do programming work.

Figure 10.7 Excerpt from a COBOL Program

This is an excerpt from a COBOL program. The purpose of this program is to calculate the average of a series of integers entered through a keyboard. The program is written in the form of sentences. The data division identifies all the data items. The procedure division starts with a control routine that shows the flow of the logic. The perform statements all refer to subordinate subroutines that carry out the individual steps.

```
****************************************************************
IDENTIFICATION DIVISION.
****************************************************************
PROGRAM-ID. AVERAGE.
* COBOL PROGRAM
* AVERAGING INTEGERS ENTERED THROUGH THE KEYBOARD.
****************************************************************
ENVIRONMENT DIVISION.
****************************************************************
CONFIGURATION DIVISION.
SOURCE-COMPUTER          H-P 3000.
OBJECT-COMPUTER          H-P 3000.
****************************************************************
DATA DIVISION
****************************************************************
FILE SECTION
WORKING-STORAGE SECTION.
01 AVERAGE          PIC ---9.99.
01 COUNTER          PIC 9(02)          VALUE ZERO.
01 NUMBER-ITEM      PIC S9(03).
01 SUM-ITEM         PIC S9(06)          VALUE ZERO.
01 BLANK-LINE       PIC X(80)           VALUE SPACES.
****************************************************************
PROCEDURE DIVISION
****************************************************************
100-CONTROL-ROUTINE.
    PERFORM 200-DISPLAY-INSTRUCTIONS.
    PERFORM 300-INITIALIZATION-ROUTINE.
    PERFORM 400-ENTER-AND-ADD
                UNTIL NUMBER-ITEM=999.
    PERFORM 500-CALCULATE-AVERAGE.
    PERFORM 600-DISPLAY-RESULTS.
    STOP RUN.
200-DISPLAY-INSTRUCTION.
    DISPLAY
        "THIS PROGRAM WILL FIND THE AVERAGE OF INTEGERS YOU ENTER".
    DISPLAY
        "THROUGH THE KEYBOARD. TYPE 999 TO INDICATE END OF DATA.".
    DISPLAY BLANK-LINE.
300-INITIALIZATION-ROUTINE
    DISPLAY "PLEASE ENTER A NUMBER".
    ACCEPT NUMBER-ITEM.
400-ENTER-AND-ADD
    ADD NUMBER-ITEM TO SUM-ITEM.
    ADD 1 TO COUNTER.
    DISPLAY "PLEASE ENTER THE NEXT NUMBER".
    ACCEPT NUMBER-ITEM.
500-CALCULATE-AVERAGE.
    DIVIDE SUM-ITEM BY COUNTER GIVING AVERAGE.
600-DISPLAY-RESULTS.
    DISPLAY "THE AVERAGE OF THE MUMBERS IS ",AVERAGE.
```

Figure 10.8 Excerpt from a C Program

This is an excerpt from a C program that performs the same processing as the COBOL program in Figure 10.7. Notice how this program is much more terse than the COBOL program, but might not be as easy to figure out.

```
/* C PROGRAM */
/* AVERAGING INTEGERS ENTERED THROUGH THE KEYBOARD */
main()
{ float average;
  int counter = 0; number = 0; sum = 0;
printf("THIS PROGRAM WILL FIND THE AVERAGE OF INTEGERS YOU ENTER\n");
printf("THROUGH THE KEYBOARD. TYPE 999 TO INDICATE END OF DATA. \N\N");
printf("PLEASE ENTER A NUMBER");
scanf("%d",&number);
while (number !=999
    {
    sum = sum + number;
    counter ++ ;
    printf("PLEASE ENTER THE NEXT NUMBER");
    scanf("%d",&number);
    }
  average = sum / counter;
  printf("THE AVERAGE OF THE NUMBERS IS ",AVERAGE);
}
```

Box 10.3 Third Generation Languages

FORTRAN (FORmula TRANslator) was introduced by IBM in 1954 as the first higher-level language. It was developed for scientific programming focusing predominantly on calculations and with relatively simple input and output requirements. Initially, it had few structured features.

COBOL (COmmon Business Oriented Language) was developed in 1959 by a committee whose goal was to produce a higher-level language for business data processing. These applications require extensive control of inputs and outputs but relatively simple calculations. Improved versions of COBOL came out in 1968, 1974, and 1985. In attempting to make COBOL programs self-explanatory, COBOL's designers permitted lengthy names of variables and subroutines and used sentencelike grammar. This design made programs extremely verbose but easier to maintain than FORTRAN programs. COBOL is the language used most commonly for business data processing today. It is a good tool for organizing programming ideas through successive decomposition and contains some features supporting structured programming.

PL/1 was introduced by IBM in 1964 as a single language that could be used for both business data processing and scientific calculations. It is extremely complicated because it incorporates and extends most of the capabilities of both FORTRAN and COBOL. PL/1 did not replace COBOL because businesses were not convinced it was worth the expense to rewrite their existing COBOL programs.

BASIC (Beginner's All-purpose Symbolic Instruction Code) was developed at Dartmouth in 1965 as a simple language for teaching introductory programming. Students learning BASIC could write small programs within an hour instead of days or weeks. The early versions of BASIC were very limited. For example, the names of variables could only be one or two characters long in the early versions. New versions of BASIC expanded its power, and it eventually became popular for programming small computers.

PASCAL was developed by Niklaus Wirth in 1971 as a tool for teaching and enforcing structured programming. It has become widely used as a teaching tool in computer science departments and has been used as an alternative for BASIC. Its input/output capabilities are too limited for most business data processing.

C was introduced by Bell Laboratories in 1972 to combine some of the low-level machine control capabilities of assemblers with the data structures and control structures of higher-level languages. It is designed to be machine independent and is used to write programs that can be used on different types of computers. It is used widely in writing new commercial software. A version of C called C++ provides capabilities related to object-oriented programming.

ADA is a language developed by the Department of Defense in 1980 to try to standardize data processing for its weapons systems and to make programs more reusable to reduce programming costs. It is a structured language that encourages modular design and facilitates testing and reusing code.

Fourth-generation languages (4GLs) are a loosely defined group of programming languages and systems that make programming less procedural than third-generation languages. The term *4GL* was closely associated with query languages and report generators for retrieving data from databases although 4GLs can also perform transactions using data in databases. Many 4GLs are subsets of larger products, such as DBMSs or integrated systems for designing and building business applications.

Query languages are special-purpose languages used to provide immediate, online answers to questions involving data in databases such as, "Which five customers in New Jersey had the highest purchases last month?" **Report generators** are special-purpose languages used to answer questions or to program reports that will be used repeatedly. The SQL in Figure 10.4 is an example of a query language. The query specification is nonprocedural. It identifies the desired output but doesn't say exactly how the computer should find the data or how the heading or body of the output should be formatted. Typical report specifications in a 4GL report generator once looked like a set of text statements but have moved to more of a graphical approach with the user using a mouse to specify options.

The benefits of 4GLs extend to both programmers and end users. Programmers need less time and effort to specify the required processing. Writing the same reporting program in COBOL might take ten times as long because of all the details that must be incorporated into COBOL programs. End users benefit because 4GLs provide a way to obtain information without requiring the direct help of a programmer. The use of 4GLs for queries and report generation reduces the pressure on programmers to write reporting programs to support immediate information needs.

Although 4GLs have been adopted widely because of their advantages, there are four reasons they have not replaced COBOL and other third-generation languages:

1. The existing investment in around 100 billion lines of COBOL code makes rewriting all these programs an enormous task with a questionable payoff. This still leaves the question of why 4GLs are not used for the development of all new systems.

2. 4GLs have limitations compared to other programming languages. Third-generation languages are more general purpose than 4GLs, which address specific parts of system development, such as defining the format of data input screens, answering queries, and generating reports. In each of these areas, 4GLs sacrifice some of the generality of 3GLs to make it easier to specify typical screen formats, queries, and reports. They cannot handle situations with the most complex formats or logic.

3. Any programming language, whether it is a 3GL or 4GL, solves only part of the the larger problem of building the sysetm and maintaining it.

4. Adopting a 4GL involves the cost of buying new 4GL software and training personnel. Since existing programs in a 3GL will not be replaced immediately, if at all, the staff must be trained to use the 4GL for some projects and 3GLs for maintaining old systems.

The four generations of programming languages define an important stream of developments, which makes programming less procedural and permits the user to be more concerned with the desired processing or outputs rather than the specific method used for performing the processing. Although Japan's Fifth Generation research project and other projects have worked toward the next generation of programming languages,[5] no fifth generation of languages is used in business today. This certainly does not mean that the four generations of languages cover all important developments, however.

REALITY CHECK **Programming Languages** The generations of programming languages illustrate progress in four directions: greater nonprocedurality, greater modularity and reusability, greater machine and data independence, and tighter links between analysis and programming.

1. Assuming you are a business professional whose job is not directly related to software development, explain why these trends might or might not matter to you.

2. As a spreadsheet user now and in the future, explain what these trends might mean to you.

Other Major Developments in Programming

The four generations of programming languages represent an important stream of developments, but certainly don't encompass all that has happened. We will now look at some other significant developments, including special purpose languages, spreadsheets, CASE systems, and object-oriented programming. DBMS would certainly belong here also, had we not covered it in Chapter 4.

Special-Purpose Languages

General-purpose programming languages have an important shortcoming. They contain no ideas about the area of business or type of problem the programmer is working on. For example, even through COBOL may be used to program an inventory system or a financial system, it contains no specific ideas about inventory or finance. If you were a programmer analyzing the cash flow from a complex real estate investment, you would prefer to use a programming language that contained financial ideas, such as net present value and return on investment. You might save more time and make fewer errors if the language contained specific ideas about real estate investments.

Modeling languages, special-purpose languages for developing models, are used extensively in decision support systems. Unlike general-purpose languages, they contain specific capabilities that make it easy to build models. Many modeling languages contain financial functions. Some contain special ways of organizing data in two-or three-dimensional arrays for easy analysis. Others include methods for drawing a picture of a model and using that picture to check the consistency of the equations in the model. Figure 10.9 shows the way the modeling language Extend can be used to create a model for analyzing the operations of a car wash. Each of the building blocks was produced in advance and stored in a module library. The programmer created this program by selecting and modifying the building blocks.

Figure 10.9 Graphical Representation of a Simulation

This is the graphical representation of a simulation developed using the Extend simulation system. The simulation was created by linking existing modules provided by the package vendor and specifying values of characteristics within those modules, such as speeds or capacities. Running this type of simulation many times generates statistics about average waiting times and other factors pertinent to improving the process.

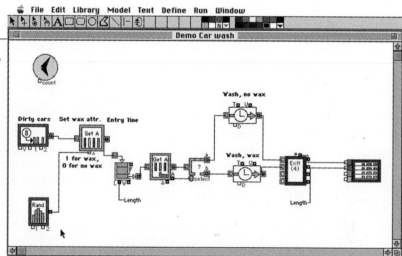

Like the 3GLs, the first modeling languages were effective only if used by programming professionals. Model building became much more practical for nonprogrammers with the advent of computerized spreadsheets in the early 1980s.

Spreadsheets

Spreadsheet products, such as Lotus 1-2-3, Excel, and Quattro, are a special type of modeling language that can be used only to describe problems that fit into a spreadsheet format. Millions of people who are not professional programmers develop programs using spreadsheet software. Several factors contribute to this widespread use. For one thing, many types of business calculations can be performed in a spreadsheet format. Since the spreadsheet format is familiar to users, they don't have to struggle with a new way of thinking about problems. Spreadsheet software also provides an easy way for users to work with the model. Instead of forcing the users to name every variable, the spreadsheet permits users to recognize what each variable means based on the cell it occupies in the grid. Focusing on the cells and their specific locations also provides a virtually automatic way of formatting the outputs for printing, making it unnecessary to master a separate report generator.

Although these factors contribute to the popularity of spreadsheets, the way they are usually handled by the software leaves users' spreadsheets inflexible and difficult to maintain. Users attempting to reorganize rows and columns run the risk of introducing errors. Since the output of a spreadsheet is related to the location of the cells, and since this is static, it is difficult to look at spreadsheet outputs in different ways. This is the same kind of problem that motivated the development of new generations of programming languages. Figure 10.10 shows how subsequent innovations tried to make spreadsheets more flexible while maintaining the benefits of the spreadsheet approach.

Figure 10.10 A New Type of Flexibility in Spreadsheets

Each of the spreadsheets formats shown here is actually just a different way of looking at the same accounting data. The data are by division (camera, VCR, CD), line item (sales, cost of goods sold, personnel, and marketing and promotion), and quarter. To convert from one format to another, the user merely switches the order and placement of the icons representing the three dimensions.

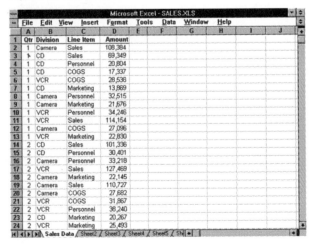

Computer-Aided Software Engineering Systems

Computer-aided software engineering (CASE) is the use of computerized tools to improve the efficiency, accuracy, and completeness of the process of analyzing, designing, developing, and maintaining an information system. CASE is based on the idea of improving quality and productivity by approaching system analysis and development in a highly structured and disciplined way. CASE systems sold by different vendors overlap in many ways but also contain certain unique features.

Users of CASE systems avoid reinventing methods that have been developed carefully and integrated into a consistent package. The CASE system establishes standard methods that must be used by the entire organization and therefore increases coordination and decreases confusion. It establishes effective methods for storing and using the data generated during systems analysis, design, and development. It also automatically checks for certain inconsistencies and errors such as inconsistent data names or formats. Finally, CASE makes maintenance more efficient because the programs are constructed based on the same structures and standards.

CASE is sometimes divided into upper-CASE versus lower-CASE. **Upper-CASE** refers to tools used by users, managers, and information systems professionals to describe business processes and the data needed by those processes. Upper-CASE techniques mentioned earlier in this text include data dictionaries, data flow diagrams for process modeling (Chapter 3), and entity-relationship diagrams for data modeling (Chapter 4).

Lower-CASE is a set of tools used by programmers to facilitate the programming process. **Screen generators** simplify programming of data input screens by making it easy to place headings, instructions, comments, and the actual data entry fields anywhere on the screen with minimal effort compared to what is required in traditional programming. Current DBMSs for personal computers contain this type of capability, which was barely available for professional mainframe programmers just a decade ago. Report generators, which are often 4GLs, make it easy to program simple listings and reports based on the fact that reports typically contain headings, subheadings, totals, and subtotals of prespecified size and format in particular locations on the page. Some CASE systems contain **code generators** that automatically generate computer programs from specifications that are not in a programming language. Code generators require a complete structured specification of exactly how the software should operate. Code generators convert those specifications into programs written in COBOL or other languages. CASE systems may contain many other tools and techniques that make system development more efficient, including the maintenance of subroutine libraries, the generation of data for testing, debugging techniques, and techniques for controlling changes in programs.

CASE tools are gradually shifting to encompass ideas from object-oriented programming, one of the major trends for computing in the future.

Object-Oriented Programming

Most software developers believe that the next major advance in programming will come with a new programming philosophy called object-oriented programming (often abbreviated OOP). This general approach was invented in the 1970s but is becoming feasible only now due to a combination of hardware and software advances. Although OOP may seem to be an extension of the structured programming techniques mentioned earlier, there is more to it than that.

Object-oriented programming treats the data and programs in a way that may seem strange to someone who has used a 3GL or 4GL. Figure 10.11 illustrates the major

Figure 10.11 Major Concepts of Object-Oriented Programming

The major concepts of object-oriented programming include classes, objects, inheritance, methods, message passing, and polymorphism. Building these ideas into the analysis and programming of an information system makes it easier to develop and maintain.

Classes and objects. Objects are the things about which data exist. Objects of the same type are grouped together into classes. Classes can include subclasses. In this example, spreadsheet models and memos are objects in the class *Documents*.

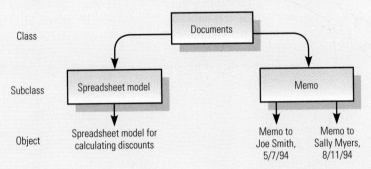

Inheritance and methods. The objects within a class inherit the methods associated with the class. The methods are functions that can be performed on the objects in the class. In this example, associated with the class Documents are a series of methods such as opening, closing, saving, and printing. All these are inherited by the objects in the subclasses.

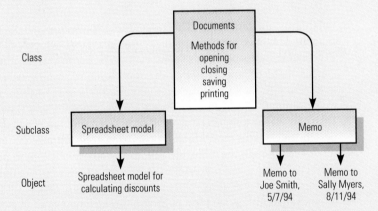

Message passing. The only way to communicate between objects is to send an explicit message.

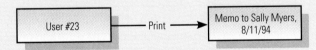

Polymorphism. The same message can be sent to objects in distinct yet related classes to start an action that may be handled in a different way depending on the characteristics of the classes. Although some aspects of printing are the same in this example, such as identifying a printer, other aspects are different, such as the need for a method to determine how to break up the spreadsheet across columns and pages.

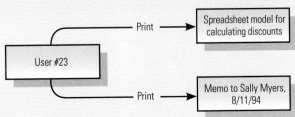

OOP concepts. OOP starts by identifying *objects*. These are the people or things about which data exist. Associated with an object are both data and actions that can be performed related to the object. For example, in a desktop computer system, the object might be a document written using a word processor. Any particular document is a member of a *class* of objects called "document." Associated with that class of objects are *actions* that can be taken, such as opening it, closing it, saving it, or deleting it. These actions all have *methods* for performing the action. All members of a class of objects *inherit* the attributes of the classes higher in the object classification scheme. A document within the subclass "memo" therefore would inherit all attributes and actions related to documents as well as additional attributes and actions related specifically to memos.

In object-oriented programming, all actions are controlled by *messages* passed between objects. For example, the object "user" could send a message to the object "Memo to A. Jones" telling it to open itself. If there are ten different types of documents and one standard way to open a document, that method for opening documents would be attached to the object class "document" and inherited by all ten types of document. To open a document of any type, it would be necessary only to send an "open" message along with any additional data required to perform this action. For example, the additional data might be the identification of the object sending the message because the method for opening documents might check whether the message came from an object permitted to open this document.

Although it may seem strange to tell a document to open itself, treating things in terms of objects, classes, actions, methods, inheritance, and messages encourages modularity and reusability. The most visible applications of object-oriented programming to date have been in graphical user interfaces, which can be described in terms of particular types of objects such as windows, menus, fields, and buttons. These same classes of objects apply whether the application is a billing system or a spreadsheet. It is therefore possible to program many methods only once and then reuse them for many different applications. Since the user interface and data handling make up a large part of many applications, OOP saves programming effort, simplifies overall system design, and creates more consistent-looking applications.

Even though the many programming tools for OOP have not yet been developed fully, OOP has proved powerful in some leading-edge applications. With the advent of object-oriented operating systems in the mid-1990s, OOP could form the basis of the long-awaited fifth generation of programming languages.

Is Natural Language Programming Possible?

Each successive generation of programming languages allowed programmers to focus less on how the machine performs its work and more on expressing the desired result. Following along this path, it might seem that programming should eventually take place in **natural language,** the spoken or written language used by people to communicate with each other. It might seem that natural language would complete the progression in Figure 10.6 because the translation from the user's ideas to machine language would be 100 percent automatic. Figure 10.4 shows how plain English can be used for queries against a defined database if the necessary background work is done in advance and if users check the response carefully to be sure the question wasn't misinterpreted. Despite the result with queries, it is highly questionable whether natural language could be used to program application systems in the near future. Even if the entire vocabulary could be defined with a dictionary, statements in everyday natural language are often ambiguous and poorly structured. Even if the sentences are clear, in combination they are often inconsistent or illogical. Furthermore, people often misunderstand each other even though they share understandings about how the world operates. Since computers do not currently understand how the world operates, these problems of ambiguity, interpretation, and inconsistency would overwhelm any current attempts to program application systems using natural language. At minimum, it would be impossible to test the resulting business application to ensure it operates correctly.

REALITY CHECK **Developments in Programming** This section mentioned a number of examples of progress that has occurred in programming. Despite that progress, many people still have trouble instructing VCRs to record television programs.

1. Based on the trends and examples, speculate about the way spreadsheet users may create spreadsheet models five years from now.

2. Based on the trends and examples, speculate about the user interfaces for VCRs, microwave ovens, and other home equipment five years from now.

Operating Systems

Thus far, the chapter has focused on business applications and end-user software, both of which are designed to support the user's business processes. It has also covered the role of system development software in translating the ideas into object code that a machine can execute. For completeness, the chapter looks at operating systems, a type of system software (rather than application software) that affects business professionals in several significant ways, starting with the fact that a computer can execute application software only if that software is compatible with the computer's operating system.

Operating systems are complex programs that control the operation of a computer by controlling (1) execution of other programs running on the computer, (2) communication with peripheral devices including terminals, and (3) use of disk space and other computer system resources. When centralized computing was the norm, it was easier to generalize about operating system functions. Today, different operating system functions are required by different computing options, which include mainframe computers, personal computers, computer networks, as well as specialized options such as parallel processing. To make things more complicated, operating systems are often intertwined with other layers of software, including DBMSs, graphical front ends such as Windows 3.1, groupware products such as Lotus Notes, and middleware products that link application programs running on client devices with programs running on servers. Table 10.2 lists characteristics of some of the major operating systems.

Operating systems differ in size and complexity. The first operating systems for personal computers were written by small groups of people. As operating systems took on new functions, the amount of development work multiplied. Microsoft's Windows NT, a completely new operating system for networked computers, cost over $150 million to develop with a team of 200 programmers, and contained 4.3 million lines of code when it was first released in 1993.[6] Our discussion of operating system functions will start with the simplest case, personal computers.

Table 10.2 Comparison of Major Operating Systems in 1994

Operating System	Single or Multiple Users	Multitasking	Platform	User Interface
MS-DOS	Single	No	IBM PCs and clones	Command language
MS-DOS with Windows 3.1	Single	No	IBM PCs and clones	GUI
OS/2	Single	Yes	IBM PCs and clones	GUI
Macintosh	Single	Yes	Macintosh computers	GUI
Novell Netware	Small to medium networks	Yes	Networked PCs	Command language but can be used with Windows 3.1
Windows NT	Networks	Yes	Networked PCs	GUI
UNIX	Many users	Yes	UNIX minicomputers, work-stations, servers	Command language or GUI
MVS	Thousands	Yes	IBM mainframes	Command language
VMS	Hundreds	Yes	VAX minicomputers and mainframes	Command language

Operating Systems for Personal Computers

The purpose of the operating system is to make it possible for you to do work on a computer by using application programs such as spreadsheets, word processors, or drawing programs. It does this by performing a variety of functions related to controlling the user interface, controlling access to data, controlling jobs in progress, and allocating resources. Here are some of the functions that affect a personal computer user:

Controlling the user interface. When you turn on a personal computer, the operating system displays startup information along with a prompt, a menu, or some other indication of what you can do. As you use the computer, the appearance of what you see on the screen is controlled by the operating system or by the interaction between the operating system and whatever application program is being used.

Controlling access to data. When you access previously stored data through an application program, the operating system uses internal directories and other internal information to determine where it can find the data. Some operating systems can update one document automatically based on data changes in another document, for example, automatically updating a document from a wordprocessor when changes are made in a spreadsheet, part of which is included in the document. In addition, if the operating system has a password mechanism for controlling data access, it asks for a password before permitting use of a restricted file.

Controlling jobs in progress. When you select an application or document to open, the operating system recognizes your inputs and takes the action you request. If you print something, the operating system controls the interface with the printer and reports problems, such as when the printer is out of paper.

Operating systems that support **multitasking** permit the user to operate two or more programs concurrently on the same computer. For example, they permit a user to switch back and forth between a spreadsheet and a word processor without turning off one application in order to use the other. Inability to support multitasking was a key weakness of the MS-DOS operating system for IBM PCs. Operating systems that supported multitasking for single-user computers by 1994 included OS/2 (for IBM-compatible personal computers), System 7 or MacOS (for Macintosh computers), and UNIX (for a variety of computers). Windows 95, the upgrade from Windows 3.1, was slated to provide this capability in 1995.

Allocating resources. When you want to save a document or spreadsheet, the operating system decides where on the diskette or hard disk the data will be stored. It makes sure that each file stored does not overlay files stored previously. If it is necessary to break the data into several blocks in different places on the storage device, the operating system keeps track of the different blocks. When you delete files, the operating system frees up the space so that it can be used again.

Operating Systems for Mainframe Computers and Networks

Operating systems for mainframe computers perform the same functions in much more complex situations. Instead of taking care of a single user, they run many jobs simultaneously for different users, taking into account the priority of different jobs. Some of the jobs involve online interaction with users. Other jobs are run in background mode with the user detached. Mainframe operating systems make sure that the users, their data, and their various jobs do not interfere with one another.

Operating systems for mainframe computers monitor the current status of the computer system and decide when to start jobs. This is necessary because computer systems have a finite computing capacity, a specific number of peripherals of each type, and a finite capacity for communicating with the peripherals. The operating system considers resource availability when it allocates resources to jobs. For example, before starting a job that requires a tape drive, it allocates a specific tape drive to that job, and it delays the job if all tape drives are currently allocated to other jobs. Likewise, before adding another online user, it decides whether the capacity is available for that user; if not, it doesn't allow the user to log on. For mainframes with multiple processors, the operating system must also make sure that work being done by one processor does not interfere with work being done by another.

In networked computer systems, the **network operating system** establishes the links between the nodes, monitors the operation of the network, and controls recovery processes when nodes go down or the entire network goes down. The network operating system must work in conjunction with the operating system for the individual workstation or other computers on the network. This adds to the complexity of establishing and maintaining computer networks because the two operating systems (for the workstation and for the network) and the application software must all be compatible.

The mere fact that another operating system is involved also affects system performance. Users of PC networks often notice that daily rituals of getting started with their work take longer on a network than on an unattached personal computer. Similarly, going through two or more operating systems to obtain data from a server may create noticeable delays compared to retrieving data from a personal computer's hard disk.

Why Operating Systems Are Important

Foremost, operating systems are important because they can lock in some applications and lock out others. With current programming methods, application programs and end-user software are written to run under a particular operating system. A program written to run under one operating system may not run under another operating system. Surprisingly, incompatibilities between even a single vendor's operating systems may cause problems. For example, Microsoft's Windows NT operating system could not run many programs written for Windows 3.1 without special software Microsoft licensed from Insignia Solutions, a small software firm.[7]

The desire for compatibility across platforms and applications is one of the reasons for the popularity of the UNIX operating system, which was developed as a standard operating system that would run on all computers. Even though UNIX might have great potential advantages as an emerging standard, moving to this operating system or any other new operating system often involves the expense of abandoning or modifying much existing software.

A 1994 survey with responses from 2,751 IS managers found growing interest in UNIX, OS/2, Windows, and Windows NT. For the data center, they were leaning toward UNIX for future systems, especially in distributed environments. Perhaps surprisingly, the same managers seemed willing to use several different operating systems for different parts of a distributed system as they migrate away from mainframes and other proprietary systems. They seemed to be embracing a variety of platforms and accepting the need to provide middleware to link the various network components.[8]

Operating systems for personal computers or for client devices in client–server computing can also present significant differences in the user interface. Macintosh computers differentiated themselves based on the graphical user interface provided by their operating system. A **graphical user interface (GUI)** uses icons to represent objects (such as programs and files), a mouse or other pointing device to select operations (such as printing or changing type font), and graphical imagery to represent and clarify relationships. Figure 1.10 compared the Windows 3.1 interface with an old MS-DOS interface. Instead of requiring the user to remember specific commands, the newer interface provides pull-down menus listing the commands. Rather than requiring the user to remember filenames, the newer interface shows the filenames and allows the user to choose a file or program by pointing with a mouse.

Use of operating systems with GUIs and interface standards within programs has had a measurable impact. A 1988 study commissioned by Apple found that it took an average of 8 hours to learn basic system operation for the GUI-oriented Macintosh versus 20 hours for a computer operating under MS-DOS without a graphical interface. The time to learn a new software application was 9 hours on the Macintosh versus 24 hours for MS-DOS. Whether or not the research was truly unbiased, effects on productivity such as these are a key reason standardized GUIs have become expected components of user interfaces.

REALITY CHECK   **Operating Systems**   Functions of operating systems include controlling the user interface, include controlling access to data, controlling jobs in progress, and allocating resources.

1. What operating systems have you used on a personal computer? What appeared to be the relationship between the operating system and the applications you ran, such as spreadsheets or word processors?

2. What aspects of the operating system could probably be improved? For example, was it extremely easy to learn, and did it do everything for you that you imagine an operating system could do?

Chapter Conclusion

SUMMARY

 What are the different types of software?

Application software processes data to structure and facilitate specific business processes. End-user software includes general-purpose tools (such as spreadsheet programs and word processors) designed for use by end users without programming assistance. System development software is used by programmers and analysts in the process of building and enhancing information systems. System software controls the internal operation of a computer system.

▶ *How is programming like a translation process?*

Programming is the process of creating instructions that a machine will execute later. Programming requires that a person organize and communicate ideas in a format that a machine can use. The use of programming languages automates part of the translation process. A programmer writes a program that expresses what the person wants. An assembler or compiler automatically translates that program into machine language instructions the machine can execute.

▶ *What aspects of programming do not depend on the programming language used?*

Regardless of the programming language used, programmers have to organize their ideas and test them. The most common technique for organizing ideas is successive decomposition, the process of breaking up a problem into smaller and smaller subproblems.

▶ *What are the four generations of programming languages?*

The generations are machine language, assembly language, higher-level language, and fourth generation language (4GL). Each succeeding generation is less procedural and permits programmers to program using concepts more related to the business situation.

▶ *What are some of the other important developments in programming?*

Other important developments include special-purpose languages for narrow types of problems, spreadsheets, CASE systems, and object-oriented programming. Special-purpose programming languages contain ideas about specific areas of business or types of analysis, such as financial calculations or queuing models. Spreadsheets are a special type of modeling language that permitted millions of people to write programs even though they are not professional programmers. CASE systems establish methods for storing and using the data generated during systems analysis, design, and development. Object-oriented programming systems treat the data and programs as if they are tightly intertwined and increase the reusability of programs.

 What are operating systems, and why should managers and users care about them?

Operating systems are complex programs that control the execution of other programs and the way computer system resources are used. The major functions of operating systems include allocating resources, controlling jobs in progress, controlling access to data, and interfacing with the user. Differences between operating systems are important to users because some provide graphical interfaces that make system use easier. Compatibility issues are also important because programs written to run under one operating system may not run under another.

INTERNATIONAL VIGNETTE

India: Motorola's Programming Group in Bangalore

Between 1985 and 1993, India's software exports soared from $24 million to $350 million. This growth is enabled by the ability to move information around the world instantaneously. It is driven by the fact that India has many highly educated English-speaking programmers and engineers who can live comfortably in India on salaries far lower than those of comparable professionals in the United States, Europe, and Japan. For example, a mid-level engineer working for Motorola in India makes about $800 per month. India's software boom is centered in the southern city of Bangalore, about 500 miles south of Bombay.

As this software boom began, many observers believed Indian programming groups were fine for doing simple programming but did not have the management skills needed to build complex systems. Motorola has come to a different conclusion. Its 2-year-old programming group in Bangalore has grown to 155 engineers, and it is programming parts of telecommunications systems ranging from cordless and cellular telephones to the Iridium system that will link 66 satellites. This team attained the highest rating in an evaluation using the Software Engineering Institute's software maturity model. No other Motorola facility in the world had attained that rating before.

> Source: Gargan, Edward A. "India Among the Leaders in Software for Computers." *New York Times,* Dec. 29, 1993, p. A1.

* Use the WCA framework to organize your understanding of this vignette and to identify important topics that are not mentioned.

* What issues (if any) make this case interesting from an international or intercultural viewpoint?

* What prevents all software development from moving to low-wage countries?

REAL-WORLD CASES

Microsoft Corporation: Building a New Operating System

David Cutler had led the development of the VMS operating system, which fueled growth in the 1970s by linking a diverse family of computers. After he resigned from Digital in 1988, Microsoft hired him to build a new operating system, eventually named Windows NT, that would run thousands of programs previously written for MS-DOS, provide powerful graphics, support multitasking, link many different types of microprocessors, and provide the types of security features corporations needed. The program eventually contained 4.3 million lines of code (the equivalent of 100,000 single-spaced pages) and cost $150 million to produce.

Cutler managed a group consisting of developers who wrote the code, testers who tried to make the code fail, and product managers who decided on features Windows NT should contain. The group was broken into three groups, each consisting of five to ten subgroups. Their work was tested separately and frequently combined to see whether the entire enterprise was proceeding consistently. Although this was a way to work efficiently toward the goal, Cutler conceded that no one person "can grasp the complexity of NT."

Because Windows NT would have little impact until applications were written that used it, in October 1991, the team published a preliminary set of code guidelines for writing programs that run on Intel microprocessors. Microsoft set a conference in July 1992 as the target date for supplying the complete design kit application developers needed. Because it would be embarrassing if the kit was full of bugs, the NT team went on what one member called a "death march." People worked Saturdays and Sundays and many began sleeping at work. Marriages were strained, and some people burned out and quit.

When a test version of Windows NT was released to some customers in October 1992, the reviews were mixed. Some familiar programs ran more slowly than they had before. Windows NT would require 12 to 16 megabytes of memory to run, rather than the 8 megabytes originally hoped for. The first general release had been delayed from late 1992 to the first half of 1993, but the enormous program still had thousands of bugs. The "show-stoppers" that could crash the system or destroy data received the most attention. Programmers had to decide whether or not to fix less serious bugs because any change might cause other problems. In the last week of April, the team fixed 1,132 bugs but found 713 new bugs serious enough to warrant fixing. By the end, some team members were looking forward to the next Windows NT release, but others were exhausted.

> Source: Zachary, G. Pascal. "Agony and Ecstasy of 200 Code Writers Beget Windows NT." *Wall Street Journal,* May 26, 1993, p. A1.

- Use the WCA framework to organize your understanding of this case and to identify important topics that are not mentioned.

- Why do you think this was such a huge project given that the original DOS operating system had been purchased by Microsoft for $50,000?

- Explain why you do or do not believe it is acceptable for Microsoft to release an operating system containing known bugs.

- Explain why you do or do not believe the personal costs described in this case were necessary.

Sante Fe Railroad: Using a 4GL for System Development

The Atchison, Topeka, and Santa Fe Railroad Company had 12,000 miles of track, 2,000 loco-motives, 52,000 freight cars, and 9,000 truck trailers. The railroad was being fined heavily because many trains were reaching their destinations without the federally mandated waybill paperwork identifying the shipments. Needing to develop a computerized information system quickly, and having no alternatives available from other railroads, it decided to build the system using the Mapper 4GL from Unisys. The firm decided to teach Mapper program-ming to railroad operations personnel (a freight scheduler and two clerical supervisors) rather than teach the details of railroad operations to programmers. The initial waybill pro-grams were completed in several months. Three linked systems completed within 18 months included the waybill system, a rail yard inventory system, and a trailer-on-flat-car system. These systems handled railroad operations involving 1.7 million transactions per day, and transmitted data to the corporate database for use in corporate reporting, accounting, and marketing.

Data processing systems were divided into two parts: the operational systems written in Mapper and the corporate database and reporting, which were kept in COBOL because of the previous programming investment. Although the two groups performed roughly equivalent work, only one-third as many people worked in the Unisys group. Mapper programmers were four to eight times as productive as COBOL programmers in new system development. Since the operational system was controlled by the operations staff rather than the IS staff, there were no complaints about the IS department.

> Source: Sprague, Ralph H., Jr., and Barbara C. McNurlin. *Information Systems Management in Practice,* 3d ed. Englewood Cliffs, N.J.: Prentice Hall, 1993.

- Use the WCA framework to organize your understanding of this case and to identify important topics that are not mentioned.

- Identify the advantages of using the Mapper 4GL.

- Explain the possible advantages and disadvantages of converting completely to Mapper given that 4GLs are usually used for the type of report generation still being handled using COBOL.

KEY TERMS

application software	syntax error	generations of programming	upper-CASE
end-user software	logic error	languages	lower-CASE
system development software	unit testing	machine language	screen generator
system software	system testing	assembly language	code generator
programming	procedural	higher-level language	object-oriented programming
computer program	nonprocedural	compiler	(OOP)
successive decomposition	modularity	source code	natural language
modules	reusability	object code	operating system
structured programming	machine independence	fourth-generation languages (4GL)	multitasking
testing	data independence	query language	network operating system
bug	computer-aided software	report generator	graphical user interface (GUI)
debugging	engineering (CASE)	modeling language	

REVIEW QUESTIONS

1. What are the four types of software, and which has the greatest potential for competitive impact?

2. Explain the significance of viewing programming as a business process.

3. In what sense is programming a translation process?

4. Why is successive decomposition important in programming?

5. Why is it necessary to test software?

6. Compare the two types of errors that can be found by debugging a program.

7. What is the difference between procedural and nonprocedural programming languages?

8. Define machine independence, and explain why it is important.

9. Why is it important to have tighter links between analysis and programming?

10. Explain the difference between machine language, assembly language, higher-level languages, and fourth-generation languages.

11. What prevents companies from abandoning COBOL in favor of 4GLs?

12. What are CASE systems?

13. Identify the basic ideas of object-oriented programming.

14. Why would it be especially difficult to program in natural language?

15. Which operating system functions affect personal computer users?

16. What are graphical user interfaces, and why are they important?

DISCUSSION QUESTIONS

1. Chapter 7 mentioned CHIPS, the Clearing House for Interbank Payments, which transfers more than $1 trillion among 120 participating banks. System developers faced a unique problem when a system upgrade was needed. They could test the programs in a simulated mode, and could do trial installations on Saturdays, but they could not test this entire, mission-critical system before putting it into operation because the banks did not have dual hardware and software. Fortunately nothing went wrong when they installed the changes on August 17, 1992, because there was no fallback.[9] Use ideas in this chapter to explain the practical and ethical issues raised by this example.

2. Studies by Microsoft show that the vast majority of spreadsheet users do little more than make lists of data and perform only simple calculations on those lists, such as adding them up. Accordingly, Excel 5.0 added new features related to managing lists of data. But the program has so many features that it barely runs acceptably on the 4 megabytes of RAM many computers had when it was introduced.[10] Explain whether you believe Microsoft is encouraging most users to keep up to date by buying software upgrades they don't really need. Explain whether doing this is different from encouraging a shopper to buy the latest fall fashions.

3. Give examples of programming you perform in everyday life. Is anything notably easy or hard about this programming? How might programming in these areas become more complex?

4. Why is it comparatively easy to get an answer to a question such as, "List all customers whose current account balance is greater than $1,000" but much more difficult to answer a question such as, "List all customers we need to call to 'remind' them to pay their bills."

5. Someone has proposed that the job of programmer will be obsolete in 20 years, when users will be able to converse with computers in natural language. Explain why you agree or disagree.

6. Read the following, answer the question, and then explain how your answer is related to the ideas in the chapter: Imagine that it is the year 2015. You have just come home after a hard day at work, and you are very hungry. As it does everyday, the home robot you purchased last year at a clearance sale says, "Good evening. I hope you have had a good day. Is there anything I can do for you?" On this particular evening, you would really like to have spaghetti and meatballs for dinner. How do you think you would communicate your request to the robot? How would the robot interpret and execute your request?

HANDS-ON EXERCISES

1. This exercise is related to the process of debugging and assumes a spreadsheet model is provided that may contain some errors.

   a. Examine the spreadsheet. Find and correct any bugs it may contain.

   b. Explain the process you used to search for the bugs.

APPLICATION SCENARIOS

Dalton Foods

Dalton Foods is a diversified food company selling cereals, canned and frozen vegetables, and frozen desserts. It has traditionally succeeded by using clever marketing techniques and having adequate products at highly competitive prices. Currently, its headquarters is in North Carolina, and there are 23 factories spread across the United States. The sales and marketing staff works out of corporate headquarters. The factories produce between 4 and 25 standard products, and it usually takes at least 6 months to develop and market a new product. Dalton ships products directly from the factories to distributors and large supermarket chains. Its packaged and frozen products have a shelf life of months, and its canned products can last for several years.

Ralph Dalton, CEO of Dalton Foods, knows little about computers and software. Recently, he attended a seminar that introduced ideas such as competitive advantage from information systems, providing better information for management, and using the latest technology. The technology discussed included 4GLs and the UNIX operating system. On returning from the seminar, Dalton called his IS director, Jim O'Malley. Dalton told O'Malley he was concerned that the company may be missing an opportunity to gain competitive advantage through the use of computers. He was especially keen about the possible use of 4GLs to reduce programming costs and the use of UNIX to permit all the company's systems to be machine independent. Computers at headquarters are currently used for all corporate-level accounting, sales, and financial information. Many of these systems were purchased from software vendors. These systems and many systems built by Dalton's programmers were mostly written in COBOL. Each plant has its own computer system for purchasing material and tracking inventory and shipments. These systems run on different brands and models of IBM and DEC computers. Most plants also have specialized process control computers linked to some food processing machines.

O'Malley felt that Dalton had come back with the erroneous belief that 4GLs and UNIX were a panacea for all the world's problems. O'Malley's staff was already looking into using a 4GL query language to make management reporting more effective. As far as O'Malley was concerned, 4GLs and UNIX were good tools for solving certain problems, but he wasn't sure those problems were of competitive significance to Dalton Foods.

1. Is there any reason to believe that switching to 4GLs and UNIX would bring competitive advantage to Dalton Foods?
2. What work would be required to switch all computer systems to 4GLs and UNIX?
3. What should O'Malley say to Dalton?

DEBATE TOPIC   *Use ideas from the chapter to argue the pros and cons and practical implications of the following proposition: It doesn't really make sense for a CEO such as Dalton to get involved in decisions about software tools such as UNIX and 4GLs.*

Palmer Publishing

Palmer Publishing publishes five regional newspapers and two magazines and has recently purchased three radio stations. It has recently completed its planning guidelines for the next five years. In general, it plans to expand 20 percent a year while increasing its staff only 10 percent by being more efficient and using information systems more heavily to offload work from people. However, the planning guidelines ask Gail Hawkins, IS director, to plan for a 50 percent reduction in staff over that period.

The rationale for this reduction is as follows: Programming is getting less and less procedural. In some areas, such as queries from a database, it has become nonprocedural. It is now possible to buy application programs from software vendors. For example, the company's payroll system was purchased from a vendor. This vendor kept up with all the changes in the tax laws and produced a better payroll system than the company could have produced because it has real experts in payroll systems building the system. Furthermore, software is moving toward being machine independent. This means that the previous effort in moving software from one machine to another will gradually fade away. In addition, the company plans to rely more on 4GLs so that nonprogrammers can do their own queries into databases to get the information they need. Maybe at some point people will be able to just describe what they want the computer to do and have the computer do it.

The programmers in the company have learned of a rumor that programming will be reduced drastically in the near future. They have come to Ms. Hawkins and want to know what is going on. They want to know whether she thinks the number of programmers should be reduced. They also want to know how she intends to protect their jobs.

1. Looking at improvements across the generations of programming languages, is it reasonable to believe that the need for programmers might decrease? Can you think of any factors that might increase the need for programmers despite the improvements in programming languages?

2. Think about the programming process and related ideas such as structured programming and testing. Will the company's need for programmers simply go away?

3. How should Ms. Hawkins handle the situation?

DEBATE TOPIC   *Use ideas from the chapter to argue the pros and cons and practical implications of the following proposition: Except when systems have very stringent online performance requirements, most future application programming will be more like revising an existing 90 percent solution provided by a software vendor.*

▓ Cumulative Case: Custom T-Shirts, Inc.

ee's technical review of Custom T-Shirt's existing systems showed that these systems were inadequate for future growth. In addition to problems with information system architecture and telecommunications, the software was inadequate. The company was relying on an application package designed for PCs used in a single-site retail business. That package contained some annoying bugs, and Custom T-Shirts had only object code and user documentation. The software vendor had the source code but was having financial problems and seemed unable or unwilling to fix the bugs and upgrade the system to fit a multisite retailer.

Lee was thinking about criteria for deciding whether to buy another package or building a system from scratch. Lee didn't care a great deal about the programming language per se but was much more concerned with the programming tools that would be used for system development, whether the work happened in-house or was done by a vendor. Regardless of whether it would be purchased or programmed by Lee's staff, the new system would have to be based on a DBMS. It would also have to operate in a networked environment. Any in-house development would use a CASE system. The operating system would have to support a graphical user interface for end users. Lee wanted to use object-oriented concepts for some of the analysis of the new system but wasn't sure whether object-oriented programming tools were far enough along and complete enough to serve as the basis for the entire programming effort.

1. Why is it a problem that Custom T-Shirts does not have the source code for their existing system?
2. What kinds of capabilities do you think Lee wants from the DBMS and CASE systems?
3. What are some of the reasons the new system might or might not be programmed in COBOL?

▓ *REFERENCES*

1. Sprague, Ralph H., and Barbara C. McNurlin. *Information Systems Management in Practice,* 3d ed. Englewood Cliffs, N.J.: Prentice Hall, 1993.

2. Andersen, Espen, and Benn Konsynski. "Brooklyn Union Gas: OOPS on Big Iron." Boston: Harvard Business School Case 9-192-144, 1992.

3. Pollack, Andrew. "2 New Efforts to Simplify Using a VCR." *New York Times,* Sept. 13, 1990.

4. Gilman, Hank, and William M. Bulkeley. "Can Software Firms Be Held Responsible when a Program Makes a Costly Error?" *Wall Street Journal,* Aug. 4, 1986, p. 17.

5. Shapiro, Ehud, and David D. H. Warren. "The Fifth Generation Project: Personal Perspectives." *Communications of the ACM,* Mar. 1993, pp. 46–101.

6. Zachary, G. Pascal. "Agony and Ecstasy of 200 Code Writers Beget Windows NT." *Wall Street Journal,* May 26, 1993, p. A1.

7. Semich J. William. "You Mean NT Can't Really Run Windows?" *Datamation,* May 15, 1994, pp. 67–68.

8. Moad, Jeff. "One True Operating System Out, Diversity In." *Datamation,* May 15, 1994, pp. 44–48.

9 Ross, Philip E. "The Day the Software Crashed." *Forbes,* Apr. 25, 1994, pp. 142–156.

10. Mossberg, Walter S. "Excel Spreadsheet Is New and Improved, But Hardly Perfect." *Wall Street Journal,* Feb. 3, 1994, p. B1.

Telecommunications and Networks

Study Questions

▶ *What aspects of the convergence of computing and communications are important for understanding telecommunications?*

▶ *What are the steps in the basic telecommunications model?*

▶ *What are the advantages and disadvantages of the different forms of wire and wireless transmission?*

▶ *What is ISDN, and why is it important?*

▶ *What are the main differences between LANs, WANs, and VANs?*

▶ *Why are telecommunications standards important?*

▶ *How is telecommunications policy related to issues faced by managers?*

Fedex (formerly Federal Express) grew to a multibillion dollar company by providing reliable overnight delivery of high-priority, time-sensitive packages and documents. Its 420 airplanes, 30,000 trucks, and 96,000 people deliver over 1.5 million packages a day. After the parcels are picked up at the customer's site or dropped off at a Fedex location, they are rushed to the local airport and flown to a Fedex hub where they are sorted by destination, loaded on planes, and shipped to the destination airport. Packages designated for overnight delivery are delivered within 24 hours.

To maintain a high degree of reliability in its shipping process, Fedex tracks each package through each step on its path from the shipper to the recipient. When the driver picks up the package, it is immediately logged using Supertracker, a portable, handheld computer containing a bar-code reader for capturing the bar-code identification on the package and a keyboard for entering additional information such as the destination's area code. On returning to the truck, the driver inserts the Supertracker into a small computer that transmits the data to the local dispatch center, which has a link to the COSMOS database. Within five minutes of initial pickup, the Fedex database contains the package's identification, location, destination, and route. The location data is updated automatically (using the package's bar code) as the package moves through each step on its way to the destination. The combination of telecommunications and computing permits Fedex to know the location of every package at any time. Perhaps more important, the tracking system makes sure that procedures are followed throughout. Any deviation would become obvious quickly.

The information in the system is used in many ways. Information about pickups and deliveries is the basis of customer billing. Detailed tracking information permits customer service agents to tell customers where their packages are at any time. Certain customers can even dial into COSMOS directly to obtain the status of a package. As a method for managing their own internal operations, Fedex developed a service quality index based on 12 types of events that disappoint customers, including late delivery, damaged or lost packages, and complaints. Even a delivery at 10:31 for a package promised for 10:30 is considered a problem. So that they will learn from past problems and mistakes, people throughout the company receive daily feedback reports identifying problems that occurred yesterday.[1]

Responding to the system Fedex built, other major package delivery and shipping companies have built or are building similar systems and are touting them to customers. A full page ad in the *Wall Street Journal* on May 18, 1993, explained how United Parcel Service (UPS) had just introduced a nationwide cellular tracking system called TotalTrack. It provides package status at all times and uses a pen-based computer to confirm delivery using the recipient's signature.

DEBATE TOPIC   *Argue the pros and cons and practical implications of the following proposition:*
Since Fedex and UPS both perform detailed tracking of packages, these information systems have become a competitive necessity in the industry and will therefore have little competitive significance in the future.

A T ONE LEVEL, THIS CASE IS ABOUT delivering packages. But at another it is about an international information system supported by a telecommunications network. The basic idea of this system is that it should "know" where each package is at all times. This requires a highly distributed but very tightly controlled system.

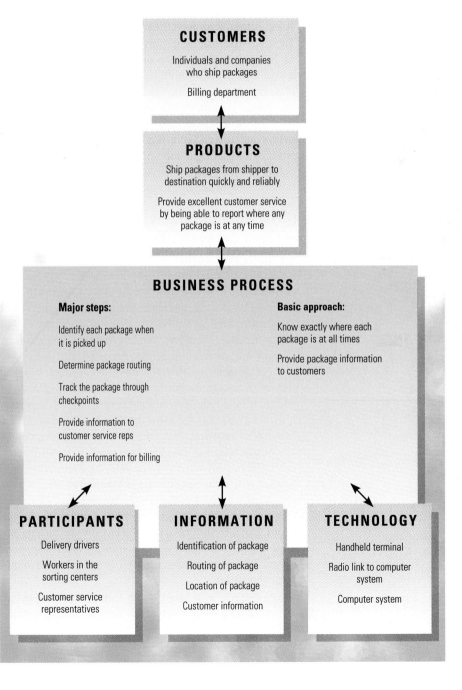

Figure 11.1 Federal Express: Tracking Customers' Packages

CUSTOMERS

Individuals and companies who ship packages

Billing department

PRODUCTS

Ship packages from shipper to destination quickly and reliably

Provide excellent customer service by being able to report where any package is at any time

BUSINESS PROCESS

Major steps:

Identify each package when it is picked up

Determine package routing

Track the package through checkpoints

Provide information to customer service reps

Provide information for billing

Basic approach:

Know exactly where each package is at all times

Provide package information to customers

PARTICIPANTS

Delivery drivers

Workers in the sorting centers

Customer service representatives

INFORMATION

Identification of package

Routing of package

Location of package

Customer information

TECHNOLOGY

Handheld terminal

Radio link to computer system

Computer system

The previous two chapters discussed computer systems, computer peripherals, and software. They mentioned distributed processing but said little about the role of telecommunications in distributed processing. In this chapter, we will look at a variety of the ways telecommunications is used and at some of the technical details business professionals need to be aware of simply to read a current business magazine such as *Business Week* or *Forbes*.

Applying Telecommunications in Business

Telecommunications is the transmission of data between devices in different locations. Typical initial experiences with telecommunications are watching television, listening to the radio, and using the telephone. In these cases, the data transmitted are sounds and images. Telecommunications applications in business include transmission of data of every type. The term **data communications** often refers to telecommunications involving files of computerized data, but not voice.

In essence, the purpose of telecommunications is to reduce or eliminate time delays and other effects of geographical separation. Telecommunications reduces the effect of geographical separation when people talk on a telephone and eliminates time delays when a customer links into a supplier's computer to order products. It provides both benefits when a system consolidates results from a company's branch offices.

Vital Role of Telecommunications

Only 20 years ago, business professionals often saw telecommunications as making telephone calls and paid little attention to it. Today, telecommunications is a requirement for business effectiveness and success. In many businesses, national or international networks are a competitive necessity for tracking inventories, taking customer orders, verifying product availability, and granting credit. Telecommunications systems have improved the effectiveness of sales and customer service work by creating immediate access to data. Moreover, telecommunications systems have changed the nature of internal communication within geographically dispersed organizations.

Telecommunications can also be a strategic business issue even if the organization resides in a single building. Consider the importance of the voice and data networks within a hospital. This infrastructure makes it possible to communicate doctors' orders, lab results, and other vital information needed to coordinate patient care. Yet hospital administrators traditionally focus on a myriad of other issues and often plan inadequately for the infrastructure needed to improve services for patients and doctors.

Telecommunications can address many different issues in a business. In some cases, the issue is operational efficiency; in others, telecommunications innovations lead to increased business effectiveness and competitive advantage. Although this chapter and many others mention competitively significant telecommunications applications, the effective use of telecommunications does not guarantee a competitive advantage. In fact, many telecommunications applications such as electronic data interchange (discussed in Chapter 6) are more like requirements for doing business in some industries.

One way to visualize the importance of telecommunications in business is to look at the value chain and identify common telecommunications applications that have competitive significance. Table 11.1 lists applications in both primary and background activities along the value chain. Telecommunications reduces delays and eliminates unnecessary work in all these applications.

Table 11.1 Examples of Telecommunications Applications

Value Chain Activity	Typical Telecommunications Applications
Product development	• Share data with other departments and with customers to make sure the product meets market needs and is manufacturable. • Work together with others who have simultaneous access to the same computerized data and drawings.
Production	• Transmit orders to suppliers' computer systems for immediate action. • Receive orders from customers for immediate action. • Transmit customer specifications to automated machines in the factory. • Collect quality data across the manufacturing process to analyze quality.
Sales	• Provide prices and production data to customers. • Obtain data from headquarters while traveling or visiting customers. • Transmit orders to the factory. • Permit customers to enter orders directly. • Transmit credit card purchase data for quick credit approval.
Delivery	• Receive delivery orders. • Track merchandise in the delivery process. • Confirm receipt of orders.
Customer service	• Receive requests for service from customers. • Transmit data to customers to help them use the product or fix problems. • Dispatch repair crews.
Management	• Receive consolidated data from across the organization. • Maintain personal communication with people throughout the organization.
Finance	• Transfer funds to suppliers. • Receive funds from customers. • Complete transactions related to financing of the organization.

Convergence of Computing and Communications

Before discussing different types of networks and telecommunications technologies, it is useful to look more deeply at the convergence of computing and communications, a widely discussed trend introduced in Chapter 1. We will discuss four aspects of this trend.

1. *Reliance of telecommunications on computers.* The earliest telephone systems included human operators who established telephone connections by plugging wires into a switchboard. Later, this work was automated using electromechanical switches that changed position to establish a circuit. Today, the long-distance connections are made electronically by computers even though some of the local connections are still made using electromechanical gear. Computers also monitor the traffic on the network and balance the loads on different parts of the network by determining which path across the network each telephone call will take. AT&T's widely publicized system failure on January 15, 1990 (mentioned in Chapter 3), was caused by a bug in a computer program that controlled part of the network.

2. *Role of telecommunications in computing.* Traditionally, people thought of computing as occurring in a specific piece of equipment called a computer. More recently, the convergence of computing and communications has made

distributed processing more practical, with the data virtually anywhere and the computing occurring anywhere. In the Fedex example, handheld computers performed some of the processing but then hooked into a computer in the truck, which transmitted data to a central database where other processing occurred. In this type of distributed system, users often do not care about the location of the computing and data as long as they can do their work conveniently. The organization cares, however, because the location of computing and data affects costs, security, control of the data, and many other important issues.

With the trend toward distributed processing, there is often some overlap between what people think of as computing and what they think of as telecommunications. Figure 11.2 illustrates that the overlap occurs as computing becomes distributed.

Figure 11.2 The Unclear Boundary Between Computing and Telecommunications

This figure shows that there is no precise boundary between computing and telecommunications.

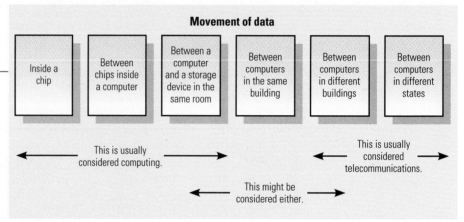

3. *Role reversal for wire and wireless transmission.* Figure 11.3 shows what might seem a surprising reversal of roles. In metropolitan areas, wireless transmission of radio and television broadcasts is being superseded by cable broadcasting, which can provide more choices and higher-quality reception. Conversely, the first telephone networks transmitted conversations only through copper wire. The inconvenience of linking all calls through wire has led to the emergence of portable telephones and data transmission through satellites.

4. *New combinations of computing and telecommunications.* Figure 1.8 showed some of the innovations that have emerged by combining certain elements of telephone, telegraph, broadcasting, and data processing. For example, electronic mail incorporates the message sending function of a telegraph but uses a computer to generate and receive the message. Voice mail uses a computer to control recording and retrieval of the voice message that might have been missed. Videoconferencing expands what would have been a telephone conversation by adding the idea of video from television broadcasting. Many new combinations of data and computing can be expected in the future.

Figure 11.3 Trend Toward Reversing Roles of Wire and Wireless Transmission

Wireless transmission of broadcasts is being superseded by transmission through cable. Correspondingly, telephone conversations are increasingly transmitted using wireless methods. (The diagram is meant to show the direction of change rather than absolute amounts.)

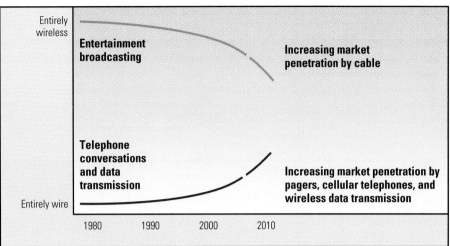

Making Sense of the Terminology and Details

Like computer systems, telecommunications systems present us with a large number of technical terms and choices. Although many business professionals may think they don't care about such things, these technical choices do determine what types of telecommunications applications are possible and at what cost. Business professionals with no understanding of the types of networks or technical options have difficulty contributing to discussions of how a telecommunications infrastructure can be used effectively and economically to support an organization's mission.

Recall how Table III.2 in the Introduction to Part III identified a series of technology performance variables under four general headings.

All the issues identified in Table III.2 apply to telecommunications just as they apply to computers, peripherals, and software. Table 11.2 shows examples of telecommunications choices related to these performance variables.

Many telecommunications decisions are difficult because these goals pull in opposite directions. For example, increasing a network's compatibility with external standards may increase its maintainability but decrease its functional capabilities by making it slower. Increasing a network's ease of use by simplifying aspects of its operation may make it incompatible with standards and may have positive or negative effects on its functional capabilities. As we introduce the technical aspects of telecommunications networks, remember that the purpose of each option is to improve some combination of functional capabilities, ease of use, compatibility, and maintainability.

REALITY CHECK **Convergence of Computing and Communications** Four aspects of this convergence include the reliance of telecommunications on computers, the role of telecommunications in computing, the changing roles of wire and wireless transmission, and new ways of combining computing and telecommunications.

1. Think about ways you have used computers and telecommunications in your everyday life. What aspects of this convergence have you felt personally?

2. Some people think that televisions will be more like computers in the future. What could this mean, and how is it related to the convergence of computing and telecommunications?

Table 11.2 Performance Variables and Related Telecommunications Choices Discussed in this Chapter

Performance Variables	Examples of Telecommunications Choices Related to Each Performance Variable
Functional Capabilities and Limitations	
Capacity	• Each transmission medium has a capacity range in terms of data transmission speeds and distances covered. • Multiplexers increase effective capacity by combining multiple transmissions and separating them when received.
Speed	• The promise of the information superhighway is limited by practical constraints on data transfer rates. • Transmitting voice communications through a satellite introduces a noticeable delay in response.
Price-performance	• Fiber optic cable has far more data-carrying capacity than twisted-pair or coaxial cable but is more expensive. • Cellular phones are more convenient than fixed-location phones but are also much more expensive.
Reliability	• Network failures sometimes call for alternative routes and other forms of backup. • Data degrades as it moves through a physical medium, motivating the use of digital transmission and calling for use of repeaters to boost the signal. • Data networks use encryption to prevent unauthorized access.
Operating conditions	• Clouds, rain, and buildings interfere with some wireless transmissions. • Weight and portability of cellular phones affect their use. • Telephone switches require uninterrupted electric supply.
Ease of Use	
Quality of user interface	• Digital transmission provides clearer transmission than analog transmission.
Portability	• Portable phones are convenient for many purposes.
Compatibility	
Conformance to standards	• Telecommunications operates based on many de facto and de jure standards.
Interoperability	• Multiple inconsistent standards exist in computer networking, such as OSI, SNA, and TCP/IP.
Maintainability	
Modularity	• Data networks are modularized so that messages can follow the least busy routing available at any time.
Scalability	• PBXs can handle particular numbers of lines and then need to be upgraded.
Flexibility	• There is often a need to upgrade or downsize networks.

Functions and Components of Telecommunications Networks

A **telecommunications network** is a set of devices linked to perform telecommunications. Each device in a network is called a **node.** The nodes of a network can include many types of devices, such as telephones, terminals, secondary storage devices, and computers. The nodes can be a few feet apart or thousands of miles apart. The data transmitted from one node to another are often divided into small chunks called *messages*. The overall amount of data transmission on a network is often called the *traffic* on the network.

Connectivity, the critical issue addressed by telecommunications, is the ability to transmit data between devices at different locations. Although connectivity refers to machine linkages, it allows people in different parts of an organization to communicate with each other and share and coordinate their work. Connectivity therefore supports business processes but has a technical side that managers must appreciate.

Basic Telecommunications Model

Figure 11.4 shows the basic functions of a telecommunications network along with the network components that perform those functions. This model is based on familiar telephone networks. We start by looking at each step briefly.

Figure 11.4 Functions and Components of a Telecommunications Network

Network components can be understood in terms of the various functions a network performs. Some functions can be performed several times by different equipment in different places during the same transmission.

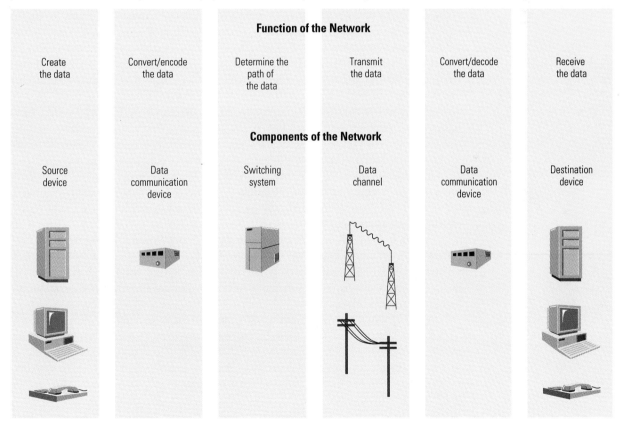

Function of the Network

| Create the data | Convert/encode the data | Determine the path of the data | Transmit the data | Convert/decode the data | Receive the data |

Components of the Network

| Source device | Data communication device | Switching system | Data channel | Data communication device | Destination device |

The first step in telecommunications is generating the data to be moved to another device. A telephone caller generates data by speaking. An ATM user generates data by keying it into the ATM terminal. A salesperson may generate data by using a push button telephone as a terminal. A computer may generate data for an overnight transfer of transactions to headquarters by copying the day's computerized transaction log.

The data must be converted from the original form into a form for transmission. This process is called **encoding.** In a telephone conversation, the telephone mouthpiece encodes sounds into electrical impulses. In transmitting a picture by fax, the original image is encoded when it is digitized by a scanner. In a system for transferring funds electronically from one bank to another, the encoding uses a secret key to make the signal meaningless to anyone intercepting it for unauthorized use.

Next comes the process of directing a signal from its source to its destination. This process is often called **switching,** and is comparable to the process of switching a train from one railroad track to another. Telephone systems require switching decisions because the data may follow alternative paths from its source to its destination. Switching is automatic in most current telephone systems. A computer assigns each outgoing telephone call to one of the firm's outgoing lines. An instant later, a computer or mechanical device in a telephone company switching station chooses among alternative physical paths to establish the circuit between the parties on the call.

A path along which data are transmitted is called a **channel.** Both wire and wireless channels are used frequently. Telephone systems once used only copper wire channels. Fiber-optic cable made of ultrapure glass is now an alternative for systems with high data volume. Air or space is the channel for wireless transmission, which eliminates some of the restrictions of wires. Telephone systems use wireless channels for many types of transmissions. Transmission to a cordless telephone in a house covers a few feet of air, whereas transmissions through a communications satellite use a channel covering 22,300 miles of space in each direction. Many applications use several different channels. For example, a single telephone call may be transmitted through several wire and wireless channels.

On arrival at the destination, the data must be converted from the coded form back to the original. This conversion is called **decoding.** In a telephone conversation, the telephone hand set decodes the data back into audible sounds. In electronic funds transfer, complex computerized procedures do the decoding using a secret key.

Finally, the decoded data are received and restored to the original form. This form may be a reproduction of the original sounds for a telephone conversation, a reproduction of the original document for fax transmission, or identical data for transmission of computer data.

To apply the telecommunications model to a specific situation, consider a telephone call from a person in a car on a freeway in Los Angeles to a person in an office in Paris. Figure 11.5 shows the steps of creating, encoding, switching, transmitting, decoding, and receiving data. Notice how several switching and transmission steps are included in this process.

Figure 11.5 shows the functions directly involved in moving data but leaves out a crucial background function. **Network management** is the process of monitoring the network's operations and reallocating work among different parts of the network so that it can handle its workload. Every large network requires major efforts in network management. Figure 11.6 shows the network management center used by AT&T for its long-distance lines.

The steps in the telecommunications model rely on technology for generating signals at precise frequencies and moving and receiving those signals with minimal data loss. Although users and managers needn't be involved in complicated technical details, they do need to recognize common telecommunications choices related to the basic functions. Next, we will cover each of the functions and components in more detail, focusing on the types of things users and managers should know.

Figure 11.5 Los Angeles to Paris by Telephone

This diagram shows one of many possible routings for a telephone call between Los Angeles and Paris.

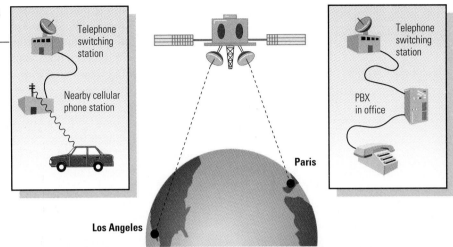

Figure 11.6 AT&T's Long-Distance Control Center

AT&T uses this control center to monitor the use of its long-distance network and to balance utilization of network resources.

Generating and Receiving Data

Telecommunications systems can use many types of telephones, terminals, secondary storage devices, computers, and other devices for generating and receiving data. In some systems, the data are generated by a handheld terminal and transmitted to a computer elsewhere. In a paging system, the data are generated by a person using a pager and received by a person using a beeper. In a large building's automatic air conditioning system, a computer receives readings from sensors and then generates commands that are sent to the cooling equipment.

The variety of terminals in computer systems that use telecommunications is expanding continually. The progression from dumb terminals to intelligent terminals was explained along with distributed computing in Chapter 9. Whether or not some of the processing is done at the terminal, the data are transmitted to a computer called the host computer. The **host computer** controls the database, checks the inputs for validity, and either accepts the transaction or sends error messages back to the terminal. A touch-tone telephone used to enter data plays the role of a dumb terminal.

Many types of special-purpose terminals are used in telecommunications applications. The special-purpose terminals for ATMs and credit card purchases permit numerical inputs and also contain a slot through which the credit card is passed for identification. Handheld terminals play a key role in applications where stationary terminals are too awkward. For example, car rental company employees use them while inspecting returned cars to enter the mileage and gasoline level. The terminals may transmit the data to the office for generating an invoice or may print a receipt using a tiny printer.

An entire computer is sometimes used as communication gear for originating and receiving network messages. A **front-end processor** is a computer that handles network communication for another computer such as a mainframe that processes the data. The division of labor between the two computers improves the efficiency of the overall system. The front-end processor is set up to send and receive network communications efficiently, whereas the mainframe is set up to update the transaction database efficiently.

Encoding and Decoding Data

Data transmission requires that data be encoded as electrical or optical signals, transmitted, and later decoded. The basic choices in encoding and decoding data are related to two factors:

1. Whether the original data are naturally analog or digital. Sounds, images, and video are naturally analog because they are continuous and depend on their shape for their meaning. Numbers, text, and other characters used in written language are naturally digital because they are discontinuous, separable codes with a specific meaning.

2. Whether the data are transmitted in analog or digital form. Transmitting data using **analog signals** means that the signal varies continuously in a wave pattern mimicking the shape of the original data. Transmitting data using **digital signals** means that the signal is represented as a series of 0's and 1's.

Analog data, analog signal. Figure 11.7 summarizes the physical method for analog encoding and decoding. The starting point is a **carrier signal** recognized by both the sending and receiving equipment. As shown in the figure, the carrier signal literally carries the encoded data and is itself a wave that swings back and forth in steady cycles. A typical telephone handset encodes sounds using the type of process shown in Figure 11.7. The handset at the receiving end decodes the signal by subtracting out the carrier signal.

Digital data, analog signal. To transmit computer-generated digital data over a standard analog telephone line, a **modem** (*Mo*dulator/*Dem*odulator) is used at each end of the transmission. The sending modem superimposes the pattern of 0's or 1's on the carrier signal. The receiving modem subtracts out the carrier signal to reconstruct the original pattern of 0's and 1's. Different modems send signals at different speeds, which are measured in bits per second (bps) or baud. (Box 9.1 explained that the term *baud* is sometimes used instead of bits per second because some devices can transmit individual signals with gradations finer than just 0 versus 1.) Early modems operated as slowly as 300 bps although modems for PCs commonly operated at 9600 or 14400 bps by 1994. At that time, online services such as America Online that still used modems operating at 2400 bps felt competitive pressure because other online services transmitted data to users at 9600 bps. By moving data at faster speeds, higher-speed modems permit more efficient use of terminals, telephone lines, and user time.

Digital data, digital signal. With digital signals, the data are not superimposed on a carrier wave. Instead they are just sent down the channel as a series of electrical or optical on–off pulses. In digital transmission, modems are replaced by other electronic devices that transmit the data in a precise pattern and recognize the data at the other end.

Analog data, digital signal. Using a digital signal to transmit analog data such as an image or sound requires that the data be digitized. As we discussed in Chapter 9, the digitized image or sound is only an approximation of the original. The quality of the image or sound received depends on the precision of the digitizing process.

Figure 11.7
Superimposing a Signal on a Carrier Wave

To encode sounds for transmission, their wave pattern is added to a carrier signal. The receiving end decodes the message by subtracting out the carrier signal.

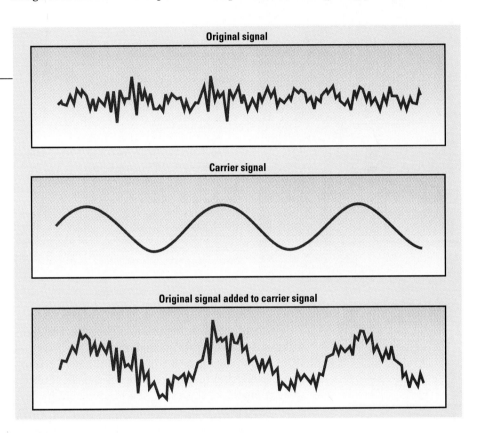

Original signal

Carrier signal

Original signal added to carrier signal

Significance of analog versus digital transmission

Table 11.3 shows that the four possibilities are not just a technical detail. The choice of type of data and type of transmission signal affects the quality of the data received, the cost of the transmission system, and the receiver's ability to manipulate the data as part of the decoding process.

The differences between analog and digital representations of data affect the quality of the transmission. The quality of analog data depends on preserving the precise shape of the wave form as it moves through a wire or through space. If the signal degrades gradually during transmission, there is no way to regenerate it. It is possible to boost the signal using a device called a repeater, but it is not possible to correct any distortions in its shape. With digital data, reconstructing the signal using a device called a regenerator requires only the ability to differentiate between the 0's and the 1's and make them sharper. Digital coding also provides many ways to use special bits for error checking and correction.

Table 11.3 Transmitting Analog or Digital Data Encoded in Analog or Digital Form

Type of Encoding / Original Type of Data	Transmission Using an Analog Signal	Transmission Using a Digital Signal
Original data in analog form, such as sounds, images, and video	**Method:** Superimpose the "shape" of the data on a carrier signal; receive the signal and subtract out the carrier wave to reconstruct the original signal **Examples:** Transmit voice using traditional telephone lines or radio broadcasting; use a fax to digitize a picture and then transmit it over a typical analog telephone line; transmit video in traditional television broadcasting **Advantages:** Basic idea of the early telecommunications applications **Shortcomings:** Signal degrades as it moves through the channel; can boost its power, but cannot restore its shape	**Method:** Digitize the sounds or images to approximate them using a stream of 0's and 1's; receive the stream of 0's and 1's and reconstruct the approximation **Examples:** Transmit voice using a digital telephone line, transmit voice via satellite, transmit television using cable **Advantages:** Can manipulate the data more effectively and can have mixed forms of data as new transmission services emerge **Shortcomings:** Greater processing requirements at the nodes and greater data transmission capacity required of the network
Original data in digital form, such as numbers and text	**Method:** Superimpose a stream of 0's and 1's on a carrier signal; receive the signal and subtract out the carrier wave to reconstruct the original signal **Examples:** Use a modem to transmit data from one computer to another using an analog telephone line **Advantages:** Permits using typical telephone lines to transmit computerized data **Shortcomings:** Not as efficient as simply sending the 0's and 1's down the channel	**Method:** Transmit a stream of 0's and 1's by sending them through the channel as a series of pulses **Examples:** Transmit computerized data in a local area network **Advantages:** Low error rate **Shortcomings:** Cannot use existing analog telephone lines for these applications

One of the most important differences between analog and digital data is that digital data can be manipulated readily. This issue underlies the struggle in the early 1990s about standards for **high definition television (HDTV),** a new standard for broadcasting and receiving television signals. If the standard were totally analog, as some competitors suggested, the result would be clearer pictures than the previous standard allowed. If the standard were digital, the result would be both clearer pictures and greater ability to manipulate the data. It would be possible to give the user new types of choices that would make television more of a controllable, interactive medium. For example, at some point, it might be possible to let the viewer of a televised baseball game decide what seat to see it from.[2] This type of thing would be possible because the data transmitted for the game would include the game itself and metadata telling the television set how to interpret the various components of the signal.

Directing Data from Source to Destination

After the signal is encoded, it must move from the source to the destination. For special applications involving high data volumes, a firm may find it cost-effective to lease a **dedicated line,** a telephone line used exclusively by that firm for transmitting voice or computerized data between two locations.

In contrast, public telephone networks are used for typical telephone communication and for lower volume computerized data. These networks often have alternative paths from a source to a destination and contain switching systems that decide what path each message will take. Figure 11.5 showed the switching steps that might occur to connect a telephone call from a car in Los Angeles to an office in Paris. Ideally, it should seem to the caller that there are only two steps: dialing the call and speaking to the person in Paris a few seconds later. The switching process therefore should be transparent to the user even though there might be a number of data transmission steps with separate switching decisions between them.

A **switch** is a special-purpose computer that directs incoming messages along a path and therefore performs switching in a network. Some types of switches control transmission across national telephone networks, whereas others control the distribution of telephone calls within a building. The first type of switch routes long-distance telephone calls through long-distance lines that cross the country. When a particular line gets very busy or is out of operation, these switches automatically assign telephone calls to other lines. Likewise, local telephone switching stations use switches to create the temporary circuits for telephone calls. These switches are still electromechanical rather than computerized in many local stations. A different type of switch called a private branch exchange (PBX) distributes calls within a customer site. Functions of PBXs are covered later in the discussion of telephone networks.

Different switching methods are used in different situations. The **circuit switching** used for telephone calls sets up a temporary circuit between the source and destination; when the telephone call is terminated, the temporary circuit is also terminated. Without circuit switching, it would be necessary to maintain permanent circuits linking all pairs of telephones. Switching for a local telephone call usually occurs in a local telephone switching facility. Switching for a long-distance call can involve several steps depending on how many different physical links are established in the temporary circuit.

Although a switching process has always been required for any telephone call, switching technology has become much faster and more highly automated over the years (see Figure 1.4). In the first telephone systems, all telephone calls required a manual switching step at a local telephone office. At that time, some forecasters estimated that the maximum number of possible telephone calls would be limited by the number of telephone operators who could be hired. Today, central telephone offices in the United States use digital switching equipment.

Packet switching is typically used when data are transmitted infrequently from a large number of nodes. In this process, a temporary circuit is not established. Instead, the message is divided into a series of segments or packets, each of which contains addressing and control instructions in addition to several hundred bytes of data in the message. These routing instructions are executed automatically as the message moves through the network. The message is reassembled when all the packets reach the destination.

Packet switching has the advantage of allowing multiple users to share the same transmission facilities because packets from different users can be interspersed on the same line. This is consistent with what can also be done for nonpacketized analog or digital data by **multiplexers,** devices that collect low-speed signals from multiple terminals and interweave these signals so that they can be transmitted more economically on a single high-speed channel. A mirror image of the interweaving process is used to separate the messages during decoding.

The basic idea of packet switching also brings disadvantages. Breaking the data into packets means that it may not be possible to reassemble them immediately at the destination. As a result, packet switching is fine for computerized data but is not currently suitable for telephone conversations because the words might arrive in garbled order. For time-sensitive applications such as telephone conversations, circuit switching is necessary.

Moving the Data through Transmission Media

The two methods for moving data from a source to a destination are wire and wireless transmission. In wire transmission, a signal moves through a "wire" such as a telephone wire, coaxial cable, or fiber-optic cable; in contrast, wireless transmission moves the signal through air or space. Different types of wireless transmission use different wave frequencies and require different types of receivers. Common categories of wireless transmission include radio and television broadcasting, microwave, radar, and satellite transmissions.

Wire and wireless transmission are currently exchanging places in many applications. Television is moving from wireless to wire transmission. In addition to the fact that it can provide more channels, cable television is becoming more popular in some areas because it can deliver a stronger and more reliable signal than broadcast television. In contrast, telephones started with wire transmission and are becoming wireless. Wireless telephones are popular because they can perform the functions of fixed telephones without the inconvenience of being anchored to one location.

Although data transmission involves many technical issues, business professionals should recognize several important characteristics of data transmission systems. For analog transmission, **bandwidth** was originally defined as the difference between the highest and lowest frequency that can be transmitted. This term is still used in relation to digital transmission, but it is usually thought of as the capacity of the channel stated in megabits or gigabits per second. In practice, systems with higher bandwidths can transmit more data. For example, voice transmission requires a bandwidth of around 4 KHz, whereas television requires a bandwidth of around 6 MHz, over 1,000 times as great. This is why television cannot be transmitted on a voice-grade telephone line. Cable television is practical because fiber-optic cable has enough bandwidth to transmit television signals for many different channels at the same time. To demonstrate the range of capacities and requirements in current telecommunications, Table 11.4 lists data rates related to topics discussed later in this chapter.

Table 11.4 Data Rates Related to Different Telecommunications Topics

Data Rate	Telecommunications Channel or Device
9.6 to 28.8 Kbps	Data transfer through a typical modem for a PC
19.2 Kbps	Data transfer to wireless terminals via ARDIS, a wireless data service using packet switching
64 Kbps	Uncompressed, digitized voice[3]
112 Kbps	Basic rate ISDN for twisted-pair wire using 2 data channels
1.5 Mbps	Primary rate ISDN for twisted-pair wire using 23 data channels
10 Mbps	Ethernet standard for a local area network using coaxial cable
100 Mbps	FDDI (Fiber Distributed Data Interface) standard for local area networks using fiber-optic cable
12 to 274 Mbps	Microwave transmission at frequencies between 2 and 18 GHz[4]
2 Gbps	Maximum data rate for a single strand of fiber-optic cable[5]

Bandwidth limitations are a major obstacle reducing the practicality of what has been called the **information superhighway,** the idea that everyone in the United States should have virtually unlimited access to information in electronic form. Consider this example to visualize the problem: Assume you have a modem that operates at 9600 bits per second and want to download a 600-page novel. Assuming the novel contained no pictures but had 300 words per page and an average of 6 characters per word (including spaces), the transmission time would be calculated as follows:

$$\text{Number of bits} = 600 \text{ pages} \times 300 \tfrac{\text{words}}{\text{per page}} \times 6 \tfrac{\text{characters}}{\text{per word}} \times 8 \tfrac{\text{bits}}{\text{per character}}$$

$$= 8{,}640{,}000 \text{ bits}$$

$$\text{Transmission time} = 8{,}640{,}000 \text{ bits} \div 9600 \tfrac{\text{bits per}}{\text{second}}$$

$$= 900 \text{ seconds}$$

$$= 15 \text{ minutes}$$

As Chapter 9 explained in the discussion of digitizing pictures, a single high-resolution picture might contain as many bits and therefore might take as much transmission time as the text of the entire novel. Since video involves 10 to 30 images per second, the amount of data required for video on demand is staggering. For example, a single copy of the movie *Jurassic Park* contains about 100 billion bytes of data. Even when compressed 25 to 1 by removing redundant background information that doesn't change from frame to frame, this is still 4 billion bytes.[6] Assuming you wanted to download the movie onto twenty 200MB hard disks, the data transmission time at 9600 bits per second would be 3.33 million seconds, or about 39 days. Although, no one intends to download movies using 9600 bit per second modems, the example shows that the promise of the information superhighway must be tempered by the capacity of current technology.

Data loss is another important characteristic of data transmission systems. **Data loss** occurs during transmission when the physical properties of the data channel or the presence of other signals weakens or distorts the signal. Causes of data loss include *noise* (due to movement of electrons in the transmission medium), *crosstalk* (interference between signals in the same medium), *echo* (reflections of signals), and *attenuation* (due to distance). Telecommunications channels may contain equipment called repeaters that amplify the signal before too much of it is lost. Since both wire and wireless systems may transmit many different signals at the same time, preventing mutual interference between signals is essential. For example, interference between signals is an important reason a geographical area can have only a limited number of television and radio stations. Using too many frequencies within the limited range of frequencies set aside for radio and television broadcasting would cause distortion.

We next explain the ways in which these characteristics and others affect the current choices in wire and wireless transmission.

Wire transmission

Wire transmission requires that wires and cables be manufactured, installed, and protected from damage. Wires and cables take up space, can be messy to install, and get in the way. However, wire can transmit vast amounts of data with high quality and little interference from other signals. Three types of wire media are illustrated in Figure 11.8.

Copper telephone wire is often called **twisted pair** because it consists of a pair of copper wires, twisted to help minimize distortion of the signal by other telephone lines

Figure 11.8 Three Types of Wire Media

Twisted-pair telephone wire, coaxial cable, and fiber-optic cable have different physical configurations because the "wire" for transmitting the data in each case has different physical characteristics.

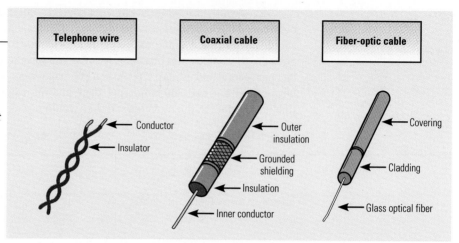

bundled into the same sheath of cable. Copper wire is used for voice transmission and for low-volume data transmission. It is the slowest medium for data transmission but can be used over long distances. Depending on the switching gear and other factors, copper telephone wire may carry from 9600 to 64K bits per second. The main advantage of copper wire is that so much wire is already in place in businesses and in telephone networks. But it also has disadvantages. It transmits data slowly and is heavier and bulkier than fiber-optic cable. What's more, it is vulnerable to unauthorized intrusion because messages traveling through telephone wire generate electrical emissions that can be detected and captured.

Coaxial cable consists of a copper data transmission wire surrounded by insulation, electrically grounded shielding, and a protective outer insulator. It is used in local area networks and for other data transmission covering less than ten miles. Its advantages include data transmission speed of 10 million or more bits per second, little distortion from external signals, and easy modification of networks without disrupting service. However, it carries signals only a short distance and is limited for secure applications because it is comparatively easy to tap into.

Fiber-optic cable contains an ultrapure glass core, a layer of "cladding," and a plastic covering. Unlike copper wire, fiber-optic cable carries data in the form of light. Its data transfer rate of 100 million bits per second or more is much higher than the rates attainable with copper wire because the frequency of light is much higher than the frequencies used with copper wire. A single strand of optical fiber can carry 8,000 telephone conversations. Fiber-optic cable carries 95 percent of the long-distance traffic in the United States. Fiber-optic cable has other advantages. It is 20 times lighter than copper wire, very difficult to tap into, and has very little data loss because the glass fiber is ultrapure. Using high frequencies also reduces the need for repeaters. However, use of light frequencies in fiber-optics transmission requires expensive, high-speed encoding and decoding. Fiber-optic cable is also difficult to splice because the glass itself is only as thick as a hair. Consequently, although fiber-optic transmission is cost-effective for high-volume applications, it is too expensive for many low-volume applications.

Wireless transmission

Wireless transmission does not need a fixed physical connection because it sends signals through air or space. Figure 11.9 shows four common types of wireless transmission.

Figure 11.9 Four Examples of Wireless Transmission

Wireless transmission ranges from cordless telephones within buildings to satellite transmission covering thousands of miles.

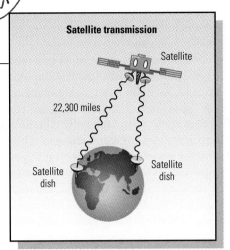

Satellite transmission

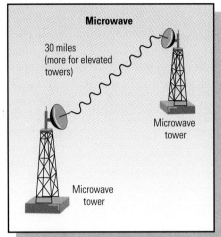

Microwave

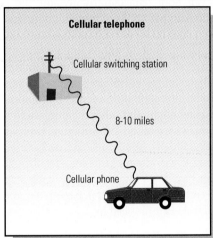

Cellular telephone

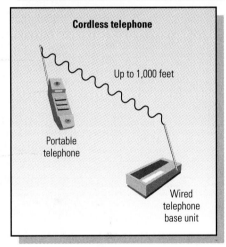

Cordless telephone

The differences in scale and complexity among these four applications are enormous. Building and launching a communications satellite costs over $100 million, whereas a cordless telephone costs under $100.

Cordless and cellular phones both achieve portability for previously non-portable telephone applications. Cordless phones for a home transmit to a base unit within 100 to 1,000 feet, depending on the surroundings. Cellular phones transmit signals to a grid of cellular stations that are linked to the wire-based telephone network. Accordingly, cellular phones operate only within metropolitan areas where the cellular stations have been built. The convenience of cellular phones is offset by several problems. First, they are expensive, often costing $.30 to $.45 per minute. In addition, the signals can be intercepted. Stories of intercepted calls abound, including purported taping of embarrassing phone conversations by Great Britain's Prince Charles and Princess Diana while their marriage was breaking up.

Although not as visible in everyday life, microwave transmission was the earliest of the four types of wireless transmission shown in Figure 11.9 to attain common use. It has been used for several decades to transmit both voice and data. Since earth-based microwave transmission is restricted to line of sight, microwave towers must be placed no more than 30 miles apart unless they are located on mountains or tall buildings.

The line-of-sight restriction limits the use of microwave transmission within city centers. Microwave transmission can also be disrupted by atmospheric conditions and is comparatively easy to intercept.

Telecommunications satellites move in geostationary orbits that remain 22,300 miles above the same part of the earth. At this altitude, the satellite can send signals to earth stations up to 11,000 miles apart. These satellites can carry 40,000 simultaneous telephone calls or 200 television channels. Satellite communication has many advantages. Because it doesn't use a wire channel and doesn't need earth-bound relay towers, it can be used in remote areas. Unlike undersea telephone cables, satellite earth stations can be placed near the people who use them and are therefore easier to maintain and repair. Unlike wire transmission, the cost of satellite communication is the same regardless of the distance between the sender and receiver on earth.

The widespread use of satellite communication became more practical in the late 1980s as the cost and size of transmission equipment decreased. Very small aperture terminals (VSATs) can even transmit and receive data from computer terminals. VSATs are used widely in both data communication and broadcasting. For example, oil drilling companies can use VSATs to transmit data from drilling platforms for analysis at headquarters. Large retailers such as Wal-Mart and Kmart use VSATs to transmit daily sales data. Unfortunately, only a finite number of satellites can operate in the 22,300-mile-high geostationary orbits. The problem is not that the satellites will collide, but rather that their signals will interfere with each other.[7]

Wireless communication provides telecommunications opportunities for emerging nations, remote rural areas, and other regions where it is impractical or inefficient to build and maintain a wire-based infrastructure. Even where a wire-based infrastructure is being installed gradually, cellular telephones have provided an important option. In Thailand, for example, the wait for installing a regular phone has been over a year, whereas cellular phones have been more readily available. Many believe Thailand's economic expansion in the early 1990s depended in part on the communication afforded by cellular phones, whose numbers multiplied by a factor of six between 1990 and 1994.[8]

REALITY CHECK   **Basic Telecommunications Model**   The basic telecommunications model includes creating data, encoding data, determining the data path, transmitting data, decoding data, and receiving data.

1. Thinking about every way you have used telecommunications, which of these steps have required your active involvement and which have basically been invisible to you?

2. Explain why and how you think this should (or should not) change in the next five years.

Types of Networks: A User's Viewpoint

The telecommunications functions and components are building blocks of various types of networks used to improve business operations and compete more effectively. The discussion of types of networks starts with the most familiar, a telephone network. It then looks briefly at broadcasting networks because everyday tasks such as ordering products, performing financial transactions, and obtaining information may merge in some ways with cable and satellite systems for delivering entertainment. Next, three types of networks that transmit data between computerized devices are discussed: local area networks (LANs), wide area networks (WANs), and value added networks (VANs). LANs and WANs are data transmission systems owned and controlled by the enterprise that uses them; VANs provide a commercial service to customers.

Telephone Networks

Americans take telephones for granted in everyday life because they are available to virtually anyone and almost always work. People in other parts of the world don't take telephones for granted because they may be unavailable, because the network isn't reliable, or because it may take years to install a telephone. For example, the lack of an up-to-date telephone system is a significant stumbling block slowing the transformation of East Germany to West Germany's level of commerce.

Telephone-related topics discussed so far include the encoding of speech, alternative transmission media, and wire and wireless telephones. We will look in detail at two aspects of telephone networks: the PBXs that perform switching and ISDN, a set of digital telephone standards whose capabilities exceed those of traditional analog telephone service. Business professionals need to recognize features of technical systems such as ISDN and PBXs because of their impact on both users in the organization and telecommunications costs.

PBXs

A **private branch exchange (PBX)** is a special-purpose computer that controls telephone switching at a company site. PBXs reside at the company site although a system called Centrex performs similar functions from a telephone company office. In its simplest form, a PBX automates functions formerly performed by switchboard operators who plugged wires into a grid. All incoming calls go to the PBX, which directs them to an attendant. The attendant answers the calls and uses a special keyboard to redirect them as is appropriate. Outgoing calls also go through the PBX, which automatically assigns each call to an available outside telephone line. Using a PBX permits a company with 50 telephones to have only 5 or 10 outside lines, depending on how frequently employees use the telephone. If all the outside lines are in use, someone trying to make a call has to wait until a line becomes free. Likewise, incoming callers get a busy signal if all the incoming lines are occupied.

PBXs have moved far beyond merely connecting telephone calls and now provide a wide range of features. Features directed at making communication more convenient and effective, include call waiting, call forwarding, and voice mail. PBX features directed primarily at decreasing costs include reducing the number of outside telephone lines, providing internal extensions, and determining least cost routings. Automatic assignment of calls to lines reduces the required number of outside lines. Providing internal extension numbers permits people to make calls within the same site using only extension numbers and without making a chargeable outside call. Least cost routing is the automatic determination of which carrier to use for each outgoing call. Although there may be no choice for local calls, long-distance calls can be routed through long-distance carriers such as AT&T, MCI, and Sprint, and through special 800 numbers. Savings from choosing the cheapest carrier for each call have paid for many PBXs.

With so many capabilities, PBXs are complex, and keeping them operating effectively takes work. For example, data tables assigning physical telephone outlets to individuals' phone extensions must be updated each time someone moves from one office to another. Deciding how to use PBXs requires a lot of planning and attention to how people can use telephones more effectively.

ISDN

ISDN (integrated service digital network) is a set of standards whose adoption provides additional telephone capabilities without scrapping existing copper telephone lines. By providing integrated service, ISDN offers consistent ways to handle voice and computer data in telephone networks. As a digital network, ISDN provides for digital transmission of both voice and computer data on the same copper telephone lines that were previously used for analog transmission. A firm switching to ISDN must install totally digital telephone gear, thereby replacing all analog on-premises telephone equipment, including even the telephone handsets.

ISDN provides a number of capabilities that reduce equipment costs and make equipment use more effective. It permits the regular telephone network to link personal computers and handle data transmission that would otherwise require expensive leased lines. The higher-volume ISDN service, called the primary rate interface (PRI), uses multiple channels for linking computers, local area networks, and PBXs into the telephone network at up to 1.5M bits per second. This ISDN service permits telephone wire to serve as cabling for small network applications. ISDN's basic rate interface (BRI) provides two voice or data channels that operate at 64K bits per second, much faster than the 9,600 or 14,400 bits per second commonly available to the desktop using telephone lines and modems.

ISDN permits connection of a voice telephone and a personal computer on the same call. Transmitting both voice and computerized data with one phone connection makes it possible for people to see and discuss the same spreadsheet or engineering drawing at the same time. This capability, called screen sharing, helps people work together on complex financial or technical topics even when they aren't in the same location. By providing higher transmission speed, ISDN can cut transmission time for fax or graphical images from 30 seconds per page to 3 seconds per page, which makes it more practical to transmit images, including x-rays, engineering drawings, and advertising designs.

ISDN has been used in trials since 1986 and is being installed for applications that require its additional capabilities today. Its national adoption requires that all telephone company switching stations use digital ISDN switches. Although it brings some important advances, ISDN's ultimate success is not assured because it may not provide adequate price-performance in many situations.

A final ISDN capability is controversial and shows some of the broad implications of adopting new technology. **Caller ID** is the capability of ISDN telephone systems to display a caller's telephone number. Box 11.1 explains why transmitting a few extra bytes of data along with a telephone call can have important implications for users of telephone systems.

Broadcast Networks

Like other parts of the telecommunications world, broadcast networks for radio and television are changing rapidly. Delivery of the signal via cable rather than through the air marked an important departure from the past. Since fiber-optic cable can carry such a vast amount of information compared to wireless broadcasting, cable television can deliver many more channels with higher-quality pictures. Instead of being restricted to whatever programs are acceptable to a wide audience, cable viewers should be more able to find programs they genuinely prefer. Beyond giving more choices of what to watch, future cable systems may make it much easier for viewers to control when they watch it. After all, why should people watch programs only at the times a broadcaster considers best for attracting the largest audience?

In addition to changing the entertainment industry, multiplying the amount of information available through a television may lead to future developments affecting many aspects of business and communication. For example, people may ask why two separate information cables should come into the house, one for telephone and one for television. Why shouldn't it be the same cable supporting both two-way telephone communication, one-way television, and possible extensions of each?

Box 11.1 The Caller ID Controversy

Caller ID is the capability of ISDN telephone systems to display a caller's telephone number automatically. In customer service and sales, this feature can be linked to computerized customer information systems. For example, when an American Express Gold Card holder calls to ask a question, the caller telephone number triggers the retrieval of account background information, the latest bill, and outstanding charges. This information is displayed as the agent picks up the call. For a time, American Express greeted callers by name based on this information, but stopped because a number of customers found it disturbing.[9] Caller ID may also reduce nuisance calls because the person receiving the call will know the source. It may also help the person receiving the call decide whether or not to answer it when otherwise busy. Caller ID could even be linked to special personal answering machines that would ring only for calls from certain telephone numbers and record all other calls. Such systems might make telephone solicitations less effective because the calls wouldn't get through as often.

The controversy about caller ID focuses on who should be protected, the caller or the person called. The person called would like to eliminate some telephone calls or respond more appropriately to others. But a caller with an unlisted telephone doesn't want that number exposed unnecessarily, and a person who anonymously calls a business to get price information doesn't want to automatically become part of that business's mailing list. The future of caller ID capabilities is unclear. In 1992, a Pennsylvania court ruled that caller ID was a form of illegal wiretapping.[10] At the same time many other states permitted it subject to various limitations and caller options.

As a project moving in this direction, in 1993 Time-Warner announced its Full Service Network, a "two-way, electronic superhighway to the home" opening up a vast range of choices, including video-on-demand, telecommunications, and a host of interactive multimedia services, such as home shopping, education, and video games.[11] More than just a better way to specify what program the viewer wants to watch, two-way cable would make it possible to play the quiz game along with the contestants or to express opinions on political issues or consumer preference surveys.

Finally, cable connections could be used for many business applications, perhaps going far beyond current capabilities for paying bills, performing financial transactions, and shopping using personal computers and modems. For example, cable's high bandwidth might permit forms of home shopping in which the consumer could get much more extensive text and image information about the product and alternatives. No one knows what will happen in this area, but it is important to recognize that today's entertainment systems may evolve into essential business and communication tools of the future.

Next we turn to LANs, WANs, and VANs, networks devoted primarily to data generated by computerized systems.

Local Area Networks (LANs)

Local area networks (LANs) connect personal computers and other equipment within a local area, such as a floor of a building. LANs are used widely in small businesses and in departments of larger businesses. They help people share equipment, data, and software, and they help them work together more effectively. They may also link to wide area networks (described later).

Applications of LANs

Chapter 9 introduced distributed computing, which permits users to have many of the benefits of both centralized computing and personal computing. LANs provide access to more computing power, data, and resources than would be practical if each user needed an individual copy of everything. They provide the benefits of personal computing, such as not being forced to do personal work through a central computer that can get bogged down by multiple users. They also provide a number of ways to make an organization more efficient and effective through sharing equipment, sharing personal files, sending messages, sharing databases, and administering software.

Sharing equipment. As shown in Figure 11.10, LANs can link multiple workstations to one laser printer, fax machine, or modem. This makes a single piece of equipment available to multiple users and avoids unnecessary equipment purchases.

Figure 11.10 A Typical Local Area Network

This LAN permits the users at workstations to share a laser printer and a fax machine. It also allows them to access a database shared through a file server.

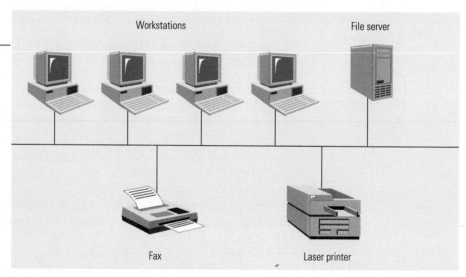

Workstations   File server

Fax   Laser printer

Sharing personal files. LAN users can select personal files that they want co-workers to see, such as engineering drawings, department plans, contracts, or drafts of memos. Co-workers can look at these files without delays for printing paper copies.

Sending messages. LANs can be used to send electronic mail instead of writing messages on pieces of paper that can be lost.

Sharing databases. LANs can be used for accessing shared databases. The LAN in Figure 11.10 is set up for this purpose because it contains a file server for retrieving data requested by the workstations. The file server is linked to a disk that contains shared databases, such as the firm's customer list and telephone directory. When a workstation needs data in a shared database, it sends a request message to the file server, which performs the retrieval from the disk and sends the data to the requesting workstation. This arrangement avoids maintaining redundant copies of data. In addition to not wasting storage, having the databases in one place avoids problems with inconsistent data.

Administering software. Instead of storing separate copies of spreadsheet or word processing software at each workstation, the file server can send a temporary copy to a workstation that needs the software. Handling software this way assures that everyone uses only the latest version of the software. Upgrading to a new software version involves only one replacement instead of finding and replacing each copy. This approach also reduces the number of copies of the software that must be purchased. For example, if no more than 10 out of 25 people on a LAN typically use a spreadsheet at the same time, the firm can purchase a license for 10 copies instead of 25 and can use the LAN to monitor the number of copies in use.

Like many other forms of wire telecommunications, LANs are becoming wireless for some applications (see Figure 11.11). Although the advantages of not having to string the wires are obvious, there are some disadvantages, such as problems in maintaining signal quality and concerns about electromagnetic radiation in the workplace. One controversial application of wireless LANs is in commodity exchanges. Floor traders in these exchanges traditionally made trades and recorded them on pieces of paper. New systems may give the traders handheld terminals for recording the trades. These terminals would be part of a wireless LAN and transmit each trade to a central computer using radio waves.

Technical aspects of LANs

Although LANs link devices rather than telephone conversations, they need to perform many of the same functions as PBXs. They route messages from source to destination, ensure the destination nodes are ready to accept the messages, and monitor network utilization. LANs are controlled by network operating systems, which control the flow of data between the devices on the network and handle requests for data. These operating systems prevent a node from sending a message until the network is ready to process it correctly and take care of busy situations where a node cannot receive a message because it is not ready.

LANs (and other networks) may be configured in a number of ways. A network topology is the pattern of connections between the devices on a network. There are many possible network topologies, each with its own advantages and disadvantages. Box 11.2 shows three representative network topologies: the star, ring, and bus.

LANs use a variety of methods for their internal communication, one of the most common of which is **token passing.** A token is a bit pattern that circulates between nodes. To transmit data, a node appends the data to the token. When the token arrives at the destination node, it adds a notation that the data has been received, and the token continues back to the sending node. The sending node removes the packet, and the token continues circulating.

Most LANs use either twisted-pair telephone wire or coaxial cable. Fiber-optic cable is used rarely for LANs because it is difficult to install and expensive. LANs use two types of data transmission: baseband and broadband. Most LANs are baseband networks. In **baseband** networks, the entire capacity of the cable is used to transmit a single digitally coded signal. Ethernet is a common baseband network that uses coaxial cable and operates at 10 Mbps. In **broadband** networks, the capacity of the cable is divided into separate frequencies to permit it to carry several signals at the same time.

It is often necessary to link LANs to other networks. This can be accomplished using a bridge or a gateway, both of which are a combination of hardware and software. A **bridge** links two compatible networks to enable data to pass between them. With a bridge in place, the two LANs operate like one from a user's viewpoint. A **gateway** links two incompatible networks. Because of the incompatibility, the gateway must convert data formats and transmission sequences before the two networks can be linked.

Wide Area Networks (WANs)

Wide area networks (WANs) are telecommunications networks that link geographically separated locations. WANs are used for many different purposes. Some are designed as

Figure 11.11 Using a Wireless LAN in Cargo Transport

Use of a wireless LAN permits instant updating of status of containers as they are transferred between ships and trucks.

a communications backbone for a large distributed organization. For example, Texas Instruments has a WAN that helps engineers around the world collaborate. It includes 23 mainframes, 2,000 minicomputers, 31,000 terminals, and 36,000 desktop computers.[12] Other WANs focus on a particular transaction processing application, such as taking orders, making reservations, or tracking packages. Many WANs are used to transfer and consolidate corporate data, such as daily transaction summaries from branches.

As Figure 11.12 illustrates, WANs can link to workstations or terminals through LANs. The LANs perform local data processing and link to the WAN for data needed or provided beyond the local environment. An example of this approach is the long-term direction of Apollo, the United Airlines reservation system. In this system, LANs are gradually being installed at travel agencies to replace dumb terminals linked to minicomputers and mainframes. The LANs maintain local copies of reservation data. New reservations are uploaded through the WAN, and travel data is downloaded to the LANs. With this arrangement, the reservationist at the travel agencies can keep working even if the WAN or one of the central computers is down.

As with LANs, important developments have occurred in wireless WANs. For example, IBM and Motorola developed the ARDIS wireless network service to reduce the separation between the office and the field and thereby improve the efficiency of field service and sales work. This service permits employees to communicate with the office using handheld terminals that use radio waves to link to a network of 1,000 base stations covering most of the United States. ARDIS permits field employees to access corporate data without using a telephone and regardless of where the data resides. For instance, a computer technician can locate the required part in the company's inventory, order it, and tell the customer when it will be available. It also permits a local office to send new instructions to a service technician driving to a service call that is now unnecessary because the customer fixed the problem. Since this system uses radio waves, users must obtain a special FCC license.[13]

Figure 11.12 A WAN That Includes Several LANs

This WAN includes several LANs, each of which links to the rest of the network through regional minicomputers.

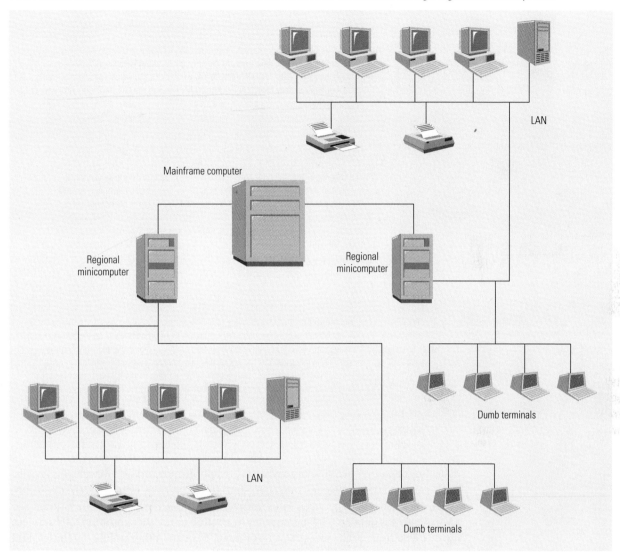

Because of their size, complexity, and response time requirements, WANs must be managed carefully by telecommunications experts. Work can grind to a halt or costs can expand if WANs are set up inefficiently or used inappropriately. The difficulty of keeping networks operating is one of several reasons for using VANs, which are described next.

Value Added Networks (VANs)

Value added networks (VANs) are public data networks that "add value" by transmitting data and by providing access to commercial databases and software. VANs are complex technical systems that use packet switching so that they can be accessible from many different types of workstations. The use of VANs is usually sold by subscription, with users paying for the amount of data they move. As a way to transmit computerized

Box 11.2 Representative Network Topologies

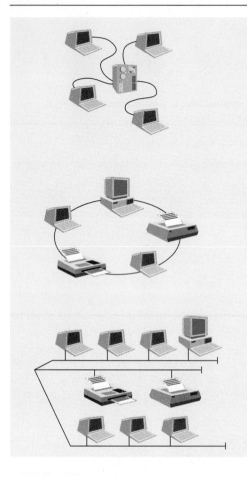

In a **star topology,** all messages go through a central node that serves as a switch, receiving messages and forwarding them to a destination node. Since every node is attached to the central node, a star network requires at most two links for a message to move from one node to another. A star network typically uses circuit switching and can integrate voice and data traffic. It provides good control because all messages go through the same node. It is also easy to expand without disrupting ongoing processing. But a star network may have reliability problems because the entire network is down whenever the central node is down. In addition, the cost of linking every node to the central node becomes excessive as the number of nodes grows and if the nodes are far from the hub.

In a **ring topology,** the nodes are linked directly without a central server, which means that messages between nodes must be retransmitted by all nodes between the source and destination. Unlike a star network, the network control and processing are distributed to each node on the network. If any node is disabled, messages must be routed around that node to keep the network operating. Adding or subtracting a node while the network is in operation requires special effort to keep the network running.

A **bus topology** attaches each node to a central channel called a *bus*. Each device on the network can access any other device directly by using its address on the bus. All messages are "heard" by every device on the network, but only the addressed device responds to a message. Bus topologies are easy to expand since the addition or loss of a node has no direct effect on any other node. As with a ring, control is distributed among the nodes. Network performance degrades as traffic increases, however, because each message requires the attention of each node. LANs commonly use bus or ring topologies. Ethernet is a common baseband network that uses a bus topology.

data, they offer a service similar to what the telephone networks do for telephone calls. VANs can send data between computers in different cities or even different countries. VANs also offer special services. For example, a personal computer in one city can use a VAN to access data on a host computer in another city. Other common VAN services include electronic mail, access to stock market data and other public databases, and access to electronic banking and other transaction processing services.

VANs are used for a number of reasons. They are a cost-effective solution for companies that need data communication services but don't want to invest in setting up their own private network. They are commonly used by companies that lack the technical expertise to maintain a network. Even small companies can enjoy the benefits of data communications by using VANs and leaving the technical details to the vendors. VANs permit companies to use part of a network instead of paying a large fixed cost for their own underutilized network. VANs also provide for easier expansion because they are set up to use their capacity efficiently and to bring in new capacity if necessary. Finally, VANs can provide convenient access to data that would not otherwise be available.

LANs, WANs, and VANs differ in scope, performance requirements, and technology. For example, the reliability and data transmission requirements for a LAN used to link three personal computers to a single laser printer are minimal compared to the requirements for a large WAN providing rapid response to any of thousands of terminals in an airline reservation system. When a VAN is down, the services provided by that VAN are essentially out of business until it comes up again.

We will complete the discussion of telecommunications by looking at telecommunications standards and policy.

REALITY CHECK   **Types of Networks**   This section discussed types of networks, including telephone networks, broadcast networks, LANs, WANs, and VANs.

1. Explain how the functions or capabilities of networks have or have not affected you in your everyday life.

2. What human and ethical issues arise from advanced network capabilities?

3. Assume that distributors of many products started offering them through computerized networks at substantial discounts because they could avoid many costs for stores, salespeople, and inventory. What kinds of products could be sold effectively this way, and what capabilities would the network need in order to serve as an alternative for stores or offices?

Telecommunications Standards

Just as people communicate best when they speak the same language, machines communicate best when they operate under consistent standards and formats. Standards make it practical to build networks containing hardware from different vendors (see Figure 11.13).

Standards involve important tradeoffs. They may disallow certain features or capabilities that are valuable in a particular situation but are inconsistent with the standard. Standards may also contradict the features vendors have built into their own proprietary products. This strikes at fundamental competitive issues because vendors often rely on their own proprietary data architectures as strategies to lock out competitors. With the proliferation of different types of computers and other devices, most large purchasers of systems are now calling for conformance to agreed-on standards.

Standards can be divided into de facto standards and de jure standards. **De facto standards** are standards established by the fact that a product dominates a particular market. Examples of de facto standards in personal computing include the Intel 486 and Pentium microprocessors, Motorola's Power PC microprocessor, and Microsoft Windows 3.1. **De jure standards** are standards defined by industry groups or by the government. Many de facto standards become de jure standards when analyzed and ratified by industry standards associations.

To appreciate the nature of networking standards, consider the **OSI** (Open Systems Interface) **reference model,** a framework for defining standards. It was created to guide the development of standards for communications between networked systems, regardless of technology, vendor, or country of origin. These standards cover all aspects of network operations and management. Developed by an industry consortium called the International Standards Organization, the OSI reference model identifies issues that specific standards should address.

At each level, the standards themselves are expressed through **protocols,** precisely defined rules, codes, and procedures for linking devices or transmitting data between devices. The various protocols needed to implement the OSI reference model cover topics such as establishing, maintaining, and terminating connections, routing information packets, controlling errors, disassembly and reassembly of messages, multiplexing and demultiplexing of messages.

Figure 11.13
Standards That Are
Visible in Hardware

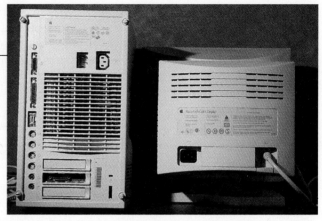

This rear view of a personal computer shows the plugs used to connect to the monitor and to other peripherals. Since these plugs all conform to common standards, many different types of peripherals can be used with this brand of computer.

The OSI model divides a network's operation into seven layers, each having well-defined and limited responsibilities. Each layer receives data from an adjacent layer, performs specific processing tasks, and passes the data up or down to the next level of the hierarchy. At the bottom, level 1 is concerned with the physical attachment of devices and looks at issues such as what type of plug to use. Intermediate levels are concerned with the formatting of messages, methods of transmission, and error correction. At the top, level 7 is concerned with the logic of the application itself. Breaking network operation into these layers makes it easier to identify and solve problems, and it simplifies bringing in enhanced capabilities since they can be added a layer at a time. Figure 11.14 explains the seven levels of the OSI reference model in more detail.

Other important networking models preceded OSI and are used widely. **SNA** (System Network Architecture) is a seven-layer model developed by IBM as a proprietary standard in 1972 and currently used by around 300,000 networks involving mainframes and minicomputers. There are important inconsistencies between SNA and OSI because SNA handles some of the details differently from the way OSI handles them. Even within the IBM world, some applications written using SNA cannot communicate with other IBM computers. **TCP/IP** (Transmission Control Protocol/Internet Protocol) was developed in the late 1960s and early 1970s to permit information sharing between different computers running incompatible operating systems. It has a five-layer reference model and is used by the Internet, which currently has millions of users.

The content and quality of telecommunications standards affect not only the commercial fortunes of individual vendors but also the long-term ability of firms to achieve desired connectivity. Governments are also involved in telecommunications issues, as we will see next.

Telecommunications Policy

This chapter closes with a brief discussion of telecommunications policy. This is a topic whose effects range from personal concerns such as what telephone service will be available at what price through regulatory issues such as who will be allowed to broadcast on which radio frequencies.

Figure 11.14 The OSI Reference Model

The OSI reference model divides network operation and management into seven layers. Layers 1 through 4 are responsible for moving data from one place to another, whereas 5 through 7 handle the exchange of data between application programs. Communicating between two programs running on two different computers requires going through each step in some way.

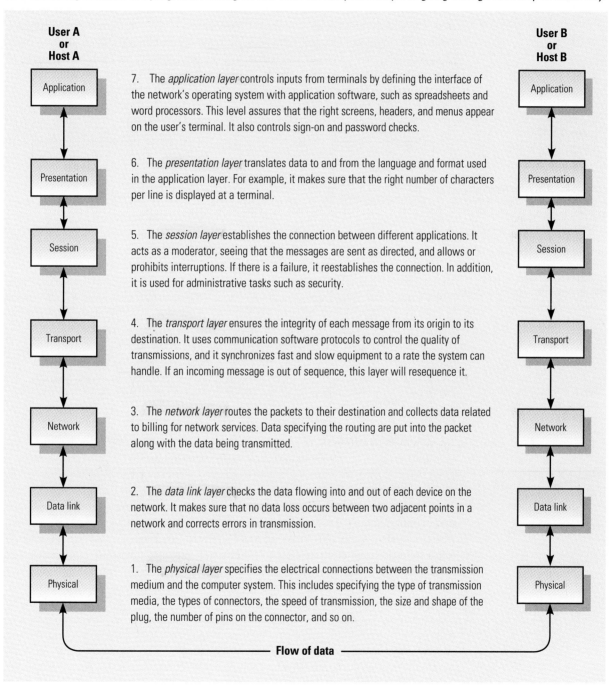

Figure 11.15 shows a framework for thinking about telecommunications policy in terms of issues and stakeholders. It shows that the issues include questions such as what products and services will be available at what prices, what level of access will be guaranteed to whom, what societal resources will be allocated to telecommunications in what ways, and how will telecommunications be regulated for efficiency and effectiveness. The stakeholders in most of these matters include telecommunications suppliers, customers, regulators or policymakers, and society in general. Since all four types of stakeholders feel each of the issues in a variety of ways in each of the areas of telecommunications, entire books have been written on this topic. We will address it by summarizing the recent history and discussing several areas of controversy.

Figure 11.15

Telecommunications Issues and Stakeholders

Customers, suppliers, regulators and policymakers, and society as a whole are all stakeholders in telecommunications issues such as what products and services will be provided at what price, what level of access will be guaranteed, what society resources will be used, and how much burden will regulation cause?

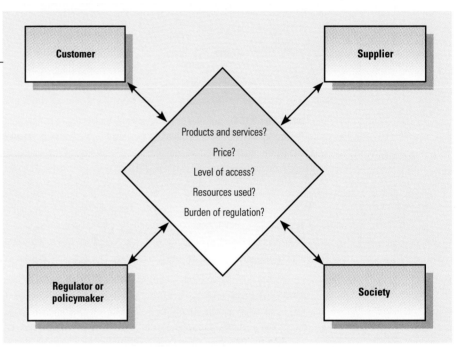

Until 1984, AT&T was a telephone monopoly servicing most of the telephones and telephone networks in the United States. A consent decree between AT&T and the Justice Department in 1984 broke up AT&T's telephone service monopoly. This change left a long-distance company (AT&T) and seven regional operating companies that handle local telephone calls. Often called the Baby Bells, the regional operating companies include Ameritech, Bell Atlantic, BellSouth, Nynex, Pacific Telesis, Southwestern Bell, and US West. The consent decree prevented the Baby Bells from selling equipment, carrying long-distance calls, and manufacturing telephone equipment. Subsequent rulings permitted them to enter new lines of business, including some information services, but these services couldn't manipulate the data they transmit. Their potential competitors in information services include cable television companies, newspapers, companies that provide VANs, and long-distance carriers such as MCI, Sprint, and the new AT&T. The broad span of companies and potential products and services raises many complex issues, such as the following:

Why should the government permit some companies, but not others, to sell products in a particular line of business? Having the original telephone monopoly avoided duplication of telephone systems and made the original investment in telephone systems less risky. The limitations on the Baby Bells were designed to prevent them from using their local telephone monopolies to freeze out competition from smaller companies. This rationale was consistent with U.S. antitrust laws but left questions about economic efficiency, customer satisfaction, taxation, and even national security. For example, why should cable television companies be able to run fiber-optic cable into a house but unable to provide telephone service? Why should a telephone company be able to provide telephone service but not television or other information?

Regulation has restricted certain types of products but permitted the development of others. For example, a number of nontelecommunications companies have entered this industry by selling systems or services they developed for internal use. Companies such as Merrill Lynch have turned their internal data communications networks into VANs by selling excess capacity to other companies that need data communications services. The question of who should be able to provide what products and services under what terms will remain contentious for many years. This issue involves major investments, affects many economic interests, and involves technical capabilities that are continually changing.

How should local, state, and federal governments control prices and levy taxes on the various competing telecommunications services? (or should they do this at all?) When AT&T agreed to purchase McCaw Cellular Communications for $12.6 billion in 1993, it told the Federal Communications Commission (FCC) that its ultimate goal was the provision of affordable, nationwide, radio-based telephones, with features and quality comparable with the wireline network and with capacities to bypass the local land-line network. As mandated by the FCC, AT&T was paying local telephone companies $14 billion to connect into their networks, funded for by a 5.5 cent-a-minute charge on interstate calls.[14] Bypassing the local telephone companies would save AT&T a great deal of money, but the Baby Bells and local telephone companies might have competitive responses of their own.

In the same year as AT&T's McCaw purchase, New York state regulators gave initial approval to a plan designed by Rochester Telephone Corp. that allows Time Warner's cable unit to provide local telephone service by linking its cable lines with Rochester Telephone's local network. In exchange, Rochester Telephone would be allowed to split into two companies: a regulated unit owning the network and providing access to its competitors and a nonregulated unit to bundle and sell telecommunications services.[15] The telecommunications world is both dynamic and highly uncertain because all the players have many options for new alliances, new services, and new types of competition, and because everything they try to do is judged by both regulators and the marketplace.

What should be the rationale for regulating telecommunications? Some observers complain that U.S. telecommunications policy is being determined by antitrust policy rather than by national telecommunications needs. In other countries where antitrust is not an issue, monopoly telephone companies are able to plan their products and services based on their view of what is needed for telecommunications. For example, Nippon Telegraph and Telephone, Japan's main telephone company, has a long-term goal of using only digital switches by the year 2000 and running fiber-optic cable to all houses and offices by 2015.[16] In contrast, telecommunications planning in the United States depends on the plans of a number of separate companies. Meanwhile, the various nations in the European Community have negotiated about a coherent plan for Europe.

Who should be able to use specific public resources, such as radio frequencies? This question shows how public issues and interests intersect with technology. All wireless transmission uses a particular frequency in the electromagnetic spectrum, whether the transmission is a television program, a cellular telephone call, or computerized data (see Figure 11.16). To prevent different uses of wireless transmission from interfering with each other, governments allocate specific frequency ranges to specific uses. Within those ranges, the governments allocate specific frequencies to individual users, including radio and television broadcasters and businesses that use certain frequencies for data communications. Since there are only a finite number of frequencies, the electromagnetic spectrum shown in Figure 11.16 can be considered a scarce resource that has been allocated by governments. Such allocations are always controversial. There is no widely accepted right way to decide that a particular radio station should own a particular frequency in a region. In the past, these frequencies were granted outright. In 1994, the Clinton administration planned to auction off 200 megahertz that was still controlled by the government. An important issue at that time was how or whether to protect the interests of small, innovative businesses that larger rivals could easily outbid.[17] On an international scale, many Third World nations have complained that the industrial world has too much control over the frequencies used for satellite communication. They argue that these frequencies are a finite resource that is allocated unfairly today.

Figure 11.16 The Electromagnetic Spectrum

Various parts of the electromagnetic spectrum have been allocated for different uses.

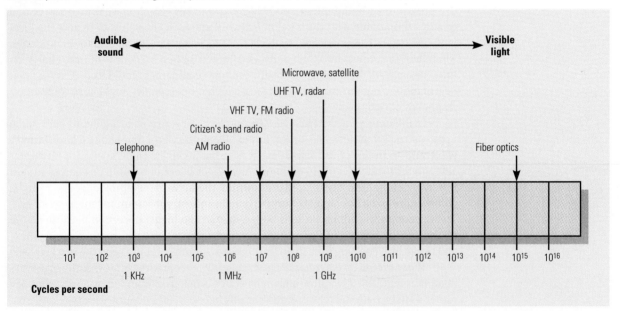

To what extent is universal access possible, and to what extent should it be guaranteed? In 1994, Vice President Gore, a key proponent of the information superhighway, told a telecommunications conference, "We cannot tolerate—nor in the long run can this nation afford—a society in which some children become fully educated and others do not; in which some adults have access to training and lifetime education and others do not. Nor can we permit geographic location to determine whether the information highway passes by your door."[18] He proposed five principles related to difficult tradeoffs between private sector and public sector concerns:

1. Encouragement of private investment (primarily by removing regulatory impediments)

2. Preservation of competition

3. Open access to the network (through uniform standards)

4. Universal service (to be assured primarily by the private sector)

5. Flexible and responsive government.[19]

Disagreements related to these principles range from questions about who will pay for universal access to concerns about whether most people want access to anything other than entertainment. Access to information and technology was one of the ethical issues discussed in Chapter 8. In a society sensitive to differences between haves and have-nots, access to new telephone, text, and video services is an important political and practical issue.

Business professionals don't confront issues such as these every day, but they need to be aware that their ability to use telecommunications will be shaped by a dynamic and unpredictable interplay of technology, business strategy, and government policy.

REALITY CHECK   **Telecommunications Policy**   This section mentioned a number of effects of telecommunications policy.

1. Explain why you do or do not believe telecommunications policy has affected you in your everyday life.

2. What human and ethical issues arise in discussions of telecommunications policy?

Chapter   Conclusion

S U M M A R Y

▶ *What aspects of the convergence of computing and communications are important for understanding telecommunications?*

Communications capabilities have become essential to many computer systems, especially with the trend toward distributed processing. Roles of computers in telecommunications include making long-distance connections, monitoring the traffic on the network, and balancing the loads on different parts of the network by determining which path across the network transmitted data will take.

  What are the steps in the basic telecommunications model?

Telecommunications is the movement of data between devices in different locations. Telecommunications starts with generating the data. The encoding step converts data from an original form into a form for transmission. The switching step directs the signal from its source to its destination. Data can be transmitted using a variety of wire or wireless channels. On arriving at the destination, data are decoded or converted back into the original form.

What are the advantages and disadvantages of the different forms of wire and wireless transmission?

Wire transmission requires that the wires be installed and protected from damage. This is difficult in remote geographical areas and where wires would take up too much space. Although a great deal of copper wire is already in place, it transmits data slowly, is heavy and bulky, and generates electrical emissions that can be intercepted. Coaxial cable is much faster but can be tapped into easily. Fiber-optic cable can transmit vast quantities of data, is very light, and generates no electrical emissions, but it requires complex electronics and is difficult to splice. Wireless transmission is the only effective method for many applications, but it can be intercepted and can be disrupted by physical objects or atmospheric conditions.

 What is ISDN, and why is it important?

ISDN (integrated service digital network) is a set of standards whose adoption provides additional telephone capabilities without scrapping existing telephone lines. By providing integrated service, ISDN offers consistent ways to handle voice and computer data in telephone networks. As a digital network, ISDN provides for digital transmission of both voice and computer data on existing copper telephone lines. By increasing data transmission speeds, ISDN eliminates some needs for expensive leased lines. It cuts transmission time for fax or graphical images, permits connection of a voice telephone and a personal computer on the same call, and provides the capability to display a caller's telephone number to the person receiving the call.

▶ *What are the main differences between LANs, WANs, and VANs?*

These three types of networks transmit data between computerized devices. Local area networks (LANs) connect computers and other equipment within a local area, such as a floor of a building; they help people share equipment, data, and software. Wide area networks (WANs) link geographically separated locations. Some WANs are used as a communications backbone for a large organization; others focus on a particular application, such as taking orders or making reservations. Value added networks (VANs) are public data networks that "add value" by transmitting data and by providing access to commercial databases and software.

▶ *Why are telecommunications standards important?*

Telecommunications standards make it practical to build networks containing hardware from different vendors. However, they may disallow valuable capabilities that are inconsistent with the standard. Standards may also contradict the features vendors have built into proprietary products. This strikes at fundamental competitive issues because vendors often rely on proprietary data architectures as strategies to lock out competitors.

▶ *How is telecommunications policy related to issues faced by managers?*

Telecommunications policy is one determinant of who owns telecommunications networks, what products come to market, and who can sell these products. The issues in this area range from economic efficiency and customer satisfaction to national security. The allocation of broadcasting frequencies, both nationally and internationally, has major impacts on business and security interests.

INTERNATIONAL VIGNETTE

Canada: Royal Bank of Canada: Linking Various Platforms

During the 1980s, the Royal Bank of Canada (RBC) had established itself among the top five banks in the world in almost every aspect of large-scale retail banking. Its vast mainframe and WAN-based transaction processing operations covered 1,600 branches with high reliability and security. Many corporate customers chose RBC because of these capabilities. In addition to supporting large-scale transaction processing, RBC had invested heavily in automating its branches and providing teller workstations. By the early 1990s, it had two platforms that did not communicate effectively. The PCs and LANs at the branches handled spreadsheets, word processing, data analysis and electronic mail, whereas the mainframes processed transactions and accessed corporate databases.

To operate more effectively, RBC needed a way to link its entire IS infrastructure. It adopted a phased migration plan to move gradually to a new internetworking architecture. It gradually started connecting to its backbone SNA network from LANs rather than network controllers. All the LANs had to be connected in a uniform way that permitted centralized network management across the LAN–WAN–LAN environment. Because downtime of even several hours would be very disruptive, RBC created a series of test environments before bringing major transaction processing systems online. Even so, in 1991, an error in a funds transfer system interrupted processing of corporate customers' payments. RBC's top officers of the bank had to cancel their scheduled work for two days to call customers to apologize. Eventually, the new architecture will increase access while reducing costs. It will eliminate hundreds of telephone lines and will increase transmission speeds by factors of hundreds.

Source: Keen, Peter G. W., and J. Michael Cummings. *Networks in Action*. Belmont, Calif.: Wadsworth Publishing, 1994, pp. 346–350.

∘ Use the WCA framework to organize your understanding of this vignette and to identify important topics that are not mentioned.

∘ What issues (if any) make this case interesting from an international or intercultural viewpoint?

∘ To what extent should RBC's top managers consider this highly technical effort strategic for the bank?

REAL-WORLD CASES

Visa International: Processing Transactions from Around the World

Visa provides credit-authorization and clearing and settlement services for thousands of member banks around the world. VisaNet, its international network, processes over 25 million transactions a day from over 7 million retail outlets worldwide, more than a million of which have automatic dial-up terminals. During peak periods, the transaction rate exceeds 1,500 per second. The system includes mainframe computers for the transaction processing and an international telecommunications network for data transmission.

More than 49 percent of Visa's transactions were generated outside the United States in 1989, when Visa began a project to upgrade VisaNet. At that time, they had major data centers in Virginia, California, and London, England, and were building a new data center in Yokohama, Japan. Although they had planned to build additional data centers, for expense and control reasons, they decided to centralize instead. They migrated to two supercenters, one in Virginia and one in Basingstoke, England, and smaller regional centers in California and Yokohama. The two supercenters have enough capacity to back each other up. Visa doesn't really need the Yokohama center now, but sees political value in serving the Asia/Pacific region from Japan instead of transmitting all these transactions to the United States.

Perhaps surprisingly, VisaNet is not currently integrated with Visa's payment system. VisaNet automates the authorizations at the point of sale to reduce credit-card fraud and make it easier for customers to use Visa cards. But building the authorization system did not change the way payments move from the card holder's bank to the merchant. A project called Payment Service 2000 is underway to create the first unambiguous tie between the credit authorization and the payment draft. It will do this by assigning a transaction identifier in the VisaNet system.

Source: "Credit Central: Interview with Visa's Rosalind L. Fisher." *Information Week,* July 5, 1993, pp. 28–29.

* Use the WCA framework to organize your understanding of this case and to identify important topics that are not mentioned.

* What are the advantages and disadvantages of the centralized mainframe architecture used here compared to a client–server architecture?

* Explain whether you think this is really a computer example rather than a telecommunications example, and whether you think this distinction matters.

Chicago Board of Trade: Pulling Out of a Worldwide Network

Globex is a futures trading network that operates around the globe 24 hours a day. In 1989, the Chicago Mercantile Exchange teamed up with London-based Reuters to build the network. In 1990, the Chicago Board of Trade (CBOT) agreed to scrap the 24-hour trading system it had been building and adopt the Merc's system. The premise of having a 24-hour international network originally seemed unassailable. It would give the Merc and CBOT a way to sell futures contracts to an international audience, would head off efforts by exchanges in Europe and Asia to introduce competing products, and would bypass some of the limitations of trading only during Chicago working hours. Globex began operation in June 1992, several years late and $25 million over its $75 million budget. It links 342 486-based PCs at trading desks, mostly in Europe and North America.

Things didn't turn out as originally hoped. The partners had estimated that Globex's worldwide volume for the Merc and CBOT would reach 50,000 contracts a day. But by March 1994, Globex carried only 3,600 contracts a day from the two exchanges. Around 25,000 Globex trades a day came from the only other exchange listing products on Globex, Marche á Terme Internationale de France in Paris. Acceptance in Asia was very limited, with only a few Globex terminals in Tokyo and Hong Kong. Globex also encountered technical problems as well, because certain products such as new types of options required tracking relationships among several hundred products, far more than the Globex screens could display. The chairman of the CBOT said, "The appetite for 24-hour markets isn't really there yet." In April 1994, the CBOT decided to drop out of the partnership.

Sources: Feder, Barnaby J. "It's Showdown Time for Globex." *New York Times,* Apr. 14, 1994, p. C1.
"Future Bleak for Globex." *Information Week,* Mar. 7, 1994, pp. 31–32.

* Use the WCA framework to organize your understanding of this case and to identify important topics that are not mentioned.

* Explain whether you think a client–server architecture would have helped in this situation.

* Explain whether you think this case demonstrates basic limitations of international trading systems.

KEY TERMS

telecommunications	digital signals	coaxial cable	ring topology
data communications	carrier signal	fiber-optic cable	bus topology
telecommunications network	modem	private branch exchange (PBX)	wide area network (WAN)
node	high definition television (HDTV)	ISDN (integrated service digital	value added network (VAN)
connectivity	dedicated line	network)	de facto standard
encoding	switch	caller ID	de jure standard
switching	circuit switching	local area network (LAN)	OSI reference model
channel	packet switching	token passing	protocols
decoding	multiplexer	baseband	SNA
network management	bandwidth	broadband	TCP/IP
host computer	information superhighway	bridge	
front-end processor	data loss	gateway	
analog signals	twisted pair	star topology	

REVIEW QUESTIONS

1. Identify some of the ways telecommunications affects value chain activities.

2. Explain how the roles of wire and wireless transmission are reversing in some telecommunications applications.

3. Identify and define the telecommunications functions included in the basic telecommunications model.

4. Describe the difference between analog and digital signals.

5. What does a modem do?

6. What is the difference between circuit switching and packet switching?

7. Why would it take a long time to transmit a movie over a telephone line?

8. Explain some of the performance differences between twisted pair, coaxial cable, and fiber-optic cable.

9. What are the advantages and disadvantages of communication via satellite?

10. Identify some of the functions performed by PBXs.

11. What is ISDN, and why isn't it used everywhere?

12. Define caller ID, and explain why it is controversial.

13. What is a LAN, and what are some common uses of LANs?

14. Identify important differences between star, ring, and bus topologies.

15. Explain why it is possible for a WAN to contain a number of LANs.

16. What is a VAN, and what are the advantages and disadvantages of using VANs?

17. Define the difference between de facto and de jure standards.

18. What is the OSI reference model, and what do its layers represent?

19. Discuss some of the issues in telecommunications policy.

20. Why is the electromagnetic spectrum a scarce resource?

DISCUSSION QUESTIONS

1. A congressional panel began a broad investigation after learning that the online service America Online, Inc. sells data on its one million subscribers to direct marketers at the rate of $100 per 1,000 names. For additional fees, direct marketers can get selections based on ZIP code, income, operating systems, and ages of users' children.[17] Given that an online service can track everything a user does, explain your view of acceptable privacy guarantees in this part of "cyberspace."

2. According to the International Telecommunications Union, 71 percent of the world's phone lines are in countries with 15 percent of the world's population. In Latin America, only 7 percent of the population has access to a phone line, and only 1 percent has access in most of Asia and Africa.[18] Explain whether disparities in telephone access have an unfair impact on global competition. What might the less-developed countries do about this situation?

3. You have just seen two commercials. In one, an executive has received an important message by pager while driving. In the other, an executive relaxing under an umbrella on an isolated beach is using a portable computer to have a videoconference with people in the Paris home office. Use ideas about data transmission to compare the situations and to explain why the second situation is not yet feasible.

4. Assume that the U.S. Congress totally deregulated telecommunications. Based on ideas in this chapter, identify five major effects this development might have.

5. Assume that you could have advanced PBX and ISDN capabilities for your home telephone. Would these capabilities make any difference in the way you use the telephone?

6. What kinds of telecommunications capabilities would be required for a large multi-national food company to provide any employee with instant access to any data in the entire company? What types of data handling capabilities would this require? Aside from technical capabilities to transmit data, explain why you do or do not believe this is practical.

HANDS-ON-EXERCISES

1. This exercise is related to the use of computerized library catalogs and indexes of periodicals. It provides background for exercise 2.

   a. Use a computerized library catalog to determine whether the library owns this textbook or other texts you are using.

   b. Use the computerized catalog to identify all the books the library owns that were written by a particular author or pertain to a particular subject, such as telecommunications.

   c. Use the computerized periodical indexes to find articles that appeared last year about a particular aspect of telecommunications or were written by a particular author.

   d. Describe what you need to know in order to use a computerized library catalog or periodical index effectively.

2. This exercise is related to the use of the Internet to obtain information from distant locations.

   a. Use the Internet to try to obtain from a library elsewhere answers to the same queries you used in the first exercise.

   b. Use the Internet to find at least one type of interesting information (not about library catalogs) from a library or other institution elsewhere.

    c. Describe what you need to know to use the Internet effectively. Is this different from what you need to know to use your library?

3. This exercise is related to calculation of data transmission requirements and assumes that a spreadsheet model is provided.

    a. Use the spreadsheet model along with any assumptions you need to make to calculate which would take longer to transmit: (1) a 5-by-7-inch photo at 200 dots per inch or (2) a 30-page book chapter containing two 2-by-3-inch photos and 5 line drawings using a drawing program.

APPLICATION SCENARIOS

Galactic Motors

"We used to be able to do all of our communications through a telephone network, but yesterday's solution can't solve today's problems." Emily Landau, the telecommunications manager of Galactic Motors, came to the point in presenting her proposal to top management. The network she proposed would cost millions of dollars, and she was sure her audience would be skeptical. The proposed system would be a private satellite network, linking company headquarters with each dealer. The dealers would need to install a VSAT dish to use the network.

Landau explained a number of areas where an improved network would improve company efficiency and effectiveness. The current use of telephone lines to link each of 5,000 dealers to headquarters was simply inefficient. The calls got through, but the overall cost was unnecessarily high. More important, the existing telephone system could not support new applications needed for better sales work, customer service, and repairs. The new network should permit dealers to give customers the earliest possible delivery dates for exactly the car they want. To do this, the dealers should be able to transmit an order for a car with specific options and get an immediate reply assigning to the order either a car currently being built or a car scheduled but not yet started. Warranty and service data for all cars sold in the last ten years should be available immediately to provide better customer service. The network should help mechanics diagnose vehicle problems and should support electronic invoicing and parts ordering systems. It should also provide business television capabilities, permitting company executives to contact all dealers simultaneously concerning sales incentives, competitive strategy, personnel changes, and other issues.

One top manager seemed to miss the point. "I don't understand," he said. "We already use a telephone network. Now you are proposing that we build our own network. We are in the automobile business, not the satellite business. Why can't we just use a network on the earth? And furthermore, I don't understand why you want to put our voice conversations and data on the same network. Does this really matter?"

1. Based on the ideas in the chapter, would an earth-bound network be possible? What are the advantages and disadvantages of a satellite network? Would broadcasting cause security problems compared to using fiber optics?

2. Are there any advantages in integrating voice and data in one network?

3. What data would you gather to quantify the system's potential costs and benefits?

DEBATE TOPIC   *Use ideas from the chapter to argue the pros and cons and practical implications of the following proposition: Executives in an auto company shouldn't be involved in this discussion. They should just set a budget, say what they want, and leave the details to their staff.*

Patton County Courts

In 1987, Patton County's entire criminal justice system was running on 30-year-old technology. All court scheduling, record keeping, and criminal information were on paper. Even the type-writers were old. The increases in drug-related arrests in the 1980s strained the system severely and led to a search for greater efficiency. A major push toward computerization was undertaken as a way to relieve some of the pressure. A computerized information system was installed for record keeping and for making scheduling more systematic.

As part of the project, a LAN was installed to link all judges to the new internal infor-mation systems and to databases for legal research. The data from the internal information system included court schedules; criminal records; and case-related documents such as motions filed, rulings on motions, case transcripts, and depositions (pretrial testimony by people involved in the case). Having a systematic way to keep track of documents was important because a large case sometimes involved thousands of documents, any of which could be lost or overlooked easily. The research database included the U.S. criminal code; federal regulations; results of cases from state and federal courts; and specialized informa-tion about bankruptcy, patents, tax, labor, and international trade law. Much of the legal information had already been available in bound volumes in the court's legal library.

After six months, secretaries and law clerks used the LAN extensively. The secretaries used it to share a laser printer, thereby producing more professional-looking legal documents. Secretaries also used the LAN for entering and checking schedules. The law clerks used it for some of their legal research although they also used the bound volumes. The judges used the LAN much less. Of 18 judges, 5 never turned on their computers, stating that the computers were helpful to other people but useless to them because they already had enough infor-mation from other sources. Several other judges occasionally used the internal database of motions and rulings but never used the computer for legal research. Five other judges found most aspects of the LAN useful: Instead of wasting someone else's time, they frequently looked up motions and rulings using the LAN and occasionally used the research database. They also used the LAN's electronic mail facility to send messages to each other.

1. What is the relationship between the technical capabilities of the LAN and business processes involving the judges?

2. Has the LAN been successful thus far? Is it important that the judges use it more? What would lead them to do so?

DEBATE TOPIC   *Use ideas from the chapter to argue the pros and cons and practical implications of the following proposition: Uneven use of the LAN raises issues about whether the Patton County courts provide equal justice for everyone.*

Cumulative Case: Custom T-Shirts, Inc.

Terry and Lee feel that the company's telecommunications system is basically a nonsystem. Currently, it consists of a telephone at each store and a small PBX at headquarters, which now has 12 people. They want to design a telecommunications system that will support planned developments in the next three years.

The product-related plans include the following: Have two to four design workstations in each store to permit customers to design their own t-shirts by modifying existing designs. Link the design computers to the printer that creates the four-layer screens used for the t-shirts. Link the stores to headquarters, both for transmitting financial data and purchasing data and for transmitting t-shirt designs and other design-related information as the product line expands beyond t-shirts into new-age boutique clothes. Link the stores to factories and warehouses that produce large orders for business customers. Devise a way to permit customers to dial in for placing orders or obtaining price lists.

The plans related to corporate functions include the following: Negotiate purchasing contracts and control purchasing centrally, while responding quickly to the specific local needs of individual stores. Analyze daily sales data to find and capitalize on trends and fads in customer preferences. Provide an integrated e-mail and v-mail system for internal communication. If possible, put television sets and video cameras in the stores and figure out how to capture an image and duplicate it using a four-layer screen.

A cable television company has approached Terry with the proposition that Custom T-Shirts should install cable into each store and use cable for all its communication needs, including voice, images, financial data, purchasing data, and television broadcasts. They even foresee the use of business television, in which the company's managers could hold one-way videoconferences.

1. Explain how the different types of networks mentioned in the chapter might be used to accomplish the aspects of the business plan mentioned here.

2. Thinking about specific business processes, such as creating the four-layer screens and performing purchasing activities centrally, identify some of the product and process performance variables (see Figure 2.10) that might be affected, and explain how they might be affected.

3. Explain why you believe the cable television proposal does or does not fit the business's needs. Whether or not it does this, explain why you believe it is or is not legal, and who should decide whether it is legal.

REFERENCES

1. Tapscott, Don, and Art Caston. *Paradigm Shift: The New Promise of Information Technology.* New York: McGraw-Hill, 1993.

2. Negroponte, Nicholas. "HDTV: What's Wrong with This Picture?" *Wired,* Vol. 1, No. 1, 1993, p. 112.

3. Stallings, William, and Richard van Slyke. *Business Data Communications,* 2d ed. New York: Macmillian College Publishing Company, 1994, p. 34.

4. *Ibid.*

5. Keen, Peter G. W., and J. Michael Cummings. *Networks in Action.* Belmont, Calif.: Wadsworth Publishing Company, 1994, p. 202.

6. Ziegler, Bart. "Building the Highway: New Obstacles, New Solutions." *Wall Street Journal,* May 18, 1994, p. B1.

7. Hudson, Heather. *Satellite Communications.* New York: Free Press, 1990.

8. Owens, Cynthia. "The Developing Leap." *Wall Street Journal,* Feb. 11, 1994, p. R15.

9. Branscomb, Anne Wells. *Who Owns Information: From Privacy to Public Access.* New York: Basic Books, 1994, p. 176.

10. "Court Blocks Caller ID." *New York Times.* Mar. 23, 1992, p. C8.

11. Time Warner. 1992 Annual Report.

12. Verify, John W., Peter Coy, and Jeffrey Rothfeder. "Taming the Wild Network." *Business Week,* Oct. 8, 1990, pp. 142–148.

13. Darrow, Barbara. "Wireless Connectivity Networking Comes of Age." *InfoWorld,* Feb. 12, 1990, p. 38.

14. Huber, Peter. "The Lessons of AT&T's Cellular Move." *Wall Street Journal,* Sept. 7, 1993, p. A14.

15. Naik, Gautam. "Hurdle Cleared in Rochester, N.Y., Plan for Wide Cable-TV Phone Competition." *Wall Street Journal,* May 18, 1994, p. B5.

16. Pollack, Andrew. "Japan Considers Creating An Optical Fiber Network." *New York Times,* June 2, 1994, p. C1.

17. Lewyn, Mark. "Airwaves for Sale: Contact Bill Clinton." *Business Week,* May 10, 1993, p. 37.

18. Pearl, Daniel. "Debate Over Universal Access Rights Will Shape Rules Governing the Future of Communications." *Wall Street Journal,* Jan. 14, 1994, p.A12.

19. Branscomb, *op. cit.,* p. 176.

20. Betts, Mitch. "Subscriber Privacy for Sale." *Computerworld,* Oct. 10, 1994, p. 149.

21. Arnst, Catherine. "The Global Free-For-All." *Business Week,* Sept. 26, 1994, pp. 118–126.

12

Steps Toward Computer Intelligence: Making Systems "Smarter"

Study Questions

▶ Why are expert systems and neural networks important for businesses?

▶ What is the relationship between artificial intelligence (AI) and systems such as expert systems and neural networks?

▶ When are expert systems useful?

▶ What are the components of an expert system?

▶ How do neural networks operate?

▶ What additional techniques related to AI are beginning to attain prominence?

▶ Why is it difficult to get a computer to understand a story for a four-year-old?

Like other credit card companies, American Express requires that merchants receive an authorization before accepting a card for a purchase. Granting credit that should be denied results in annual losses of several hundred million dollars. Incorrectly denying credit reduces sales commissions and annoys customers who choose the American Express card to avoid having a preset credit limit.

Credit requests go from a merchant to an authorization center. Most requests can be granted automatically through a computerized system that uses statistical criteria to detect unusual activity on the card. The 5 percent of requests that require direct human attention go to credit agents who have 90 seconds to make a decision (the response time guaranteed by American Express). Prior to 1988, the agents had to decide by quickly looking at information in up to 12 different databases.

American Express implemented an expert system called the Authorizer's Assistant to improve the authorization process. (An expert system is an information system that supports or automates decision making in well-defined situations requiring expert knowledge.) The Authorizer's Assistant analyzes the 5 percent of requests requiring human attention, using over 800 rules to simulate the decision process of experienced credit agents. Within 4 seconds, the agent sees a recommendation plus an explanation of the reasoning behind it. The remaining 86 seconds is available to think about the situation and ask any necessary questions. The system has increased credit agents' productivity by 20 percent, recommended 33 percent fewer credit denials, and improved the accuracy of predictions of credit and fraud losses.[1, 2] Although the Authorizer's Assistant is widely cited, it is only one part of a large business process that includes a large-scale transaction processing system for receiving credit requests from merchants, processing those requests, and transmitting the approval or denial back to the merchant.

DEBATE TOPIC   *Argue the pros and cons and practical implications of the following proposition:*
Although this system demonstrates a modicum of intelligence by the way it uses information, it is not as intelligent as any alternative system that would provide positive identification of the card holder.

THE AUTHORIZER'S ASSISTANT IS PARTLY BASED on ideas from research about artificial intelligence (AI), a controversial and ill-defined area of computer science. Although people have dreamt of machine intelligence for centuries, the term *artificial intelligence* first achieved prominence at a small conference of AI pioneers at Dartmouth in 1956. **Artificial intelligence** is the field of research related to the demonstration of intelligence

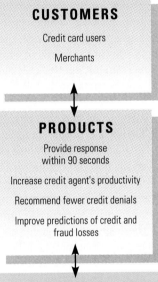
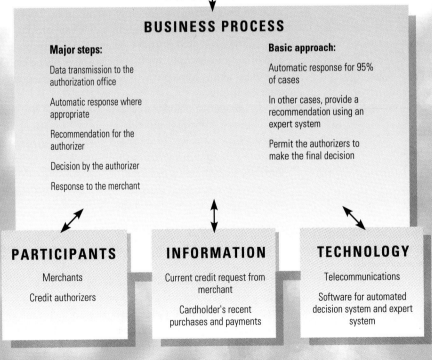

Figure 12.1 American Express: A Computerized Assistant for Credit Agents

CUSTOMERS

Credit card users

Merchants

PRODUCTS

Provide response within 90 seconds

Increase credit agent's productivity

Recommend fewer credit denials

Improve predictions of credit and fraud losses

BUSINESS PROCESS

Major steps:

Data transmission to the authorization office

Automatic response where appropriate

Recommendation for the authorizer

Decision by the authorizer

Response to the merchant

Basic approach:

Automatic response for 95% of cases

In other cases, provide a recommendation using an expert system

Permit the authorizers to make the final decision

PARTICIPANTS

Merchants

Credit authorizers

INFORMATION

Current credit request from merchant

Cardholder's recent purchases and payments

TECHNOLOGY

Telecommunications

Software for automated decision system and expert system

by machines. This includes, but is not limited to, the ability to think, see, learn, understand, and use common sense. The controversy about AI concerns whether it is possible for machines to do these things, regardless of whether they can execute predefined programs.

Presenting the Authorizer's Assistant as a component of a larger system is consistent with the view of most developers of real-world expert systems. In a 1994 article, the CEO and president of Teknowledge noted that, "Practical experience has made it clear that KBS [knowledge-based systems] are rarely more than 20% of a complete solution to real-world problems."[3]

The usefulness of systems like the Authorizer's Assistant shows why business professionals care about artificial intelligence. They want to improve business results by improving business processes; they want to maximize benefits from the firm's information and knowledge; they want people to use the firm's best knowledge even if it resides in the heads of a few experts; they want new members of the organization to become productive quickly; and they want to make sure knowledge will not disappear when experts move to other jobs.

These goals are sometimes obscured because the general topic of machine intelligence has spawned a great deal of hype, confusion, and speculation. As illustrated in Figure 12.2, people sometimes exaggerate computer intelligence and think of computers as gigantic brains. People often say a computer "knows" something, when they really mean that the computer program has access to that information. People often give undeserved credit or blame to computers, almost assuming that the computer took responsibility for something that happened in business or government. And people often use the terms *smart* or *intelligent* to describe computer systems even though these systems don't come close to showing many types of intelligence that the least intelligent human employee shows every day.

Business professionals need to understand something about AI because they may find opportunities to apply techniques developed from AI research and because they need a realistic understanding of what computers can and cannot do. Accordingly, this chapter has two primary goals: (1) to introduce expert systems, neural networks, and other successfully applied techniques based on ideas from AI research, and (2) to use ideas about AI as a way to explain both the power and the limitations of computerized systems.

A single issue about machine intelligence reappears in different guises throughout the chapter. Although we can program machines to perform impressively complex procedures in particular areas of knowledge, our present understanding of intelligence is the fundamental factor limiting current attempts to create machine intelligence. Particularly difficult areas include interpreting ambiguous or incomplete information and executing or suggesting appropriate actions that cannot be determined using prespecified formulas or procedures.

Applying Expert Systems to Use Knowledge More Effectively

An **expert system** is an information system that supports or automates decision making in an area where recognized experts do better than nonexperts. Expert systems do this by storing and using expert knowledge about a limited topic, such as authorizing credit or analyzing machine vibrations. These systems produce conclusions based on data they receive. They are used either as interactive advisors or as independent systems for converting data into recommendations or other conclusions. A system that performs calculations the same way that anyone would do them is not an expert system. For

Figure 12.2 Images and Dreams of Machine Intelligence

The two pictures illustrate some of the questions underlying this chapter: What does artificial intelligence mean, and what are its current limits?
(a) People sometimes think of computers as giant brains. Election day 1952 was one of the first situations in which computer intelligence was widely reported. Hours before the newscasters were willing to predict the outcome, a computer projected that Eisenhower would win. This was publicized as a demonstration of computer intelligence even though the projection was based on statistical formulas that are covered in undergraduate statistics courses today and can be used on any personal computer. (b) People may subconsciously believe part of the dream of humanlike robots. This dream may inspire an image of computers that fuels some of the confusion about what computers can do today.

example, a computer program that converts Fahrenheit temperatures to Centigrade temperatures is not considered an expert system.

The first expert systems were developed in the 1970s as part of AI research about developing ways for computers to "understand" situations in order to translate between languages and respond to queries from people. That research did not achieve its direct objectives, but spawned techniques that were applied to many business problems within a decade.

By now, thousands of expert systems have been used successfully. Du Pont's 600 small expert systems saved $75 million per year. Digital Equipment Corporation's 50 major expert systems contributed $200 million in annual savings.[4] Box 12.1 identifies a number of important expert systems, some of which are mentioned elsewhere in this book to illustrate various ways to improve decision making, execution, or competitive position. Table 12.1 lists some of the different types of problems for which expert systems have been used.

Table 12.1 Types of Problems Addressed by Expert Systems

Problem Type [5]	Examples
Interpretation	• Determining molecular structure from technical data • Helping geologists understand seismic data for oil prospecting • Interpreting text messages in funds transfer systems
Prediction	• Predicting abnormal conditions in a blast furnace • Predicting how long it will take to construct a building • Predicting when armed conflicts will occur
Diagnosis	• Finding faulty components of computer systems • Diagnosing medical problems • Helping analyze coal mine disasters to find trapped miners
Design	• Designing cooling systems in cars • Designing the paper path in copy machines • Designing new molecules
Planning	• Creating personal financial plans • Developing plans for discharging and loading container ships • Developing television advertising campaigns
Monitoring	• Identifying excess charges by physicians • Identifying suspicious money transfers • Continuous monitoring of signals from space vehicles
Debugging	• Analyzing problems with oil well operations • Helping mechanics identify problems with automobiles • Finding faults in telephone networks
Instruction	• Training technicians to repair computer disks • Training space shuttle flight controllers • Providing advice to taxpayers about tax rules
Control	• Controlling the operation of desalinization plants • Controlling throughput in semiconductor plants • Making sure all paperwork is complete in real estate contracts

Current expert systems are often built using commercial software products called **expert system shells.** Similar to special-purpose software in other areas, they make it more efficient to create expert systems. They do this by providing preprogrammed modules for entering rules and data, performing calculations, and presenting information to users.

Expert systems are often called **knowledge-based systems** because they represent knowledge in an explicit form so that it can be used in a problem-solving process. Knowledge is a combination of instincts, ideas, rules, and procedures that guide actions and decisions. In this sense, a person may remember a lot of facts or a database may contain a lot of facts without having much knowledge.

Many expert systems represent knowledge in the form of **if–then rules** stated in the form: *If* certain conditions are true, *then* certain conclusions should be drawn. An example of an if–then rule that might appear in an expert system for loan analysis is:

If: The applicant is current on all debts, and the applicant has been profitable
for two years, and the applicant has strong market position,
Then: The applicant is an excellent credit risk.

A rule such as this would be used as part of the analysis of whether to grant a loan. The expert system might use several approaches for determining whether each of the three conditions is true. It might find the answer in a database or use data from the database plus other rules to conclude that the applicant is current on all debts. It might ask the user a direct question such as, "Is the applicant current on all debts?" It might also ask the user questions and use other rules to conclude that the applicant is current on all debts. Regardless of how it found the data required by this if–then rule, the rule would be part of the knowledge that it uses systematically to support a decision process.

Like a human expert working on a problem, an expert system uses knowledge to draw interim conclusions based on whatever incomplete information is currently available about the situation. When it cannot reach a conclusion, it uses the knowledge to figure out what questions to ask or what information to retrieve in order to make more progress. In many situations, the expert system has enough information to draw partial conclusions but may not have enough information to resolve the situation completely. This is typical of what happens with human experts such as oil prospectors, advertising consultants, and doctors. Unlike human experts, however, expert systems do not truly understand the data and knowledge they are manipulating. This is why it is risky to trust expert systems to make decisions independently.

Expert systems can play several different roles in a decision process. In an idealized expert system, the user and expert system engage in a dialogue during which the expert system structures an analysis of the situation and drives toward a conclusion. The expert system serves as an assistant to a human decision maker rather than as a replacement. The role of the assistant is to provide suggestions, ensure that all typically salient factors have been considered, and keep track of how intermediate conclusions were reached. This form of expert system usage doesn't apply to all expert systems, however. The chapter opening American Express case and the Digital Equipment Corporation example in Box 12.1 involve little or no user interaction and use hundreds or thousands of rules to analyze data in an existing database. Others, such as a factory management systems built by IBM, operate as part of real-time control systems. They obtain their data from a real-time database and must respond so quickly that extensive user interaction is infeasible.

Although there are many impressive success stories about expert systems, don't be misled. For every widely reported success, there are probably many unpublicized expert system projects that fail because of poor problem selection, lack of necessary knowledge, fear or lack of interest by experts, and other technical or organizational problems.

Purposes of Expert Systems

There are many potential reasons for building expert systems, including recording and disseminating expert knowledge; ensuring consistent, accurate, and complete problem solving; and helping rookies learn new jobs. Early expert systems in the 1970s were built partially to solve a problem and partially to do research about expert system techniques. A key issue in this research was to try to capture knowledge in an active form, rather than in a passive form, as it would exist in a book. Dendral and MYCIN are well-known examples of this research. Dendral was developed to analyze molecular structures using outputs of mass spectrometers, devices that record a spectrum of frequencies by vaporizing a sample of the unknown molecule. After years of development effort, Dendral could analyze mass spectrometer outputs as well as an expert chemist. MYCIN was developed for diagnosing and treating infectious blood diseases. In several tests, it performed as well as experienced doctors in diagnosing these diseases.

Box 12.1 Expert Systems with Major Impacts

A number of expert systems are listed here along with the benefits they provide.

Campbell's Soup developed an expert system to capture the knowledge of a long-time plant engineer who was about to retire. He was the company's best expert on soup sterilizers. The system preserved some of his knowledge in a form in which it could be used by other engineers. Months of work led to an interactive expert system containing 151 rules for diagnosing problems and recommending specific solutions. The difference between the readily available data in this situation and the knowledge needed to use that data reinforces the difference between data, information, and knowledge.

Digital Equipment Corporation developed an expert system called XCON to ensure that properly configured computers were shipped for installation at customer sites. Starting with a customer order and configuration guidelines, XCON adds or deletes components necessary to make the order complete and correct. It eventually grew to 10,000 rules, 40 percent of which changed each year. Based on previous configuration error rates and increases in order levels, this system saved $40 million per year. This is an example of using an expert system to improve execution of a repetitive task.

Coopers & Lybrand, a leading accounting firm, developed an expert system called ExperTAX^sm to help relatively junior auditors work with small-to medium-sized client firms on tax planning. This analysis uncovers decisions that will affect the client's tax liability for the year. Later, a senior auditor prepares a written report making recommendations about the issues uncovered. Although it uses over 3,000 rules to help identify issues needing clarification, ExperTAX leaves the final recommendations to human experts.

N. L. Baroid, a supplier of drilling mud used in oil wells, developed an expert system to help customers decide how to adjust the drilling mud used in specific sites. The muds are pumped into wells to lubricate the drilling process and carry away rock shavings. The system helps the customers avoid expensive mistakes. This is an example of using an information system to differentiate what is otherwise a commodity product.

Many expert systems have been developed to record and disseminate the knowledge of recognized experts. The Campbell's Soup and Coopers & Lybrand examples mentioned in Box 12.1 served this purpose. Recording experts' knowledge allows the use of knowledge even when the experts aren't available. This can be especially significant in preventing the loss of their knowledge when they eventually change jobs or leave the organization.

Many other expert systems are built to ensure consistency in problem solving, to ensure that a situation is analyzed thoroughly, or to ensure that all appropriate procedures have been followed. The Digital Equipment Corporation system mentioned in Box 12.1 has over 10,000 rules. Such systems attempt to protect against human shortcomings such as fatigue, selective attention, sloppiness, and limited ability to process and remember information.

Other reasons for building expert systems are to help people new to a job learn how to do the job correctly and to prevent them from making serious omissions or errors of judgment while they are still novices. By codifying the organization's work practices, expert systems help rookies and more experienced individuals avoid oversights and errors.

When Are Expert Systems Useful?

Expert systems have been used in a wide range of applications. These go from complex analytical tasks such as interpreting seismic data to procedure-oriented tasks such as making sure that the right paperwork goes out with an order or contract (see Table 12.1). Despite the breadth of possibilities, the characteristics that determine whether it is practical to build an expert system in a situation are the availability of knowledge and the nature of the task (see Table 12.2).

Table 12.2 When Expert Systems Are Applicable?

Nature of the task	• Experts can do better than nonexperts. • The task involves reasoning and knowledge, not intuition or reflexes. • The task can be done by a person in minutes or hours. • The task is concrete enough to codify. • The task is commonly taught to novices in the area.
Availability of knowledge	• Recognized experts exist. • There is general agreement among experts. • Experts are able and willing to articulate the way they approach problems.

Expert systems are worth building only if experts perform the task better than nonexperts. They can be built successfully only where recognized experts exist. These experts must be willing to work with knowledge engineers to create the knowledge base and must be able to articulate the rules. Since the development of an expert system requires many iterations and is time consuming, lack of a committed expert reduces the chances of success. The practicalities of using expert systems also require reasonable agreement about the knowledge itself.

Expert systems are applicable for tasks performed based on reasoning and knowledge rather than intuition or reflex. Playing basketball or driving a race car therefore wouldn't be good problems for using an expert system. Expert systems work best for tasks performed by a person in a time span ranging from a few minutes to a few hours. It may not be worthwhile to build expert systems for tasks taking less time; tasks that take longer are probably too complicated for this approach to succeed today. Expert systems also have a better chance for success when used for tasks that are routinely taught to novices. Such tasks are concrete enough to codify based on rules that use specific information.

Current expert systems cannot exercise common sense. **Common sense** is a general shared understanding of how things work in everyday life. For example, an expert system for designing buildings might contain many rules about the structure and function of buildings but might not include a rule about not placing a building in the middle of a road. This might seem so obvious to anyone in our society that no one would think of including it in an expert system. And if the expert system designer did try to include all conceivably relevant common sense knowledge, the expert system would become unmanageably huge.

Because they lack common sense and because they don't really understand the rules they use, expert systems don't recognize when they have reached the limits of what they "know." Unlike people, they also don't know how to break rules when it is necessary to do so. With these limitations, expert systems should be used only for the parts of tasks that can be described in terms of information and rules and that require no common sense. Except in problems that are totally understood, appropriate uses of expert systems divide responsibilities between the expert system and a person. The person is responsible for making the decision and exercising common sense. The expert system structures the analysis, makes sure that important factors haven't been ignored, and provides information that helps the person make a good decision.

By trying to capture and use the knowledge of experts, expert systems attempt to do something that may seem extraordinary compared to what other systems try to do. Expert systems use rules or other knowledge representations to draw conclusions and interact with users. The next sections look at ways to represent knowledge and ways expert systems use this knowledge.

Representing Knowledge

Representing knowledge and creating ways for computers to use knowledge remains a major research topic. Two of the many possible ways to represent knowledge are if–then rules and frames. If–then rules focus on the logic of making inferences. Frames focus on the important characteristics of situations.

If–then rules

 If–then rules are the most common way to represent knowledge in knowledge-based systems. Such rules are rules stated in the form: If certain conditions are true, then certain conclusions should be drawn. The rules in many knowledge-based systems are steeped in the jargon of the particular area of knowledge. Consider the following rule from MYCIN, a knowledge-based system for assisting in diagnosing infectious diseases:[6]

> If: The stain of the organism is grampos, and the morphology of the organism
>   is coccus, and the growth conformation of the organism is chains,
> Then: There is suggestive evidence (0.7) that the identity of the organism is
>   streptococcus.

In addition to containing conditions and conclusions, this rule from MYCIN contains a certainty factor (0.7), indicating that the conclusion is likely but uncertain. Knowledge-based systems for assisting experts often include uncertainty of this type because uncertainty is inherent in much of the work experts do.

A knowledge-based system that uses if–then rules starts with a list of facts about a particular situation. It uses rules to draw conclusions or take actions based on these facts. These conclusions or actions create other facts. These additional facts are added to the list of current facts, and the system continues using the rules to draw additional conclusions or take additional actions. Some systems also use the facts and rules to decide what additional questions to ask. For example, a medical diagnosis system might look at its current set of facts, draw a tentative conclusion, and ask additional questions that would confirm or disconfirm that conclusion.

Knowledge-based systems that use if–then rules have been applied to a wide range of diagnosis, planning, and analytical tasks. They have been used in business situations from factory production and medical diagnosis to oil drilling and real estate sales. Despite the wide range of applications, all practical systems to date have one thing in common: They focus on a limited area of knowledge, such as the maintenance of boilers or procedures for granting credit.

The second type of knowledge representation we will look at is frames, which organize the information about a situation to make sense of it and to identify any unexpected features that are present.

Frames

Frames provide a way to organize data about specific situations. When you walk into a room, your mind somehow processes the visual data it receives almost instantaneously, compares this to what it expects or believes, and identifies what it must attend to. Your expectations are different in different types of rooms. When you walk into a kitchen, you expect to see a refrigerator, stove, sink, and cabinets. When you walk into a personal office, you expect to see a desk, chairs, a bookcase or bookshelf, perhaps a computer, and possibly some pictures on the wall. You don't expect to see a stove or refrigerator in an office although either might be there in some form in some offices.

As shown in Table 12.3, a **frame** is a data structure for representing a specific entity, such as a concept, item, or class. The frame consists of slots that identify the attributes for that particular kind of entity. Table 12.3 shows a frame for an office. The frame's slots identify the important attributes of an office. Each slot has an entry or value for each specific attribute being considered. For example, Table 12.3 shows that Fred Harwood's office has a northern exposure and two file cabinets. The data in a frame can be used to identify which aspects of a situation are pertinent, to organize the data, and to identify surprises. For example, the table shows how the frame has helped identify the surprising observation that the office has no telephone. Any of the slots in a frame could have default (typical) values or references to other frames.

Table 12.3 Frame for Fred Harwood's Office

Slot	Entry
Owner	Fred Harwood
Location	Atkins Building, 1488 Main Street
Window exposure	Northern
Desk	Large, wooden, in middle of room
Chairs	One desk chair, two side chairs
Bookcase	One large built-in bookcase opposite the window
Books	Mostly about marketing and management
File cabinet	Two tan four-drawer file cabinets, mismatched in color
Computer	One IBM PC with large screen
Telephone	None
Pictures	Child's drawing plus several prints

Although less commonly used than if–then rules, frames have been used in some knowledge-based systems. The Coopers & Lybrand system mentioned in Box 12.1 uses a combination of frames and rules to identify situations and important tax planning information. Another expert system that uses frames is the Gate Assignment and Display System (GADS) developed by United Airlines to help gate controllers reassign incoming airplanes to gates at airports when planes arrive. Before GADS, the gate controllers moved magnetic pieces around on a wall-sized scheduling board to try out alternative assignments. Now they use individual computer displays to visualize the assignments of planes to gates and use a mouse to try out alternatives long before traffic problems develop. GADS handles the routine mechanics of gate assignments and lets the gate controller concentrate on the problems that crop up when assignments must be changed due to delays and other problems.

Other forms of knowledge representation have been proposed and used in research. For our purposes, if–then rules and frames suffice. The main point is that there must be some way to represent knowledge in order to use it in knowledge-based systems. The next question is how an expert system actually uses the knowledge as part of a problem–solving process.

Components and Operation of Expert Systems

Although real expert systems are customized to the needs of a particular situation, Figure 12.3 presents a common idealization of how expert system components interact. This section describes each of the components and summarizes the types of reasoning expert systems perform.

Components

The five major components of an expert system are the knowledge base, database, inference engine, interface, and explanation module. The **knowledge base** is a set of facts and if–then rules supplied by an expert. A consultant who helps the expert produce the knowledge base is often called a **knowledge engineer.** Knowledge engineers must

Figure 12.3 Basic Components of an Expert System

An idealized expert system can be described in terms of five components.

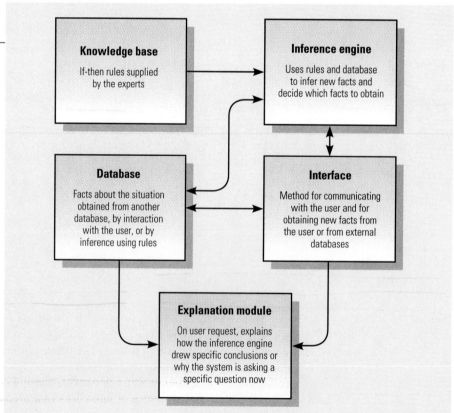

understand both the process of getting experts to explain how they analyze situations and the logic by which expert systems operate internally. Knowledge engineers may or may not start a project knowing much about the subject matter covered by the expert system. The knowledge engineer's job is to work with the expert through a series of iterations aimed at developing the if–then rules in the system. This process starts by understanding the factors generally considered in making decisions of the type being analyzed. It eventually produces a fine-tuned set of rules along with the preferred sequence for using these rules.

The *database* of facts may start as a blank slate each time the system is used or may begin with data that were gathered previously. For example, American Express's Authorizer's Assistant uses its database to retrieve all recent credit card charges by a customer as the starting point for its analysis of whether to approve the purchase. While analyzing a situation, many expert systems obtain additional facts by asking questions to the user or by querying other databases. For example, expert systems assisting in medical diagnosis may ask the doctor about particular conditions that would confirm or rule out possible diagnoses.

The **inference engine** uses rules in the knowledge base plus whatever facts are currently in the database to decide what question to ask next, either to the user or to other databases. Which questions are asked next depends on the current goal of the inference engine. For example, if the inference engine has identified five different facts that all must be true in order to confirm the current working hypothesis, it may ask those five questions in turn. If one of the responses is negative, the inference engine may then abandon the current line of reasoning in favor of a more promising one.

The *interface* is the way the expert system interacts with the user. The user interface may operate as a set of text questions and answers, or it may be highly graphical if more effort is put in to make the interface easier to use. Figure 12.4 shows the user interface of the GADS system mentioned in the discussion of frames.

Figure 12.4 User Interface of an Expert System Used at Airports

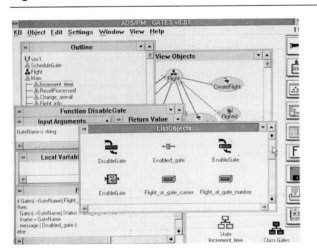
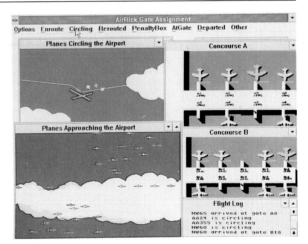

The **explanation module** is available to the user as a way to find out how a particular fact was inferred or why a particular question is being asked. The explanation either confirms the sequence of inferences that produced a conclusion or explains how a question may eventually lead to a conclusion.

Contrary to the idealized illustration in Figure 12.3, many systems that are often considered expert systems don't contain all these components. For example, some expert systems don't contain an interactive interface for carrying on a dialogue with the user. Other expert systems don't have an explanation module but are still considered expert systems because they use knowledge to derive a conclusion.

How expert systems perform reasoning

Understanding expert system reasoning processes helps visualize where and how these systems can be applied. As illustrated in Figure 12.5, the two main types of reasoning in expert systems proceed in opposite directions and are called forward chaining and backward chaining. In any particular situation, an expert system might use forward chaining and backward chaining in combination.

Figure 12.5 Forward Chaining versus Backward Chaining

An emergency room physician examines a 3-year-old injured in an automobile accident. The child has a bump on his head, has vomited, and seems disoriented. Although the physician would immediatley decide to perform tests to rule out a brain hemorrhage, an expert system might go through intermediate forward chaining steps.

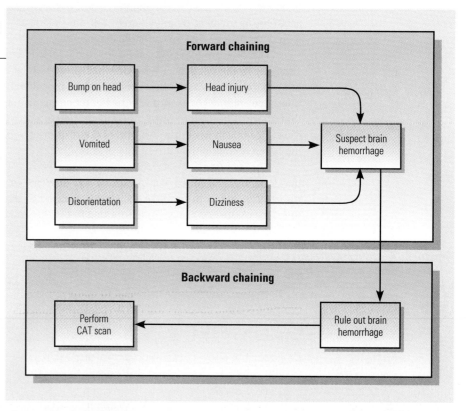

An expert system using **forward chaining** starts with data and tries to draw conclusions from the data. Forward chaining is often used when there is no clear goal and the system is just attempting to determine all the conclusions implied by the data. For example, the expert system Dendral uses forward chaining to identify all possible compounds that conform to data from mass spectrographs.

An expert system using **backward chaining** starts with a tentative conclusion and then looks for facts in the database that support that conclusion. As part of backward chaining, the expert system may identify facts that would confirm or deny the conclusion and then look up these facts in a database or ask the user questions related to these facts. Backward chaining is used when an expert system has a specific goal, such as ruling out hepatitis as a possible diagnosis or deciding whether a business applying for a loan has a strong balance sheet.

Controlling the order in which rules are used and questions are asked to the user is a key design issue in building expert systems. Imagine a medical expert system that has thousands of rules about medicine but starts with no facts about a patient. If the system asks questions in an arbitrary order, it could pose an enormous number of questions. Doctors avoid this problem by asking only those questions that are likely to affect diagnosis and treatment in the situation at hand. They ask those questions in an economical way by starting with broad screening questions. For example, determining that a patient has never had a heart problem can rule out an entire line of questions.

A doctor's typical analysis process is a combination of forward and backward chaining. The doctor starts with a brief medical history and draws some tentative conclusions, such as the hypothesis that the patient might have a particular disease. The doctor then uses backward chaining to confirm or deny this hypothesis. The doctor obtains the necessary information by asking questions, performing physical examinations, or obtaining laboratory results.

The need to combine forward and backward chaining and the need to control the order of the analysis implies that inference engines must be customized to the logic of particular problem areas. Expert systems differ in this regard from mathematical optimization techniques such as linear programming, which can solve a wide range of problems that share the same structure.

Treatment of uncertainty

The knowledge in many situations involves probabilities rather than certainties. For example, a set of symptoms including severe pain in the lower right side of the abdomen point to a diagnosis of appendicitis. However, these same symptoms are sometimes caused by other medical problems. In the same way, the results of a seismic survey for oil can be related to many different types of underground formations. To handle situations such as this, the expert system must be able to draw conclusions about the relative likelihood of different conclusions based on the facts. The likelihood of alternative conclusions is crucial in many situations. Consider a case in which the symptoms could suggest either a bad cold or meningitis. A diagnosis with probabilities of 70 and 0.00001 percent, respectively, is different from a diagnosis with probabilities of 70 and 15 percent. In the latter case, the doctor might well prescribe drugs for meningitis because the risk and consequences of making a mistake are too great, even if a bad cold is the most likely illness.

The treatment of uncertainty in expert systems raises many issues, starting with how to describe uncertainty. Many expert systems use **certainty factors** that describe the likelihood of a rule's conclusion given that its premises are true. For example, if certainty factors go from 0 to 1 in a particular system, a certainty factor of 0.5 on a rule would say that the conclusion is true about half the time.

The difficulty in using certainty factors is in combining the certainty factors from separate inferences. For example, consider a situation in which symptom A is linked to meningitis 45 percent of the time, and symptom B is linked to meningitis 75 percent of the time. If both A and B are observed, what is the probability of meningitis? In some cases, the two symptoms might be independent; in others, they might be mutually reinforcing; in yet others, they might be somewhat contradictory. The handling of uncertainty is a difficult challenge because there are no foolproof ways of combining certainty factors.

Are Expert Systems Equivalent to Human Experts?

The term *expert system* sets the expectation that a computer system will operate as well as a human expert. Whether or not this is realistic depends on the difference between what a human expert can do and what an expert system can do.

Comparing human experts with expert systems

Although expert systems can mimic human experts by solving problems and explaining the logic used to reach the solution, human experts have many characteristics that cannot be duplicated in expert systems today. Human experts learn by experience, restructure their knowledge, break the rules when necessary, determine the relevance of new facts, and recognize the limits of their knowledge. As human experts start encountering situations they are not familiar with, they understand they are approaching the limits of their expertise and become more cautious.[7] Although their performance usually degrades as they move into unfamiliar territory, human experts can perceive situations where the existing knowledge does not apply well and can decide what rules to break in order to solve a problem. They can apply common sense by noting that data is probably erroneous or that a particular rule or procedure was designed for one situation and doesn't really apply in another.

Expert systems have no way of showing this type of common sense and operate totally within the realm of the rules in their knowledge base and the facts they can obtain from a database or user. The only facts recognized by existing expert systems are the facts related to the "if" portions of the if–then rules in their knowledge base. Expert systems tend to either quit or make bad mistakes when they encounter situations not included in their knowledge base. It is possible to add new facts and new rules to an expert system, but each upgrade is like a program enhancement. A person must debug the revised system to ensure that the addition doesn't interfere with the rest of the system's logic.

Looking at how experts actually work

Even though expert systems are built based on rules provided by human experts, it is important to ask whether expert systems actually mimic what human experts do. Box 12.2 uses the example of learning to drive to illustrate a five-stage model of how people acquire and use knowledge. People start as novices and learn the rules and important features of the situation. Advanced novices begin to notice different types of situations and how to handle them. Competent individuals focus on achieving goals rather than executing rules. They can concentrate on pertinent aspects of a situation and ignore other aspects. Proficient individuals and experts recall many situations they have been involved in. Their knowledge is so ingrained that many of their actions and responses are automatic. Although the model works for many types of knowledge, it fits less well in situations that involve complex reasoning instead of second-by-second performance.

The five-stage model was originally proposed to support the claim that real experts work in a totally different way than expert systems do. These differences would cast doubt on whether expert systems mimic experts. Notice how novices have to think about rules explicitly, whereas experts work with the accumulated knowledge of thousands of individual cases that they have experienced deeply. To verify whether this model makes sense, think about how you have mastered activities such as driving a car, playing tennis, writing a paper, or cooking a meal. In each case, you can probably identify a number of rules that you learned as a novice but that you rarely thought about once you became deeply involved with the activity.

Box 12.2 Five Stages of Becoming an Expert

In a critique of artificial intelligence and expert systems, Dreyfus and Dreyfus proposed a five-stage process of becoming an expert. They used the five-stage process to claim that expert systems operate more like advanced novices than like experts.[9]

Novice. As novices, people learn the important features of whatever is being mastered and learn the rules for doing things. They learn the features and rules explicitly and think about them when they practice. Novices often do not know which aspects of situations need attention and which are unimportant. Everything they do requires conscious attention as they learn to identify various aspects of the situation and think about how to respond. In the novice stage of learning to drive a car, the driver learns the rules and gets a feel for the response of the steering wheel and brakes.

Advanced novice. Advanced novices begin to notice different types of situations in which basic rules and skills must be mastered, such as driving in the rain or on a highway in fast-moving traffic. They begin to notice how to handle these situations. Advanced novices are still operating at a very conscious level.

Competent. People who are competent in an area know enough about the basic skills and common situations to identify important issues and have a plan for dealing with them. Competent individuals focus on pertinent aspects of the situation as they arise and ignore irrelevant aspects. A competent individual starts to make real choices and take risks and has an emotional involvement in what is happening. A competent driver has enough control to choose among alternative responses in unexpected driving situations.

Proficient. Proficient individuals exercise many of the skills in the area without a great deal of thought because these skills have been internalized. Where making a left turn in traffic might have required careful concentration for a novice, a proficient driver can make the left turn while having a conversation and thinking about something else. People become proficient as a result of working through many situations and receiving vivid feedback about their performance in those situations.

Expert. The expert's skills are sufficiently ingrained that an expert may not have to think very much when using these skills. In particular, an expert does not work based on explicit rules. Instead, an expert works according to an accumulated knowledge of thousands of individual cases that were experienced deeply.

This model also explains why experts may find it difficult to explain how they do their work. If the retiring plant engineer mentioned in Box 12.1 really analyzed soup sterilizers based on the ingrained experience of thousands of cases, he may not be aware of all the ideas he uses. The model also shows why the term *expert system* is a misnomer. What we call expert systems may actually be "advanced novice systems" or "competent systems."

Although the model raises issues about how people become experts and about why experts may have trouble explaining what they do, the issue about expert systems not mimicking experts is probably beside the point. For example, a robot for driving a car would need to respond to the same conditions that a human driver must respond to but might operate very differently from the way a human drives. It might drive a car successfully without knowing exactly what a human driver knows about driving. It also might acquire knowledge in a different way because special types of knowledge representation might be effective for computers, but not for people.

There is no question that expert systems have proved useful in many situations. There are even a few cases in which expert systems have been compared directly to humans performing the same task. For example, a system called Internist contained information about 500 diseases when its developers tested it using cases from the *New England Journal of Medicine*. On 43 diagnostic questions, Internist was right 25 times, physicians who had tended the patients were right 28 times, and clinical experts were right 35 times.[8] Performing nearly as well as physicians is a great accomplishment, even if the system could not match the clinical experts.

The general conclusion to date is that some expert systems perform as well as experts in limited knowledge domains, but most do not. However, many expert systems can provide important benefits if they perform at only a "competent" level and mainly help novices. Furthermore, in many situations such as codifying procedures and rules for performing business operations in a new way, there are no real experts because the situation is being invented. In such situations, it is still possible to use expert system technology to develop systems that control and improve business process performance.

R E A L I T Y   C H E C K   **What Can We Trust Expert Systems to Do?**   This section explained some of the strengths and weaknesses of expert systems. Use these ideas to consider the following:

1. You are a passenger on an airplane and have just learned that it will be landed automatically by an expert system. How would you feel about that? Why?

2. You are a pilot and have just learned that the airline plans to buy airplanes containing an expert system that controls takeoffs and landings. How would you feel about that? Why?

Applying Neural Networks to Recognize Patterns

A **neural network** is an information system that recognizes objects or patterns based on examples that have been used to train it. Each training example is described in terms of a number of characteristics, each of which is the input to a separate "neuron." The neural network combines these inputs in a way that distinguishes between different objects or patterns included in the training examples. Because they perform identification and discrimination tasks by giving numerical weights to many different characteristics, neural networks often operate well even if some information is missing. They are used for tasks that people can perform even though they cannot define formulas or procedures for performing these tasks. If a discrimination task could be performed using known procedures, there would be no reason to build a neural network.

To visualize the type of problem neural networks solve, consider the task of recognizing individuals based on physical appearance. People (and animals such as dogs) can do this readily, but it is hard to say how they do it. For example, people can usually recognize acquaintances even if part of their typical appearance is obscured because they are facing in different directions or are wearing sunglasses, hats, or heavy coats. Recognizing an individual involves much more than matching a few measurable characteristics such as height, shape, and coloring. Somehow our minds combine many different characteristics to recognize familiar individuals almost instantaneously even when some of the information is incomplete.

Although neural networks emerged from a branch of AI, they operate based on a totally different approach than expert systems. Expert systems rely on an expert's ability to capture knowledge in the form of a knowledge representation such as rules. In contrast, neural networks are built assuming that no such explicit knowledge exists. Instead, they use statistical techniques to "learn" how to recognize a particular type of pattern by combining the features from a set of training examples.

Neural networks were originally conceived as a way to study learning and intelligence. The idea of an evidence-weighing machine called a *perceptron* was invented by Frank Rosenblatt in 1959, but perceptrons went out of favor as a research area in the late 1960s. After several decades of relative neglect, neural networks are being applied in pattern-related recognition tasks, such as recognizing spoken words or predicting the likelihood of different outcomes based on many pertinent examples of past performance.

The term *neural network* comes from seeing these systems as models of how the human brain operates. Although scientists know which areas of the brain control vision, hearing, balance, and other functions, they are still trying to figure out how the human brain performs thinking. Understanding the brain is overwhelming because it consists of up to 100 billion cells called neurons, each of which is linked to 1,000 or more neurons. The artificial neural networks described here usually contain only tens or hundreds of neurons and are tiny compared with what we might imagine as the neural networks in the brain.

Operation of Neural Networks

Neural networks take many different forms. One common form contains three or more layers of nodes called neurons. These layers include:

- A layer of input nodes representing each of the inputs to the recognition task

- A layer of output nodes representing the particular objects or patterns being recognized

- One or more intermediate layers, usually called hidden layers, representing the associations between the input nodes and the output nodes

To visualize how neural networks operate, consider a simplified system for deciding whether to approve mortgage loans. As shown by Figure 12.6, loans are approved or denied based on applicant characteristics: years at the current address, years at the current job, the ratio of salary to the loan amount, health, and credit rating. The input layer contains a separate neuron for each characteristic. Each of these neurons is linked to each of 7 neurons in the hidden layer, and each of those neurons is linked to the 2 neurons in the output layer. In all, this neural network contains 14 nodes and 49 links. Each of the links has a numerical weighting represented in the picture by the thickness of the line. The stronger the relationship between two nodes, the stronger the weighting.

The neural network learns by adjusting these weightings based on examples. As a starting point, each of the weightings is assigned randomly. This means that some of the initial weightings may make sense, whereas others are totally wrong. Next the network receives a training example that includes the five input characteristics and whether the loan should have been approved or denied (based on whether a problem was ever observed in the payments for the actual loan). A mathematical procedure adjusts all the weights to minimize the error the network would have made. Then the network receives the next example and performs the adjustment again. In real cases, a network might have 1,000 examples, and the entire sequence might be repeated 50 times to make sure the weightings converge to the best representation of the data. In some ways, this process resembles how a child learns to speak by making sounds and gradually adjusting them into clearly pronounced words.

Figure 12.6 Using Neural Networks

The process of using neural networks starts by defining the network's structure. This is done by identifying the nodes in the input and output layers, creating the links to and from the hidden layer(s), and deciding on the mathematical technique that will be used for learning. The next steps are creating a starting point for its training, training it, and then using it.

Create a starting point for training: The starting point for the learning process is a neural network with random weights assigned to all the associations between the hidden layer and the input and output layers. Some of these initial weights may not make much sense since these initial values are an arbitrary starting point. They are eventually washed out by exposure to numerous repetitions of examples that contain the information the neural network is learning.

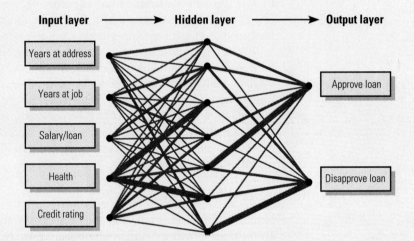

Adjust the weights based on each example: This step is repeated for every example in the training set. The mathematical techniques for modifying the weights (and hence, learning) involve changing the weights in a way that minimizes the overall error that would occur when all the examples thus far are considered. You can see that a number of the weights have changed. For example, the links emanating from *years at job* and *ratio of salary to loan* have increased in weight because these two variables must be strong indicators of good loans in the training set.

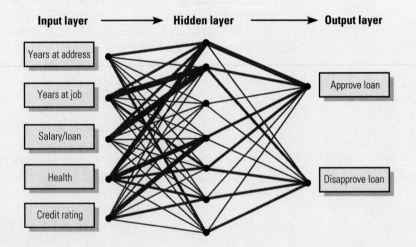

Use the neural network: Once the neural network is trained, it can be used for making decisions. If a loan application arrived from someone with long job tenure and a high ratio of salary to loan amount, this neural network would probably approve the loan.

In contrast to the hidden layer, the nodes in the input and output layers have an assigned meaning. The nodes in the hidden layer have no meaning in advance but make it possible for the neural network to absorb the patterns in the examples.

After the training, the neural network would be ready to assist in mortgage loan decisions. Whether it served as an advisor or actually made the decision would depend on the desired business process. Because it uses a weighting scheme involving many inputs, the neural network might give reasonably good results even for slightly novel examples, such as a combination of characteristics that had not been used in the training. The weighting process is also less sensitive to missing or inaccurate data than other types of classification schemes.

Applications of Neural Networks

The applications of neural networks are five or ten years behind the applications of expert systems. Nonetheless, neural networks have been applied in many business and research settings, such as predicting business failures, rating bonds, predicting stock prices, trading commodities, preventing fraud, generating forecasts, and generating near-optimal schedules and routings in manufacturing and transportation.[10] Neural networks are especially applicable in situations where a large database of examples is available and where even experts cannot give rules for combining a large number of inputs to recognize patterns.

Research on neural networks has yielded some impressive results. A neural network for converting text to speech was trained using around 1,000 words spoken by a child. After 50,000 presentations, it was able to speak words with around 95 percent accuracy. When presented with a 439-word continuation of the same child's text (including some novel words), it spoke with 78 percent accuracy. This showed that the neural network could generalize beyond the specific words it was trained with.[11] In another language-related research project, a neural network learned the past tense of verbs. Originally, it made mistakes like saying "bringed" instead of "brought" and "tooked" instead of "took." Eventually, it built up a set of links for irregular verbs and learned the past tense.

The impressive results are not limited to the research, however. Here are some of the application results obtained so far:[12,13]

- In an experiment, a neural network for analyzing electrocardiograms and other data in emergency rooms outperformed emergency room doctors. On 331 patients suffering from chest pain, the neural network recognized 35 of 36 heart attacks (97 percent) whereas the emergency room doctors identified 28 (78 percent).[14]

- Spiegel, Inc. uses a neural network to determine which customers should receive their catalogs. Spiegel's director of market research expects savings of $1 million per year.

- Mitsubishi Electric uses a neural network in refrigerators. It divides the day into two-hour blocks and records the frequency of door openings in each. Using a neural network to decide when to defrost, precool, and perform other functions has reduced temperature variations in food by 2.2°C.

- Siemens uses neural networks to predict failure of large induction motors, claiming the system achieves 80 to 90 percent prediction accuracy compared to 30 percent with previous techniques.

- Using a neural network between 1989 and 1993, the Fidelity Investments Stock Selector fund averaged 30 percent return, one and a half times that of the overall market.[15]

Neural networks have also been used in a number of military or militarylike applications involving the recognition of obscure patterns. One neural network seems to be better than humans at using sonar waves to recognize undersea mines on a rock-strewn ocean floor in shallow water.[16] A civilian application is the detection of plastic explosives in airplane luggage. Plastic explosives cannot be detected by x-rays but can be detected by a gamma-ray frequency distribution generated when the baggage is exposed to a beam of neutrons.

It appears likely that neural network applications will attain increasing importance in finance and many other areas. For a realistic understanding of what may happen, it is necessary to look at the limitations of neural networks.

Limitations of Neural Networks

Like expert systems, neural networks are applicable to certain types of tasks in certain types of situations. Their limitations are related to the need for experts, the need for a training database, vulnerability to training errors, and the necessity of focusing on a limited type of problem.

Need for experts. At first blush, a computerized system that learns automatically might seem like magic. Like expert systems, neural networks are not magic. Even though neural networks do not try to capture rules from experts, the people who set them up should be experts who understand the important factors in the problem area and the techniques for defining, training, and validating these systems. They must decide what factors to use as input nodes and output nodes, how to arrange the hidden layers, and what mathematical learning technique to use for adjusting the weights within the network. They must also gather a large set of representative training examples. The neural network's ultimate performance depends on how well it is designed and on how well the training examples capture the patterns the neural network is trying to learn.

Need for a representative training database. Neural nets are good for discrimination and generalization tasks where a large number of examples exist that define the things being studied. If the training database is too small or if it is not representative, the neural network will not "learn" how to perform its task properly.

Notice that learning through repetition, trial, and error is one of many ways that people learn things. Children learn language and reading this way. But an adult learning a second or third language may combine several different learning approaches. Instead of using only trial and error, he or she may learn the language's vocabulary and grammatical rules by memorizing patterns explained in a book. Notice also that people learn many things through single examples, such as not to touch a hot stove or not to do specific things that bother one's parents. Imagine what it would be like if people had to use 50,000 repetitions to learn things like that.

Vulnerability to training errors. The lack of explicit knowledge makes neural networks vulnerable to learning the wrong conclusions from training cases. For example, a prototype of a loan approval system often approved loans for applicants with low income and rejected loans for applicants with high income. The training data had contained a number of loans for which certain low-income individuals were good credit risks. The neural network's weighting scheme eventually treated low income as a favorable characteristic.[17]

Other aspects of the training data can cause problems. In one case, a neural network was trained to distinguish between tanks, rocks, and other battlefield objects. But all the pictures of the tanks had been taken with one camera and were slightly darker than the pictures of the other objects, which had been taken by another camera. The neural network had actually learned to distinguish between the cameras, not between tanks and other objects.[18]

People are also vulnerable to training errors, even from a single example. As happens when a child touches a hot stove, people are both able and extremely willing to classify and generalize based on just a few examples. Think of how we set up stereotypes in our minds, even as adults. For example, think how easy it is to conclude that people from Chicago are helpful after receiving one example of special help while in Chicago.

Necessity to focus on a limited type of problem. Like expert systems, neural networks are used in highly focused situations involving a limited problem area. For neural networks to be practical, the problem area must be defined in terms of a limited number of specific inputs and outputs. This implies that current neural networks cannot solve the kinds of broadly defined problems people solve in their everyday lives.

Neural networks approach AI from a totally different viewpoint than expert systems. Expert systems require that knowledge exists and can be recorded in a form such as rules or frames. Neural networks do not start with explicit knowledge about a problem domain, but instead learn to recognize patterns by adjusting the weights of associations between nodes. Although learning through experience is a plausible description of how people learn many things, current neural network computers with hundreds of "neurons" trained on thousands of presentations of examples are a far cry from human brains, which have billions of interconnected neurons and learn from many fewer separate presentations of examples. Both expert systems and neural networks are useful in important applications. How and whether either approach (or other approaches) will eventually mimic human intelligence remains to be seen.

REALITY CHECK **Vulnerability to Training Errors in Neural Networks** This section mentioned that neural networks are vulnerable to training errors but that people are also vulnerable because they establish stereotypes based on just a few examples.

1. Identify some of the stereotypes you have heard people talk about that are probably based on just a few examples that may be unrepresentative.

2. Explain whether you think it is healthy or unhealthy to form stereotypes this way. For example, is it unhealthy to conclude that ice is dangerous after slipping once or that people from Chicago are helpful after you were helped once?

Additional AI-Related Techniques

Fuzzy logic, case-based reasoning, and intelligent agents are three additional AI-related techniques that have important business applications. Fuzzy logic uses rules but assumes that the conditions and conclusions of rules are stated in an approximate way without forcing people to pretend their perceptions and beliefs are unrealistically precise. Case-based reasoning provides guidance to decision makers by searching a database of past cases and displaying previous cases most similar to the current case. Intelligent agents permit a user to create an automatic process that operates in the background to find information or create danger warnings while other foreground processes are taking place.

Fuzzy Logic

Fuzzy logic addresses a problem that occurs in expert systems and in many types of precise, formal reasoning. One of the expert system rules cited earlier included the condition "if the applicant has been profitable for two years." The problem with performing detailed reasoning based on this type of condition is that it permits only two states, making it either true or false that the applicant has been profitable for two years. For example, this rule would treat a large company with $1 profit differently from the way it would treat the same company with a $1 loss. A trivial distinction might result in a large difference in the decision. To avoid this type of problem, the reasoning could use a richer set of conditions, such as being very profitable, somewhat profitable, slightly profitable, slightly unprofitable, and so on. Furthermore, it could treat adjacent conditions as though they overlapped to some degree. For example, instead of forcing a precise cutoff between "somewhat profitable" and "slightly profitable," the reasoning system could treat these categories as somewhat overlapping, thereby reasoning in manner similar to the way a person would reason. Better decisions might result from recognizing a range of conditions for the relevant factors and doing the analysis using logic based on shades of inclusion rather than just either–or categories.

 Fuzzy logic is a form of reasoning that makes it possible to combine conditions stated in an imprecise form similar to the way people think about many things. The term *fuzzy logic* was coined in 1964 by Lofti Zadeh, a professor at Berkeley. The basic idea of fuzzy logic is to describe characteristics as a range of values rather than a point value and then to have a good way to combine rules that use these ranges of values.

Figure 12.7 shows that fuzzy logic makes it unnecessary to describe a variable such as temperature using mutually exclusive categories, such as cool versus cold. Instead, a temperature might have some degree of membership in coldness and some degree of membership in coolness. With fuzzy logic, it is not necessary to state rules as though coldness and coolness are mutually exclusive. Instead, a rule about coolness can apply at the same time a rule about coldness or another characteristic applies. The fuzzy controller comes to a decision by combining all the rules based on the relative degree of coldness, coolness, and other characteristics. This type of logic avoids artificial cutoffs and state transitions that make control using either–or rules difficult.

A famous fuzzy logic application is the controller of the subway in Sendai, Japan. This controller was built by observing the factors a human brakesman used to control the train using a manual brake. A key breakthrough in developing the system was the realization that the human brakesman knew the route and therefore began to apply the brake before the subway came to a downhill section. Eventually, the controller could control the trains so precisely that people standing on the train do not need to hold straps when the train starts or stops.

Fuzzy logic has also been used effectively in many Japanese home appliances such as washing machines and vacuum cleaners and consumer electronics items such as video cameras. Matsushita's fuzzy washing machines use sensors and fuzzy rules to automatically adjust the wash cycle to the kind and amount of dirt (muddy or oily) in the wash water and the size of the load.[19] The applications in video cameras include automatic focusing, automatic exposure, automatic white balancing, and image stabilization. The autofocus technique reduces the amount of time needed to hunt for the right focus by using 13 rules, such as "If the sharpness is high and its differential is low, then the focus motor speed is low." The image stabilization detects unwanted movements caused by bumping and bouncing of platforms and jitters caused by shaking hands, and then corrects the shaken image as much as possible.[20]

Figure 12.7 Example of Fuzzy Variables, Fuzzy Rules, and How They Are Combined

Instead of saying that 72° is either comfortable or warm, the fuzzy membership function shown here says that 72° gives a comfortableness rating of about 0.7 and a warmness rating of about 0.5.

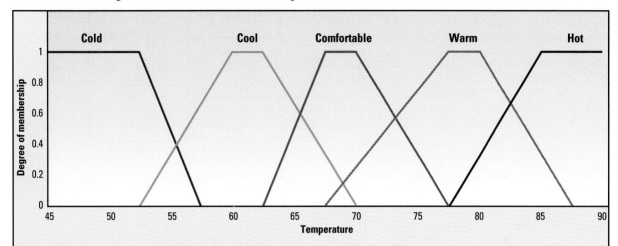

If an air conditioner were based on crisp rules, it would have to decide whether the current temperature was comfortable or warm. Only one case could apply. But a fuzzy controller could use the following two rules simultaneously:

1. If it is comfortable, then continue the current cooling level.

2. If it is warm, then increase the cooling a little.

> At a temperature of 72°, both rules would fire, but their effect would be weighted by the degree of comfortableness (from the first rule) and the degree of warmness (from the second rule). Many other rules might fire at the same time. The fuzzy controller could weight all these results to decide whether to increase, decrease, or leave the cooling constant.

The use of fuzzy logic in household appliances in Japan became such a fad that appliances are labeled fuzzy or not, and people argue about whether a particular appliance truly deserves the label. Even with its commercial success in Japan, some observers believe that the use of fuzzy logic was much less important than simply building in sensors that monitor whatever process is being performed.

Fuzzy logic caught on in Japan but received comparatively little attention in the United States until the early 1990s when the success of Japanese fuzzy appliances became apparent. A book popularizing fuzzy logic[21] contains a number of possible explanations. One is that philosophers and mathematicians at leading American universities were interested in other approaches or found the basic ideas of fuzzy logic unacceptable on theoretical grounds. Another explanation is that fuzzy logic fits better with the Japanese language and view of the world. From this viewpoint, the Western tradition stresses clarity and precision in language, whereas the Japanese speech is full of qualifiers, such as "more or less" or "I think," that make statements more ambiguous.

Case-Based Reasoning

Assume you were working at a manufacturer's customer service help desk. Calls come in every day about many different models of many different products. Although there are shelves of manuals for each of the products, looking things up in those manuals takes a

Figure 12.8 Logic of Case-Based Reasoning

Case-base reasoning operates by finding a case in a database that is most closely related to the user's problem. When a new problem is solved, the information about that case is added to the database.

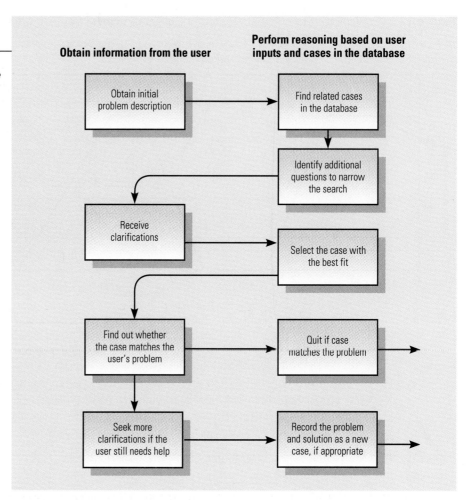

long time. Worse yet, the manuals explain how the product is supposed to work but often say very little about the types of things that go wrong and the way the customer could solve these problems. When Compaq Computer installed a case-based reasoning system to support the people at its help desk, the system paid for itself within a year.[22]

Case-based reasoning (CBR) is a decision support method based on the idea of finding past cases most similar to the current situation in which a decision must be made. CBR systems therefore maintain a history of cases related to the topics under consideration. When a new situation arises, or a new call comes to the help desk, the decision maker identifies the characteristics of the situation and receives a list of related situations that have been analyzed in the past. Often the past solutions provide important clues or directly answer the current question. When the issue is resolved, the decision maker can add the case just solved as an additional instance in the database. In this way, a case-based reasoning system starting empty or with just one case can gradually be expanded to make it a valuable resource (see Figure 12.8).

Case-based reasoning resembles neural networks in one important way. Instead of operating based on rules, it operates based on past cases and their characteristics. Instead of trying to find the relationships in the data, however, CBR merely attempts to display the most similar case.

Like other systems using AI-related techniques, the systems based on CBR are not magic and have the same dependence on human infrastructure as systems unrelated to AI. Before a CBR application is set up, someone must study the situation to identify the initial categories of cases and the way the cases will be compared and retrieved. Although a CBR system can go into operation with only a few cases in its database, such systems achieve their potential as the database of cases grows to several hundred examples. Building the database of cases requires someone to play the administrative role of receiving reports of newly encountered cases, verifying these cases differ from cases currently in the database, and coding and indexing the new cases for inclusion and retrieval. Using CBR without this type of administrative effort undermines the system because the database fills up with redundant and confusing entries.

Intelligent Agents

Truly intelligent machines will require some version of the amazing capability of our nervous systems to control multiple simultaneous processes at different levels of conscious awareness. Consider the different processes being controlled simultaneously by your nervous system as you drive a car to a familiar destination while chewing gum and having a strenuous political argument with a passenger. The argument might be at the highest level of consciousness, followed by awareness of the familiar driving route, and by the sensation of gum in your mouth, A simultaneous process of watching out for traffic hazards is going on in the back of your mind. In addition, body regulation processes, such as maintaining your heart beat and focusing your eyes are also continuing at a totally unconscious level. Suddenly a ball bounces into the street. Immediately the traffic hazard process takes over, and you temporarily forget about the political argument. Seconds later your heart is racing from the jolt of adrenaline as you slam on the brakes.

Truly intelligent machines would require a capability to operate many simultaneous foreground and background processes and bring background processes into the foreground immediately when necessary. Although the question of how to control such a system is an important research challenge for computer science and AI, merely stating the problem this way helped computer scientists invent the idea of intelligent agents.

An **intelligent agent** is a computerized process that can be launched into a computer system or network to perform background work while other foreground processes are continuing. An intelligent agent is a background process that sleeps until it wakes up on a schedule or until a trigger sets it into motion.

Consider three examples of possible intelligent agents, each of which operates in the background performing information-related tasks that save time or increase the usefulness of information:

E-mail agent: This might scan incoming e-mail to identify the comparatively few incoming messages that call for the recipient to be interrupted instead of just going on a list to be read at the recipient's convenience.

Data-mining agent: This might sort and filter data in a database to identify trends, surprises, and other new information a user might want.

Interface agent: This might scan articles on a computerized news service to create a personalized daily news bulletin containing only articles of interest to a particular individual. Ideally, this type of agent would be able to learn about the individual's changing interests instead of being told to what to do by programming or check-off lists.[23]

Although the idea of intelligent agents is related to past AI research, such as Marvin Minsky's book *The Society of Mind*,[24] the initial techniques used to implement intelligent agents look more like mainstream programming than AI. For example, an intelligent agent might be launched into a network to interrogate various travel providers to find the vacation that most closely suits someone's desires. A general capability that could perform this and similar tasks would involve many programming issues about data definition, standards, and telecommunications but very little about intelligence in the AI sense. Whether more intelligence can be programmed into intelligent agents remains to be seen.

REALITY CHECK **Additional AI-Related Techniques**   This section identified fuzzy logic, case-based reasoning, and intelligent agents as three additional techniques with important current or potential application.

1. Identify examples of situations you have encountered or might encounter in which each of these techniques might be used currently or in the future.

2. For each example, explain why the interpretation of ambiguous or incomplete information is or is not important.

How Smart Is "Computer Intelligence"?

Expert systems, neural networks, and the other techniques mentioned in this chapter are often grouped with robotics, computer vision, language translation, and a number of other topics under the general heading of AI (see Figure 12.9). The common thread among these topics is the attempt to program computers to use and interpret ambiguous or incomplete information about a topic that cannot be described using known formulas or procedures.

Seeing both the strengths and the limitations of expert systems, neural networks, and other AI-related techniques provides context for thinking about this topic. Business professionals need to understand it because they frequently encounter magazines, consultants, and system vendors making claims and promises about intelligent systems, intelligent machines, intelligent databases, and even intelligent enterprises.

Why Can't Intelligent Systems Understand Stories for Four-Year-Olds?

Questions about artificially created intelligence existed long before the first computers were developed. With the advent of the computer, researchers saw new possibilities for progress toward intelligent machines. A great deal of progress occurred. For example:

- Computers have played chess at a grandmaster level.

- Computers have solved mathematical problems that challenge expert mathematicians.

- Computers have constructed accurate three-dimensional representations from two-dimensional satellite photos.

- Computers have controlled guided missiles and airplanes.

Although these examples are impressive, and might have seemed like science fiction 40 years ago, people today would question whether they are examples of intelligence. This leads to an interesting question: How can we decide that a computerized system is intelligent?

Figure 12.9 Computer Vision

Computer vision systems can identify objects by taking a picture and then analyzing the image to find the edges and other features.

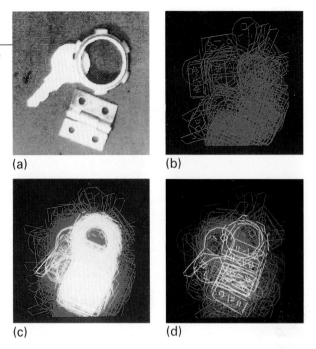

(a)   (b)

(c)   (d)

In 1950, the English mathematician Alan Turing suggested the following test: An interrogator should use a computer terminal to ask questions to something—a person or machine—that is in another room. If the interrogator cannot tell from the typed responses whether the questions are being answered by a person or a machine, the machine would be judged intelligent. Turing's test does not ask whether the machine can perform impressive tasks using preprogrammed mathematical procedures. It asks whether a machine could answer questions well enough to be indistinguishable from a person. Let's look at two examples to think about Turing's test. The first is chess played by computer. The second involves attempts to get a computer to understand stories for four-year-olds.

One of the most successful chess computers to date was developed by a team of researchers at Carnegie-Mellon University. The computer, which defeated a well-known grandmaster shortly after winning the 1989 world computer chess championship, uses a specially designed microprocessor to evaluate 720,000 alternative board positions in a second. Each evaluation is performed by assigning a value to the possible positions of each piece. For example, the computer assigns 6,274 points for a knight in the middle of the board, and 4,738 for a knight in a corner where it is less effective. These values were fine-tuned by analyzing 900 games played by expert human players. The program contains procedures for considering only plausible moves and countermoves. It often goes through 15 levels of moves and countermoves before deciding what to do. It is especially strong on defense because it can look deep enough to identify real threats. It is not as good on offense because it cannot plan long-term strategies. None of the designers can defeat the system they built.[26]

AI researchers have made enormous progress in solving complex problems such as playing chess. Surprisingly, their most difficult challenge is to replicate abilities that everyone has. Consider the problem of getting a computer to understand stories that four-year-old children can understand, such as:

> Billy was invited to Sally's party. He asked his mother if she would like a kite. She said that Sally already had a kite and would return it.

Even a simple story like this requires interpretation. We assume that Billy and Sally are young children (but not infants) and that Billy thinks Sally would like a kite as a birthday present. The word *she* in the second sentence refers to Sally because it is unlikely that Billy would be asking his mother if she (his mother) would like a kite, especially since the previous sentence referred to Sally's party. Even though the word *gift* did not appear in the story, we assume the kite is to be a gift because we know that children usually bring gifts to birthday parties. Apparently Billy's mother believes he understands that if Sally already had a kite she wouldn't want another. (But if Sally already had a $50 bill, she probably would want another, especially as she got older.)

Children can interpret a story like this easily because of their understandings about how the everyday world operates. Although computers have been programmed to play chess, no methods currently exist for teaching computers how to obtain and use the knowledge a four-year-old uses to understand a simple story.

As an example of what a computer might have to know to understand a story for children, Box 12.3 lists some of the real-world knowledge about piggy banks that one researcher compiled for use in early research on understanding children's stories. If this is just part of what a child knows about piggy banks, imagine how difficult it would be to compile everything a typical child knows about everything. Notice also that ideas about piggy banks are culture specific. Although many children in the United States may have piggy banks, children in other countries may have never heard of the idea. Even in the United States the idea of piggy banks may not be general knowledge.

Box 12.3 Common Facts About Piggy Banks

These facts about piggy banks are excerpted from a Ph.D. thesis that focused on understanding children's stories. This thesis helped AI researchers understand how difficult it would be to capture the knowledge needed for a computer to show common sense.

"Piggy Banks (PBs) come in all sizes and shapes, though a preferred shape is that of the pig. Generally the size will range from larger than a doorknob to smaller than a breadbox. Generally, money is kept in PBs, so when a child needs money he will often look for his PB. Usually, to get money out you need to be holding the bank, and shake it (up and down). Generally holding it upside down makes things go easier. There are less known techniques, like using a knife to help get the money out. If, when shaken, there is no sound from inside, it usually means that there is no money in the bank. If there is a sound, it means that something is in there, presumably money. You shake it until the money comes out. We assume that after the money comes out it is held by the person shaking, unless we are told differently. If not enough comes out you keep shaking until you either have enough money, or no more sound is made by the shaking (i.e., the bank is empty)."

Source: Charniak, Eugene. *Toward a Model of Children's Story Comprehension.* Cambridge, Mass.: MIT Ph.D. Thesis, 1972.

The difference between playing chess and understanding children's stories helps us visualize how much "intelligence" has been built into current computer systems. Certain computer systems would pass as intelligent if we consider only a limited, well-understood domain such as playing chess, and if we asked only the specific types of questions they are designed to answer. The Carnegie-Mellon chess computer would seem intelligent if it were evaluated on its ability to create chess moves better than most human chess players. It would not seem intelligent if it were judged on how well it could converse about its strategy. Current computer systems would all fail the test for intelligence if they were evaluated by asking enough questions to see whether they understood a simple story as well as a child.

As with expert systems, knowledge of the world is an essential issue for machine intelligence. We use that knowledge to decide that Billy is thinking about a birthday gift for Sally even though the word *gift* or *present* is never mentioned. Just putting together the knowledge to answer questions about children's stories would be such a formidable task that no one has done it.

To date, the most ambitious effort in this direction is the CYC project at the Microelectronics and Computers Consortium (MCC) in Austin, Texas. The project has tried to identify real-world knowledge people use to interpret things that happen in the real world. Between 1984 and 1994, the project generated 4 million assertions such as "a child can't be older than its parents."[27] The project was called CYC because it was trying to develop a unique form of encyclopedia containing the commonsense knowledge not found in regular encyclopedias because it is too obvious to include. The ultimate usefulness and success of this project remains to be seen.

Assuming the knowledge could be compiled, how would it be used? In addition to having the knowledge, there must be a way to sift through the knowledge, interpret any situation, and decide what to do about it. AI researchers have worked on rules, frames, and other ways to do this but have not yet come up with a technique that is powerful enough. They face a big challenge. Until major breakthroughs occur in the representation and use of commonsense knowledge, expert systems, neural networks, and other information systems will not be able to pass Turing's test on any area of knowledge other than the specific rules they contain.

Why Must Intelligent Systems Interpret Ambiguous or Incomplete Information?

From the outset, this chapter has portrayed computer intelligence in relation to the use of computers to interpret ambiguous or incomplete information and either execute or suggest appropriate actions that cannot be determined using formulas or provable procedures. Expert systems and the other four approaches to machine intelligence described in this chapter all encompass part of this view. Since terms such as smart machines and intelligent databases are bandied about frequently, it is important to recognize meanings of these terms that are less related to machine interpretations of ambiguous situations.

In common speech, terms such as smart machine or smart system often mean "having useful features" or even "not having features that seem poorly designed or inappropriate." Table 12.4 identifies three ways to make computers "smarter" in this sense. These three approaches include making application systems more powerful, embedding data processing capabilities in new places, and making programming and problem-solving tools more powerful. While looking at each in turn, notice how the term *smart* has much less to do with the type of intelligence discussed in this chapter and much more to do with just having appropriate features and capabilities.

Make application systems more powerful

Making application systems more powerful makes them "smarter" in most user's eyes. The issue here is to provide system features that help the user perform work efficiently and effectively. Table 12.5 uses common examples to show how adding better features

Table 12.4 Three Approaches for Making Computerized Systems "Smarter" Without Making Them Intelligent.

Approach	Meaning of the Term "Smarter"
Make application systems more powerful	This approach is used whenever an information system is improved to help users do their work more effectively. Examples: improved inventory systems or design systems.
Embed data processing capabilities in new places	This means integrating microprocessors or sensing devices into things that once had no data processing capabilities. Examples: intelligent terminals or intelligent buildings.
Make programming and problem-solving tools more powerful	This approach is used when creating tools end users or programmers can use in writing programs or developing models. The process of problem solving is improved because the tool contains more powerful features for solving the problem. Examples: spreadsheets, special-purpose languages, or object-oriented programming.

Table 12.5 Examples of Making Application Systems "Smarter" by Making Them More Powerful

Useful	Smarter	Even smarter
Word processor		
• Provide different types of formatting • Provide different fonts	• Check documents using spelling and grammar checkers • Provide starting points of different types of documents	• Check that the document makes sense
System for Ordering Merchandise		
• Check that orders received by mail contain valid customer and product numbers	• Accept orders by computer and immediately warn the customer of obvious errors such as invalid product number	• Warn the customer about possible errors when items do not match their buying profile • Alert customers of possible needs based on past usage rates
System for Designing Buildings		
• Provide tools for drawing pictures of the components • Store the drawings in an organized form	• Evaluate the design to identify likely building code violations • Use design data to calculate predictable costs for paint and carpeting	• Evaluate the design to determine structural soundness • Evaluate the building based on aesthetics

to an application system can make it smarter in this sense. For example, any word processor today would have capabilities related to formatting and use of different fonts. A smarter word processor might contain a spell checker and grammar checker. But it might be possible to have an even smarter word processor, for example, one that contained many different sample business letters to use as a starting point for a new letter. An even smarter word processor (of the distant future) might read the completed letter to make sure it made sense.

The principles for making application systems smarter in this sense start with removing obvious obstacles that get in the way when people try to do work. These obstacles are program features that force the user to do things that seem unnecessary or illogical or that may lead the user to wonder what the system designers were thinking about. Making systems smarter in this sense usually requires a detailed knowledge of how the users do the work and what aspects of the work could be improved.

Embed data processing capabilities in new places

Embedding data processing capabilities into systems is another way to make them smarter in this sense. An example is intelligent terminals. Chapter 9 explained that the early centralized computer systems performed all the data processing in a central computer and used dumb terminals that did little more than serve as input and output devices. In contrast, intelligent terminals are workstations that can perform a great deal of processing.

Other examples of embedding data processing in new places include smart cards and smart buildings. Smart cards are like credit cards except they have an electronic memory that can be updated. They can be used to store an individual's medical history or to pay for copies at copy machines or food in a college cafeteria. The data processing built into smart buildings includes temperature controls for heating and air conditioning, energy controls for turning lights on and off, and access control systems that track entry and exit from particular areas.

Make programming and problem-solving tools more powerful

Chapter 10 surveyed progress that has occurred in programming languages. Each step in that progress made programming languages or problem-solving tools more powerful, which ultimately resulted in systems that were more powerful. Two especially noteworthy steps mentioned in Chapter 10 were special-purpose languages and object-oriented programming.

Special-purpose languages attain their power by incorporating ideas directly related to a specific type of situation, such as calculating financial plans or simulating the operation of factories. These tools seem smarter to users because they help the users think about the problem in the terms in which the problem is stated. This means that the users have to do less work to express their ideas. Although this would not be seen as intelligence in anything like Turing's sense of the word, it certainly seems smarter to the users because it helps them more directly.

Object-oriented programming seems smarter because it permits people to define a class of objects once and then assume that characteristics for that class will be inherited by all members of the class. The efficiency gains from OOP result from greater ability to reuse programming work that has already been done. Although OOP is usually thought of as a new programming approach rather than an aspect of AI, many of the ideas of OOP are intertwined with ideas from AI research. At minimum, the research helped people see more clearly the benefits of OOP as a way to handle some of the programming knowledge built into programming systems.

Has Artificial Intelligence Succeeded or Failed?

Almost since the term *AI* was coined in 1956, it has been the subject of dreams, speculation, and unmet promises. Early research on computer intelligence led to great optimism, such as a program that proved a mathematical theorem in a novel way using a computer much less powerful than a current laptop. Extrapolating on early advances, Herbert Simon predicted in 1965 that by 1985 "machines will be capable of doing any work that a man can do."[28]

Even after the depth of the problem became clear to Simon and others, the early 1980s saw predictions of a multibillion-dollar AI industry by 1990. A number of AI software firms went public, only to disappoint their employees and investors. Despite the use of thousands of expert systems in industry, the predicted $4 billion market for AI products and services was probably closer to $600 million in 1990.[29] Headlines in the popular media helped fan the hype about artificial intelligence. With expert systems solving problems, neural networks showing how computers can learn, and intelligent machines doing impressive things, the immense possibilities for artificial intelligence may seem closer than they really are today.

Although AI research has not found the silver bullet that solves all the mysteries of intelligence, it has contributed to developments in many areas. In addition to expert systems and other techniques explained in this chapter, practical applications of this research include natural language processing (see Figure 4.5 and the case opening Chapter 9), automated translation of technical journals, computer vision (see Figure 12.9), and robotics (see Figure 6.10).

AI research has also had important impacts other than direct practical applications to date. It has provided viewpoints for studying language, learning, and human intelligence. It has contributed to programming techniques such as OOP by generating alternative methods for building knowledge into systems. It has helped people appreciate the complexity of capturing knowledge, especially commonsense knowledge that everyone shares. Knowing how hard it is to capture commonsense knowledge and understanding has helped clarify the limitations of what computers can do. These contributions will continue to influence practical developments in the future.

Although AI researchers care about AI for its own sake, business professionals care about AI techniques primarily as one of many ways to improve business processes. The business issue is not whether to use AI or expert systems or neural networks. The business issue is whether systems using these techniques will be more effective than systems using other techniques.

REALITY CHECK   **How Smart Is "Computer Intelligence"?**   This section discussed the challenges related to computer intelligence and showed the range of different meanings people attach to terms such as smart system.

1. Think of making a system smarter in terms of making it more useful and powerful. Identify some of the application areas in which it would be valuable to make systems smarter in this sense.

2. Think of making a system smarter in terms of making it more able to interpret and use ambiguous and incomplete information. Identify some of the application areas in which it would be valuable to make systems smarter in this sense.

Chapter Conclusion

SUMMARY

▶ *Why are expert systems and neural networks important for businesses?*

Expert systems improve the use of knowledge in organizations by making the best knowledge available even if it resides in the heads of a few experts. They also help new members of the organization become productive quickly and reduce the knowledge lost when experts switch jobs or leave the organization. Neural networks improve decision making in discrimination and pattern recognition tasks in which experts cannot say exactly how to perform the task even though a large number of examples exist.

▶ *What is the relationship between artificial intelligence (AI) and systems such as expert systems and neural networks?*

Artificial intelligence is the demonstration of intelligence by machines. This includes, but is not limited to, the ability to think, see, learn, understand, and use common sense. Expert systems, an offshoot of AI research about understanding language and the world, are information systems that store and use expert knowledge to support or automate decision making in a limited area where recognized experts do better than nonexperts. Neural networks, also offshoots of AI research, are information systems that perform discrimination tasks based on what they learn statistically from examples.

▶ *When are expert systems useful?*

The existence and availability of expertise and the nature of the task determine whether expert systems are useful. Expert systems are worth building only if experts do better at the task than nonexperts, if recognized experts exist who are willing to work on the system, and if there is reasonable agreement about the knowledge itself. Expert systems are applicable for tasks routinely taught to novices and performed based on reasoning and knowledge rather than intuition or reflexes.

▶ *What are the components of an expert system?*

The components include the knowledge base, database, inference engine, interface, and explanation module. The knowledge base is a set of facts and if–then rules supplied by the expert. The database is the set of facts that are used in drawing conclusions in a situation. The inference engine uses rules in the knowledge base plus whatever facts are currently in the database to draw conclusions and to decide what question to ask next. The interface is the way the expert system interacts with the user. The explanation module explains how a fact was inferred or why a question is being asked.

▶ *How do neural networks operate?*

Neural networks use statistical techniques to "learn" how to recognize a particular type of pattern by combining the features from a set of training examples. Common neural networks contain an input layer, output layer, one or more hidden layers, and links between the nodes in successive layers. The strength of each link is initially set randomly and is adjusted to minimize the error that would occur for the examples in the training set. After multiple repetitions of the training set, the weightings of the links may converge to represent whatever pattern is present.

▶ *What additional techniques related to AI are beginning to attain prominence?*

Fuzzy logic, case-based reasoning, and intelligent agents are three techniques that are beginning to attain prominence. Fuzzy logic uses rules but assumes that the conditions and conclusions of rules are stated in an approximate way without forcing people to pretend their perceptions and beliefs are unrealistically precise. Case-based reasoning provides guidance to decision makers by searching a database of past cases and displaying cases most similar to the current case. Intelligent agents permit a user to create an automatic process that operates in the background to find information or create warnings while other foreground processes occur.

▶ *Why is it difficult to get a computer to understand a story for a four-year-old?*

Even simple stories require interpretation based on real-world (sometimes culturally determined) understandings, such as the fact that children usually bring gifts to birthday parties. Children can interpret stories when they have these understandings. Although computers have been programmed to play chess, no methods currently exist for teaching computers how to obtain and use the knowledge a four-year-old uses to understand a simple story.

INTERNATIONAL VIGNETTE

Denmark: Using Fuzzy Logic to Make Cement

The first commercial application of fuzzy logic occurred in Denmark at the cement manufacturer F. L. Smidth & Company and addressed a common problem in that industry. Cement is produced by mixing and heating calcium silicates and other chemicals in enormous, slowly rotating kilns until they form pebble-sized chunks called clinker. The clinker is later pulverized into the cement that is sold. The problem is that controlling cement kilns is more an art than a science. If the heating and mixing aren't applied correctly, the clinker may not form properly or may come out too hard to grind. Monitoring a cement kiln for eight hours at a time is not a fascinating job, however, and inattention or human error can result in ruined batches and wasted energy.

In 1974, an engineer working for F. L. Smidth attended a conference in Zurich on automatic control and found a paper related to fuzzy logic. The use of rules to control a kiln seemed straightforward because the people who did the work could learn to do it in just eight weeks. In 1980, the company installed a fuzzy logic system that controls a cement kiln automatically although the operator can override it if necessary. In 1982, the engineers working on the project installed a similar system in Oregon. The system has been refined since that time, and an estimated 10 percent of the world's cement kilns now use fuzzy logic.

Source: McNeill, Daniel, and Paul Freiberger. *Fuzzy Logic: The Revolutionary Computer Technology* That Is Changing the World. New York: Touchstone, 1993.

⁕ Use the WCA framework to organize your understanding of this vignette and to identify important topics that are not mentioned.

⁕ What issues (if any) make this case interesting from an international or intercultural viewpoint?

⁕ Explain why it does or doesn't appear that there is a special need to use fuzzy logic when making cement.

REAL-WORLD CASES

Otis Elevator: Combining Fuzzy Logic and Neural Networks to Minimize Waiting for Elevators

Since long waits for elevators are one of the aggravations of working or living in a high-rise building, Otis Elevator and its competitors such as Hitachi, Toshiba, and Mitsubishi have tried to improve their automatic dispatchers. These are the programs that decide which elevator to send when a person presses an elevator call button in a hallway. In a simple example, one person is in an elevator going down from the 16th floor, nine are in an elevator going down from the 12th floor, and someone presses the call button to go down from the 8th floor. With older dispatching systems, the elevator nearest the new call would pick up that person, even though this choice would delay nine people rather than just one who is in the higher elevator. With a fuzzy logic system, it is easier to use additional variables, such as how full the cars are or how inconvenienced the people in different cars would be from extra waiting or from being crammed together excessively.

Fuzzy logic alone is not enough to wring the best performance from an elevator dispatcher, however. Buildings have their own idiosyncrasies, such as different office schedules in different parts of the building or the fact that a cafeteria may be on the 27th floor. To get the best performance, the dispatcher needs the ability to learn the building's idiosyncrasies. This is an ideal application of an neural network because extensive data can be captured easily.

The first Otis Elevator using a fuzzy dispatcher was installed at a Hyatt Hotel in Osaka, Japan, in 1993. During this installation, the Otis team learned about some factors in elevator dispatching that go beyond mere logic. They concluded that in Japan people care more about causing an extra delay for someone else, whereas in New York people simply don't want to wait, period.

> Source: Pinder, Jeanne E. "Fuzzy Thinking Has Merits When It Comes to Elevators." New York Times, Sept. 22, 1993, p. C1.

* Use the WCA framework to organize your understanding of this case and to identify important topics that are not mentioned.

* Identify some of the characteristics of elevator location that the dispatching system might consider.

* Explain why you believe fuzzy logic is or is not important in the elevator system.

Compaq: Case-Based Reasoning Packaged with a Printer

After successfully applying case-based reasoning to support its help desk, Compaq Computer decided to develop what is apparently the first attempt to use case-based reasoning in a consumer market. Starting in 1992, purchasers of Compaq Pagemarq printers received three additional diskettes containing case-based reasoning software plus a database of cases related to analyzing and solving common printer problems. In effect, Compaq took the war stories from the help desk and put them online for use by customers.

In a typical situation, the PC user might type "blurry and smeared pages." The case-based reasoning software would look through the database of cases, ignoring those related to paper jams or incorrect printer fonts, and coming back with a case related to blurry copies. It might propose a solution, such as "Check the laser scanner window for dirt or contamination," or might ask for additional information to better distinguish between several cases that fit reasonably well but may not be a match. This is effective frequently enough that Compaq has seen significant reductions in customers' calls to its help line. It estimates that the case-based reasoning approach will save it $10 to $20 million per year in customer service operations, in addition to helping the customer avoid waiting on hold.

> Source: Chartrand, Sabra. "Compaq Printer Can Tell You What's Ailing It." New York Times, Aug. 4, 1993. p. C4.

- Use the WCA framework to organize your understanding of this case and to identify important topics that are not mentioned.

- Identify other areas where a case-based reasoning system might be enclosed with a product, and explain what the system might do. Would it be possible to use case-based reasoning if the product being sold does not involve a computer?

KEY TERMS

artificial intelligence	common sense	explanation module	fuzzy logic
expert system	frame	forward chaining	case-based reasoning (CBR)
expert system shell	knowledge base	backward chaining	intelligent agent
knowledge-based system	knowledge engineer	certainty factors	
if–then rules	inference engine	neural network	

REVIEW QUESTIONS

1. Use the WCA framework to explain why it made sense for the CEO of Teknowledge to say that knowledge-based systems are rarely more than 20 percent of a complete solution to real-world problems.

2. Define expert systems, and explain how they improve the use of knowledge.

3. What are expert system shells?

4. Describe roles an expert system can play in a decision process.

5. When are expert systems useful, and why can't they exercise common sense?

6. Describe two ways to represent knowledge in expert systems.

7. Identify the components of an idealized expert system.

8. What are the two basic methods expert systems use to perform reasoning?

9. Discuss the way experts actually work, and explain why the term *expert system* often is a misnomer.

10. What is a neural network?

11. Explain how a neural network operates.

12. Describe the limitations of neural networks.

13. What are the advantages of reasoning using fuzzy logic?

14. Define case-based reasoning and explain how a CBR system typically operates.

15. Define intelligent agent, and explain why it should or should not be grouped with the other techniques related to artificial intelligence.

16. Why can't current computerized systems understand stories for four-year-olds?

17. How can you decide whether a machine is intelligent?

18. Why should business professionals care about artificial intelligence?

DISCUSSION QUESTIONS

1. The manager of a $100 million company pension fund at Deere & Co. used a neural network to outperform common stock market indicators. At one point, the neural network suggested the fund should invest 40 percent of its assets in bank stocks. The manager's boss overruled the neural network, but in retrospect the boss was

wrong.[30] Explain why this experience should or should not convince people not to overrule the neural network.

2. There has been a great deal of speculation about medical applications of expert systems and neural networks. These systems have demonstrated many impressive characteristics but have been used only in research settings. Explain the legal and ethical questions that might apply to their use. Would these questions be different depending on whether they served as an aid to a human doctor versus making decisions automatically?

3. What would have to be done to build an expert system for coaching a basketball team? Why do you believe it is or is not possible to build such a system?

4. Describe the process of attaining knowledge in anything you have ever studied outside school, such as how to play baseball, play an instrument, or dance. Explain why it would or would not be possible for an expert system or neural network to learn how to do these things.

5. Did this chapter contain any examples that you consider to be machine intelligence? If so, what are the examples, and why do you believe these are examples of machine intelligence? If not, identify examples in the chapter that are closest to machine intelligence, and explain how the examples would be different if they truly demonstrated machine intelligence.

HANDS-ON EXERCISES

1. This exercise is about the operation of expert systems and assumes that an expert system example is provided.

   a. Use the expert system example provided to draw conclusions about a situation and to explain how the expert system came to its conclusion.

   b. Examine the expert system in more detail. Identify the rules. Explain whether the database changes as the problem is being solved.

2. This exercise is about the operation of neural networks and assumes that a neural network example is provided.

   a. Use the neural network provided to categorize several new examples that were not used to train the neural network.

   b. Present several training examples to the neural network, and observe how its parameters change.

APPLICATION SCENARIOS

Associated Financial Planners

Associated Financial Planners (AFP) is a national firm specializing in financial planning for individuals. Unlike a stock brokerage, AFP receives no commissions from selling stocks, bonds, or other investment products. Advice is all that it sells. A typical client wants help in developing a long-range financial plan to take care of retirement, college educations, aging parents, and other needs. AFP planning counselors produce written plans after studying a client questionnaire and meeting with clients for several hours. AFP urges clients to come back for an "annual financial checkup" to see how the plan is working and whether it should be adjusted.

William Waters, president of AFP, is concerned about AFP's long-term future and is looking for new ways, to improve services and increase profitability. He is considering asking a firm that builds expert systems to build an expert system for personal financial planning. It would use rules developed by AFP's five best planning counselors. The system would accept standard data about financial resources and personal goals, and would produce a 20- to

40-page printed financial plan. The planning counselors would study these plans and try out additional options before meeting with clients. For example, they might change a goal, such as level of retirement income, and see how the system's recommendations would change. The system would decrease the paperwork involved in producing a financial plan. It would also eliminate many oversights and other human errors and would produce more consistent plans.

Waters was surprised by the reaction when he discussed his idea with several planners. Although he said he believed that planners usually did a good job, they wanted to know why he distrusted them so much that he wanted to bring in an expert system. They also wondered how the clients would react if they believed that the plan was produced by a computer. If the system were introduced, they believed that most planners would rely on it more and more and would eventually lose their skills. Finally, they argued that this system would open the door for clients to use computerized planning systems themselves and totally bypass AFP.

1. Write 3 rules that might appear in such a system.

2. Explain why you believe it is or is not feasible to build this expert system.

3. If you were a potential AFP client and knew that an expert system was being used, would this sway you toward or away from AFP? Why? Would you have the same response if you knew it was a computer system but didn't know it was an expert system?

4. If you were Waters, how would you react to the planning counselors' comments?

DEBATE TOPIC   *Use ideas from the chapter to argue the pros and cons and practical implications of the following proposition: It would be unethical to modify this system to make it a freestanding expert system designed to give personal financial advice over a computer network, thereby bypassing the human financial advisor altogether.*

Northridge High School

Harold Barber was adamant about the use of the Writer's Assistant. As principal of Northbridge High School, he felt it was his job to produce literate graduates. He felt that the Writer's Assistant program should not be used at the school because the students needed to learn how to write English rather than having a computer look over their shoulders to tell them whether they were making sense. He believed spelling checkers had already reduced the student's ability to spell. With the yearend standardized tests coming up, he was especially concerned about not making things worse.

Several of the teachers thought he was totally wrong, arguing that the Writer's Assistant program wouldn't tell students how to write and certainly wouldn't tell them whether they were making sense. It would only check students' writing to help them identify likely errors in spelling, grammar, and word usage. Students would still have to decide whether these were errors and how to correct them. To make their point, they found a memo signed by Barber and typed it into the Writer's Assistant, which found four likely errors.

Later, Barber admitted that he didn't understand what the Writer's Assistant could really do. Like most people, he could easily imagine how spelling checkers identify some possible misspellings: find a word, look it up in a dictionary, and warn the writer if it doesn't appear there. This process cannot identify all misspellings because it looks only at a word at a time rather than at the word in its context. For example, it would see nothing wrong with the sentence "All the world is a stages" because *stages* is a word. To identify that error, it would have to recognize enough basic grammar to determine that a singular form is called for rather than a plural form.

The Writer's Assistant goes far beyond that, however. It dissects sentences to identify the subject, verb, and object, and uses this analysis to identify likely errors. Using a library of over 10,000 rules, it identifies mismatched subject and verb forms, awkward language, nonstandard punctuation, unnecessary uses of passive voice, excessive sentence length, ambiguous pronoun references, and some inappropriate word choices. When it finds a possible problem, it highlights the words involved, explains the possible problem, and sometimes suggests a correction.

1. Explain why you believe it is or is not feasible to build this expert system.

2. How do you feel about Barber's point? Are there any human or ethical issues related to using a tool like the Writer's Assistant in a school setting? What is your opinion about those issues?

3. Explain what you believe currently available systems of this type can and cannot do. Explain why you believe systems five to ten years in the future will have essentially similar or greatly expanded capabilities and what it would be like to use them.

DEBATE TOPIC   *Use ideas from the chapter to argue the pros and cons and practical implications of the following proposition:* Within 10 to 20 years, most newspaper articles will be written by computers based on audio or video input from the field.

■ Cumulative Case: Custom T-Shirts, Inc.

Dale came back from a Management of the Future seminar wondering whether Custom T-Shirts needed artificial intelligence. At that seminar, a speaker had discussed the importance of artificial intelligence and the fact that it had been applied in many situations.

It seemed to Dale that there were a lot of problems artificial intelligence might help with, starting with the decision about where to place new stores. Results thus far from new stores had been very inconsistent. With artificial intelligence, maybe they would have better results. Another area was matching of colors between the fabric and the custom image in the t-shirts and new sweatshirt products. When nonartists wanted to customize their own t-shirts, the resulting color combinations were often ugly. Perhaps AI could help with this situation by warning them. AI might also be used to help them design the pattern itself since nonartists' patterns often came out looking as though a fourth grader had produced them.

On hearing these suggestions, Lee was unusually sarcastic. "You're always optimistic, but this time you're just dreaming. What the guy at the seminar must not have said, or at least what you don't understand is that AI is not a product. You can't go somewhere and just buy it like a t-shirt. AI is a research area that has produced some useful things in particular areas where its techniques fit well. Looking for AI applications will get us nowhere. Instead, let's make a list of important business problems, rank them in order of importance, and try to solve them in that order. If something from AI is the solution to those problems, great. But I bet it won't be."

1. For each of the problems cited, explain what aspects of expert systems might be pertinent. What aspects might be pertinent for neural networks? For case-based reasoning?

2. Explain why it does or does not seem to you that AI might be a solution to the problems Dale cited.

3. Explain why you agree or disagree with Lee's statement that AI is not a product and that looking for AI applications will get them nowhere.

▍*REFERENCES*

1. Dzierzanowski, James M. et al. "The Authorizer's Assistant: A Knowledge-Based Credit Authorization System for American Express." In Herbert Schorr and Alain Rappoport, *Proceedings of the First Annual Conference on Innovative Applications of Artificial Intelligence.* Menlo Park, Calif.: American Association for Artificial Intelligence, 1989, pp. 168–172.

2. Leonard-Barton, Dorothy, and John J. Sviokla. "Putting Expert Systems to Work." *Harvard Business Review*, Mar.–Apr. 1988, pp. 91–98.

3. Hayes-Roth, Frederick, and Neil Jacobstein. "The State of Knowledge-Based Systems." *Communications of the ACM*, Mar. 1994, pp. 27–39.

4. Meador, C. Lawrence, and Ed G. Mahler. "Choosing an Expert System Game Plan." *Datamation*, Aug. 1, 1990, pp. 64–69.

5. Waterman, Donald A. *A Guide to Expert Systems.* Reading, Mass.: Addison-Wesley, 1986.

6. Waterman, Donald A. *op. cit.*

7. Davis, Randall. "Amplifying Expertise with Expert Systems." In Patrick H. Winston and Karen A. Prendergast, eds. *The AI Business: Commercial Uses of Artificial Intelligence.* Cambridge, Mass.: MIT Press, 1984, pp. 17–39.

8. Shurkin, Joel. "Expert Systems: The Practical Face of Artificial Intelligence." *Technology Review*, Nov.–Dec. 1983, pp. 72–78.

9. Dreyfus, Hubert, and Stuart Dreyfus. "Why Computers May Never Think Like People." *Technology Review*, Jan. 1986, pp. 42–61.

10. Sharda, Ramesh. "Neural Networks for the MS/OR Analyst: An Application Bibliography." *Interfaces*, Mar.–Apr. 1994, pp. 116–130.

11. Cowan, Jack D., and David H. Sharp. "Neural Nets and Artificial Intelligence." In Stephen R. Graubard, ed. *The Artificial Intelligence Debate: False Starts, Real Foundations.* Cambridge, Mass.: The MIT Press, 1988.

12. Widrow, Bernard, David E. Rumelhart, and Michael A. Lehr. "Neural Networks: Applications in Industry, Business, and Science." *Communications of the ACM,* Mar. 1994, pp. 93–105.

13. Asakawa, Kazuo, and Hideyuki Takagi. "Neural Networks in Japan." *Communications of the ACM,* Mar. 1994, pp. 106–112.

14. Alexander, Michael. "Neural Network Bests Doctors at Diagnoses." *Computerworld*, Dec. 16, 1991, p. 22.

15. Kuhn, Susan E. "The New Perilous Stock Market." *Fortune*, Dec. 27, 1993, pp. 48–58.

16. Campbell, Jeremy. *The Improbable Machine: What the Upheavals in Artificial Intelligence Research Reveal about How the Mind Really Works.* New York: Simon & Schuster, 1989, p. 170.

17. Stipp, David. "Computer Researchers Find 'Neural Networks' Help Mimic the Brain." *Wall Street Journal*, Sept. 9, 1988, p. 1.

18. Loofbourrow, T. H. "Expert Systems and Neural Networks: The Hatfields and the McCoys?" *Expert Systems,* Fall 1990.

19. McNeill, Daniel, and Paul Freiberger. *Fuzzy Logic: The Revolutionary Computer Technology That Is Changing the World.* New York: Touchstone, 1993.

20. Munakata, Toshinori, and Jani Yashvant. "Fuzzy Systems: An Overview." *Communications of the ACM*, Mar. 1994, pp. 69–76.

21. McNeill, Daniel, and Paul Freiberger. *op. cit.*

22. Allen, Bradley P. "Case-Based Reasoning: Business Applications." *Communications of the ACM,* Mar. 1994, pp. 40–42.

23. Negroponte, Nicholas. "Less Is More: Interface Agents as Digital Butlers." *Wired*, June 1994, p. 142.

24. Minsky, Marvin. *The Society of Mind.* New York: Simon & Schuster, 1986.

25. Hayes-Roth, Frederick, and Neil Jacobstein. "The State of Knowledge-Based Systems." *Communications of the ACM*, Mar. 1994, pp. 27–39.

26. Byrne, Robert. "Chess-Playing Computer Closes in on Champions." *New York Times*, Sept. 26, 1989.

27. Ditlea, Steve. "Silent Partners." *Byte*, May 1994, pp. 160–169.

28. Herbert A. Simon. *The Shape of Automation for Men and Management,* New York: Harper & Row, 1965, p. 96.

29. Bulkeley, William M. "Bright Outlook for Artificial Intelligence Yields to Slow Growth and Big Cutbacks." *Wall Street Journal*, July 3, 1990.

30. Bylinsky, Gene. "Computers That Learn by Doing." *Fortune*, Sept. 6, 1993, pp. 96–102

PART IV

Planning, Building, and Managing Information Systems

The first three parts of the book have presented a framework for thinking about information systems and have looked at each part of the framework in some depth. Part IV closes the book by looking at processes related to building these systems and keeping them operating. This part introduction focuses on three themes underlying the material in these chapters:

1. Planning, building, and managing information systems are business processes that can be described and evaluated like any other business processes.

2. A number of general management principles apply to most situations in which information systems are planned, built, and managed.

3. Despite the general principles, planning, building, and managing information systems brings many difficult challenges.

Chapter 13 begins Part IV by summarizing information system planning, the process by which a firm decides how to allocate its resources among different information system projects. Most of these projects involve maintaining or upgrading existing systems rather than building new ones. Since firms build information systems based on these planning decisions, Chapter 14 explains and compares different types of processes for building and maintaining information systems. Chapter 15 completes the book by looking at system control and security, the things that must be understood and done to assure that information systems are used effectively, efficiently, and without fraud or crime.

The Business Processes of Planning, Building, and Managing Information Systems

Planning, building, and managing information systems are business processes. They can be described, evaluated, and improved just like any other business process because the same issues apply. Recalling the original discussion of the WCA framework, these issues include identifying the customer and product of the business process and finding a balance between the business process, participants, information, technology, and the results expected by the customer.

For example, assume that a computer-aided software engineering (CASE) system is used as part of the process of building an information system. Merely buying the software tool does not mean that the business process of building systems will generate better results. A common problem with CASE systems is that the software is purchased but not adequately integrated into the business processes of building and maintaining systems. Key steps in the before-and-after analysis of the CASE investment should include looking at the desired product of the business process, describing the way the business processes will produce those results, and deciding what role the CASE system should play.

Chapters 13, 14, and 15 directly or indirectly mention many other situations in which the WCA framework can be used to think about how the work should be done. For example, there are a variety of IS planning methods, but there is often a question about whether the payoff is worth the time and effort expended. Likewise, there are many ways to create financial justifications of IS investments, but participants often wonder whether these justifications have much bearing on actual decisions. There are also various ways to build systems, each with its own advantages and disadvantages. And there are many methods for controlling and protecting systems, each with its own costs, benefits, and risks. Approaching Chapters 13, 14, and 15 with the WCA framework in the back of your mind will help you use the ideas when you participate in planning, building, or managing systems.

Management Principles

A series of management principles apply across the ideas in Chapters 13, 14, and 15 related to planning, building, and managing information systems. These include:

- Support the firm's business strategy with appropriate technical architecture, standards, and policies.

- Evaluate technology as a component of a larger system.

- Recognize life cycle costs, not just acquisition costs.

- Design systems to be maintainable.

- Recognize the human side of technology use.

- Support and control the technical system.

Each will be introduced briefly here. Although certain points are stressed in particular chapters, each management principle applies to all three chapters in some way.

Support the Firm's Business Strategy with Appropriate Technical Architecture, Standards, and Policies

Finding the right balance between what should be decided centrally and what should be decided locally is one of the major issues related to planning, building, and managing information systems. If people or departments plan, build, and manage their own systems their own way, opportunities for coordination and economies of scale are lost. In large companies, immense amounts of time and effort have been wasted trying to bridge technical gaps and inconsistencies between multiple systems that all do roughly the same thing, such as generate paychecks or keep track of purchases. If central authorities make too many decisions about systems, some of the best knowledge about differing local needs and conditions will be ignored. Individuals or departments with genuinely different needs will then have to do extra work to get around the shortcomings of whatever was decided centrally.

Although different firms have come to different conclusions about the balance between centralization and decentralization, most have concluded that some issues should be decided centrally. The key issues involve tools for building and maintaining systems, the general architecture for information, and technical standards such as what personal computers and operating systems to use. In today's world of rapid organizational change, consistent decisions in these areas make it much easier to keep systems operating effectively even as the business reorganizes.

Evaluate Technology as a Component of a Larger System

Specific hardware and software products should always be evaluated in their own right and as a component of an overall system. Consider what a highway engineer said about the rebuilding of certain highway overpasses after the 1994 San Fernando Valley earthquake: "When we strengthen some of the older structures using the newest highway technology, what we are basically doing in many cases is moving the likely point of failure from one place to another." In a similar way, having the latest microprocessor may not change system performance at all if the system continues using old software whose internal design cannot take advantage of the new microprocessor's speed.

As this book's first two chapters pointed out, the human and technical infrastructure surrounding an information system is also essential for success. The latest hardware and software may have little impact if the training and support for participants is inadequate. Similarly, the best data analysis software may be useless if the right data cannot be provided from external systems.

Recognize Life Cycle Costs, Not Just Acquisition Costs

The discussion of a customer's view of a product in Chapter 7 was based on a customer involvement cycle in which the customer perceives costs and benefits across the entire cycle of learning about a product, customizing it, using it, and maintaining it. In a similar way, the costs of any information system typically far exceed the cost of acquiring the hardware and software. For example, a typical large company's costs related to personal computers and their use is at least $10–$15 thousand per machine, a significant multiple of the $3,000 the computer itself might cost. The difference consists of costs incurred to install the computer and use it effectively. These costs are related to wiring the computer to a network, buying software, training users, and providing support for users.

Design Systems to Be Maintainable

Anyone who has ever tried to remodel a house recognizes the value of designing systems to be maintainable. The difficulty of doing the home improvements depends on what you find when you tear open the wall. And the work is much easier if you have an accurate blueprint or wiring diagram telling you where to look and what to expect.

System users whose main computer experience is with their own spreadsheets often have trouble understanding why it takes so long to build and implement information systems. Unlike spreadsheet models developed for temporary, personal use in analyzing a current situation, many information systems must last for years and must be maintainable long after the original system builders have moved to other jobs. This requires that the systems be constructed and documented carefully, and that the documentation be updated whenever the system is changed. In general, it is also easier to maintain systems if the parts are simpler and are designed as modular components meant to be plugged into other components built consistent with accepted industry standards.

Recognize the Human Side of Technology Use

A point made repeatedly throughout this book is that people are part of the system. A technically spectacular system may still fail if its human participants are unwilling or unable to play their part effectively. Similarly, even technically primitive systems can often be very successful when supported and understood by active participants.

The human side of technology use is one of the reasons the process of designing systems and implementing them in organizations requires involvement and commitment by system participants and their management. Processes for planning, building, and managing systems should be designed accordingly.

Support and Control the Technical System

Important as the human side of the system is, the technical side should also be supported and controlled. Information systems need care and maintenance in much the same way as cars or houses. If care and maintenance are ignored, systems gradually degrade and become more prone to failure from overloaded databases, incorrect data, faulty documentation, or human error.

The need for care and maintenance leads to the question of who should do that work. The trend toward decentralization and outsourcing leaves less of this work in the hands of centralized groups. These groups often have greater technical depth than individual functional departments and greater company allegiance than outsourcing vendors who have their own external business agendas. Consequently, the support and control of technical systems is just as much a planning issue as deciding what new information systems to build.

Challenges of Planning, Building and Managing Information Systems

Sometimes hidden in the explanation of procedures, policies, and standards related to information systems are the challenges that led to some of these procedures and policies. These challenges include:

- Difficulty foreseeing and assessing opportunities

- Difficulty assuring consistency with organizational plans and objectives

- Difficulty building systems

- Difficulty maintaining system performance

- Difficulty collaborating with system builders

Difficulty Foreseeing and Assessing Opportunities

It is sometimes said that information system strategies become apparent only after they have been accomplished. Consider what happened with the Sabre reservation system, which is often considered a major factor in American Airlines' competitive success. That system was not initially designed as a major competitive strategy. Rather, it evolved through four distinct stages over 30 years. It began in the early 1960s as a response to American Airlines' inability to use manual methods to monitor its inventory of available seats. Although a technical achievement for the time, it was a far cry from the powerful system later accused of presenting biased displays to travel agents so that they would see and select American Airlines flights for their clients.[1] A similar story applies for the order entry and inventory control system American Hospital Supply (later acquired by Baxter International) built for its customers in hospital supply departments. That system started as a simple way to keep track of orders and evolved into a major competitive tool by providing such complete service that customers found it expensive to switch to other suppliers.[2] But competitors eventually offered similar systems, leading to frustrating situations in which a hospital might have to use different systems, including different terminals, for different vendors. In 1994, Baxter abandoned the proprietary system strategy and teamed up with three competitors to create an industrywide EDI system for entering orders.[3]

The point of both examples is that it is usually difficult to foresee the way information system innovations will develop. As with many complex products, users typically identify new uses and possible improvements that the inventor never imagined. Consequently, information system plans should be reviewed periodically, and systems should be designed to be flexible and extendible.

Difficulty Assuring Consistency with Organizational Plans and Objectives

A fundamental problem with information systems planning is that individual departments within companies have their own priorities and business practices and often have difficulty working toward a mutually beneficial plan. This issue is especially significant if a business or government organization attempts to develop an information architecture and infrastructure that spans departmental boundaries. Even if mutual benefits seem likely, the process of developing the plans takes a lot of time and effort, and the rewards may be distributed unevenly.

Difficulty Building Systems

Large information systems are complex creations that often take years to build and involve many organizational, political, and technical tradeoffs. In many system development efforts only a small cadre truly understands what the system is trying to do and how it will operate both organizationally and technically. It is not surprising that even major business organizations such as American Airlines, Bank of America, Chemical Bank, and the London Stock Exchange have suffered costly project failures. For every failure reported in the press, many smaller failures were never reported. And for every unreported failure there have been many semi-failures, systems that were developed and installed but never came close to accomplishing their goals. The difficulty of building systems is one of the reasons information system investments require management attention.

Difficulty Maintaining System Performance

Each of the six elements of the framework points to things that can go wrong with information systems. Whether or not the system performs as it was designed, the customer may be dissatisfied for a variety of reasons. The products and services produced by the information system may not have the cost, quality, responsiveness, reliability, and conformance expected by the customers. The business processes within the system may lag in productivity, flexibility, or security. Participants can cause problems through anything from inattention to criminality. The information in the system can cause problems due to anything from occasional inaccuracy to fraud. And the technology can impede or stop the business process by degrading or failing. Each of these problems can be anticipated to some extent, and a preventive response can be planned, but at the cost of more effort, more attention, greater expenditures, and less flexibility.

Difficulty Collaborating with System Builders

Business professionals and system builders sometimes talk past each other as if they come from different worlds. Anyone who has dealt with lawyers, doctors, or math teachers recognizes the resulting frustrations. Specialists may have trouble translating their specialized knowledge and world view into terms nonspecialists genuinely understand. Nonspecialists may feel they can't speak the lingo and can't even explain their concerns, no less engage in a genuine dialogue about alternatives. Even if they trust the specialists, they are left with a queasy feeling of operating too much on trust and too little on mutual understanding.

Attaining a genuine dialogue is important because the business professionals and the system builders each bring knowledge and understanding essential for system success. The system builders have paid attention to many different types of system applications and may be able to suggest approaches the business professionals would not have imagined. They know what is easy and what is difficult to do with computers. They know how to analyze, design, program, and debug computerized systems. They know what it takes to make a system maintainable over time. Business professionals have the most direct experience with the business problem but may not have much experience articulating the problem systematically. They may have some idea about how to create small spreadsheet models but usually know little about building maintainable information systems for supporting business processes. They typically want a quick solution to their business problem and lack patience for the delays required to build robust systems. This book was designed to help you regardless of which type of role you will play.

REFERENCES

1. Hopper, Max D. "Rattling SABRE —New Ways to Compete on Information." *Harvard Business Review*, May–June 1990, pp. 118-125.

2. Gibson, Cyrus F., and Barbara Bund Jackson. *The Information Imperative.* Lexington, Mass.: Lexington Books, 1987.

3. Winslow, Ron. "Four Hospital Suppliers Will Launch Common Electronic Ordering System." *Wall Street Journal.* Apr. 12, 1994, p. B7.

Information System Planning

Study Questions

▶ *What is an information system plan?*

▶ *Why do users and managers have to participate in information system planning and development?*

▶ *How is information system planning linked to business planning?*

▶ *What are some of the strategic issues in information system planning?*

▶ *What are the key issues in balancing centralized versus distributed processing and control?*

▶ *How is cost–benefit analysis used in making investment decisions about information systems?*

▶ *What are the basic elements of project management for information system projects?*

In 1989, Eastman Kodak Co. made a decision that startled the information systems profession. Kodak decided to dismantle part of its systems staff by farming out its data center operations to IBM, its networking to Digital Equipment Corporation, and its personal computer supply and support operations to Businessland. As part of the ten-year agreement, Kodak turned its mainframes and storage equipment over to IBM, which agreed to build a 140,000-square-foot data center, consolidating four previous Kodak mainframe sites. These computers would handle financial transactions, payroll, personnel, customer records, and manufacturing data. IBM would provide new hardware and software as needed, as well as disaster recovery and security for information processing.

Kodak's strategy was consistent with a corporate trend of focusing resources and energy on a company's core business and outsourcing the other activities (hiring another firm to perform functions formerly done in-house). According to Kathy Hudson, Director of Information Systems, Kodak made this decision because "IBM is in the data processing business, and Kodak isn't." Kodak's 1989 plan was to eventually reduce its central IS staff from 2,000 employees to fewer than 200. Around 800 programmers were moved into user departments to provide support closer to them and to focus on linking information technology to the business strategy.

By 1991, the strategy had generated results. Kodak took a $225 million restructuring charge against its earnings in 1989, but its capital spending for computing dropped 90 percent and operating expenses dropped 10 to 20 percent. Kodak also became more frugal in handling data processing. Previously, users had not taken data processing expenses as seriously because data processing was an internal cost. Now Kodak's departments actually paid IBM, and this led them to attend to costs more closely.[1, 2] But by 1993, Kodak had layoffs and needed to restructure its business operations. It renegotiated its outsourcing contracts with IBM and with JWP, a New York service conglomerate that had acquired Businessland but was itself having business difficulties and laying off employees.[3] Meanwhile, a lawsuit by former Kodak employees who had been transferred to Digital Equipment Corporation in the outsourcing had not been settled. They claimed that they did not receive the benefits and job security they had been promised.[4]

DEBATE TOPIC   *Argue the pros and cons and practical implications of the following proposition:*
Outsourcing information system functions is a bad idea because it stifles innovation and gives vital resources and company knowledge to external vendors.

T HE DECISION TO OUTSOURCE INFORMATION CENTER OPERATIONS was the result of long-term IS planning by Kodak executives. They made the decision based on their perception of the best way to develop and maintain the information systems Kodak needed to accomplish its corporate business plans. IS planning didn't stop with the outsourcing decision, however. That decision was one of many higher-level decisions leading to much additional work creating a detailed plan of action to move from the current way of doing things to the new way.

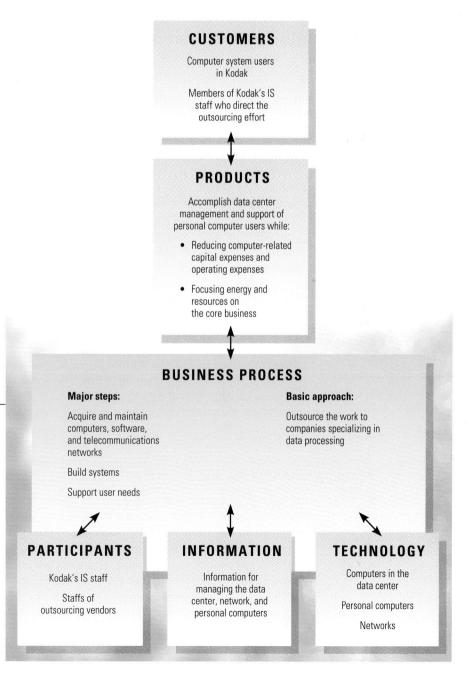

Figure 13.1 Kodak: Outsourcing Data Processing

CUSTOMERS

Computer system users in Kodak

Members of Kodak's IS staff who direct the outsourcing effort

PRODUCTS

Accomplish data center management and support of personal computer users while:

- Reducing computer-related capital expenses and operating expenses

- Focusing energy and resources on the core business

BUSINESS PROCESS

Major steps:

Acquire and maintain computers, software, and telecommunications networks

Build systems

Support user needs

Basic approach:

Outsource the work to companies specializing in data processing

PARTICIPANTS

Kodak's IS staff

Staffs of outsourcing vendors

INFORMATION

Information for managing the data center, network, and personal computers

TECHNOLOGY

Computers in the data center

Personal computers

Networks

This chapter introduces many issues related to IS planning that every firm should do in some way. Regardless of whether the firm has one employee or 100,000, it is still necessary to decide what will be done, who will do it, when they will do it, how it will be done, and what are the desired results.

This is the first of three chapters about building and maintaining information systems. Aspects of these topics such as alternative processes for building and maintaining systems were introduced briefly in Chapter 1 and will now be explained in more depth. This chapter covers information system planning at both the strategic and project levels. Chapter 14 covers alternative approaches for building information systems, and Chapter 15 covers information system security and control.

Introduction to Information System Planning

What Is an Information System Plan?

Planning is the process of deciding what will be done, who will do it, when they will do it, how it will be done, and what are the desired results. Table 13.1 shows that these questions can be addressed at several levels when thinking about information systems. At the strategic level, the questions are about the firm's overall priorities and goals for information systems and the technical and organizational approaches that will be used. At the project level, the questions boil down to two types of concerns: first, what specific capabilities are required in each system, and second, who will do what and when will they do it to produce the specific results needed in a specific project, such as building a new sales tracking system or retraining users of a customer service system that has been changed.

Information system planning should be an integral part of business planning. Business planning is the process of identifying the firm's goals, objectives, and priorities, and developing action plans for accomplishing those goals and objectives. **Information systems planning** is the part of business planning concerned with deploying the firm's information systems resources, including people, hardware, and software. Figure 13.2 illustrates the similarity between information system planning and planning in various functional areas. The goals, objectives, and priorities of the business should drive all the plans. Furthermore, although each plan is produced by specialists in a particular department, all the plans should support the same strategy and goals. From this viewpoint, the unique aspect of the information system plan is that it concentrates on information system projects.

Planning Role of the IS and User Departments

A firm's information systems department is usually responsible for producing the IS plan in conjunction with the user departments, such as marketing and finance. As happens in other departments, managers in the IS department start the planning process by reviewing their progress on the existing plan. They look at special problems, such as systems approaching obsolescence. They confer with managers in the user departments to learn about user priorities and needs for system improvements, new systems, and user support. IS department managers also look at the needs of their own department such as training, hiring, and personnel development.

Table 13.1 Planning Questions for Information Systems

Issue	Strategic Level	Project Level
Who?	• What are the responsibilities of the IS department and the user departments? • Which vendors will perform major functions that are outsourced?	• Who will work on each project? • Who will decide how the business process should operate? • Who will manage and support the system after it is in operation?
What?	• What are the major things that the IS department must do so that the firm can accomplish its goals?	• What specific capabilities are required in the system? • What will be the individual steps in each project?
When?	• What are the major completion dates that the firm can rely on?	• When will the individual steps in each project be completed?
How?	• What technology will be used to do the work? • What technology must be available so that the work can be done well? • What capabilities must the firm have to compete in the future?	• How will system development techniques be used to produce the desired results? • How will the IS department and user departments work together on the project?
Desired results?	• How will business processes change in terms of detailed operation and controllable results?	• What deliverable results will each step in each project produce?

Figure 13.2 The Information System Plan as Part of the Business Plan

The plan for each functional area (and for information systems) should be based on the firm's goals, objectives, and priorities. The individual plans in each of the areas are part of the business plan and should be consistent with it and support it.

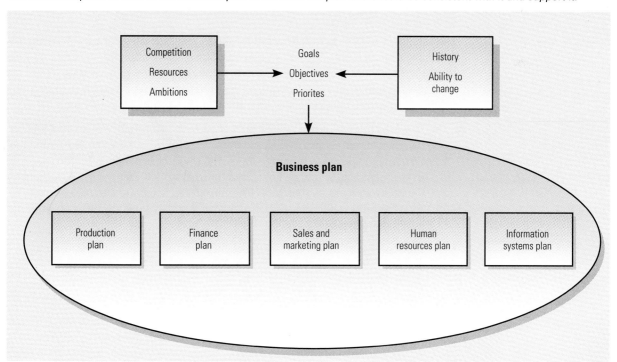

Many questions and issues arise as an initial IS plan is produced and reviewed. Users are often frustrated by how long it takes to build new systems and how much effort it takes to make what might seem like small changes to existing systems. The IS department often feels frustrated by its inability to keep up with many of the business's pressing problems.

It is important to allocate resources carefully because most firms don't come close to having the IS resources needed to develop all the systems that people in the company say they need. It is not unusual for a central IS department to have over a two-year backlog of committed projects, with many other requests simply turned down or never submitted formally because of the minimal chance that they would be acted on.

Chief information officer

Recognizing the importance of information systems in corporate success, some firms have designated the head of the IS department the **chief information officer (CIO),** just as the head of finance is the CFO and the chief executive of the company is the CEO. By leading the IS function, the CIO has special responsibility for making sure that the IS plan supports the firm's business plan and provides long-term direction for the firm's system-related efforts.

The role of CIO calls for a rare mix of business skills and technical knowledge. CIOs too focused on computer technology may have trouble being seen as business-people working for the overall good of the firm. CIOs too focused on general business issues may have trouble resolving the technical issues related to adopting new technologies essential for future business practices. In the early 1990s, career turmoil among CIOs was so common that some claimed CIO stood for "career is over." Regardless of whether individuals succeeded in filling an ambitious role, the strategic nature of IS leadership is increasingly clear.

User roles in IS planning

Even though the IS department compiles the IS plan, members of user departments also have responsibilities related to IS plans. Since information systems exist to help them do their work, they have to ensure that the right systems are developed and are used effectively and efficiently. Members of user departments participate in IS planning in various roles, including sponsor, champion, and steering committee member.

- **Sponsors** are senior managers who recognize the importance of an information system and make sure resources are allocated for building and maintaining the system. In addition to funding, the crucial resource is people from the user department who would be doing their normal work if they were not working on the information system project. For example, an accounting manager might spend months as the user representative in a project building a new accounting information system.

- **Champions** are individuals who recognize the importance of an information system and exert effort to make sure that the system is recognized as important by others in the organization. Champions may not have direct control of resources for the system even though they promote its success.

- **IS steering committees** meet to make sure the IS effort reflects business priorities. These committees typically include knowledgeable representatives from user groups plus members of the IS department. Responsibilities of these committees range from identifying problems to reviewing system proposals and long-term IS plans (see Figure 13.3).

Figure 13.3 IS Steering Committee Discusses the IS Plan

IS steering committees typically include knowledgeable representatives from user departments and members of the IS department.

Since IS planning efforts inevitably face questions about resources for maintaining existing systems versus resources for building new systems, we will look at this issue next.

Allocating Resources Between New and Old Systems

An IS plan allocates resources such as money and programmer time between different possible uses of those resources. Major uses of those resources include maintaining existing systems, developing new systems, supporting users, and trying out new ideas and techniques.

Maintaining existing systems and supporting users

Keeping existing systems operating efficiently and effectively as business conditions change often absorbs 60 to 80 percent of the planned work in an IS plan. This work can be split into three categories: direct user support, system enhancements, and bug fixes.

User-support projects include helping users with applications developed by the IS department, with applications purchased from outside vendors, and with individual work performed on personal computers. The individual work typically involves personal use of tools such as spreadsheets, word processors, and presentation graphics. Given the ongoing nature of user-support projects, many firms have staffed **information centers,** separate groups devoted to helping users develop and maintain their own applications, especially applications that extract data from corporate databases. Ideally, an information center should reduce costs and increase effectiveness by standardizing on a few types of hardware and software, offering training programs for users, and helping users analyze and solve their own problems.

Enhancements are improvements in an existing system's function without changing its fundamental concepts or operation. Active users who care about what the system does are often able to suggest many desired enhancements. The list of suggestions usually grows as users learn what the system can and cannot do in its current form and as they think up new ways to use it to greater advantage. Many IS departments could assign every programmer to enhancements and barely make a dent in the list of suggestions from their users.

Bug fixes are projects directed at correcting bugs in existing systems. Bugs are flaws in systems that cause them to produce incorrect or inappropriate results. All large information systems (and most small ones) contain bugs. The planning issue is to decide how much effort should go into fixing them. Since important bugs may be recognized during the period covered by the plan, IS plans should reserve time and effort for bug fixes even though the specific bugs to be fixed may not be known in advance.

Bugs are usually divided into priority-based categories. Bugs that prevent people from doing their work or prevent departments from operating effectively receive the highest priority and usually preempt other scheduled work. Bugs that cause minor problems for the user are typically fixed when convenient. Minor bugs having little impact on users' ability to do their work may never be fixed.

New development, infrastructure, and other projects

Resources not assigned to maintaining existing systems and supporting users can be allocated to a variety of other projects, including new application development, information infrastructure projects, and research projects.

Major new application projects provide new types of capabilities for users rather than small improvements in existing application systems. New application projects can be divided further into projects that require new technology, knowledge, and methods, versus systems for which existing knowledge and methods suffice. Projects that require new technology, knowledge, or methods are usually riskier than those applying currently used approaches. To reduce the likelihood of high visibility failures, only a limited number of high-risk projects should be undertaken at any time.

Information infrastructure projects install and maintain the hardware, software, and human support organizations that are used by application systems. Installing and maintaining computers and telecommunications hardware is the type of infrastructure project users see most directly. Infrastructure projects emphasizing software include installing a new DBMS or new system development software. Installation and maintenance of networks involves work on both the network hardware and the software controlling the network.

Research projects evaluate new methods or technology to determine how they might be used. The research may involve finding out about the existence of new tools and trying them out. When a new technology seems applicable, the firm typically does a **pilot project,** a limited, experimental application to get experience with the new technology. Pilot projects are usually done with users who are particularly interested and wish to be innovators. Although these projects use a small percentage of a firm's IS resources, they are important because they help bring about innovation and change. An IS department that does no research may be stagnating.

Merely looking at the different types of projects helps you see that IS planning involves much more than just making a list of the new systems to be developed. Many IS professionals feel frustrated that so little of their effort can go into new system development.

Project Roles of Information System Professionals

IS projects vary greatly in size and complexity. In small system development projects, a single person or several people may play all the necessary roles without defining them explicitly. For example, if a small business buys and uses an accounting package, a user or IS professional may purchase it from a computer store, install it on a personal computer, train other users, and consult the vendor's customer support staff for questions. Various roles may be combined into a single person's job responsibilities in this way.

In large projects involving hundreds, or even thousands, of people, many distinct roles are assigned to individuals. Box 13.1 briefly defines common roles in typical major projects, such as developing online transaction processing systems used for day-to-day operation of large companies. Teams of analysts, programmers, and programmer-analysts produce such systems. Technical writers produce the user documentation. Computer operators keep the systems running and make sure the reports are produced at the right times. The system manager makes sure that the computer system itself is maintained. The user support staff makes sure that the users are trained and are receiving benefits from the system.

Many of the same roles apply even if the project involves acquiring and installing an application package sold by a software vendor. For example, systems analysts still need to determine the requirements, and the user support staff still has to train the users. Programming may also be required to tailor the purchased system to the firm's needs or to link the purchased system to the firm's other internal systems.

Box 13.1 Roles of Information System Professionals in Building and Maintaining Information Systems

---

Large system development projects involve many roles such as the following:
- *Project managers* manage the people doing the work to make sure that project goals are accomplished. Among other things, project managers develop schedules, monitor work for completeness and quality, and help resolve conflicts and questions that arise. Project managers in IS departments typically started as programmers or systems analysts and showed they could take responsibility for larger parts of projects.

- *Application programmers* convert a general understanding or written description of a business problem into a set of programs that accomplish the required computer processing. Their jobs include designing the programs and database, coding and testing the programs, and producing the related program documentation.

- *Systems analysts* perform the analysis to decide how a new or updated system can help solve a business problem or exploit a business opportunity. They communicate the results to programmers who write the programs.

- *Programmer-analysts* play the role of both programmer and analyst in situations where it is more effective to combine these roles.

- *Technical writers* produce user documentation and training material.

- *Computer operators* make sure that a computer is running, that tapes and removable disks are loaded and unloaded, and that jobs such as backups and database reconfigurations are performed on time.

- *Database administrators* control the definition of all items in a shared database and monitor the performance of the database.

- *System managers* manage computer installations and make sure that the hardware is configured properly and that the operators do their jobs.

- *Systems programmers* write programs related to the operating system and internal operation of the computer system. This is a more specialized job than programmer, which generally refers to someone who produces programs related to business applications.

- *User support staffs* help the users use the system by providing training, answering questions, and collecting change requests.

REALITY CHECK **Issues in Planning** A plan is a statement of what will be done and how and when it will be done. Strategic-level plans and project-level plans address different concerns.

1. Identify any project you have worked on (preferably with other people). Whether or not a plan existed for that project, summarize some of the things that could have been included in the strategic-level plan and in the project-level plan.

2. Explain why you agree or disagree with this statement: Information systems plans should be fundamentally similar to any other type of plan since a plan is just a statement of what will be done and how and when it will be done.

Strategic Issues

Strategic planning issues related to information systems combine business, technical, and organizational concerns. Optimal use of information systems requires appropriate technology applied to the right business problems in a way that is effective in the organization. This section looks at six types of strategic concerns: consistency with business priorities, IS architecture, IS infrastructure, centralization versus decentralization, outsourcing, and international issues.

Consistency with Business Priorities

Since information systems exist to support business processes that carry out a company's plans, it might seem obvious that a company's IS plan should be linked to its business plan. Obvious or not, this has not always happened. Only 36 percent of the CEOs interviewed in a 1989 survey[5] believed that the deployment of information system resources in their firm supported their company's business plan.

With the enormous amount of attention information technology has received in the late 1980s and early 1990s, many companies are now more careful that information system plans truly reflect business needs. Two rallying cries used to focus these efforts are critical success factors and business process reengineering.

Critical success factors

The **critical success factors** (CSF) method is an approach for identifying the factors that are critical to a business operation's success. Information systems that support these factors should have the highest priority and should provide important information needed by executives. The CSF method encourages executives to identify what is important to them in their business. It builds on that dialogue to identify what information systems are most needed.

The CSF method uses four steps. First, the executives identify the firm's primary mission and the objectives that define satisfactory overall performance. Next, they identify critical success factors, the things that must go right for the business to succeed. Most businesses have relatively few critical success factors. CSFs typically come from sources such as the structure of the industry, the firm's competitive strategy, its industry position or geographic location, environmental factors surrounding the firm, and temporary operating problems or opportunities.[6] Examples for one firm included improving customer relationships, improving supplier relationships, making the best use of inventory, and using capital and human resources efficiently and effectively.

The third step is to identify the pertinent indicators or measures of performance for each CSF. For example, customer relations might be measured in terms of trends in customers lost, new customers, the ratio of customer inquiries to customer orders, or on-time delivery. The fourth step is to decide which measures are most important and then make sure that IS plans provide means for collecting and using this information.

The benefits of using the CSF method start with a shared understanding of what is critical to a company. This influences not only the design of systems but also the priorities for system development. Explicit identification of CSFs also aids executive-level communication about important company issues.

Although the CSF method provides a useful framework in many situations, like any technique it should be applied with care and has some important weaknesses. It is more effective when used with senior managers rather than middle managers who focus more on their own areas and are less aware of the organization's overall CSFs. Furthermore, some managers who focus on day-to-day operations rather than planning may have difficulty dealing with the conceptual nature of CSFs.[7]

Business process reengineering

According to Michael Hammer, the consultant who popularized the term, **business process reengineering (BPR)** is "the fundamental rethinking and radical redesign of business processes to achieve dramatic improvements in critical contemporary measures of performance, such as cost, quality, service, and speed."[8] Highly publicized examples such as Ford's accounts payable system (opening case in Chapter 3) made business process reengineering a guiding principle for projects aimed at changing key business processes such as the way insurance companies handle claims and the way manufacturers design products.

This approach starts from the belief that nothing about an organization or business process is sacred. The way things are done today may reflect nothing more than many years of trying to do things the same way even though the business environment and customers changed. Therefore, the business process of tomorrow may be completely different. Common outcomes of business process reengineering include combining several jobs into one, permitting workers to make more decisions themselves, defining different versions of processes for simple cases versus complex ones, minimizing the number of jobs devoted to checking someone else's work, and reorganizing jobs to give individuals more understanding and more responsibility.[9] Many reengineering efforts also result in significant staff reductions.

The promise of business process reengineering captured the imagination of American managers in the early 1990s, and many impressive successes were announced. But it was also seen in many quarters as a slogan or umbrella term under which any important project might be explained and as a convenient excuse for layoffs. For example, *Fortune* quoted a telephone company executive who said, "If you want to get something funded around here— anything, even a new chair for your office—call it reengineering on your request for expenditure."[10] The author Paul Strassmann is even more skeptical: "There's nothing new or original about business process reengineering. It's just a lot of old industrial methods, recycled and repackaged to seem like the latest in management science. ... Reengineering excels more in its packaging than in its substance. Its purpose is to make the purging of past staffing gluttony more palatable."[11]

Because of the radical restructuring it calls for, most firms attempting major BPR projects have found them difficult and risky. Robert Rubin, President of SIM, the leading organization for IS executives, expressed part of the problem as follows: "One way to judge if you are reengineering: The first time you bring it up, if no one screams,

'Are you crazy?' then it is not a reengineering project." The same article cited a report co-authored by Michael Hammer speculating that the failure rate for reengineering projects is likely on the order of 70 percent.[12] A 1994 survey of 350 executives by the consulting firm Arthur D. Little concluded that more than 85 percent of the respondents were dissatisfied with the results, and 60 percent encountered unanticipated problems or unintended side effects related to turf battles, lack of management buy-in, and inadequate implementation skills.

Both CSF and BPR are approaches for thinking about what information systems should do. CSF focuses on providing information about the things that the business needs to do to succeed. BPR focuses on using information systems to totally change the way important business processes operate. In both cases, the analysis leads to information system priorities that should be in line with business priorities. Next, we look at strategic issues that must be considered while deciding how to put the results of the CSF or BPR analysis into operation in an organization.

Information System Architecture

The WCA method in Chapter 2 used the term *architecture* as one of five perspectives for thinking about a specific system. This perspective involved defining the system's components and the way those components operate together. The term is also used in a more general way in IS planning.

A firm's **information system architecture** is the basic blueprint showing how the firm's data processing systems, telecommunications networks, and data are integrated. It is a highly summarized answer to the following questions:

- What data are collected?

- Where and how are the data to be collected?

- How are the data to be transmitted?

- Where are the data stored?

- What applications use the data, and how are these applications related as an overall system?

Monsanto faced a typical IS architecture problem when attempting to track actual versus projected costs on engineering projects. One database contained the hours each employee worked on each project, whereas another summarized project expenses in dollar amounts according to engineering discipline but not project. Simply moving data from one computer to another was also a problem. For example, there was no direct link between the computer at Monsanto's Hawaii refinery and its database in California. Even in today's seemingly networked world, data transfer required copying data from a DEC PDP-11 computer onto a diskette, walking to a personal computer, uploading the data to an IBM 3090 mainframe in California, and then downloading it to the server running the database.[13]

Although IS architecture may seem like a technical issue, it is actually a strategic, managerial view of how an organization operates. IS architecture is strongly linked to a firm's business strategy because it determines the practical range of business and product strategies the firm can employ.[14] Consider a bank whose new business strategy is based on combining checking accounts, savings accounts, credit cards, and loans into a simplified account relationship. This strategy can be used only if customer IDs in each of the separate areas can be grouped into single combined accounts. In addition, the bank can provide 24-hour response to customer queries only if all the data is in an immediately accessible database rather than on paper files at branches. The wrong IS architecture would doom the business strategy.

Enterprise modeling

Enterprise modeling is a technique used to summarize a firm's current information system architecture and to design a new architecture for data processing. Enterprise modeling starts with analyzing current business processes and the data they use and share. A new set of systems is proposed, clustering around groups of shared data. For instance, customer-oriented systems such as order entry, billing, accounts receivable, and service contract management are grouped around the central customer database. Figure 13.4 shows a simplified example of the type of process–data matrix that is produced by enterprise modeling.

Figure 13.4 A Process–Data Matrix for a Manufacturing Firm

A process–data matrix such as this simplified example can be used in enterprise modeling to summarize current data processing systems and to help visualize desired changes. In the matrix, C and U stand for "creates" and "uses." For example, the sales planning uses the market forecast and creates the sales plan.

Processes \ Data	Market forecast	Sales plan	Work-in-process	Inventory	Purchase plan	Open orders	Vendor quality	Vendor history	Engineering data	Equipment data
Sales planning	U	C								
Production planning		U	U	U						
Daily scheduling		U	U	U						
Vendor qualification							C			
Ordering					C	C	U	C		
Receiving						C		C		
Inventory control				C						
Manufacturing			C	U					C	C
Process engineering									U	U
Product engineering									U	
Equipment maintenance										U

Specifying a new IS architecture is a big job usually done only when major system revisions are planned. It often takes six to eight weeks or more to define business processes, define the data used by the processes, summarize the current IS architecture, and recommend a new architecture.[15] This project requires concentrated effort by experienced analysts and knowledgeable user representatives. The payoff is greater understanding and a longer-lasting IS architecture than would be likely if each application were built independently.

Information System Infrastructure

Like a city's infrastructure, information system infrastructure goes beyond the blueprint and includes the technical and human systems that are shared by different applications. A city's infrastructure includes physical things such as streets, public buildings, and telephone lines. It also includes shared services such as police, fire fighting, education, and public health. These services use various technical means but are delivered by people who are an essential part of the city's infrastructure.

A firm's **information system infrastructure** is its IS architecture plus the technical and human resources for building, operating, and maintaining systems. Just as the fire department is part of a city's infrastructure, the IS department is part of a firm's IS infrastructure. For an IS plan to be feasible, the IS department staff must be willing and able to perform the required development and maintenance. Four aspects of infrastructure will be discussed: platforms, tools and methods, legacy systems, and IS staff.

Platforms

Computerized information systems cannot exist without the computer and other hardware. The term **platform** is used to describe the basic type of computer and network that an information system uses. A small business that needs only a personal computer might choose between a platform based on an Intel 486 chip, a Pentium chip, or a Motorola Power PC chip. The decision would depend on characteristics of the application, including the processing required, database size, and the availability of software that runs on that chip. After deciding on the platform, the company could choose among various brands of computers using the chip that was selected. If needs were underestimated, upgrading to a more powerful chip in the same family would cost money but should not be difficult in principle. Going to a different family, such as from a Motorola Power PC to an Intel Pentium would be more difficult because software written for the Power PC would not run on the Pentium and would have to be replaced.

In larger companies, the choice of a platform is much more complicated because the platform often includes mainframes, departmental computers, and workstations that must work together using networks. Sharing information and applications while using different platforms is often a waste of resources and can become a nightmare if incompatibilities are serious. Consolidating from multiple platforms to a unified platform to make the infrastructure more efficient is rarely a prized project. The benefits are in the background and are often less visible to users than direct benefits from application enhancements. Consequently, the choice of a platform for large shared applications has long-term implications and should be considered carefully.

Tools and methods

IS infrastructure also includes the tools and methods used to build and maintain information systems. The entire discussion of programming and software in Chapter 10 was about the evolution of better methods for building and maintaining systems. COBOL was the basis of most business data processing systems built before the 1980s. Relational DBMSs, and CASE systems became common in the last decade. Object-oriented programming is newer and now often at the pilot project stage. These technical developments are important to business because an inability to build or enhance systems quickly and reliably reduces any firm's competitiveness.

Although programming languages receive a lot of attention, they are only part of the tool kit since the coding process is only 10 to 15 percent of the work in many projects. Programming languages become effective in business only when they are surrounded by systems that help programmers store, modify, and document program modules, and test programs and systems. Acceptance of DBMS, CASE, and more recently object-oriented programming has been delayed by the lack of these tools that make it possible to use the language effectively and efficiently in a system development process.

Legacy systems

Legacy systems are a crucial challenge to any effort to improve IS architecture and infrastructure. **Legacy systems** are systems that have been passed down to the current users and IS staff. They are old, often technically obsolete systems that perform essential data processing such as accounting and customer billing in many firms. Many of these systems were initially built in the 1960s or 1970s and have been enhanced many times but still use programming methods that are 20 years out of date. The many changes to these systems are often poorly documented, and the people who made the changes have often left for other jobs.

An example was Aetna Life and Casualty's Fastline claims processing system. Originally built in the 1970s and eventually consisting of 1.75 million lines of COBOL code, it had been modified many times and had become a nightmare for the 28 programmers required to maintain it. In 1986, Aetna restructured it totally. By 1990, 70 percent fewer programmers could support the same number of maintenance requests.[16]

Like many legacy systems, Aetna's Fastline had reached the point where it was essential to business operations but difficult to change as business needs evolve. Such systems are a major stumbling block because they are complicated, technically fragile, and poorly understood. Nonetheless, it may be hard to get the funds to overhaul them because the benefits from doing the overhaul are indirect and largely related to greater flexibility and reliability in the future. Other large projects that could use the same funds often generate greater immediate business benefits.

The IS staff

In information-intensive companies, such as financial institutions, it is especially important to maintain a highly skilled IS department capable of developing competitively significant systems. In less information-intensive companies, it is cost effective to rely much more on commercially available application packages. This approach is less challenging for the IS staff. A team that only installs predeveloped packages provides a useful service but may be less able to build a new major system if it were needed.

The match between the IS plan and the IS staff's capabilities and aspirations often is a key issue. Retaining top-quality programmers and systems analysts often requires an IS plan including some substantial development projects. Ambitious programmers and systems analysts often find the greatest challenge, enjoyment, and professional recognition in developing new systems. They are less interested in installing commercially available packages and providing small enhancements and troubleshooting for existing systems.

Changing to a newer technology can also cause staffing problems when staff members are unwilling to learn the new technology or feel that it threatens their personal expertise. For example, Kash 'n Karry Food Stores, a $1.2 billion grocery chain in Tampa, Florida, saw a 70 percent exodus from its mainframe computing staff in the first six months of its migration to client–server computing.[17]

Centralization versus Decentralization

The balance between needs for centralization and decentralization strongly affects the success of information systems. As with many other organizational endeavors, over-centralization results in overly rigid systems that cannot handle local variations.

Similarly, excessive decentralization creates systems that may solve local problems but may not conform or interface well enough to solve problems that cross departments. Decisions involving centralization and decentralization often hinge on debates about efficiency (using the least resources to produce a given output) and effectiveness (producing the right output). Centralization is often more efficient because it eliminates redundant resources and effort. If decentralization is technically feasible, it is often more effective because it allows people to make the right decisions for their own local situations.

Centralization versus decentralization is an especially difficult issue for international firms because every aspect of IS management has more variations and surprises, such as differences in country infrastructure, culture, and laws. International issues are discussed later.

In information systems, the term **distributed processing** is often used to describe the dispersion of information system location, ownership, and control to different parts of the organization. Organizations that have more distributed processing also have a more decentralized IS function. Key factors in centralization and decentralization include configuration of the hardware, location of data, standards, and ownership and management control (see Table 13.2).

Table 13.2 Centralization versus Decentralization

	Highly Centralized	**Intermediate**	**Highly Decentralized**
Hardware configuration	Central computer, remote terminals	Distributed network linking local data centers	Independent local data centers, personal computers
Data location	Centralized database	Central database plus local databases	Local databases
Hardware and software choices	Central decisions	Central guidelines, local choices	Local choices
Ownership and control	Central information systems group	Central services, system ownership by user departments	User departments
Organizational affiliation of IS staff	Central IS group	Highly technical IS roles affiliated with central group, less technical roles in user organization	Most IS roles affiliated with user organization (except infrastructure and planning)

Location of hardware and data

Computer hardware can exist at any or all of the following levels: corporate headquarters, regional processing centers, site processing centers (for individual factories or offices), department processors, work group processors, and individual workstations. The most centralized approach is to have all the computers in a centralized computer center, with telecommunications links to terminals at other locations. The least centralized approach is to provide employees with their own personal computers and allow them to perform and control their own data processing.

Figure 13.5 show how most large firms use intermediate configurations that combine a centralized data processing facility with local data processing centers and networked personal computers for individuals or offices. Centralized locations process data that must be shared across the company or that can be processed most efficiently in a centralized way. Local data centers process data that should be shared within a division or geographical location but are not needed elsewhere in the company. The personal computers are used for individual data processing.

Figure 13.5 Intermediate Degree of Distributed Processing

Most large firms use intermediate degrees of centralized data processing, with local data processing centers and personal computers for individuals or offices.

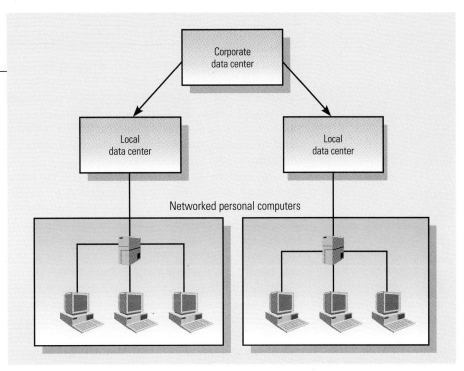

In distributing data, the most centralized approach is to have all the data at a centralized location; the least centralized is to allow individuals to maintain their own data. Intermediate configurations employ a centralized database for data that must be accessed across the organization, plus local or individual databases for data pertinent only to an office or individual. Centralized databases are used for corporate accounting, corporate inventories, and other data that must be controlled at the corporate level and accessed broadly. Firms frequently compromise between convenience and accessibility of local data and control and maintainability of centralized data. They do this by performing daily downloads of locally relevant portions of the central database to the local users. Many companies have developed extensive telecommunications networks for moving data to and from centralized databases.

Standards, ownership, and guidelines for action

Establishing corporate standards is essential for efficiency, even if the hardware and data are physically decentralized. Corporate standards determine which hardware and software can be purchased and what procedures to use in deploying the systems. Standards for hardware and data make it easier for people to share their work. They are also necessary for economies of scale in purchasing equipment, training personnel, and using data. Without standards, individuals and departments can make independent decisions about which hardware and software to buy, often resulting in incompatible systems. The existence of incompatible systems may not affect individuals doing their own individual work but is grossly inefficient when data or models must be shared by many users. Having standards doesn't guarantee that systems will be consistent but does increase the chances of realizing economies of scale.

Regardless of where hardware and data reside, the question of ownership is always an issue. For example, who should own a division's sales forecasting system: the marketing department or the IS department? With a centralized approach, a central department owns and controls all information systems, and a request to change a system would go to that department. A decentralized approach would say that whoever owns the products forecasted by the system should own the system itself. Permitting decentralized ownership of systems leads to greater responsiveness to change requests but may result in systems that are not well controlled. For example, a company with extremely decentralized systems found that one of its important systems had absolutely no documentation. The developer, a flamboyant individual who liked helping users but hated writing documentation, had left the company. Had the system been under central control, it probably would be documented but might not have had as many of the features users wanted.

Whether or not a central IS group owns the information systems, there are still important reasons to have general guidelines for building and administering systems. At minimum, such guidelines reduce the organizational inefficiency of learning how to install, interface, and manage unnecessary variations on the same basic technologies. But the guidelines can go further by talking about the way the organization's systems should be justified and built. For example, the guidelines might say that a formal cost–benefit analysis must be done for any system beyond a particular size or that data should be captured when first created. To support interoperability even when different types of hardware or software are used, the guidelines can cover things such as eliminating redundant data definitions, defining uniform transmission standards, limiting the different types of graphical interfaces, separating data definitions from the programs that use them, and establishing uniform CASE environments.[18]

Issues concerning location, ownership, and control of resources are by no means unique to information systems. Questions about centralization versus decentralization occur in all business functions whether or not computerized systems are involved. In sales, the question is often whether several product divisions will share the same sales force or distribution channels. In production, it is whether product divisions will share factories and research labs. In each case, the decision incorporates historical precedent in the company; economies of scale from centralization; advantages of focus from decentralization; and other personal, political, and economic issues.

Issues about centralization or decentralization are often even more complicated for information systems because the technology itself adds a layer of professional expertise, details, inertia, and confusion. Each approach has its advantages. Centralization may enhance the IS department's effectiveness and long-term potential. It also increases the ability to maintain standards for quality, consistency, and maintainability. Decentralization may avoid bureaucracy and lengthy system development backlogs. Decentralization also makes it possible to experiment locally and grow in smaller increments and to continue processing work even when one computer is down.

Position of the IS staff

The division of labor between user and IS departments is based on a combination of organizational history and practical tradeoffs. With a highly centralized approach, the programmers, analysts, and support personnel are in the IS department. This maintains professional affiliations with systems activities and may lead to greater professional depth in their discipline. But it may also separate them from the users and reduce responsiveness to user needs. In a decentralized approach, the programmers and analysts are in the user department, which tends to generate greater loyalty to the user department and greater understanding of the application. It also reduces their affiliation with other professionals in their field, however, and may ultimately reduce their technical depth. Table 13.3 lists some of the commonly cited differences between IS professionals and typical system users. Like most generalizations about groups of people, there are many counterexamples to the differences listed in the table. No individual should be treated on the basis of a stereotype.

The balance between centralizing and decentralizing the information systems staff may affect the success of information systems. With too much centralization, users often feel that they don't receive enough support and that the IS department doesn't appreciate their needs. With too much decentralization, servicing of small requests may be fine, but there is less of the centralized focus and planning needed to develop strategic systems.

Table 13.3 Commonly Cited Differences Between IS Professionals and Typical Users

Type of Difference	Tendency of IS Staff	Tendency of User Department
Professional orientation	Allegiance to profession	Allegiance to firm
Language	Language of computers	Language of business
Interests and recognition	Technical elegance	Practical solutions produced quickly
Project goals	Long-term maintenance	Practical solutions produced quickly
Work style and content	Analytical work related to computers	Work through people

Outsourcing

The term **outsourcing** can be used in a general way to denote any product or service that is purchased from another firm. For example, all major auto companies outsource manufacturing of many components. Likewise, many firms outsource their cafeteria to food service companies. In general, companies outsource the products and services they do not want to or are unable to produce themselves. Competitive pressures of the 1990s have increased outsourcing across all industries by forcing companies to focus on the unique functions they do best, such as manufacturing at the lowest cost or providing excellent customer service in retailing.

Outsourcing of computer hardware, telecommunications services, and systems software such as operating systems and DBMSs is a long-standing practice in IS departments. These departments also purchase end-user software such as spreadsheets and word processors because there is no reason to reinvent tools a software company specializing in these products can provide much more cheaply. Although these examples involve products and services bought from other firms, they are not the type of IS outsourcing that has become controversial.

The controversial side of IS outsourcing involves hiring outside organizations to perform system-related functions often performed by IS departments. Business application software was one of the first areas for this type of outsourcing, with many firms purchasing commercial systems for common functions such as keeping track of inventory, purchase orders, and customer orders. Buying commercially available application software makes sense when there is nothing unique or competitively significant about the way the firm wants to perform the business function. Firms attempting to attain competitive advantage from a unique way of performing a business function typically cannot buy readily available commercial software to support the function.

Operating computer centers and telecommunications hardware is another common area for outsourcing. Companies deciding whether to do this look for reasons why they can perform these functions more efficiently than firms whose main business is in this area. By performing these functions for many customers, outsourcing vendors may have more experience doing the work and greater ability to negotiate quantity discounts with hardware and software vendors. They may also be more able to pick up the slack if key staff members at a particular site leave.

Taken to an extreme, outsourcing of IS activities would mean having a very small IS department limited to developing IS plans and negotiating with outsourcing vendors. This is risky because of the reliance on an outside firm to perform essential functions, including building and maintaining application systems. Since the outsourcing vendor would have so much of the knowledge about the company's systems, the company might end up lacking the staff and vision needed to produce competitively significant systems. If the outsourcing vendor developed business problems of its own, the company's basic data processing could be thrown into chaos. Even without a calamity, a ten-year outsourcing contract might spawn other problems by not anticipating evolving business requirements.

A careful study of outsourcing in the early 1990s concluded that public information sources are often overoptimistic about outsourcing, that outsourcing vendors are not necessarily more efficient than internal IS groups, and that internal IS groups can often achieve similar results. The study argued against the belief that IS is just a commodity or utility, and noted that the outsourcing phenomenon is closely related to the difficulty of demonstrating the value of IS. Since the outsourcing vendors have their own separate profit motives and business issues, the study urged companies considering outsourcing not to be enticed by slogans about outsourcing vendors as "partners" and to write the outsourcing contract with the utmost care.[19]

International Issues

As business becomes more international and competition more global, information systems crossing national boundaries have proliferated. Some of these are internal management and control systems of multinational companies. Others are links between companies in one country and customers, suppliers, and agents elsewhere. The significance of these systems is growing because they provide a way to reduce the limitations of time and geography.

International issues start with a basic fact that things just work differently in different places, especially when different histories, cultures, and languages are involved. These differences appear at many different levels and make it necessary to retest basic assumptions about how things work. Shirts may button differently, paper may be a different size, doors may open differently, people may drive on the other side of the street, and, as shown in Figure 13.6, a power cord made in one country may not fit another country's wall sockets.

Technical incompatibilities in hardware, software, and data standards often make it difficult to transfer or share software between countries. An example is the international differences in the formats of numbers and dates. The date 6/8/95 means June 8, 1995, in the United States and August 6, 1995, in Europe. The same date would be written 95/6/8 in Japan. This simple discrepancy necessitated changes in hundreds of programs when the software company Consilium first installed its manufacturing system at Siemens in Germany.

Figure 13.6 American and French Electrical Plugs

American appliances need special adapters in order to use French electrical outlets.

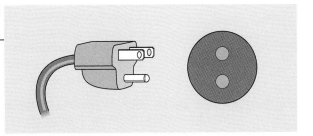

Social and political issues cause many types of confusion and inefficiency in systems used in more than one country. These problems start with incomplete personal communication caused by speaking different languages. At a deeper level, differences in laws, work rules, accounting practices, and general expectations of workers may make information system practices from one country impractical in another.

Telecommunications is an area where regulation, economics, and quality are especially intertwined. In the United States, telecommunications is highly competitive, and there is a tradition of high quality, customer orientation, and rapid service. In many other countries, telecommunications is controlled by government monopolies that are less customer oriented, and it may take a year or more to install a telephone. A British bank had to write off $10 million in the mid-1980s when it tried to move some of its transaction processing to Paris using packet switching over a leased telephone line. According to the French government telephone monopoly, sending packets via private network was illegal, and the system had to be scrapped.[20] Reliability was an issue when Kentucky Fried Chicken wanted to operate its corporate distribution system in Mexico. They could not use the system because the phone lines available through Telmex could not provide enough reliability in transferring sales information from individual stores to KFC headquarters.[21]

Economic issues in international information systems are obvious to any international traveler who has noticed how much more a phone call costs when it goes from Europe to the United States rather than in the reverse direction. A number of "callback services" have been formed just to exploit this imbalance. Callers from Europe can dial a U.S. number and hang up. This triggers a telephone switch that returns the call and provides a U.S. dial tone. The caller from Europe enters the desired telephone number and is connected. Since the bill at the end of the month is calculated at U.S. rates, it may be 50 to 70 percent lower than it would have been at European rates. Needless to say, the telephone monopolies in many nations are not pleased with these callback systems. The Kenyan government took out newspaper ads warning callback users they could be prosecuted. Japanese telephone companies pressed regulators for a ban on this service.[22]

Economic issues also arise in regulatory attempts to protect domestic computer firms by limiting imports of products and services. For example, one executive reported that in Indonesia "all equipment must be purchased by a local distributor; if the local distributor does not sell a particular product, it cannot be used in the country."[23]

A final international issue is the laws some countries have passed concerning the handling of data linked to individuals, especially in transborder data flows. For example, in 1989, France temporarily stopped Fiat from transferring its French personnel records to Italy because privacy laws there did not meet French regulations.[24] Any company wishing to transmit personnel records, credit card data, and customer data across national borders must take into account the laws of all nations that might be affected.

International issues are the last of the strategic IS issues, which started with the IS plan's consistency with the business plan, and included IS architecture, IS infrastructure, centralization versus decentralization, and outsourcing. Analyzing these issues helps clarify the firm's approach to building and maintaining information systems. These guidelines are useful when deciding what systems to invest in and what capabilities to include in those systems.

REALITY CHECK   **Strategic Issues for IS Planning**   This section discussed strategic issues, including consistency with the business plan, IS architecture, IS infrastructure, centralization versus decentralization, and outsourcing.

1. Consider any major purchase you or your family have made in the last few years, such as a car, a computer, or a college education. Explain the extent to which that purchase did or didn't fit into a strategic plan.

2. Explain why strategic planning is or isn't relevant for the decision you identified.

Selecting Systems to Invest In

The decision to build an information system is an investment decision, as is the decision about which capabilities to include in the system. The strategic issues from the previous section provide guidelines for these investments, such as building systems that are consistent with the business plan, the architecture, and the company's approach to distributed processing and outsourcing.

Although these ideas provide some guidance and eliminate some options, there is no ideal formula for deciding which systems and capabilities to invest in. Many IS departments could double and still not have enough people to do all the work users would like. In practice, many IS departments allocate a percentage of their available time to different project categories, such as enhancements, major new systems, and user support. But within each category, they still need to decide which systems to work on and what capabilities to provide. Cost–benefit analysis may help with these decisions.

Cost–Benefit Analysis

Cost–benefit analysis is the process of evaluating proposed systems by comparing estimated benefits and costs. Cost–benefit analysis should occur only after the proposed system has been described in enough detail to clarify key issues in areas such as system architecture and performance.

Cost–benefit analysis requires that estimated benefits and costs be expressed in monetary terms. If the benefits are substantially greater than the costs, the project may be worth pursuing. Cost–benefit analysis can be used in several ways. First, it is a planning tool to help in deciding whether the new system is a worthwhile investment compared to other possible uses of resources. In addition, it may be used as an auditing tool to determine whether a project actually met its goals.

Although the idea of comparing estimated benefits with estimated costs sounds logical, it has limitations. It is most appropriate when the system's purpose is improving efficiency. If its purpose is providing management information, transforming the organization, or upgrading the IS infrastructure, predicting either the benefits or the costs is more difficult. Furthermore, since cost–benefit analyses are usually done to justify someone's request for resources, the numbers in a cost–benefit study may be biased and may ignore or understate foreseeable project risks. Key issues for cost–benefit analysis include the difference between tangible and intangible benefits, the tendency to underestimate costs, and the effect of the timing of costs and benefits.

Tangible and intangible benefits

Benefits are often classified as either tangible or intangible. **Tangible benefits** can be measured directly to evaluate system performance. Examples include reduction in the time per phone call, improvement in response time, reduction in the amount of disk storage used, and reduction in the error rate. Notice that tangible benefits may or may not be measured in monetary terms. However, using a cost–benefit framework requires translating performance improvements into monetary terms so that benefits and costs can be compared.

Intangible benefits affect performance but are difficult to measure because they refer to comparatively vague concepts. Examples of intangible benefits include:

- Better coordination
- Better supervision
- Better morale
- Better information for decision making
- Ability to evaluate more alternatives
- Ability to respond quickly to unexpected situations
- Organizational learning

Although all these goals are worthwhile, it is often difficult to measure how well they have been accomplished. Even if it is possible to measure intangible benefits, it is difficult to express them in monetary terms that can be compared with costs. All too often, project costs are tangible and benefits are intangible. Although hard to quantify, intangible benefits are important and shouldn't be ignored. Many of the benefits of information systems are intangible.

Tendency to understate costs

A common flaw of cost–benefit studies is the understatement of costs. Careless cost analysis often includes the cost of hardware, software, and programming but omits other costs related to problem analysis, training, and ongoing operation of the system.

Table 13.4 separates some of the more apparent costs of information systems from some of the costs that are easy to overlook. Notice how the time and effort of user management and staff is easy to overlook in each of the four phases of an information system (see Figure 1.15). This is because their salary and overhead is already accounted for in the work they normally do.

For many systems, training, implementation, and troubleshooting absorb so much time and effort that their cost exceeds the original cost of the hardware and software. A study of ten large companies by a unit of KPMG Peat Marwick found that time spent by personal computer users helping other users cost $6,000 to $15,000 per year for every computer. A participant in the study said, "We just about fell out of our chairs when we saw that amount of mutual support."[25]

Table 13.4 IS Costs that Are Easy to Overlook in a Cost–Benefit Analysis

Phase	Costs Easily Assigned to a Project	Costs Easily Overlooked
Initiation	• Salary and overhead for IS staff • Cost of communication and travel related to the project • Consulting fees (if any)	• Salary and overhead of user staff and management involved in the analysis • Other work that is displaced in favor of work on the project
Development	• Salary and overhead for IS staff • Equipment purchase and installation costs • Purchase (if any) of system or application software	• Salary and overhead of user staff and management involved in the analysis • Site modifications such as wiring offices
Implementation	• Salary and overhead for IS staff and trainers • Cost of communication and travel related to the project	• Salary and overhead of user staff and management involved in the implementation • Disruption of work during implementation process • Salary of users during training and initial usage
Operation and maintenance	• Salary and overhead for IS staff • Software license fees (if any) • Depreciation of hardware	• Salary and overhead of user staff and management involved with system maintenance activities

Timing of costs and benefits

The cost and benefit streams from an information system project occur at different times. The timing of costs and benefits in the customer service system in Figure 13.7 is typical in that many costs precede any benefits. The shape of the cost curve reflects different staffing levels at different points in the system building process. The figure shows that the benefits start in month 6 and increase to a high level when implementation is complete. If these estimated cost and benefit streams actually are accomplished, the cumulative net benefit of having the system will become positive during month 11. If development takes longer than planned or if the benefits accrue more slowly than originally anticipated, net benefit becomes positive later.

The cost of any system includes the cost of building or buying the system plus the cost of ownership. The **cost of ownership** includes the cost of implementing, operating, and maintaining it. For many information systems, the cost of only the implementation is much higher than the cost of the original development since training and conversion require work by all the users. Cost of ownership is therefore a key characteristic for any system.

Risks

A surprisingly large percentage of information system projects either fail to attain their goals or attain them only after the expenditure of more time and effort than was initially anticipated. Common disappointments include:

- Desired benefits are not achieved.

- The project is completed late or over budget.

- The system's technical performance is inadequate.

- There is lack of user acceptance.

- Shifting priorities reduce the project's importance.

Figure 13.7 Estimated Benefit and Cost Streams

In these estimated costs and benefits of a new system, costs are incurred before benefits are attained. The cumulative net benefit (total benefits minus total costs) is negative until month 11 even though the benefits start in month 6. Monthly costs decrease after the system goes into operation but continue for the life of the system. This estimate includes minimal maintenance. Costs will be higher if more maintenance is needed.

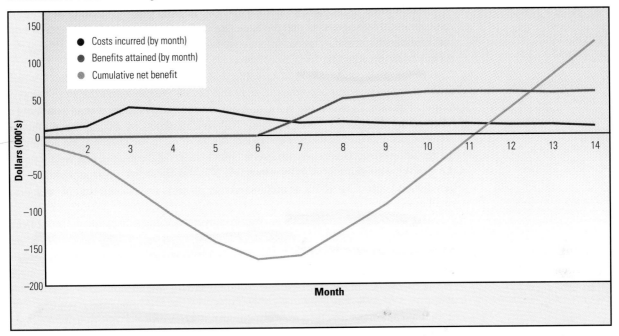

Since information system development is a risky endeavor, the risks should be considered in some way while deciding which projects to undertake. To anticipate the risks inherent in a proposed system, it is possible to compare the proposed system to a situation with minimum risk:

The system is to be produced by a single implementor for a single user, who anticipates using the system for a very definite purpose that can be specified in advance with great precision. Including the person who will maintain it, all other parties affected by the system understand and accept in advance its impact on them. All parties have experience with this type of system, the system receives adequate support, and its technical design is feasible and cost effective.

The further a system development situation deviates from this ideal situation, the greater are the inherent risks. This does not mean that only low-risk systems should be developed. Companies developing only low-risk systems are not learning much in this area and are probably attaining much lower benefits from systems than they might. The appropriate use of comparisons with this ideal situation is to identify areas of risk and then determine implementation strategies for managing those risks.

Financial Comparisons

IS steering committees often select among proposed IS projects by reviewing formal proposals and deciding how to allocate resources among them. The proposals usually include a formal justification stated in terms of the likely monetary costs and benefits.

Expressing costs and benefits in dollars provides a useful way to compare and rank projects even though dollar benefits are hard to estimate for projects involving major changes of business processes or IS infrastructure. Going through a formal justification process also eliminates some projects because their sponsors cannot devise a plausible justification that satisfies cost–benefit criteria.

Common criteria used for comparing and ranking projects include net present value, internal rate of return, and payback. These three measures take into account the cost and benefit streams that go into a cost–benefit analysis. All three are thoroughly explained in introductory finance courses.

Net present value (NPV) is the estimated amount of money the project is worth to the firm, taking into account the cost and benefit streams and the time value of money. The ratio between the value of a dollar today and a dollar a year from now is reflected by the *discount rate* applied. NPV is calculated by taking the difference between benefits and costs in each period, discounting to the present, and adding up the resulting terms. Given two otherwise equally beneficial projects, one would prefer the project with the higher NPV. However, NPV favors larger projects (with higher benefits and costs). The NPV of mediocre large projects can exceed that of very good small ones.

Internal rate of return (IRR) is a way to convert NPV into a form that makes projects more directly comparable. A project's internal rate of return is the interest rate one would have to receive on its cost stream to produce the same ultimate return as the project. IRR is computed by treating the discount rate in the NPV formula as a variable, setting NPV to 0, and solving for the discount rate. Many organizations use internal rate of return as a *hurdle rate* by funding only projects whose IRR is at least 12 or 15 percent.

Payback period is the length of time until the project's net benefit becomes positive. Given two projects with roughly equivalent long-term benefits, the one with a shorter payback period is preferred. A shorter payback period reduces the risk that the project will miss its targets. The division head of a large bank that often missed system deadlines decided to use payback as a primary criterion for selecting projects. Until system development performance improved, no systems with a payback of over six months would be approved. The division could not even consider large projects involving significant change, but its development efforts were brought under control.

Although NPV, IRR, and payback can serve as useful controls on resource allocations, use of these criteria is ineffective when they are applied to the wrong projects. They are most applicable for projects with easily estimated benefits and costs, such as projects that automate part of a well-understood process. Since major changes often generate unanticipated benefits and costs, the financial return on highly innovative systems is often hard to estimate. Managers realize that proposals for these projects are based on unreliable guesses and that purely financial criteria may provide insufficient insight for choosing among them.

Strict adherence to guidelines such as requiring an estimated rate of return over 15 percent may eliminate innovative projects that are worth the risk. Viewing this as a problem, American Express allocated $5 million in 1984 for innovative high-risk projects. One of the resulting projects was the Authorizer's Assistant described at the beginning of Chapter 12. This highly publicized expert system improved the decisions of agents who approve credit card use for large or unusual purchases. Although not undertaken based on NPV or IRR, it paid for itself many times over.[26]

REALITY CHECK   **Cost–Benefit Analysis**   This section discussed costs, benefits, risks, and several financial criteria that can be used to compare projects.

1. Consider any major purchase you or your family have made in the last few years; a car, a computer, or a college education. Identify the costs, benefits, and risks of several alternatives you considered or should have considered.

2. Explain why cost–benefit analysis would or wouldn't have helped in that decision.

Project Management Issues

A project plan outlines initial answers to the who, what, how, and when questions summarized in Table 13.1. Answering these questions before starting a project helps organize the work and helps keep it on track. A project plan is especially important in IS projects because unanticipated technical and organizational problems often arise. At minimum, having a plan helps in identifying surprises and evaluating their impact. This section will look at two types of issues related to project plans: division of labor between the IS department and users, and keeping a project on schedule. Chapter 14 will look at alternative approaches for building systems.

Division of Labor Between the IS Department and Users

There are many ways to allocate IS personnel and responsibilities between the IS department and user departments. Mixed results with projects totally led by IS departments have encouraged giving user departments responsibility for the systems they use. Even many technical roles for application systems have been moved into user departments.

As an example, Figure 13.8 shows how a food company divides work between the user departments and the IS department. The two dimensions in Figure 13.8 show that jobs closer to the application and user tend to be in the user department, whereas those closer to the machine and technology tend to be in the IS department. Jobs in the shaded area are in the user departments, whereas those in the unshaded area are in the IS department. The location of jobs shown in Figure 13.8 is actually a change from the way this company operated previously, when programmer-analysts and systems analysts were in the IS department. These jobs were moved into the user departments to increase responsiveness to user needs.

Figure 13.8 Possible Boundary between User and IS Departments

Many of the jobs in this figure could be in either the user department or the information systems department. The shading indicates one possible way to divide the work. Jobs in the shaded area are assigned to the user department, and the others are assigned to the IS department.

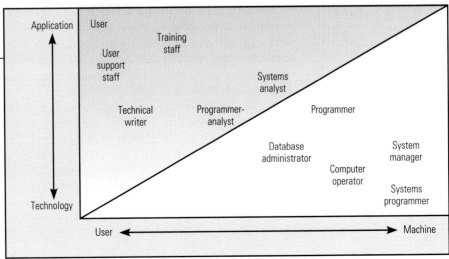

However the work is divided, people in both the IS department and the user department should recognize staffing issues mentioned in the section on centralization versus decentralization. These issues make it all the more important to keep projects on schedule.

Keeping the Project on Schedule

Information system projects have an unfortunate tradition of exceeding budgets and missing schedules. Project participants and users can help avoid these problems by appreciating the need for project goals, deliverables, and schedules, and by recognizing some of the special challenges in IS projects.

Goals, deliverables, and schedules

Effective project management requires clear, measurable goals. A **project goal** is a result that should occur if the project is carried out successfully. For example, a project's goal might include staying within a $450,000 budget; project completion by June 30, 1996; average order confirmation time of 15 minutes; and average customer satisfaction rating of 4.7 six months after system installation. The first two goals involve the process of building the system; the last two involve the organization's operation after system installation. Each goal is specific enough to measure. Without such goals, it is impossible to evaluate project completion or success.

In addition to their own unique goals, IS projects share commonsense goals in the back of any project manager's mind: creating the right system, creating it efficiently, making sure it works properly, and making sure it can be maintained and enhanced. Although these goals might seem obvious, too many system development efforts create the wrong system, create it inefficiently, fail to make sure it works properly, or create it in a form that is difficult to maintain. Systems miss the mark frequently enough that the picture in Figure 13.9 has become a cliché for system developers.

The essence of project management is controlling tasks that occur in a particular sequence and have an expected duration. Dividing a project into steps, or subprojects, clarifies what needs to be done and helps the people doing the project understand exactly what they have to do and how their work fits into the overall project. This approach also supports a project management process of monitoring progress and recognizing problems early enough to make midcourse corrections.

Each step in an information system project produces one or more deliverables. **Deliverables** are tangible work products, such as documents, plans, or computer programs. Specifying the deliverables expected with each step is a way to make sure the work is progressing. The steps simply aren't finished until deliverables are completed. In combination, the deliverables in IS projects provide a running history of what was done, when it was done, and why it was done. The deliverables for each step in a project form the basis for work done in subsequent steps.

The deliverables are produced according to a schedule. A **project schedule** is a terse project description identifying the timing of major steps and who will do the work. Many project management tools have been developed to record and update schedules and track progress versus schedules. Most IS projects use **Gantt charts,** illustrated in Figure 13.10. Gantt charts represent a schedule visually by displaying tasks along with their planned and actual start and completion times and resource requirements. The tasks may or may not overlap in time and may or may not have mutual dependencies. Resource requirements may be stated in terms of person-months, dollars, or time allocations for specific individuals.

Gantt charts are excellent tools for communicating with project groups, identifying problems, and deciding what corrective action to take. A quick glance at a Gantt chart

Figure 13.9 Why Is It Hard to Develop the Right System?

This figure illustrates a dilemma that has frustrated a generation of system developers.

shows whether a project is ahead of or behind schedule. In team meetings, Gantt charts are effective in reviewing progress, identifying problems, and explaining why resources must be shifted.

Gantt charts and similar management techniques depend on the quality of schedule data. If the tasks are stated vaguely, it is difficult to say when they are completed. If people are reluctant to report problems or if they say tasks requiring more polishing are "almost complete," the Gantt chart will display and amplify misleading data.

Managing IS projects involves balancing system scope and quality against schedule performance. Participants are often overoptimistic about how long the work will take, especially since these projects often hit unanticipated complexities. Possible responses to problems and slippages include maintaining the project's scope and schedule, changing the project's scope, changing the schedule, or adding more resources. Maintaining an unrealistic schedule causes morale problems and staff turnover. Reducing the scope may create a feasible project that doesn't solve the user's problem; extending the schedule may cause unacceptable delays. Making up for delays and other problems is often difficult because of the learning required if the staff is expanded. Losing a key individual from an IS project is an especially difficult problem because of the loss of knowledge.

Figure 13.10 Gantt Chart

This Gantt chart shows the planned sequence and timing of the different steps in an information system project. Among other things, it shows that physical design will start about half way through logical design, that programming will start just before a design walkthrough, and that installation will take almost three months.

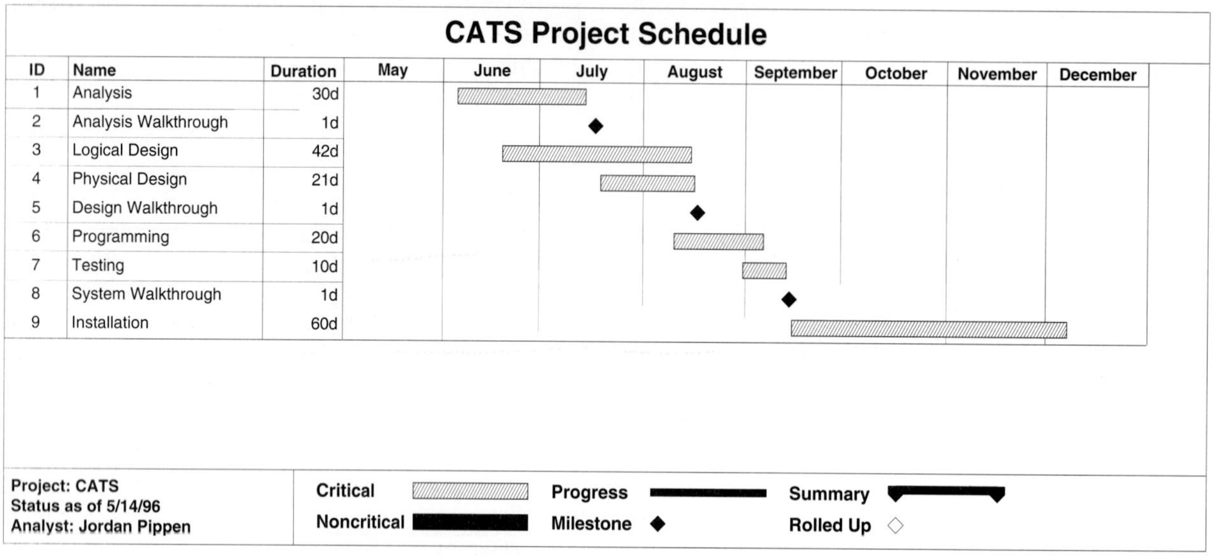

CATS Project Schedule

ID	Name	Duration	May	June	July	August	September	October	November	December
1	Analysis	30d								
2	Analysis Walkthrough	1d			◆					
3	Logical Design	42d								
4	Physical Design	21d								
5	Design Walkthrough	1d				◆				
6	Programming	20d								
7	Testing	10d								
8	System Walkthrough	1d					◆			
9	Installation	60d								

Project: CATS
Status as of 5/14/96
Analyst: Jordan Pippen

Critical	Progress	Summary
Noncritical	Milestone ◆	Rolled Up ◇

Challenges in information system projects

Many of the challenges of project management mirror those of any other form of management: assigning the right people to the right jobs, getting people to do high-quality work, getting people to report their progress realistically, and resolving issues and disputes. Especially important in project-oriented work are estimating project scope and duration, minimizing rework on completed steps, and recovering from delays.

Estimating project scope and duration. It is difficult to estimate the scope and duration of projects for a number of reasons, including uncertain project scope, changes in scope, individual differences in productivity, and the way work is distributed in projects. Since the first phase of an IS project is basically a research project to appreciate the true nature of the problem and to identify a cost-effective solution, project scope is only partially known when the first project estimates are made. Even after this research is finished, important details involving both the business situation and the technical solution may remain poorly understood. Projects also change in scope because the business situation changes or the users learn that their original understanding of the situation was off the mark. Both of these issues often cause **requirements creep,** continual increases in project scope that make project completion a moving target. A survey of 160 IS professionals found that 80 percent believed requirements creep "always or frequently" affected schedule performance.[27]

Vast productivity differences between individuals doing information system work cause additional estimating problems. An often-cited study of programming productivity factors found that a mediocre team developing software often takes over four times as long as a superior team.[28] Even when the development team is known in advance, such wide productivity differences make it difficult to estimate what any individual will accomplish.

The combination of estimation difficulties, requirements creep, and individual differences often results in difficult practical and ethical dilemmas, starting with the common reluctance to pass on the bad news to the managers. People who are evaluated on the basis of meeting schedules are tempted to underplay problems that endanger schedules, even if this means that the result of the work will be less useful.

Minimizing rework on completed steps. Although some steps of an IS project may be performed simultaneously, many steps build on the outputs of previous steps. Ideally, it should not be necessary to return to previous steps to correct errors and omissions that become apparent later. In reality, each succeeding step tests the feasibility of conclusions from previous steps. Conclusions or outputs from previous steps may have to be changed because more is understood now or because the previous work contained errors. Consequently, there is often some rework even though a project is described as a sequence of successive steps.

Recovering from delays. The most natural unit for estimating the size of system development projects and tracking their progress is the *person-week* or *person-month.* A manager therefore might describe a new application as a 20 person-month project, meaning anything from 1 person for 20 months to 20 people for 1 month. If this 20 person-month project falls behind schedule by the equivalent of 5 person-months, it might seem possible to bring in the equivalent of 5 additional person-months of work to get back on schedule. This tactic often fails for IS projects, even if it might work for other projects.

In the early 1970s, Fred Brooks summarized the difficulty of getting IS projects back on schedule by coining the term the **mythical man-month.**[29] (The more current term *person-month* is used here.) Brooks deemed the man-month (person-month) mythical because it implied people are interchangeable and can be added to a project at any time. In fact, people are interchangeable only in projects that require little knowledge, communication, or learning.

Participants in each step of an IS project must understand its goals and strategy, the plan for doing the work, and the technology used; they must coordinate with other workers. A great deal of effort must go into training and communication. Bringing a new worker into a project requires a knowledgeable worker to spend less time doing productive work while bringing the new worker up to speed. Adding many new workers to an ongoing project can temporarily halt progress. The mythical person-month is therefore one of the reasons it is so important to keep projects on schedule. Since involving more people in a project means that communication and training will absorb more effort, successful system builders avoid allowing a project to get too large too soon.

REALITY CHECK **Project Management** This section discussed project management issues related to the division of labor between users and technical specialists and keeping the project on schedule.

1. Consider a significant project you or your acquaintances have been involved in during the last few years. Identify any important issues related to the division of labor or related to keeping the project on schedule.

2. Explain any special issues in the project that were unrelated to division of labor or keeping the project on schedule.

Systems Analysis Revisited

Chapter 2 defined systems analysis as a general process of defining a problem, gathering pertinent information, developing alternative solutions, and choosing among those solutions. By covering many different facets of information systems, this book's main purpose is to help you understand how to analyze these systems from a business professional's viewpoint. This is why tools such as the WCA framework, data flow diagrams, and entity-relationship diagrams were introduced in the first few chapters.

This last section looks at the process of gathering information during systems analysis. The discussion is equally applicable to IS planning and to building and maintaining information systems (covered in the next chapter).

Information Sources for Analyzing Systems

Common sources of information for analyzing information systems include interviews, inputs, outputs, and documentation of existing systems, on-site observation, questionnaires, and examination of similar systems.

Interviews. Interviewing users and their managers is probably the most obvious method for gathering information about a system. After all, who should understand the situation better than the people who will use the system?

Inputs, outputs, and documentation of existing systems. An existing system's input screens and output reports can give a good idea of what data are available and what data people use. System documentation often helps explain why the system exists, what business problems it solves, and how it solves them. However, documentation may be so detail oriented that it doesn't explain the purpose of system features. What's more, if the system has been modified many times, it is likely that the documentation will be outdated.

On-site observation. One of the best ways to understand how a system operates is to go to the site and observe it for several days, or even weeks. If possible, an analyst should even try to perform the job the system will support. Analysts who never observe the current system in action often misunderstand the problem they are trying to solve.

Questionnaires. Questionnaires can be used to gather information from users, managers, and other stakeholders in the project. This method is especially useful when there are many geographically dispersed stakeholders, making it impractical to interview everyone. Although questionnaires sometimes bring in ideas that would otherwise be missed, people often fill them out perfunctorily because they are busy with other things and feel uninvolved in the project.

Benchmarking. **Benchmarking** is the analysis of similar systems in other companies to provide both perspective and new ideas about the situation being analyzed. Many companies use this approach in their total quality management (TQM) efforts. In addition to new ideas, interviewing users of similar systems may produce insights into why particular system features are effective or ineffective.

Each of these methods provides a way to obtain information needed when analyzing a system. Using different methods is important because systems analysts often discover that things said in interviews are inconsistent with what they find when they observe systems in action. Because interviews are used so commonly, we will look at the interviewing process in more detail.

Performing Interviews

Although talking to users might seem like a simple task, a surprising number of problems may reduce interview effectiveness. Table 13.5 summarizes some of these, which include missing viewpoints, superficial information, and distorted information. Minimizing these problems involves careful preparation, execution, and follow-up, including an insistence on understanding the situation rather than just making a list of what the users apparently want.

Table 13.5 Common Problems Encountered by Analysts Interviewing Users

Problem	Typical Cause	Preventive Action
Missing viewpoints	Users unwilling or unable to participate	Make involvement of key users a condition for doing the project
	Stakeholders who are not invited to participate	Include all groups affected by the system
Superficial information	Lack of preparation by the analyst	Learn about the business setting; prepare before the interview
	User's assumption that only minor changes are possible.	Don't just ask for the user's wish list; understand the reason for the user's problem rather than just the suggested solution
Distorted information	User responses based on user aims other than the system, such as political position in the organization	• Obtain multiple viewpoints to confirm data and conclusions • Be sure users know the purpose of the interview
	Analyst misunderstanding or biasing the user's response	• Learn about the business setting • Prepare before the interview

Careful preparation for an interview includes gathering background information before the interview and going to the interview with a clear goal and a list of key questions. Conducting an interview without a clear goal, such as understanding a user's problems or information requirements, wastes time and leads to garbled conclusions. Having a list of questions helps you focus the discussion and helps the respondent understand the interview's purpose. Although the discussion may move to unanticipated topics that are important, starting with a list of questions helps keep the interview on track and helps you recognize important observations. Prior knowledge of the organizational setting, business process, and other aspects of the situation helps you understand what the user means. It also avoids giving the user the impression of wasting time explaining things you should know. Being prepared keeps you focused on receiving information and helps you avoid putting words in the user's mouth.

Although interviews differ in content and feeling, there are common rules of thumb for interviewing:

- Make sure that the interviewee knows the reason for the interview. In too many cases, the interviewee is unclear about the purpose and may withhold information or cooperation as a result.

- Ask **open-ended questions,** which invite the interviewee to provide more information than a yes or no. For example, ask "How do you use the customer file?" rather than a yes–no question such as, "Is the customer file useful?"

- Validate responses by restating them and by comparing responses from others. Different People often disagree about problems, causes, and priorities. The greater the disagreement, the more difficult it will be to design and implement a successful system.

- Pay attention to body language (both yours and the interviewee's). Uninterested or antagonistic interviewees often project a different feeling from those who genuinely want the project to succeed.

• Close the interview by reviewing some of the main points covered, thanking the respondent, and requesting permission to call back if you need clarification or additional information.

Follow-up after an interview is also important. Avoid the strong temptation to file your notes and go on to other work without analyzing what was said. In complex projects, it may even be worthwhile to rewrite your notes. If you neglect doing this, weeks later you may not understand much about what was said or why. Reviewing your notes also encourages you to follow up on unclear responses or on questions you hadn't raised during the interview. It is much better to ask more questions than to develop a system based on a misunderstanding.

These guidelines for gathering information are useful in information system planning, in system development projects (discussed in the next chapter), and in many other areas of business. The guidelines help project participants stay focused and help them avoid unnecessary difficulties in projects that already have many challenges.

Chapter Conclusion

SUMMARY

▶ *What is an information system plan?*

A plan is a statement of what will be done, who will do it, when they will do it, how it will be done, and what are the desired results. At the strategic level, IS plans focus on priorities and goals for information systems and the technical and organizational approaches that will be used. At the project level, they focus on specific capabilities required in each system and on who will do what and when will they do it to produce specific results.

▶ *Why do users and managers have to participate in information system planning and development?*

Even though the IS department compiles the IS plan, members of user departments have to ensure that the right systems are developed, are used efficiently and effectively, and have the desired impact.

▶ *How is information system planning linked to business planning?*

IS planning is the part of business planning concerned with deploying the firm's information system resources. Like plans in all business functions, the IS plan should support the strategy and goals in the business plan and should be linked to the plans in other functional areas.

 What are some of the strategic issues in information system planning?

These issues include consistency with business priorities, IS architecture, IS infrastructure, centralization versus decentralization and outsourcing. To support a firm's business processes its IS plan should be linked to its business plans and priorities. A firm's IS architecture determines the practical range of business and product strategies the firm can employ. Its IS infrastructure is its IS architecture plus the technical and human resources for building and maintaining systems. Key aspects include platforms, tools and methods, legacy systems, and the IS staff. The way information systems are centralized or decentralized should be consistent with the way the firm is organized. Outsourcing is hiring outside organizations to perform system-related functions often performed by IS departments.

What are the key issues in balancing centralized versus distributed processing and control?

The key issues involve the extent to which information system location, ownership, and control should be dispersed to different parts of the organization. Excessive centralization often results in rigid systems that cannot handle local variations. Excessive decentralization often solves local problems but often doesn't solve problems that cross departments and misses opportunities for economies of scale.

▶ *How is cost–benefit analysis used in making investment decisions about information systems?*

Cost–benefit analysis is the process of evaluating proposed systems by comparing their estimated monetary benefits with their estimated costs over a time horizon. Key issues for cost–benefit analysis include the difference between tangible and intangible benefits, the tendency to underestimate costs, and the effect of the timing of costs and benefits.

 What are the basic elements of project management for information system projects?

Like any business project, information system projects have goals, deliverables and schedules, and roles and responsibilities. The essence of project management is controlling tasks that occur in a particular sequence and have an expected duration. Dividing a project into steps with specific deliverables clarifies what needs to be done and helps project participants understand exactly what they have to do and how their work fits into the overall project.

INTERNATIONAL VIGNETTE

Switzerland: Nestle's Information Technology Strategy

Headquartered in Vevey, Switzerland, Nestle is a multinational company with food and pharmaceutical sales of $40 billion, 300 operating companies, 80 separate IS organizations, and 220,000 employees worldwide. The company's three official languages are English, French, and Spanish. Despite the challenges of the company's huge size and decentralized operations, its central IS group is trying to attain the benefits of standardization in those areas that can be standardized without imposing unnecessarily on local business operations.

In the past, various units in the company have used a wide range of proprietary and open systems from different vendors. In the early 1990s, it decided to move toward a set of standards that support distributed client–server systems. The standards include UNIX systems from IBM, Digital, and HP; Oracle's Version 7 relational DBMS; the German firm SAP's integrated material, distribution, and accounting applications; Powersoft's PowerBuilder application development system; and Ernst & Young's Navigator CASE product. At one point, headquarters tried to suggest a single PC vendor, but the outcry from the business units was so great that there is now a list of recommended PCs.

Although the central IS staff is able to block the budget of any local IS organization that does not conform to standards, it generally pushes responsibility to the local groups because Vevey is simply too far from the rest of the world to know what is right in all situations. Instead, Vevey recommends standards and supports the development of core applications that can be used across multiple business units even if they need some customization for individual units. This approach mirrors efforts throughout the company to improve margins by generating improvements in logistics and operations and then adapting those improvements to other parts of the business.

Source: Greenbaum, Joshua. "Nestle's Global Mix." *Information Week,* Apr. 25, 1994, pp. 44–46.

- Use the WCA framework to organize your understanding of this vignette and to identify important topics that are not mentioned.

- What issues (if any) make this case interesting from an international or intercultural viewpoint?

- What difference would it make to Nestle if its centralized IS group were disbanded?

REAL-WORLD CASES

McKinsey's Client–Server Project Encounters Common Setbacks

The most important resources for an international consulting company such as McKinsey & Co. are its people. Accordingly, McKinsey set out to develop PeopleNet, a companywide human resources information system to keep track of staffing assignments and related information about the firm's employees. During the project, McKinsey encountered many of the common setbacks consultants often help their clients with. As a first foray into client–server computing, the project was a departure from the company's previous focus on mainframes and PCs, and some of the people in the IS group never agreed with the technical approach. The expected infrastructure based on a $20 million telecommunications project was not available because that project was later judged too expensive. Consequently, the PeopleNet project had to bear the unexpected burden of building infrastructure incrementally.

McKinsey's highly independent branch offices worried that a uniform set of guidelines would reduce their traditional local control over staffing. After many meetings, control of the part of PeopleNet related to tracking staff assignments was given to local offices, which agreed to share with headquarters only a limited amount of personnel data, such as languages spoken, skills, and experience. There were also problems with data discrepancies between the Scandinavian offices and headquarters in New York, resulting in a massive cleanup. Originally seen as a 12-month, $4.9-million project, the revised projections were that it would run 30 months, cost $12 million, and produce a system somewhat different from the one originally envisaged.

Source: Caldwell, Bruce. "Consultant, Heal Thyself." *Information Week,* June 21, 1993, pp. 12–13.

- Use the WCA framework to organize your understanding of this case and to identify important topics that are not mentioned.

- Explain why you do or do not believe the problems encountered were related to the system's use of a client–server architecture.

- Explain why you do or do not believe the outcome was optimal from the viewpoint of McKinsey as a complete enterprise.

Du Pont: Developing a Global Infrastructure

A global firm's value-chain activities are influenced by two types of factors: the diversity in individual country markets and the need for global integration to coordinate among activities in different countries. Du Pont is divided into nine separate business units, each having its own IS resources to maximize responsiveness to end users and involve business unit management in decision making. Du Pont's objectives for IS include providing a functioning worldwide infrastructure at lower cost than that of the competition, providing education to motivate and enable the use of information technology, introducing new technology faster than the competition, and providing overall stewardship for IS activities.

To minimize costs and eliminate unnecessary variation, Du Pont constrains its technology base to particular hardware and software products from particular vendors. In traditional general-purpose computers, these include IBM 370s, Digital VAXs, and certain HP systems. Pilot tests of newer open systems have been directed at taking advantage of open architecture. Even its 800 PC-based expert systems, which are used for manufacturing, marketing, and scheduling, are limited to standard platforms to simplify training. The network layer conforms to similar limits. For example, there are three data networks (IBM's SNA, DEC's DecNet, and HP's X.25), plus one voice network and one video network. To provide competitive advantage, Du Pont has many automated interfaces with customers and suppliers. Around 800 companies have some degree of direct access to a Du Pont internal database or otherwise communicate with Du Pont electronically.

> Source: Konsynski, Benn R., and Jahangir Karimi. "On the Design of Global Information Systems." In Stephen P. Bradley, Jerry A. Hausman, and Richard L. Nolan. *Globalization, Technology, and Competition.* Boston: Harvard Business School Press, 1993, pp. 81–102.

* Use the WCA framework to organize your understanding of this case and to identify important topics that are not mentioned.

* Explain which ideas in this chapter seem most and least pertinent to this discussion of Du Pont's global infrastructure.

KEY TERMS

information systems planning	pilot project	distributed processing	project goal
chief information officer (CIO)	critical success factor (CSF)	outsourcing	deliverables
sponsor	business process reengineering	cost–benefit analysis	project schedule
champion	(BPR)	tangible benefits	Gantt chart
IS steering committee	information system architecture	intangible benefits	requirements creep
user support	enterprise modeling	cost of ownership	mythical man-month
information center	information system infrastructure	net present value (NPV)	benchmarking
enhancement	platform	internal rate of return (IRR)	open-ended questions
bug fix	legacy system	payback	

REVIEW QUESTIONS

1. Describe the difference between strategic-level and project-level plans for information systems.

2. What is information systems planning, and how should it be related to other planning in a business?

3. Identify important user roles in information systems planning.

4. How much of a typical IS group's work is usually involved with keeping existing systems operating, and what types of projects does this include?

5. Identify some of the roles of IS professionals in building and maintaining information systems.

6. What are critical success factors, and how are they used in IS planning?

7. Explain why business process reengineering is a controversial topic.

8. What is a firm's information system architecture?

9. How are platforms, tools and methods, legacy systems, and IS staff related to a firm's information system infrastructure?

10. Describe the advantages and disadvantages of centralization versus decentralization of computer hardware and data.

11. In relation to centralization versus decentralization, what are the major issues related to standards and ownership?

12. What are the different degrees of outsourcing, and why is extensive outsourcing controversial?

13. Describe some of the problems that often arise when systems span two countries or are moved from one country to another.

14. Explain the difference between tangible and intangible benefits.

15. Why is the timing of costs and benefits important in evaluating proposed information systems, and how does it affect financial measures such as NPV, IRR, and payback?

16. Describe the characteristics of information system projects with minimal risks.

17. Why are goals, deliverables, and schedules important in project management?

18. What limits the effectiveness of Gantt charts and other project management methods?

19. Explain the idea of the mythical person-month.

20. Describe some guidelines for interviewing during information system projects.

DISCUSSION QUESTIONS

1. Assume that you have been an IS manager at XYZ Corp. for the past 12 years and have just been informed that the outsourcing contract signed yesterday transferred all major IS operations to a leading outsourcing vendor. As part of the deal, you and your staff are to become employees of the vendor, which has different salary scales, different benefits, and a different culture. Ignoring any laws that might apply to this situation, what economic or ethical responsibilities did XYZ Corp. have toward you and your colleagues as it negotiated this contract?

2. A noted software expert has stated that "the introduction of new CASE tools may cause a short-term productivity problem that will impact the current project. ...Most organizations have found that productivity typically declines for the first 3 to 6 months after the introduction of CASE tools, and sometimes by as much as 25 percent during the first year."[30] Explain how this phenomenon is related to IS planning topics covered in this chapter.

3. To improve customer responsiveness in its consumer banking group in the early 1980s, Citibank decided to "decentralize its information process capabilities quickly to as low a level of responsibility and control as possible. ...Instead of increasing responsiveness, Citibank soon found itself drowning in a sea of systems, unable to collect, store, disseminate, or analyze vital information." Citibank quickly recentralized its information management processes.[31] Explain how Citibank's experience is related to issues covered in this chapter.

4. "When a company budgets $1 million to develop a new software system it is, in fact, committing to spend more than $4 million over the next five years. Each dollar spent on systems development generates, on average, 20 cents for operations and 40 cents for maintenance. Thus, the $1 million expenditure automatically generates a follow-on cost of $600,000 a year to support the initial investment."[32] Explain whether this quotation seems surprising to you and how it is related to topics covered in this chapter.

5. In talking about information system planning, this chapter mostly takes the viewpoint of a large firm. Which topics in the chapter seem equally applicable to a small firm or individual? Which topics seem less applicable?

6. You are nearing the end of a seven-month system development project. Last week, the leader of one of your teams estimated his group was 95 percent finished. This week, he says he may have been a bit optimistic, and his team is probably only 85 percent finished. He asks you to assign two more programmers to his team to help him finish. What ideas from the chapter would you think about before responding?

HANDS-ON EXERCISES

1. This exercise is about cost–benefit analysis and financial comparisons between alternative projects. It assumes a spreadsheet model of a system development project is provided.

    a. Use the spreadsheet model to graphically show the impact on cumulative net benefits of a six-month delay in system implementation (assuming the cost stream is unchanged over a two-year time horizon).

    b. Show the changes in payoff, NPV, and IRR over two years if this delay occurs.

APPLICATION SCENARIOS

Zylotech Semiconductors: What Are the Requirements?

As president of Zylotech Semiconductors, Len Snider was concerned that the company's internal systems weren't able to support the types of growth he had promised his board of directors. At this point, Zylotech had acceptable systems for individual functions such as developing production schedules, tracking work-in-process, billing customers, and calculating costs. Len thought the missing element was the types of systems that coordinate work across the functional areas such as sales, design, manufacturing, and finance. Two months ago, he had put together a task force to study this issue. Unfortunately, each individual on the task force came up with a recommendation focusing on issues in his or her own department.

    Vice-president of manufacturing. He believed that the current system for planning work in the plant and tracking work-in-process should be improved. According to him, this would increase yields and improve machine utilization, thereby leading to better customer service and lower prices.

    Vice-president of design. He thought that Zylotech was using antiquated design techniques. In his opinion, Zylotech could cut design time in half with better design tools.

    Vice-president of sales. She considered the current system for making delivery commitments to customers a major drawback for sales because there was no way of directly influencing the priority of customer orders after they were launched into manufacturing.

    Vice-president of finance. According to her, the current system for determining the cost of material produced was extremely inaccurate. More detailed cost data would help in establishing more appropriate prices for the various products.

    Vice-president of information systems. He believed it was impossible to go much further in any direction without building an integrated company database. This would require months of analysis to find out what data items should go into the integrated database and how it should be retrofitted into the hundreds of existing programs. Regardless of what the various departments wanted, in his opinion they wouldn't be able to get it without an integrated database.

    Len's immediate response to these comments was that although he believed that each of these department-focused proposals could be beneficial, he wanted to see some proposals about how the different departments would work together.

    1. Explain how the following ideas from the chapter are or are not pertinent to this situation: critical success factors (CSFs), business process reengineering, information system infrastructure, distributed processing, and cost–benefit analysis.

    2. How do you think Len should proceed?

DEBATE TOPIC   *Use ideas from the chapter to argue the pros and cons and practical implications of the following proposition: Len identified the wrong issue. The right issue is to define the company's overall direction and then ask how systems could support that direction.*

Dawson Paints: Working Successfully with Top Managers

Terry Castile, CEO of Dawson Paints, looked at Alan Crossetti, the new IS manager and felt his blood pressure go up. Why were these guys always bothering him about information systems? Castile felt he received adequate information and was tired of being asked whether he needed more. Of course he supported the use of information systems for transaction processing. That was necessary for any business, in the same way that doing personnel reviews and making promises to customers were necessary. He decided to let the information systems manager have it:

"Take a look at our supposed management information system, and I'll tell you what you will find: It's for clerks, not management; it contains tons of data and very little information; and it is a bunch of unrelated applications rather than an overall system. And don't ask me about all the information I use because it will take me all day to tell you about it, and I already use it anyway, regardless of what you try to do. And for sure, don't tell me about how you are going to try to capture my knowledge so that my successor can do a better job because some computer told him what I would normally do under some circumstances."

Crossetti was not surprised by this harangue. He had been hired by the vice-president of finance to try to improve the company's information systems despite the CEO's general lack of interest, plus the CEO's rejection of the previous IS manager. Crossetti had a new approach:

"As CEO, you appreciate the organization's information needs and feel that your own needs are adequately served. As IS manager, I'm concerned about our information system plan. I don't know whether any system we build could help you in your job, but I don't think that is the most important issue right now. You seem satisfied with the information you have. I am concerned that some of the systems we are currently building for sales, production, and finance may be off target. I want your help in making sure we are making the right information system investments."

This caught Castile's attention. In today's tough competitive environment, he certainly didn't want to waste money. But he wasn't sure how he could help Crossetti.

1. Use ideas from the chapter to identify some of the problems Dawson Paints faced.

2. Castile has had little involvement with information systems in the past, but Crossetti needs his help now. What should Castile ask Crossetti to do?

DEBATE TOPIC   *Use ideas from the chapter to argue the pros and cons and practical implications of the following proposition: Since Castile is not really interested in information systems, he probably cannot help Crossetti even if he tries.*

▩ Cumulative Case: Custom T-Shirts, Inc.

"I'm not a complainer, Terry," said Lee Turner, Director of Information Systems, "but I really am concerned that I'm out of the loop. I have been here for ten months and think our systems are basically under control now. But I'm not always clued in on the big picture. It always seems to me that you, Dale, and Pat get together and decide what will really happen and I only get a small part of the story. I think I could contribute much more if I got in on some of the original planning discussions. At minimum, it would help me make sure that our IS plans are really linked to the business plan. In addition, I think I could add some good ideas since we rely so much on information systems both as part of the service we offer and as a way to keep the organization organized."

Terry mentioned this conversation at the next management meeting with Dale and Pat. Of course the idea of linking the IS plan to the business plan made sense, but there were just a few problems. First, the company didn't really have a well-worked-out plan. Terry, Dale, and Pat had been struggling with that issue for years. It was hard to know what the competitors would do next month, much less next year, and the important improvements in customer service and product quality often came from doing experiments, seeing what worked in a few stores whose managers were interested in the idea, and then trying it out with more stores after it was tested.

There was also a bit of disagreement about Lee. The way Dale's programmer friend seemed to be shoved aside when Lee came on board was still a sore point. Although Terry trusted Lee and believed a great deal of progress had been made in the last ten months, Pat wasn't as convinced and thought Lee had tried to control things too much. For example, the decree that Lee would personally approve every computer, software, or telecommunications purchase in the company seemed excessive to Pat.

Terry also wondered whether the company really needed the type of IS staff Lee was trying to build. Lee had recently asked for four new programmers plus three months of training for each of them in new technologies such as object-oriented programming. The company wasn't using these technologies yet, but Lee believed that programmers who wanted to do things the 1980's way just didn't belong in a company that intended to grow during the 1990s. Unfortunately for Lee's argument, one programmer who had just received this training recently quit to join another company that could use these new skills immediately.

Going further in thinking about the future of the IS group, Terry wondered whether outsourcing would be a more effective way to do the company's computer-related work. "After all," Terry thought, "we aren't in the computer business. Why shouldn't we give that work to someone who is?" Terry was reluctant to get into this conversation with Lee. Since Lee already felt out of it, a discussion of outsourcing might raise fears of having less power, and Terry didn't want Lee to get that impression at this point.

1. Based on the chapter and your understanding of the company, identify some of the choices Lee might make about information systems and information technology if the company were to centralize or decentralize its IS efforts as much as possible.

2. Considering the ideas in the chapter, make a recommendation about the extent to which Lee should be integrated into the company's long-range planning efforts and the general direction Lee should take for building the IS staff.

REFERENCES

1. Scott, Robert. "Kodak Hands MIS to IBM, Businessland." *MIS Week*, July 31, 1989, p. 12.

2. Kirkpatrick, David. "Why Not Farm Out Your Computing?" *Fortune*, Sept. 23, 1991, pp. 103–112.

3. Caldwell, Bruce. "New Image for Outsourcing." *Information Week*, Feb. 22, 1993, pp. 12–13.

4. Horwitt, Elizabeth. "Outsourcing Hits Human Snag." *Computerworld*, Feb. 8, 1993, p. 15.

5. Goff, Leslie, and Michael Puttre. "Business Strategies Misaligned with MIS Resources." *MIS Week*, Nov. 6, 1989, p. 38.

6. Rockart, John F. "Chief Executives Define Their Own Data Needs." *Harvard Business Review*, Mar.–Apr. 1979, pp. 81–92.

7. Boynton, Andrew C., and Robert W. Zmud. "An Assessment of Critical Success Factors." *Sloan Management Review*, Summer 1984, pp. 17–27.

8. Hammer, Michael, and James Champy. *Reengineering the Corporation: A Manifesto for Business Revolution*, New York: Harper Business, 1993.

9. Ibid.

10. Stewart, Thomas A. "Reengineering: The Hot New Management Tool." *Fortune*, Aug. 23, 1993, pp. 41–48.

11. Strassmann, Paul A. "Re-engineering: An Emetic in a Perfume Bottle?" *Computerworld*, Aug. 16, 1993, p. 33.

12. Cafasso, Rosemary. "Rethinking Re-engineering." *Computerworld*, Mar. 15, 1993, pp. 102–105.

13. *Forbes ASAP*. "Liberate Your Data." Feb. 28, 1994, pp. 58–68.

14. Keen, Peter G. W. *Every Manager's Guide to Information Technology*, Boston: Harvard Business School Press, 1991.

15. Flaaten, Per O., et al. *Foundations of Business Systems*, 2d ed. Fort Worth, Tex.: The Dryden Press, 1992.

16. Weinman, Eliot D. "CASE Studies in Implementation." *Information Week*, Dec. 10, 1990, pp. 32–41.

17. Johnson, Maryfran. "Showstoppers?" *Computerworld Client/Server Journal*. Aug. 11, 1993, pp. 17–20.

18. "Preparing a Technology Battle Plan: Interview with Paul Strassmann." *Beyond Computing*, May–June, 1994, pp. 52–54.

19. Lacity, Mary Cecelia, and Rudy Hirschheim. *Information Systems Outsourcing: Myths, Metaphors, and Realities*. Chichester, UK: John Wiley & Sons, 1993.

20. Keen, Peter. *Shaping the Future: Business Design through Information Technology*. Boston: Harvard Business School Press, 1991, p. 88.

21. Hecht, Laurence, and Peter Morici. "Managing Risks in Mexico." *Harvard Business Review*, Jul.–Aug. 1993, pp. 32–40.

22. Moffett, Matt. "Callbacks Cut Telephone Bills of Users Abroad." *Wall Street Journal*, June 21, 1994, p. B1.

23. Ives, Blake, Sirka Jarvenpaa, and Richard Mason. "Global Business Drivers: Aligning Information Technology to Global Business Strategy." *IBM Systems Journal*, Vol. 32, No. 1, 1993, pp. 143–161.

24. Cespedes, Frank V., and H. Jeff Smith. "Database Marketing: New Rules for Policy and Practice." *Sloan Management Review*, Summer 1993, pp. 7–22.

25. Bulkeley, William M. "Study Finds Hidden Costs of Computing." *Wall Street Journal*, Nov. 2, 1992, p. B6.

26. Feigenbaum, Edward, Pamela McCorduck, and Penny H. Nii. *The Rise of the Expert Company*. New York: Times Books, 1988.

27. Anthes, Gary H. "No More Creeps!" *Computerworld*, May 2, 1994, pp. 107–110.

28. Boehm, Barry W. "Improving Software Productivity." *Computer*, Sept. 1987, pp. 43–57.

29. Brooks, Frederick P., Jr. "The Mythical Man-Month." *Datamation*, Dec. 1974, pp. 44–52.

30. Yourdon, Edward. *Decline & Fall of the American Programmer*. Englewood Cliffs, N.J.: Yourdon Press, 1992, p. 162.

31. Boynton, A. C., B. Victor, and B. J. Pine, II. "New Competitive Strategies: Challenges to Organizations and Information Technology." *IBM Systems Journal*, Vol. 32, No. 1, 1993, pp. 40–64.

32. Keen, Peter G. W. *Shaping the Future: Business Design through Information Technology*. Boston: Mass.: Harvard Business School Press, 1991, p. 141.

14

Methods for Building Information Systems

Study Questions

▶ *What are the four phases of information system projects?*

▶ *What types of issues are addressed by the different system development processes?*

▶ *How does the traditional system life cycle solve the control problem of keeping a project on track?*

▶ *What are the advantages and disadvantages of prototypes?*

▶ *What are the advantages and disadvantages of application packages?*

▶ *What are the advantages and disadvantages of end-user development?*

▶ *What are the major issues in supporting end users?*

▶ *How is it possible to combine system development approaches into a system's life cycle?*

Atelephone company's billing system is the heart of its business, and Pacific Bell was paralyzed by its system, which had been built 20 years earlier to handle the limited products and services that were available then. Telephone technology and the competitive and regulatory environment had changed greatly, and Pacific Bell could now offer businesses and homes many new products and services, such as call waiting, unlimited calls to a certain area code, and many others. But they couldn't bring all these products and services to the market because the billing system couldn't handle them. In some cases, they had to redesign the products and services to fit the billing system's limitations.

Pacific Bell's project team did extensive research to find out what customers would like in terms of both phone services and billing arrangements. After deciding the basic requirements, they hired Andersen Consulting to help build the system using CASE tools and COBOL. Working in Pacific Bell's human factors laboratory, user representatives from the groups that answer Pacific Bell's service lines tried out the system before it was implemented in the organization. The lab even videotaped the users to find the rough spots and confusions in the user interface. The system preview was fortunate because it identified important problems that the developers fixed before trying to implement the system in the organization. The new system provides flexibility that was previously impossible. Making a simple change to a bill used to take months. Now changes can be entered immediately.

Other old systems at Pacific Bell had similar problems. Troubleshooting problems with a customer's account often involved logging into several legacy systems related to customer accounts, service commitments, pricing schemes, and so on. After analyzing the legacy systems a customer service representative might have to access, Pacific Bell developed a way to keep parts of the old systems but change the interface so that customer service representatives could do their work more effectively. The new approach was to surround the old systems using a client–server front end for handling data communications and data retrieval.[1, 2]

DEBATE TOPIC   *Argue the pros and cons and practical implications of the following proposition:*
The idea of surrounding poorly understood legacy systems with better interfaces is fundamentally flawed because the end result is a bad system with a good interface. Pacific Bell should rebuild the old systems from scratch.

Pacific Bell's work on rebuilding systems raises many issues related to building systems. How did the systems get to the state they were in? Why were they so inflexible? Was it really necessary to build a billing system and try it out with the users instead of doing it right the first time? Are there any processes for building systems that would have avoided some of the problems that led to these reengineering projects?

The outright failure of many systems is another reason to look carefully at how the system building process is performed and managed. For example, a survey of 300 large companies by KPMG Peat Marwick, a Big Six accounting firm, discovered that 65 percent had at least one project that went grossly over budget, was extremely late, and ultimately produced results of little value. Peat Marwick called such a project a **runaway,** as in a "runaway train."[3]

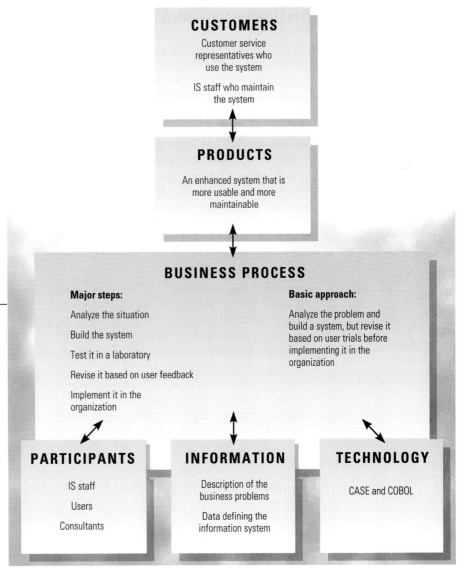

Figure 14.1 Pacific Bell: The Process of Rebuilding a Billing System

This chapter discusses four alternative models for building and maintaining information systems that were originally summarized in Chapter 1. These alternative approaches include the traditional system life cycle, prototypes, application packages, and end-user development. The chapter starts by reviewing the four information system phases summarized in Chapter 1 as a least common denominator for discussing and comparing the alternative models. Since each approach has advantages and disadvantages, system builders need to decide on the combination of these approaches that makes the most sense in any particular situation.

As you read this chapter, remember that building an information system is a business process. Like other business processes, it has an architecture that ultimately affects its internal performance and the product it produces for customers. Product performance can be evaluated in terms of cost to the customer, quality, responsiveness, reliability, and conformance. Internal process performance can be evaluated in terms of capacity, consistency, productivity, cycle time, flexibility, and security.

Phases of Any Information System

The starting point for most systems is a business problem or opportunity that gives someone the idea that some kind of system might provide desired benefits. Next, someone refines that idea into a specific statement of what the system will accomplish. Analysts or designers decide how to convert this description of desired system functions into a set of programs that accomplish these functions on specific hardware. These participants acquire whatever hardware they need and either write programs or buy them. They test the programs to ensure the correct functions are performed in the correct manner. A team implements the system in the organization through a process involving user training and conversion from the previous system. The system then goes into operation and is modified as necessary. Eventually, the system may be absorbed into other systems or terminated.

Whether the software was produced by the IS department, the user department, or an outside vendor, this general process can be summarized in terms of four system phases introduced in Chapter 1: initiation, development, implementation, and operation and maintenance.

Various authors use the terms *development* and *implementation* in different ways. In this book, the term development refers to the phase concerned with designing, programming, and testing a computer system. This is the second of four phases for any successful system. Consistent with common usage, the verb *develop* is also used here in a general sense, as in "Acme developed a sales system." For programmers, the term *implementation* often refers to the process of designing and programming a computer system. Since this is a book for business professionals, the word *implementation* is used in the way they typically use it, namely, to refer to making the system work in the organization. Defined this way, implementation is the third phase of the system life cycle. We will discuss each of the four phases in turn.

Initiation

Initiation is the process of defining the need for a system, identifying the people who will use it or be affected by it, and describing in general terms what the system will do to meet the need. This phase may occur in response to obvious problems, such as unavailable or incorrect data. It may be part of a planning process searching for innovations even if current systems pose no overt problems. This phase concludes with a verbal or written agreement about the desired system's general function and scope, as well as a shared understanding that it is technically and organizationally feasible.

A key outcome of this phase is an understanding of a proposed system's purposes and goals. Errors in this phase may result in systems that work on the computer but don't support the organization's goals. Since it is possible to change a system even after it goes into operation, design errors in the initiation phase may not be fatal to the project. However, they are especially expensive because the subsequent work on the system builds on these errors. Figure 14.2 demonstrates the importance of identifying design errors early in a system development process by showing how the cost of design errors escalates the later they are discovered.

Figure 14.2 Costs in Design Errors Detected at Different Times

The later a design error is detected, the more expensive it is to correct because so much rework and retesting is required.

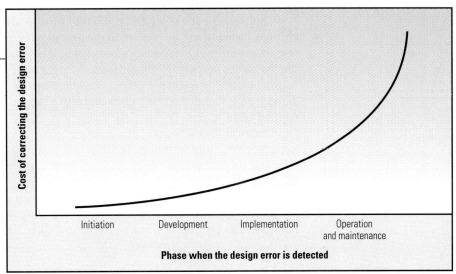

Some system projects never go beyond the initiation phase. For example, the analysis in this phase may show that the likely costs outweigh the likely benefits or that the system is technically or organizationally impractical. Other systems are abandoned because people cannot agree on system goals or because too few people in the organization care about the problem the system addresses. Although no one wants to invest time and effort in a project and then stop it, stopping a project at this phase is far better than pouring time and effort into something that probably won't succeed.

Development

Development is the process of transforming general system requirements into hardware and software (and related documentation) that accomplish the required functions. This phase includes deciding exactly what the system will accomplish and exactly how its computerized and manual parts will operate. If the hardware isn't already in place, development also includes purchasing and installing hardware. Purchasing an application package from an outside vendor reduces this phase to clarifying objectives, choosing a vendor product, testing the product's adequacy, and deciding exactly how to use it. Completion of development does not mean that "the system works." Rather, it means only that the computerized parts of the system operate on a computer. Whether or not the system works will be determined later by how it is used in the organization.

A key goal of the development phase is assuring that system features really solve problems the users want solved. This is sometimes difficult because many users are unable to describe exactly how a new system might help them. They also may not realize that a system could help them in some ways but might become a hindrance in other ways. Another key goal is to perform the technical work in a way that makes it easier to modify the system as new needs arise.

Implementation

Implementation is the process of putting a system into operation in the organization. This phase starts when tested software runs on the computer. Activities in implementation include planning, user training, conversion to the new system, and follow-up to ensure the system is operating as it should.

Implementation of a new system may involve major organizational or personal changes. Conversion from the old to the new must be planned and executed carefully to prevent errors or even chaos. Conversion of transaction processing systems often requires some users to do double work during a pilot test, operating simultaneously with the old and new systems. Running two systems in parallel helps identify unanticipated problems with the new system that might require changes before the system can be used fully.

Political issues related to power and control within the organization often become visible during implementation. For example, implementing an integrated sales and production system might make computerized production scheduling data directly accessible to a sales department. Ideally, this data should help sales and production work together. However, it might also permit sales to exert new pressure on production, which previously had sole access to the data. The new system's cooperative rationale might be replaced with a win–lose feeling. Such issues should be identified and discussed as early as possible.

Operation and Maintenance

Operation and maintenance is the ongoing use of the system after it has been installed, as well as work to enhance it and correct bugs. Minimally, system operation requires someone responsible for ensuring that it actually works and provides benefits. System changes are often needed to address the current business situation rather than what existed when the system was first built.

People tend to overlook the significance of this phase. To the IS staff, building new systems often seems more challenging and creative than keeping old ones effective as needs change. Perceiving this phase as less creative, users may assume that upgrades should be easy. In fact, the operation and maintenance phase is often challenging. For example, consider the response time and uptime requirements of systems companies rely on for taking customer orders or managing factories. Once a system is in operation, users expect it to work. Downtime and bugs must be dealt with immediately, which requires the ability to diagnose and correct problems under time pressure.

Furthermore, the longer a system has been in operation, the harder it is to change. Original developers who understood it best may have different jobs; documentation becomes outdated; infrequently used parts of the system fall into disrepair. Programmers become justifiably wary of changing the system because a change in one place is more likely to cause a bug elsewhere. In turn, the users are less likely to get the changes they want and start to complain about the IS department's unresponsiveness and the system's ineffectiveness. Ideally, the business process chosen for building a system should minimize these problems.

We have now described the four phases of any information system. This model serves as a least common denominator for understanding and comparing different types of business processes used for building and maintaining systems. Figure 14.3 shows how the end product of one phase is the starting point of the next. It also shows some of the reasons for returning to a previous phase even though the four phases ideally occur in sequence.

Figure 14.3 Links between the Four Phases and Reasons for Rework

This diagram shows how the end product of the first three phases is the starting point of the next phase. It uses italics to show why it is sometimes necessary to return to a previous phase.

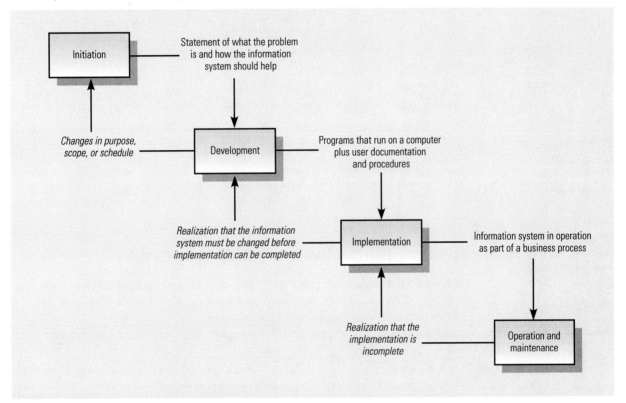

Table 14.1 summarizes problems and issues that must be dealt with in order for each phase to succeed. Different business processes are used to perform the individual phases depending on the type of system, the problem it attempts to solve, and the situation in which it will operate. In some situations, the requirements are clear and easily agreed on; in others, no one may be able to describe the requirements clearly until they have a system to try out. In some cases, existing technology will be used; in others, new technology must be mastered and used for the first time in the organization. In yet other situations, buying an application system may be a better choice than building one from scratch. The next section explains and compares alternative processes used in these different situations.

Table 14.1 Common Issues and Problems in Each Phase of an Information System

Phase	Common Issues and Problems
Initiation	• Can we agree on the purposes and goals of the proposed system? • Are the requirements unnecessarily elaborate and expensive?
Development	• Can we assure that the system genuinely solves the user's problems? • Can we get users to participate effectively in the design process?
Implementation	• Can we convert effectively and painlessly from the old system to the new system? • Can we solve political issues related to changes in power relationships?
Operation and maintenance	• Can we keep system performance and uptime at acceptable levels? • Can we correct bugs and enhance the system to keep it focused on current business problems?

REALITY CHECK   **Project Phases**   This section explained four phases of an information system project and explained why it is sometimes necessary to return to a phase that was previously considered complete.

1. Think of a project or team effort that you or your family members have been involved in. Explain how well each of the four phases applied in that project.

2. Explain which of the issues in Table 14.1 are most related to important aspects of your project. (Since your project might not have involved an information system, you may have to restate the issues.)

Overview of Alternative Approaches for Building Systems

Chapter 1 introduced the idea that there is no best method for building information systems. It identified four alternative approaches summarized in Table 14.2 (same as Table 1.2) and explained in depth in this chapter.

Table 14.2 Differences between Four System Life Cycle Approaches

Life Cycle Approach	Issue Addressed	Summary of Method
Traditional system life cycle	Control	Go through a fixed sequence of steps with signoffs after each step and careful documentation
Prototype	Knowledge	Quickly develop a working model of the system; use the model to gain experience and decide how the final system should operate
Application packages	Resources and timing	Purchase an existing information system from a vendor; customize the system if necessary
End-user development	Responsiveness	Provide tools and support that make it practical for end users to develop their own systems

The **traditional system life cycle** uses a prescribed sequence of steps and deliverables to move reliably from user requirements to a system in operation. These deliverables are related because each subsequent step builds on the conclusions of previous steps. The traditional system life cycle tries to solve a *control* problem by keeping the project on track. This type of process became popular in response to numerous system development efforts that went out of control and either failed to produce a system at all or produced a system that did not solve the users' problem effectively. Accordingly, the traditional system life cycle establishes tight controls to guarantee that technical and organizational issues are addressed at each step. The controls are project deliverables ensuring that each step is completed in turn and documented carefully.

A **prototype** information system is a working model of a system built to learn about the system's true requirements. Firms build prototypes to solve a *knowledge* problem of not knowing exactly what the system should do to address an important issue. In this situation, the user needs some way to get a feeling for how the system should operate. Accordingly, a prototype is built quickly to help the user understand the problem and determine how a system might help in solving it.

An **application package** consists of commercially available software that addresses a specific type of business application, such as sales tracking, general ledger, or inventory control. Firms acquire application packages to solve a *resource and timing* problem by using commercially available software that performs most of the functions desired. The IS department installs and operates this software instead of building customized software from scratch. This approach reduces the delays in developing custom software, reduces risks due to technical uncertainties and possible changes in the business problem, and reduces the resources needed to solve the problem.

End-user development is the development of information systems by end users rather than IS professionals. Firms apply end-user development to solve a *responsiveness* problem involving the inability of information systems groups to keep up with individuals' changing information needs. The idea is to allow end users to produce their own applications systems without requiring development by programmers. This is accomplished by giving end users spreadsheets, database packages, report generators, analytical packages, and other tools that can be used by nonprogrammers. End-user development is effective only for systems that are small enough that a systems professional is not needed for system design, programming, testing, and documentation.

We will now explain each of the four alternatives in more detail.

Traditional System Life Cycle

The goal of the traditional system life cycle is to keep the project under control and assure that the system produced is what the user requested. The traditional system life cycle divides the project into a series of steps, each of which has distinct deliverables, such as documents or computer programs. These deliverables are related because each subsequent step builds on the conclusions of previous steps. Some deliverables are oriented toward the technical staff, whereas others are directed toward or produced by users and managers. The latter ensure that users and their management are included in the system development process.

Although there is general agreement about what needs to be done in the traditional system life cycle, different authors name the individual steps and related deliverables differently. Many versions of the traditional system life cycle emphasize the building of software and deemphasize what happens in the organization before and after software development. Since this book is directed at business professionals, its version of the traditional system life cycle emphasizes implementation and operation in the organization in addition to software development.

Initiation

The initiation phase may begin in many different ways. A user may work with the IS staff to produce a written request to study a particular business problem. The IS staff may discover an opportunity to use systems beneficially and then try to interest users. A top manager may notice a business problem and ask the head of IS to look into it. A system crash or other operational problem may reveal a major problem that can be patched temporarily but requires a larger project to fix it completely. However this phase begins, its goal is to analyze the scope and feasibility of a proposed system and to develop a project plan. This involves two steps, the feasibility study and project planning, which produce the functional specification and a project plan.

The **feasibility study** is a user-oriented overview of the proposed system's purpose and feasibility. A system's feasibility is typically considered from economic, technical, and organizational viewpoints.

Economic feasibility involves questions such as whether the firm can afford to build the system, whether the system's likely benefits substantially exceed its costs, and whether the project has higher priority than other projects that might use the same resources.

Technical feasibility involves questions such as whether the technology needed for the system exists and whether the firm has enough experience using that technology.

Organizational feasibility involves questions such as whether the system has enough support to be implemented successfully, whether it brings an excessive amount of change, and whether the organization is changing too rapidly to absorb the system.

If the system appears to be feasible, the initiation phase produces a functional specification and a project plan. The **functional specification** explains the importance of the business problem; summarizes changes in business processes; and estimates the project's benefits, costs, and risks. The **project plan** breaks the project into subprojects with start and completion times. It also identifies staffing, dependencies between work steps, and resource requirements.

The functional specification is approved by both user and IS personnel. It clarifies the purpose and scope of the proposed project by describing the business processes that will be affected and how they will be performed using the system. Functional specifications once consisted primarily of prose. With the advent of diagramming tools such as data flow diagrams and entity-relationship diagrams (Chapters 3 and 4), functional specifications have become much easier to read and understand. These visual representations help explain how work will be done and what general role the computerized parts of the system will play. Functional specifications typically do not explain exactly what data, reports, or data entry screens will be included. This more detailed description is produced in the development phase.

Development

The development phase creates computer programs (with accompanying user and programmer documentation) and installed hardware that accomplish the data processing described in the functional specification. This is done through a process of successive refinement in which the functional requirements are translated into computer programs and hardware requirements. The purpose of the various steps and deliverables in the development phase is to ensure that the system accomplishes the goals explained in the functional specification. These steps are summarized in Figure 14.4.

Figure 14.4 Steps in the Development Phase of the Traditional System Life Cycle

The development phase of the traditional system life cycle starts with the detailed requirements analysis based on the functional specification from the initiation phase. The resulting external specification is used for internal design, which outlines the structure of programs and specifies hardware requirements. System testing occurs on completion of hardware installation, programming, and documentation. The development phase ends with a system that operates on the computer according to the specifications.

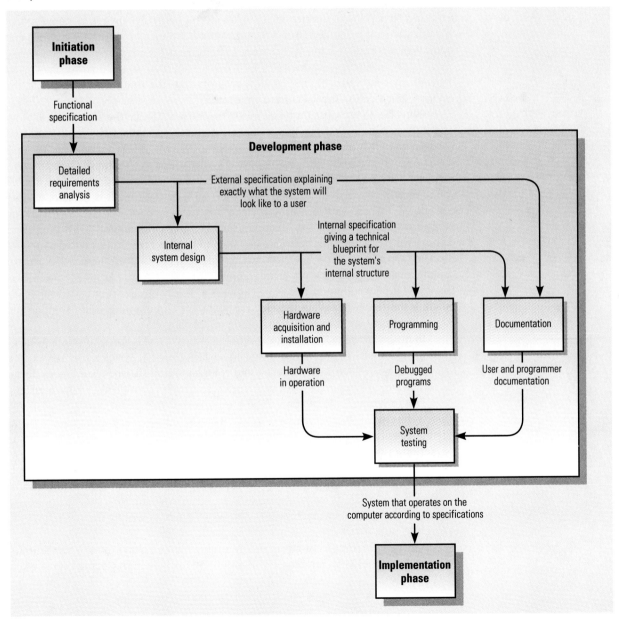

The first step in the development phase is the **detailed requirements analysis,** which produces a user-oriented description of exactly what the system will do. This step is usually performed by a team including user representatives and the IS department. It produces a document called the **external specification.** Building on the functional specification, the external specification shows the data input screens and major reports and explains the calculations to be performed by the system. It shows what system users will see rather than explaining exactly how the computer will perform the required processing. Users reviewing this document focus on whether they understand the data input screens, reports, and calculations, and whether these will support the desired business process. By approving the external specification, the users and IS staff signify their belief that the system will accomplish what they want.

The next step is **internal system design,** in which the technical staff decides how the system will be configured on the computer. This step produces the **internal specification,** a technical blueprint for the system. It documents the computer environment the system will operate in, the detailed structure and content of the database, and the inputs and outputs of all programs and subsystems. System users do not sign off on the internal specification because it addresses technical system design issues. Instead, the IS staff signs off that the internal specification accomplishes the functions called for in the external specification the users have approved.

Thus far, the discussion has focused on software. Since the software will work only if there is hardware for it to run on, an essential step in the development phase is **hardware acquisition and installation.** For some systems, this is not an issue because it is a foregone conclusion that the new system will use existing hardware. Other systems require a careful analysis to decide which hardware to acquire, how to acquire it most economically, where to put it, and how to install it by the time it is needed. Factors considered in hardware acquisition decisions include compatibility with existing hardware and systems, price, customer service, and compatibility with long-term company plans. Computer hardware can be purchased or rented through a variety of financing arrangements, each with its own tax consequences. A firm's finance department usually makes the financing arrangements for significant hardware purchases. Especially if new computer hardware requires a new computer room, lead times for building the room, installing the electricity and air conditioning, and installing the computer may be important factors in the project plan.

In firms with large IS staffs, users rarely get involved with the acquisition, installation, and operation of computer hardware. Much like telephone systems, users expect the hardware to be available when needed and complain furiously whenever it goes down. This is one reason computer hardware managers sometimes consider their jobs thankless.

Programming is the creation of the computer code that performs the calculations, collects the data, and generates the reports. It can usually proceed while the hardware is being acquired and installed. Programming includes the coding, testing, and documentation of each program identified in the internal specification. Coding is what most people think of as programming. The testing done during the programming step is often called **unit testing** since it treats the programs in isolation. The documentation of each program starts with the explanation from the internal specification and includes comments about technical assumptions made in writing the program, plus any subtle, nonobvious processing done by the program.

A number of improvements in programming methods have made programming faster and more reliable. Structured programming (explained in Chapter 10) is often used to make the programs more consistent, easier to understand, and less error prone. Fourth-generation languages (4GLs) also expedite programming for some systems.

However, as should be clear from all the steps leading up to coding and following coding, coding often accounts for less than 20 percent of the work in developing a system. This is one of the reasons improved programming tools, such as 4GLs, do not drastically shrink the system life cycle for large systems, even when they slash programming time.[4]

Documentation is another activity that can proceed in parallel with programming and hardware acquisition. Both user and technical documentation is completed from the material that already exists. The functional specification and external specification are the basis for the user documentation, and the internal specification and program documentation are the basis for the programmer documentation. With the adoption of CASE tools described in Chapter 10, more of the documentation is basically a compilation of data and diagrams already stored on a computer. Additional user documentation is usually required, however, because different users need to know different things depending on their roles. People who perform data entry tasks need to understand the data entry procedures and what the data mean; people who use data from the system need to understand what the data mean and how to retrieve and analyze data, but they may not need to know about data entry details.

After the individual programs have been tested, the entire system must be tested to ensure that the programs operate together to accomplish the desired functions. This is called the **system testing,** or integration testing. System tests frequently uncover inconsistencies among programs as well as inconsistencies in the original internal specification. These must be reconciled and the programs changed and retested. Although system testing may seem an obvious requirement, inadequate system testing often leads to serious problems. A new trust accounting system put into operation prematurely by Bank of America on March 1, 1987, lost data and fell months behind in generating statements for customers. By January 1988, 100 institutional customers with $4 billion in assets moved to other banks, several top executives resigned, and 2.5 million lines of code were scrapped.

An important part of testing is the creation of a **testing plan,** a precise statement of exactly how the system will be tested. This plan includes the data that will be used for testing. Creating a testing plan serves many purposes. It encourages careful thought about how the system will be tested. In addition, having a thorough plan increases the likelihood that all foreseeable contingencies will be considered and that the testing will catch more of the bugs in the system.

It should be clear that the development phase for a large information system is a complex undertaking, quite different from sitting down at a PC and developing a small spreadsheet model. Explicitly separating all the steps in the development phase helps ensure that the system accomplishes the desired functions and is debugged. Such an elaborate approach is needed because the system is a tool of an organization rather than an individual. An individual producing a spreadsheet is often trying to solve a current problem and has no intention to use the spreadsheet next month, much less that someone else will need to decipher and use it next year. In contrast, the traditional system life cycle assumes that the system may survive for years, may be used by people who were not involved in its development, and may be changed repeatedly during that time by people other than the original developers. The steps in the traditional life cycle try to make the long-term existence of the system as efficient and error-free as possible.

Implementation

Implementation is the process of putting a system into operation in an organization. Figure 14.5 shows that it starts with the end product of the development phase, namely, a set of computer programs that run correctly on the computer, as well as accompanying documentation. This phase begins with **implementation planning,** the process of creating plans for training, conversion, and acceptance testing. The training plan explains how and when the user will be trained. The conversion plan explains how and when the organization will convert to new business processes. The acceptance testing plan describes the process and criteria for verifying that the information system works properly in supporting the desired business processes.

Training is the process of ensuring that system participants know what they need to know about the system. The training format depends on user backgrounds and the system's purpose and features. Users with no computer experience may require special training. Training for frequently used transaction processing systems differs from training for occasionally used analysis systems. Systems performing diverse functions require more extensive training than systems used repetitively for a few functions. Training manuals and presentations help in the implementation by explaining what will be different with the new system. After the previous system has receded into history, other types of training material are more appropriate.

After the training comes the carefully planned process of **conversion** from the old business processes to new ones using the new information system. Conversion is often called *cutover* or *changeover*. It can be accomplished in several ways, depending on the nature of the work and the characteristics of the old and new systems. It is possible to simply choose a date, shut off the old system, and turn on the new system. This is risky, though, because it doesn't verify that the new system works properly and that the users understand how to use it.

Consider the following example: The State of California installed an optical disk system to streamline the process of doing title searches (establishing ownership and identifying indebtedness on a property) for borrowers who wished to purchase property. Previously, there was a two- to three-week delay between the borrower's loan request and the bank's receipt of a confirmation that the title was clear. The new system was to reduce this delay to two days. Both the vendor and several state officials recommended that the old manual system remain in full operation during the conversion in case of problems. However, the secretary of finance rejected the request for an additional $2.4 million, and the manual system was simply shut down when the optical disk system came up. Unfortunately, software bugs plagued the new system, and the resulting logjam of 50,000 loan requests delayed title searches for up to ten weeks. The new system was shut down for repair, and the old manual system reinstated. The assistant secretary of state stated that some banks almost went out of business because of the slow turnaround.[5]

To minimize risk and wasted effort, most conversions occur in stages, which can be done in several ways. A **phased approach** uses the new system for a limited subset of the processing while continuing to use the old system for the rest of the processing. If something goes wrong, the part of the business using the new system can switch back to the old system. The simultaneous use of the old system and the new system is called **running in parallel.** Although this involves double record keeping for a while, it verifies that the new system works properly and helps the users learn to use it effectively.

Conversions from one computerized system to another are often far more difficult than users anticipate. Computerized data in the old system must be converted into the formats used by the new system. Inconsistencies between the two systems frequently lead to confusion about whether the data in either system are correct. Furthermore, programs that convert the data from one system to another may have their own bugs, thereby adding to confusion and delays.

Figure 14.5 Steps in the Implementation Phase of the Traditional System Life Cycle

The implementation phase starts with a system that operates on the computer but not in the organization. Implementation planning creates the plan for three other steps, training the users, converting to new business processes, and formal acceptance by the users.

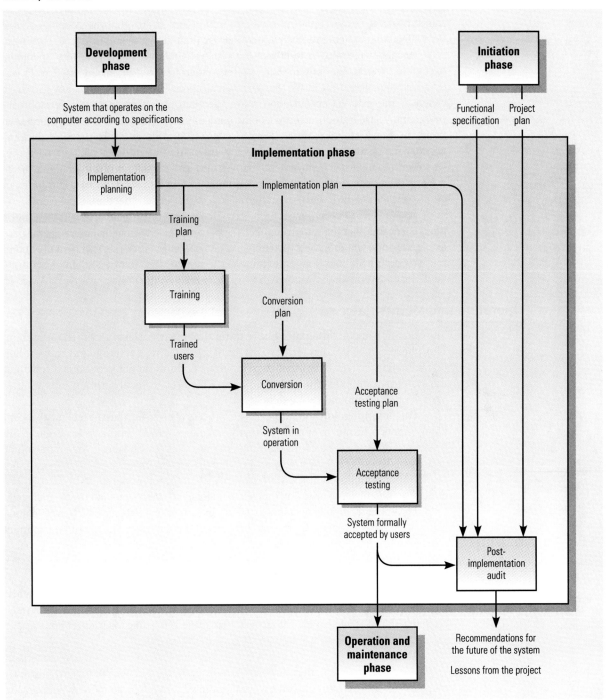

Conversion requires careful planning because even minor problems can be blown out of proportion by people who don't want the new system and use the problems as an opportunity to complain. For these reasons, it is often wise to do a **pilot implementation** with a small group of users who are enthusiastic about the system. Ideally, their enthusiasm will motivate them to learn about the system and to forgive minor problems. After a pilot implementation demonstrates that the system works, it is usually much easier to motivate everyone else (including the skeptics) to start using it.

Acceptance testing is testing of the system by the users as it goes into operation. Acceptance testing is important because the system may not fit, regardless of what was approved and signed off in the external specification. The business situation may have changed; the external specification may reflect misunderstandings; the development process may have introduced errors; or the implementation may have revealed unforeseen problems. For all these reasons, it makes sense to include an explicit step of deciding whether the system is accepted for ongoing use. If the system doesn't fit user needs, for whatever reason, installing it without changes may lead to major problems and may harm the organization instead of helping. Acceptance testing also solidifies user commitment because it gets people in the user organization to state publicly that the system works.

The **post-implementation audit** is the last step in the implementation phase even though it occurs after the system has been in operation for a number of months. Its purpose is to determine whether the project has met its objectives for costs and benefits and to make recommendations about the future of the system. This audit is also an opportunity to identify what the organization can learn from the way the project was carried out.

Operation and Maintenance

The operation and maintenance phase starts after the users have accepted the system. This phase can be divided into two activities: (1) ongoing operation and support and (2) maintenance. Unlike the other steps in the life cycle, these steps continue throughout the system's useful life. The end of a system's life cycle is its absorption into another system or its termination.

Ongoing operation and support is the process of ensuring that the technical system components continue to operate correctly and effectively. This process is similar to the process of making sure a car or building operates well. It works best when a person or group has the direct responsibility for keeping the system operating. This responsibility is often split, with the technical staff taking care of computer operations and a member of the user organization ensuring that users understand the system and use it effectively.

Day-to-day computer operations typically include scheduled events such as generating summary reports for management and backups of the database. The **operations manual** specifies when these jobs should be done. For transaction processing systems essential to business operations, a technical staff member also monitors computer-generated statistics about response times, program run times, disk space utilization, and similar factors to ensure the system is running efficiently. When the database becomes too full, or when response times start to increase, the technical configuration of the computer system must be changed. This is done by allocating more disk space, unloading (backing up onto tape or discarding) data that are not current, or changing job schedules.

Maintenance is the process of modifying the system over time. As users gain experience with a system, they discover its shortcomings and usually suggest improvements. Most shortcomings involve ways that the system might do more to support the organization's work, regardless of the system's original design goals. Some shortcomings are bugs. Important shortcomings must be corrected if users are to continue using the system enthusiastically.

Handling of enhancement requests and bug fix requests is both a technical challenge and a delicate political issue for IS departments. The technical challenge is ensuring that changes don't affect other parts of the system in unanticipated ways. The traditional life cycle helps here because system documentation and internal design methods enforce modularization and make it easier to understand the scope and impact of changes. The political issue for most IS departments is their inability to support even half the enhancement requests they receive. For new or inadequately planned systems, some departments have more enhancement requests than they can even analyze. In this environment, it requires both technical and political skill to keep users satisfied. Users are often frustrated by how long it takes to make changes. What might seem to be a simple change to a person who "programs" spreadsheets is often vastly more complex in a large information system. Changes often require retesting of other parts of the system and spawn changes in several levels of documentation.

The steps in each of the four phases of the traditional system life cycle have now been introduced. Table 14.3 outlines the steps in each phase and makes two major points in addition to the details it presents. It shows that users are highly involved in three of the four phases. In other words, building information systems is not just technical work done by the technical staff. It also shows that each step has specific deliverables that document progress to date and help keep the project under control.

The traditional system life cycle is a tightly controlled approach designed to reduce the likelihood of mistakes or omissions. Despite its compelling logic, it has both advantages and disadvantages. Adherence to fixed deliverables and signoffs improves control but guarantees a lengthy process. Having specific deliverables due at specific times makes it easier to monitor the work and take corrective actions early if the work starts to slip. But the schedule of deliverables sometimes takes on a life of its own and seems as important as the real project goals. Going through the motions of producing deliverables on schedule, participants may be tempted to turn in work that is incomplete and to approve documents they do not truly understand.

The traditional system life cycle is the standard against which other approaches are compared. Project managers who want to bypass some of its steps still need a way to deal with the issues these steps raise. The chapter looks next at three alternative approaches based on different assumptions and priorities: prototypes, application packages, and end-user development.

REALITY CHECK **The Traditional System Life Cycle** This section mentioned that the traditional system life cycle is organized around a sequence of steps and deliverables.

1. Assume you were buying or renting a house or apartment that you plan to live in for five years. You want to make a plan for this process. What will the steps be, and what will be the deliverable for each step?

2. Explain the ways your process reflects some of the ideas in the traditional system life cycle. (Since this is a different problem, your process should differ from the traditional life cycle in many ways.)

Prototypes

The traditional system life cycle enforces tight controls to ensure that the resulting system performs according to requirements and is maintainable. The prototype approach emphasizes a different issue. Prototypes are used when the precise requirements for a new system are difficult to visualize and define because the business process will change substantially.

Table 14.3 Steps and Deliverables in the Traditional System Life Cycle

Step	Degree of User Participation	Key Deliverable, Plan, or Document	Key Participants
Initiation Phase			
Feasibility study	High	Functional specification	User representatives, management, and technical staff
Project planning	Medium	Project plan	User representatives, management, and technical staff
Development Phase			
Detailed requirements analysis	High	External specification	User representatives, management, and technical staff
Internal system design	None	Internal specification	Programmers and technical staff
Hardware acquisition and installation	None	Hardware plan Hardware operational	Technical staff Technical staff
Programming	None	Individual programs debugged	Programmers
Documentation	Medium	User and programmer documentation	Technical staff and users
System testing	Medium	Test plan Completed system test	Programmers and users
Implementation Phase			
Implementation planning	High	Implementation plan	Training staff, users, and management
Training	High	Training materials	Trainers and users
Conversion	High	System in use	Users and project team
Acceptance testing	High	System accepted	Users and project team
Post-implementation audit	High	Audit report	Users and management
Operation and Maintenance Phase			
Ongoing operation and support	Low Low High	Operations manual Usage statistics Enhancement requests and bug fix requests	Technical staff Technical staff and users Technical staff and users
Maintenance	Medium	Maintenance plan	Technical staff and users
Absorption or termination	— —	— —	— —

A prototype information system is a working model built to learn about the system's true requirements by testing features of a proposed system. Instead of asking users to imagine how a proposed system might operate, the prototype approach allows them to work actively with a model of the system. This helps them identify the features they need. It also helps identify impractical features that originally seemed to be beneficial.

A prototype system's purpose is similar to that of a prototype automobile. For example, assume that an automobile designer wants to test out a new type of steering. A prototype would be designed specifically to test the steering. The steering system and suspension would be produced carefully, but the prototype might not have a paint job, back seat, or radio. These features would be put in later when the design is completed.

The prototype information system might contain a rough model of the data entry screens but might lack error checking because this would not be necessary to demonstrate the concept of the system. Since only a small sample database would suffice for a demonstration, no effort would go into making the prototype efficient. If the system contained a model, it might calculate approximate results just to show the types of outputs the system would produce. Later versions would check the inputs, make the model more elaborate, and make its outputs look more complete.

Prototype information systems are sometimes classified as throwaway prototypes or evolutionary prototypes.[6] A **throwaway prototype** is designed to be discarded after it is used to test ideas and is especially useful for comparing alternative designs for parts of a system. These prototypes might be programmed for a PC even though the final system might use a different computer. An **evolutionary prototype** is designed to be adapted for permanent use after the ideas are clarified and must be built using the programming tools that will be used for the final system.

The phases of building and using a prototype are covered next. Table 14.4 summarizes important characteristics of each phase.

Table 14.4 System Life Cycle Based on a Prototype

Phase	Characteristics
Initiation	Users and developers agree to develop a prototype because they need experience with a working model before designing a final system.
Development	Working iteratively with users, a prototype is developed or improved. Later, decide whether to complete the prototype or switch to a traditional life cycle.
Implementation	Accomplish parts of implementation along with development as users work with the prototype system. Dispel skepticism about whether the system will meet user's needs.
Operation and maintenance	May be similar to a traditional life cycle. May require less maintenance because the system fits users' needs more accurately. May require more maintenance because the system is not constructed as well.

Phases

The phases of a prototype approach differ from those of a traditional system life cycle because the approaches have different assumptions. The traditional system life cycle assumes that users understand the requirements and that the main issue is to guarantee requirements are followed in a disciplined way. Prototyping assumes that users either cannot say exactly what the proposed system should do or would have difficulty evaluating a written specification. Using a highly iterative approach, it proceeds by building a succession of "quick and dirty" versions of the system. The users look at each iteration and suggest improvements, continuing this way until they know what they want. At this point, they and the technical staff decide how to complete the project. Figure 14.6 shows the iterative process used in the prototype approach.

Figure 14.6 Using a Prototype Approach

Building an information system using a prototype is an iterative process. It involves evaluation and revision of a model system until the users and system builders understand the problem well enough to decide how to complete the project.

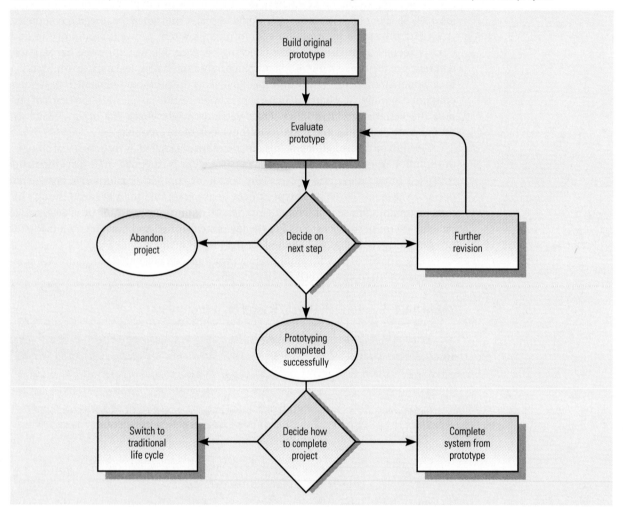

Initiation

The initiation phase begins with a request to build an information system in response to a business problem or opportunity. Since the problem isn't well understood, or since the users are unable to say exactly what they want, users and developers start by building a prototype instead of writing a functional specification. For this approach to succeed, the users must be willing and able to enter an iterative design process. Issues about completeness and consistency of the requirements are dealt with as the users study successive versions.

Development

The development process emphasizes speed and rapid feedback. It begins by developing an initial prototype that demonstrates some of the desired processing but is far from complete. Next come a series of iterations, each modifying the prototype based on user comments about the most recent version. The technical approach for this process differs from what would be used in a traditional life cycle. Instead of using a programming language that would support high-volume transaction processing, a prototype might use a 4GL or DBMS for personal computers.

Building prototypes is much easier today than it was in the past because programming technology is much better. In particular, DBMSs, 4GLs, and CASE systems all contain screen generators (see Figure 14.7), report generators, and data dictionaries that make it easier to set up a model application quickly. Furthermore, since these same tools may be used for building the production version of the system, the transition from a prototype to a running system is much easier than it once was.

Figure 14.7 Creating a Data Input Screen Using a Screen Generator

This screen generator permits a programmer to set up a data entry screen with minimal effort by placing headings, instructions, and data entry fields anywhere on the screen. It is an example of the programming advances that have made prototyping much easier.

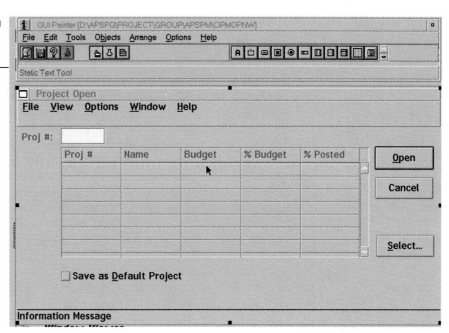

Once the requirements are clear, the users and technical staff must decide how to proceed. They might conclude that the project should be abandoned. Although no one wants to start a project only to abandon it, the prototype reduces the time and resources absorbed by a project that won't succeed. If the project is to continue, one approach is to complete the prototype using the code that has been generated thus far. Another is to shift to a traditional system life cycle by writing a functional specification and external specification based on what has been learned and then doing the internal design based on the desired level of system performance. The shift to a traditional system life cycle is especially appropriate for a system that will have a long life or will be critical to the business. If the system is primarily for management reporting, or if business problems are changing rapidly, extending the prototype might be a better choice.

Implementation

When using a prototype, part of the implementation is done in parallel with development. Users try out the system during successive iterations and become familiar with what it does and how it can help them. Systems developed this way may require less user training in the implementation phase. Active user participation in the development phase may offset skepticism about whether the system will be beneficial. For users who didn't participate in the prototyping, the training should be similar to the training they would have received in the traditional system life cycle. The conversion step should be similar to that of the traditional approach.

Operation and maintenance

The operation and maintenance phase of a system developed using a prototype should be similar to that of a system developed with the traditional life cycle. However, the characteristics of the development process contribute to both advantages and disadvantages during the operation and maintenance phase.

Advantages and Disadvantages

The advantages of prototyping come from creating a more accurate idea of what the users really need. Starting from a better understanding has effects on each remaining phase. During development, users have a tangible system to work with instead of abstract specifications that may be difficult to visualize. This helps them provide useful feedback and may terminate an infeasible project before too much effort is wasted. During implementation, the system may be more on target than it would have been otherwise. Early user involvement may also reduce skepticism and create a climate of acceptance about the new system. The impact during the operation phase may be a reduced number of changes because the initial system matches user needs.

Using prototypes has disadvantages, however. The process of developing a prototype may require greater involvement and commitment by key users who are already busy with their regular work. Continual changes while analyzing succeeding versions of the prototype may be difficult for these users. The succession of rapid changes may also require an unusual level of skill and commitment by the IS professionals. This process can be frustrating because the users are often saying that the system is not right. It can also be stressful because rapid iterations imply frequent deadlines in producing the next version. On the other hand, system developers often find developing prototypes exciting because they produce tangible results quickly and get immediate feedback about their accomplishments.

Building prototypes is much easier today than it was in the past because programming technology is much better. In particular, DBMSs, 4GLs, and CASE systems all contain screen generators (see Figure 14.7), report generators, and data dictionaries that make it easier to set up a model application quickly. Furthermore, since these same tools may be used for building the production version of the system, the transition from a prototype to a running system is much easier than it once was.

The shortcuts that make rapid prototyping iterations possible sometimes undermine the completed system's technical foundations. This is a problem for prototypes put into use without being revamped technically. Internal design, programming, and documentation are not as sound for these systems as they would have been under the traditional life cycle. As a result, these systems may have worse performance and reliability and may require more maintenance than if the traditional life cycle had been used.

System users sometimes fail to appreciate the fragility of prototypes and don't understand why the IS staff may insist on revising a system that appears to work properly. Prototypes are built to demonstrate ideas. Even if the final system is to have the general appearance of the prototype, much more work must be done to assure reliability and adequate performance in real use. Regardless of whether a system looks good, it is not helpful if it operates ten times too slowly, shuts down because of internal flaws, or has inadequate backup and recovery capabilities.

Prototypes are not the only alternative for bypassing parts of the traditional life cycle. Another is to purchase an application system previously developed by a software vendor.

Application Packages

Although every company is unique in some ways, many information systems are similar across groups of companies. For example, the payroll systems in two small construction firms could be quite similar. Since there are thousands of such firms, this similarity leads to a business opportunity to develop and sell a payroll system that many firms can use. Such systems typically start with custom work done for one or several firms. When the system works well for the original users, the software vendor markets it to other firms with similar requirements. The software vendor gradually builds more features into the software to support the needs of more customers. Such systems often contain a number of modules and are therefore called application packages. Figure 14.8 shows relationships between the modules of a type of system that is commonly purchased as an application package.

The potential customers for most application packages have similar size and are in a particular market segment. For example, an appointment scheduling system sold to clinics with several doctors might not fit large clinics, which need different business processes for scheduling appointments.

Purchasing an application package reduces the time delay until a system can be operational. It also reduces the amount of development work that is needed. However, as will be apparent by looking at the phases of acquiring and using an application package, the life cycle for these systems still requires a great deal of effort and commitment. Table 14.5 shows some of the special characteristics of the phases of using an application package.

Figure 14.8 Example of a Commercial Application Package

Manufacturing resource planning (MRP) systems such as this one are often application packages rather than internally built systems. The complexity of these systems gives software vendors competitive advantage versus in-house IS groups in building and maintaining these systems.

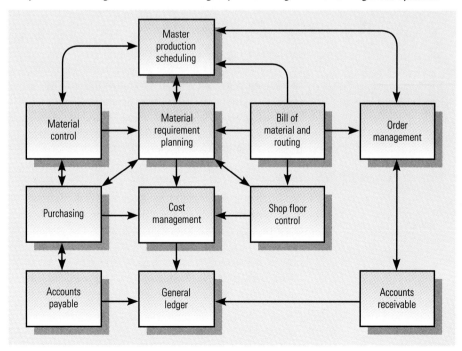

Table 14.5 System Life Cycle for Using an Application Package

Phase	Characteristics
Initiation	May start with a user's or manager's recognition of a business problem or with a sales call from a vendor.
Development	The vendor sells software built previously for other customers. The purchaser still performs some typical development activities, such as determining detailed requirements. Additional development activities by purchaser or vendor may include customization of the software and user documentation.
Implementation	Implementation starts by deciding exactly how the package will be used. It often relies on the vendor's staff since they have the greatest knowledge of the system.
Operation and maintenance	Operation occurs as it would with a traditional life cycle. Maintenance is different because the vendor maintains the software based on requests from customers and demands of the market.

Phases

It might seem that buying an application system from a vendor would bypass most of the work of system building and maintenance. In fact, the company's staff must still work on all four phases of the system to ensure that the right application package is selected and is set up and supported properly. For large applications such as factory management systems, several years of effort may pass before the system is fully operational and delivering benefits.

Initiation

The initiation phase may occur much as it would in the traditional life cycle, with a business problem or opportunity motivating a proposal to develop a new system. It may also start with a vendor's sales call trying to convince the firm's management that the firm could use the vendor's system.

Regardless of how the project begins, it is often useful to produce a functional specification just as is done in the traditional life cycle. The functional specification represents the firm's perception of the problem and the required capabilities. It helps in deciding which vendors to consider and in selecting an application package. Failure to produce a functional specification can give vendors too much leeway in shaping the firm's view of its own problems.

Development

Although purchasing pre-existing software changes the development phase, many development activities are still required. It is still necessary to decide exactly what features are needed, to test the software, and to tailor parts of the documentation for use within the firm. The process of clarifying user requirements and evaluating alternatives involves the same issues as the first part of the development phase in the traditional life cycle. Instead of writing a formal external specification, the project team invites vendors to present their products and to provide live demonstrations.

These demonstrations may be set up like prototype installations, with a small number of users using the system on real data to understand how it works.

The firm may perform benchmark testing. **Benchmarking** an application package involves running a test application with the same volumes of input, output, data access, and data manipulation that the final application will have. Benchmarking sometimes reveals that an application package performs the right processing but operates too slowly. To compare products systematically, the project team may issue a **request for proposal (RFP),** which converts the ideas in the functional specification into a checklist of required capabilities and features. The vendors respond by explaining how their products meet the requirements.

Choosing among competing application packages is often difficult because each has advantages and disadvantages, and few satisfy all user requirements. It may be unclear which features are or are not important. Business factors also matter, such as the vendor's financial strength and long-term viability. The selection process is based partially on information from vendors who emphasize their strengths and deemphasize weaknesses. Good vendors avoid selling poorly matched solutions, however, since unhappy customers usually hurt a vendor's reputation. Poorly matched solutions also have implementation problems that often waste vendor time and resources.

In competitive situations with large, expensive systems, vendors often try to be the first one in the door and try to "help" the buyer analyze the business problem. They do this to influence the problem statement so that the vendor's solution appears to be a better fit than a competitor's solution. For example, if vendor A's software runs on an IBM computer and vendor B's runs on Tandem, vendor A may try to influence the company to require an IBM platform. Simultaneously, vendor B might try to include features that are difficult to obtain on IBM.

When all is said and done, it is always possible to argue about the requirements. In fact, they are the result of a process of learning about alternative ideas and deciding which ones seem most important. Different people doing the same task might come up with different requirements.

However the requirements are developed, it is necessary to select a vendor and system. Consider a retailer deciding what payroll system to purchase. To make the selection, it has identified a series of important characteristics under various headings, including application features, technical features, vendor comparison, and economic comparison. The retailer wants to decide by evaluating each alternative in terms of each characteristic and then combining these scores. The more important characteristics have a higher weighting in the final score. Box 14.1 illustrates this type of analysis. It weights each characteristic between 0 and 3 based on importance, evaluates each characteristic between 0 and 10 for each alternative, and calculates an overall score. System B is preferred, but not by much.

In reality, the type of analysis in Box 14.1 is only an input to the decision and is often used as a sanity check to make sure that a significantly less preferable alternative is not chosen. One of many problems with overreliance on a numerical comparison is that both the weightings and the ratings can be manipulated to some extent to give either of two close alternatives a slightly better score. Frequently, the real decision hinges on just several characteristics, such as whether the software runs on the right type of computer, whether the vendor is financially sound, and whether the vendor seems willing to change the product to suit the customer.

Box 14.1 Selecting an Application Package

The table shown here illustrates a common method for evaluating and comparing application packages. The results of this analysis are one of many types of information used in the selection. The table compares competing packages A, B, and C based on four groups of characteristics. Each alternative has a score for each characteristic. For example, A has a score of 9 for completeness. Each characteristic also has a weight. For example, completeness has a weight of 2.5. The weighted score for each characteristic is the weight times the score. For example, the weighted score for completeness for A is $9 \times 2.5 = 22.5$. The total score for each alternative is the sum of its weighted scores. In this example, B is the preferred alternative with a total weighted score of 172.9.

Characteristic	Weight	Score			Weighted Score		
		A	B	C	A	B	C
Application Features							
Completeness	2.5	9	7	8	22.5	17.5	20.0
Quality of reports	1.0	9	5	9	9.0	5.0	9.0
Ease of use	2.3	5	9	6	11.5	20.7	13.8
Documentation	2.8	3	9	7	8.4	25.2	19.6
Technical Features							
Use of DBMS	2.8	8	7	3	22.4	19.6	8.4
Transportability	0.8	2	5	6	1.6	4.0	4.8
Expandability	1.2	4	5	5	4.8	6.0	6.0
Vendor Comparison							
Financial strength	2.0	9	7	5	18.0	14.0	10.0
Management strength	1.3	6	9	8	7.8	11.7	10.4
Commitment to product	2.6	4	7	9	10.4	18.2	23.4
Economic Comparison							
Purchase price	2.0	7	5	7	14.0	10.0	14.0
Maintenance contract	1.5	7	7	8	10.5	10.5	12.0
Consulting charges	0.6	5	6	8	3.0	3.6	4.8
Conversion cost	2.3	5	3	5	11.5	6.9	11.5
Total weighted score					155.4	172.9	167.7

Implementation

The implementation phase begins by deciding exactly how the application package will be set up and used. This decision is necessary because most application packages contain a broad range of options to satisfy different customers' needs. A typical approach is to compare the alternatives using trial installations.

System documentation provided by the vendor must often be extended with a training manual tailored for a specific setting. For example, the vendor's manual may show how an order-entry system works for a paper distributor. A hardware distributor's users will learn about it most easily if the examples in the training manual are about hardware products.

The conversion from the existing system to the new system requires the same types of planning and training needed in a traditional life cycle. One key difference is related to knowledge since the main experts on the system are employees of the vendor rather than the firm using the system. Someone expert on the system should be available during the implementation. The expert could be a vendor employee or a company employee who knows enough to troubleshoot problems that occur during implementation.

Operation and maintenance

Operation and maintenance for application packages is similar to this phase in the other processes. Someone must be responsible for ensuring the software operates efficiently on the computer and is used effectively in the organization. There must be a process for collecting enhancement requests and acting on them, and there must be a process for installing new software releases, starting with an analysis of their possible impact on users.

Application packages are unique because the vendor has the greatest expertise about the software and owns the responsibility for enhancing it. Most vendors enhance their products based on customer feedback and their own long-term plans. They typically send out new releases every six to nine months. A **release** is an upgraded version of the software the customer must install. Ideally, the vendor and customer should cooperate closely. The vendor should be available for questions and should base future enhancements on product usage. The vendor should respond quickly when bugs are found, especially if the bugs prevent users from doing their work. Figure 14.9 shows how the vendor's responsibilities fit into the phases of the system life cycle.

Product enhancements are a delicate issue in vendor–customer relationships. As happens with in-house development, vendors of software used in multiple sites soon have long lists of enhancement requests. Some of these require major product changes. Vendors usually work with their customers to identify the genuinely important enhancements. They also explain that many desired enhancements cannot be done. Managing relationships with vendors requires business and negotiation skills. These relationships require the ability to exert pressure to get the vendor to do what you want but without having direct management authority over vendor personnel.

To protect themselves and their customers, vendors usually provide software under license agreements allowing the customer to use it but not change it. To minimize dissatisfaction about receiving information in the wrong format, vendors usually provide database formats and links to 4GLs. These features help customers program their own reports, even if they are not permitted to change the transactions or database structure. Limiting customer changes prevents the customer from contaminating the database.

Figure 14.9 Vendor
Responsibilities for
Application Packages

*When an application package
is used, the vendor's staff
plays major roles at each
phase of the system life cycle.*

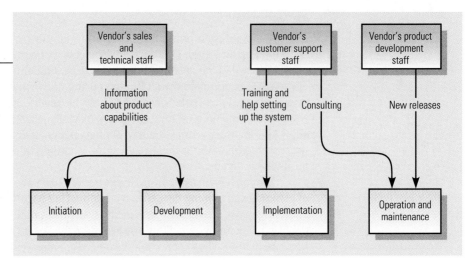

Advantages and Disadvantages

There are many reasons to purchase application packages. Benefits accrue sooner, and the risks of cost and schedule overruns drop because the purchased software is available immediately rather than months or years from now. Purchasing software helps a firm focus its resources on producing and selling whatever product or service it provides. Since the software is the vendor's business, it will usually be documented and maintained better than in-house software. Vendors may also produce a better solution because they study the same problem in many companies. Finally, the firm's IS department may not have the knowledge, experience, or staffing necessary to build the software.

With these advantages, purchasing software might usually seem a good choice. Unfortunately, application packages may not fit well. Firms using vendor software often have to compromise on the business processes they want. Alternatively, they can purchase application software and then modify it to suit their requirements. Modifying a vendor's software has its own risks, however, because application vendors usually won't maintain software modified by customers. Even without customized changes, users of major application packages typically pay 10 to 15 percent of the package's purchase price per year for maintenance, support, and new releases.

Control of the system is also an issue because the vendor decides its product's long-term direction. Since many customers provide inputs about desired enhancements, individual customers may have little control over software that controls their business processes. In addition, there is the risk that the vendor will go out of business, leaving no reliable way to maintain the software.

Application packages require the IS staff to analyze, install, and maintain software developed elsewhere instead of developing new systems themselves. Many IS professionals recognize that these evaluation and maintenance roles require knowledge and professionalism and are critical to the organization. However, these roles sometimes receive less professional credit and fewer accolades in the organization. Some IS staff members and users resent having to conform to software developed elsewhere. NIH ("not invented here") is often cited as a reason purchased software encounters problems.

Although application packages can support specific data processing needs, they rarely provide sustainable competitive advantage because any competitor can usually buy the same package. Some firms have a strategy of using application packages for functions that don't provide competitive advantage but are necessary for running the business, such as accounting, payroll, and human resources. Acquiring application packages in these areas frees up resources for other applications that help differentiate the firm in its market.

The alternatives described thus far all assume that professional programmers will develop a system for users. The next process assumes that the users are able to develop their own systems.

End-User Development

In the 1980s, the term **end-user computing (EUC)** became popular as a description of computing that was truly the tool of the end user. EUC was originally viewed as the direct, hands-on use of computer systems by end users whose jobs go beyond entering data or processing transactions. The personal computer revolution of the 1980s made end-user computing possible through the use of personal productivity tools such as word processors, spreadsheets, online appointment calendars, electronic mail, and presentation graphics. Linkage of PCs into networks later permitted end-user computing to evolve and include many forms of everyday access to corporate data. Some observers even called this the convergence of end-user and corporate computing.[7]

End-user development is a form of EUC in which users rather than programmers develop small data processing systems or models. Typical tools for end-user development include spreadsheets, DBMSs, 4GLs, and data analysis software. Figure 14.10 shows how an end user can define a database within an end-user development process that uses 4D.

Figure 14.10 A Tool for End-User Development

The end user is using the relational DBMS 4D to define the database for a small application.

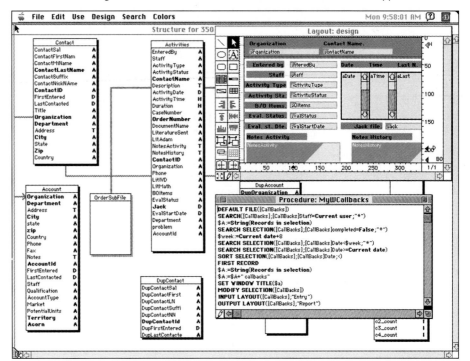

End-user development became possible with the advent of spreadsheets and small DBMSs that could be used and controlled by people not trained as programmers. It is a partial solution to a severe overload problem in most IS departments, many of which have two-year backlogs of scheduled work. In this situation, users may feel it is pointless to request additional changes to existing application software, and the IS staff feels frustrated at not being able to provide good service. If the users could just change report formats or build small data processing systems, they would get more of what they want, and the IS department's backlog would shrink. The technical staff would be more able to focus on major problems and opportunities rather than continually changing old systems. Table 14.6 outlines important aspects of this approach.

Table 14.6 System Life Cycle for End-User Development

Phase	Characteristics
Initiation	Since the user will develop the system, a formal functional specification is unnecessary.
Development	The user develops the system using tools that do not require a professional level of programming knowledge. Mission-critical systems and multi-user systems require more extensive testing, documentation, and usage procedures.
Implementation	Implementation is simplified because the developer is the user.
Operation and maintenance	End users are responsible. Long-term maintenance and technical quality become larger issues because end users have other work to do and are not professional programmers.

End-user development applies only where requirements for response time, reliability, and maintainability are not stringent; where the project is limited to a department and not on a critical path for other projects; and where proven technology is used.[8] Unassisted end-user computing may be inappropriate even if high performance levels aren't needed. For example, the error rate in even simple spreadsheet models is high because users often lack knowledge of testing methods and other programming disciplines needed to debug spreadsheet models.

Phases

The phases of end-user development are based on the fact that the end user does the work and is responsible for the results.

Initiation

The user identifies a problem or opportunity that can be addressed with end-user technology. For example, a sales manager might need a system for keeping track of sales prospects. Support staff may help in defining the problem more clearly and in identifying how the available tools can help. A functional specification is bypassed because the problem scope is small and because an explanation required for someone else's approval is unnecessary.

■ *Development*

End users take responsibility for their own systems, deciding what they need and doing development using tools appropriate for them. Successful end-user development often depends on the availability of IS staff who support the end-user developers with training and consulting. In most firms, end users must use computers and software supported by a central IS department. Figure 14.11 shows the various roles that the IS department plays in end-user development.

Figure 14.11 Roles in End-User Development

Although end users develop and maintain information systems, the IS staff plays many crucial roles in end-user development.

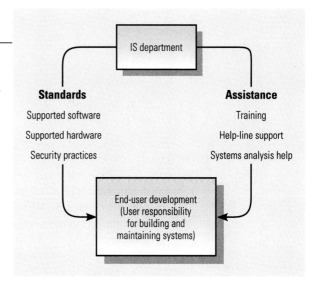

IS department

Standards
Supported software
Supported hardware
Security practices

Assistance
Training
Help-line support
Systems analysis help

End-user development
(User responsibility
for building and
maintaining systems)

■ *Implementation*

End-user development simplifies the implementation phase since the end user doesn't need training about the application. Training of other system users is easier because an end user is an expert on both the information system and how it fits into the department's business processes. Likewise, system acceptance may be less of an issue because end-user developers are so attuned to what is needed.

■ *Operation and maintenance*

End users are totally responsible for the operation and maintenance of information systems developed through end-user development. They decide when and how these systems will be used and create whatever documentation is needed. They perform backups and are responsible for system security. End users also determine what enhancements and corrections are needed and make those changes. When those systems are critical to the company, controls must be enforced to establish system security and to maintain the systems.

Supporting the Users

Successful end-user computing must deal with a number of issues involving hardware, software, training, data availability, data security, and systems analysis (see Table 14.7).

Table 14.7 Common Approaches to Issues in End-User Computing

Issue	Common Approach
Hardware selection and maintenance	The IS staff selects the types of hardware that can be purchased and maintains the hardware.
Software selection	The IS staff selects the spreadsheets and other end-user software that can be purchased and used.
Training	The IS staff provides training for end users on selected hardware and software.
Data availability	End users control their own data and share it using LANs. Corporate data are downloaded from central computers.
Data security	Users can access only the data they need.
Systems analysis	The IS staff helps end users with systems analysis and design where necessary. They also provide help lines and other types of support.

Since end users are not hardware experts and have other work to do, the IS department typically supplies and manages computers and workstations. The IS staff produces guidelines about what equipment will be supported, thereby reducing costs for computer acquisition and service. Instead of buying computers and LANs one at a time, firms can get volume discounts. Rather than trying to keep different types of computers operating, the firm's hardware staff can concentrate on one or several types.

Similar issues arise for software. Although individuals might have their own favorite spreadsheet or word processor, using many different products is inefficient. Firms often arrange **site licenses,** blanket contracts covering the use of a particular software product at a particular site by a particular number of users. (The number of simultaneous users can be controlled through LANs that supply the software when needed.) Using only compatible software also makes it easier for users to work together. At minimum, it eliminates obstacles to teamwork.

Training is an area where restricting the hardware and software available to end users has important advantages. End-user training is often required for successful end-user computing. It is much easier to offer training and assistance for a small number of hardware and software choices.

Data availability is crucial when end-user applications need data residing on other computers. For example, consider a human resources manager who needs data to analyze a proposed benefit program. Some of the data may reside elsewhere on a network. Transferring data from a central computer to a personal computer is called **downloading.** The ability to download data or access data on other workstations is one of the reasons for using LANs.

Greater access to data raises questions about data security. End-user computing entails security risks because end users have individual control over what they do with data. Downloading data to a workstation with a floppy disk drive makes it easier to steal data. Consequently, the data available to end users must be limited to what they legitimately need. This limitation is far from foolproof, however, because many users need sensitive data, such as customer lists, pricing arrangements, and product design data.

End users often lack the system-related experience of IS professionals and need help in analyzing and designing systems and troubleshooting problems. Firms provide this help in various ways. Many deploy internal consultants to help end users by providing advice but not developing systems themselves. Many have set up a **help line,** a small group that answers telephone questions related to computers and systems. Many IS departments have established user support organizations called information centers, which support end-user development by selecting and maintaining hardware and software, training end users, and providing consulting.

Advantages and Disadvantages

Compared to the complexity of the traditional life cycle, end-user development almost sounds too good to be true. It reduces the need for programmers and minimizes the problem of explaining requirements to people unfamiliar with the business. It eliminates the delays and political negotiations in resolving requirements and in implementing the system once it is developed.

Unfortunately, end-user development applies only to a limited set of situations. It works best where problems can be isolated from each other so that users can take full responsibility for both data and programs. Among other factors, the limitations of end-user development are related to the development tools used, the technical quality of the system, and the need for long-term maintenance.

Since end users have other work to do and little time for learning to program, their tools are not the same as those designed for professional programmers. Many end users can use spreadsheets, small DBMSs, 4GLs, and statistical packages. Almost none can use programming languages or complex DBMSs requiring a professional level of involvement and understanding. Tools for trained programmers are needed to produce maintainable systems with shared databases and stringent response time or security requirements.

Technical quality is another issue for systems built by end users. These systems are often less well designed and constructed than systems built by IS professionals. They are also more prone to bugs because end users are inexperienced in debugging. These issues may not be a problem in systems built for temporary, personal use by an individual but matter greatly for systems with many users over a sustained period.

Long-term maintenance is an especially important issue for complex applications involving many users. End-user developers may also find that long-term maintenance interferes with their primary job responsibilities. Like it or not, the support staff may be drawn into system maintenance roles when these situations occur.

REALITY CHECK   **End-User Development**   This section explained end-user development and some of its advantages and disadvantages.

1. Think about your personal experience in developing spreadsheet models or doing other work related to computers. How comfortable would you feel if you had to develop a small system by yourself for keeping track of customers or calculating customer bills?

2. What kind of help do you think you would need?

Deciding Which Combination of Methods to Use

The four life cycle approaches described so far are idealized models, each involving different processes and emphasizing different issues. Understanding these issues helps in deciding what methods to use for a project. After comparing the advantages and disadvantages of the four alternatives, this section will conclude with ways to combine their features into an approach appropriate for a particular situation.

Comparing Advantages and Disadvantages

Table 14.8 compares the advantages and disadvantages of the four alternatives. Many of the principal disadvantages of each approach are the mirror image of its principal advantages.

Table 14.8 Advantages and Disadvantages of Four System Life Cycle Approaches

Life Cycle	Advantages	Disadvantages
Traditional system life cycle	• Forces staff to be systematic by going through every step in an idealized process • Enforces quality by maintaining standards and reinforcing the expectation that the system will be produced to spec • Higher probability of not missing anything in the requirements analysis	• May produce excessive documentation; users feel buried in paperwork • Users often unwilling or unable to study the specs that they approve • Takes too long to go from the original ideas to a working system • Users have trouble describing requirements for a proposed system
Prototype	• Helps clarify user requirements before the design is cast in concrete • Helps verify the feasibility of the design • Promotes genuine user participation in design • May produce part of the final system	• May encourage inadequate problem analysis • User may not give up the prototype • May require "superprogrammers" • May generate confusion about whether or not the system is complete and maintainable
Application package	• Software exists and can be tried out • Software has been used for similar problems elsewhere • Reduces delays for analysis, design, and programming • Has good documentation that will be maintained	• Controlled by another company, which has its own priorities and business considerations • The package's limitations may prevent desired business processes • May be difficult to get needed enhancements if other companies using the package have different needs • Lack of intimate knowledge about how the system works and why it works that way
End-user development	• Bypasses the IS department and avoids delays • User controls the application and can change it as needed	• Systems are fragile since programming is done by an amateur • Many systems eventually require consulting and maintenance assistance from the IS department

The traditional system life cycle emphasizes control to avoid developing systems that miss the mark or are difficult to maintain. But the controls are sometimes burdensome and may take on a life of their own. When this happens, the project team starts going through the motions of producing deliverables but puts less effort into responding to the users' changing needs.

Prototypes focus on helping the user identify the requirements based on real understanding. Rapid iterations of prototypes support this but often produce programs that are more difficult to maintain than programs designed carefully before programming begins. When the prototype takes shape, the users often wonder why they cannot put it into operation immediately. In addition, the process of developing ideas and coding simultaneously requires programmers and users who are willing and able to work iteratively.

Application packages keep company resources focused on the company's business rather than on building systems to support the company's business. But the company does not have complete control over how the package works. Business processes may have to change to conform to the logic built into the package. Furthermore, desired enhancements may never appear because the vendor's other customers may not find these enhancements important.

End-user development may be more responsive to end-user needs because it bypasses the IS department and avoids delays. However, it is appropriate only for systems that are limited in organizational scope, easy to debug, require little maintenance, and can be built using tools appropriate for end users.

Combining System Life Cycle Approaches

Although the four life cycle models might seem mutually exclusive, it is possible to combine their features into the approach for a given situation. Here are some ways to combine their features:

- Use a prototype as part of a traditional system life cycle. It may be difficult to produce a good functional specification or external specification without providing some hands-on experience. Therefore, include a prototyping phase in the original project plan, but insist that an internal specification be written as the basis for the internal design of the final system.

- Use a small application package as a prototype. Shortcut the analysis process by purchasing an inexpensive application package and determining why it would or would not solve the problem. Identify required features it contains or lacks, as well as its unnecessary features. If it is well documented, use its documentation as a reference for clarifying business terminology and even helping the programmers understand an unfamiliar business situation.

- Adopt aspects of a traditional life cycle to purchasing an application package. Start with a functional specification. This makes it easier to evaluate alternative vendor systems. Purchasers of a packaged system can use appropriate parts of the traditional life cycle to be sure the problem is understood, the system well tested, and the implementation well organized.

- Add an end-user development component to the traditional life cycle. Use the traditional life cycle to create the core of the system based on a solid internal design and carefully controlled data updates. Develop user reports or inquiries using a 4GL that can be taught to users. Let the users develop their own reports using the original report programs as starting points and as demonstrations of good programming style. This maintains control of data while providing some of the advantages of end-user development. For complicated reporting requirements, use a programmer.

Other variations on the four life cycle models have been used but won't be covered in detail here. In the **phased approach,** the system is built through a sequence of iterations of development, implementation, and operation. The idea is to produce a solution to a small and manageable part of the problem, observe how the system works, and then identify another small project that would lead to improvements but not have the risk of a lengthy project.

Joint application development (JAD) is another important variation. Its distinguishing feature is a carefully prepared two-to four-day meeting bringing together user representatives and IS staff members. At this meeting, they analyze the business problem and come to a shared understanding of what must be done. JAD tries to eliminate misunderstandings that often persist despite lengthy user interviews during the analysis needed for functional specifications and external specifications. Bringing people together this way increases user participation and gives the user community a greater feeling of ownership for the system. Some believe JAD also saves a lot of time that would be spent in a lengthy analysis.

However, some research on JAD has also found that it may not live up to its promise. In a genuine problem-solving dialogue, both business professionals and the system builders freely express their opinions, understandings, and concerns about the situation. One exploratory study found that JAD workshop activities were focused on system developers' models and terminology and that the business area personnel were expected to participate on those terms with little or no training.[9]

There are clearly many ways to build systems. The four life cycle models are just that, models that express a particular approach. System builders applying any of these approaches should be aware of their advantages and disadvantages, and they should develop a project plan that truly fits the situation.

Chapter Conclusion

SUMMARY

▶ *What are the four phases of information system projects?*

Any information system, regardless of how it is acquired, goes through four phases. Initiation is the process of defining the need for a system, identifying potential users and stakeholders, and summarizing the way the system will meet the need. Development involves transforming general requirements into hardware and software that accomplish the required functions as well as documentation for programmers and users. Implementation involves making a system operational in the organization. Operation and maintenance is the ongoing use of the system after it has been installed, along with the work done to enhance it and correct bugs.

▶ *What types of issues are addressed by the different system development processes?*

The traditional system life cycle tries to solve a control problem by using a prescribed sequence of steps and deliverables. A prototype information system is a working model built to address a knowledge problem of not knowing how a system should solve an important problem. Firms acquire application packages to solve a resource and timing problem by using commercially available software that performs most of the functions desired. Firms use end-user development to solve a responsiveness problem involving the inability of IS departments to keep up with changing information needs of individuals.

▶ *How does the traditional system life cycle solve the control problem of keeping a project on track?*

The traditional system life cycle establishes a series of phases and steps with specific deliverables. For the initiation phase these include the functional specification and project plan. For development, they include external and internal specifications, hardware plan, programs, testing plan, completion of system testing, and user and technical documentation. For implementation, they include the implementation plan, training materials, formal system acceptance, and post-implementation audit report. For operation and maintenance, they include the operations manual, maintenance plan, and completion of specific enhancements.

▶ *What are the advantages and disadvantages of prototypes?*

The advantages of prototyping come from creating a more accurate idea of what the users need based on a tangible working model instead of abstract specifications that may be difficult to visualize. The number of changes following development may be reduced. However, developing a prototype may require exceptional developers and excessive involvement by users already busy with their regular work. Users may not appreciate the incompleteness and technical fragility resulting from technical shortcuts during prototyping.

▶ *What are the advantages and disadvantages of application packages?*

Application packages reduce system development work, thereby reducing delays and helping a firm focus its resources on products or services it provides. They are often documented and maintained better than software built in-house and may provide better solutions. However, they often fit a firm's work practices only partially, and the firm lacks long-term control of the system's direction.

▶ *What are the advantages and disadvantages of end-user development?*

End-user development reduces the need for programmers, avoids the communication overhead of explaining requirements to a technical staff, and eliminates some delays and political negotiations. However, it applies only to a limited set of situations and works best where problems can be isolated from each other so that users can take full responsibility for both data and programs. The resulting systems are often less well designed and more prone to bugs than systems built by IS professionals.

▶ *What are the major issues in supporting end users?*

Hardware and software issues start with supplying and managing personal computers, LANs, and software upgrades and distribution. Many end-user applications become multiuser systems, immediately generating questions about standards, controls, and training. Data availability is crucial when end-user applications need data that reside on other computers. End-user computing entails many security risks because the end users have individual control over sensitive data. Many end users also need help in analyzing, designing, and troubleshooting systems.

▶ *How is it possible to combine system development approaches into a system's life cycle?*

A prototype can be used as part of a traditional system life cycle. A small application package can be used as a prototype to shortcut the analysis process. A structured approach can be used when purchasing an application package. An end-user development component can be added to the traditional life cycle.

INTERNATIONAL VIGNETTE

United Kingdom: Integrating Global Commercial Operations at BP Chemicals

In 1985, BP Chemicals, a $4 billion division of British Petroleum, embarked on an ambitious project to integrate all aspects of its commercial operations. Its corporate strategy was to emphasize service to avoid competing on price alone, yet its ordering and distribution systems could not support excellent service because they were fragmented by country and operating unit. A customer desiring several products from BP Chemical might have to place separate orders with different sales offices. Information about customer creditworthiness, inventory availability, potential delivery dates, and sales history information were often incomplete or unreliable. That 50 percent of all orders had to be filled from another country compounded the problem.

The Commercial System Project (CSP) was to develop a new, fully networked system linking all BP Chemical locations. With the help of Scicon, BP's wholly owned software subsidiary, separate project teams were established for stock, distribution, sales, and database design. Based on the initial results in early 1986, the company's Executive Committee formally gave its full support to the project and said it was probably the most important business systems project in the next two years. At this point, Scicon replaced its existing team with a new team that lacked the skills necessary to do the project. Generating schedules became an exercise in frustration because unanticipated tasks kept cropping up, and no change request was ignored. As the project continued, the need to interface with existing systems became a difficult issue because most sites did not fully understand the function and scope of their existing systems, no less the new system that was being built. With installation of a partial system in sight, a training program was begun, including a video, but most users forgot what they had learned by the time the first version of the system was installed at some sites in 1987. Despite running several years late and going over budget, the Commercial System eventually became operational in Europe even though many issues were never resolved about standardizing business processes across countries. Several competitors offered to buy the system, but the company declined the offers. In 1991, a new project to redesign order-processing procedures began.

> Source: Jelassi, Tawfik, and Soumitra Dutta. "Integrating Global Commercial Operations with Information Technology at BP Chemicals." *Journal of Strategic Information Systems*, Vol. 2, No. 1, Mar. 1993, pp. 77–95.

- Use the WCA framework to organize your understanding of this vignette and to identify important topics that are not mentioned.

- What issues (if any) make this case interesting from an international or intercultural viewpoint?

- Use ideas about alternative system life cycle approaches to explain why this project took so long.

REAL-WORLD CASES

Revlon: Shut Down by a Billing Dispute with a Vendor

In February 1989, the cosmetics manufacturer Revlon purchased a customized information system for real-time processing of customer orders and matching inventory to orders. The vendor was Logisticon, a software firm with 16 years of experience building such systems. The $1.2 million system was to be delivered in two phases, starting in January 1990. Bugs and delays led to a dispute between Revlon and Logisticon. Revlon claimed that bugs prevented them from generating accurate inventory receipts. Logisticon said that software-related bugs had been fixed and that the remaining problems involved Revlon's computer hardware.

On October 9, 1990, Revlon sent a letter to Logisticon stating that it was withholding a $180,000 payment for the first phase and canceling the second phase. Logisticon responded on October 16 by "repossessing" the software by disabling it using a telephone dial-in system. Workers at two Revlon distribution centers stayed home for three days because the distribution centers needed this software to operate. After three days, Logisticon reactivated the software pending further discussions. Revlon sued Logisticon for extortion, stating that disabling the software prevented shipping orders worth $20 million. Three months later, the lawsuit was settled out of court. Revlon and Logisticon refused to comment on the settlement.

Sources: Davis, Fred. "Could the Repo Man Grab Your Invaluable Software? *PC Week*, Nov. 12, 1990, p. 266.
"Revlon Settles Contract Suit Against Logisticon, Inc." *Wall Street Journal*, Jan. 8, 1991.

* Use the WCA framework to organize your understanding of this case and to identify important topics that are not mentioned.

* Explain how this case is related to the choice among different system life cycle approaches.

California Department of Motor Vehicles: A System Development Project That Failed

In 1987, the California Department of Motor Vehicles (DMV) hired Tandem Computers and the consulting company Ernst & Young to replace its aging mainframes and merge its massive drivers license and vehicle registration databases. Seven years and $44 million later, the DMV threw in the towel, leaving it tracking 50 million vehicle registrations and driver's licenses and $5.2 billion of fees per year using vehicle and driver's license software first written for RCA computers in 1965. These applications now ran on IBM ES/9000 mainframes and had a 220 GB database. According to the Automobile Club of Southern California, which had 5,000 terminals tied to these mainframes, retrieval of data worked acceptably for them although insufficient communication ports were a problem. The DMV had to start with reengineering business processes throughout the department to conform with new legislative mandates such as a motor/voter program. Technical challenges included moving the 220 GB database to a relational database so that flexible reporting would be possible, rewriting ancient, poorly written programs, replacing around 300 communication computers, and replacing 40,000 dumb terminals whose maintenance contracts would expire in several years.

The California legislature approved a $500,000 expenditure to find out what had happened. Tandem claimed that its $20 million of computer gear and relational database software were operating, but that no applications had been loaded. Ernst & Young had withdrawn from the project in 1990 citing differences with the DMV about project direction. DMV staffers had tried to develop applications themselves using the Texas Instruments CASE tool called IEF but were surprised at how difficult the learning curve was. The programs written so far couldn't perform some basic functions and operated ten times slower than the old system.

Sources: Bozman, Jean S. "DMV Disaster: California Kills Failed $44M Project." *Computerworld*, May 9, 1994, p. 1.
King, Ralph T., Jr. "California DMV's Computer Overhaul Ends Up as Costly Ride to Junk Heap." *Wall Street Journal*, Apr. 27, 1994, p. B5.

* Use the WCA framework to organize your understanding of this case and to identify important topics that are not mentioned.

* Use the traditional system life cycle to explain some of the things that went wrong in this case.

▮ *KEY TERMS*

runaway	project plan	implementation planning	throwaway prototype
initiation	detailed requirements analysis	training	evolutionary prototype
development	external specification	conversion	benchmarking
implementation	internal system design	phased approach	request for proposal (RFP)
operation and maintenance	internal specification	running in parallel	release
traditional system life cycle	hardware acquisition and installation	pilot implementation	end-user computing (EUC)
prototype	programming	acceptance testing	site license
application package	unit testing	post-implementation audit	downloading
end-user development	documentation	ongoing operation and support	help line
feasibility study	system testing	operations manual	phased approach
functional specification	testing plan	maintenance	joint application development (JAD)

REVIEW QUESTIONS

1. Identify the four phases any system goes through and some of the common issues and problems that occur in each phase.

2. Why is it sometimes appropriate for a system project never to go past the initiation phase?

3. What are the links between the four phases and some of the reasons for rework of a previous phase?

4. Describe the four alternative approaches for building systems and the main issues addressed by each.

5. What different types of feasibility are considered in a feasibility study?

6. Identify the main deliverables from the development phase, and explain why other phases are necessary after development.

7. When in the traditional life cycle is user involvement greatest? Least?

8. What are the different approaches for converting from a previous system to a new system?

9. Explain reasons for using pilot implementations, acceptance testing, and post-implementation audits.

10. How is using a prototype different from using a traditional system life cycle?

11. What are the two types of prototypes?

12. Why is it still necessary for a firm to do a lot of systems analysis work when it purchases an application system?

13. What types of characteristics are considered when selecting among several application packages?

14. Explain what a firm may expect to receive from an application package vendor with an established product during each of the four phases.

15. What are the advantages and disadvantages of using application packages?

16. Under what circumstances is end-user development appropriate?

17. Why do firms arrange site licenses with software vendors?

18. How is it possible to combine features of different life cycle models into the approach for building any particular system?

DISCUSSION QUESTIONS

1. A code of ethics developed by three Swedish trade unions that organize computing personnel stated that computer professionals only take part in projects with the time and resources to do a good job, only develop systems in close collaboration with the user, and refrain from tasks aiming at control in ways that can be of harm to individuals.[10] Explain why you do or do not believe any computer professional would conform to these rules at all times.

2. Assume that your entire class had two months to write a single combined term paper. Within a broad guideline that the paper must be about some topic related to information systems, the class must decide on the topic and produce the paper. The class has asked you to decide how to do the project, what the steps will be, and who will do what work. What process would you propose? What problems or difficulties are likely to occur in this project as you have outlined it? Compare your approach to the traditional system life cycle, explaining major similarities and differences.

3. In the 1970s, IBM developed a system to automate portions of newspaper production. Although a lengthy analysis produced a 2,400-page requirements document, the developers and customers interpreted it differently when they attempted to use it to

settle questions about what had been promised.[11] How is the difficulty in using the requirements document related to the ideas in the chapter?

4. The information systems manager at Balboa Hardware decided to take a stand. "We have had too many system failures. As of today, don't even think about a new system unless you use a traditional system life cycle." Use the ideas in the chapter to explain the implications of this statement.

5. Should the development process for the different types of systems identified in Chapter 5 be different? If so, explain what the differences should be. If not, explain why there should be no differences.

6. Explain any relationships between the critical success factors method described in Chapter 13 and the various life cycles described in this chapter. If the relationships are unimportant, explain why.

HANDS-ON EXERCISES

1. This exercise is about the use of ranking and weighting to compare alternative software packages. It assumes a spreadsheet model for comparing a particular set of alternatives has been provided.

   a. Use the spreadsheet provided to show how the preferred result could be changed just by changing some of the weightings.

   b. Use the spreadsheet to show how the preferred result could be changed through relatively small changes in both weightings and ratings.

APPLICATION SCENARIOS

Whisler Industries: How Can We Salvage This Project?

As manager of system development since early 1994, Paul Olafson had inherited a project from his predecessor and had not succeeded in turning it around. Whisler had a broad product line of different building materials, including certain types of semicustom tiles, moldings, and flooring. It sold both to distributors and retail stores. The project was an attempt to develop an integrated system that salespeople could use for entering orders, negotiating discounts for multiple products ordered simultaneously, and making delivery commitments. This project was seen as an important way to provide better service to customers and increase sales. The project had encountered many problems:

A key departure. In 1993, during negotiations about system functionality, the lead analyst accepted a job from a competitor at a 25 percent salary increase.

Accommodation to the departure. The new lead analyst came to an informal agreement about the scope of the project and told his staff to start working on the data structure and program design.

Change in scope. Late in 1994, Whisler acquired one of its competitors and began to sell through distributors for the first time. Olafson informed the heads of information systems and sales that this would make it necessary to go back to the drawing board because the data structures and basic logic of the system would have to be changed. They responded that delays in this crucial system were unacceptable.

Divide and conquer. Fearing demotion if he made a big fuss, Olafson decided to break the project into two parts. The first part would be the completion of a system that satisfied only the needs of sales to retailers; the second part would expand that system to include additional functions needed for sales to distributors.

Another departure. At this point, one of the two lead programmers quit. Already working 50 hours a week, he thought it was impractical to try to retrofit one relatively untried system to two sets of requirements.

Dissension in the ranks. This departure led to a near revolt of the programming staff. The programmers insisted on an absolute freeze on the specifications to avoid continual rework to accommodate shifting goals.

Refusal to freeze the spec. The IS director decided it was unacceptable to produce something that was not what the internal customer wanted, especially in a firm priding itself on customer service.

At this latest development, Olafson concluded that the current project would surely crash and burn. He decided it was time for a heart-to-heart talk with his wife and two high-school-age children. He felt he was in an impossible situation. He could probably keep his job because he now had the best understanding of how the company's systems supported the sales and order commitment process. But his job was no joy, and he was ready to go somewhere else, even at substantially lower pay, before he went crazy in this situation.

1. Compare the analysis and development process thus far with the traditional system life cycle.

2. What might have been done earlier to prevent the project from getting to where it is now?

3. What should Olafson and the IS director do?

DEBATE TOPIC   *Use ideas from the chapter to argue the pros and cons and practical implications of the following proposition: The refusal to freeze the spec is a betrayal of the people working in the IS department.*

Hope Software: Responding to an RFP

Jack Rostin, Vice-President of Development for Hope Software, looked at a 59-page RFP and shook his head. Hope Software was one of the leaders in packaged software for managing factories. Judy Mikulski, Sales VP, had just brought him the RFP. Hope had two weeks to respond.

"Let me get this straight," Rostin said, "The government has worked with a consulting firm for several months analyzing this defense factory. Because the factory makes military gear and we don't have security clearances, all we know about the situation is that they assemble and test something very complicated and very expensive. We have this 59-page RFP that includes over 200 questions about our system, which they have never seen or used. The questions ask us to rate on a scale from 1 to 5 whether we have specific features they need, such as planning calculations that can cover a 6-month time horizon and a component numbering scheme that permits 15-digit part numbers. They need our response fast because they need to have a system running in ten months. The instructions say they can sue us if we misrepresent the system."

"Meanwhile," he continued, "we have a major new release of our product coming out in three months. Our customers have complained for two years about our data collection system, and the new version is just about ready. We need two months to test it and are working overtime to get new features into the release. Who is going to analyze all these questions? Who is going to swear that our answers even make sense when we haven't seen their plant? I can truthfully say that our variable time horizons can support ten years of plans if they want. What I can't say is whether our software will really solve their problem."

Mikulski had heard this story with the last RFP. Rostin had convinced system experts to spend four days working on it. Hope had received a huge contract, and it seemed likely that the customer would be pleased even though the users had not understood exactly what they were requesting. Mikulski wanted to convince Rostin to try for a repeat performance. She was sure Hope had the best commercially available software for the defense factory's requirements and thought Hope could back out without a lawsuit if the software didn't fit. She knew Rostin was a cautious person and would not lie in the numerical responses.

1. Analyze this situation using ideas about the traditional system life cycle and any of the three alternative life cycles that are pertinent.

2. Mikulski wants Rostin to produce answers to 200 complex questions within 2 weeks. Are there any ethical, legal, or practical problems with what she wants?

3. What should Rostin and Mikulski do? Why should they or should they not bid on this contract?

DEBATE TOPIC *Use ideas from the chapter to argue the pros and cons and practical implications of the following proposition: The consulting firm was unethical in taking the contract to write the RFP. Any competent consulting company would know that the answers to a questionnaire would not indicate whether the software really fits.*

Cumulative Case: Custom T-Shirts, Inc.

L ee Turner, Director of Information Systems, was trying to decide what to do next. Lee had started the job by suspending a scheduled 5-month system development project that was far from finished 14 months after it began. Lee's first ten months on the job were devoted to stabilizing existing systems. This involved correcting existing data that was often wrong, establishing consistent procedures for running the systems, controlling system inputs, taking backups, and finally, making sure all store personnel understood the procedures and followed them. The company's basic information systems for accounting and purchasing were based on a commercial application package designed for running individual stores. This package omitted many of the requirements of a single company with 50 stores. Now it was time to revamp the existing systems and build new ones.

Lee did not want to produce a lot of software and hoped a commercially available package would provide the capabilities needed for all the standard business functions, such as payables, receivables, purchasing, inventory control, payroll, and financial planning. This would leave more of the programmers to work on services the company used to differentiate itself, such as better artwork, better customization, and faster response to customer requests through electronic links for taking customer orders and sending and receiving customer artwork.

Unfortunately, no commercially available package seemed to handle the company's various specialized needs. Ordering was to involve a combination of central procurement and swapping between stores. It was to use special formulas developed by tracking sales at each store by day for the last three years. The company wanted to pay store managers based on a combination of store profitability, company profitability, and special corporate goals such as high utilization of the artists and large-order production facility at headquarters. Artists were to be paid on a sliding scale related to the use and reuse of their work. Commercial packages did not handle these and other special requirements adequately.

Lee was also concerned about several key programmers who were unhappy with the standardization efforts of the last ten months. They saw programming as a creative activity and wanted to write programs their own way. Lee saw programming as a relatively mechanical step within a much larger process of developing and implementing systems. For Lee, the creativity was in identifying the capabilities the company needed and then building a system that was both maintainable and bulletproof.

1. What system life cycle was used for the existing accounting and purchasing systems? What appear to be the advantages and disadvantages of that life cycle in this situation?

2. What approach do you think Lee should use in revamping these basic information systems? Think about the advantages and disadvantages of the various system life cycles and how Lee can best use the experience to date with the existing systems.

3. What should Lee do about the programmers who resisted the standardization effort?

REFERENCES

1. LaPlante, Alice. "Pacific Bell Becomes More Responsive to Its Customers' Needs." *InfoWorld*, Sept. 7, 1992, p. 58.

2. Cafasso, Rosemary. "From Old to New with Just a 'Click.' " *Computerworld*, May 3, 1993, p. 115.

3. Cringely, Robert X. "When Disaster Strikes IS." *Forbes ASAP*, Aug. 29, 1994, pp. 58–64.

4. Yourdon, Edward. *Managing the System Life Cycle*. Englewood Cliffs, N.J.: Yourdon Press, 1988.

5. Greenstein, Irwin. "Imaging System Snafu Snarls Calif. Banks." *MIS Week*, June 19, 1989, pp. 1+.

6. Fournier, Roger. *Practical Guide to Structured System Development and Maintenance.* Englewood Cliffs, N.J.: Yourdon Press, 1991.

7. McLean, Ephraim R., Leon A. Kappelman, and John P. Thompson. "Converging End-User and Corporate Computing." *Communications of the ACM*, Dec. 1993, pp. 79–92.

8. Flaaten, Per O., et al. *Foundations of Business Systems*, Chicago: The Dryden Press, 1989.

9. Davidson, Elizabeth J. "An Exploratory Study of Joint Application Design (JAD) in Information Systems Delivery." In Degross, Janice I., Robert P. Bostrom, and Daniel Robey, *Proceedings of the Fourteenth International Conference on Information Systems*, Orlando, Fla., 1993, pp. 271–283.

10. Dahlbom, Bo, and Lars Mathiassen. "A Scandinavian View on the ACM's Code of Ethics." *Computers and Society,* Vol. 24, No. 2, June 1994, pp. 14–15.

11. Fox, J. *Managing Software*, Englewood Cliffs, N.J.: Prentice-Hall, 1980.

15

Information System Security and Control

Study Questions

▶ What are the main types of risks of accidents related to information systems?

▶ What are the different types of computer crime?

▶ What issues magnify the vulnerability of information systems to accidents and crime?

▶ What measures can be taken to minimize accidents and computer crime?

▶ What are the different ways to control access to data, computers, and networks?

The systems for controlling landings and takeoffs at airports are among the most critical computerized systems in today's society. Their purposes include minimizing delays, maximizing airport efficiency, and ensuring the safety of passengers and crews. Any system failure literally endangers hundreds of lives. The Federal Aviation Administration (FAA) information system currently used at large airports has been recognized as obsolete and sometimes dangerous for over a decade. It uses obsolete computers and obsolete workstations. It displays only part of the potentially available information that air traffic controllers might be able to use in normal situations and emergencies. Although computer failure is totally unacceptable in this type of system, computer failures have occurred at control centers, leaving air traffic controllers with little to work on but guesses and projections from last-known locations.

The air traffic problems over Dallas on the morning of the 1989 Texas–Oklahoma football game demonstrate the problem. Hundreds of small planes were flying into Dallas's old airport, Love Field, because it is near the Cotton Bowl. Many of these planes were arriving at the same time as the morning rush of flights into and out of the new Dallas–Fort Worth airport (DFW), one of the nation's busiest. The 1960-vintage Univac 8300 computer had been overloaded and stopped operating for ten minutes the day of the previous year's Texas–Oklahoma game. Determined not to let this happen again, the FAA had programmed a software "patch" to bypass some nonessential functions and reduce the workload on the overloaded processor. Unfortunately, the computer center specialist who activated the patch on the morning of the 1989 game entered the instructions from a terminal not authorized to give such commands. The computer overloaded again, sounded an alarm, and went down.

When the computer came back a few seconds later, it showed partially scrambled information. Some was obviously wrong, and some might be right, but the controllers could not know for sure. DFW halted all departures, and incoming planes were diverted if possible. For 20 minutes, air traffic controllers used paper and pencil to keep track of planes in the air. Once air traffic was generally under control again, technicians shut off the computer completely and rebooted the system. Two minutes later, the system was operating normally, but it took hours to untangle the hundreds of delayed and diverted flights. Four months later, the FAA upgraded the computer equipment.[1]

In 1982, the FAA had proposed starting a project to overhaul the entire air traffic control system, with the new system scheduled for initial installation in Seattle in 1992. In 1984, IBM and Hughes were chosen as finalists for the contract. After three years and $500 million of FAA expenditures on prototypes, the FAA selected IBM's $3.6 billion fixed-cost contract in 1988. The Government Accounting Office (GAO) warned that this was unrealistically low. In 1990, air traffic controllers visited a demonstration center built by IBM and proposed hundreds of changes, causing rework and an announced 19-month delay. Attempting to catch up, IBM's middle managers skipped IBM's formal software-review process, resulting in serious bugs. In 1993, the FAA finally froze system specifications, and IBM transferred its four project managers, putting the head of its Federal Systems Division in charge of the project. Estimated completion was nine years away, and the project was already $1.5 billion over budget.[2] Later in 1993, IBM sold its Federal Systems Division to Loral. An independent review of the project in 1994 estimated that 6,000 workdays would be required to fix the 3,000 known bugs in the IBM software, leaving the FAA with a difficult decision about how to proceed.[3]

DEBATE TOPIC   *Argue the pros and cons and practical implications of the following proposition:*
The FAA should place severe limits on air traffic until a safe, reliable air traffic control system can be built.

EVEN THOUGH THIS BOOK'S FIRST **14** CHAPTERS mentioned some of the problems that have occurred with computerized systems, those chapters emphasized the great progress that has been made not only in technology, but also in attaining personal and organizational benefits through information systems. To round out the picture, this chapter focuses on problems that may occur with these systems and on approaches for minimizing these problems.

The air traffic control system exemplifies the risks of relying on these systems and of building them in the first place. This example shows that even systems that lives

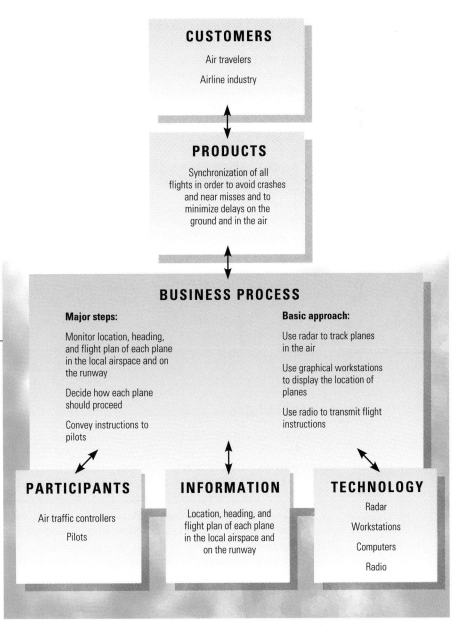

Figure 15.1 Federal Aviation Administration: Controlling Flights into and out of Airports

depend on may not work properly because of a combination of hardware, software, and human limitations. Furthermore, it may take years to upgrade complex systems because of a combination of their technical complexity and the difficulty of defining the requirements and adapting to changing needs.

This chapter's many examples illustrate the reality of the threats and the need for system security and careful management. No system is foolproof, but careful use of established methods reduces the risks substantially and increases the likelihood of enjoying the benefits.

Threat of Project Failure

The first threats to any computerized system occur while the system is being built. Table 15.1 lists common reasons for failures at each of the four major phases. Although the previous chapter covered some of the problems that occur during information system projects, this brief section serves as a reminder that development failures and implementation failures are serious threats. In development failures, the system never runs successfully on the computer. In implementation failures, the system runs on the computer but fails to attain the hoped-for benefits when used by the organization.

Table 15.1 Common Reasons for Project Failure at Different Project Phases

Phase	Common Reasons for Project Failure
Initiation	• The reasons for building the system have too little support. • The system seems too expensive.
Development	• It is too difficult to define the requirements. • The system is not technically feasible. • The project is too difficult for technical staff assigned to it.
Implementation	• The system requires too great a change from existing work practices. • Potential users dislike the system or resist using it. • The implementation receives too little effort.
Operation and maintenance	• System controls are insufficient. • Too little effort goes into supporting effective use. • The system is not updated as business needs change.

Development Failures

The air traffic control project mentioned in the introductory case was late and over budget, but the project was continuing. A complex project abandoned during the development phase was the Confirm reservation system, a strategic system being built as a partnership between AMR (parent of American Airlines), Hilton and Marriott hotel firms, and Budget Rent-A-Car. In 1992, the project dissolved into accusations and lawsuits, with AMR writing off $109 million. AMR claimed that the three partners deviated from an agreed-on plan to build a common reservation system and pressed AMR to build three separate systems within Confirm. AMR said that its partners "bombarded it with an unending flurry of change requests," failed to provide necessary information, and made poor staffing assignments. But the project had also encountered technical design problems making it impossible to integrate its transaction processing component with its decision support component. Some AMR IS managers had delayed notifying upper management as these problems emerged.[4, 5]

The air traffic control project, the Confirm project, and several project failures mentioned previously (Blue Cross and Blue Shield of Massachusetts in Chapter 2 and the London Stock Exchange in Chapter 7) had a number of things in common. These projects had none of the characteristics of the idealized low-risk project described in Chapter 13. They were complex both technically and organizationally. They required inputs from many stakeholders in business situations with new information and new priorities emerging continually. Projects of this type often encounter a combination of unreasonable expectations, insufficient resources, technological risk, and inadequate project methodology and staff.

Implementation Failures

Many information system projects that survive the development phase limp through an ineffective implementation and never generate the planned benefits. For example, in the late 1980s the Postal Inspection Service found that only one-third of project savings were realized from installing newer sorting machines. At 20 of 22 sites reviewed, mail that should have been processed by the new machines was diverted to less efficient machines or manual processing. In most cases, this was done to keep clerks and mail handlers busy. The General Accounting Office (GAO) blamed archaic work rules for unnecessarily high expenses, but the president of a postal workers' union felt that workers were being blamed unfairly.[6]

Regardless of who is to blame, this example hints at common causes of disappointing implementations: inconsistent priorities, incomplete communication between the developers and the users, and inadequate follow-up to make sure the system is used effectively. Many types of systems have encountered related problems. For example, LANs are often sold based on the claim that they help people work together. But many LANs generate only modest benefits because they have little impact on the way people work together even though they may be useful for sending electronic mail and sharing printers.

Implementation problems such as these are sometimes cited as an important reason for what is sometimes called the "productivity paradox," in which companies with substantial investments in information technology often have no better competitive success than similar companies without those investments.

The remainder of this chapter will focus on system problems and failures that occur or become evident in the operation and maintenance phase.

Threat of Accidents and Malfunctions

Many people assume that information systems will work as they are designed to work. They assume that the system will operate reliably and that the information generated will be correct. When these assumptions are proved wrong, the consequences can be disastrous. This section looks at seven types of risks related to accidents: operator error, hardware malfunctions, software bugs, data errors, damage to physical facilities, inadequate system performance, and liability for system failure.

To help you see the range of risks from accidents, Figure 15.2 assigns each type of risk to one element of the WCA framework. Do not assume that each type of accident is totally caused by the element it is associated with, however. For example, saying that a particular accident involved operator error might seem to imply participants are at fault. But the technology might have been difficult to use and the business process might have been designed based on unrealistic assumptions about human capabilities. Interactions between causes of accidents is a key point as we look at each type of accident in turn.

Figure 15.2 Seven Types of Risks Related to Accidents

Seven types of risks related to accidents can be associated with individual elements of the framework although the cause of the problem is often a combination of factors.

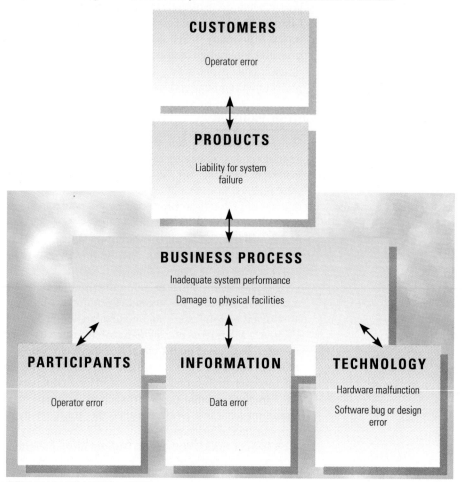

Operator Error

A prime cause of accidents is **operator error,** a combination of inattention, nonconformance to procedures, or other error by participants in a system. A dramatic example occurred in 1979, when a test tape was accidentally mounted on the wrong tape drive in a missile defense facility. The test tape contained simulated attack data used to test the missile warning system. The incorrect tape drive fed the simulated data into a defense computer connected to the operational missile alert system. The software in the computer had no way to distinguish a real attack from the simulation designed to test the system's response. During the ensuing six-minute alert, ten tactical aircraft were launched from bases in the northern United States and Canada. Luckily, the commanders chose to ignore indications of a full-scale attack.[7]

A careful study of accidents in complex systems such as nuclear plants, dams, tankers, and airplanes found that 60 to 80 percent of major accidents were attributed to operator error but that many factors other than operator carelessness contributed to the problems. These factors included flawed system design, poor training, and poor quality control.[8] One of that study's main examples was the partial meltdown at the

Three Mile Island nuclear plant in Pennsylvania. A commission blamed the problem on operator error, but the operators were confronted with enormously complex technical systems, incomplete or contradictory information, and the necessity to make decisions quickly. The nature of the system created a high likelihood of operator error.

Several factors magnify the risk of operator error. It is often difficult to anticipate how systems will really work in practice and how users will adapt to them. User adaptations and shortcuts may cause errors the designers never imagined. In addition, people tend to become complacent when a system seems to operate correctly. They begin to assume it will continue to operate correctly and put less energy and care into checking for errors. Who would anticipate that a tape would be mounted on the wrong tape drive in a defense facility? Obviously, "the system" should have prevented this from happening. The main point is that all systems are vulnerable to errors by people.

REALITY CHECK **Operator Error** This section mentioned that 60 to 80 percent of major accidents in one study were attributed to operator error but that many factors other than carelessness contribute to operator error.

1. Identify times you or your acquaintances have been guilty of operator error in everyday life, for example, by accidentally erasing an audiotape or by backing up when intending to go forward.

2. What factors caused the operator error in these cases? Was it ever caused by poor equipment design that somehow encouraged the operator error?

Hardware Malfunctions

Although significant hardware malfunctions are becoming more and more infrequent as computer technology improves, these problems do occur occasionally. A highly embarassing hardware flaw was publicized in late 1994 when Intel acknowledged that the division function of its Pentium microprocessor occasionally calculated incorrect answers on divisions involving more than five significant digits. Consider the following calculation:

$$(4,195,835 \div 3,145,727) \times 3,145,727$$

Basic algebra says that A - (A ÷ B) × B should be zero, but the flawed Pentiums gave the answer 256. Intel had known about this problem for months before it became public, but had downplayed it since most users don't do division calculations with five significant digits. Intel eventually took a $475 million write-off to account for replacing defective chips. The previous 386 and 486 chips also had math errors that were corrected.[9]

More frequent and noticeable sources of hardware malfunctions are electrical power and telecommunication networks that cause computers to go down because of fires, accidentally cut cables, and other problems. For example, the entire NASDAQ stock exchange went down for 34 minutes on August 1, 1994, because a squirrel shorted out a power line despite the local electric utility's previous attempts "to improve the squirrel-proofing of power lines in the heavily wooded area" near the computer center.[10]

Vulnerability to hardware malfunctions is magnified by user disbelief that hardware can malfunction. As occurred several times in airplane and nuclear plant accidents, it may be unclear whether the malfunction is in the hardware or in the warning system. Furthermore, as software functions are integrated into hardware, what is seen as hardware can have bugs just like software.

Interference between electronic devices has also become an important cause of hardware malfunctions. Between 1986 and 1993, the Federal Aviation Administration received 24 complaints that passengers' electronic devices such as notebook computers, CD players, and electronic games interfered with a plane's electronic control systems. Most airlines have now banned use of these devices below 10,000 feet.

Software Bugs

A **software bug** is a flaw in a program that causes it to produce incorrect or inappropriate results. Software bugs have caused significant financial losses even in large, well-run businesses. Chapter 10 explained a transaction processing bug that cost the Bank of New York $5 million and a spreadsheet bug that cost a construction company $254,000. The first bug existed unnoticed for a long time and had its effect only when the transaction load peaked. The other resulted from inattention by an inexperienced spreadsheet user.

Software bugs are a fundamental problem with computerized systems because there are no infallible methods for proving that a program operates correctly. The best-tested software may still have bugs after testing is complete. Even if it were possible to prove that a program operates correctly relative to its design specs, there is no guarantee that it will operate correctly under unanticipated circumstances. Some of the factors overlooked by computerized systems seem bizarre in retrospect. On October 5, 1960, a missile warning system indicated that the United States was under a massive attack by Soviet missiles with certainty of 99.9 percent. The early warning radar at Thule, Greenland, had spotted the rising moon, but nobody had thought about the moon when specifying how the system should perform.

The IS staffs of large companies with aging legacy systems look forward to the year 2000 with trepidation because the transition from 1999 to 2000 may reveal previously undetected bugs in undocumented, decades-old programs. Consider what might happen when a program written in 1973 calculates an employee's age by subtracting the last two digits of the employee's year of birth from the current year. If the year is 1975 and the year of birth is 1951, the program calculates 75 - 51 = 24 and uses an employee age of 24 years in programs related to the company's insurance and pension plans and government reporting. But if the year is 2000 and the employee was born in 1976, the program would calculate the employee's age as -76 by subtracting 76 from 00. No one knows what kinds of chaos might ensue from a spate of errors of this type.

Data Errors

Data errors are another source of risk since information systems are no better than the data they contain. Information systems in everyday life frequently contain errors such as incorrect phone numbers or addresses. It is possible to check for some errors automatically, such as determining whether a number is within a specified range or whether a zip code is valid. Unfortunately, validity checks such as these cannot detect many common errors. For example, a system that checks whether an employee's age is between 18 and 70 usually cannot determine that 12/10/54 was accidentally entered instead of 10/12/45. Many errors due to carelessness and inattention therefore cannot be detected automatically.

Seemingly small data errors sometimes have major impacts. On March 25, 1993, a clerical error caused a 12-point drop in the New York Stock Exchange's Dow Jones index in the last few minutes of trading. An institutional investor had sent Salomon Brothers a computerized order to sell $11 million of stock spread over 400 companies. A Salomon Brothers clerk entered this order incorrectly, typing 11,000,000 in the "shares" box rather than the "dollars" box on a data entry screen. The system automatically allocated the 11 million shares among the companies and generated individual sell orders. The sell orders for under 99,999 shares of individual stocks on the New York Exchange were handled automatically by SuperDot, the Exchange's small-order system. Larger orders and orders for stocks on the NASDAQ exchange went to traders who looked at the size of the orders, concluded they were mistakes, and canceled them. The estimated cost of the error for Salomon Brothers was at least $1 million to repurchase shares sold erroneously and make up for lower prices received.[11]

Some data errors are related to incentives that motivate people to enter incorrect data. One manufacturer developed a system that consolidated all records by customer number. Late in the project it discovered that salespeople created a new customer number for each sale, even to existing customers, because they received larger commissions for opening new accounts. The company scrapped the project after discovering the database contained more than 7,000 customer numbers for McDonnell Douglas, a single large customer.[12]

Damage to Physical Facilities

Physical facilities and equipment may be vulnerable to a wide range of environmental threats and external events. In the last few years, computer facilities have been damaged by fires, floods, hurricanes, and earthquakes. Computer and telecommunications equipment may be disabled by power failures and network breakdowns occurring far from the site.

Damage to physical facilities doesn't require a natural catastrophe. In 1991, a telephone maintenance crew accidentally cut a fiber-optic cable that provided 40 percent of New York City's long-distance service. Because an AT&T operations center had not been notified that the work was being done, computers had not been programmed to give priority to data transmissions for air traffic control. Consequently, New York's three main airports lost their long-range radar for 102 minutes. Several days later, a U.S. Sprint cable broke, disrupting calls to and from Chicago.[13] In both cases, businesses were affected by an event miles from their facilities. Firms relying on information systems need to protect their own facilities and need to prepare for the effects of problems elsewhere.

Inadequate System Performance

Inadequate system performance occurs when a system cannot handle the task that is required of it. A highly visible example occurred during the stock market crash of October 19, 1987. The New York Stock Exchange's "real-time" information system of stock prices ran 2 hours late as more than 500 million shares of stock were traded, three times the average daily volume at that time.

Inadequate system performance also occurs in many mundane situations. For example, an overloaded computer may provide poor response time for interactive users or may generate the summary report on yesterday's production too late for this morning's production meeting. The need to maintain adequate performance is one reason to build information systems carefully and monitor their performance.

Liability for System Failure

Liability is legal responsibility for one's actions or products. Every type of accident mentioned thus far can result in a liability claim against a firm or individual. This is an especially serious potential problem in medical systems. Chapter 2 described how a bug in a computer program controlling an x-ray machine caused a patient's death by setting the machine to deliver 100 times the prescribed exposure to radiation. Potential liability is one of the reasons medical expert systems have largely remained research tools rather than common tools for doctors. Whoever created or sold such a system might be held liable if it produced an incorrect diagnosis.

Liability is also an issue in business systems. In 1994, Kane Carpet Co. of Secaucus, N.J., was in court trying to prove that after 22 consecutive profitable years and growth up to $90 million in sales, it had gone out of business because of flaws in an inventory system it purchased from McDonnell Douglas. Although the system seemed to work well at a flooring company in Houston, within a week of its installation in 1989, Kane experienced severe problems filling orders and quoting correct prices and credit terms.[14]

Liability related to information systems is complex because so many different things can go wrong. Given the potential for product liability lawsuits, software vendors are usually careful to avoid claiming their software is bugfree. Their license agreements usually state that any problems resulting from the use of the software are the user's fault.

The seven types of risk mentioned thus far are all related to things that go wrong accidentally. Before going on to security measures that reduce these risks, we will look at computer crime, which is anything but accidental.

REALITY CHECK   **Risks Related to Accidents**   This section gave examples of seven different types of risks related to accidents.

1. Look at the categories and identify an example of each type of problem or something similar that you have personally encountered, regardless of whether a computer was involved.

2. Explain why you do or do not believe there is anything unique about the way these problems arise in relation to computerized systems.

Threat of Computer Crime

Computer crime is the use of computerized systems to perform illegal acts. It can be divided into two main areas: theft, and sabotage and vandalism. Computer pranks are included as illegal activities because they often have at least the potential for significant harm. Further, they may be difficult to differentiate from sabotage and other forms of destructive behavior.

Computer crime is growing more worrisome as computerized systems become more pervasive. The potential for significant damage to commercial interests and national defense through computer viruses and other forms of computerized sabotage has been demonstrated clearly. Weaknesses exploited often involve technical gaps between what a computer system is capable of enforcing and what it is expected to enforce. Other weaknesses involve gaps between computer policies, social policies, and human behavior.

There is no single profile for computer criminals. They range from application programmers and clerical personnel to managers and accountants. In general, perpetrators of computer crime can be divided into employees, outsiders, and hackers. *Employees* use their knowledge of how a business operates to identify opportunities for theft or sabotage and to obtain easy access to the resources they need for their criminal activity. *Outsiders* often have a more difficult task of learning how to penetrate a system without having easy access to information about how it works. **Hackers** are less concerned about personal gains or damage they might cause. Instead, they commit computer crime for the "fun" or intellectual challenge of breaking into a computer.

Despite its seriousness, computer crime is not treated in the same way in our society as other types of crime. Perhaps this is because the perpetrators seem less physically threatening to victims than other criminals. Perhaps it is because companies victimized by computer crime are hesitant to suffer adverse publicity. Regardless of the cause, to date many convicted computer criminals have received mild treatment. In some cases, they have even taken jobs as security consultants after receiving minor punishments.

As illustrated in Figure 15.3, the vulnerable points in computerized systems include people and procedures in addition to hardware, software, and data. A detailed look at many cases that are called computer crime reveals that the computer played a relatively small role compared to the role of bypassed procedures and forged transaction documents. Most of the following examples might have been stopped through better organizational procedures and safeguards.

Figure 15.3 Threats Related to Computer Crime

Various types of threats related to computer crime can be associated with individual elements of the framework although computer crimes often involve a combination of factors.

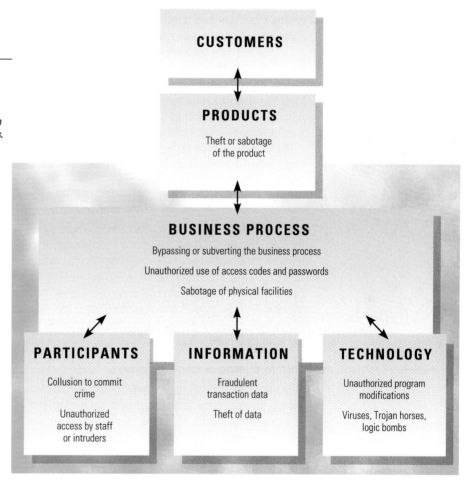

Theft

Theft via computer can be divided into four categories: unauthorized use of access codes and financial passwords, theft by entering fraudulent transaction data, theft by stealing or modifying data, and theft by modifying software.

Unauthorized use of access codes and financial passwords

Telephone credit card numbers, PBX access codes, ATM passwords, and regular credit card numbers have all become major targets of criminals. AT&T's manager of corporate security estimated that fraud costs the telephone industry, and hence its customers, $2 billion per year.[15] Many companies have been victimized by criminals stealing PBX access codes used to route telephone calls through the company's PBX to get reduced corporate rates and simplify accounting. Until the theft is detected and the access code switched off, it is used to make foreign long-distance calls from pay phones and to arrange drug deals and other illegal activities at home.

Criminals steal telephone credit card numbers and PBX access codes in many ways. "Shoulder surfers" use binoculars, video cameras, or just good eyesight and number memory to spy on people entering telephone credit card numbers while making long-distance calls at pay phones. Company insiders may also steal these codes. For example, an MCI Communications employee was arrested in 1994 for stealing 60,000 calling-card numbers and selling them to an international crime ring. MCI officials estimated the entire loss was more than $50 million.[16]

Many schemes have been used to steal PIN (personal identification) numbers for ATMs. Criminals have scanned cordless and cellular telephone signals looking for people using bank-by-phone services. It is also possible to steal data using wire taps, thereby capturing data moving from one location to another. A former consultant to a telephone company used this approach in conspiring with several others to pull PIN numbers from phone lines transmitting transactions from ATMs. They then made 5,500 fake ATM cards by encoding the data in magnetic strips on pieces of cardboard. They might have stolen millions of dollars from a cash-machine network had the police not been tipped off.[17]

Theft by entering fraudulent transaction data

Entering fraudulent transaction data is the simplest and most common method of theft in computer-related crime. Box 15.1 lists major categories of fraud using transaction data. Such frauds are perpetrated by forging documents, bypassing procedures, or impersonating someone. Often this can be done by criminals who know little about computers. In these cases, what is commonly called computer crime often relies much more on knowledge of how business systems operate than on a knowledge of computers. Many businesses have easy targets for this type of crime because their internal systems are managed carelessly.

Theft by stealing or modifying data

Stealing or modifying data is yet another form of computer crime. One way to steal data is by removing physical media such as paper documents, tapes, or diskettes. There are many stories of salespeople taking a customer list on leaving a job. The pervasive use of personal computers and diskettes makes this easy to do. Product and process specifications are another valuable type of data that can be stolen this way. Unlike other forms of theft, it is often possible to steal computerized data without changing or moving it.

New communication technologies such as cellular telephones, electronic mail, and voice mail have created new possibilities for theft. In a 1993 federal court case in Boston, Standard Duplicating Machines (SDM) accused its rival Duplo Manufacturing of "a prolonged and surreptitious campaign of business espionage" by stealing voice-mail messages to steal business. The evidence involved recorded product inquiries on SDM's voice-mail system that were answered the next day by Duplo's salespeople. The lawsuit zeroed in on an employee hired by Duplo shortly after he was fired by SDM and is based on after-hours calls into SDM's toll-free 800 number from Duplo and from his home. Apparently, SDM had not terminated telephone passwords for the terminated employee.[21]

Box 15. 1 Examples of Fraud Committed Using Transaction Processing Systems

Listed here are some of the many ways to commit fraud using transaction processing systems.[18] These types of fraud are usually perpetrated by insiders who generate fraudulent transaction data.

Forgery. The criminal produces fraudulent checks, ID cards, or even money. Desktop publishing technology such as scanners, drawing programs, and laser printers have made forgery easier than ever before. Figure 15.6 shows an example of this type of forgery. The American Bankers Association estimated that counterfeiters aided by laser printers and color copiers forged $2 billion worth of checks in 1992.[19]

Impersonation fraud. The criminal impersonates someone else, accesses that person's account electronically, and steals money or information. One criminal recognized that bank computers handle deposits based on the magnetic account number at the bottom of deposit slips and not by the depositor's signature. This thief substituted specially coded deposit slips in the place of general deposit slips available in the bank lobby for customers who forget their own personalized slips. For the next three days, all deposits made with these fraudulent deposit slips were credited to the thief's account. The thief withdrew the money and vanished before the depositors' checks started to bounce.

Disbursements fraud. The criminal gets a company to pay for products or services it never received. This is often done by learning the procedures and paperwork through which purchases are made, and the receipt of material is verified. Pinkerton Security and Investigation Services suffered this type of fraud when an accounting employee transferred money out of a company bank account into accounts set up for bogus companies at another bank. This employee needed a superior's approval before making a transfer but was once asked to cancel a former superior's approval code. Instead of canceling it, she started using it herself. Normally, the reconciliation of different accounts would have caught the discrepancies, but she was also supposed to do these reconciliations. Eventually caught in an audit, she pleaded guilty to stealing over $1 million and was sentenced to prison.[20]

Inventory fraud. The criminal modifies inventory records or causes inventory to be shipped to a location where it can be stolen. In one case, employees of a railroad changed the boxcar inventory file to indicate that over 200 boxcars were scrapped or destroyed. These boxcars were then shipped to another railroad company's yard and repainted.

Payroll fraud. The criminal pads an organization's payroll with nonexistent employees or leaves former employees on the payroll after termination. In one example, an employee of a welfare department's data center stole $2.75 million by creating a fictitious work force. He used fake social security numbers and created input data that generated weekly checks through a payment system. He and several collaborators intercepted the checks and cashed them.

Pension fraud. The criminal embezzles funds from pension payments. Typically, the criminal keeps a deceased person on the file but sends that person's pension check to his own account. To test the existence of this problem, the State Retirement Board in Boston asked 14,500 pension recipients to submit proof they were still alive. They received responses from only 13,994.

Cashier fraud. Cashiers steal part of the cash payments received from customers. For example, a ticket clerk at the Arizona Veterans' Memorial Coliseum was caught issuing full-price basketball tickets, selling them, and then recording the transactions as half-price tickets by entering incorrect codes into the computer.

Theft by modifying software

Some programmers have committed computer crime by modifying software so that it performs differently when it encounters a particular account number or other triggering condition. One technique is to accumulate fractions of pennies on financial transactions and add them to a personal account. Presumably no one would notice and no one would be harmed. Since this technique involves shaving thin slices from transactions, it is sometimes called a *salami swindle.* In one case, the modified program put the money in the account of the programmer's father, who was stunned to see an unexpected $100,000 in his account at the end of one month. The crime was uncovered when the programmer's father went to the bank to report the error.[22]

Figure 15.4 Check Forgery

A number of flaws suggest that a check may be forged.

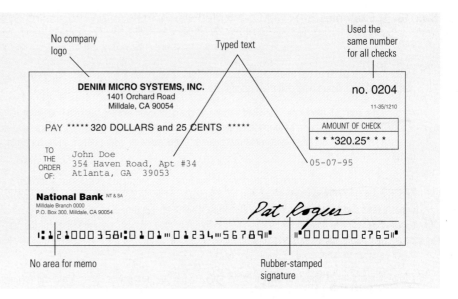

Unlike that solitary crime, software modifications sometimes involve collusion with business executives. In what was called the largest criminal tax case in Connecticut history, top executives of Stew Leonard's, a sprawling dairy store that had received awards for entrepreneurship and customer service, pleaded guilty to conspiracy. They had stolen $17.5 million in cash receipts between 1981 and 1991 and used a computer program to modify the company's records so that auditors would not discover the discrepancies. The investigation began not through auditors' efforts, but when U.S. Customs agents stopped Leonard as he boarded a flight to a vacation home in the Caribbean with $80,000 in undeclared cash.[23]

Sabotage and Vandalism

Perpetrators of sabotage and vandalism try to invade or damage system hardware, software, or data. They may range from hackers to disgruntled employees to spies. Although some hackers may not intend to cause harm, sometimes they do so by making mistakes. Chapter 2 cited an example in which a graduate student was convicted of a felony for accidentally disrupting 6,000 computers while trying to demonstrate a security weakness in the Internet.

Disgruntled employees who understand a computer system's operation and its weak points are especially dangerous perpetrators of computer crimes. Disgruntled employees have erased, modified, and even kidnapped both data and programs. Although little is said about sabotage by spies, the fact that 14-year-olds have penetrated military networks says there are possibilities for computer system sabotage by spies. A number of programming techniques have been used for sabotage and vandalism:

A **trap door** is a set of instructions that permits a user to bypass the system's standard security measures. Trap doors are frequently put into programs by system developers to make it easier for them to modify the system. The Internet worm that disrupted 6,000 computers operated through a trap door left by system developers.

A **Trojan horse** is a program that appears to be valid and useful but contains hidden instructions that cause damage. For example, a Trojan horse could identify a particular account number and bypass it or could accumulate differences due to rounding and place them in a particular account.

A **logic bomb** is a type of Trojan horse whose destructive actions are set to occur when a particular condition occurs, such as reaching a particular clock time or the initiation of a particular program. Logic bombs are sometimes used for computerized vandalism and revenge. In such use, the logic bomb is designed to go off long after the programmer has left the organization. One logic bomb that did not succeed was designed to go off at 6 p.m. on May 24, 1991, and wipe out programs related to the availability and cost of parts used by General Dynamics in building the Atlas missile. It would then erase itself. Fortunately, on April 10, a co-worker of the programmer accused of planting the bomb discovered it accidentally and notified federal agents.[24]

A **virus** is a special type of Trojan horse that can replicate itself and spread, much like a biological virus. A virus attached to a program is loaded into the computer's memory when the program is loaded. The virus is programmed to insert a copy of itself into programs or files that do not contain it. When those programs are executed, the copy of the virus starts up and attempts to replicate itself again. A 1993 survey of corporations estimated the year's virus damage costs at almost $2 billion, with the average virus attack affecting 142 personal computers and taking more than 2 days to eradicate.[25] Six years after the Chernobyl nuclear disaster contaminated an area the size of Delaware, a disgruntled employee inserted a virus into the computer system used to monitor a nuclear plant in Lithuania. Fortunately, control room engineers saw indications that fuel rods were overheating. Whether or not this virus could have led to a meltdown, the mere fact that it could be introduced into the computer system shows the potential danger from lax security.[26]

Viruses are introduced into company computer systems in many different ways. Of sites reporting viruses in a National Computer Association survey of 602 sites, 61 percent reported viruses from disks from home, 10 percent from computer bulletin boards, 8 percent from sales demo disks, and 8 percent from repair or service people.[27]

Several companies have unknowingly shipped hardware or software infected by viruses. In 1991, Novell sent letters to 3,800 customers warning them that its network support encyclopedia had been infected with the Stoned III virus. Around the same time, Leading Edge Products sold 500 computers whose hard disks were infected with the Michelangelo virus.[28]

Earlier speculation that viruses might be used for warfare were proven out in the Persian Gulf War. U.S. Intelligence agents in Amman, Jordan, replaced a computer chip in a French-made computer printer with a chip designed by the U.S. National Security Agency to disrupt a mainframe computer when the printer was used. The printer was attached to a mainframe used by Iraq's air defense system and caused data to vanish from computer screens.[29]

Theft, sabotage, and vandalism are intentional threats to information systems, whereas accidents (covered earlier) are unintentional threats. Many of the intentional and unintentional threats result from characteristics of systems, people, and the business environment. These causes of vulnerability are discussed next to lay the groundwork for the subsequent overview of measures to maintain system security.

Factors That Increase the Risks

Many examples of system-related accidents and crime have been presented to demonstrate the reality and breadth of the threat that must be countered by management and security measures. Although each example involved a unique situation, interrelated conditions such as carelessness, complacency, and inadequate organizational procedures increased the vulnerability to both accidents and crime. Table 15.2 shows particular conditions that increase vulnerability to each type of accident or crime. Behind the conditions in Table 15.2 is a combination of issues related to three themes: the nature of complex systems, human limitations, and pressures in the business environment.

Table 15.2 Conditions That Increase Vulnerability

	Type of Threat	Conditions That Increase Vulnerability
Threats from unintentional occurrences	Operator error	• Difficulty in anticipating how systems will really work in practice and how users and others will adapt to them • Complacency in assuming the system will operate as it is supposed to • Lack of energy and care in assuring systems work properly
	Hardware malfunction	• Disbelief that hardware can malfunction • Difficulty deciding whether the hardware or the warning system is malfunctioning
	Software bugs	• Inadequate design and testing • Unanticipated factors that affect system operation • Inability to prove software is correct
	Data errors	• Flaws in procedures • Inability of software to detect many types of errors • Carelessness and inattention
	Damage to physical facilities	• Inadequate backup • Inadequate physical security related to natural phenomena • Inadequate protection against failure of important external systems
	Inadequate system performance	• Inadequate design • Unanticipated peak loads or demand variations
	Liability for System Failure	• Inadequate limitation on liability • Inadequate system quality
Threats from intentional actions	Theft	• Inadequate design of computer system or human processing • Existence of many easy targets for theft • Distributed systems
	Vandalism and Sabatage	• Inadequate prevention of unauthorized access • Inadequate software change control • Inadequate organizational procedures

The Nature of Complex Systems

Many complex systems rely on numerous human, physical, and technical factors that all have to operate correctly to avoid catastrophic system failures. Consider how a simple power outage at a New York City AT&T switching station at 10 a.m. on September 19, 1991, was magnified by a combination of power equipment failure, alarm system failure, and management failure. When workers activated backup power at the station, a power surge and an oversensitive safety device prevented diesel backup generators from providing power to the telephone equipment, which automatically started drawing power from emergency batteries. Workers disobeyed standard procedures by not checking that the diesel generators were working. Operating on battery power was an emergency situation, but over 100 people in the building that day did not notice the emergency alarms for various reasons: Some alarm lights did not work; others were placed where they could not be seen; alarm bells had been inactivated because of false alarms; technicians were off-site at a training course. At 4:50 p.m., the batteries gave out, shutting down the hub's 2.1 million calls-per-hour capacity. Because communication between the region's airports went through this hub, regional airport operations came to a standstill, grounding 85,000 air passengers.[30, 31]

In addition to relying on everything to work correctly, computerized systems are often designed to hide things users don't want to be involved in, such as the details of data processing. Although usually effective, this approach makes it less likely that users will notice problems. In addition, users often try to bypass systems by inventing new procedures that are convenient but that may contradict the system's original design concepts. The more flexible a system is, the more likely that it will be used in ways never imagined by its designers.

System decentralization and multivendor connectivity also affect security. As networked workstations become more common, the ability to access, copy, and change computerized data expands. Electronically stored data in offices are highly vulnerable because many offices are low-security or no-security environments where people can easily access and copy local data and data extracted from corporate databases. Storage media such as diskettes, and even the computers themselves, are easy to move. Data channels such as electronic message systems and bulletin boards are largely uncontrolled. These areas of vulnerability all result from the worthwhile goal of making systems available and readily usable.

Human Limitations

To make things worse, many users of office systems are unsophisticated about system security and ignore it. Other human limitations increasing system vulnerability include complacency, carelessness, greed, and limited ability to understand complex systems.

Complacency and carelessness lead users and managers to assume systems work correctly. Pepsi-Cola's managers in the Philippines were certainly surprised when a "computer error" in their Numbers Fever promotion generated 800,000 winning numbers inside bottle caps instead of 18. With a promised prize of one million pesos ($40,000) for each winner, Pepsi-Cola found itself in a public relations and legal nightmare. It certainly did not have $32 billion to pay the claimants, and tried to appease them by spending $10 million to give 500 pesos ($20) to each claimant with a winning number.[32]

Complacency and carelessness also lead to lax enforcement of security systems. Controls designed to prevent disasters in systems are often ignored by the people who are supposed to enforce them. A U.S. General Accounting Office (GAO) audit of the top U.S. stock markets turned up 68 security and control flaws. Three of the exchanges had no computer backup facilities; two had no alternative power supplies for trading floors; two had telecommunications equipment that could be used to modify data; one had combustible materials in a computer room.[33]

Greed and other human frailties increase vulnerability because they provide a motive for computer crime. People having personal problems related to drinking, drugs, gambling, or other difficulties may see computer crime as a way to solve their problems. People who want revenge on their employer or supervisor may also resort to computer crime.

Human limitations of system developers also have an impact. Even with the best CASE techniques, it is sometimes difficult to visualize exactly how a complicated system will work. Many individuals understand parts of systems, but few understand everything about a complex system. Inability to anticipate how the system will operate under all circumstances leads to accidents and increases the chances of computer crime.

Pressures in the Business Environment

The business environment increases vulnerability by adding pressures to complete systems rapidly with limited staffs. System vulnerability may not be considered adequately when development decisions are driven by needs to maximize return on investment. In the rush to meet deadlines with insufficient resources, features and testing that reduce vulnerability may be left out. Hallmarks of careful systems work may be curtailed, such as thorough documentation, careful design reviews, and complete testing. These things happen not only in information systems, but also in many other large projects. For example, after years of delays, the billion dollar Hubble space telescope was launched into orbit with a warped mirror that had not been given a standard final test on earth.

The competitive environment has even pushed companies to reduce their executive level attention to security. Despite the argument that having a high-level security expert is more important to many organizations today than it ever was in the past, a number of high-profile businesses have shifted these responsibilities to their end-user departments. For example, First Boston Corporation eliminated its corporate executive position for data security and recovery as part of its attempt to eliminate layers of management and give more local control to end users.[34]

Methods for Minimizing Risks

We have covered many threats related to accidents and computer crime to demonstrate why positive action to minimize these threats is essential. Figure 15.5 represents these actions as a series of business processes in a value chain for establishing and maintaining system security and control. The remainder of the chapter will use the following order to explain the basic sequence of developing the system properly, establishing security, controlling operations, and anticipating problems:

- Build the system correctly in the first place.

- Train users about security issues.

- Once the system is in operation, maintain physical security.

- Given that it is physically secure, prevent unauthorized access to computers, networks, and data.

- Having controlled access, make sure transactions are performed correctly.

- Even with transaction controls in place, motivate efficient and effective operation and find ways to improve.

- Even if the system seems secure, audit it to identify problems.

- Even with continuing vigilance, prepare for disasters.

None of the methods mentioned in the remainder of the chapter are foolproof because many problems cannot be foreseen. However, consistent and thorough attention to the security and control value chain reduces the likelihood of accidents, computer crime, and ineffective usage.

Figure 15.5 Value Chain for System Security and Control

System security and control involves a number of separate business processes that combine to reduce the risk of accidents, crime, and ineffective use.

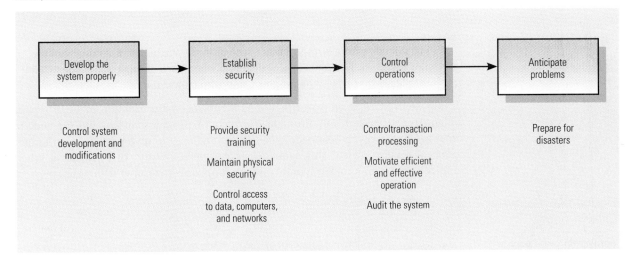

Controlling System Development and Modifications

Software quality control is the process of making sure that software is developed efficiently, debugged completely, and maintained carefully and efficiently. Software quality control usually implies careful adherence to a structured system life cycle, whether the system was built in-house or by a vendor. The use of CASE is becoming an accepted discipline for controlling system quality.

Maintaining software quality also calls for careful testing of any vendor-supplied software before it is distributed in the organization. Although this may seem unnecessary because the software and computers should work properly, we have already seen many systems that did not work as intended. Problems and vulnerabilities of many systems are linked directly to bugs and design flaws that can be found through testing.

Another aspect of maintaining software quality is to prevent contact with computer viruses. Although there is no foolproof way to do this, effective measures include controlling access to computerized systems, using only authorized, vendor-supplied software, and using vaccine programs to identify and eliminate known viruses. It is particularly dangerous to use programs from any sources that may not have been controlled carefully, such as public bulletin boards, public domain (free) software, pirated software, and any diskettes that may be infected.

Software change control systems separate the duties of different individuals to provide a procedural approach for maintaining software quality and preventing unwarranted changes. Figure 15.6 illustrates the sequence that occurs whenever a program is changed:

1. The programmer documents the change to be made and then checks out the programs to be changed. When these programs are checked out, no one else can check them out or change them.

2. The programmer changes the programs and tests them.

3. The programmer transfers the modified programs to another person authorized to check them. That person reads the documentation of the desired change, studies the before and after versions of the programs, tests them, and signs off that they are correct.

4. The system administrator replaces the old versions of the programs with the new revisions. A journal is kept detailing when each change was made, what it entailed, who revised the program, and who checked it.

Many variations on this sequence have been used. For example, many IS organizations use structured walk-throughs in which the programmer explains the code to other programmers to be sure it is consistent and easy to understand. As with other forms of quality review, this sequence is cumbersome and isn't foolproof. When enforced, however, it makes it more difficult for people to tamper with programs.

Figure 15.6 Software Change Control

Software change control creates a division of responsibility in which one person modifies and tests a program and others check the changes and move the changes back into the program library.

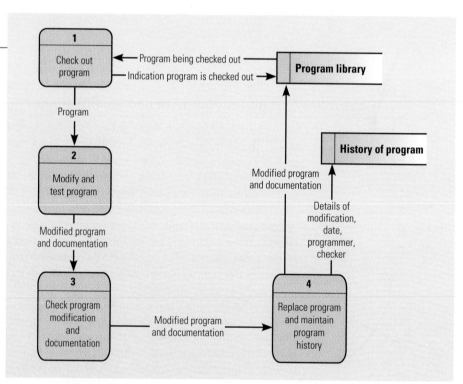

Training Users About Security

Complacency, carelessness, and lack of awareness all increase the likelihood of accidents and computer crime. Companies should train users to be aware of security concerns and to understand how these concerns are related to rules and procedures. Every employee who uses a computer or is at all involved with transaction processing should be familiar with the issues this chapter raises. They should also know some of the signs of suspicious activity and the company's procedures for reporting that activity.

Although the many examples presented here and the huge costs of telephone fraud and viruses show why this type of training and awareness is important, many companies do not follow through adequately. Large losses are not surprising when employees are unaware of the risks or know that company management doesn't care.

Maintaining Physical Security

Maintaining physical security is essential for protecting computing and communication facilities. Physical security measures should take into account threats including accidents, uncontrollable external events, and attack by intruders. Physical security starts with simple measures, such as forbidding eating, drinking, and smoking near computer equipment. Just dropping a cup of coffee can damage equipment and erase data.

Physical access controls guard against physical access to computer facilities and data. The general guideline is to keep unauthorized people out of computer rooms, communication centers, and places where data is stored. Contrary to that guideline, one author recalls a security consulting assignment in which his elevator accidentally stopped at the floor of a large casino's computer center at 11:00 p.m. He and an associate walked up to a locked door marked "Computer Center—No Admittance." They rang the bell, were admitted by a computer operator without saying a word, and wandered through the computer center for ten minutes before leaving. If they had been disgruntled heavy losers rather than security consultants, they might have done substantial damage.[35]

Firms go to great lengths to protect critical data processing facilities and rightfully so. Concerns about physical security for its reservation system led American Airlines to build an underground facility in Tulsa, Oklahoma. With its extreme reliance on that system, foot-thick concrete walls and a 42-inch ceiling seemed justified.

Controlling Access to Data, Computers, and Networks

After providing for physical security, the next set of measures involves controlling access to data, computers, and networks. Security measures should restrict access to confidential information and enforce mandatory ground rules. Table 15.3 summarizes four aspects of access control: enforcing guidelines for manual data handling, defining access privileges, enforcing access privileges, and encrypting data to make it meaningless to anyone who bypasses access controls.

Table 15.3 Controlling Access to Data, Computers, and Networks

Control Technique	Example
Enforce manual data handling guidelines	• Lock desks • Shred discarded documents and manuals
Define access privileges	• Give different individuals different levels of privilege for using the computer. • Give different individuals different levels of access to specific data files.
Enforce access privileges	
What you know	• Password • Special personal data
What you have	• ID card • Key to physical facility
Where you are	• Call-back system
Who you are	• Fingerprint or handprint • Retina pattern • Voice pattern
Make data meaningless to anyone lacking authorization	• Data encryption

Guidelines for manual data handling

The way people handle data manually can constitute a security risk. Consider the common practice of going home and leaving work on top of your desk. Confidential or proprietary information lying on a desk is an easy target. Consequently, organizations may require people who work with sensitive information to lock it in their desks at night or whenever they leave.

Surprisingly, the handling of garbage also can be a security risk. Many organizations are careful to shred discarded documents and manuals instead of throwing them in the trash. Failure to do this led to a commonly repeated story about computer crime and security. In 1971, a 19-year-old operated an illegal business based on information he obtained from a trash bin. The trash bin belonged to a supply office of Pacific Telephone and Telegraph (PT&T). In it, he found discarded equipment, which he refurbished. He also found manuals and the detailed operating and ordering procedures used by installation and repair crews. After posing as a freelance writer to get a plant tour, he impersonated a PT&T employee dialing orders into the PT&T computer. He drove to a PT&T facility in an old PT&T truck he had bought at an auction, picked up the equipment he had ordered, and sold it to other companies at discounted prices. Caught after stealing over $1 million in inventory, he served 40 days in jail, paid an $8,500 fine, and later went to work as a security consultant.[36] If PT&T had shredded their operating procedure manuals instead of throwing them in the trash, this incident probably would not have happened. Although it is excessive to shred every document and printout that is no longer used, dumping ordering manuals, customer lists, and company plans into a trash bin invites unauthorized access to proprietary information.

Access privileges

Locking desks and shredding obsolete documents are security measures related to manual data handling. Security measures for computerized systems start with defining access privileges. **Access privileges** are precise statements of which computers and data an individual can access and under what circumstances. The simplest way to define access privileges is with a list of all authorized users of a system. Access lists are effective only if organizations enforce them strictly. Security-conscious organizations are especially concerned that all computer-related records and privileges are up to date for all employees. Such organizations ensure that all access to computers is canceled when an employee leaves.

The fact that someone can log onto a computer system doesn't mean he or she should have access to all data in the system. Many systems use file access lists that grant individual users or groups of users different levels of access to specific files. Typical levels of access include none, read only, read and copy, or read and update. For example, almost all users would have no direct access to the list of passwords. Some users would have read and copy access to a customer list. All users would have read and update access to files produced in their own personal work.

Whether the focus is physical facilities or computer networks, access lists require enforcement. We will look at ways to enforce access control based on four concepts: what you know, what you have, where you are, and who you are.

Access control based on what you know

A **password** provides a simple form of protection. After logging on with an account number or user ID, the user enters a confidential password. The user can use the system only after the computer checks that this password goes with this account. Businesspeople today may have separate passwords for electronic mail, voice mail, and several different computer networks, not to speak of PIN numbers for ATMs and credit cards.

Unfortunately, password schemes have a variety of weaknesses. People who connect to many different systems often have to remember many different passwords. Because it is hard to remember infrequently used passwords, people are tempted to use short passwords or passwords that can be guessed easily, such as the person's account number, a child's name, pet's name, or middle name. If a password is simple enough, it is easy to figure out by trial and error. This is especially true if a computer generates each trial password and tries it out automatically. Employers may forget to cancel passwords after employees leave a company. Where security is sloppy, terminated employees may be able to dial into an employer's computer months after being dismissed. Since the password list is just a file inside a computer, it may be possible to find and copy this list by working around the standard file security routines in the system. With all these shortcomings, passwords are certainly not foolproof. Nonetheless, they are useful as one part of an overall security system.

One of the most important shortcomings of passwords is that people literally give them away, such as by writing passwords on the side of a workstation or by letting other people look over their shoulders. Many computer system break-ins occur because an operator has divulged a password to someone who appears to be authorized to receive it. The impostor often telephones, pretends to be a repair person, gains the unsuspecting operator's confidence, and then asks the operator to say or type the password as part of a supposed repair process. Some computer hackers cynically call this **social engineering.**[37] Stealing a password this way is similar to the way purse-snatchers pretend to be police officers and ask for ATM PIN numbers for an official sounding reason, such as "verifying your account." All users of networked systems should be trained to recognize social engineering scams.

Access control based on what you have

ID cards provide some security by making it more difficult for people to enter a physical facility or computer system. Simple ID card systems have many problems similar to those of passwords, however. The cards may be lost. The organization may fail to insist they be returned when an employee leaves. The card may be stolen or forged, as happens occasionally with driver's licenses and passports. The technology for ID cards is becoming more powerful, and ID cards themselves can store data other than a name, number, and picture. ID cards that can be read by scanners can be used in combination with definitive personal identification to provide more advanced security methods.

Access control based on where you are

One way to prevent unauthorized access to computer systems is to make sure that a given user can access the system only from that user's terminal. This is accomplished using a **call-back system,** with which the user enters an account number and password and is then disconnected automatically. If the numbers match, the system then calls the user back at a phone number listed in an internal system directory. This prevents access by people who have stolen a password unless they are using the password from the password owner's location. Extending this idea, a device has been patented that instructs the person calling back to repeat several words over the phone. Access would be granted only if the voice matches a stored voiceprint.

Access control based on who you are

For more definitive identification than is possible with passwords and ID cards, specialized equipment can sense a person's unique physical characteristics, such as fingerprints, voiceprints, and blood-vessel patterns on the retina. These are all forms of **biometric identification** because they use the individual's personal, biological characteristics. These systems are becoming competitive with magnetic card systems for restricting entrance to buildings. Hand and fingerprint identification are used to control access to high-security areas ranging from government facilities and nuclear research labs to jewelry vaults and are now even available for unlocking car doors (see Figure 15.7). American Airlines uses a retina scanner as part of the security system for its underground computer facility. The Cook County Jail in Chicago has used retina scanners to make sure prisoners don't attempt to exchange identities by memorizing each other's names, addresses, and personal information.[38]

Figure 15.7
Using Handprints for Identification

To reduce waiting time for frequent international travelers, the U.S. Immigration and Naturalization Service permits travelers at some airports to identify themselves using a hand scanner and an identification card.

All the access control methods, even biometric identification, can be undermined by carelessness after the access control check is completed. For example, merely walking away from a computer terminal logged into a network can provide an opportunity for unauthorized access to data. A simple way to reduce this risk is to log off whenever you leave a terminal. To minimize unauthorized access, some systems apply an **automatic log off** to any terminal left unused for a fixed amount of time, such as ten minutes.

Making the data meaningless to unauthorized users

Another way to protect data is to make it meaningless to unauthorized users. As introduced in Chapter 9, encryption is the encoding of data so that it can be understood only when a user has access to an automatic decoding method. Simple encryption schemes such as substituting one letter for another or reversing the letters in words are easy to figure out. Real encryption schemes are much more complicated and often require that some part of the encryption rule change frequently.

Thus far, ways to control access to data have been described. Since insiders are responsible for most computer crime, it is clear that even people with authorized access may cause problems. The next level of control tries to make sure transactions are processed correctly.

Controlling Access to Computers, Networks, and Data In this section, we described many ways to control access to computers, networks, and data.

1. Assume you have been hired in the patent office of an extremely security-conscious company. On your second day at work, you see someone across the room who appears to be copying a password that is written on the side of a workstation. Do you think you have a responsibility to do anything in this situation?

2. Several weeks later, the company brings in a retina scanner to check the identity of anyone entering the patent office. How would you feel about undergoing a retina scan every time you enter the office?

Controlling Transaction Processing

Control of transaction processing starts with data collection and includes the way computers process the data and the way errors are corrected. The control points we will look at include data preparation and authorization, data validation, error correction, and backup and recovery.

Data preparation and authorization

Data preparation and authorization creates the transaction data that will be entered into a transaction processing system. The story of Equity Funding Corporation shows the importance of controlling data preparation. Over the course of ten years, officers and computer programmers of Equity Funding colluded to make the company appear to be on a rapid growth path by issuing 60,000 fake insurance policies, accounting for about 65 percent of the company's total. The fake policies were sold to reinsurance companies. When the premiums were to be paid, Equity Funding generated more fake policies, sold them to reinsurers, and used the proceeds of the sale to pay premiums for policies sold earlier. In creating the fake policies, the programmers used statistical data from the company's legitimate policies to ensure that the fakes had the same profiles in coverage, premiums, policy cancellations, and benefits paid. When federal investigators asked to audit the files, the company delayed until it could forge health reports, contracts, and supporting documents. This fraud eventually cost investors $1 billion.[39]

Collusion on the scale of the Equity Funding case is extraordinary because it requires the cooperation of so many people. Crime through fraudulent transaction data is much easier to perpetrate if it can be done by one person. Segregation of duties is a control method that makes it more difficult to perpetrate such crimes. **Segregation of duties** is the division of responsibilities among two or more people to reduce the likelihood of theft or accidental misprocessing. For example, one person in an accounts payable department might write the expense voucher, while another person authorizes it, and a third actually writes the check. Segregation of duties does not assure honesty and accuracy, but it makes dishonesty and carelessness more difficult.

Segregation of duties is used extensively in both computerized and noncomputerized systems. It is just as applicable in system development groups as it is in finance departments. Some computer frauds were possible only because an individual working in isolation from others could modify a program to put money into a particular account or perform other improper processing. IS organizations use software change control techniques (mentioned earlier) to improve software quality and avoid this problem.

Although segregation of duties has advantages for security, it has disadvantages for efficiency because it requires multiple authorizations and the involvement of many people in processes that could be handled by one person. The extent of segregation of duties is a management choice based on this tradeoff.

Data validation

Data validation refers to checking transaction data for any errors or omissions that can be detected by looking at the data. Common computerized validation procedures include checking for missing data (such as a missing social security number), invalid data (such as an impossible zip code), and inconsistent data. As an example, Figure 15.8 shows a transaction screen from a hypothetical registration system at a college. Some of the validation checks are obvious, such as matching the student's name and social security number or checking that the student's financial account is current. Others require more complex processing, such as determining whether the student has taken the prerequisite courses or whether the sequence of courses will permit graduation on time.

Although it is essential to validate transaction data to keep the database accurate and avoid wasting time correcting past errors, it is impossible to validate all the data in a system. For example, transpositions such as 56 instead of 65 are often difficult to catch because there may be no reason to suspect that 65 is more likely than 56. An army clerk who made such an error on a 13-digit part number ended up ordering a 7-ton anchor instead of a $6 incandescent lamp.[40] Better system design might have prevented this error. Instead of requiring the clerk to type a 13-digit number, a system built today could easily permit the clerk to choose the item from a list of existing part numbers plus item descriptions.

Figure 15.8 Validation Checks for a Course Registration Transaction

This figure shows a transaction screen from a hypothetical registration system and a list of automatic validation checks that might be used.

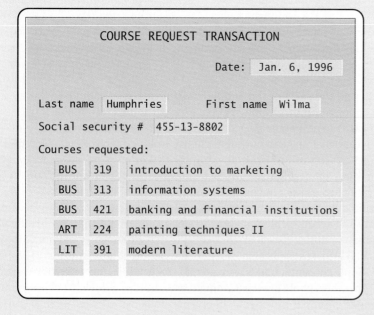

Error correction

Error correction is an essential component of any transaction processing system because it is impossible to assure that all data in the system are correct, regardless of how carefully the data were validated when first entered. Error correction in many TPSs is surprisingly complicated because of the possibility of fraud. If erroneous data could be corrected by editing the data values (as would be done using a word processor), correct data could also be changed using the same techniques. Embezzlement would be rampant and the validity of most databases in doubt.

To control TPSs involving data related to financial accounting, error correction is usually handled as a separate transaction that is recorded and accounted for. The transaction history from the TPS therefore includes each normal transaction that occurred, such as payment of a bill or receipt of an order, as well as each error correction transaction, such as changing a customer's account balance because a bill contained the wrong price or because the merchandise was unsatisfactory.

Backup and recovery

The last step in controlling transaction processing is to make sure that regular processing will resume with minimal pain and inconvenience if the computer system goes down. The typical method for doing this was illustrated in Figure 4.11, which shows the logic of performing periodic backups and using those backups to restore the transaction database to the point at which a disruption occurred. Since the topic of backup and recovery was explained in Chapter 4, it will not be repeated here.

Motivating Efficient and Effective Operation

Topics already discussed, such as developing the system properly, maintaining security, and controlling transaction processing are all aspects of system management. Another side of system management is creating incentives for efficient and effective operation, especially by monitoring system usage and by using chargeback to motivate efficiency.

Monitoring system usage

Since it is difficult to manage things without measuring them, well-designed information systems contain measures of performance both for the business process being supported and for the information system itself. Consider a telemarketing firm's customer service information system. It might include measures of business process results, such as sales per hour and customer waiting time before speaking to an agent. It might also contain measures of information system efficiency, such as downtime, average response time for database inquiries, and weekly operating cost. Patterns of suspicious activity might also be recognized with the help of credit card companies.

Because of the prevalence of telephone fraud, all three types of monitoring are important for PBXs. User waiting time and cost savings on outside calls routed through the PBX are measures of the business process. PBX costs and downtime describe the information system's performance. Peculiar patterns of using one access code for frequent calls or unusual foreign calls could be a warning that an access code has been stolen.

Whether the monitoring concerns business process performance, information system performance, or unusual activity, it has little value unless users and managers are willing and able to use the information. This is one of the reasons graphs of key measurements are often posted in the corridors going into factories. Posting the indicators makes sure that everyone knows they are important and that everyone recognizes how well the factory is doing.

Encouraging efficiency by charging users

The lack of publicized measures for many computerized systems leads users to ignore their costs, use them inefficiently, and sometimes tolerate misuse. This is one of the reasons for charging users to encourage efficiency. **Chargeback systems** try to motivate efficient system use by assigning to user departments the costs of information systems. Effects of chargeback systems on behavior are apparent in the way offices operate. If the telephone is treated as corporate overhead and therefore appears to be free to users, people will use the phone more than if they or their departments are charged in proportion to usage. Likewise, disk storage on departmental computers is filled much more quickly if the users incur no storage charges. Even if resources aren't free, the way they are charged out affects how they are used. Consider a laser printer charged at 10¢ per page and a copier charged at 5¢ per page. If you had to make 45 copies, you would probably print one copy on the laser printer and make the other copies on the copier. But if the laser printer cost 5¢ or less, you would make all the copies there. Ideally, chargeback schemes should motivate people to use resources efficiently by reflecting the organization's true costs.

The key issue in charging for using information system resources is to affect people's decisions. If, for example, total computer costs are charged to departments based only on headcount, the charges probably won't affect decisions because the charges are the same regardless of how people use the computers. Instead of using this type of broad-brush allocation, chargeback schemes should use recognizable units of output that correspond closely to business activities. Directly controllable chargeable items include pages printed, transactions performed, and amount of data stored.

Some charging schemes also reflect resource scarcity to motivate usage only when those resources are needed. For example, most computer facilities are especially busy at particular times such as late morning and midafternoon and are underused other times. Rate differentials are sometimes used to shift some of the work to times of low use, thereby making it unnecessary to buy more capacity to cope with the peaks. With rate differentials, users are charged more when resources are scarcer. Resources such as CPU cycles or telephone minutes during busy periods could cost two or more times as much as they cost during slack periods. Although some users have no choice, rate differentials succeed in shifting some of the demand to times when resources would be underused.

REALITY CHECK   **Chargeback**   Charging people for use of computer resources is one of the ways to motivate efficient usage.

1. Identify situations in your everyday life in which the way you are charged for something determines how efficiently you use it.

2. How do you think a university should encourage efficient usage of its internal telephone system and computers?

Auditing the System

Auditing standards and controls are designed to ensure that financial operations are neither misrepresented nor threatened because of defective procedures or accounting systems. With the advent of computer systems, the scope of auditing expanded to encompass both general controls over computer installations and application controls for assuring that the recording, processing, and reporting of data are performed properly.

Methods for verifying the phases of processing can be categorized as either auditing around the computer or auditing through the computer. In **auditing around the computer,** the auditor typically selects source documents, traces associated entries through intermediate computer printouts, and examines the resultant entries in summary accounts. This approach basically treats the computer itself as a black box. Although it is useful in finding some errors, and is often cost-effective, it may not provide enough detail to catch crimes such as stealing a fraction of a penny on certain transactions.

In **auditing through the computer,** the auditor attempts to understand and test the computer's processing in more detail. A common technique is to create test data and process the data through the system to observe whether the expected results occur. An important shortcoming of this approach is that only preconceived conditions are tested. Furthermore, it is impractical for the test data to represent every possible situation. If a program illegally transfers money every Thursday and the test data are processed on Tuesday, the problem will be missed.

An auditor's responsibility goes much further than just looking at how transactions are processed. Auditors must examine issues such as unauthorized access, controls on computerized data files, controls on data transmission, and procedures for recovering when the system goes down unexpectedly.

Preparing for Disasters

You don't need to look at computer systems to understand the importance of genuine preparedness for possible disasters. Consider the oil tanker accident that polluted Prince William Sound in Alaska with 10 million gallons of oil. A large oil terminal was permitted in this area because a major accident seemed unlikely. Just in case, there was a 1,800-page contingency plan for handling a major spill. But when the accident occurred, almost nothing was done to contain and clean up the spilled oil during the first two days of calm seas, and almost nothing could be done after fierce winds spread the oil on the third day. Exxon, Alyeska Pipeline Service Co., and state officials blamed each other, citing reasons such as not having equipment ready or delaying authorization to use chemical dispersants. This example illustrates the necessity of genuine preparedness for disasters, not just having a plan on paper.

A **disaster plan** is a plan of action to recover from occurrences that shut down or harm major information systems. The nature and extent of an information systems disaster plan for a business depend on the role of information systems to the day-to-day operation of the business. Reliable online transaction processing systems are essential for banks, distributors, and airlines. For businesses such as these, any unplanned computer downtime can cut into customer service and revenues. These businesses may go to great expense maintaining redundant real-time databases in different locations, with several databases updated simultaneously whenever a transaction occurs. Even businesses that use information systems primarily for accounting and management reporting still need definitive plans for recovering from unexpected downtime, however. A 1993 survey of Fortune 500 companies showed that 95 percent had a recovery plan in place for mainframe computers, but only 29 percent had a plan for voice networks, and only 27 percent had a plan for personal computers.[41]

Businesses rely on computerized information systems so heavily today that disaster planning and recovery has become a small industry. The companies in this industry provide backup computer centers at remote sites and help their customers develop action plans in case their own systems suddenly become inoperable. Disaster preparedness was crucial to Midwestern companies affected by the summer floods of 1993 (see Figure 15.9). Comdisco, Inc., a firm offering disaster recovery services, helped a Des Moines, Iowa, company that was not flooded, but whose mainframe computers were down because of an infrastructure problem, the inability to get water needed to cool the computers. The Comdisco customer flew 1,000 pounds of computer tapes on a chartered jet to Comdisco's Illinois site at 5:30 p.m. on Sunday and was back in full production by Monday morning. Around the same time, the city government's computers and PBX were shut down for days because a flood in a subbasement disrupted electric power. The city's administrator of data processing admitted that the city didn't have a recovery plan.[42]

Figure 15.9 A Flood Creates a Data Processing Disaster

Many firms lost their data processing capabilities temporarily when the Mississippi River flooded in 1993.

Chapter Conclusion

SUMMARY

▶ *What are the main types of risks of accidents related to information systems?*

The main types of risks of accidents include operator error, hardware malfunction, software bugs, data errors, damage to physical facilities, inadequate system performance, and liability for system failure.

▶ *What are the different types of computer crime?*

Computer crime is the use of computerized systems to perform illegal acts. Computer crime can be divided into theft, sabotage, and vandalism. Thefts can be perpetrated through unauthorized use of access codes, fraudulent transaction data, theft or modification of data, and modification of software. Entering fraudulent transaction data is the simplest and most common method of computer-related theft. Even without much computer knowledge, fraudulent data can be entered by forging documents, bypassing procedures, or impersonating someone.

▶ *What issues magnify the vulnerability of information systems to accidents and crime?*

This vulnerability is magnified by the nature of complex systems, human limitations, and the business environment. Complex systems have many vulnerable points that may be difficult to identify in advance. Decentralization within systems decreases control. Human limitations such as complacency and carelessness increase opportunities for accidents and crime. Greed provides a motive for crime. Difficulty in visualizing how complex systems work makes it harder to anticipate accidents or guard against crime. The business environment's pressures for limiting staff and attaining immediate financial results reduce the time and effort devoted to making systems secure.

▶ *What measures can be taken to minimize accidents and computer crime?*

The value chain for security starts by building the system right the first time, typically by adhering to a structured system life cycle and using software change control. The next step is training users about security issues to reduce carelessness. Once the system is in operation, maintain physical security and prevent unauthorized access to computers, networks, and data. Having controlled access, make sure transactions are performed correctly and monitor system usage to ensure effectiveness and find ways to improve. Even if the system seems secure, audit it to identify problems and also prepare for disasters.

▶ *What are the different ways to control access to data, computers, and networks?*

Access control includes enforcing guidelines for manual data handling, defining access privileges, enforcing access privileges, and using encryption to make the data meaningless to anyone who bypasses access controls. Guidelines for manual data handling range from rules about leaving work on top of desks to procedures for shredding sensitive documents. Access privileges are precise statements of which computers and data an individual can access and under what circumstances. Access control can be enforced based on four concepts: what you know (such as passwords), what you have (such as ID cards), where you are (such as permitting access only from a particular terminal), and who you are (such as biometric identification).

INTERNATIONAL VIGNETTE

Germany: Penetrating a U.S. Network for Espionage

The first hint about a highly publicized episode of espionage through computer networks occurred when Clifford Stoll, an astrophysicist at the University of California's Lawrence Berkeley Laboratory (LBL), discovered a mysterious $0.75 charge on an accounting report. His curiosity led him to try to find its source, and he concluded that someone had broken into the network. Searching through system records led him to an unauthorized user named Hunter, and to other mysteries, such as use of an inactive account of someone known to be away traveling. The intruder had also broken in by using a guest account and password occasionally provided for guests to LBL. The account name and password were easy to guess because both were the word *guest*. Stoll concluded the intruder had originally broken in through the guest account and had managed to find a way to copy the password file, which provided access through many other accounts.

Since the intruder seemed more determined and curious than a student hacker, Stoll carefully tracked the intruder's use of the system, along the way creating an electronic record of everything the intruder did. Stoll set a number of traps to entice the intruder to search through files on the system, thereby staying attached long enough for federal law enforcement agents to trace the incoming call. Eventually, they found the computer hacker was in Germany. Further investigation after the hacker was arrested by German authorities found that he was being paid by the KGB, the USSR's spy organization. Stoll wrote his story in the 1990 book *The Cuckoo's Egg*, and received national notoriety.

> Source: Stoll, Clifford. *The Cuckoo's Egg*. New York: Pocket Books, 1990.

- Use the WCA framework to organize your understanding of this vignette and to identify important topics that are not mentioned.

- What issues (if any) make this case interesting from an international or intercultural viewpoint?

- How is this case related to the potential commercial application of computer networks for exchanging information or transacting business?

REAL-WORLD CASES

New York Telephone: Giving Away Personal Identification Numbers in a Sweepstakes Promotion

New York Telephone, an operating unit of the Baby Bell Nynex, was looking for a way to promote local usage of telephone credit card calls. These calls are made by dialing 0 and the recipient's telephone number, waiting for a beep, entering the caller's telephone number, and then entering a four-digit personal identification number (PIN) used to prevent unauthorized people from charging calls to someone else's number. To promote these calls, New York Telephone created a sweepstakes with $150,000 in prizes. The winners would be selected from people who had used phone credit cards for local telephone calls between April 4 and May 31, 1994. To publicize the sweepstakes and to remind people about the PINs, which are easy to forget if they aren't used, New York Telephone mailed three million letters, each of which contained a punch-out card with the telephone customer's PIN printed on it.

People concerned with telephone fraud were aghast. Whenever any form of password security is used for bank ATMs, computer networks, or other purposes, the people who will use the passwords are sternly admonished to be careful, not to write them in the same place as their account number or phone number, and not to leave them where others can see them. And now three million letters with these numbers were sitting in mailboxes in New York. Nynex said it had reviewed the mailing materials with postal authorities and would change the PIN of anyone who complained.

> Source: Elliott, Stuart. "Phone Promotion Miscue Raises Concerns of Fraud." *New York Times*, Apr. 6, p. A1.

- Use the WCA framework to organize your understanding of this case and to identify important topics that are not mentioned.

- Explain how this case is related to the chapter's ideas about things that can go wrong with systems.

Chapman & Cutler: Failing to Validate Billing Data

James Spiotto, a top partner at the Chicago law firm of Chapman & Cutler, billed clients $2,336,784 for 6,022 hours of work in 1993. That adds up to 16.5 hours per day, seven days a week, for every day of the year. Big law firms usually expect lawyers to bill 1,700 to 2,000 hours per year, and billings of 3,000 hours or more are very rare. Unless clients agree otherwise, a lawyer's billable time consists only of time spent on the client's work and doesn't include other things law firm partners spend time on, such as sleeping, taking breaks, performing internal law firm management, and developing client relationships.

According to legal ethics specialists, intentionally overbilling is a form of fraud and would be prosecuted as theft by deception. Although partners at most law firms have access to the billing records of other attorneys, it is not clear whether anyone reviewed Mr. Spiotto's billings carefully. Several lawyers in the firm said that he had a reputation for very high billings but that they were reluctant to confront him because he was very powerful.

> Source: Stevens, Amy. "Top Chapman & Cutler Partner Chalked Up Astronomical Hours." *Wall Street Journal,* May 27, 1994, p. B1.

- Use the WCA framework to organize your understanding of this case and to identify important topics that are not mentioned.

- How is it possible that this kind of thing could happen at a major law firm?

- Does this example have any implications for information systems in general?

KEY TERMS

operator error	Trojan horse	password	data validation
software bug	logic bomb	social engineering	error correction
liability	virus	call-back system	chargeback system
computer crime	software change control	biometric identification	auditing around the computer
hacker	physical access controls	automatic log off	auditing through the computer
trap door	access privileges	segregation of duties	disaster plan

REVIEW QUESTIONS

1. What are common reasons for project failure at each of the four phases of an information system project?
2. Identify the seven types of risks related to accidents rather than computer crime.
3. What factors make operator error more likely?
4. Why do software bugs occur?
5. Why does the year 2000 raise fears about problems with old computerized systems?
6. How do software vendors limit their legal liability for software they sell?
7. What are the different types of computer crime, and which is most common?
8. Describe different ways to steal through fraudulent transaction data.
9. What programming techniques have been used to commit sabotage and vandalism?
10. How is system vulnerability related to the nature of complex systems, human limitations, and pressures in the business environment?
11. Identify the steps in the value chain for system security and control.
12. How does software change control operate?
13. What techniques are used for controlling access to data, computers, and networks?
14. Explain some of the shortcomings of passwords.
15. What do computer hackers mean when they use the term *social engineering?*
16. Describe the main methods for controlling transaction processing.
17. How do chargeback systems encourage efficiency?
18. Why is it important to have a disaster plan for information systems?

DISCUSSION QUESTIONS

1. The Business Software Alliance, a software-industry trade group, announced plans to offer a bounty of up to £2,500 ($3,900) to anyone in Great Britain who informs on companies using unlicensed software. Since around half the software used in Great Britain is thought to be unlicensed, many large firms will probably be named. Information about unlicensed use will be obtained through a toll-free number dubbed the Software Crimeline. The chairman of the Computer Users of Europe complained that this was "like the old East Bloc process of informing" and that he "could not see anyone who has any desire to continue his career feeling he could turn in his boss."[43] Explain how this example is related to this chapter's ideas about computer crime and system security.

2. A 20-year-old MIT junior was indicted for managing a computerized bulletin board allegedly used for illegal distribution of copyrighted software. He was not accused of posting software to it or of profiting from the alleged illegal activities. His defense revolves around the assertion that a computerized bulletin board is just a conduit for information and is not responsible for the information posted on it.[44] What are the ethical responsibilities of a person who runs a computerized bulletin board?

3. Your friend has been given a wonderful game program and wants to show you how it operates. He has used it on his computer without problems. Under what circumstances should you allow him to run it on your computer?

4. The night before the Space Shuttle Challenger blew up, killing the astronauts aboard, several engineers at Morton-Thiokol tried to have the launch delayed. They thought that the cold weather at Cape Canaveral might affect critical joints on the body of the booster and thereby endanger the spacecraft, but they were overruled. Identify any ideas in this chapter that might help explain why the Challenger was allowed to take off.

5. You are seated on an airplane about to take off and hear the following announcement after the instructions about fastening seat belts and the location of emergency exits: "This is your pilot. I want to congratulate you as the first group of passengers to benefit from our new autopilot system, which will control the entire flight from take-off to landing. But don't worry, I'm still here just in case." How would you react to this announcement?

HANDS-ON EXERCISES

1. This exercise is about the use of security measures in any computer work you do.

   a. Explain how often you do backups, how you do them, and how you keep track of what information is backed up where. If you do not do backups, explain why you do not and what risks you are encountering.

   b. Explain the virus protection method you use for your own personal computer. Explain what you understand of the virus protection method used by your computer facility.

   c. Explain how passwords are handled in the computer facility you use. Is anything lax about the way they are handled? Is anything overly awkward or time consuming about the way they are handled?

APPLICATION SCENARIOS

Oakdale Bank: Thwarting the Programmer's Revenge

Everyone knew that Warren Smathers was on his way up in Oakdale Bank. His grandfather had founded the bank in 1945, and now his father was the president. After receiving an undergraduate degree in computer science, Warren had been hired as a teller and had rotated through several positions before his latest position as manager of information system applications in the consumer banking division.

Just as everyone knew Warren was on his way up, everyone knew that Larry Argol was on his way nowhere. Larry had been a programmer in the bank for seven years. He was strong technically but had trouble getting along with people. Despite numerous coaching sessions with managers in the bank, he tended to be abrupt and sometimes cruel in his interactions with less-talented employees. For this reason, he had been overlooked for promotions several times. Losing out to the president's son seemed to upset Larry greatly. When Warren tried to clear the air with Larry, Larry acted evasive. Then he suddenly stopped, looked Warren in the eye, and said, "You guys are going to be sorry."

Warren was worried because he could easily imagine the ways Larry could make them sorry. Of the people in the department, Larry had the best understanding of Oakdale Bank's consumer banking information systems. Several of these systems were badly designed and poorly documented. Backup systems existed but were also badly designed. The bank's computer operations were loose and would probably be vulnerable to tampering.

Warren thought about the situation and met with his father the next day. Recounting the history with Larry, Warren recommended that Larry be fired immediately before he did disastrous damage to the bank's operations. Warren's father replied that was out of the question and said that you just don't fire someone for being angry about not getting a promotion. Warren responded that you also just don't leave angry people on your staff who could shut the bank down with a few lines of code that no one would ever see.

1. Explain the conditions that make the bank vulnerable in this situation.

2. Identify things that might have been done to keep the situation from getting to the present point.

3. What would you recommend?

DEBATE TOPIC *Use ideas from the chapter to argue the pros and cons and practical implications of the following proposition:* It is unethical to fire someone because of a suspicion that they might be angry enough to do something harmful to the company.

Aberdeen Pharmaceuticals: Is It Red Tape or Security?

In her role as user support manager, Jane Zirpel really enjoyed her working relationship with the end users in the product development group at Aberdeen Pharmaceuticals. They were avid computer users and genuinely appreciated the help they received from the information center. In the last year, they had worked with the user support staff to develop a proposal to link their individual workstations using a network. Soon after this proposal was approved, the product development staff could share its work more effectively than ever before. For example, it was now possible for a researcher in one building to produce a model, send it to a colleague in another building for comments, and get it back that day without wasting 15 minutes walking each way. Although this might seem minor, little conveniences such as this added up to a much better way to work.

Unfortunately, one researcher had done more networking than anyone anticipated. Because of sloppy network security, he had been able to use the network to snoop around in other people's files. He had discovered and secretly copied a series of models built over the course of three years as crucial steps in developing four new drugs. (One drug might eventually reverse baldness in men; the others fought hepatitis, hypertension, and diabetes.) It was only by chance that a technical system manager came in to work on Sunday morning to test a new version of the network software. The system manager noticed unusual activity on the network and used several tracing techniques to make a list of the transfers that were happening. After calling the division vice president, he warned the company's security guards, who seized the researcher's briefcase containing the stolen models.

The following Monday, Jane called a meeting with the product development group to discuss this incident and try to come up with a realistic security scheme that would protect against this type of situation in the future. Saying that management would simply remove the network unless they came up with something, Jane listed some of the obvious security ideas that might be adapted to this situation. The response from one of the most effective network users was, "Jane, you helped us get this system and now you want to tie us up in red tape so we can't use it."

1. What are some of the alternative approaches for improving security?

2. Is the complaint about red tape justified?

3. If you were the system manager, how could you know whether the unusual transfers were suspicious enough to seize a researcher's briefcase?

4. What would you suggest Aberdeen's managers do to improve security without making it too awkward to get work done?

DEBATE TOPIC   *Use ideas from the chapter to argue the pros and cons and practical implications of the following proposition: The system manager should have an announced practice of intercepting and inspecting anything sent over the network.*

Cumulative Case: Custom T-Shirts, Inc.

Pat always hated sloppiness in anything, and this story revealed sloppiness that shouldn't have occurred in a successful business. A long-time employee working in store 28 had sent the central production facility an order for 500 t-shirts for Stopwhistle, Inc.'s company picnic. But the order somehow ended up with last year's "Ready, Aim, Hire" motto on this year's picture. When the t-shirts arrived one day before the picnic, Stopwhistle wouldn't accept them. Aside from the mere fact of the error, that motto had been used in a disastrous hiring campaign that ended with a layoff when the anticipated upturn in business evaporated. Pat estimated the price of the fiasco at $3,000 in direct costs and at least three times that much in lost business if Stopwhistle's human resource manager went to another t-shirt company with next year's orders for several events.

An even worse problem happened when a customer brought in a diskette containing not only a t-shirt design, but also a virus that scrambled screen displays. Although every computer in every store had antivirus software to check each diskette before it was read, either a new virus had been created or the antivirus software had not been used in that case. Since the problem could not be diagnosed immediately, to be on the safe side every piece of computer equipment at that store was reinitialized and all the data reloaded from backups that seemed to be virus-free. After two days of computer work and some disruption of sales, the store was now totally back in operation. One recommendation for minimizing problems with viruses in the future was to route all input of customer artwork from diskettes through a central computer at headquarters. It would make it impossible to bypass the antivirus software.

Another disturbing problem had occurred in which a long-time employee in a Denver store went to work for a competitor in Houston and apparently left after making electronic copies of up to 2,000 pieces of t-shirt artwork. The reason for the suspicion was the sudden drop in business in Houston and the appearance of many t-shirts that resembled t-shirts that Custom had produced over the last two years. The competitor claimed innocence, said the similar patterns were a coincidence, and basically dared company management to try to prove anything.

1. Based on the chapter, describe the types of things that might have caused the sloppiness problem, and give some suggestions for reducing the likelihood of a repeat.

2. Explain the advantages and disadvantages of the antivirus recommendation of filtering all artwork inputs through a computer at headquarters.

3. Explain how the theft of artwork could have occurred. Explain why it might be difficult to prove the artwork was stolen, and what the competitor might do to make the alleged theft even more difficult to prove.

■ *REFERENCES*

1. Lee, Leonard. *The Day the Phones Stopped*. New York: Donald I. Fine, Inc., 1991.

2. Lewyn, Mark. "Flying in Place: The FAA's Air-Control Fiasco." *Business Week*, Apr. 26, 1993.

3. Pearl, Daniel, and Jeff Cole. "Loral's Proposal to Save Big Job May Be in Peril." *Wall Street Journal*, June 2, 1994, p. A3.

4. Halper, Mark. "AMR Sues Partners Over Failed Venture." *Computerworld*, Oct. 5, 1992, p. 1.

5. Halper, Mark. "AMR Calls Confirm Partners Selfish," *Computerworld*, May 24, 1993, p. 4.

6. Lewyn, Mark. "The Post Office Wants Everyone to Pay for Its Mistakes." *Business Week*, Mar. 5, 1990, p. 28.

7. Roberts, Eric, and Steve Berlin. "Computers and the Strategic Defense Initiative." In Bellin, David, and Gary Chapman, *Computers in Battle: Will They Work?* Boston: Harcourt, Brace, Jovanovich, 1987, pp. 149–167.

8. Perrow, Charles. *Normal Accidents: Living with High-Risk Technologies*. New York: Basic Books, 1984.

9. Markoff, John. "Flaw Undermines Accuracy of Pentium Chips," *New York Times*, Nov. 24, 1994, p. C1.

10. Getler, Warren. "Errant Squirrel Causes Another Nasdaq Outage." *Wall Street Journal*, Aug. 2, 1994, p. C1.

11. Norris, Floyd, "Salomon's Error Went Right to Floor." *New York Times*, Mar. 27, 1993.

12. Bulkeley, William M. "Databases Are Plagued by Reign of Error." *Wall Street Journal*, May 26, 1992, p. B6.

13. Bradsher, Keith. "How AT&T Accident Snowballed." *New York Times*, Jan. 14, 1991, p. C1.

14. Ross, Philip E. "The Day the Software Crashed." *Forbes*, Apr. 25, 1994, pp. 142–156.

15. Blumenthal, Ralph. "Officers Go Undercover to Battle the Computer Underworld." *New York Times*, Jan. 26, 1993, p. B14.

16. Booker, Ellis, and Gary H. Anthes, "Toll Fraud Rings in High Cost." *Computerworld*, Oct. 10, 1994, p. 1.

17. Cole, Patrick. "Are ATMs Easy Targets for Crooks? *Business Week*, Mar. 6, 1989, p. 30.

18. Allen, Brandt. "Embezzler's Guide to the Computer." *Harvard Business Review*, Jul.–Aug. 1975, pp. 79–89.

19. Fenyvesi, Charles. "Washington Whispers: Forging Ahead." *U.S. News & World Report*, Aug. 3, 1992. p. 20.

20. Carley, William M. "Rigging Computers for Fraud or Malice Is Often an Inside Job." *Wall Street Journal*, Aug. 27, 1992, p. A1.

21. Bulkeley, William M. "Voice Mail May Let Competitors Dial 'E' for Espionage." *Wall Street Journal*, Sept. 28, 1993, p. B1.

22. Sheridan, John H. "Is There a Computer Criminal Working for You?" *Industry Week*, Jan. 8, 1979, pp. 69–79.

23. Levy, Clifford. "Founder of Renowned Store Pleads Guilty in Fraud Case," *New York Times*, July 23, 1993. p. A11.

24. Alexander, Michael. "Feds Arrest 'Logic Bomber,'" *Computerworld*, July 1, 1991, p. 10.

25. Daly, James. "Virus Vagaries Foil Feds," *Computerworld*, July 12, 1993, p. 1.

26. Reichlin, Igor. "Many Chernobyls Just Waiting to Happen." *Business Week*, Mar. 16, 1992.

27. Alexander, Michael. "Mac Virus Busters Help Nab Two Suspects." *Computerworld*, Mar. 2, 1992.

28. Alexander, Michael. "If You Catch a Virus, See Your Attorney." *Computerworld*, Mar. 9, 1992.

29. *U.S. News & World Report*, "The Gulf War Flu." Jan. 20, 1992, p. 50.

30. Horwitt, Elizabeth. "N.Y. Sites Unfazed by Outage." *Computerworld*, Sept. 23, 1991, p. 1 +.

31. Anthes, Gary H. "FCC Basts AT&T for New York Blowout." *Computerworld*, Nov. 18, 1991, p. 58.

32. Edwards, Tamala M. "Numbers Nightmare: A Pepsi Promotion Misfires in the Philippines," *Time*, Aug. 9, 1993, p. 53.

33. Anthes, Gary H. "GAO Finds Security Lax at U.S. Stock Exchanges," *Computerworld*, Sept. 2, 1991, p. 99.

34. Caldwell, Bruce. "Security Czars Get Locked Out." *Information Week*, June 21, 1993, p. 16.

35. Ball, Leslie D. "Computer Crime." *Technology Review*, Apr. 1982, pp. 21-30.

36. Time-Life Books. *Computer Security*. Alexandria, VA: Time-Life Books, 1986.

37. Cheswick, William R. and Steven M. Bellovin. "Repelling the Wily Hacker." *Computerworld*, May 16, 1994, pp. 113–116.

38. Booker, Ellis. "Retinal Scanners Eye-Identify Inmates." *Computerworld*, Mar. 23, 1992, p. 28.

39. Time-Life Books. *Computer Security*. Alexandria, VA: Time-Life Books, 1986.

40. "A 7-Ton Clerical Fluke: Anchor Arrives Instead of Lamp," *Washington Post*, Apr. 13, 1985.

41. Kay, Sheryl. "Hot data? Hot site," *Computerworld,* July 19, 1993, p. 101.

42. Booker, Ellis. "Data Dowsed in Midwest Floods," *Computerworld*, July 19, 1993. p. 6.

43. Hudson, Richard L. "Know Anybody Using Pirated Software? That's Information Worth Some Money." *Wall Street Journal,* Oct. 11, 1994, p. B5.

44. Braudel, William. "Licensing Stymies Users." *Computerworld*, April 18, 1994, p. 12.

Longer Cases

The Internet: Information Source and Shopping Mall of the Future?

THE INTERNET IS A NETWORK that links computer networks. Originally created in the early 1980s to help military installations share information even if a nuclear war knocked out any particular computer on the network, the Internet grew from a network of 586 in 1982 to over 2,000,000 in 1994. By the mid-1990s it was being used for purposes far beyond its original scope, and had attained what sometimes seemed a cult status, with people from many parts of society talking about "cruising the Net" and "surfing the Net."

It was the subject of enormous hype and speculation. For example, according to a search of the news information service Nexis, the word *Internet* appeared in 2,475 newspaper stories in November, 1994, a 309% increase from the previous year.[1] Although electronic mail and electronic bulletin boards dominated Internet usage by the general public, much of the speculation focused on the possibility that the Internet would become a key information source and shopping mall of the future.

Although no one knew exactly what the Internet would become just a few years in the future, the possibility that it would play a major role in commerce was not just a technologist's pipe dream. In May, 1994, Edwin Artzt, chairman of the consumer products giant Procter & Gamble, had warned a convention of advertising executives that "Our most important ad medium, television, is about to change big time. And from where we stand today, we can't be sure that advertising-supported TV programming will have a future in the world being created." Artzt went on to describe a "burgeoning riot of cable, satellite, and telephone-delivered television, of virtual home shopping malls and interactive CD-ROMs; a world where pay-per-view programming, video games, movies-on-demand and subscription services would dramatically alter viewing habits, make commercial television untenable." An example of the changes that might occur in advertising is the approach taken by ProductView Interactive, which planned an interactive service allowing consumers to view product brochures online. ProductView intended to charge advertisers for broadcasting in to the ether, but rather, for each time a customer accessed their server to request product information.[2]

No one knows whether the Internet will eventually play a direct role in broadcast television or compete with it. By 1995, however, uses of the Internet to provide both product awareness information and in-depth answers to customer questions were well established. It was also technically feasible to complete credit card purchase transactions using the Internet, even though Internet security was not yet tight enough to fend off cyberspace thefts. Expansion and wide diffusion of such capabilities would have far-reaching implications for many aspects of product marketing. Whether or not the Internet could be part of this future depended in part on its history, management, current capabilities, and on the directions it might develop.

History of the Internet

The enormous attention the Internet receives in public media today probably would have been a great surprise to its original developers. The Internet grew out of research on computer networking done by ARPA, the Advanced Research Projects Agency of the U.S. Department of Defense in the 1970s and 1980s.

Incompatibility between different types of computers and networks is one of the basic problems the Internet had to solve. It did this using an approach very different from that of a telephone system, which creates a temporary circuit that carries a two-way conversation until it is completed. In contrast, the Internet uses a technique called packet switching to subdivide all data transmissions into packets, small blocks of data packaged with the network address of their destination. The software that runs the Internet controls transmission of each packet to the computer it is addressed to, and then performs any necessary reassembly of messages that have been divided into packets for transmission. This software runs on a special purpose computer called a router whose job is to connect a LAN or WAN to the Internet backbone. A key technical breakthrough at the heart of packet switching software was TCP/IP (Transmission Control Protocol/ Internet Protocol), which is still used for transmitting and receiving messages.

By 1982, a prototype Internet linked computers at several dozen academic and industrial research sites. The number of computers on the Internet approximately doubled every year from 1982 to 1994, going from several hundred computers to over two million. Responding to continual increases in network traffic, in the mid-1980s the National Science Foundation (NSF) funded capacity increases and created NSFNET, which became the Internet's data transmission backbone in 1988. In 1991, IBM, MCI, and MERIT, the three contractors that had built the NSFNET, formed a nonprofit company called Advanced Networks and Services (ANS). ANS created a new privatized Internet by building a backbone with 30 times the capacity of the NSFNET that it replaced.[3]

The transmission of data as packets is the part of the microscopic view of how the Internet operates. At the level of applications, the Internet is organized to perform client-server computing, which permits a program running on one computer (the client) to request a service from a program running on another computer (the server). In a commercial example, the client might request information about a particular product or might request that payment be credited to a particular account. The server would then respond to that request. Viewing the Internet in terms of client-server computing is important when thinking about this type of usage because it shows that the server must be accessible and able to perform the requested service whenever the client requests it. Anyone wanting to provide shopping or information services through the Internet must provide a server with enough capacity to take care of the service requests it will receive. The client device must also have enough capacity to receive the response. This is important for home users because the modems in personal computers often operate at 9,600 or 14,400 bits per second. At these rates, transferring a page of text takes 10 seconds or more, and transferring a picture can take several minutes. Even as PC modems speeds double to 28,800 bps, data transmission speed will limit the information retrieval that can be performed using the Internet. Greater bandwidth to any particular site could be attained using ISDN or cable.

Consistent with its client-server architecture, the Internet has no central computer or focal point through which all activities operate. In a somewhat similar fashion, although it has various advisory boards and some parts of it are privately owned, as a totality it has no central business organization that controls its evolution over time. It is designed to serve as part of a non-profit infrastructure for a huge number of distributed activities. In contrast, a totally commercial network would probably make explicit planning choices about which customers to serve, which products to allow, and how to provide a consistent view point for customers. Instead, the Internet often seems so amorphous that users may not know whether they are using it or the commercial or research networks that link to it. This is one of the reasons why the Internet of 1994 did not have an accessible directory of user addresses.

Individuals wanting to use the Internet directly can do so for free if they have access through a university, government agency, or company that has an electronic gateway into the Internet and pays for Internet access. They can also sign up with Internet service companies that have their own gateways and provide this access for a fee such as $20 per month for the first 20 hours of connect time.

Traditional Internet Services

The original users of the Internet were researchers who had a relatively limited number of uses. Most of these were concerned with sending messages or documents between computers attached to different computer networks. Unlike users in shopping or customer service applications, researchers were often frequent users who were willing to learn the terminology and grammar of computer-related commands. The flavor of their original uses remains in some of the Internet capabilities that are used frequently today, including electronic mail, bulletin boards, file transfer, remote login, and browsing.

Electronic mail involves sending an electronic message to another person identified by a computer address such as smithj@uiowa.edu or billg@microsoft.com. (The general format is *[person's name]@[business establishment].[type of establishment]*. With this type of format, the Internet software directs the message to the right network, such as uiowa.edu, and the account directory at that node is used to direct the message to the right user.) Although the Internet supports many different programs that send or receive e-mail, the lack of an easily usable e-mail directory for the 20 or 30 million addresses makes it more difficult to send e-mail to anyone other than immediate colleagues and friends.

Bulletin boards provide the ability to post a message or document that can be accessed later by anyone who knows the bulletin board exists and is interested in the topic it covers. The Internet contains bulletin board capabilities for automatically notifying users if new items on a bulletin board have not been read. Bulletin board services are also available through commercial online services such as Compuserve and America Online.

File transfer is the ability to send a file from one computer to another. The file could be a working draft of a research paper, a computer game, or data collected in the course of research. File transfers can be requested by computer programs as well as online users.

Remote login is the ability to log in to another computer elsewhere. This can be valuable in many ways, such as permitting someone to use a program without transferring the program to that person's computer. The Internet's remote login service makes it possible for someone using one brand of computer to log into a computer of a different type.

Browsing services make it possible to look for information on remote computers. One Internet service that supports browsing is called gopher because it was developed at the University of Minnesota, whose football team is the gophers, and because *gofer* is a slang term for someone who does odd jobs on request. Gopher is a multi-level menu system. The user sees a menu, selects one item, and then sees another menu of choices related to that item. For example, the sequence of choices for finding information about a volleyball tournament at MIT might be universities (versus other options), Massachusetts (versus other states), MIT (versus other universities in

Massachusetts), athletic events (versus other choices at MIT). Having made all these choices, the user would receive information about the tournament only if someone at MIT had posted the information in the right place.

The Internet of the 1980s and early 1990s had characteristics that were adequate in many research and hobbyist environments, but quite unsuited to commercial environments, where many users would be unwilling or unable to learn a lot of computer system details that seem arbitrary. For example, someone interested in retrieving files offered by the Electronic Frontier Foundation would have to type

ftp ftp.eff.org.

Doing this would require that the person know that *ftp* performs file transfers, and also that the information could be accessed at the address *ftp.eff.org*.[4] Knowing the right commands was a small issue compared to the fact that the Internet gave the appearance of having no clear organization, and seemed to infrequent users more like a vast library without a usable catalog. The appearance was worse than the reality because many different Internet directories existed, but it remained awkward to find the directories unless a user knew where and how to look for them.

Commercial Online Services

As the Internet was developed to accomplish research and military goals in the 1980s and early 1990s, the idea of providing online services to consumers was starting to receive attention elsewhere. Developers of these services assumed consumers didn't think of what they wanted in terms of computer commands, such file transfers and remote logins, but rather, about user applications such as sending messages, shopping, and obtaining specific types of information.

The first extensive experience in this arena involved the French Minitel system, originally subsidized and developed to promote France's telecommunications infrastructure starting in the mid-1970s. It is the computer network with the most extensive history of penetration into consumer and commercial markets. As of 1993 it was by far the world's largest network of its type. It had around six million subscribers and provided 20,000 services. Around 50% of the French working population had access to it at home or at work. It could also be accessed in most of Western Europe. Its consumer services included entertainment and transportation schedules, classified ads, interactive games, home banking, home shopping, and comparative pricing. It had an estimated 95% penetration into businesses with more than 500 employees, and had significant impacts on some industries. For example, a telerouting system permitted trucking businesses to post drop-off schedules, thereby helping them find loads for trucks that would otherwise return home empty after the drop-off. Almost every French bank had a home banking system permitting customers to check account balances and pay utility bills. Many retailers had electronic catalog services that were expected to be used more actively as soon as the network could be used for direct payment. Travel agents, insurance companies, and firms in other industries provided other services.

Prodigy was one of the first American online services directed at the consumer market. Its original business concept looked to television and radio and borrowed the idea of displaying paid advertising as consumers moved toward the content they wanted. Prodigy offered its first service after three years of development, but was unsuccessful as an early online shopping mall. In 1992, Prodigy started charging for e-mail because many users were more interested in using it for e-mail than for shopping.

By the mid-1990s, Prodigy, Compuserve, America Online, and other commercial online services were competing in the consumer market by providing electronic mail, bulletin boards, access to news articles from newspapers and magazines, access to multi-party interactive games, access to financial databases, and even transaction oriented services such as purchasing airline tickets. Aside from its own unique mix of services, each competitor in this market had its own pricing structure. For example, Prodigy charged $15 per month with unlimited use, whereas America Online charged $10 per month for up to five hours of use, and $3.50 for each additional hour. By early 1995, America Online and CompuServe had 1.6 million paying accounts compared to Prodigy's 1.35 million.

The importance of the Internet for the online services in the near term future is reflected in the way Prodigy changed its strategy after failing to generate profits from online shopping and advertising. Its new strategy included updating its interface to the same look and feel as Microsoft Windows and Apple Macintosh, aggressively wooing outside content providers, and scrapping the proprietary technology that made it slow and inefficient to create content for Prodigy. It would switch instead to an open systems approach by using industry standards such as the hypertext markup language (HTML) used in the part of the Internet called the World Wide Web (discussed next). Moving even further in that direction, Prodigy's new operating philosophy is to be "totally intermingled with the Internet."[5] This strategy may not turn out to be distinctive, however, because the other online services also planned to expand access to the Internet.

The World Wide Web

First used in 1993, a part of the Internet called the World Wide Web made it more practical for consumers and other information users to access information provided on servers linked to the Internet. Previously the Internet's external appearance had been too technical and cumbersome for most occasional users to stomach. The World Wide Web had made it practical for infrequent users to retrieve product-related multimedia information using convenient point-and-click methods.

The World Wide Web organizes information into "pages." Authors of these pages set them up as hypertext, with links to other pages indicated by bold type. The key to accessing information through a sequence of pages is standardization of the components of those pages. The hypertext markup language that is interpreted by the browser software identifies specific elements such as the headline, byline, body of the text, graphic elements, and key words that link to other pages. An Internet user using software called a Web browser can click on any underlined word or phrase and to go automatically to the desired Web page. Consistent with the Internet's client-server architecture, the information on a Web page can be on any server attached to the Internet.

This type of capability makes it comparatively easy for a company to use the Internet for distributing anything from advertising to customer service information. The customer needing information accesses the company's home page, clicks to identify the type of information needed, and then reads it or downloads it. This approach can also be used to request specific information, subscribe to future information distributions, and even to purchase products. The information accessed through the World Wide Web can be any combination of text, images, and sound, although there is always the caveat that images and sound take longer to transmit. By September 1994 there were 3,223 home pages in the United States, most of which were set up by universities for distributing information to students and professors. Silicon Graphics, Digital Equipment, Alberto's Nightclub and Fresh Flowers were among the first companies to set up home pages to provide information for their customers.

The overnight success of the World Wide Web through early 1995 was based on the availability of browser software, much of which was given away free. A program called Mosaic was the first Web browser to enable even casual computer users to use point-and-click methods to tap into information available through the Internet. This program was originally developed at the University of Illinois, and later licensed to Spyglass, Inc. James Clark, founder of Silicon Graphics, a leading workstation manufacturer, later hired most of the Mosaic developers and established a new company called Netscape Communications. It quickly captured a majority of the browser "market" by downloading over three million copies of its Netscape Navigator software for free via the Internet. The company initially stated it hoped to make money by charging between $1,500 and $2,000 per server for the software an information provider would need to link servers into the Internet.[6] This strategy could certainly change and Netscape and its competitors could charge fees as new browsers are developed.

Security Concerns

Although the Internet has great potential for distributing information, highly publicized security flaws have raised questions about whether it could serve as a reliable electronic shopping mall of the future. The Internet's basic mission is to provide connections between millions of computers linked to thousands of computer networks. What prevents unauthorized uses that steal information during transmission, that sabotage computers on the network, or that even steal information stored in those computers? These risks are not as far fetched as one might hope. Two highly publicized incidents involve the Internet worm that penetrated 6,000 computers in 1988 (see Chapter 2) and the Clifford Stoll's sleuth work in tracking down a spy who used the Internet to break into the University of California's computers from Germany.

A more recent example was the early 1995 arrest of Kevin Mitnick, a convicted computer felon who had been on the run from Federal law enforcement officials since November, 1992. The great media attention to this event stemmed partially from the way his capture seemed to end a cyberspace duel between himself and Tsutornu Shimomura, a computer security expert whose home computer in San Diego Mitnick had broken into on Christmas Day, 1994. After working for six weeks starting with traces of Mitnick's break-in, Shimomura determined that Mitnick was operating through a computer modem connected to a cellular telephone somewhere near Raleigh, North Carolina. He was present when the FBI apprehended Mitnick shortly thereafter in North Carolina.[7]

A less publicized aspect of this story is the fact that Mitnick's escapades had nearly destroyed the Well, a small online service near San Francisco that had around 11,000 users. Mitnick had penetrated into the Well, had read confidential e-mail messages of its subscribers, and was using accounts there as camouflage for attacks on computers across the Internet. After these activities were discovered, Well officials permitted Mitnick to continue so that investigators could monitor and capture him. The last time he logged in he erased all of the Well's accounting records, although Well officials concluded Mitnick had actually done this through an accidental typing error.[8]

The investigation also found that Mitnick had stolen 20,000 credit-card numbers from Netcom On-Line Communication Service, Inc., a company that provides Internet link-ups to 90,000 customers. Netcom officials said that they discovered someone had tampered with their computers several weeks earlier, but hadn't realized the credit-card data had been stolen until the Well discovered those files stored on its computers. The director of technology assessment for MasterCard International, Inc. said "It's very unsettling. We wouldn't use the Internet as it is today to conduct electronic commerce." At the time, MasterCard was working with Netscape Communications Corp. to develop a secure payment system for online traffic. Visa International was working on a similar effort with Microsoft.[9]

Just a few days after Mitnick was captured, the Wall Street Journal reported a security problem in the Mosaic software that first made the World Wide Web broadly accessible. The flaw was in the server software (rather than the browser software for the users), which incorrectly allowed a computer to run command strings that are too long, thereby allowing an intruder to sneak in an extra line of damaging commands that the server would not catch. Exploiting this flaw might permit hackers to gain control of these servers and then access or destroy information they contain. The University of Illinois group in charge of Mosaic quickly generated a software patch that verifies the length of command strings, and said that no known security breaches have occurred as a result of the problem. However, the mere fact that the details of the flaw were publicized probably increased the short term threat.[10]

The many break-ins and other security problems that have occurred thus far with the Internet demonstrate some of the risks of linking to it. Many firms have tried to reduce the danger using what are called firewalls, computers that intercept incoming transmissions and check them for dangerous content. One company even adopted the stance that incoming transmissions would be copied onto a diskette that would then be moved to another computer that would check it for viruses. Maneuvers like this might reduce the risk, but they also reduce the effectiveness of a networked environment.

The mere process of downloading information across the Internet may entail hidden risks. For example, when a graphics file is downloaded to a PC, the server basically seizes a portion of the PC's hard disk and deposits data in it. As this is happening, what prevents it from obtaining more information, such as the size of the hard disk or the type of word processor that is available? This type of snooping might seem unethical, but it has occurred. For example, the electronic registration form Central Point Software included with its PC Tools for Windows automatically collected the type of microprocessor being used, the version of DOS and Windows, the type of display and mouse, and the amount of free space on the computer's hard disk. Some of Central Point's customers complained after discovering a small file on their hard disks containing this information. Central Point said it was registration software developed by another company and was not aware of the snooping function. Although the Central Point situation seems not to have caused harm, it also leads one to wonder whether people browsing through home pages on the World Wide Web may open themselves up for being browsed.[11]

How Might the Internet Overcome Obstacles to a Commercial Future?

The powerful trend toward a networked society has many components, starting with the fact that use of online networks is exploding. Millions of people have used networks for business and personal uses. E-mail is becoming commonplace in leading businesses and universities. Electronic bulletin boards are used for purposes ranging from answering customer service inquiries to exchanging views about personal topics and politics. Many corporations are linked for electronic transactions using EDI systems. Reinforcing these trends, hardware and software suppliers are building network capabilities into their products. Modems are becoming standard, built-in features of personal computers. Operating systems such as Windows 95 contain built-in networking capabilities presented in a format much more palatable than the older generation of interfaces that required command languages and attention to grammar.

Looking specifically at the role of the Internet, many observers see the World Wide Web as an important turning point for commercial opportunities because it has made the Internet so much more accessible to non-technical users. A number of obstacles are apparent, however, when one looks at the possibility that the Internet will become an electronic shopping mall and a major source of product and company information in the future. These are related to organization, security, online performance, freedom and control, competition, and flash versus substance.

organization: Based on the way it has evolved, the Internet lacks the type of clear organization that would make it easy to use as an electronic shopping mall or as an information source. Although the Internet's former appearance was daunting and unfriendly, however, the advent of multimedia

browsers has made it far easier to use and sometimes even enjoyable.

security: The many break-ins and other security problems that have occurred thus far with the Internet demonstrate some of the risks of linking to it. Many firms have tried to reduce the danger using what are called firewalls, computers that intercept incoming transmissions and check them for dangerous content. One company even adopted the stance that incoming transmissions would be copied onto a diskette that would then be moved to another computer that would check it for viruses. Maneuvers like this might reduce the risk, but they also reduce the effectiveness of a networked environment. On the other hand, many observers believe that effective use of encryption and firewall techniques could eliminate much of the risk related to unauthorized access and data theft.

online performance: Current modems and phone lines limit data transmission rates and therefore make multimedia communication through the Internet less attractive. However, some cable companies had already started providing Internet access, and the trend toward deregulating telecommunications may imply that data rates will become a much less important restriction in the near future.

freedom versus control: The Internet's history includes many incidents that raise issues about freedom and control. E-mail messages, postings to bulletin boards, and other forms of electronic distribution of information have raised most of the common issues about free speech, such as false advertising, libel, racism, pornography, and promotion of violence. Legislation has been proposed related to criminal penalties for transmitting pornography through networks. There have even been issues about whether various forms of advertising are permissible on the Internet, as evidenced by the enormous furor when two immigration lawyers used e-mail to post an advertisement for their services on thousands of usergroups. Although the Internet has been unregulated in the past, it is possible that future events will result in legislation or other controls limiting the Internet's role in commerce.

competition or cooperation with online services: The rapid growth of the World Wide Web raises serious questions about the business model used by online services such as Prodigy, America Online, and Compuserve. These services need links to the Internet to provide global e-mail service, but also need to differentiate themselves by providing content that other online services do not provide. Linking more extensively to the Internet could help them provide more services, but could also reduce the public's ability to see them as separate from the Internet.

flash versus substance: Although surfing the Net was enticing to hobbyists, in fact the Internet may not provide the substance that makes it valuable for shopping and commercial information access, rather than e-mail and bulletin boards. For example, an early 1995 article questioning the business opportunities with the Internet claimed that more money was being made writing books about the Internet than by selling products and services using the Internet directly. It seemed that users of the Internet were more interested in looking than in buying.[12] The author of a letter responding to that article said there is no way he would allow unbridled access to it in a business because it would be like putting a television on every desk.[13] Whether the great potential of the Internet will prevail over these skeptical views remains to be seen. Almost no one would have anticipated the rapid developments stemming from the World Wide Web, and it is highly likely that today's users and providers will invent new ways of using the Internet that would be difficult to anticipate today.

Questions

1. If you have access to the World Wide Web, log in and find a specific piece of information that is important to you (or explain why you couldn't find something important). Estimate how much you would be willing to spend for that information if it were not available for free.

2. Assume you owned a distribution business that sold music CDs and were considering advertising by placing a home page on the World Wide Web.

    a. What do you think the advertisement would look like to a potential customer if you could only use text ? If you could use text and graphics? Full multimedia including sound and video?

    b. Explain what you believe would be the steps in the entire process of creating and placing the advertisement.

    c. Assume one person in the firm was in charge of all advertising and marketing work. What percentage of that person's effort do you think you would allocate to the following four areas: magazine and newspaper advertising, direct mail using the postal service, advertising through the World Wide Web, and marketing through alliances with other businesses? (The percents should add up to 100 to indicate the relative allocation for each area.)

    d. Explain why you probably would or wouldn't want to advertise by placing a home page on the World Wide Web.

3. Explain how your answer to the four parts of question #1 would be different if your business were: an auto dealership, a university, a medical clinic, a gourmet food store.

4. Assuming the following capabilities were available to you through the Internet, which do you think you would use if they were available for free? How much would you be willing to pay to use such capabilities? Which capabilities do you think you would not use even if they were free? (Give reasons for your answers.)
- electronic mail
- purchasing airline reservations
- bulletin board about automobiles or other topics of interest
- downloading books or movies
- reading a daily newspaper.

5. Explain why you do or do not believe the Internet should be regulated by the U.S. government, even if it does not receive government funding.

References

1. Churbuck, David C. "Where's the Money?" Forbes, Jan. 30, 1995, pp. 100-107.
2. Rapaport, Richard. "Digitizing Desire," Forbes ASAP, Apr. 10, 1995, pp. 66-76.
3. Comer, Douglas E. The Internet Book, Englewood Cliffs, NJ: Prentice-Hall, 1994.
4. Tetzeli, Rick. "The Internet and Your Business," Fortune, Mar. 7, 1994, pp. 86-96.
5. Eng, Paul M. "Prodigy Is in that Awkward Stage," Business Week, Feb. 13, 1995, pp. 90-91.
6. Lewis, Peter. "Netscape Knows Fame and Aspires to Fortune," New York Times, Mar. 1, 1995, p. C1.
7. Markoff, John. "A Most-Wanted Cyberthief Is Caught in His Own Web," New York Times, Feb. 16, 1995, p. A1.
8. Markoff, John. "Hacker Case Underscores Internet's Vulnerability," New York Times, Feb. 17, 1995, p. C1.
9. Sandberg, Jared. "Undetected Theft of Credit-Card Data Raises Concern about On-Line Security," Wall Street Journal, Feb. 17, 1995, p. B10.
10. Sandberg, Jared. "Internet Web Found to Have Security Lapse." Wall Street Journal, Feb. 21, 1995, p. B3.
11. Hutheesing, Nikhil. "Big Modem Is Watching," *Forbes,* Feb. 13, 1995, p. 186.
12. Churbuck, op. cit.
13. *Forbes.* "Internet: fans and flames," Feb. 27, 1995, p.128.

Resumix, Inc.:
Automation of Résumé Processing

DID **YOU EVER WONDER** what happens when a job applicant sends a résumé to a large company that has placed an advertisement in a newspaper? Who actually looks at it? If 100 résumés arrive on the same day, how do they decide which applicants to interview? If a similar job opening occurs three months later, how does the company find the many applicants who are still interested, regardless of whether they see the next newspaper advertisement?

While an engineering manager at TRW's artificial intelligence research center in northern California, Steve Leung saw these issues from a different viewpoint. He was totally frustrated by the responses he was getting when he called job applicants who had submitted their résumés in response to TRW's advertised job openings. The problem was that the best applicants were no longer available by the time he called them. When he went to the human resources department to complain, he found four people sitting there reading résumés from weeks-old piles.

A year later, in 1988, he founded Resumix, a company devoted to solving problems related to the processing of résumés. He received initial funding in the form of purchase orders from Sun Microsystems and Advanced Micro Devices, and later received an additional $2.5 million in venture capital.

A New Way to Process Résumés

The traditional approach for processing résumés and matching them to requisitions for new employees was slow and paper intensive. The human resources department received and processed however many résumés job applicants sent, mostly in response to a job posting or newspaper ad. The résumés were date-stamped and passed on to the internal recruiters who coded the résumés, categorized them by job grouping, and filed them. Individual recruiters sometimes did this for several hundred résumés in a day.

Matching the résumés to job requisitions was also very paper intensive, with the recruiter identifying the résumés that seemed appropriate for a particular job requisition, copying those résumés, and forwarding them to the hiring managers for review. They then tracked the results manually to see what happened with each résumé and whether letters were sent to the applicants either setting up an interview or thanking the applicants for their interest and telling them their résumés would remain on file for subsequent review. These manual processes were often so slow and paper intensive that neither the hiring managers nor the applicants were satisfied with the results. The human resources professionals often felt overwhelmed in paper and frustrated that they couldn't provide better service.

With the Resumix system, which is in use at many major companies, universities, and government organizations, résumé processing is performed quite differently. The first step is to capture the résumé in electronic form using a scanner if it has come in by mail or by fax. Next, an optical character recognition program finds the text in these images. The OCR software can find this information regardless of the résumé's format, font, or style.

A patented program analyzes the text to extract key résumé information and then inputs that information into an applicant database. The information in the résumé summary includes name, addresses, telephone numbers, degrees, schools, grade point averages, and work history, including dates, companies, job titles, and up to 80 skills. With high-volume optical scanners, it is possible to scan and process up to 2,000 pages a day per scanner.

Searching for eligible applicants is easy once the applicant data is in the applicant database. The recruiter or manager simply identifies skill and experience criteria and clicks on a search button. Resumix responds with a prioritized list of qualified candidates for review. Instead of looking through a large number of résumés, the recruiter or manager examines only the résumés of the applicants who fit reasonably well based on the criteria given. Based on the results of a search, the manager will either be satisfied enough to start calling the current "short list" of candidates or may choose to sharpen the categories and do another search. Since searching even a 100,000 applicant database takes only seconds because of the way the database is organized, it is easy to do several iterations to find the best applicants.

The most distinctive aspect of Resumix is the way it converts the scanned image into data in a structured database. Although many current OCR systems can identify the text in a scanned image, it is far more difficult to convert that text into data items that fit in a preformatted database. Resumix does this using a knowledge base of over 85,000 rules and concepts defining skill terms and phrases, abbreviations, acronyms, and even common misspellings. After working for years developing this knowledge base in cooperation with its clients, Resumix, Inc. claims that the product contains the most extensive library of recruitment-and industry-specific terminology in existence, and that this provides the most thorough and accurate extraction of information from résumés. The knowledge base also contains comprehensive data on universities, degrees, majors, corporations, and industries. This makes it possible to identify candidates from specific schools, with specific educational backgrounds, employment backgrounds, and employment histories at specific companies.

Three notable software capabilities within Resumix include résumé blocking, context-sensitive recognition, and automatic categorization. Resume blocking is the ability to recognize discrete blocks of résumé text that deal with the common categories of résumé information, such as biographical, educational, and experiential. For example, Resumix can determine whether the word *Berkeley* is being used as an applicant's address, name, school, or employer. Context-sensitive recognition recognizes identifiers within discrete blocks of text. For example, it can make the distinction between having an MBA and working toward an MBA. Automatic categorization permits Resumix to assign an individual to as many as six professional categories based on skills and experience in the résumé.

Resumix operates using a client/server architecture with a UNIX server that supports a wide range of client desktops, including workstations, IBM-compatible PCs, x-terminals, and Macintosh. Because it supports multitasking, the UNIX server can run multiple processes such as scanning, skills extraction, and printing while executing multiple desktop processes such as report-writing or database query. Additional capabilities include a Windows 3.1 interface, capabilities to access the organization's other human resources databases, and capabilities to extract and write data from Resumix into SQL databases for data analysis, summarization, and reporting.

Typical Applications

National Semiconductor

National Semiconductor, which employs over 25,000 people worldwide, receives over 50,000 résumés each year. When a position opened before Resumix was available, an internal recruiter often spent days, or sometimes weeks, sorting through hundreds of color-coded files to find applicants who seemed worthy of an interview. National has used Resumix since 1989 and has built a database of 84,000 résumés. Now, a manager can get an immediate response to a request such as "a person with an MBA but not a PhD. who speaks English and Japanese and has 10 years of semiconductor experience." Once the résumé of a qualified applicant is on the screen, a recruiter can send it to the hiring manager by e-mail or fax. Resumix has helped the human resources department reduce its hiring cycle from over 100 days to fewer than 50, has helped it find better employees, and has helped it process more work using its existing staff.

Vanguard Group

The Vanguard Group is a mutual fund company with over 4,000 employees. In 1992, its human resources department analyzed the company's hiring system and found that approximately 8,400 hours were required to log in, sort, and circulate the 21,000 résumés it received that year. The analysis also showed that thousands of dollars were spent on recruitment advertising because staff were unable to locate résumés already in-house.

The company installed Resumix, and by 1994 résumés were logged in and processed 75 percent more quickly than in 1992. Incoming résumés are scanned, matched to existing needs, and routed to the appropriate manager in 24 hours. Several recruiters can simultaneously review the same résumé, and résumés are kept alive indefinitely instead of disappearing into file cabinets never to be found again.

The ability to perform automatic screening of résumés that do not fit desired job profiles has been a great boon to the human resources group, whose productivity has increased because the staff does not have to personally read all the résumés the company receives each year.

The system has other advantages as well. Fewer résumés are lost, and less human error occurs in overlooking important qualifications. The system can automatically generate rejection letters and invitations to come for an interview. In addition, the system helps circumvent discrimination in the screening process because race and religion are unlikely to be coded into the system's rejection process.

United Parcel Service Airlines

With 11,500 employees, United Parcel Service Airlines is the largest private employer in Kentucky. Rapid matching of people's skills with job opportunities is vital because the company receives around 30,000 résumés a year and because the company has a very strong policy of promoting from within.

Until mid-1993, the company had five separate employment functions in Louisville. With the existing manual system for handling résumés the hiring cycle was too long, and it was difficult to track the disposition of a résumé or the status of a job application. There was also an embarrassing duplication of efforts, such as when a recruiter called applicants who already had been hired elsewhere in the company.

After installing Resumix, the human resources department processed almost 3,000 résumés in a few days after 145 new job openings were announced. In addition, new uses of the system were soon invented, such as smoothing the job transfer process for 5,000 union employees in Louisville. With 29 different work assignments, a contract allowing employees up to two transfers per year, and giving preference based on seniority, the job transfer system prior to Resumix was paperwork nightmare. With Resumix, the human resources department could immediately identify the union workers bidding for any job.

Extensions of the Original Idea

As new technologies are implemented and used, system participants often find new uses that may not have been imagined initially. Resumix is no exception. Extensions of the original idea include reverse matching, uses for in-placement, integration with larger human resources systems, uses for regulatory reporting, and links to internal communication systems.

The idea of reverse matching is to start with the candidate and look for openings rather than start with the openings and look for candidates. For example, applicants looking for a job at Motorola's new plant in Bathgate, Scotland, can fax a résumé to the human resources department, which uses Resumix to see whether the applicant is qualified for any current openings. Resumix can then generate letters inviting the applicant to come for an interview or saying "thanks, but no thanks."

The same idea has been applied for in-placement of both current employees who want to switch jobs for career advancement and current employees whose jobs are being eliminated in downsizing or reengineering efforts. In both cases, the employee initiates a search that looks for openings within the firm.

Uses for in-placement raise questions about the degree to which Resumix is integrated with other human resources systems within the firm. In an example moving in that direction, Bell Atlantic uses Resumix to keep a record of all staff qualifications and job vacancies, current and prospective, and to match people with opportunities. Because job details as well as staff qualifications are on the database, employees can pick up a touch-tone phone, dial their employee identification number, and the system guides them through all the current vacancies for which they are qualified. This type of use supports staff morale in difficult downsizing situations because the staff may feel it is more likely that they can find other positions within a large organization even if their own position is eliminated.

Resumix has potential applicants in regulatory reporting because it can create a history of which résumés were received, which searches were performed, and who was hired. This information can help the company prepare reports that demonstrate Equal Employment Opportunity compliance.

Since the résumés are digitized, linking Resumix to internal communication systems is an ideal way to transmit résumés to hiring managers. To move further in that direction, Resumix, Inc. established an alliance with Lotus Development Corporation related to linking Resumix with Lotus Notes, a leading groupware package that can be used to distribute job requisitions and résumés.

Impacts and Limitations

Resumix has generated significant benefits related to speedier processing of résumés and more effective use of information related to job openings and applicant qualifications. The types of jobs for which it is most effective involve specific technical knowledge or skills.

Resumix also has potential effects on job applicants. Since the résumés are processed and screened by computer, the effort of producing a distinctive résumé may become less effective. Resumix has not gone unnoticed by résumé-writing services, some of which have had to adapt their work to make résumés more likely to be selected in automatic screening processes. Since Resumix is usually used to find specific facts and skills rather than intentions, résumés that will be read by Resumix should highlight specific experience and skills.

Questions

1. Explain the ways Resumix changes the processing of résumés.

2. Explain how Resumix expanded from a résumé processing system toward a more general employee information system.

3. Explain the impact of Resumix on human resources departments.

4. Explain the impact of Resumix on internal and external job applicants.

5. Explain whether you believe people who work in human resources departments should be worried that Resumix will automate their work.

6. Explain whether you believe future extensions of Resumix might hire people automatically.

7. Assume the company is primarily concerned with matching résumés to job requisitions. How should the company perform the economic analysis to decide whether to purchase Resumix?

8. Does anything surprise you about Resumix's capabilities? Which of its capabilities would increase the usefulness of other computerized systems you are familiar with?

References

Dyson, Esther. "What to Do with That Stack of Résumés." *Forbes*, Oct. 15, 1990, p. 200.

Greengard, Samuel. "New Technology in HR's Route to Reengineering." *Personnel Journal*, July 1994.

Howe, Kenneth. "Firm Turns Hiring into a Science." *San Francisco Chronicle*, Sept. 19, 1992, pp. B1–B2.

Odom, Maida. "Words Perfect: Optical Scanners Are the New Corporate Gate Keepers." *Philadelphia Inquirer*, June 14, 1994.

Resumix, Inc. *Reengineering the Workforce with Human Skills Management: An Executive Briefing.* Marketing brochure, 1994.

The Denver International Airport: Baggage System Blues

ORIGINALLY SCHEDULED TO OPEN on October 31, 1993, the new Denver International Airport (DIA) was to be the first major airport opened in the United States since the Dallas-Fort Worth Airport opened in 1974. The new airport was designed to support projected air travel increases well into the next century and would be one of the world's largest. Six times larger than the 65 year old Stapleton Airport on the edge of downtown, DIA would cost more than $3.2 billion, and would be financed largely on bonds sold to private investors. Twice the size of Manhattan, it would cover 53 square miles of prairie 23 miles northeast of Denver. Major airlines such as United and Continental would each have separate terminals. It would have five parallel 12,000 foot runways, permitting 1,750 planes to take off and land every day. The facility would be able to handle 99 landings an hour in bad weather, an increase over the maximum of 25 per hour at Stapleton.[1]

On May 2, 1994, Denver's mayor, Wellington Webb, announced that DIA would miss its fourth publicly announced deadline by failing to open on May 15. The airport was already more than $1 billion over budget, and further delays would cost around $1 million per day. At this point, the mayor was unwilling to "hazard a guess" about when the airport would open. A number of problems had caused delays, but most of the public attention was directed at a state-of-the-art, $193 million baggage handling system that was not yet operational.

The initial trials of the new baggage handling system were a public relations nightmare. Although system developers typically assume that complex systems will have bugs in their first tests, in March, Denver officials had invited the news media to attend an initial test of the baggage handling system. It was not a pretty sight. The system smashed bags together, tore them apart, and even sliced one in half. The second-to-second synchronization required to direct thousands of bags to their destinations automatically on separate baggage cars was more difficult than anyone had imagined it would be. The software had not been debugged totally. There were also additional problems related to seemingly simple but troublesome issues such as power surges and dirt on the sensors resulting in false readings.

Gene Di Fonso, President of Dallas-based BAE Automated Systems, which built the system, saw himself becoming a media star against his wishes after defending the company on television talk shows. He said the airport's failure to open on March 8, its third deadline, was not BAE's fault. His main arguments were that Denver officials kept changing their plans, left too little time for testing, failed to fix electrical flaws, and then turned the whole system over to inexperienced managers. City officials only partly denied his version of the story.[2]

The Baggage System

DIA's baggage system was designed to meet the needs of an enormous airport with three main concourses, one of which is a mile away from the terminal. The system's goal was to move luggage between the terminal and the gate in 10 minutes, usually before the passengers could go this distance. Speed was especially important to United Airlines, which saw DIA as a showcase hub where planes could land, transfer passengers and baggage, and take off quickly. To meet its business goals, it wanted to move luggage between any two gates on its 3,300-foot-long concourse B in 6 minutes.[3] This level of performance would help it compete in today's airline industry, where minimizing the time a plane sits on the ground is an important determinant of profits.

Although BAE was the world leader in baggage systems, the DIA system was a special challenge because it moved the company into largely uncharted waters. BAE had installed systems for individual airlines in many major airports, but had not installed an integrated system to serve an entire airport and move bags between airlines. Most of its previous systems had been based on conveyor belts, but this system used a Telecar system, which resembled a computer controlled railroad with an individual fiberglass car for each piece of luggage. The system could meet the airport's projected load of up to 150,000 bags per day by moving luggage to its destination in 10 minutes. A similar system used only by United Airlines at the San Francisco Airport had less than a tenth of the new system's capacity. In addition to size, the DIA system brought a number of firsts. It was the first baggage system anywhere in which the cars only slowed down but did not stop to pick up and drop off bags. It was the first run by a network of PCs rather than a mainframe computer, the first to use radio links, and the first with a subsystem for oversized bags, such as skis.[4]

The Telecar system has 6 miles of conveyor belts, 22 miles of tracks, and 10,000 motors propelling 4,000 cars up to 20 miles per hour, five times faster than a conveyor belt. The Telecar system identifies the bag in the car using either photocells or bar codes printed at the check-in counter and attached to the bags. It scans the bar code or photocell every 150 to 200 feet in the bag's progress toward its destination and uses that identification information to look up the gate the bag is moving toward. When the bag arrives at the gate, a computer gives the order to tip it onto the conveyor belt for that gate or baggage carousel. Although this might not sound too difficult for an individual car, synchronizing 4,000 cars moving up to 20 miles per hour turned out to be a difficult challenge.

The computer system that controls the Telecar system was designed as a distributed network. Its technical configuration was originally based on 18 486 33-MHz PCs from Texas Microsystems, each running under version 2.0 of OS/2. The PCs were in eight control rooms where routing decisions for different sections of track were made. The PCs sent commands to 92 programmable logic controllers (PLCs), which controlled the motors and track switches to shunt cars to their proper places. The baggage system operated on its own fiber-optic network, which sits apart from another fiber-optic FDDI network that acts as a backbone for the airports client/server systems.[5, 6] The heart of the control system is a complex program called the Empty Car Management System, which dispatches empty cars to any input point where they are needed. It also coordinates the flow of cars to ensure that empty queues of cars are replenished in time for arriving bags. This program was written over 2 years by 20 programmers.[7]

Problems

Unfortunately, the routing subsystem turned out to be more complicated than anyone had anticipated. During public trials, cars crashed into each other at intersections or dumped the baggage in the wrong locations. Sometimes cars were sent out too early or too late, resulting in too much time sitting empty instead of being where they were needed. To fix these software problems, programmers wrote new logic for both the OS/2-based car-routing application and the PLCs that carry out the commands. The software for establishing communication with United's reservation system also contained many bugs that had to be fixed.

Other problems occurred in the physical environment. Smudged bar codes caused two thirds of the bags in one test to be shunted off to a special area for sorting by hand. Some optical sensors became coated with dirt or knocked out of alignment, and therefore could not detect cars going by. Faulty latches caused cars to dump luggage on the track between stops or become jammed against the side of the tunnel.[8] Even jams due to incorrect loading of garment bags caused problems.

In September 1993, BAE also noticed that power surges were tripping circuit breakers that shut down the system's motors. Delays in ordering special filters to maintain an even power supply resulted in delays in testing the system, which in turn contributed to the embarrassing results of early tests.

Project Background

The problems and delays in 1994 received a great deal of publicity and generated a lot of fingerpointing. The project had been approved by the voters in 1989, with a projected completion date of October 1994. Federico Pena, who was then mayor, decided to move up the opening date to 1993 to hasten construction.[9]

According to Mr. Di Fonso, United originally contacted BAE in the fall of 1991 to build a baggage system just for that airline. He says United was concerned that the airport project had been going on for several years, but the city had not yet contracted for a baggage system. Ginger Evans, DIA's former chief engineer said that the airport had expected each airline to build its own baggage system but that only United came forward with plans. Mr. Di Fonso says that the city then decided that an integrated baggage system for the entire airport would be more efficient but that none of the 16 companies contacted would even make a bid on the project because there was not enough time to complete it before the deadline. (Evans says three companies actually did bid but that their designs would not meet the airport's needs.) Technical advisors to Munich, Germany's new airport agreed there was not enough time. That airport had an automated baggage system far less complex than Denver's, yet they had spent two years just testing the system, which had been operating 24 hours per day for six months before that airport opened.

In early 1992, the city asked BAE to build the integrated baggage system. Di Fonso says BAE accepted the project with the proviso that BAE would be given top priority for access to any part of the airport and that there would be specific freeze dates for mechanical design, software design, permanent power requirements, and other details that had to operate together. The plans did change, however. United decided to reduce its costs $20 million by going from two tracks to one, Continental requested a larger baggage link, and outside stations were relocated. Other problems that delayed construction or testing of the baggage system included overloaded motors due to faulty power supplies and radio transmission dead spots that prevented ongoing communication between engineers working in the terminal and in the concourses. Evans argued that the construction was actually completed by the summer of 1993 and that programming problems caused most of the delays.[10] Larry Port, the testing manager for BAE in Denver, saw the basic problem differently, saying "This kind of system normally takes three and a half years to build, and we were asked to do it in two. We hadn't completed the debugging."[11]

DIA Opens

In August 1994, the city of Denver announced that it would spend about $50 million to build an alternative baggage handling system to serve as fall-back for the automated system, thereby assuring the airport would open by February 28, 1995. The alternative system used conventional carts like those used in most airports. In its first public split with the city over a major airport issue, United Airlines opposed the decision to build the alternative system. Observers suspected the disagreement could end up in court because the contract between United and the city specifies the airport would open with a functioning automated baggage system. At the time, United was not sure whether the alternative system would move bags fast enough to meet its needs.[12]

In October 1994, United Airlines was designated as the systems integrator in charge of fixing the baggage system. United's initial suggestions involved reducing the load on the individual computers that control the cars. As many as 60 cars were on a track at a given time, and United planned to cut that to 30 by adding new tracks and reducing the number of cars per track. At the time, there was still uncertainty about when the work could start because of disputes between the city of Denver and BAE about payment of delay costs. Denver mayor Wellington Webb urged BAE to work with United to repair the automated baggage system for United's concourse B and to permit use of the alternative baggage systems to make the February 28, 1995 opening feasible.[13]

The airport finally did open on February 28, 1995, 16-months late and $2 billion over budget. The baggage handling system performed adequately except for some soiled luggage. During that day, three jetliners landed simultaneously in bad weather, something possible nowhere else in the world. Boosters of the airport thought it was great, but detractors still wondered whether it was absolutely necessary to build a new airport so far from downtown, more than doubling the cab fare to $35 and adding three quarters of an hour to skiers' trips to the mountains. United and other major airlines serving Denver announced that airfare into and out of Denver would increase an average of $20 each way, in part because the landing fee per passenger was $18, up from $6 at the old Stapleton Airport.[14] Whether the high hopes for the airport will be realized eventually remains to be seen.

Questions

1. Assume a version of this case appeared in a newspaper with the heading "Computer problems delay multi-billion dollar airport." Identify facts of the case that support this headline, and other facts that make it seem misleading. Suggest a single headline that you think would be both balanced and informative.

2. Use the traditional system life cycle as a model to outline what happened and what went wrong. Identify any additional insights from the prototype and packaged-system life cycles.

3. Assume you were managing the baggage system after it went into operation. What measures of performance would you monitor?

4. Explain the significance of infrastructure, context, and risk issues in this case.

5. Assume you were the mayor of a city contemplating a new airport or other major project. How do you think you would obtain a realistic estimate of how long the project would take and how much it would cost?

References

1. Johnson, Dirk. "Denver Delays Opening of Airport Indefinitely." *New York Times*, May 3, 1994, p. A9.
2. Myerson, Allen R. "Automation Off Course in Denver." *New York Times*, Mar. 18, 1994, p. C1.
3. Rifkin, Glenn. "What Really Happened at Denver's Airport." *Forbes ASAP*, Aug. 29, 1994, pp. 111–114.
4. Myerson, Allen R. "Automation Off Course."
5. Scheier, Robert L. "Software Snafu Grounds Denver's High-Tech Airport." *PC Week*, May 16, 1994, p. 1, 11.
6. Bozman, Jean S. "Denver Airport Hits System Layover," *Computerworld*, May 16, 1994, p. 30.
7. Rifkin, Glenn. "What Really Happened." *Forbes ASAP*, Aug. 29, 1994, pp. 111-114.
8. Scheier, Robert L. "Software Snafu." *PC Week*, May 16, 1994, p. 1, 11.
9. Johnson, Dirk, "Denver Delays Opening." *New York Times*, May 3, 1994, p. A9.
10. Rifkin, Glenn. "What Really Happened." *Forbes ASAP*, Aug. 29, 1994, pp. 111-114.
11. Bartholomew, Doug. "Rocky Start for Airport." *Information Week*, Mar. 21, 1995, p. 15.
12. Charlier, Marj. "Denver to Build Backup System for Luggage." *Wall Street Journal*, Aug. 5, 1994, p. A6.
13. Bozman, Jean S. "United to Simplify Denver's Troubled Baggage Project." *Computerworld*, Oct. 10, 1994.
14. Ayres, B. Drummond, Jr., "Finally, 16 Months Late, Denver Has a New Airport." *New York Times*, Mar. 1, 1995, p. A8.

The Wellington Education Board: Converting to a New Payroll System

Written by Michael Myers. Originally published in James Sheffield, et al. Australian and New Zealand Cases in Information Systems. *Auckland, New Zealand: Pagination Publishers, 1992. Reprinted by permission of Michael Myers and Addison-Wesley Publishing Company.*

GRAHM WILSON, THE GENERAL MANAGER of the Wellington Education Board, was starting to panic. Payday for the board's hundreds of teachers was just two days away, and the new payroll system was turning out to be "a complete and utter shambles." Wilson feared that in 48 hours time he would be inundated with complaints from teachers who found that they had the wrong pay or none at all. What was worse, they would probably hold the board and Wilson responsible.

Wilson's payroll staff had spent many long hours preparing for the introduction of the New Zealand Education Department's new centralized payroll system. The board had just received the processed pay slips from the new centralized computer system only to find that a lot of data his staff had submitted had been omitted or wrongly punched in. Board staff now had to re-check each teacher's pay slip before mailing them to schools. Both of these tasks were made more difficult by the fact that the slips had arrived from the Education Department in one large batch, sorted in alphabetical order, by surname. The pay slips would have to be manually sorted by school before they could be checked and delivered to the waiting teachers.

Wilson was furious. In the newspapers, he pleaded for calm from teachers who found they had no pay or the wrong pay on Wednesday, February 10, the first pay day for 1993.

The Education Department, a government department based in Wellington, had decided to introduce a new centralized payroll system. All payroll processing would be done in Wellington, processing over 50,000 per fortnight [every two weeks]. Previously, the payroll processing for pre-school, primary, secondary, and technical institute teachers had been done manually by 28 separate salary units, the largest ones being the regional education boards.

The new system, when fully complete, would allow for each of the 28 salary units to input salary data directly into the Education Department's system. For most of 1993, however, it was planned that all data would be entered at the Education Department's head office in Wellington. Each of the 28 salary centers, which had previously done all the payroll processing themselves, would have to send details of each teacher's pay to the Education Department for input to the computer system. The pay details for each teacher would include data such as appointments, promotions, resignations, and transfers.

Malcolm McDonald, the Education Department's Director of Management Services, believed that the new system would save the government "millions" of dollars. The system would eliminate pre-holiday payments covering 10 weeks over the summer holidays, and three to four weeks in May and August, saving "huge amounts" of interest lost to the government. Under the previous system, employees received all their holiday pay by check, which saved the employees from having to come into the office during the holidays. Under the new system, employees would be paid fortnightly regardless of holidays, and money could be directly credited to a bank account.

The First Pay Day for 1993

Wednesday, February 10, was supposed to be the first pay day for teachers for 1993. This would be the teacher's first pay since holiday packets had gone out to teachers in December of the previous year.

Unfortunately, a lot of data which had been submitted by the salary centers of the Education Department for processing had been omitted or incorrectly keyed in, which meant that staff in all 28 salary centers had to re-check the pay slips before mailing them to schools. The Education Department offered to make extra staff available and approved the use of couriers to get pay slips to schools on time.

Thousands of teachers found that they had been paid incorrectly, and hundreds did not get paid at all. The regional education boards found themselves in the firing line for complaints from teachers. In Auckland, for example, the board's payroll staff fielded telephone calls from agitated teachers who had been unable to meet financial commitments when their salary did not arrive. The Auckland board called for the resignation of Malcolm McDonald, the man in charge of the computer changeover.

By Friday, February 12, the updated pay details for teachers would have to be sent to the Education Department for processing in Wellington; thus, salary staff in the regional education boards now had just two days to correct errors before the next fortnight's pay run.

The Second Pay Day for 1993

Wednesday, February 24, the second pay day for 1993, was not an easy day for any of the 28 salary units. In Auckland, for example, at least 100 primary school teachers found they had not been paid at all. As an emergency measure, Auckland Education Board staff had to write 744 checks for teachers wrongly paid or not paid at all.

The salary clerks in board offices were starting to lose ground—correcting errors in the previous paysheet left less time for the following one. An Auckland Education Board spokesman said errors were being made at both ends—the board staff who provided information and the Education Department payroll data entry operators. Bad communication between the Department and education boards was hindering the error-checking process. The *New Zealand Herald* blamed the problems on a computer jinx.

Lionel Devaliant, Chairman of the Post Primary Teachers' Association, blamed the delays and errors in teachers' pay on the State Services Commission, which had failed to provide adequate resources for the project. The State Services Commission was the employer of people in the state education system. Devaliant said, "We appreciate the work done by clerical workers in the department and in the boards, who are struggling under extreme difficulties. The buck stops with the commission which should have provided enough staff for the job."

Malcolm McDonald said that most delays would disappear once pay staff became used to the new system's requirements and the new system was completed with online terminals for each of the groups preparing teachers' pay records. This time of the year had usually been a difficult one with delay and errors on some teachers' pay, but the introduction of the new system had added to the problems. "But in a few months this will be just an unpleasant memory." McDonald said a proposed meeting between the Department of

Education and salaries officers from the regions should remove most misunderstandings about the new system.

The Problems Continue

Rosslyn Norman, the National Secretary of the Educational Institute, said that the Institute was going to seek compensation for teachers for the cost inflicted by problems associated with the new payroll system. Many teachers had been forced to pay bank charges for bounced checks, and some had been hit with penalties on late mortgage payments, overdraft charges, and other late payment costs because their pay had not arrived.

Meanwhile, Graham Wilson, the Wellington board's general manager, said that Education Board staff dealing with teachers' pay problems were under so much pressure that they were "breaking down and crying at work." One senior officer was ordered home to see a doctor and had to receive psychiatric counseling. In many cases, staff were in "the terminal stage of stress-related health problems," according to a *New Zealand Herald* article.

Education Board staff in all centers were working 12-hour days as well as one or two days every weekend.

Wilson explained that the Education Department had to decide to switch to the new computer system after Christmas, even though all 28 salary units did not have the computer equipment needed to input the information directly into the central computer. Salary units had to mail this information to the Education Department. However, if information was wrong or "rejected by the computer" for being in the wrong format, the Department staff then had to send it back to salary units for correction. "If all salaries offices had been able to input pay details directly into the central system they would have been able to correct mistakes as they were made." As things stood—it was now over two weeks since the system went live—"the whole thing was snowballing" as staff were having to correct massive errors and at the same time prepare the next lot of pay.

Two Months Later

Two months after the central computer system was introduced, up to a quarter of some schools' staff were still affected by teachers' pay errors. Relieving teachers and some part-time teachers had not been paid by mid-April.

School principals in Auckland now believed that there was something wrong with the software running the system and that these were not just temporary problems as claimed by the New Zealand Education Department. For example, most of the staff at one West Auckland school had received net pay of less than $1.00! At a central Auckland school, a teacher found the pay slip details were not too far astray, except no money had actually been paid into the bank account.

The President of the Auckland Secondary School Principals' Association, Brother Pat Lynch, said school boards were having to dip into their own funds to advance money to help staff with financial problems because of the payroll errors. Principals were becoming convinced that the computer systems' software was just not right for the job.

The Education Department, however, said that most of the problems were teething problems which involved salaries staff who were not used to the new system. The equipping of all regional offices with terminals would be a phased operation and would be completed in September.

Malcolm McDonald denied that the software was not suited to the needs of the Education Department. He said it was not a software or a hardware problem. The payroll software was an international package used throughout New Zealand and the world called International Payroll and Personnel by MSA Software. The Department was running the software package on a VAX minicomputer supplied by Digital Equipment Corporation. The fundamental problem, according to McDonald, was the proficiency of the salaries personnel in the salaries unit. These staff had had difficulty in adjusting to the procedural differences of the new system. The payroll problem was "a purely human problem," exacerbated by an underestimation of the training required for payroll staff. Additionally, many of the previous manual records were inaccurate and outdated. While these records were benign in the old system, the inaccuracies became malevolent in a computerized system. Also, whereas staff were used to taking shortcuts to get things done in the old system, the new computer system rejected shortcuts. McDonald said that staff would have to learn that the new system was more exacting and demanded accuracy.

By June 1993, McDonald was able to announce that the Education Department's new computerized payroll system was on target to meet its objective of saving the government millions of dollars. The first regular payments during holiday time had gone out correctly in May. However, a spokesman for the Post Primary Teachers' Association said teachers had complained about the new system, even though it was now working correctly. "Big payments were useful for those who, say, went overseas for holidays," he said.

Questions

1. Use the WCA framework to summarize the way the payroll system should operate.

2. Use a data flow diagram to explain the changes in system architecture.

3. Assuming you were Graham Wilson, what level of performance would you expect from a payroll system, and how would you measure its performance?

4. Explain why it is or is not possible to attribute the problems in this case to each of the following causes:
   a. Faulty hardware
   b. Faulty software
   c. Human error
   d. Insufficient training
   e. Inaccurate data

5. Explain why you do or do not believe the system development life cycle used in this project was one of the causes of the problems encountered. Identify any changes in the system building process that might have averted these problems.

6. What do you see as the main lessons from this case?

911: The System behind the Phone Number

by Richard Oyen

IN 1991, BOULDER COUNTY, COLORADO, installed a new 911 system. The first day the system was in operation, an elderly man with a speech impediment reported a fire at his house. Emergency dispatchers could not understand him when he gave his address, but the new 911 system automatically determined his location based on the telephone number he was calling from. Had he called a day earlier, it would have taken 45 minutes to trace the call and locate its origin, possibly resulting in greater destruction of his property, and maybe even his death.

Most Americans take 911 emergency phone systems for granted, and many have used them at least once. In elementary schools, children are trained to call 911 in an emergency, even if they are at a pay phone without money. Current 911 systems provide great improvements over the way people made emergency calls prior to their inception in 1968, but problems still occur. For example, in 1994, a New York City caller (who ironically was a 911 technician for the city) died because he was unable to give his address when he called 911, and the operator was unable to trace his location. Much like a city's infrastructure, 911 systems receive little public attention until they malfunction. Overloaded and busy phone lines, too many nonemergency calls, and inability to trace calls from cellular phones are but some of the problems that have led to mounting criticism of these systems. Even though the vast majority of calls are handled without incident, 911 systems seem to receive the greatest public attention when mishandled calls result in tragedies or fail to prevent them.

The Original 911 Systems

Until the 1960s, a person needing emergency help could either dial the local police or fire station or dial a local telephone operator to be linked to them. With the telephone technology of that time, this process was too slow and led to numerous accidental deaths that might have been avoided. This problem led to a 1967 recommendation of the Presidential Committee on Law Enforcement that a single, nationwide emergency service telephone number be implemented. In 1968, AT&T introduced a three digit emergency number that could be used to reach public local safety agencies throughout the country. It would only be necessary to dial 9-1-1 to gain access to switchboards operated by individual communities. These Public Safety Answering Points (PSAPs) consisted of regular telephone equipment and manual switchboards. The operator answering the call would determine the appropriate department to transfer the call to and would do so manually.

Known as basic 911 or B911, this original 911 system was better than the prior method of obtaining emergency help, but it still had shortcomings. The elapsed time before help arrived was slower than anticipated, and operators were sometimes unable to locate the caller. Consequently, the Presidential Committee on Law Enforcement joined with the National Academy of Engineering and the National Institute of Law Enforcement and Criminal Justice in requesting that AT&T develop an enhanced 911 system called E911. It would have three new features: Automatic Number Identification (ANI), Automatic Location Identification (ALI), and Selective Routing. By 1971, AT&T had developed these new capabilities and implemented a test program in 20 communities across the United States.

How 911 Operates Today

The E911 system was refined further, and in 1980 the current version of E911 was introduced throughout most of the country. The telephone number for the incoming call is automatically captured using methods later applied for commercial caller ID service. A computer uses this telephone number to look up the street address in a database, identify the PSAP assigned to that location, and transfer the call to that PSAP. Seconds after the operator starts talking to a caller, the location and phone number information appears on the operator's screen.

The PSAP operator classifies the call and takes appropriate action based on information from the caller. Training helps the operator determine whether the situation being described by the caller is a hoax, a nonlife-threatening emergency, or a life-threatening emergency. Many callers become impatient while they are on the phone answering questions from PSAP operators because they incorrectly think all the questions are delaying the police response. In fact, the proper public safety office is being notified and is being provided all available information as the 911 call continues.

The demands and expectations placed on today's 911 systems are somewhat different from the goals of the original 911. The original intent was for faster, universal emergency service, and a reduction in the crime rate due to faster police responses. Emergency response time has decreased significantly, but the success of 911 systems created the sometimes unrealistic expectation that calls should be answered instantly, and an emergency response should arrive within minutes. The original goal of reducing the crime rate through faster response proved unattainable, in part because rapid response cannot lead to rapid arrest if, as usually happens, the emergency call is received long after the crime has occurred.

Public safety agencies are now requesting additional caller information beyond the phone number and address that was provided by E911. This additional information includes exact location, the room number, area within the city, district and jurisdiction information, nearest hospital, and medical information about the caller (such as if they are deaf or have high blood pressure). These requests are basically about extending the content of the database a 911 system can access.

Many suburban communities and rural areas are centralizing their 911 services. By using a single office, communities can more efficiently utilize computer systems and still have fast, reliable 911 service. E911 service is less common in rural areas than in urban areas because of the large costs associated with a small population. For example, in northern Iowa, a proposed telephone rate increase to fund a new E911 was as high as 600 percent. However, by purchasing comparatively inexpensive 911 packages offered by small software companies, these counties have actually reduced their emergency costs by 14 to 26 percent.

The discussion of technical components of future 911 systems focuses primarily on digital technology. Current analog systems handle calls at a comparatively slow rate and are unable to perform complex switching if there is a flood of 911 calls. Digital switches, digital PSAPs, and new transmission technologies should improve the speed, flexibility, efficiency, and cost effectiveness by managing more aspects of the calls directly. Attaching more complex databases could provide more information to the PSAP as the 911 call proceeds. Extra operators help might also be employed from the operator's homes during emergency situations by using the digital interface technology.

New Jersey introduced a statewide 911 system in 1993 that is reportedly one of the best in the country. This new system covers all three New Jersey area codes and uses three Specialized Communication Exchanges (SCXs) located throughout the state. A caller's initial request for help is routed by using a digital cross-connect switch (DCS) to one of the three SCXs. The DCS also provides an alternative routing of the call in case of a failure in the first transfer. By using different lines and different switches, the call can go to any PSAP in the event that the primary one is busy. The redundancy and backup created makes for greater efficiency. The new network approach has resulted in reduced time and payroll costs for New Jersey Bell. The centralization makes monitoring and maintenance much easier. There is less downtime for the system, specifically the PSAPs, so technicians do not need to spend a lot of time repairing them, and the training time is greatly reduced as well.

Problems with the 911 System

Fundamental problems with 911 still exist despite the great improvements in telecommunication technology in the last decade. One huge problem is the misuse of the system. Despite education programs for the general public, the majority of 911 calls are not for emergency or life threatening situations. Statistics for some large metropolitan areas demonstrate the size of the problem. In Los Angeles, only 30 percent of the calls were judged top priority; in Houston, 10 to 30 percent were life threatening; and in Boston, this was less than 10 percent. The nonlife-threatening calls include nonemergency calls, wrong numbers (such as misdialing 411 information), and prank calls by children. In Washington, a new nonemergency number was created to reduce this problem. It has received 2,000 calls a day but has not decreased the number of 911 calls. Some cities are actually starting to "demarket" 911, that is, to discourage use for anything except life-threatening emergencies.

Such caller overuse and abuse bogs down 911 services and outrages the public. Being put on hold during heavy 911 call usage periods makes the caller feel as if an emergency call is being handled like a call to order concert tickets. A study in Los Angeles showed that the elapsed time to connect a 911 call with the right public safety agency ranged from 10 seconds to 10 minutes.

Most 911 systems are also unable to locate cellular phone users, which are beginning to make up a greater number of calls. In 1990, the California Highway Patrol estimated that they received over a million 911 calls. Approximately 50 percent of those calls were from cellular phones, and none of those could be located using the automated location identification capabilities available at the time. Although difficult, this problem may not prove totally insurmountable. In cooperation with cellular phone companies, a 911 capability was being developed in Houston that utilizes triangulation to find the location of a cellular caller. Although such sophistication may sound unnecessary, a Los Angeles study found that 25 percent of cellular callers were unable to identify their location when placing a call to 911. As cellular phones become more affordable, the number of users will increase. Therefore, the ability to locate these callers will become more important.

The training and capabilities of 911 operators are limiting factors in any attempt to reduce 911 response times further. The job stress felt by 911 operators has been compared to that of air traffic controllers. Theirs is a high-pressure position, in which a misunderstanding or misinterpretation could

result in the death of the caller. The stress is even greater during peak hours when many calls are generated. In Oakland, California, the dropout rate for new 911 operators is so high that 50 percent quit before they go on active duty.

The problems of overworked and undertrained 911 operators came to national attention in Philadelphia in 1994. In this case, a neighborhood fight ended with several youths beating one youngster with baseball bats. Despite some 20 calls by frantic callers, it took over 40 minutes to notify the police. Once notified, the police were on the scene within five minutes, but it was too late, and the boy died the next day. Most of the blame was directed at the operators who had received only 5 to 7 days of training. Seven of the operators were disciplined by the mayor for their handling of the incident, citing their rude and abrupt behavior on the phone, and their downplaying of the seriousness of the beating. This incident highlights challenges related to inadequate training and excessive work, a combination that leads to poor communication and improper responses. The expectations placed on the operators are very high, yet they are often ill-equipped to deal with some of the situations they encounter.

Many cities recognize the importance of establishing operator skills and keeping their stress at a reasonable level. In San Francisco, future operators initially go through stringent testing on performance and typing, as well as oral and medical examinations and polygraph tests. Once they pass these tests, they enter a rigorous and lengthy training program. They learn how to handle incoming calls during five weeks of training at the police academy. They then have 12 to 16 weeks of on the job training. Next, they go back to the police academy, and spend another two weeks learning about dispatching. This is followed up with 12 to 14 more weeks of on the job training. This total of over 31 weeks of training has led to better performance. They receive over 80,000 calls a month but average fewer than 10 complaints per month from callers complaining that the calls were mishandled or that they were treated rudely. The operators are frequently monitored, and observation reports from supervisors are used to maintain high performance levels. The response to job stress starts by having operators work only six and a half of the eight hours on their shift, and by having them switch positions every two hours. The same counseling that is available to police officers is available to the operators. Counseling and group sessions are also used to address the job burnout problems that many operators feel.

Questions

1. Summarize the way the architecture of emergency response systems has improved over the last 30 years. Identify any technical advances that have made 911 systems more effective or less effective during this period.

2. Assume you were managing a 911 system. What measures of performance would you track? What do you think would be appropriate targets for each of these measures of performance?

3. Explain how infrastructure and context issues are significant for 911 systems.

4. What policies might reduce the misuse of 911 systems?

5. Explain how risk affects the various components of current 911 systems.

References

Abelson, Reed. "Rescuing 911." *Forbes*, Mar. 2, 1992, p. 103.

AP. "Seven Facing Punishment in 911 Case" *New York Times*, Nov. 29, 1994, Sec. A, p. 20.

Depaola, John. "NJ Bell Answers Call for Help with a Unique E-911 System." *Telephony*, Jan. 11, 1993, pp. 36–37.

Joint Interim Hearing on the 911 Emergency Response System. California Legislature, Senate Committee on Energy and Public Utilities, Nov. 21, 1990.

Kroupa, Doug. "911: What's Emerging in Emergency Phone Service." *Telephony*, May 2, 1994, pp. 132–140.

Petromilli, Karen. San Francisco Police Communications Manager, Interview by Richard Oyen, Mar. 6, 1995.

Study for Alameda County 911, Law Enforcement Assistance Administration, U.S. Department of Justice, Oct. 1974.

Turque, Bill. "The Curse of 911." *Newsweek*, Nov. 5, 1990, pp. 26–27.

Tyler, Steve. "Advanced Technology Brings Enhanced 911 Services to Rural Environments." *Telecommunications*, June 1993, p. 69.

The CONFIRM Project:
A Failed Strategic Alliance

Extracted from Effy Oz, "When Professional Standards are Lax: The
CONFIRM Failure and its Lessons." *Communications
of the ACM*, Oct. 1994, Vol. 37, No. 10, pp. 29–36. Reprinted with
permission of the Communications of the ACM.

IN 1988, A CONSORTIUM COMPRISED OF Hilton Hotels Corporation, Marriott Corporation, and Budget Rent-A-Car Corporation subcontracted a large-scale project to AMR Information Services, Inc., a subsidiary of American Airlines Corporation. The consulting firm was to develop a new information system (IS) called CONFIRM, which was supposed to be a leading-edge comprehensive travel industry reservation program combining airline, rental car, and hotel information. A new organization, Intrico, was especially established for running the new system. The consortium had grand plans to market the service to other companies, but major problems surfaced when Hilton tested the system. Due to malfunctions, Intrico announced an 18-month delay. The problems could not be resolved, however, and three and a half years after the project had begun and a total of $125 million had been invested, the project was canceled.

In a letter to employees, Max Hopper, American Airlines Information Services chief, wrote: "Some people who have been part of CONFIRM management did not disclose the true status of the project in a timely manner. This has created more difficult problems—of both business ethics and finance—than would have existed if those people had come forward with accurate information. Honesty is an imperative in our business—it is an ethical and technical imperative." Apparently, the clients were misled into continuing to invest in an operation plagued with problems in database, decision-support, and integration technologies[1].

Background

In 1987, a potential market caught the attention of AMR: centralized hotel reservations. As the company discovered, only 20 percent of hotel reservations were made through a centralized service, while in the airline business 80 percent of the reservations are made through a central system like AMR's SABRE. The company decided to take advantage of this situation in the form of a new, comprehensive system.

CONFIRM was the name given to an IS that was supposed to be the most advanced reservation system in the combined industry of travel, lodging, and car rental. The clients relied on the professionalism of the specialists who developed the highly successful airline reservation system SABRE. SABRE was a classic example of how an IS can gain strategic advantages for its user organization.

There are more than 85 hotel companies in North America. The major national hotel chains are Marriott, Hilton, Hyatt, Westin, and ITT Sheraton. The ease with which travelers can make reservations is vital to this industry. Over the past 16 years, each of these chains acquired a computer-based reservation system. The systems provide information to travel agents throughout the world. Some chains developed their own systems; others had vendors develop their systems. The systems varied in efficiency and effectiveness. For example, Marriott's MARSHA has been recognized as one of the best in the industry, while Hilton's NORTH, dated from the early 1960s, was inadequate and inefficient.

Like the major hotel chains, airlines, too, have acquired reservation systems. The most notable are SABRE and APOLLO. SABRE was developed by AMR, the parent of American Airlines Corporation; APOLLO was developed by United Airlines Corporation. The former has gained acclaim as the world's most successful airline reservation system. The system was installed in 1976 and has since been continually upgraded.

In 1986, AMR formed AMRIS, the information systems arm of the corporation. AMR's chairman hired Max Hopper to head AMRIS and offered him "a chance to combine running the SABRE business … and expanding it into other businesses, really leveraging it." AMRIS was to exploit its success with SABRE for business in other areas. But, unfortunately, the success of one system does not always guarantee the good fortune of a more advanced system. What follows is the chronicles of the events that led to the CONFIRM "disaster." The information is taken from media reports and the lawsuit filed by Marriott[2].

The CONFIRM Chronicles

On March 13, 1987, AMRIS representatives made a presentation to Marriott executives about a new reservations system they were preparing to develop. The system, named CONFIRM, would be superior to any existing reservation system in the industry. The representatives claimed it would be a state-of-the-art reservation system meeting all business needs of hotel and car-rental partners in the joint venture. According to the proposal, AMRIS, as a managing partner, would be in charge of the design and development of the system. The hotels would pay for this effort and would input the necessary data.

The partners, hotels, and car-rental businesses would use the system for their daily operations. In addition, they would join AMR in an effort to market customized versions of the systems to other hotel and car-rental companies for profit. AMRIS was to operate the data processing center of the system.

From May through August of 1987, Marriott and other potential partners met with AMRIS executives to negotiate the deal. AMRIS people repeatedly assured the partners that CONFIRM would be superior to any current reservation system, while not more costly to use. They also promised that the project would be completed in time to outpace the competition in the hotel and car-rental industries.

On September 2, 1987, Marriott, a major partner in the venture, agreed to consider the AMRIS proposal although it already had an excellent system. The company's vice-president emphasized: "Marriott is pleased with its current reservation system... we have one of the best reservation systems in the industry in terms of both functionality and cost." Thus, he said his company would join the venture if "the joint venture can develop a reservation system that is functionally richer than the system we intend to operate [and that Marriott costs] will be less than the costs to operate our proposed system."

The first three partners to the joint venture were Marriott, Hilton, and Budget Rent-A-Car. In October 1987, they formed a consortium and named it Intrico. In late 1987 and early 1988, technical representatives from the four partners started to plan detailed performance capabilities of the new system. On May 24, 1988, AMRIS issued a press release announcing the commencement of the CONFIRM design process. In the meantime, the Intrico partners funneled large sums of money into the project. By September of 1988, Marriott alone spent more than $1.45 million on the preliminary design.

In September 1988, after a year of negotiations, Marriott, Hilton, and Budget signed a partnership agreement with AMRIS. According to the agreement, the objectives of the joint venture were:

- To design, develop, operate, and maintain a new "state-of-the-art" reservation-processing system to be marketed worldwide
- To design and develop "interfaces" with airline computer reservation systems so consumers could make airline, hotel, and car rental reservations through a single, computerized system
- To market the reservation system and other communication services to customers for a profit
- To convert each of the partners' reservation systems to the newly developed system

AMRIS was designated "Managing Partner, Development" of CONFIRM. The agreement made the company responsible for all aspects of the design and development of the new system. The four partners undertook to pay AMRIS $55 million for the development. Each partner was to appoint a professional team that would be stationed in Dallas, at AMRIS headquarters, so that the partners would provide input as to what functions were needed and also test and evaluate the system as it was developed.

The agreement stated two phases: the design phase and the development phase. The design phase was to take 7 months, and the development phase was to be completed within 45 months after the agreement was signed. Thus, the deadline was the end of June 1992.

The contract provided that the total expenditure to develop CONFIRM would not exceed $55.7 million. AMRIS warranted that it had "no reason to believe" that the development costs would exceed this amount. The company also undertook to develop the system so that operation costs would be limited to $1.05 per reservation.

On December 30, 1988, AMRIS presented a "base design" of the system. Marriott claimed the functional specifications were not adequate. A 1992 internal audit by AMR's SABRE personnel stated that "these documents describe the expected functionality in general terms; they do not provide sufficient detail for a developer to understand what the user is expecting."

In March 1989, AMRIS declared the functional and technical specifications were complete. Late that month, the company circulated a preliminary development plan. The plan was unacceptable to the partners. The next six months were devoted to revision of the plan. During this time, AMRIS executives reassured the partners that the system would comply with all the requirements and that it would be ready on time.

AMRIS completed the design phase in September 1989 and circulated a proposed development plan for partners' review. At this time, the company increased the price of the project from $55.7 million to $72.6 million. It also stated that the cost per reservation would be $1.30 (instead of the original $1.05) in the first year of full operation and decline to $0.72 and $0.40 in the fourth and fifth years, respectively.

According to the partnership contract, the three client-partners could withdraw when the development plan was presented. (A penalty of $1 million was involved.) The partners had to make the decision at this point. The per-reservation cost was crucial information in their decision making.

On August 8 and 15 of 1989, AMRIS representatives met with those of Marriott, Hilton, and Budget to review AMRIS's pro forma financial statements. Two years later, in August 1991, Marriott found that the statements were false. AMRIS understated the costs of personnel and other operating costs. The company also used numbers that overstated the total number of reservations. The actual processing cost per reservation was then estimated at $2.00.

Based on these statements, the client-partners decided not to exercise their option to withdraw. To Marriott, for instance, the value of the project

declined by $1 million but still promised a net present value of more than $3 million. In September 1989, the partners accepted the development plan. The deadline was revised from June 1992 to July 1992.

The contract outlined four major development phases: the business area analysis (BAA) to develop business models, the business system design (BSD) to enumerate detailed descriptions of the application systems, construction of the system's code (construction), and testing activities (testing).

On October 16, 1989, AMRIS assured the partners that the project was on time and on budget. However, in January 1990, the company missed the contractual deadline of completing the terminal-screen design. In February 1990, AMRIS missed the completion milestone of the BAA phase. Apparently, the developers redefined the unfinished work of this phase to become a part of the next phase.

In February 1990, AMRIS admitted it was more than 13 weeks behind schedule, but claimed it could catch-up and recapture much of that lag. In March 1990, the company began a six-week "replanning" effort.

Millions of dollars kept flowing into the project. On May 15, 1990, AMRIS made a presentation to the partners saying the project was still on time and that the system would be ready by its deadline. At the same time, major players in the development effort were chastised for delays.

During the summer of 1990, both Budget and Marriott expressed concerns that the project was behind schedule and that its management was ineffective. While employees at the project office estimated CONFIRM would not be ready in time, they were instructed by management to change their revised dates so that they reflected the original project calendar. In August of that year, AMRIS declared the first phase complete and entered the second major phase (BSD). When Marriott representatives asked to see some "deliverables" of the completed phase, and developers refused to show or explain their status. In October, the company admitted to the partners it was one year behind schedule. But company executives claimed they would still meet the deadline.

In February 1991, AMRIS presented a "Re-Plan" to replace the original development plan. According to the Re-Plan, only Hilton would be using the system by June 1992, and Marriott would not receive all the features it was promised before March 1993. Marriott later claimed that AMRIS executives knew they could not meet the new schedule. The hotel company said AMRIS forced employees to artificially change their timetable to reflect the new schedule, and that those who refused either were reassigned to other projects, resigned, or were fired. The Re-Plan attached a new price tag: $92 million, far above the original $55 million and the previously revised $72 million. The AMRIS president resigned in October 1991, and during the end of that year and the beginning of 1992 about 20 additional employees resigned.

AMRIS employees were dissatisfied with the way management handled the project. They believed their managers kept stating unrealistic schedules and lied about the project status. Many realized the "schedule" could not be met even with nine-hour workdays and work on weekends. By the summer of 1991, about half of the people assigned to CONFIRM (slightly more than 180 employees) were looking for new positions. A consultant was hired by AMRIS to evaluate the project. Dissatisfied with his findings, a vice-president "buried" the report and dismissed the consultant.

An evaluation by Marriott concluded that the developers could not complete the project. However, the hotel chain still gave them a chance: "As a partner, we hope that you will be able to perform as promised. However, as a user, we do not, based on experience to date, believe you can"[3]. AMR, the developers' parent company responded that CONFIRM's development was on target and that the system would be fully functional. AMRIS continued to bill Marriott at a rate of more than $1 million per month.

Finally, in April 1992, AMRIS admitted it was approximately two to six months behind schedule. Like Marriott management, Hilton management was still hopeful that "whatever has been broken can be fixed to meet the original schedule"[4]. But there was no basis for these hopes. That month, major problems surfaced when Hilton tried the system as CONFIRM's first beta-test user[5]. On April 29, 1992 the AMRIS chairperson wrote to the three partners:

"Unfortunately, things have not gone as planned. Specifically: (1) The individuals whom we gave responsibility for managing CONFIRM have proven to be inept. Additionally, they have apparently deliberately concealed a number of important technical and performance problems. (2) The technical staff, while skilled, has failed in the construction of the very demanding interfaces between the systems, and the extensive database, which will both be part of the completed CONFIRM system. The bottom line, gentlemen, is that in our best current judgment they system is 15 to 18 months from completion ...".[6] The company promised to repay 100 percent of the investment to any partner who wished to withdraw from the joint venture. A senior officer of AMRIS blamed employees for lying and the project management of concealing problems. The project, he said, was actually two years behind schedule.

On April 28, 1992, AMRIS fired 8 top executives and replaced another 15 employees. On May 1, 1992, the company's vice-chairperson circulated a letter to employees acknowledging that CONFIRM's "system interfaces and databases are inadequate to provide the necessary performance and system reliability." He explained: "Our CONFIRM RS problem has many roots—one more serious than the other. Some people who have been part of CONFIRM RS management did not disclose the true status of the project in a timely manner. This has created more difficult problems—of both business ethics and finance—than would have existed if those people had come forward with accurate information."[7]

In July 1992, after three and a half years, and after spending $125 million of the project, the Intrico consortium disbanded. Technically, the developers' main problem was to tie CONFIRM's transaction-processing facility-based central reservation system with its decision-support system. AMRIS's president admitted: "We found they were not integratable." Further, it was later discovered that the database was irrecoverable in the event of a crash.

Apparently, some of the failure was due to bad management practices of all four partners in the Intrico consortium. The client—partner teams met with the developer's representatives just once a month. An AMRIS executive said: "You cannot manage a development effort of this magnitude by getting together once a month. Had they allowed the president of Intrico to function as CEO in a normal sense and empowered their senior reps [to] work together with common goal and objective, it would have worked."[8]

AMR filed a countersuit against Marriott, Budget, and Hilton in September 1992. On May 14, 1993, AMR amended its suit to suggest that its partner-clients changed an approved plan to determine specifications for the common reservation system. Instead of a single system, AMR claims, the developers were encouraged to create three individual systems under CONFIRM. The company accused its clients of being "selfish."[9] By January 1994, AMRIS had reached out-of-court settlements with all its partners for undisclosed amounts. Some sources say the firm was facing damages of more than $500 million and therefore agreed to pay about $160 million.[10]

Questions

1. Explain how the problems in this situation might be attributed to each of the following causes:
   a. unforeseen and insurmountable technical difficulties
   b. underestimation of costs and completion dates
   c. failure of the developers to understand the system's requirements
   d. changing requirements after the project started
   e. unprofessional conduct

2. Explain why you do or do not believe the system development life cycle used in this project was one of the causes of the failure. Identify any changes in the system building process that might have averted failure.

3. Explain your view about why experienced system developers such as the AMRIS team could have misrepresented the situation to their management.

4. Assume a large company is embarking on a system development alliance with several other large companies. What guidelines would you suggest to help avoid the problems that occurred in this situation?

References

1. Halper, M. "IS Cover-Up Charged in System Kill. *Computerworld*, Aug. 10, 1992, p 1.
2. *Marriott v. AMR*, Filed with the Circuit Court for Montgomery County, Maryland (Case No. 96336), Sept. 26, 1992.
3. *Marriott V. AMR.*
4. Ibid.
5. Halper, M. "IS Cover-UP."
6. *Marriott v. AMR.*
7. Ibid.
8. Halper, M. "Too Many Pilots." *Computerworld* Oct. 12, 1992, p 8.
9. Halper, M. "AMR Calls CONFIRM Partners Selfish." *Computerworld*, May 24, 1993, p 4.
10. Zelner, W. "Portrait of a Project as a Total Disaster." *BusinessWeek*, Jan. 17, 1994, p 36.

Photo Credits

Company Index

Author Index

Glossary/Index